The Secret★Sakura Shares

AKIRA HAGIO

The Secret Sakura Shares

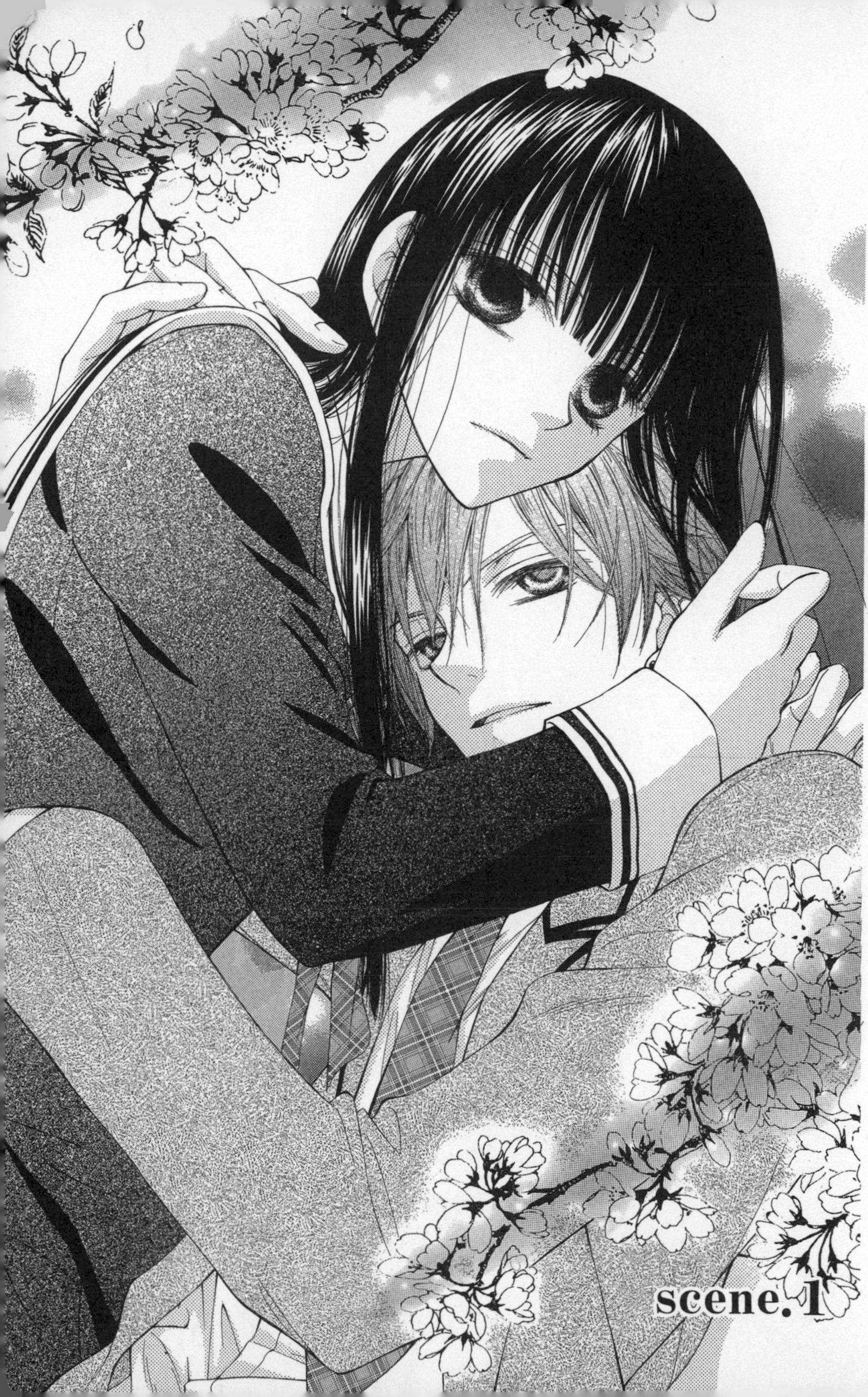
scene.1

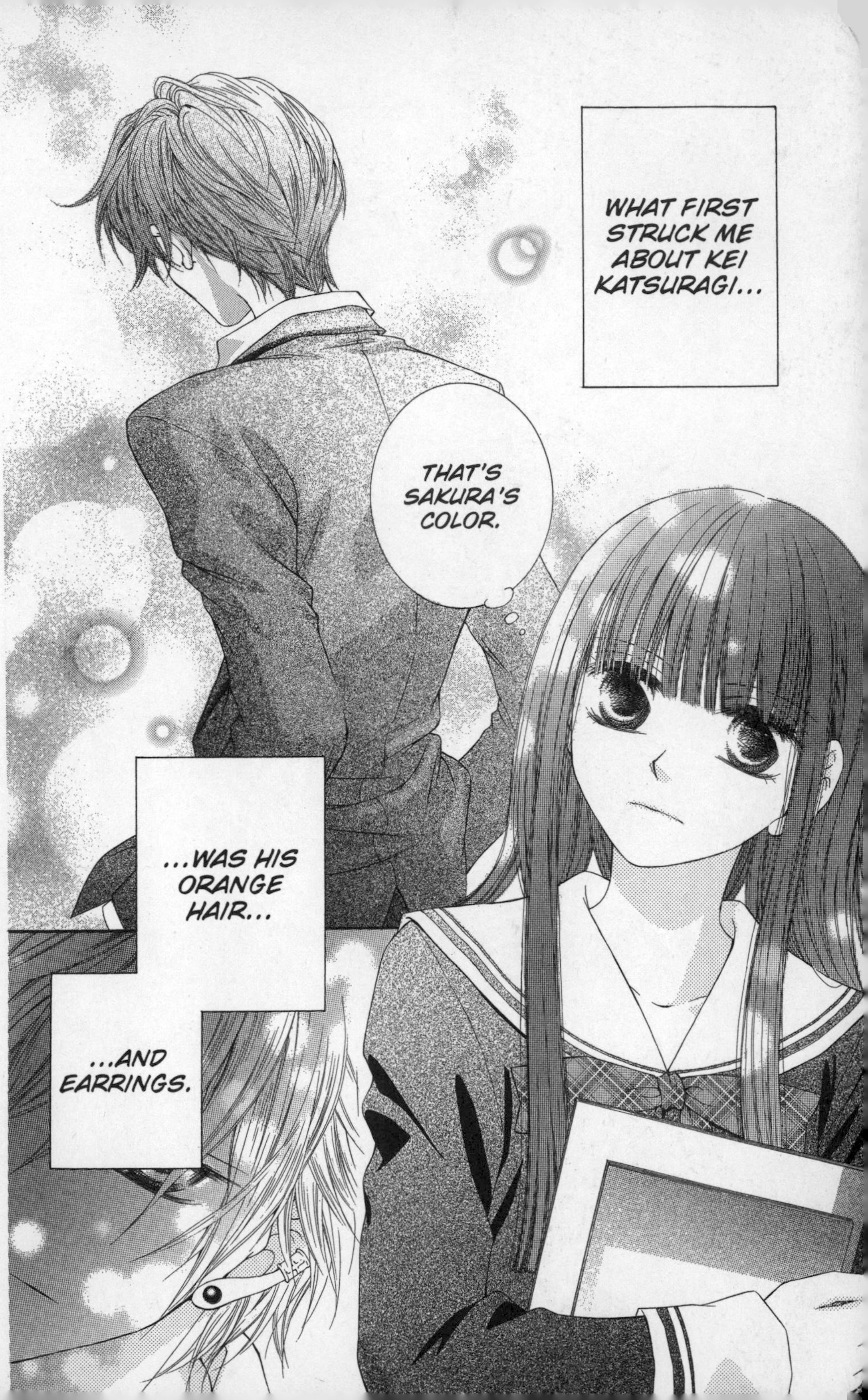
WHAT FIRST STRUCK ME ABOUT KEI KATSURAGI...
THAT'S SAKURA'S COLOR.
...WAS HIS ORANGE HAIR...
...AND EARRINGS.

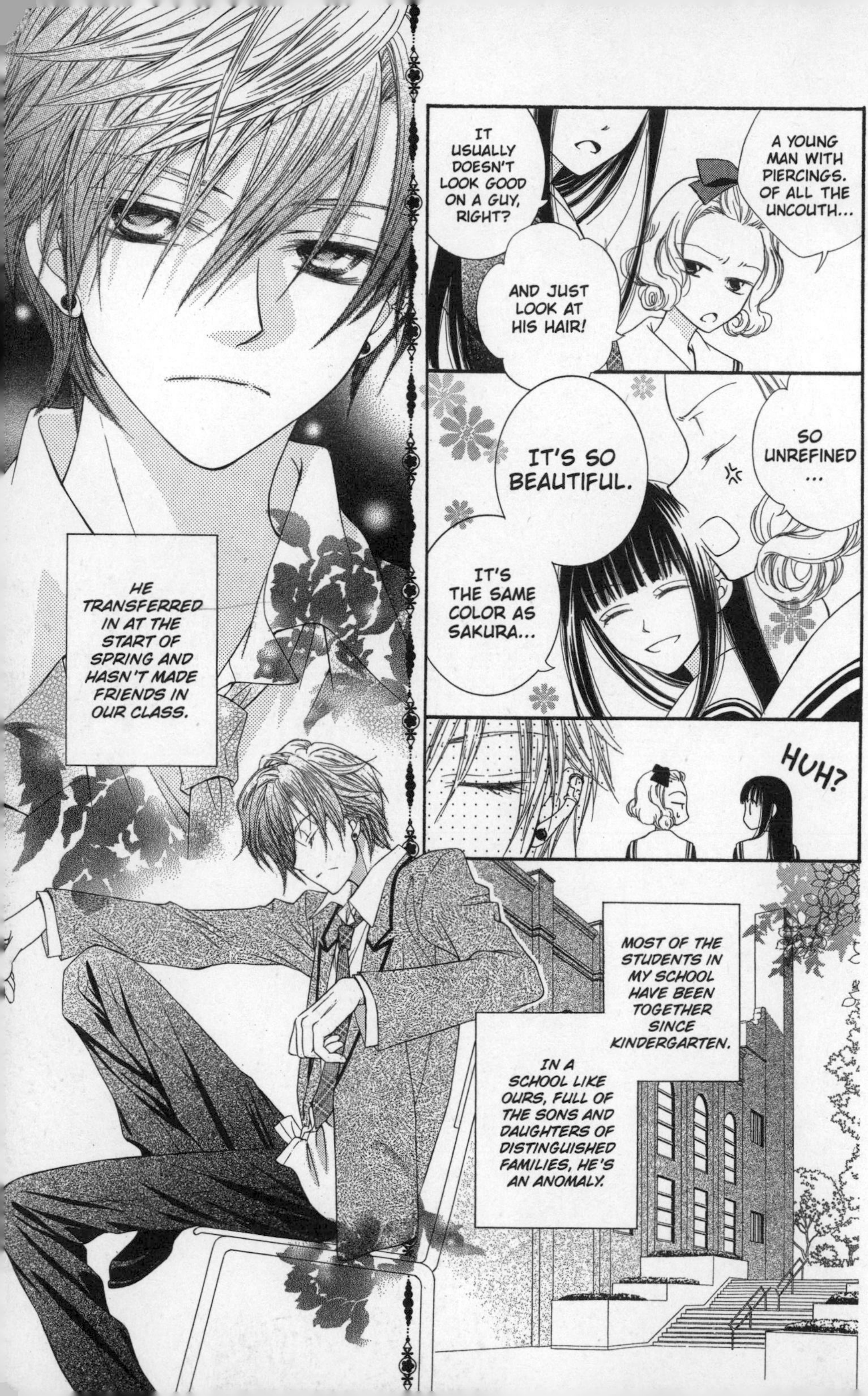
A YOUNG MAN WITH PIERCINGS. OF ALL THE UNCOUTH...
IT USUALLY DOESN'T LOOK GOOD ON A GUY, RIGHT?
AND JUST LOOK AT HIS HAIR!
SO UNREFINED ...
IT'S SO BEAUTIFUL.
IT'S THE SAME COLOR AS SAKURA...
HUH?
MOST OF THE STUDENTS IN MY SCHOOL HAVE BEEN TOGETHER SINCE KINDERGARTEN.
IN A SCHOOL LIKE OURS, FULL OF THE SONS AND DAUGHTERS OF DISTINGUISHED FAMILIES, HE'S AN ANOMALY.
HE TRANSFERRED IN AT THE START OF SPRING AND HASN'T MADE FRIENDS IN OUR CLASS.

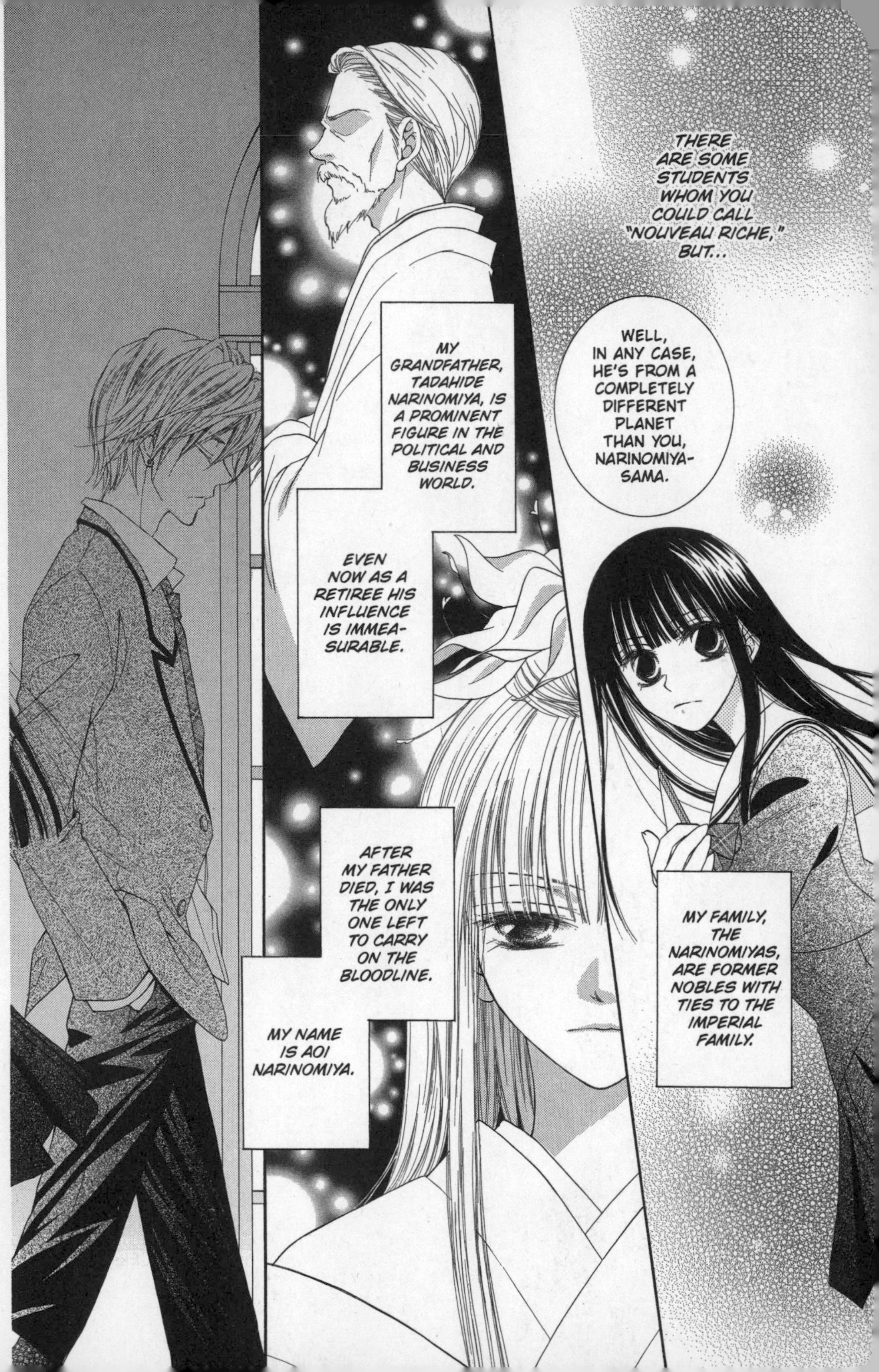
THERE ARE SOME STUDENTS WHOM YOU COULD CALL "NOUVEAU RICHE," BUT...
WELL, IN ANY CASE, HE'S FROM A COMPLETELY DIFFERENT PLANET THAN YOU, NARINOMIYA-SAMA.
MY FAMILY, THE NARINOMIYAS, ARE FORMER NOBLES WITH TIES TO THE IMPERIAL FAMILY.
MY GRANDFATHER, TADAHIDE NARINOMIYA, IS A PROMINENT FIGURE IN THE POLITICAL AND BUSINESS WORLD.
EVEN NOW AS A RETIREE HIS INFLUENCE IS IMMEA-SURABLE.
AFTER MY FATHER DIED, I WAS THE ONLY ONE LEFT TO CARRY ON THE BLOODLINE.
MY NAME IS AOI NARINOMIYA.

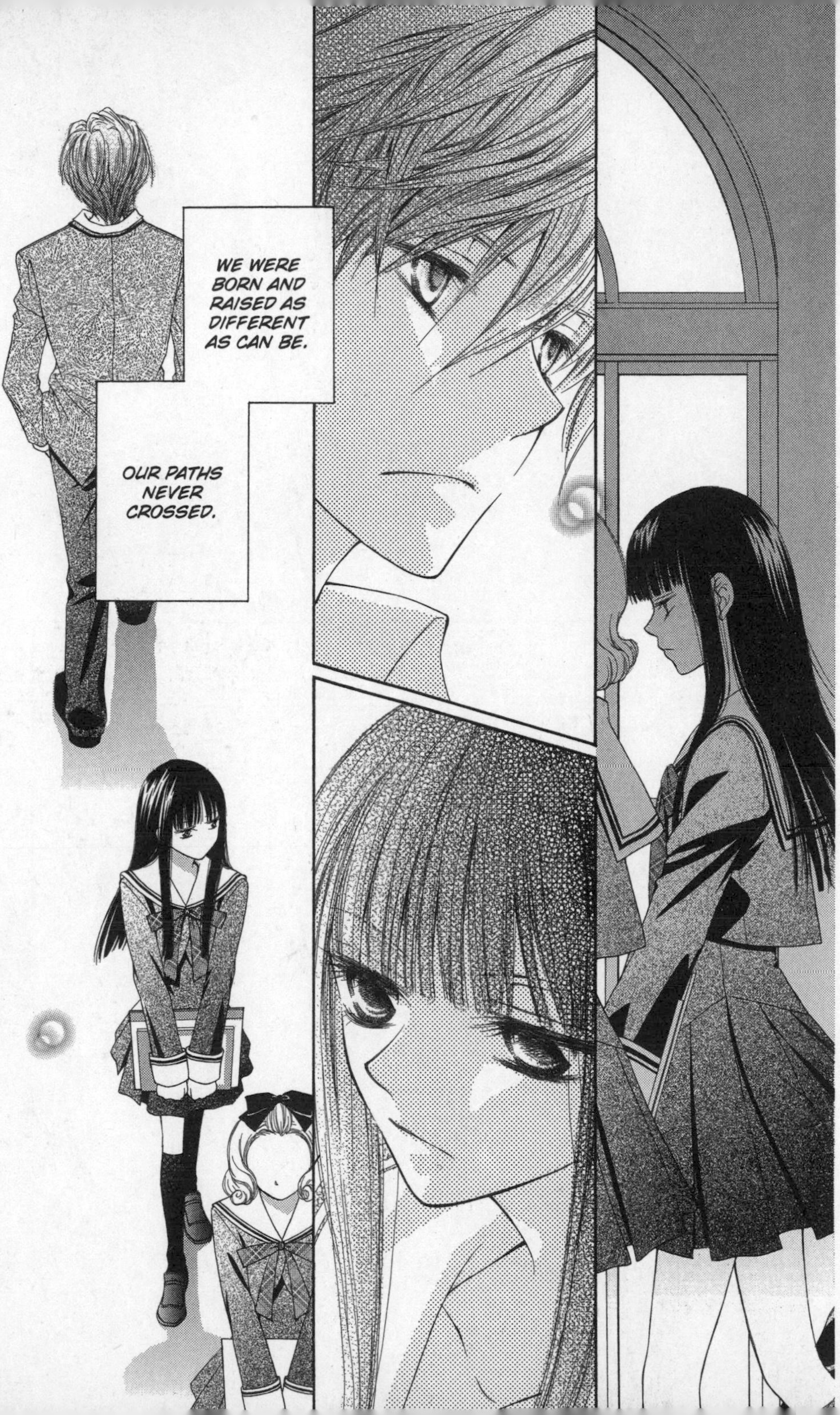
WE WERE BORN AND RAISED AS DIFFERENT AS CAN BE.
OUR PATHS NEVER CROSSED.

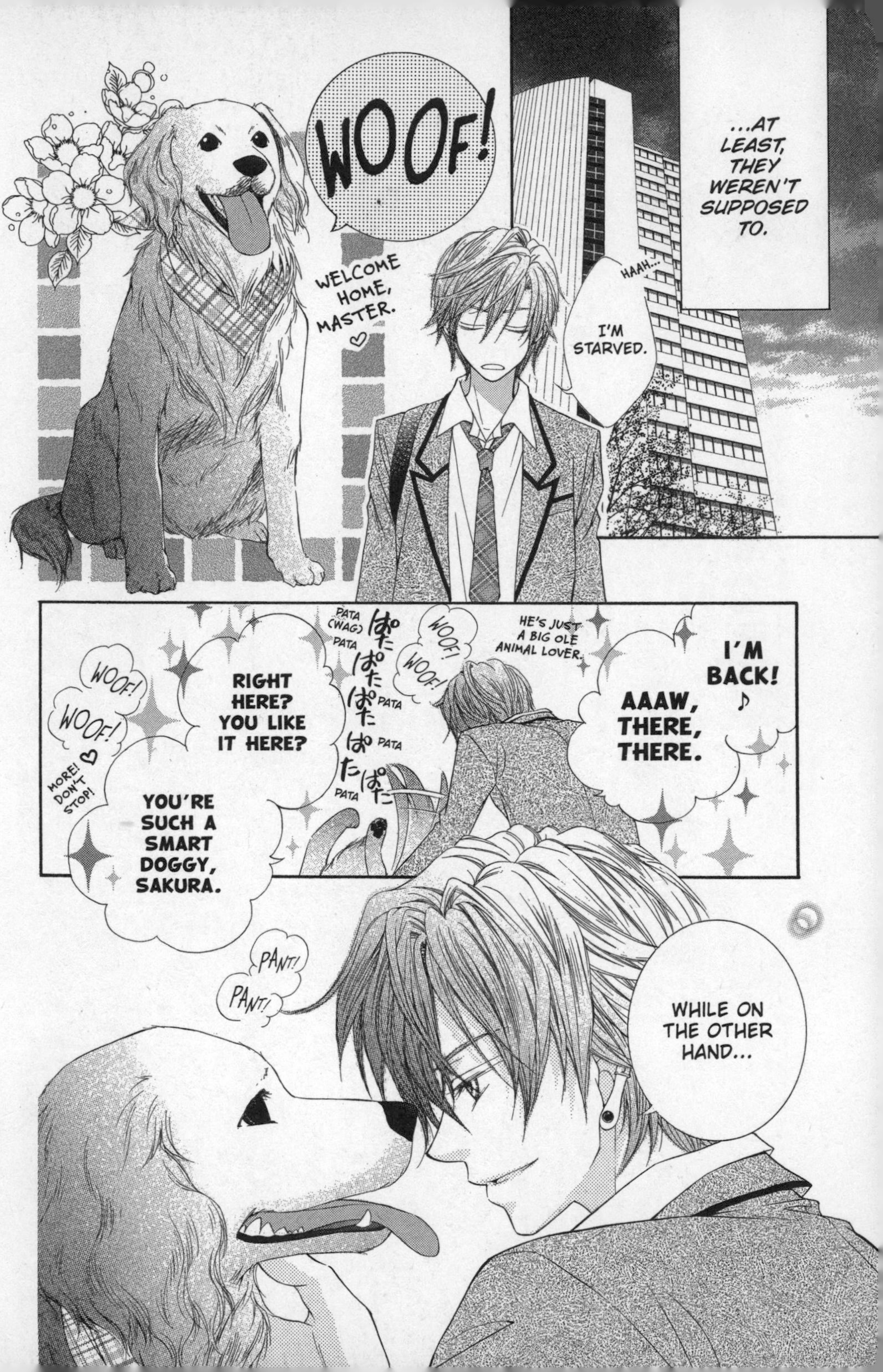
...AT LEAST, THEY WEREN'T SUPPOSED TO.
HAAH...
I'M STARVED.
WOOF!
WELCOME HOME, MASTER. ♡
I'M BACK! ♪
AAAW, THERE, THERE.
HE'S JUST A BIG OLE ANIMAL LOVER.
WOOF! WOOF!
PATA (WAG) PATA PATA PATA PATA
ぱたぱたぱたぱたぱた
RIGHT HERE? YOU LIKE IT HERE?
WOOF! WOOF! ♡
MORE! DON'T STOP!
YOU'RE SUCH A SMART DOGGY, SAKURA.
WHILE ON THE OTHER HAND...
PANT! PANT!

ONE いち

TO THOSE I'M MEETING FOR THE FIRST TIME AND THOSE I'VE MET COUNTLESS TIMES ALREADY, HELLO!
MY NAME IS AKIRA HAGIO.

THANK YOU FOR PICKING UP VOLUME 1 OF *THE SECRET SAKURA SHARES*. IT'S BEEN OVER A YEAR SINCE CHAPTER 1 WAS SERIALIZED, BUT IT'S FINALLY ALL COMPILED INTO A BOOK.

YAY! ♪

WELL, I HOPE YOU ENJOY THE WORLD OF OUR TWO MAIN CHARACTERS AS THEY WAVER WITHIN THE NARROW SPACE BETWEEN LOVE AND PERVERSION. ♥

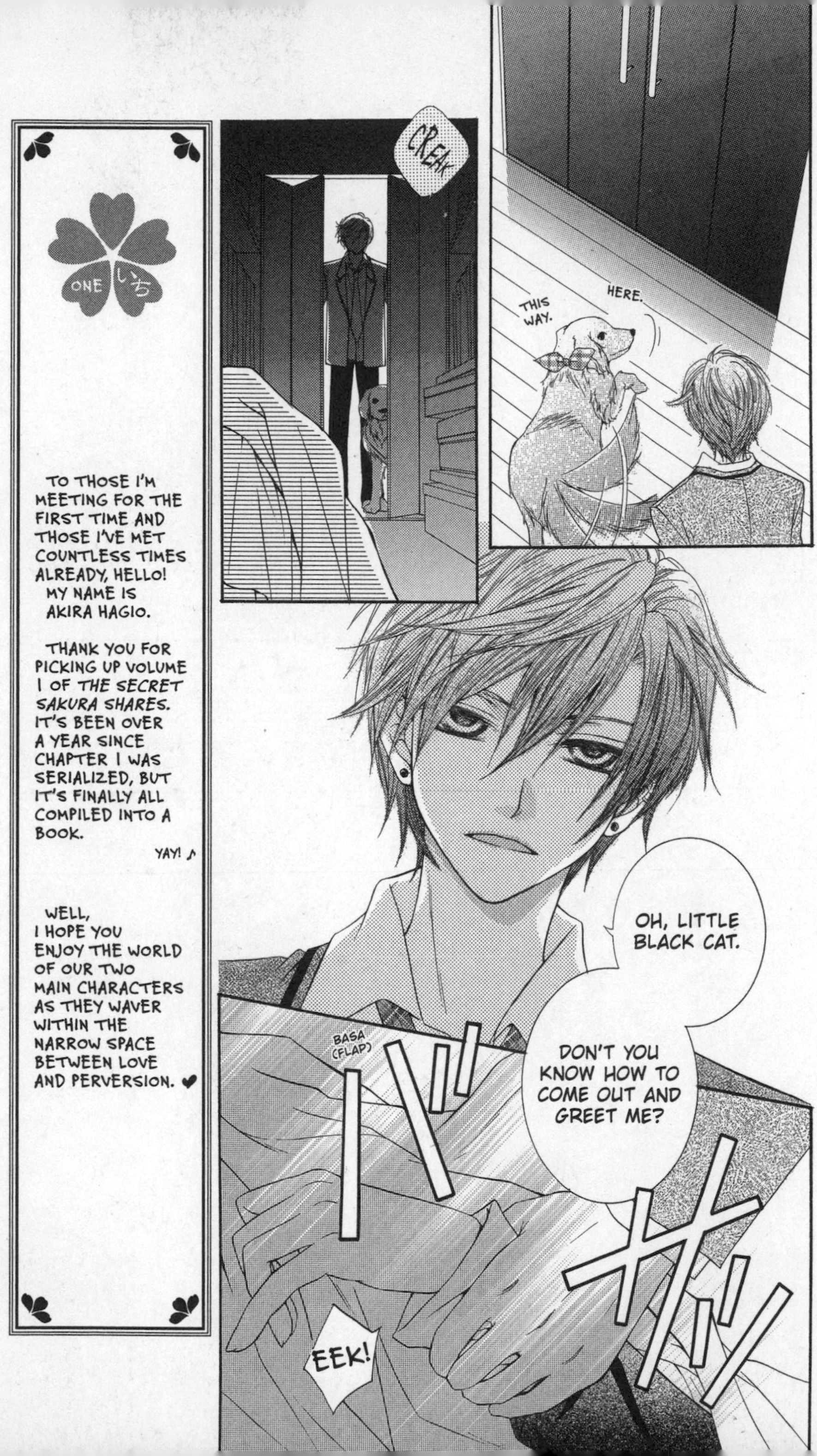
HERE.
THIS WAY.
CREAK
OH, LITTLE BLACK CAT.
DON'T YOU KNOW HOW TO COME OUT AND GREET ME?
BASA (FLAP)
EEK!

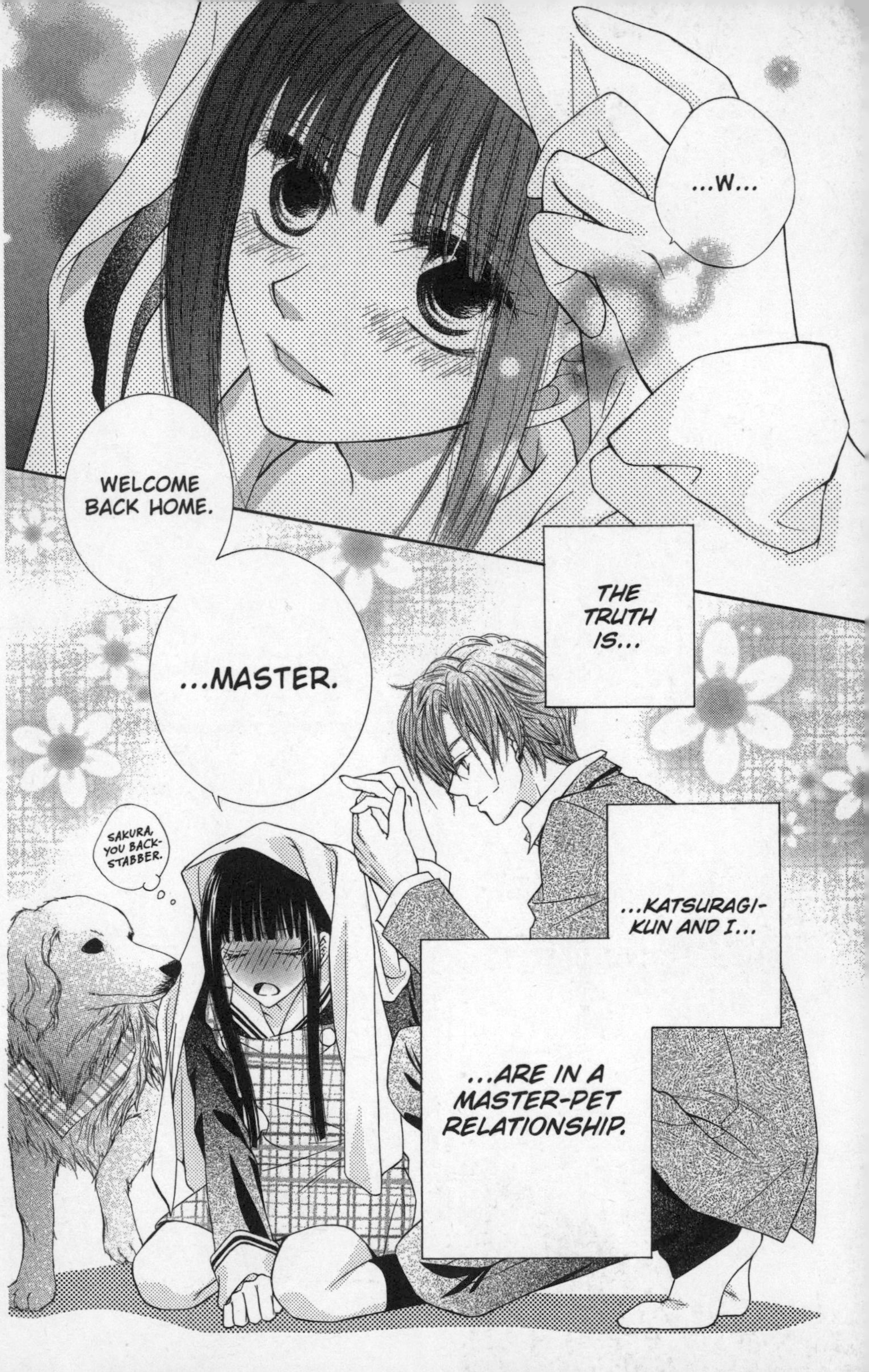
...W...
WELCOME BACK HOME.
...MASTER.
THE TRUTH IS...
SAKURA, YOU BACK-STABBER.
...KATSURAGI-KUN AND I...
...ARE IN A MASTER-PET RELATIONSHIP.

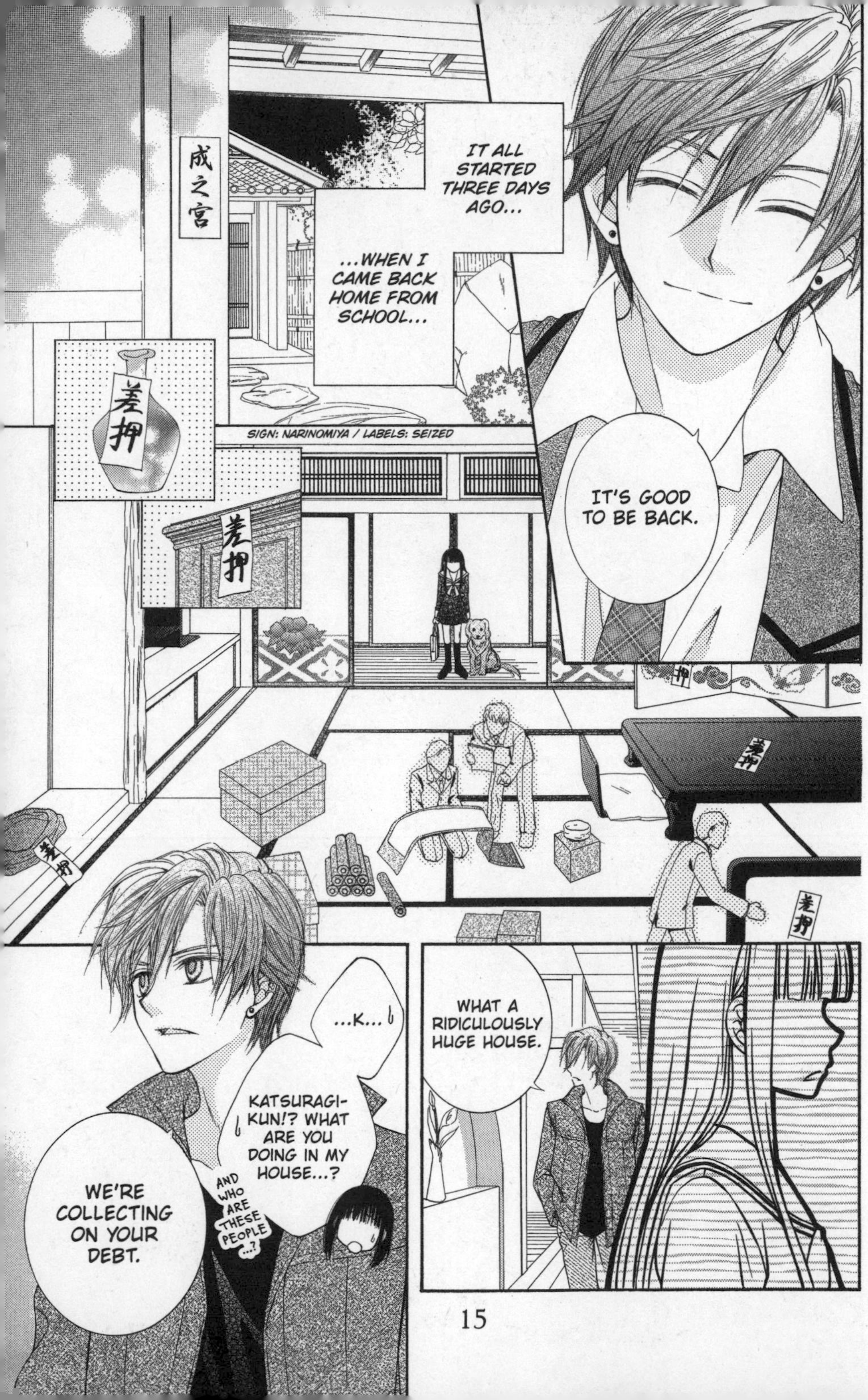
IT ALL STARTED THREE DAYS AGO...
...WHEN I CAME BACK HOME FROM SCHOOL...
IT'S GOOD TO BE BACK.
成之宮
差押
SIGN: NARINOMIYA / LABELS: SEIZED
差押
差押
差押
差押
WHAT A RIDICULOUSLY HUGE HOUSE.
...K...
KATSURAGI-KUN!? WHAT ARE YOU DOING IN MY HOUSE...?
AND WHO ARE THESE PEOPLE...?
WE'RE COLLECTING ON YOUR DEBT.

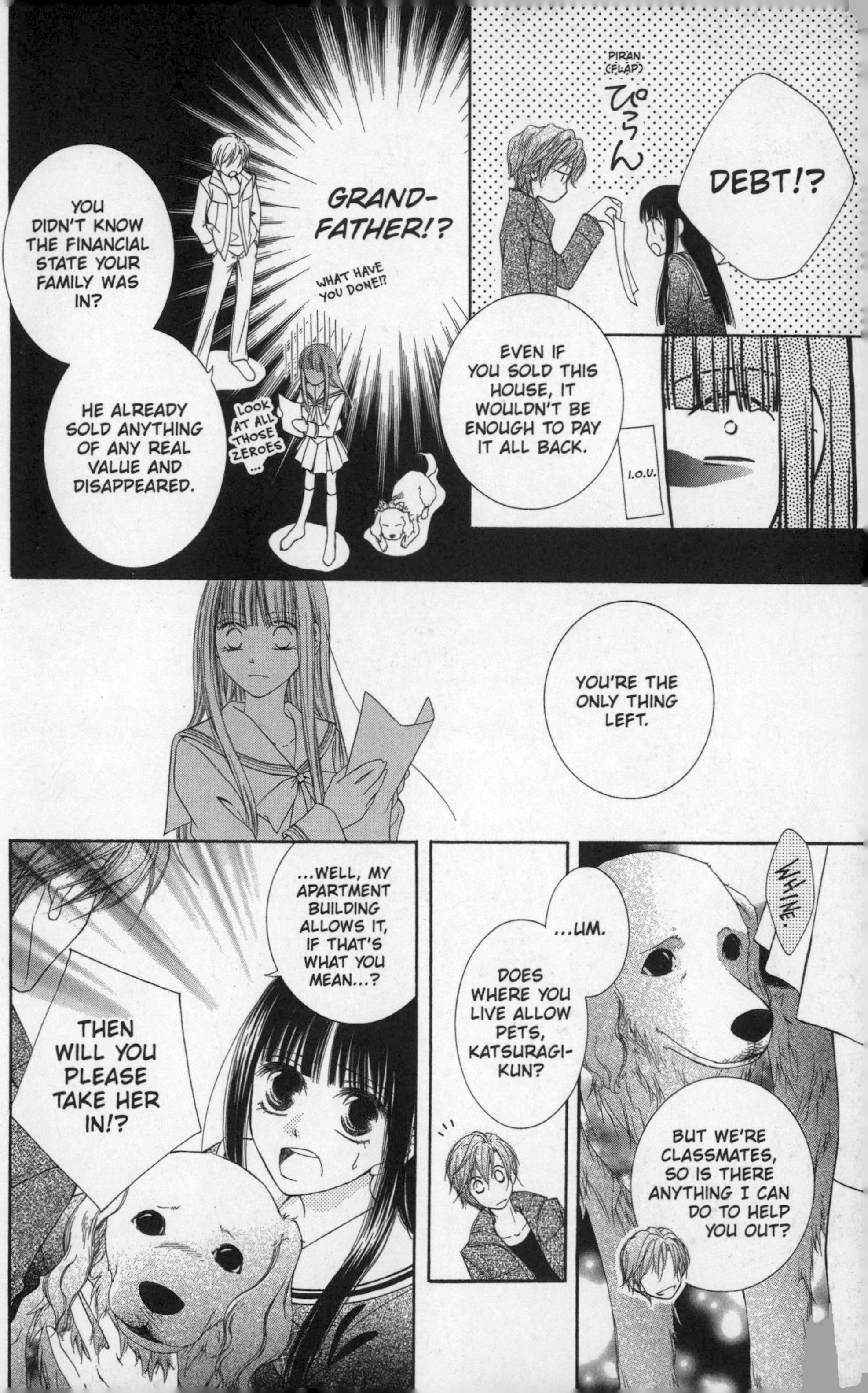
PIRAN (FLAP)
ぴらん
DEBT!?
I.O.U.
EVEN IF YOU SOLD THIS HOUSE, IT WOULDN'T BE ENOUGH TO PAY IT ALL BACK.
GRAND-FATHER!?
WHAT HAVE YOU DONE!?
YOU DIDN'T KNOW THE FINANCIAL STATE YOUR FAMILY WAS IN?
HE ALREADY SOLD ANYTHING OF ANY REAL VALUE AND DISAPPEARED.
LOOK AT ALL THOSE ZEROES...
YOU'RE THE ONLY THING LEFT.
WHINE.
BUT WE'RE CLASSMATES, SO IS THERE ANYTHING I CAN DO TO HELP YOU OUT?
...UM.
DOES WHERE YOU LIVE ALLOW PETS, KATSURAGI-KUN?
...WELL, MY APARTMENT BUILDING ALLOWS IT, IF THAT'S WHAT YOU MEAN...?
THEN WILL YOU PLEASE TAKE HER IN!?

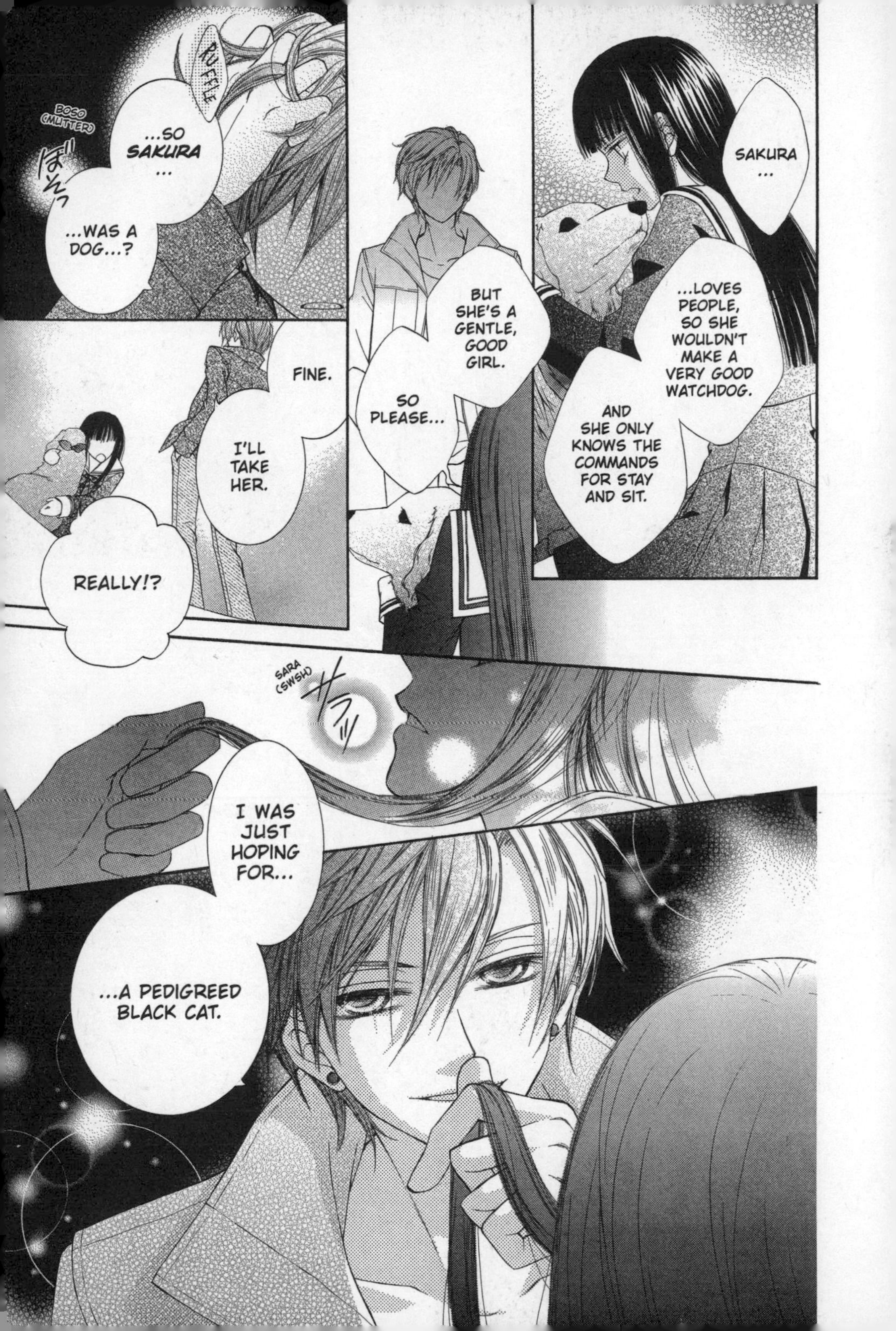
SAKURA ...
...LOVES PEOPLE, SO SHE WOULDN'T MAKE A VERY GOOD WATCHDOG.
AND SHE ONLY KNOWS THE COMMANDS FOR STAY AND SIT.
BUT SHE'S A GENTLE, GOOD GIRL.
SO PLEASE...
RUFFLE
...SO SAKURA ...
BOSO (MUTTER)
ぼそっ
...WAS A DOG...?
FINE.
I'LL TAKE HER.
REALLY!?
SARA (SWSH)
サラッ
I WAS JUST HOPING FOR...
...A PEDIGREED BLACK CAT.

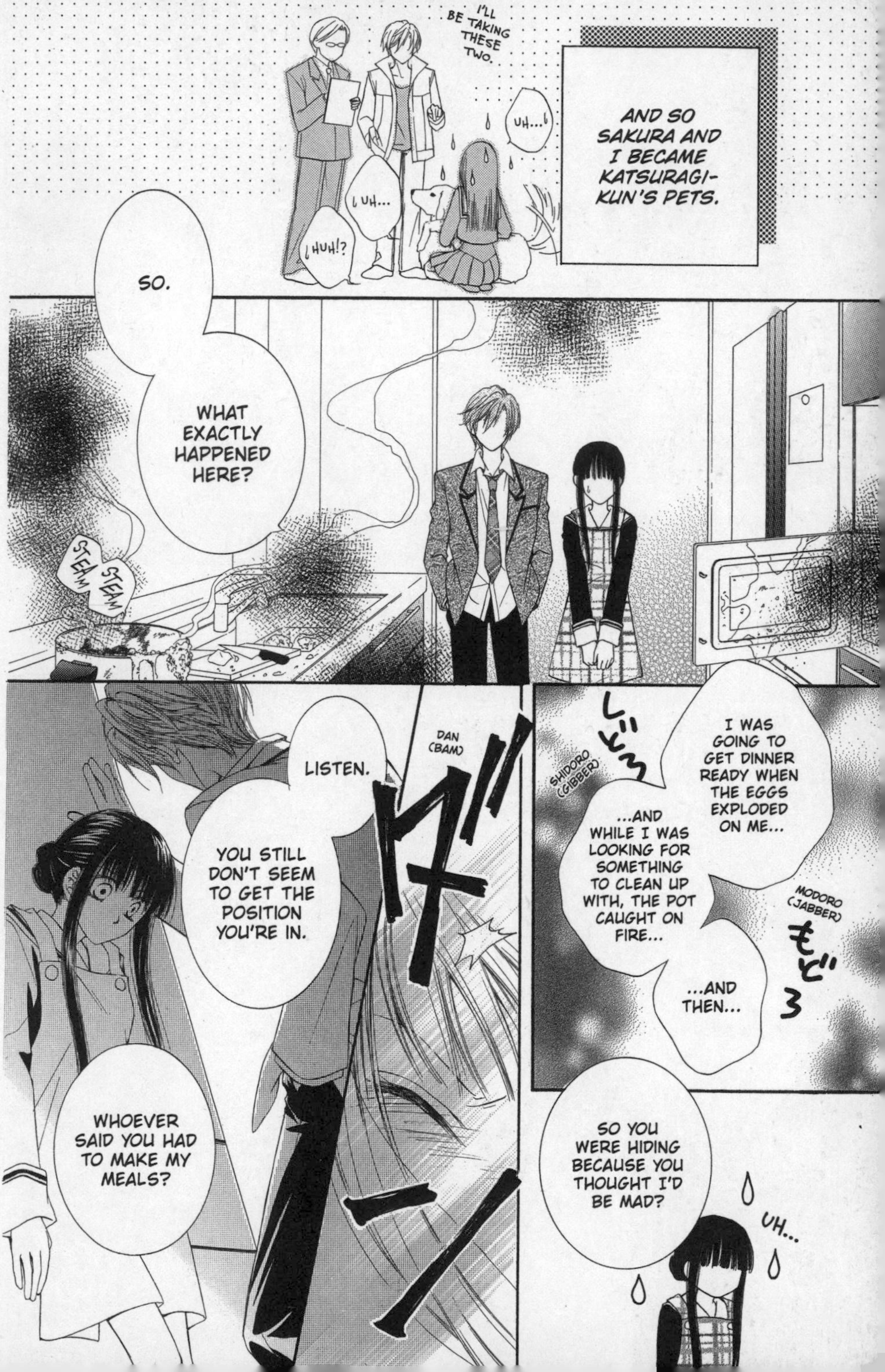
AND SO SAKURA AND I BECAME KATSURAGI-KUN'S PETS.
I'LL BE TAKING THESE TWO.
UH...!
¿ UH...
¿ HUH!?
SO.
WHAT EXACTLY HAPPENED HERE?
STEAM
STEAM
しどろ
SHIDORO (GIBBER)
I WAS GOING TO GET DINNER READY WHEN THE EGGS EXPLODED ON ME...
...AND WHILE I WAS LOOKING FOR SOMETHING TO CLEAN UP WITH, THE POT CAUGHT ON FIRE...
MODORO (JABBER)
もどろ
...AND THEN...
SO YOU WERE HIDING BECAUSE YOU THOUGHT I'D BE MAD?
UH...
DAN (BAM)
LISTEN.
YOU STILL DON'T SEEM TO GET THE POSITION YOU'RE IN.
WHOEVER SAID YOU HAD TO MAKE MY MEALS?

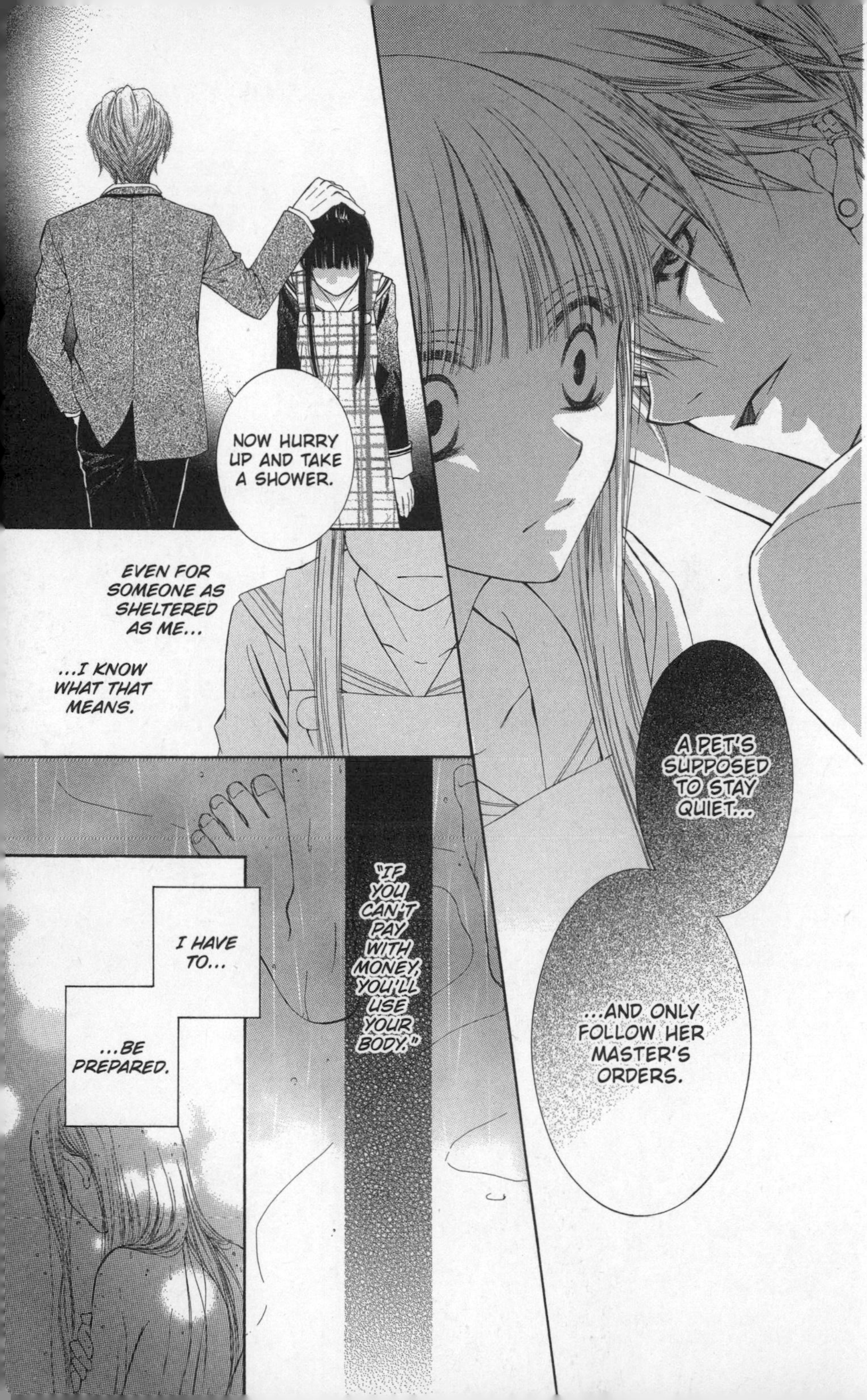
A PET'S SUPPOSED TO STAY QUIET...
...AND ONLY FOLLOW HER MASTER'S ORDERS.
NOW HURRY UP AND TAKE A SHOWER.
EVEN FOR SOMEONE AS SHELTERED AS ME...
...I KNOW WHAT THAT MEANS.
"IF YOU CAN'T PAY WITH MONEY, YOU'LL USE YOUR BODY."
I HAVE TO...
...BE PREPARED.

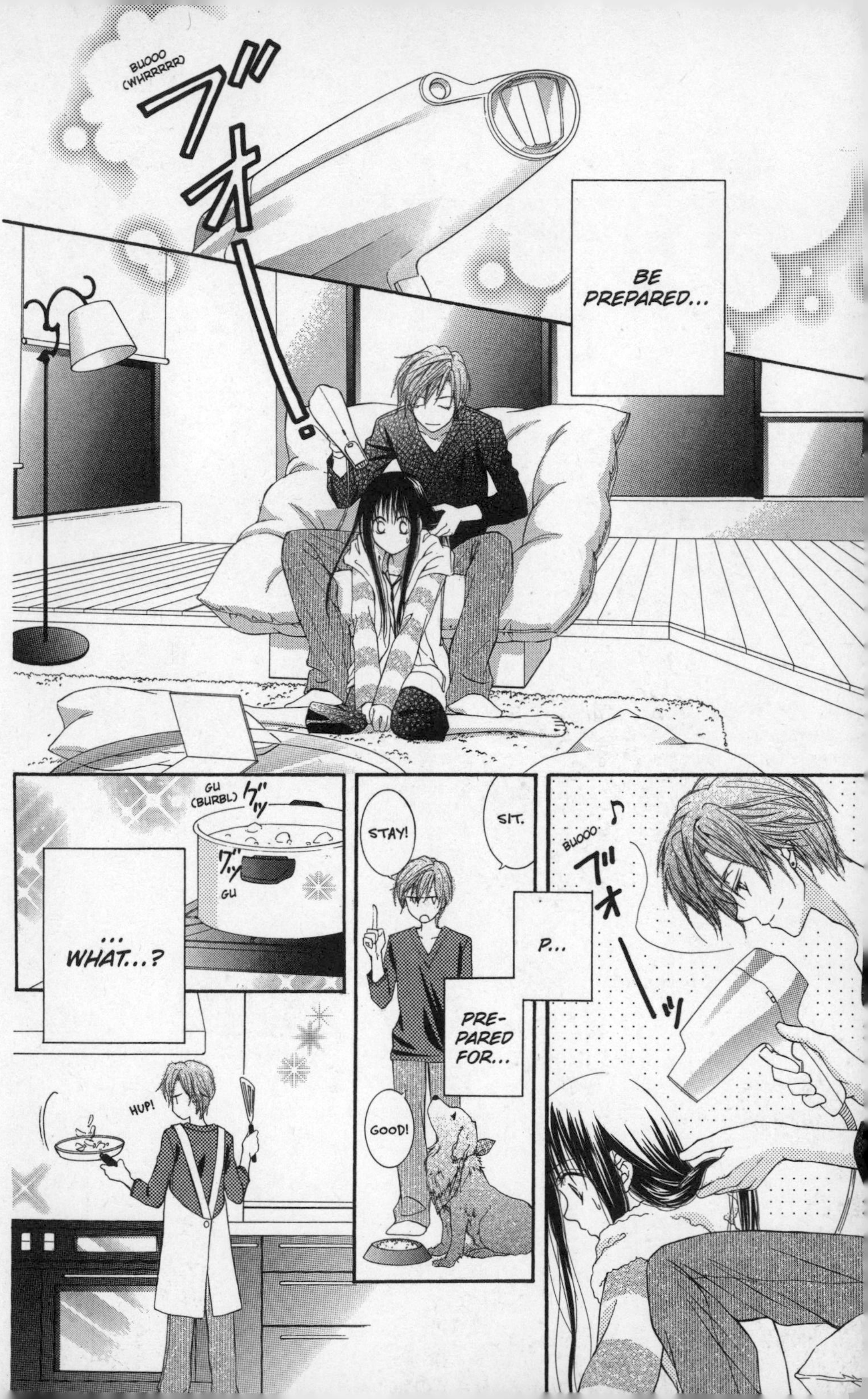
BE PREPARED...
BUOOO (WHRRRRR)
BUOOO
P...
PRE-PARED FOR...
SIT.
STAY!
GOOD!
GU (BURBL)
GU
... WHAT...?
HUP!

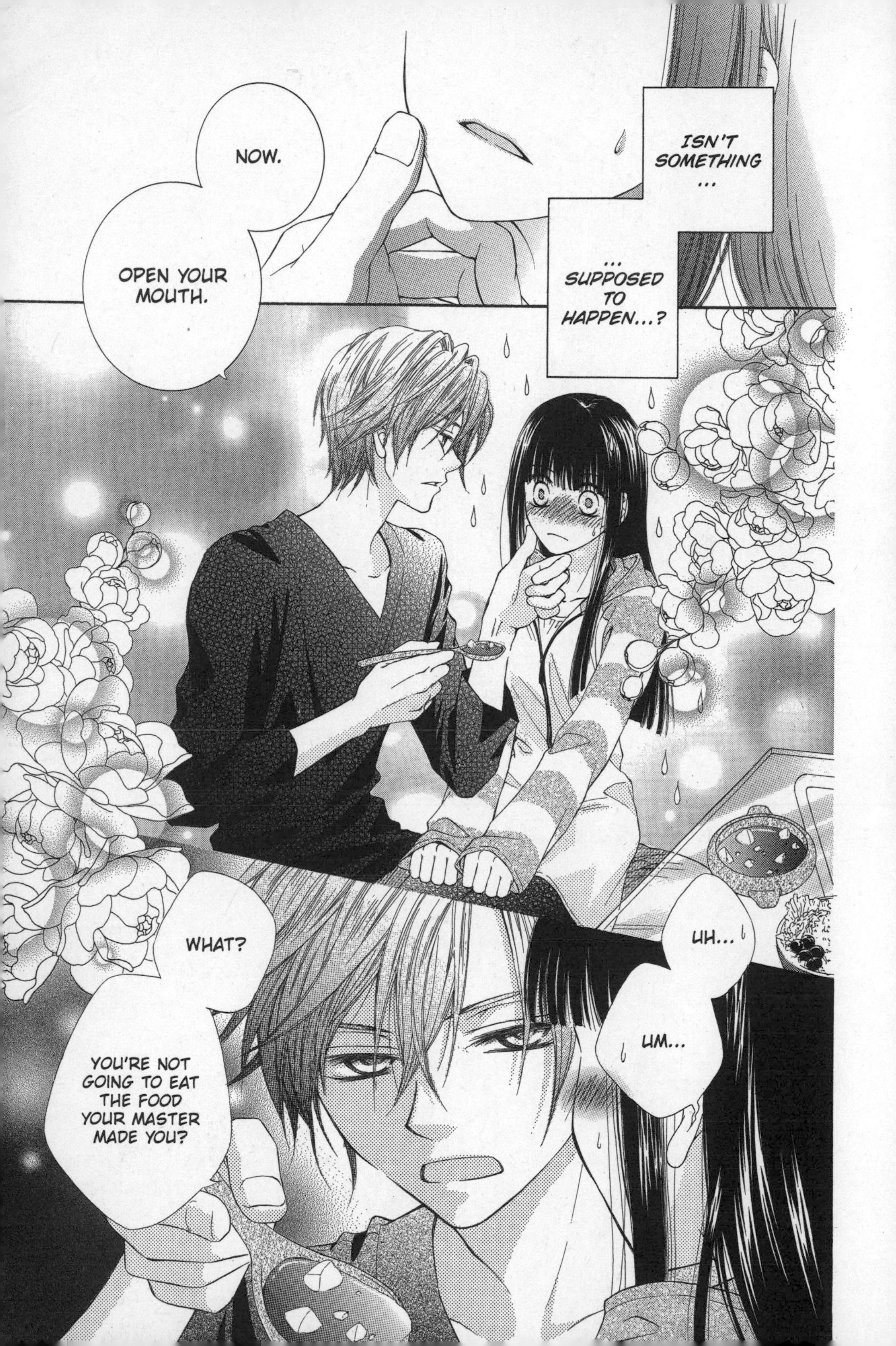
ISN'T SOMETHING ...
... SUPPOSED TO HAPPEN...?
NOW.
OPEN YOUR MOUTH.
UH...
UM...
WHAT?
YOU'RE NOT GOING TO EAT THE FOOD YOUR MASTER MADE YOU?

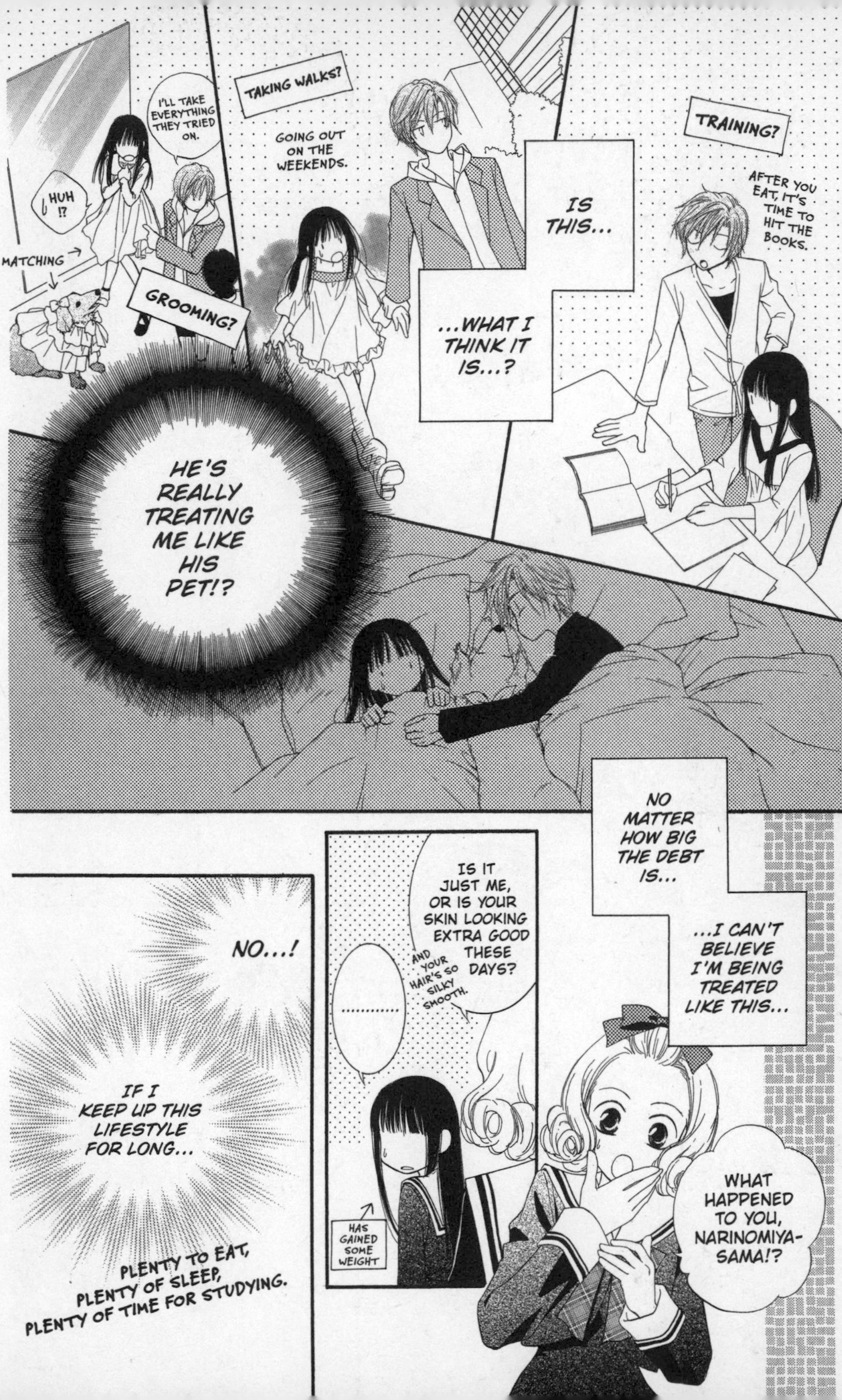
TRAINING?
AFTER YOU EAT, IT'S TIME TO HIT THE BOOKS.
IS THIS...
...WHAT I THINK IT IS...?
TAKING WALKS?
GOING OUT ON THE WEEKENDS.
GROOMING?
I'LL TAKE EVERYTHING THEY TRIED ON.
HUH !?
MATCHING
HE'S REALLY TREATING ME LIKE HIS PET!?
NO MATTER HOW BIG THE DEBT IS...
...I CAN'T BELIEVE I'M BEING TREATED LIKE THIS...
WHAT HAPPENED TO YOU, NARINOMIYA-SAMA!?
IS IT JUST ME, OR IS YOUR SKIN LOOKING EXTRA GOOD THESE DAYS?
AND YOUR HAIR'S SO SILKY SMOOTH.
....
HAS GAINED SOME WEIGHT
NO...!
IF I KEEP UP THIS LIFESTYLE FOR LONG...
PLENTY TO EAT, PLENTY OF SLEEP, PLENTY OF TIME FOR STUDYING.

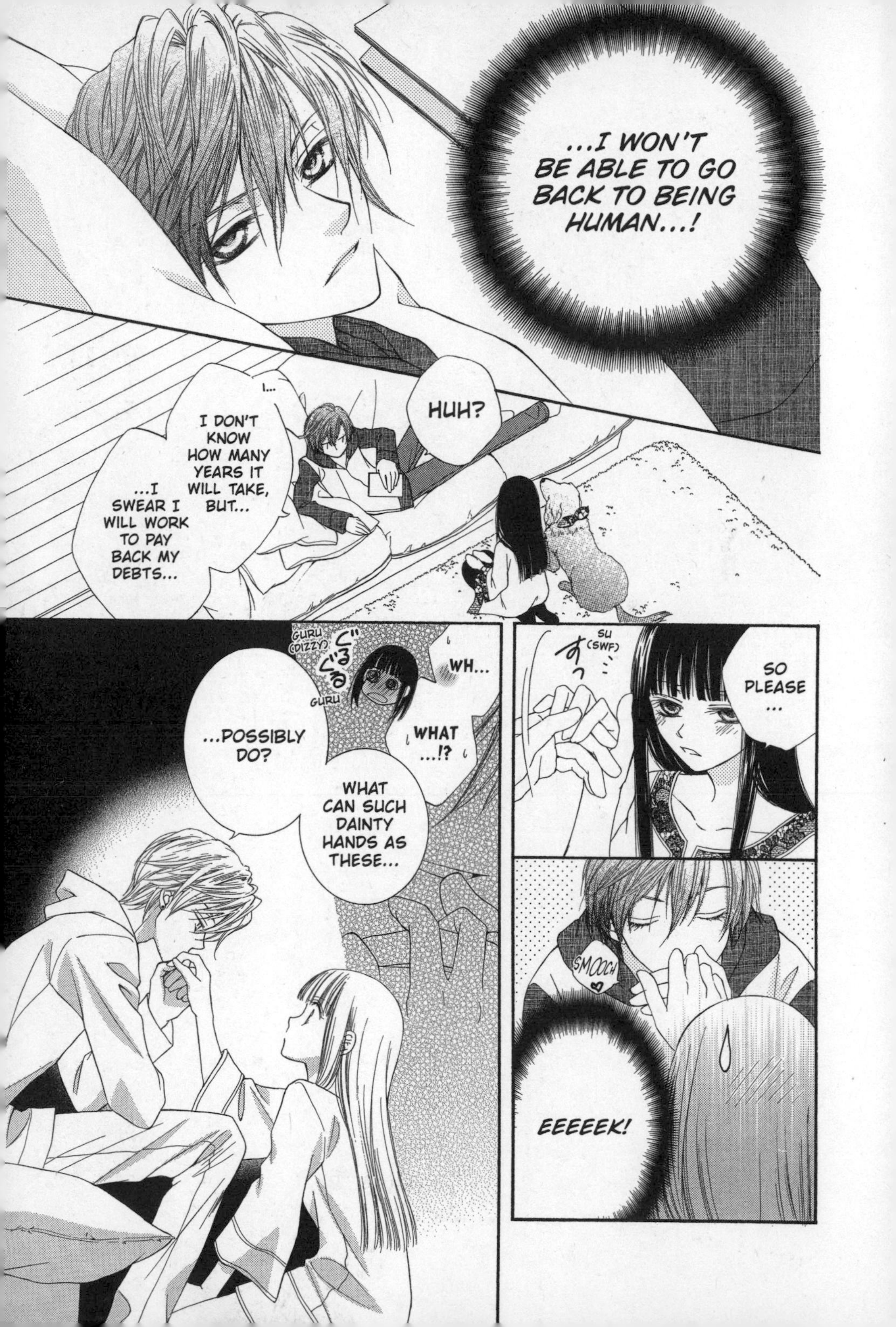
...I WON'T BE ABLE TO GO BACK TO BEING HUMAN...!
HUH?
I...
I DON'T KNOW HOW MANY YEARS IT WILL TAKE, BUT...
...I SWEAR I WILL WORK TO PAY BACK MY DEBTS...
すっ
SU (SWF)
SO PLEASE ...
SMOOCH
EEEEEK!
WH...
WHAT ...!?
ぐるぐる
GURU (DIZZY)
GURU
WHAT CAN SUCH DAINTY HANDS AS THESE...
...POSSIBLY DO?

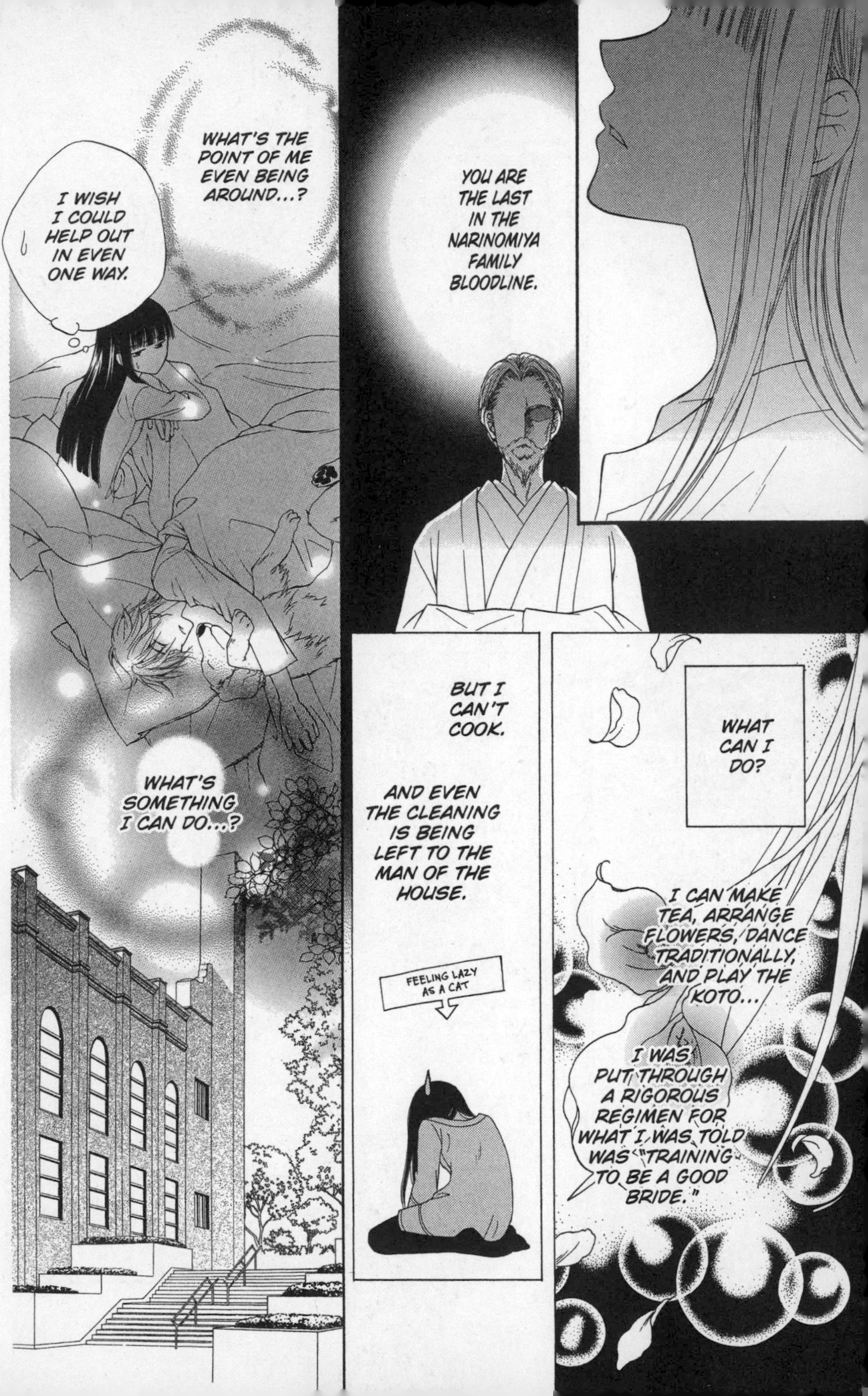
YOU ARE THE LAST IN THE NARINOMIYA FAMILY BLOODLINE.
WHAT CAN I DO?
I CAN MAKE TEA, ARRANGE FLOWERS, DANCE TRADITIONALLY, AND PLAY THE KOTO...
I WAS PUT THROUGH A RIGOROUS REGIMEN FOR WHAT I WAS TOLD WAS "TRAINING TO BE A GOOD BRIDE."
BUT I CAN'T COOK.
AND EVEN THE CLEANING IS BEING LEFT TO THE MAN OF THE HOUSE.
FEELING LAZY AS A CAT
WHAT'S THE POINT OF ME EVEN BEING AROUND...?
I WISH I COULD HELP OUT IN EVEN ONE WAY.
WHAT'S SOMETHING I CAN DO...?

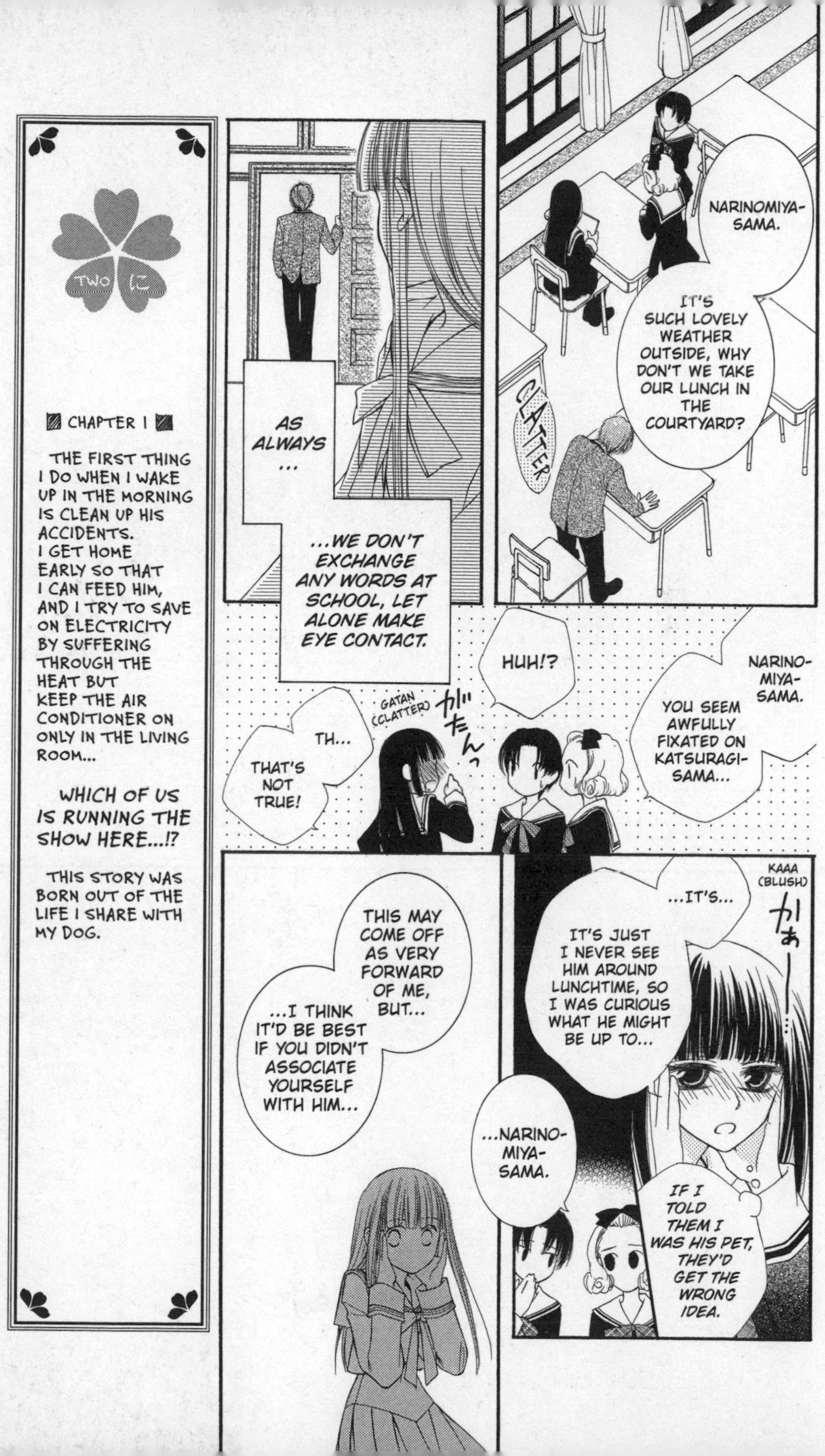
NARINOMIYA-SAMA.
IT'S SUCH LOVELY WEATHER OUTSIDE, WHY DON'T WE TAKE OUR LUNCH IN THE COURTYARD?
CLATTER
AS ALWAYS...
...WE DON'T EXCHANGE ANY WORDS AT SCHOOL, LET ALONE MAKE EYE CONTACT.
NARINOMIYA-SAMA.
YOU SEEM AWFULLY FIXATED ON KATSURAGI-SAMA...
HUH!?
GATAN (CLATTER)
TH...
THAT'S NOT TRUE!
KAAA (BLUSH)
...IT'S...
IT'S JUST I NEVER SEE HIM AROUND LUNCHTIME, SO I WAS CURIOUS WHAT HE MIGHT BE UP TO...
IF I TOLD THEM I WAS HIS PET, THEY'D GET THE WRONG IDEA.
...NARINOMIYA-SAMA.
THIS MAY COME OFF AS VERY FORWARD OF ME, BUT...
...I THINK IT'D BE BEST IF YOU DIDN'T ASSOCIATE YOURSELF WITH HIM...

TWO に

CHAPTER 1

THE FIRST THING I DO WHEN I WAKE UP IN THE MORNING IS CLEAN UP HIS ACCIDENTS. I GET HOME EARLY SO THAT I CAN FEED HIM, AND I TRY TO SAVE ON ELECTRICITY BY SUFFERING THROUGH THE HEAT BUT KEEP THE AIR CONDITIONER ON ONLY IN THE LIVING ROOM...

WHICH OF US IS RUNNING THE SHOW HERE...!?

THIS STORY WAS BORN OUT OF THE LIFE I SHARE WITH MY DOG.

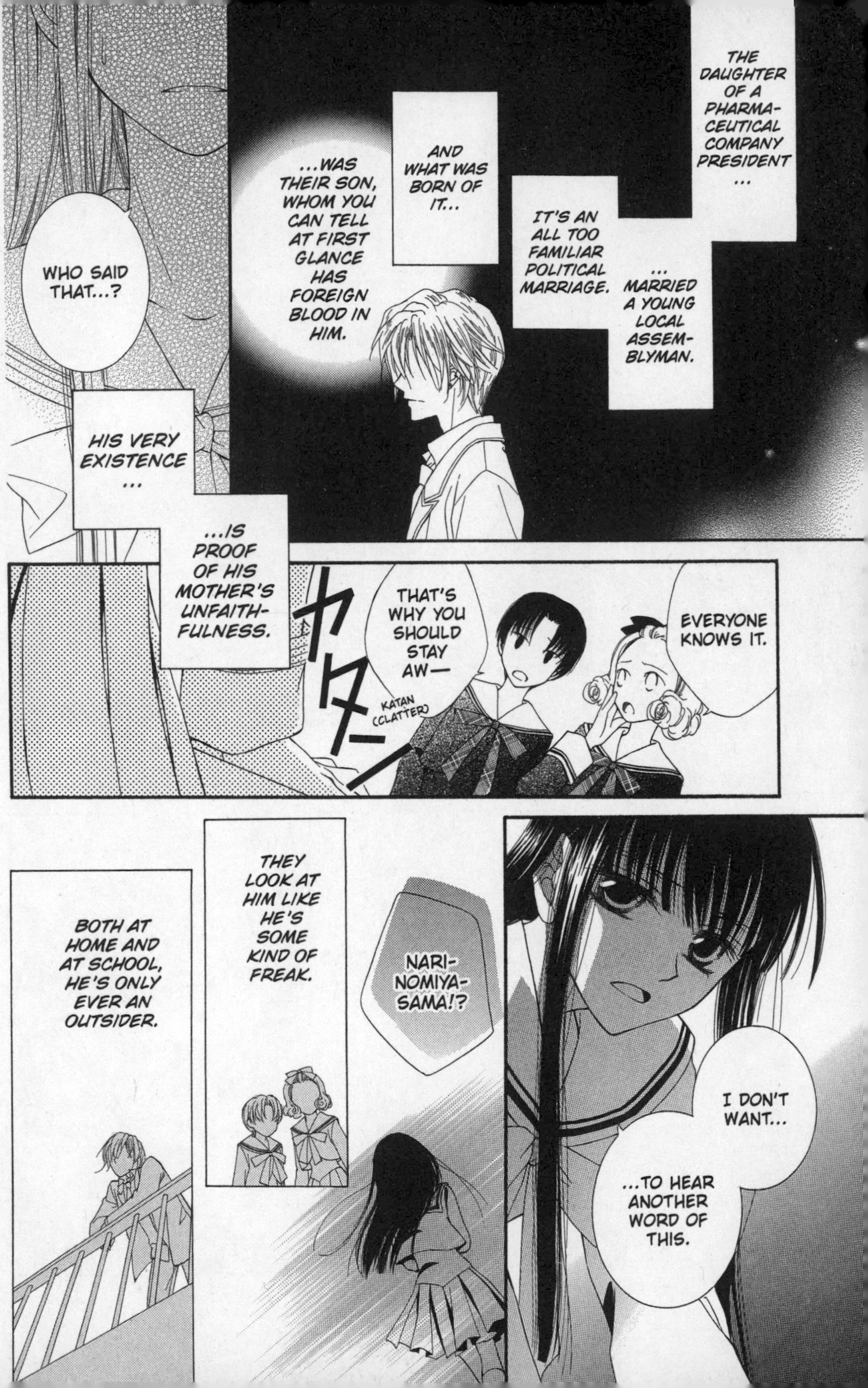
THE DAUGHTER OF A PHARMA-CEUTICAL COMPANY PRESIDENT...
...MARRIED A YOUNG LOCAL ASSEM-BLYMAN.
IT'S AN ALL TOO FAMILIAR POLITICAL MARRIAGE.
AND WHAT WAS BORN OF IT...
...WAS THEIR SON, WHOM YOU CAN TELL AT FIRST GLANCE HAS FOREIGN BLOOD IN HIM.
WHO SAID THAT...?
HIS VERY EXISTENCE...
...IS PROOF OF HIS MOTHER'S UNFAITH-FULNESS.
EVERYONE KNOWS IT.
THAT'S WHY YOU SHOULD STAY AW—
KATAN (CLATTER)
I DON'T WANT...
...TO HEAR ANOTHER WORD OF THIS.
NARI-NOMIYA-SAMA!?
THEY LOOK AT HIM LIKE HE'S SOME KIND OF FREAK.
BOTH AT HOME AND AT SCHOOL, HE'S ONLY EVER AN OUTSIDER.

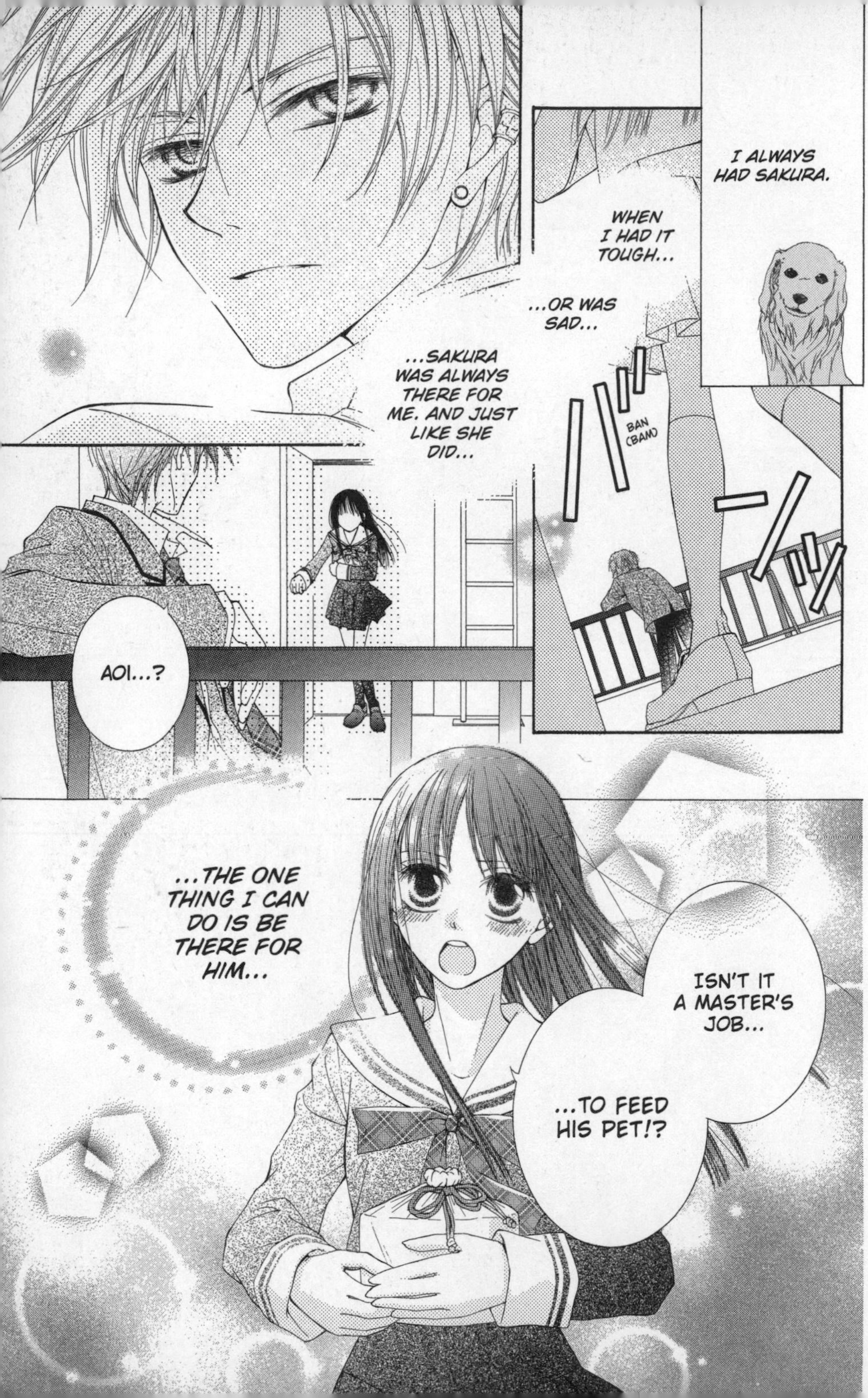
I ALWAYS HAD SAKURA.
WHEN I HAD IT TOUGH...
...OR WAS SAD...
BAN (BAM)
...SAKURA WAS ALWAYS THERE FOR ME. AND JUST LIKE SHE DID...
AOI...?
...THE ONE THING I CAN DO IS BE THERE FOR HIM...
ISN'T IT A MASTER'S JOB...
...TO FEED HIS PET!?

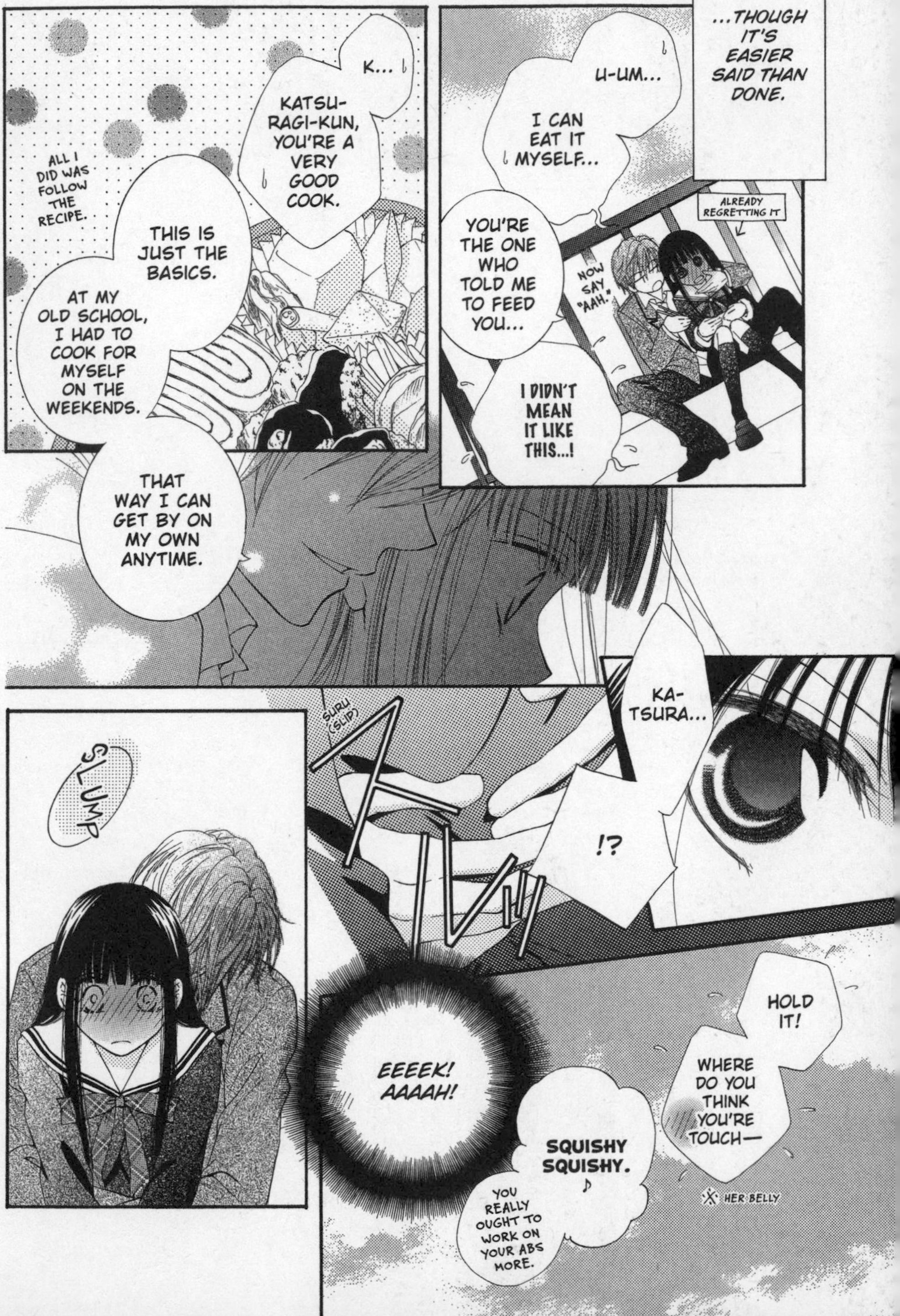
...THOUGH IT'S EASIER SAID THAN DONE.
U-UM...
I CAN EAT IT MYSELF...
ALREADY REGRETTING IT
NOW SAY "AAH."
YOU'RE THE ONE WHO TOLD ME TO FEED YOU...
I DIDN'T MEAN IT LIKE THIS...!
K...
KATSURAGI-KUN, YOU'RE A VERY GOOD COOK.
ALL I DID WAS FOLLOW THE RECIPE.
THIS IS JUST THE BASICS.
AT MY OLD SCHOOL, I HAD TO COOK FOR MYSELF ON THE WEEKENDS.
THAT WAY I CAN GET BY ON MY OWN ANYTIME.
KA-TSURA...
!?
SURU (SLIP)
HOLD IT!
WHERE DO YOU THINK YOU'RE TOUCH—
※ HER BELLY
SQUISHY SQUISHY. ♪
YOU REALLY OUGHT TO WORK ON YOUR ABS MORE.
EEEEK! AAAAH!
SLUMP

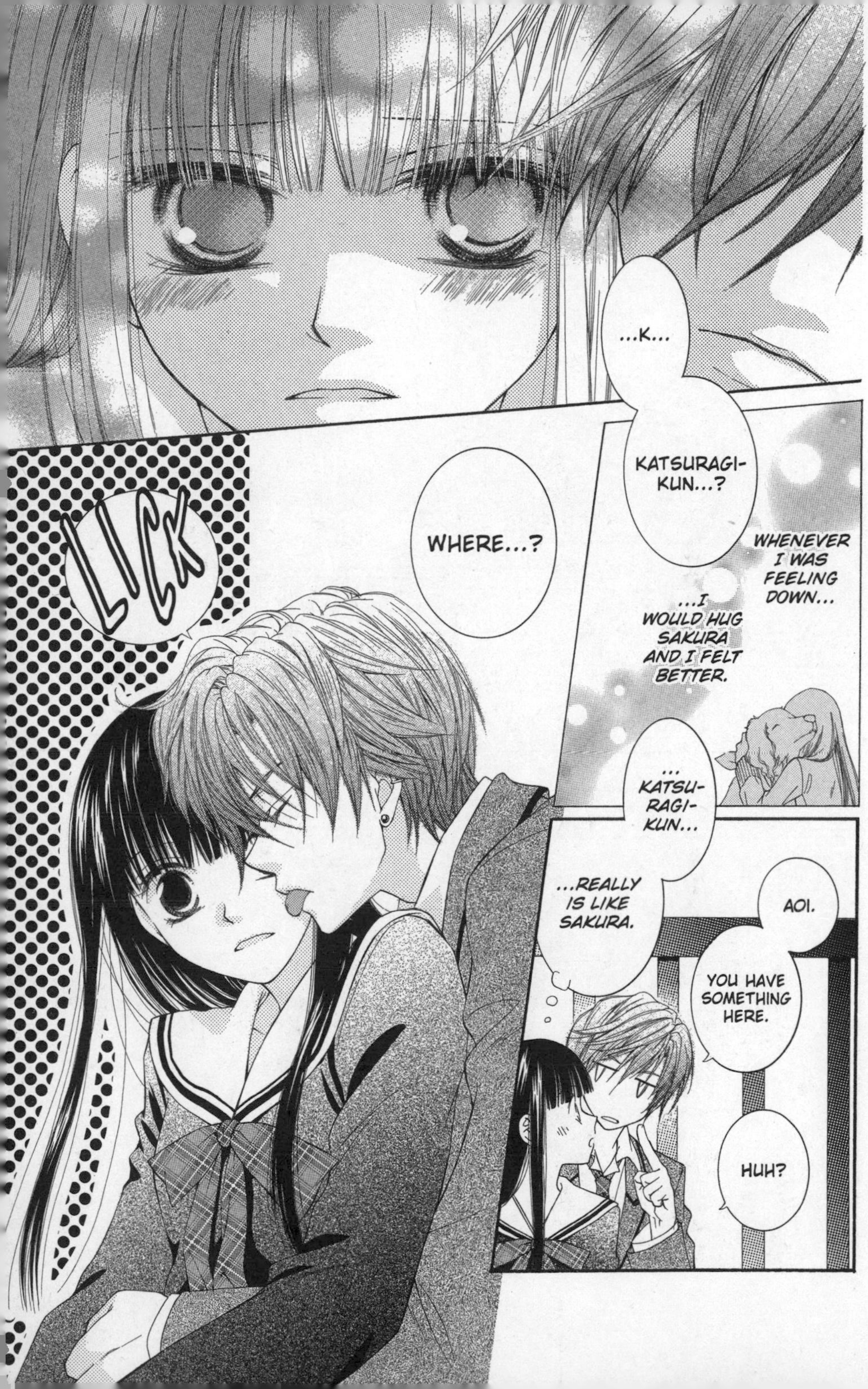
...K...
KATSURAGI-KUN...?
WHENEVER I WAS FEELING DOWN...
...I WOULD HUG SAKURA AND I FELT BETTER.
...KATSURAGI-KUN...
AOI.
...REALLY IS LIKE SAKURA.
YOU HAVE SOMETHING HERE.
HUH?
WHERE...?
LICK

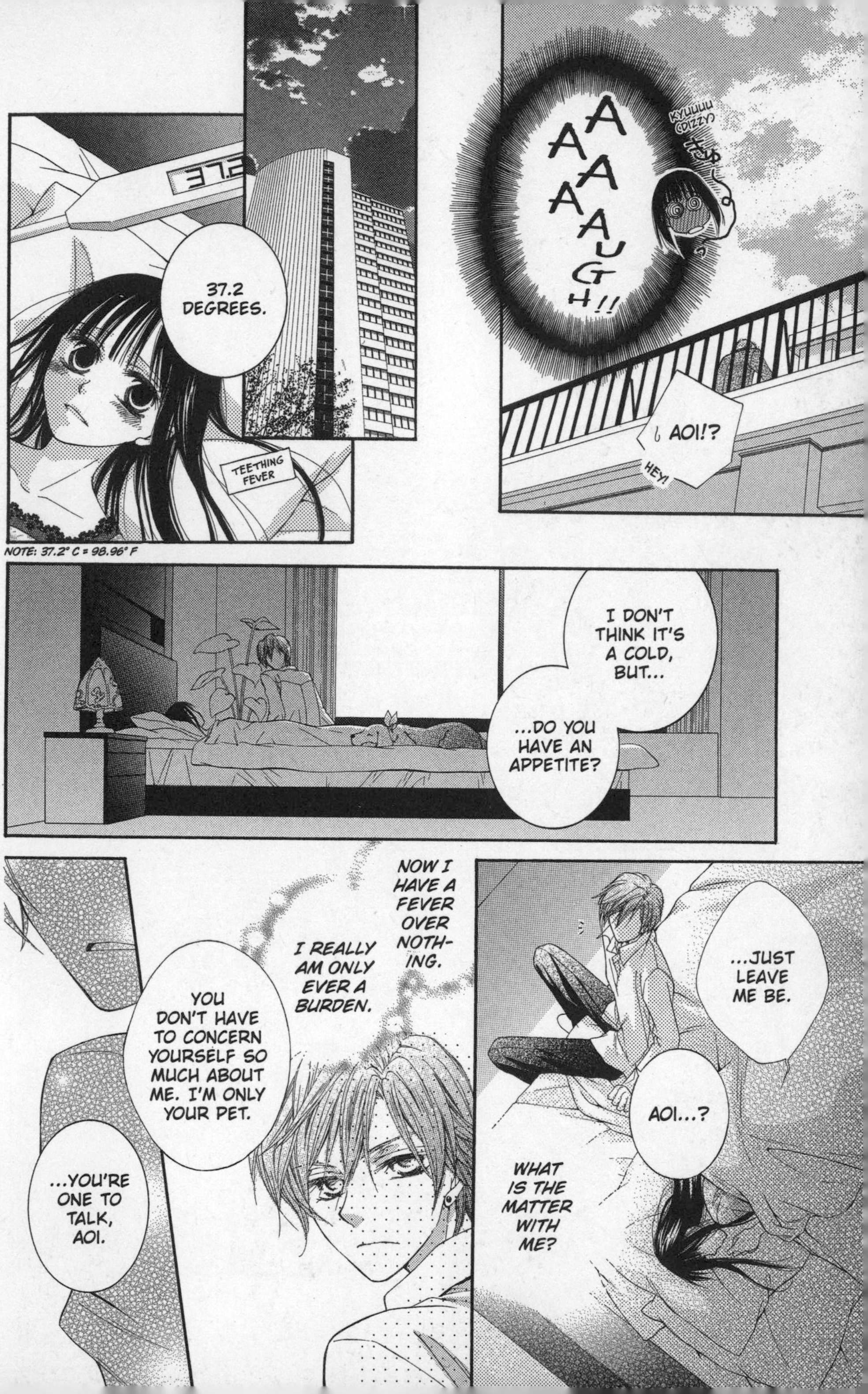
AAAAAUGH!!
KYUUUU (DIZZY)
AOI!?
HEY!
37.2 DEGREES.
TEETHING FEVER
I DON'T THINK IT'S A COLD, BUT...
...DO YOU HAVE AN APPETITE?
...JUST LEAVE ME BE.
AOI...?
WHAT IS THE MATTER WITH ME?
NOW I HAVE A FEVER OVER NOTH-ING.
I REALLY AM ONLY EVER A BURDEN.
YOU DON'T HAVE TO CONCERN YOURSELF SO MUCH ABOUT ME. I'M ONLY YOUR PET.
...YOU'RE ONE TO TALK, AOI.
NOTE: 37.2° C = 98.96° F

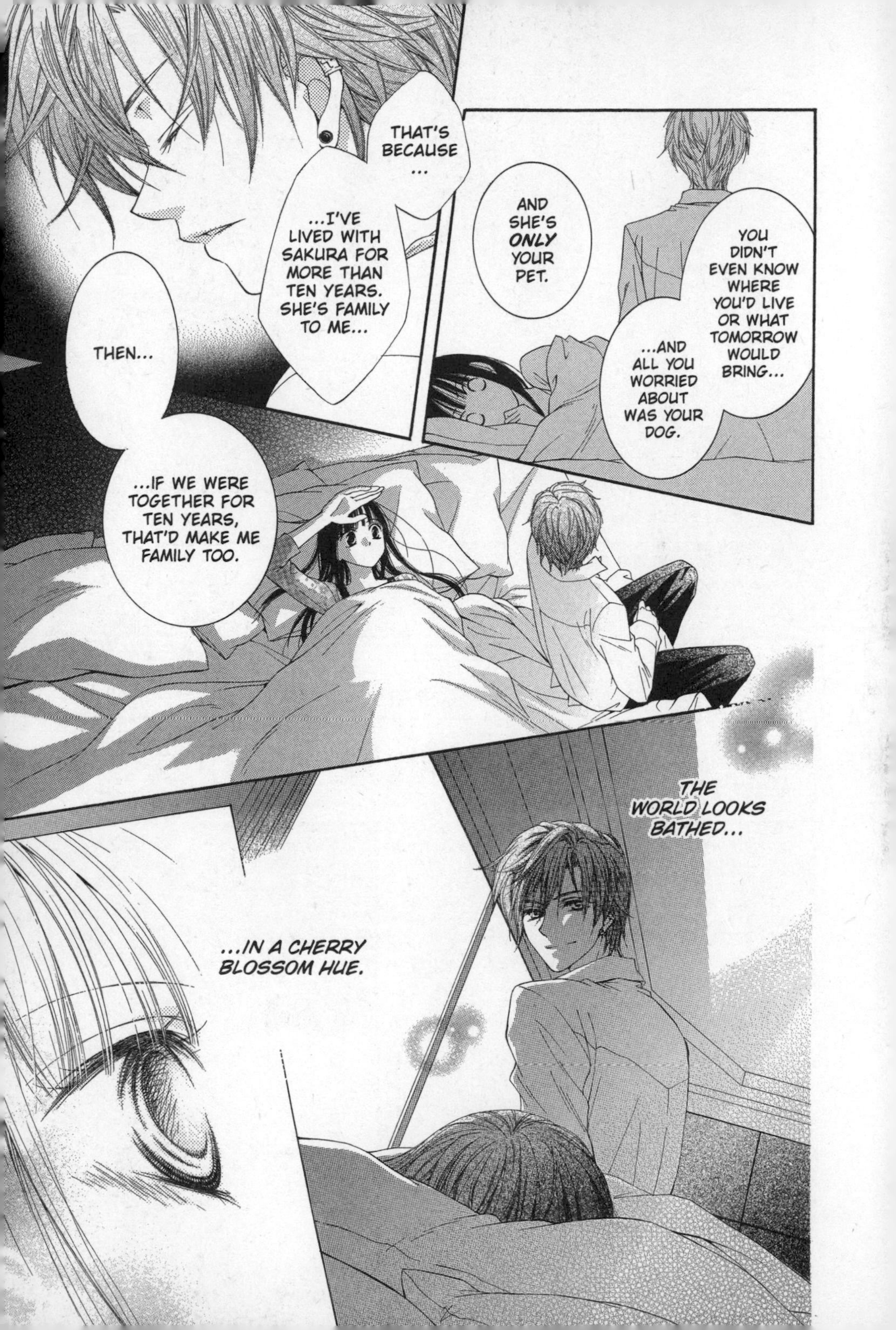
YOU DIDN'T EVEN KNOW WHERE YOU'D LIVE OR WHAT TOMORROW WOULD BRING...
...AND ALL YOU WORRIED ABOUT WAS YOUR DOG.
AND SHE'S *ONLY* YOUR PET.
THAT'S BECAUSE ...
...I'VE LIVED WITH SAKURA FOR MORE THAN TEN YEARS. SHE'S FAMILY TO ME...
THEN...
...IF WE WERE TOGETHER FOR TEN YEARS, THAT'D MAKE ME FAMILY TOO.
THE WORLD LOOKS BATHED...
...IN A CHERRY BLOSSOM HUE.

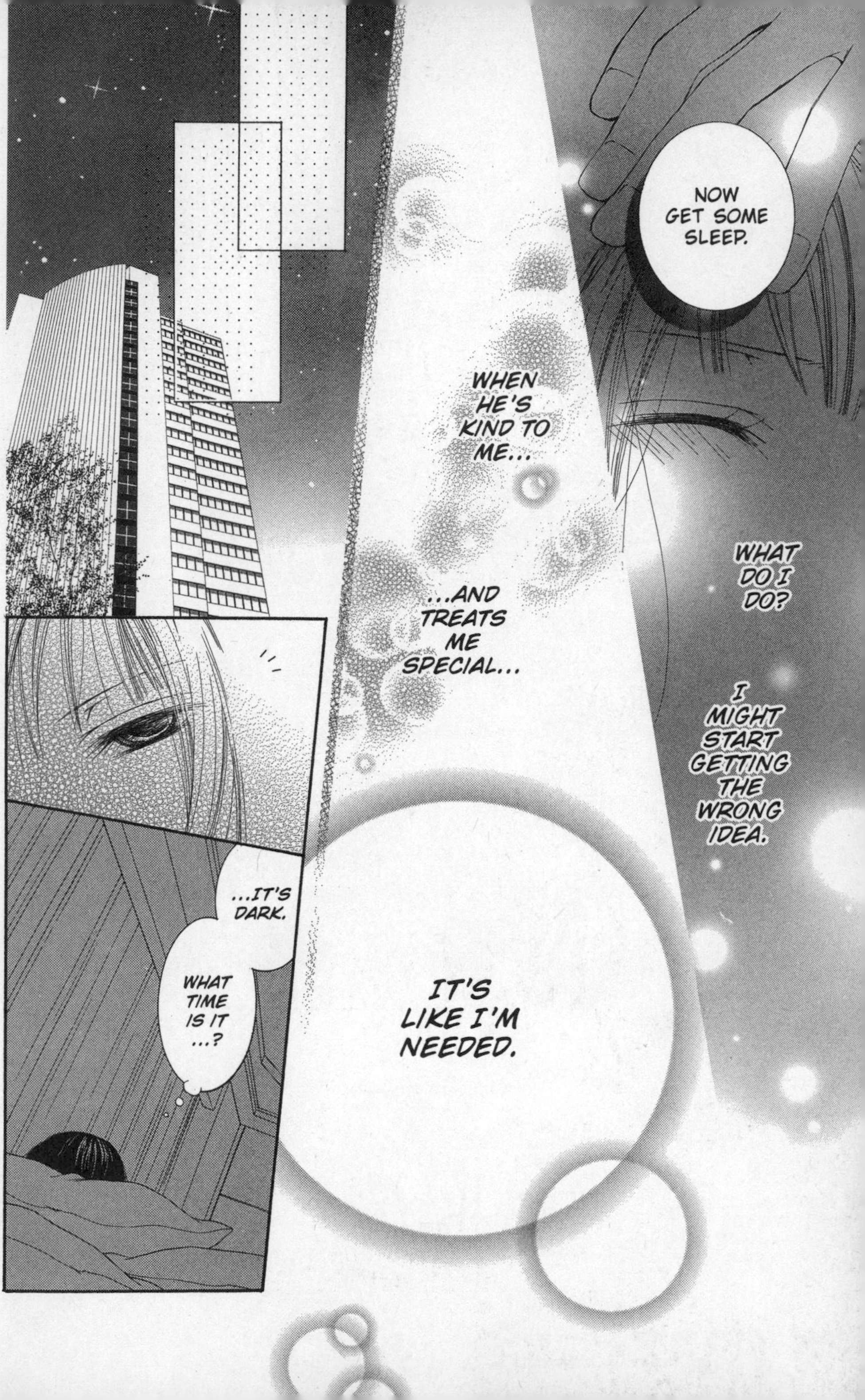
NOW GET SOME SLEEP.
WHEN HE'S KIND TO ME...
...AND TREATS ME SPECIAL...
IT'S LIKE I'M NEEDED.
WHAT DO I DO?
I MIGHT START GETTING THE WRONG IDEA.
...IT'S DARK.
WHAT TIME IS IT ...?

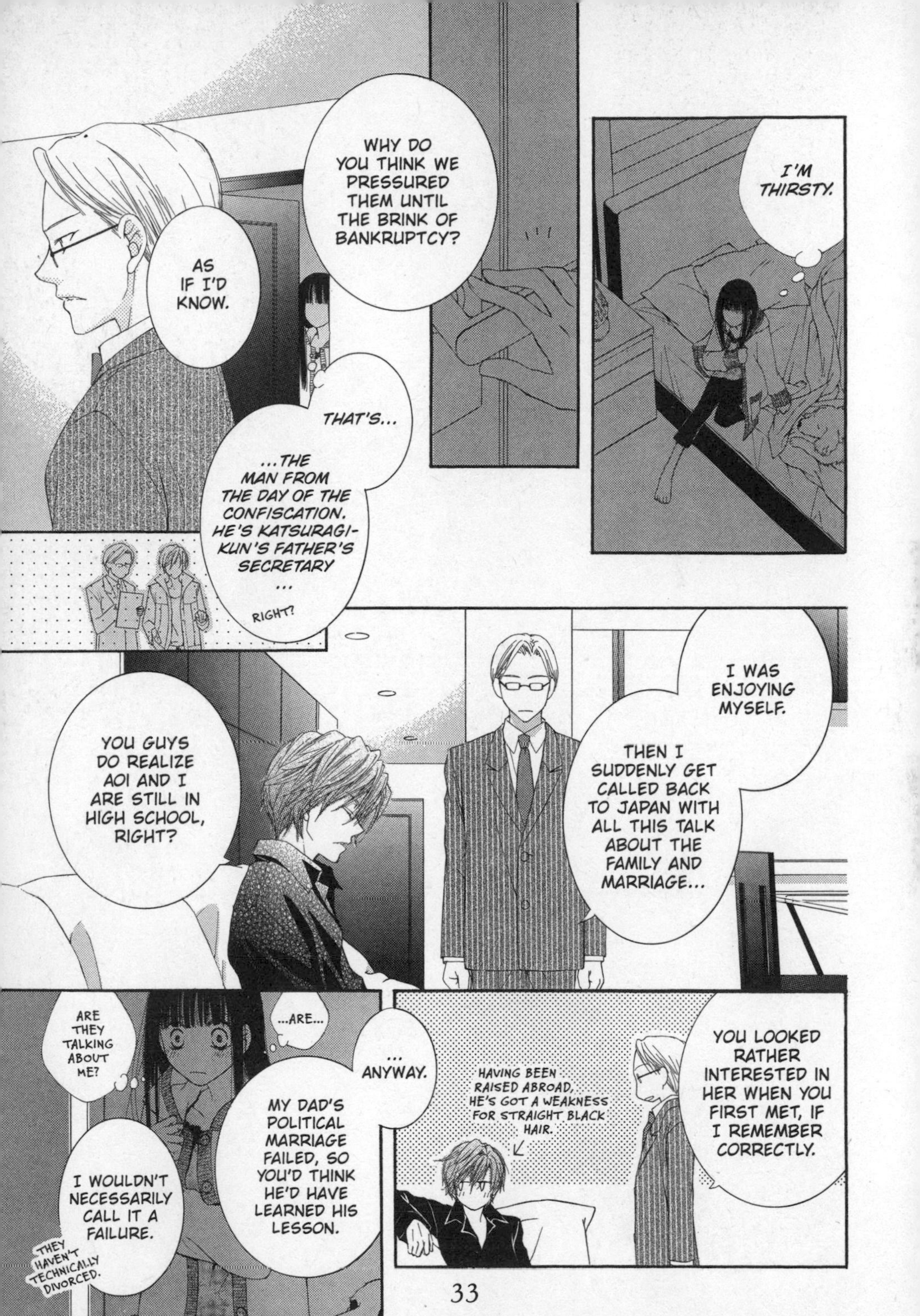
I'M THIRSTY.
WHY DO YOU THINK WE PRESSURED THEM UNTIL THE BRINK OF BANKRUPTCY?
AS IF I'D KNOW.
THAT'S...
...THE MAN FROM THE DAY OF THE CONFISCATION. HE'S KATSURAGI-KUN'S FATHER'S SECRETARY...
RIGHT?
I WAS ENJOYING MYSELF.
THEN I SUDDENLY GET CALLED BACK TO JAPAN WITH ALL THIS TALK ABOUT THE FAMILY AND MARRIAGE...
YOU GUYS DO REALIZE AOI AND I ARE STILL IN HIGH SCHOOL, RIGHT?
YOU LOOKED RATHER INTERESTED IN HER WHEN YOU FIRST MET, IF I REMEMBER CORRECTLY.
HAVING BEEN RAISED ABROAD, HE'S GOT A WEAKNESS FOR STRAIGHT BLACK HAIR.
...ANYWAY.
...ARE...
ARE THEY TALKING ABOUT ME?
MY DAD'S POLITICAL MARRIAGE FAILED, SO YOU'D THINK HE'D HAVE LEARNED HIS LESSON.
I WOULDN'T NECESSARILY CALL IT A FAILURE.
THEY HAVEN'T TECHNICALLY DIVORCED.

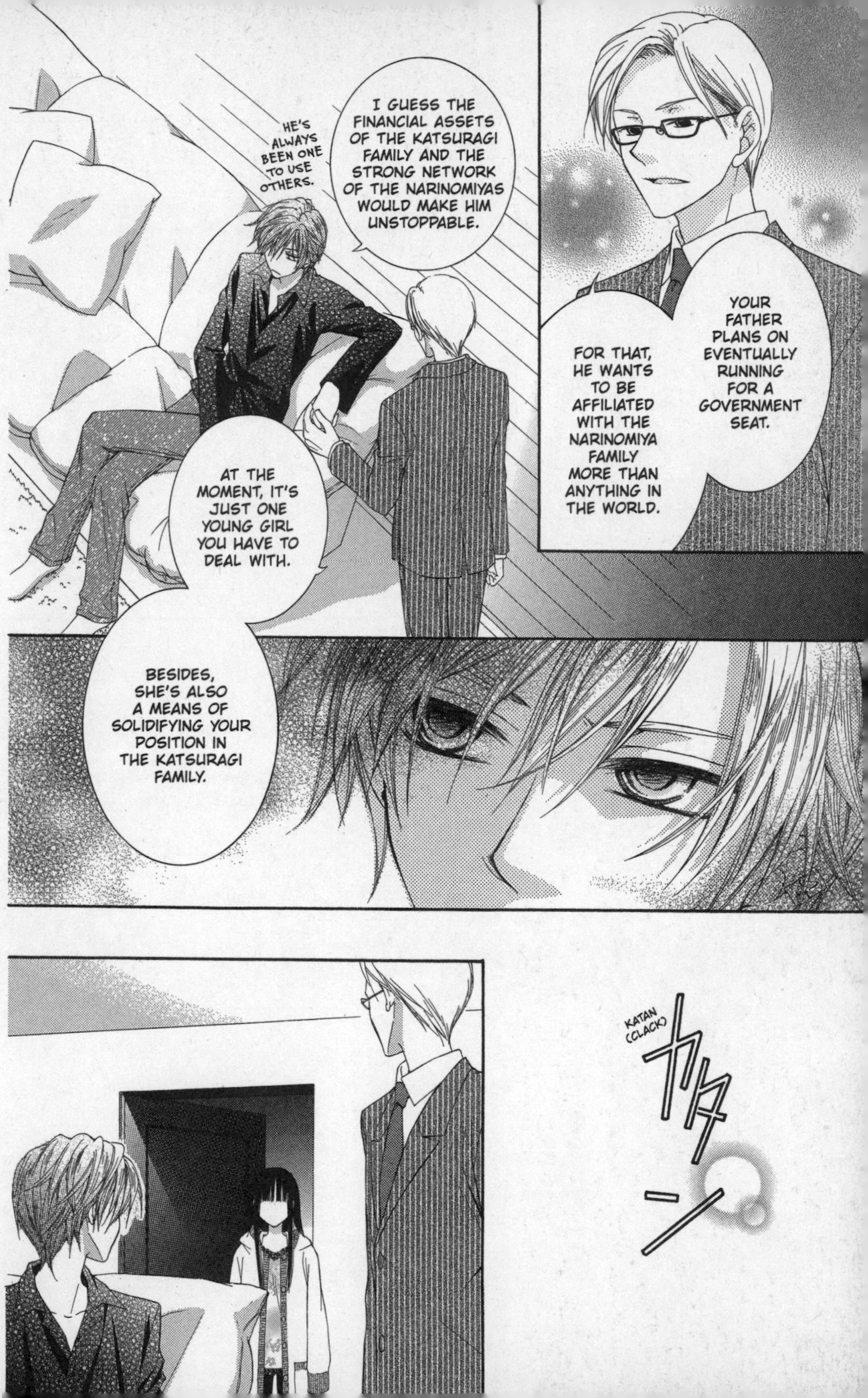
YOUR FATHER PLANS ON EVENTUALLY RUNNING FOR A GOVERNMENT SEAT.
FOR THAT, HE WANTS TO BE AFFILIATED WITH THE NARINOMIYA FAMILY MORE THAN ANYTHING IN THE WORLD.
I GUESS THE FINANCIAL ASSETS OF THE KATSURAGI FAMILY AND THE STRONG NETWORK OF THE NARINOMIYAS WOULD MAKE HIM UNSTOPPABLE.
HE'S ALWAYS BEEN ONE TO USE OTHERS.
AT THE MOMENT, IT'S JUST ONE YOUNG GIRL YOU HAVE TO DEAL WITH.
BESIDES, SHE'S ALSO A MEANS OF SOLIDIFYING YOUR POSITION IN THE KATSURAGI FAMILY.
KATAN (CLACK)

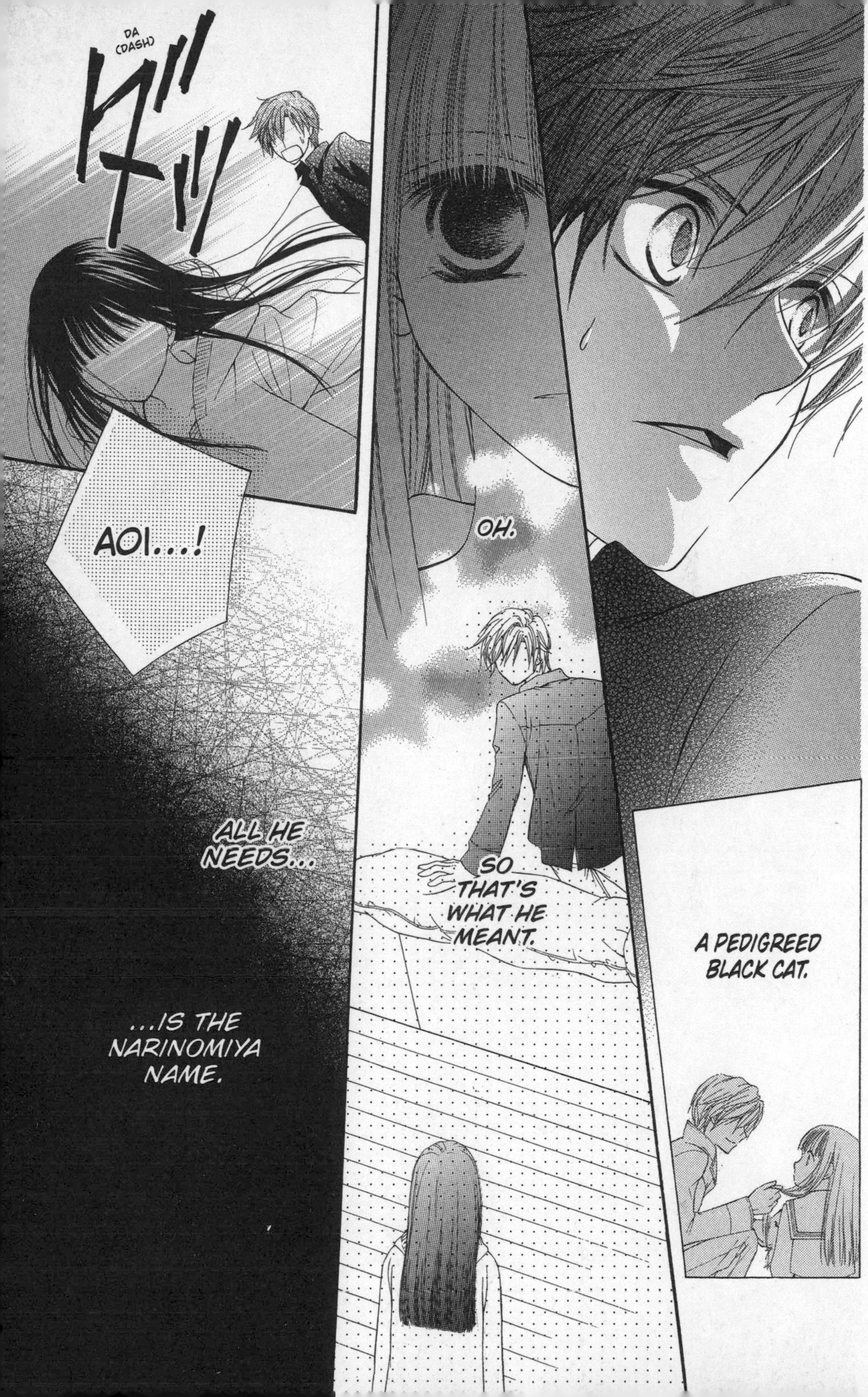
A PEDIGREED BLACK CAT.
OH.
SO THAT'S WHAT HE MEANT.
DA (DASH)
AOI...!
ALL HE NEEDS...
...IS THE NARINOMIYA NAME.

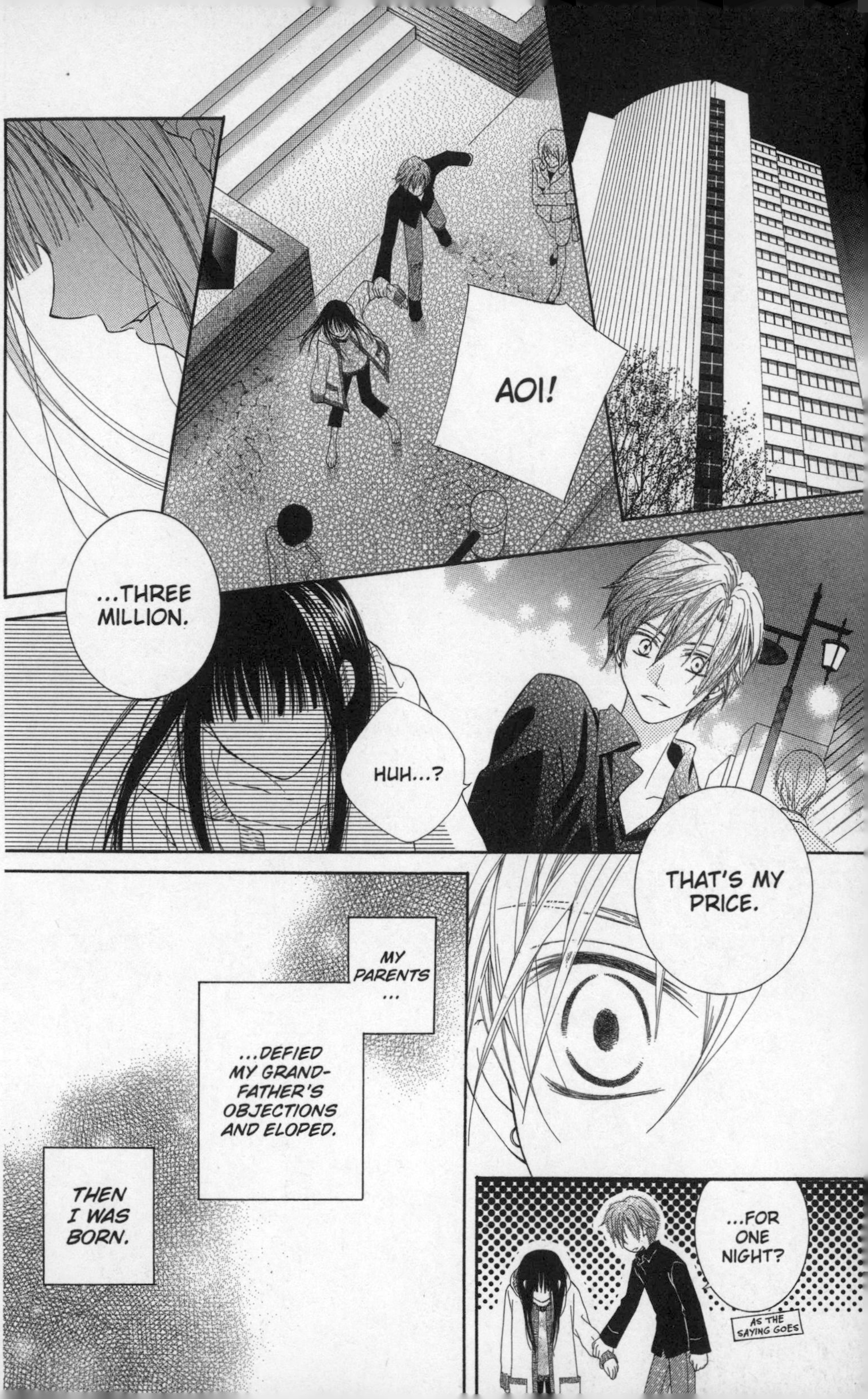
AOI!
...THREE MILLION.
HUH...?
THAT'S MY PRICE.
...FOR ONE NIGHT?
AS THE SAYING GOES
MY PARENTS ...
...DEFIED MY GRAND-FATHER'S OBJECTIONS AND ELOPED.
THEN I WAS BORN.

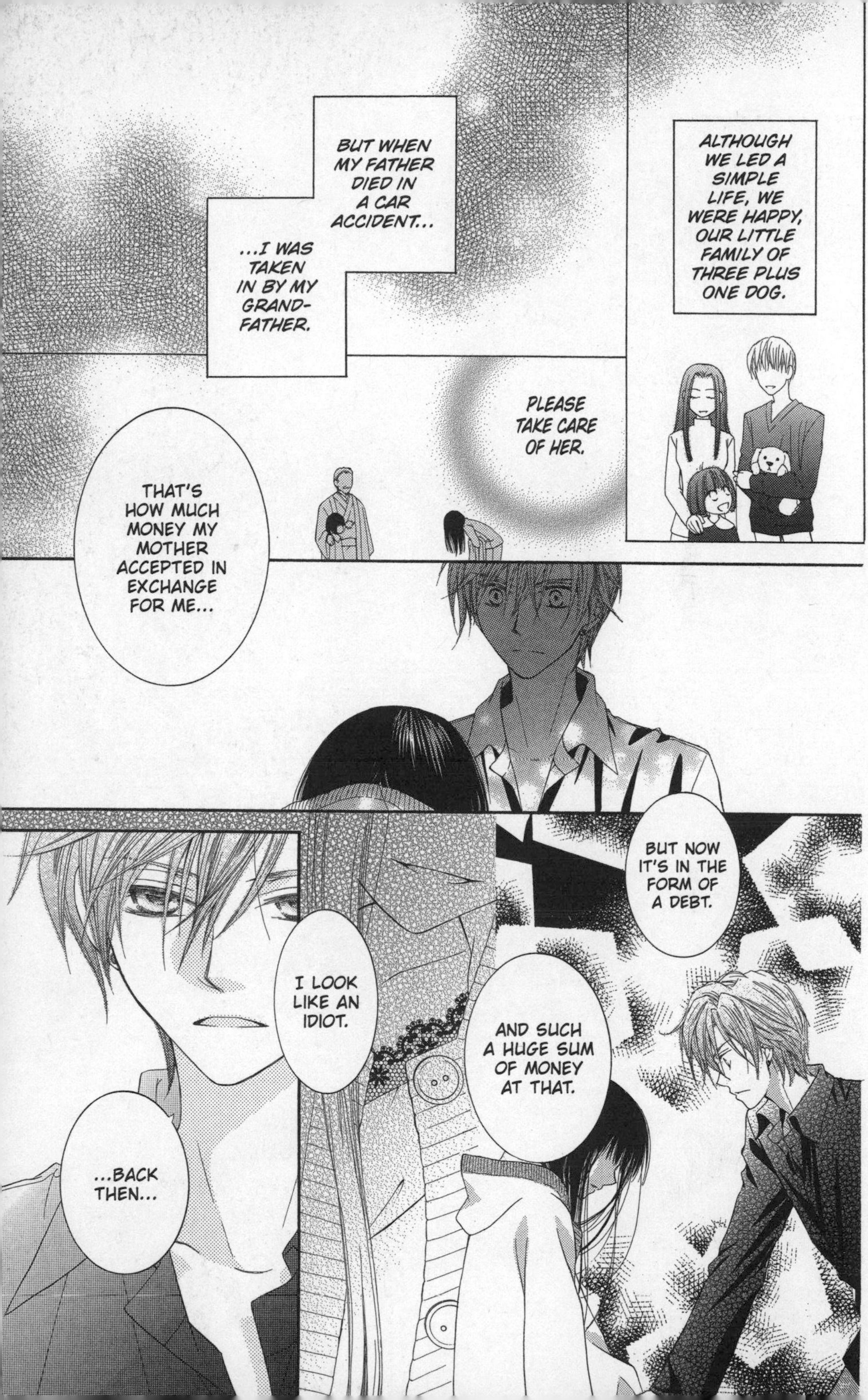
ALTHOUGH WE LED A SIMPLE LIFE, WE WERE HAPPY, OUR LITTLE FAMILY OF THREE PLUS ONE DOG.
BUT WHEN MY FATHER DIED IN A CAR ACCIDENT...
...I WAS TAKEN IN BY MY GRAND-FATHER.
PLEASE TAKE CARE OF HER.
THAT'S HOW MUCH MONEY MY MOTHER ACCEPTED IN EXCHANGE FOR ME...
BUT NOW IT'S IN THE FORM OF A DEBT.
AND SUCH A HUGE SUM OF MONEY AT THAT.
I LOOK LIKE AN IDIOT.
...BACK THEN...

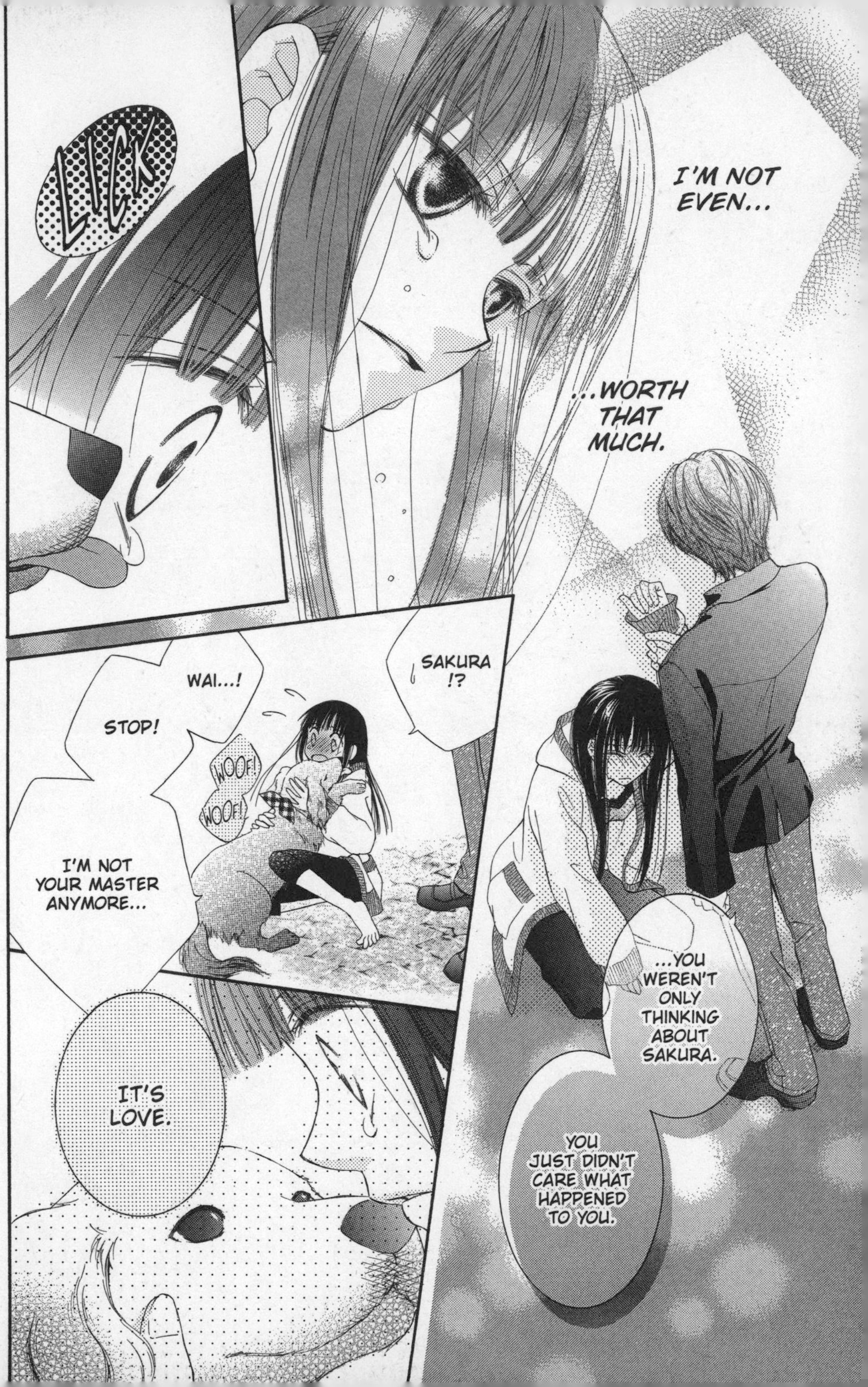
I'M NOT EVEN...
...WORTH THAT MUCH.
LICK
SAKURA !?
WAI...!
STOP!
I'M NOT YOUR MASTER ANYMORE...
IT'S LOVE.
...YOU WEREN'T ONLY THINKING ABOUT SAKURA.
YOU JUST DIDN'T CARE WHAT HAPPENED TO YOU.

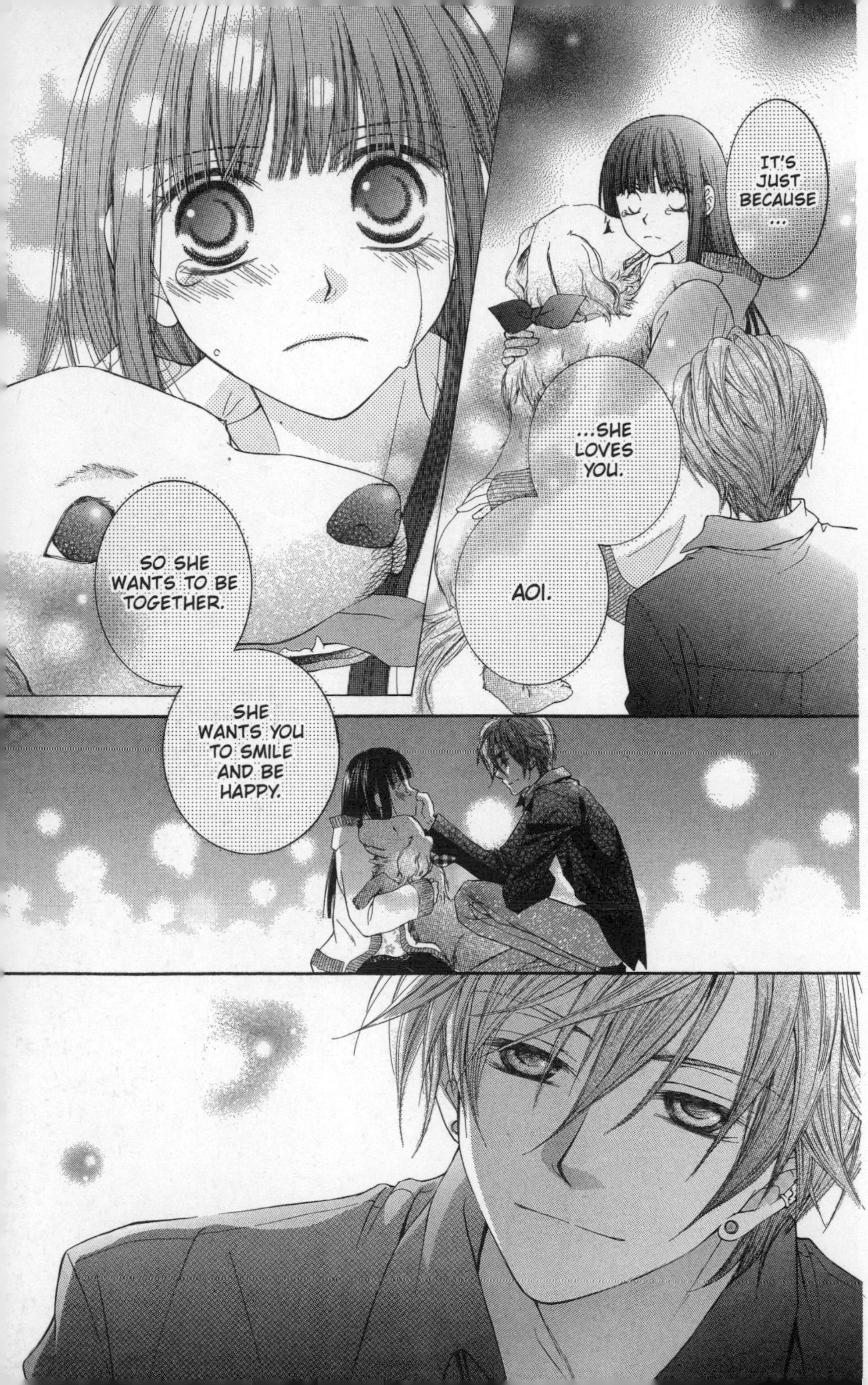
IT'S JUST BECAUSE ...
...SHE LOVES YOU.
AOI.
SO SHE WANTS TO BE TOGETHER.
SHE WANTS YOU TO SMILE AND BE HAPPY.

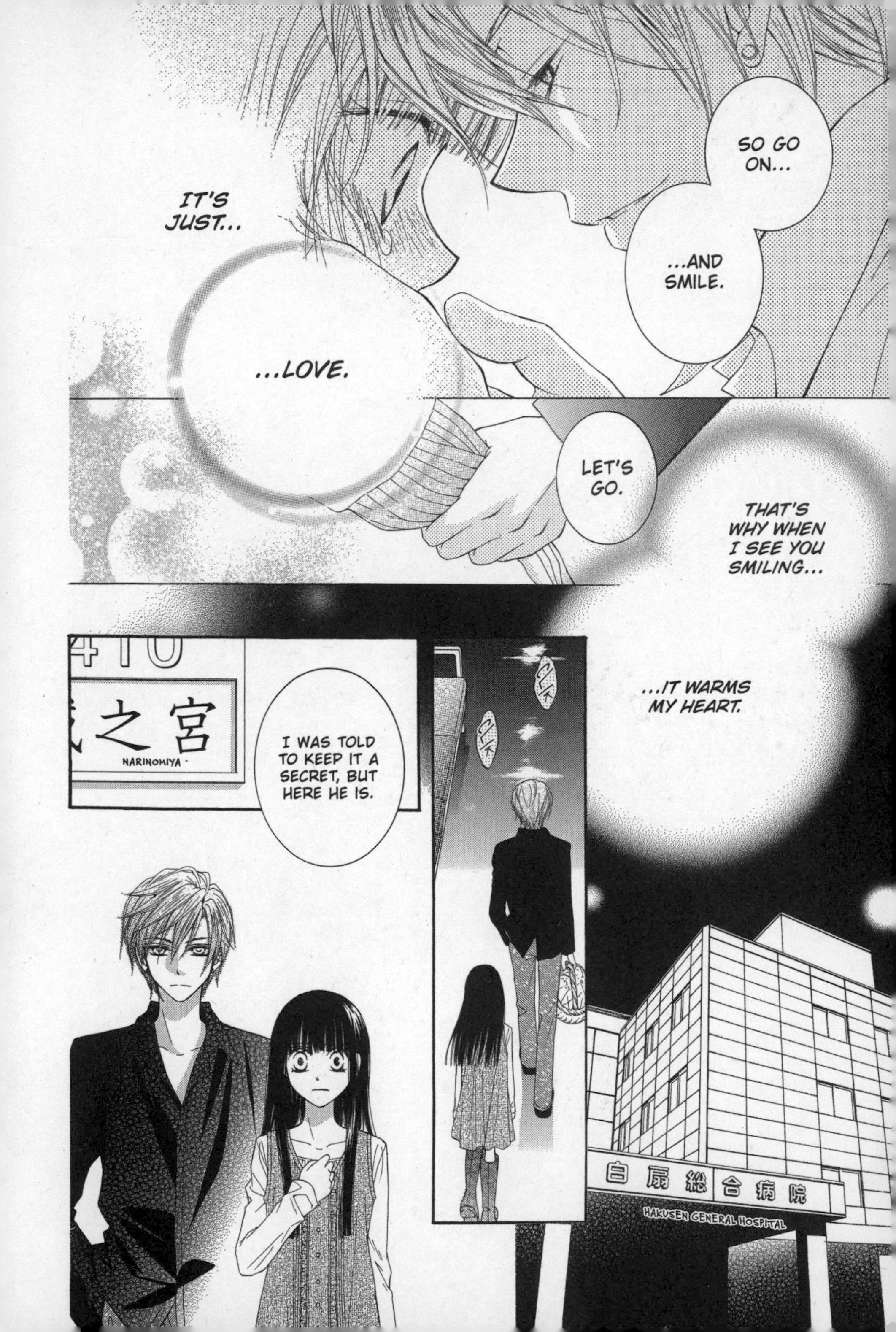
SO GO ON...
...AND SMILE.
IT'S JUST...
...LOVE.
LET'S GO.
THAT'S WHY WHEN I SEE YOU SMILING...
...IT WARMS MY HEART.
白扇総合病院
HAKUSEN GENERAL HOSPITAL
CLK
CLK
410
之宮
NARINOMIYA
I WAS TOLD TO KEEP IT A SECRET, BUT HERE HE IS.

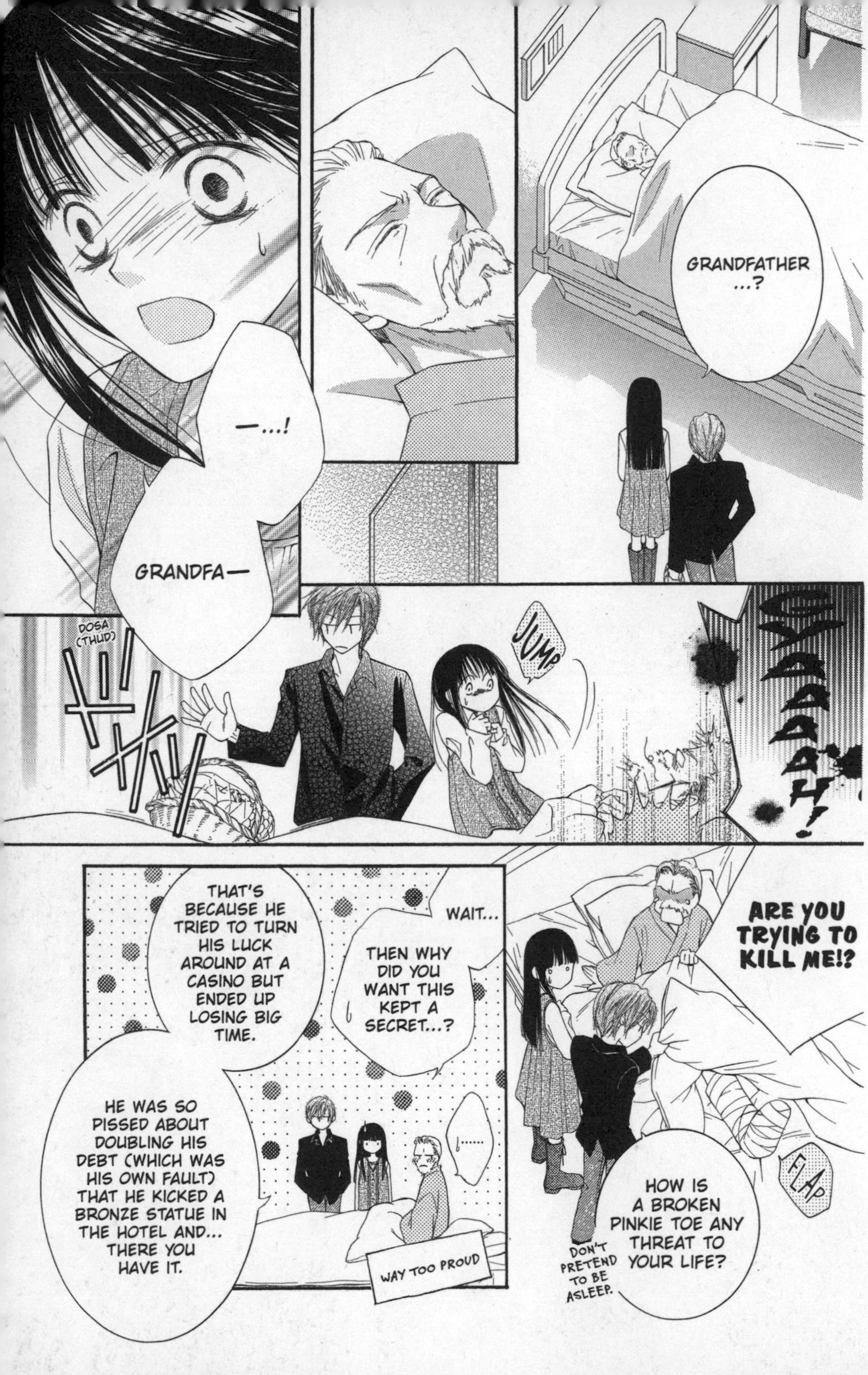
GRANDFATHER ...?
—...!
GRANDFA—
GYAAAAH!
JUMP
DOSA (THUD)
ARE YOU TRYING TO KILL ME!?
FLAP
HOW IS A BROKEN PINKIE TOE ANY THREAT TO YOUR LIFE?
DON'T PRETEND TO BE ASLEEP.
WAIT...
THEN WHY DID YOU WANT THIS KEPT A SECRET...?
THAT'S BECAUSE HE TRIED TO TURN HIS LUCK AROUND AT A CASINO BUT ENDED UP LOSING BIG TIME.
......
HE WAS SO PISSED ABOUT DOUBLING HIS DEBT (WHICH WAS HIS OWN FAULT) THAT HE KICKED A BRONZE STATUE IN THE HOTEL AND... THERE YOU HAVE IT.
WAY TOO PROUD

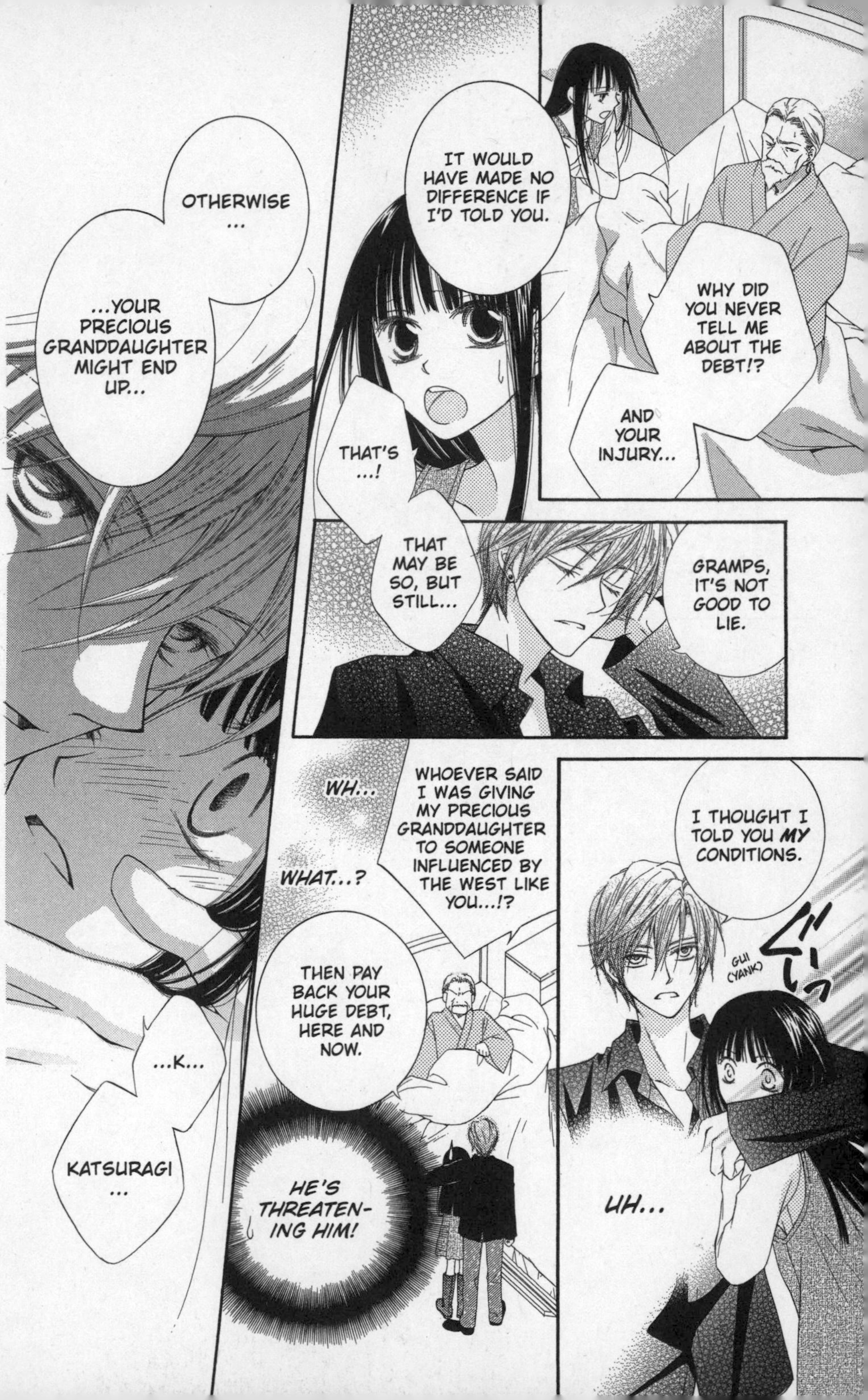
WHY DID YOU NEVER TELL ME ABOUT THE DEBT!?
AND YOUR INJURY...
IT WOULD HAVE MADE NO DIFFERENCE IF I'D TOLD YOU.
THAT'S ...!
GRAMPS, IT'S NOT GOOD TO LIE.
THAT MAY BE SO, BUT STILL...
I THOUGHT I TOLD YOU *MY* CONDITIONS.
GUI (YANK)
UH...
WHOEVER SAID I WAS GIVING MY PRECIOUS GRANDDAUGHTER TO SOMEONE INFLUENCED BY THE WEST LIKE YOU...!?
WH...
WHAT...?
THEN PAY BACK YOUR HUGE DEBT, HERE AND NOW.
HE'S THREATEN-ING HIM!
OTHERWISE ...
...YOUR PRECIOUS GRANDDAUGHTER MIGHT END UP...
...K...
KATSURAGI ...

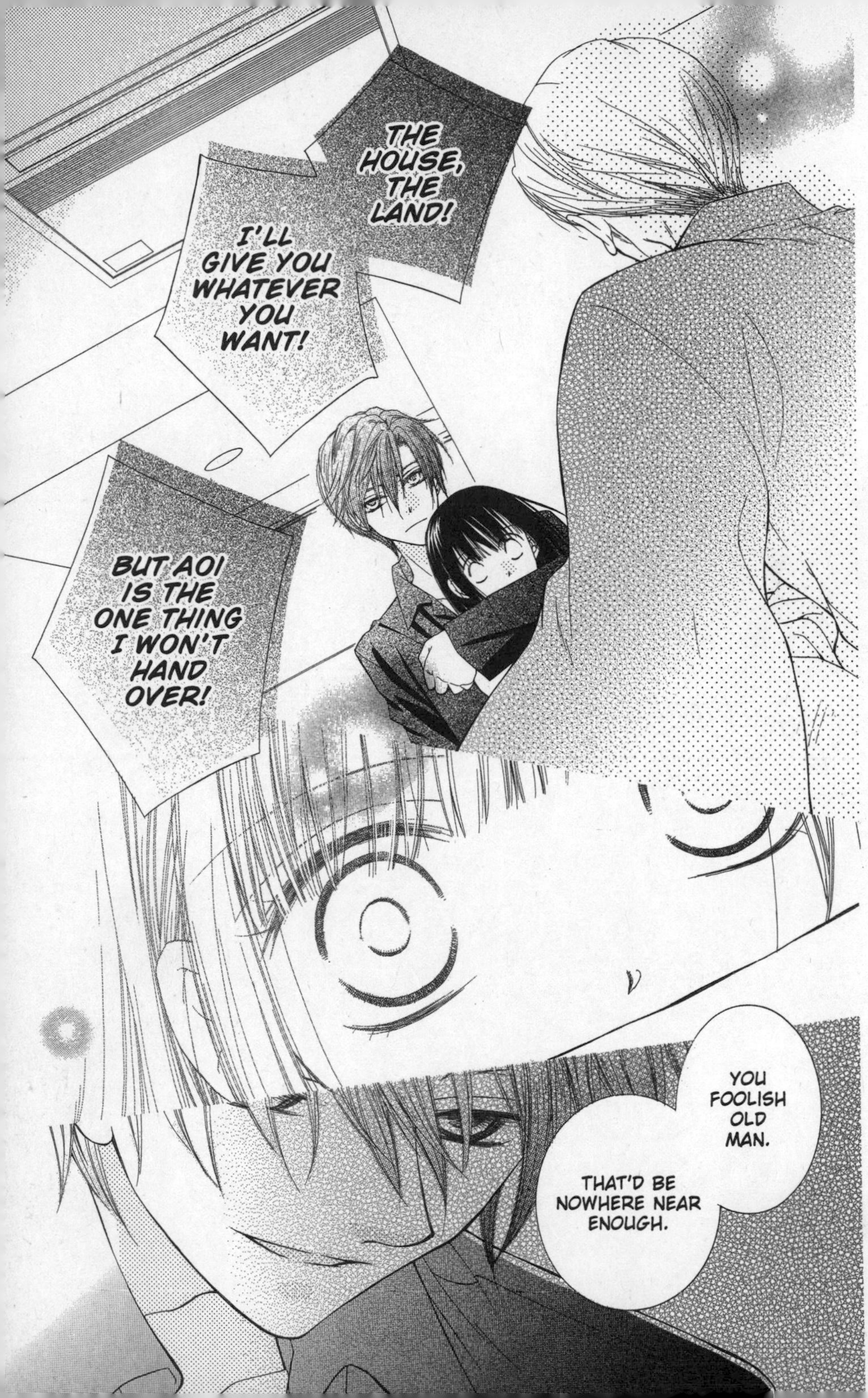
THE HOUSE, THE LAND!
I'LL GIVE YOU WHATEVER YOU WANT!
BUT AOI IS THE ONE THING I WON'T HAND OVER!
YOU FOOLISH OLD MAN.
THAT'D BE NOWHERE NEAR ENOUGH.

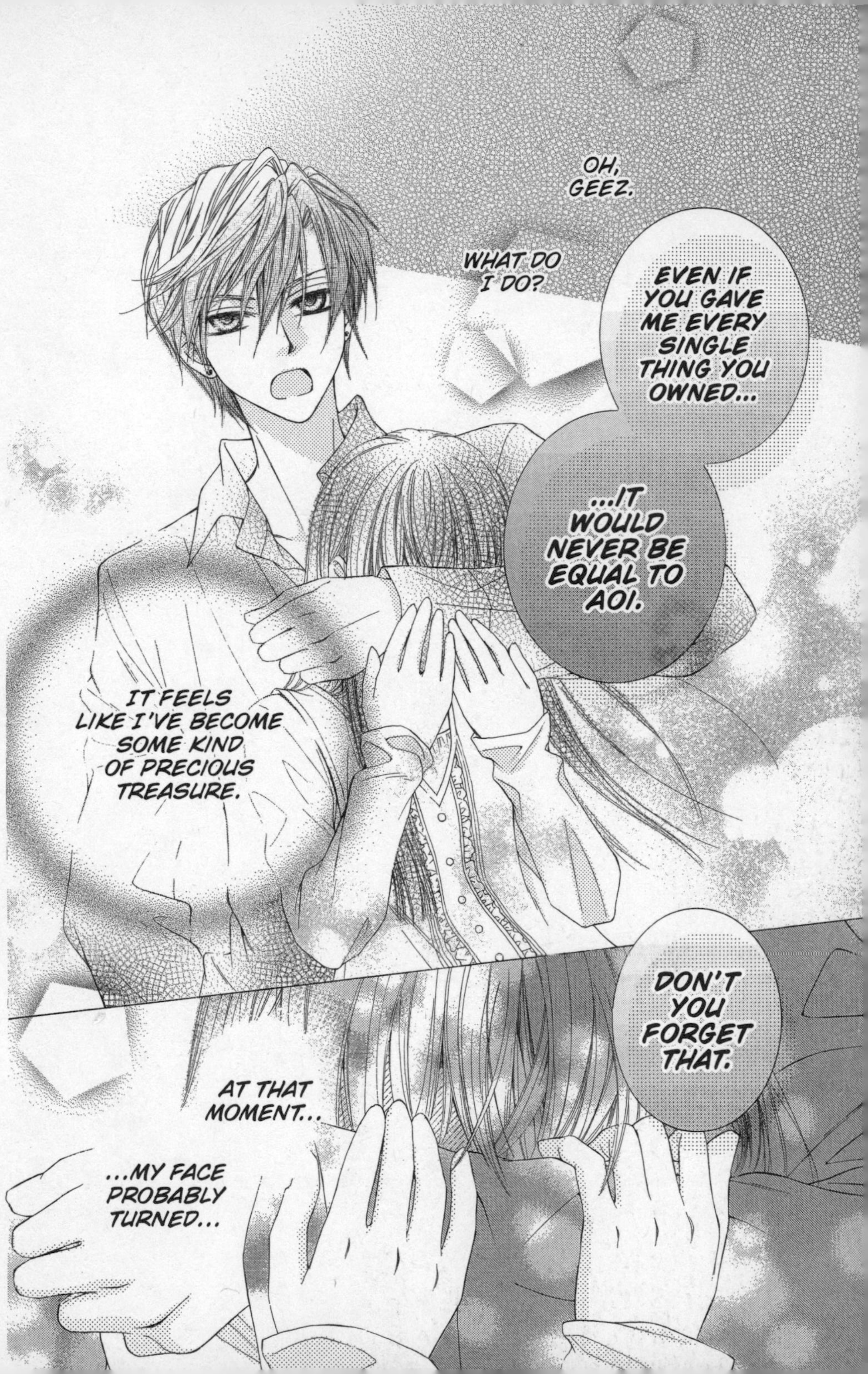
OH, GEEZ.
WHAT DO I DO?
EVEN IF YOU GAVE ME EVERY SINGLE THING YOU OWNED...
...IT WOULD NEVER BE EQUAL TO AOI.
IT FEELS LIKE I'VE BECOME SOME KIND OF PRECIOUS TREASURE.
DON'T YOU FORGET THAT.
AT THAT MOMENT...
...MY FACE PROBABLY TURNED...

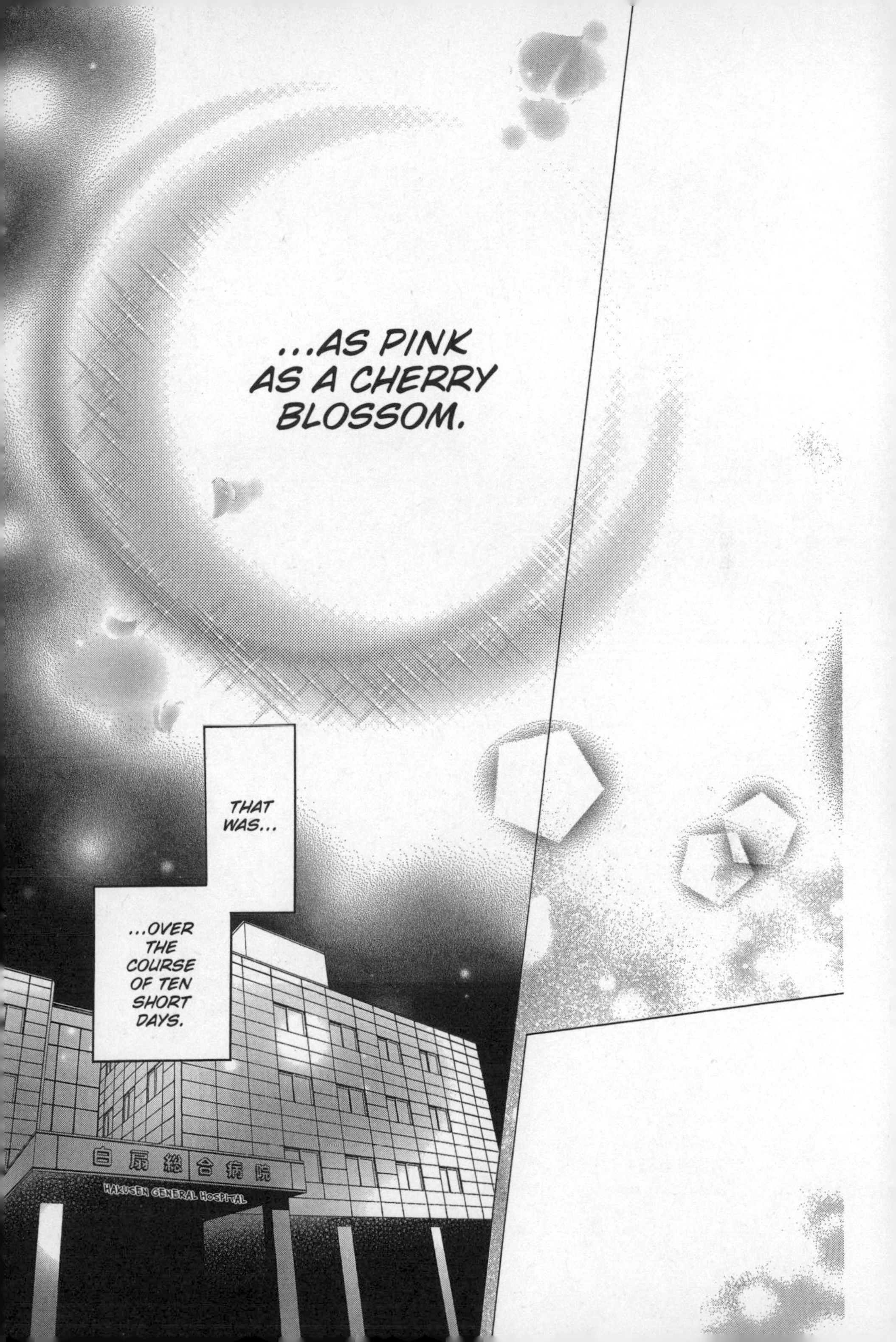
...AS PINK AS A CHERRY BLOSSOM.
THAT WAS...
...OVER THE COURSE OF TEN SHORT DAYS.
白扇総合病院
HAKUSEN GENERAL HOSPITAL

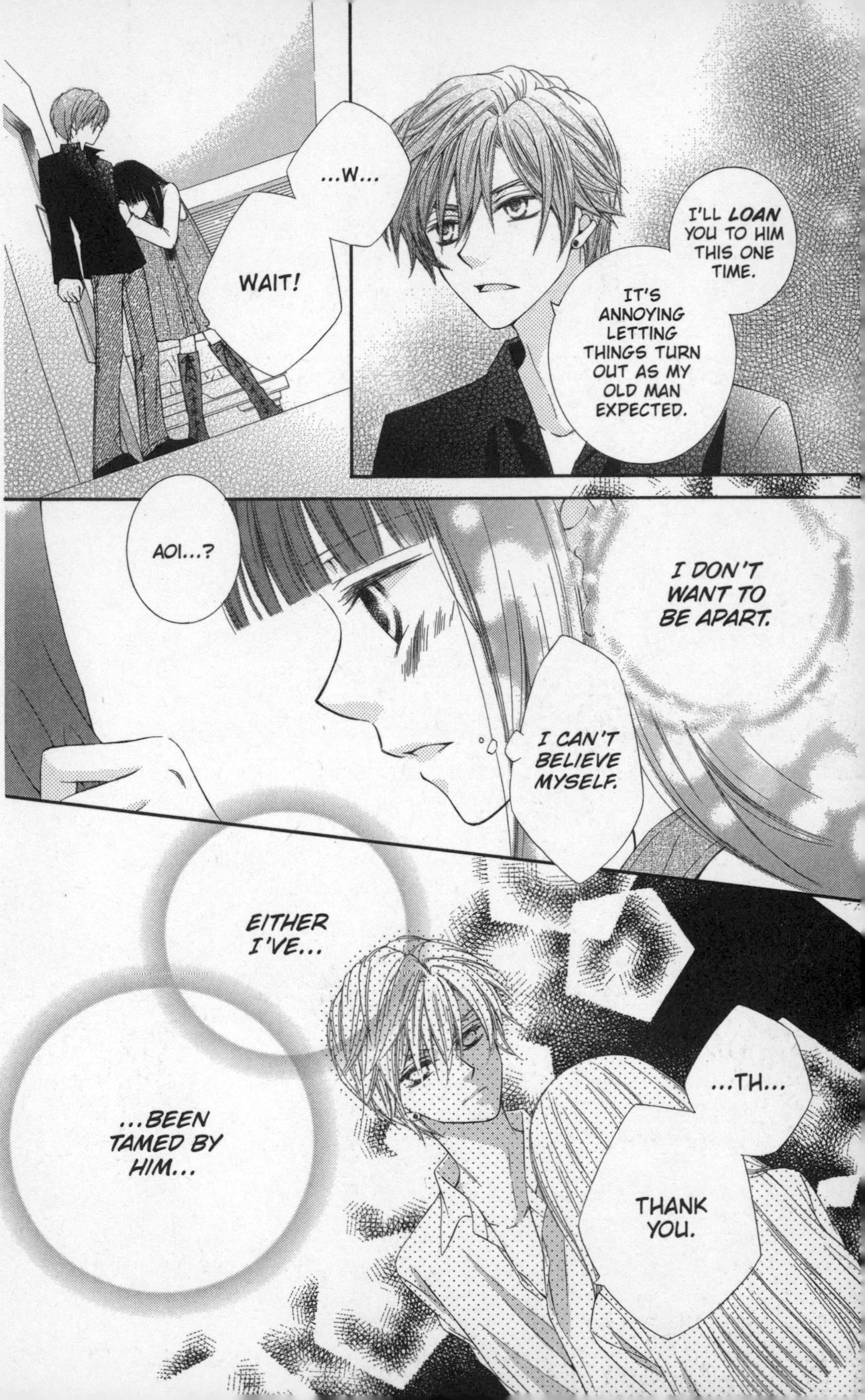

I'LL *LOAN* YOU TO HIM THIS ONE TIME.
IT'S ANNOYING LETTING THINGS TURN OUT AS MY OLD MAN EXPECTED.
...W...
WAIT!
AOI...?
I DON'T WANT TO BE APART.
I CAN'T BELIEVE MYSELF.
...TH...
THANK YOU.
EITHER I'VE...
...BEEN TAMED BY HIM...

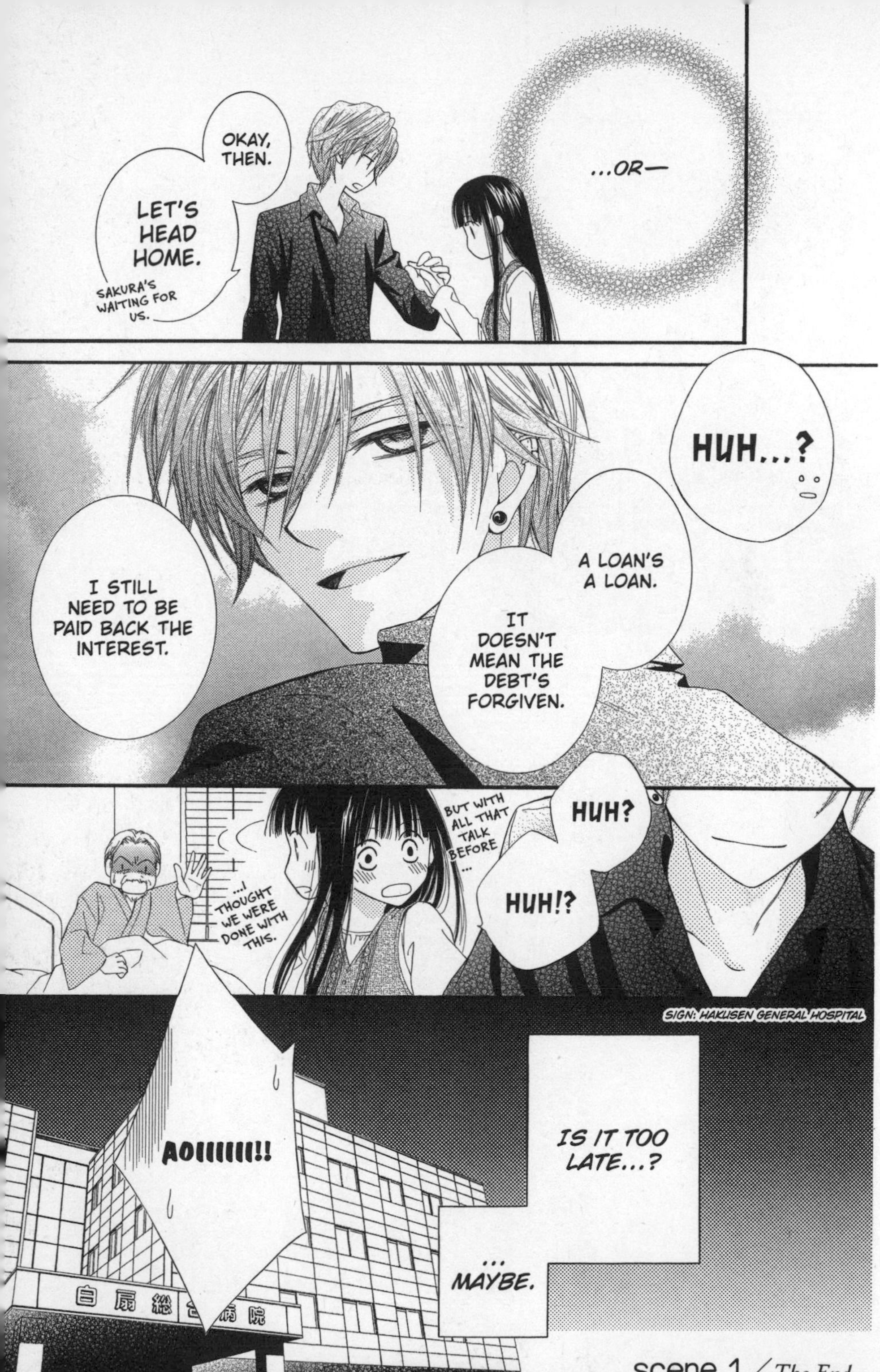
...OR—
OKAY, THEN.
LET'S HEAD HOME.
SAKURA'S WAITING FOR US.
HUH...?
A LOAN'S A LOAN.
IT DOESN'T MEAN THE DEBT'S FORGIVEN.
I STILL NEED TO BE PAID BACK THE INTEREST.
HUH?
HUH!?
BUT WITH ALL THAT TALK BEFORE...
...I THOUGHT WE WERE DONE WITH THIS.
SIGN: HAKUSEN GENERAL HOSPITAL
IS IT TOO LATE...?
...MAYBE.
AOIIIIIII!!
白扇総合病院

scene.1 / *The End*

Illustration for Preview
of Chapter 1

Illustration for Preview
of Chapter 2

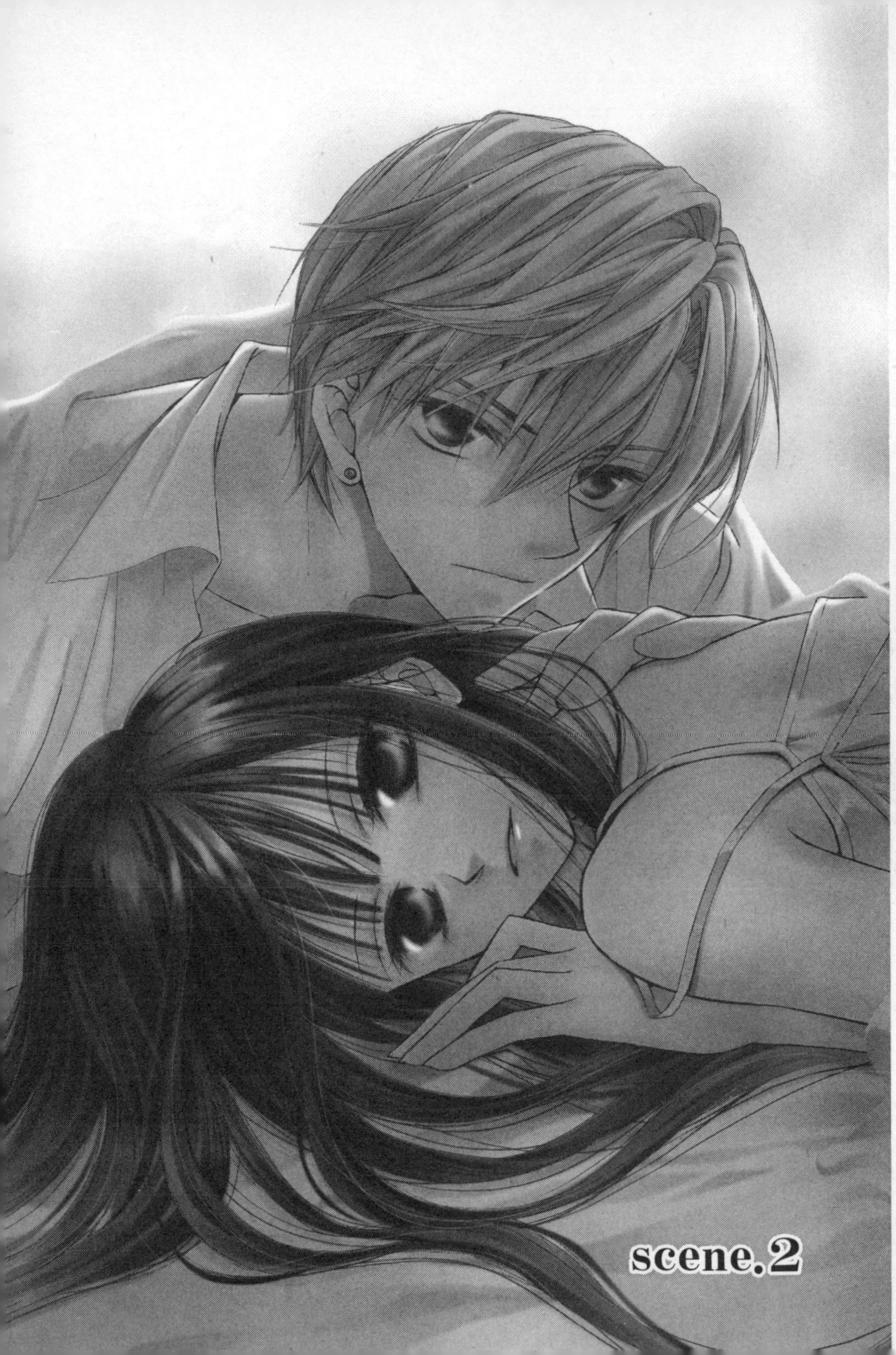
scene.2

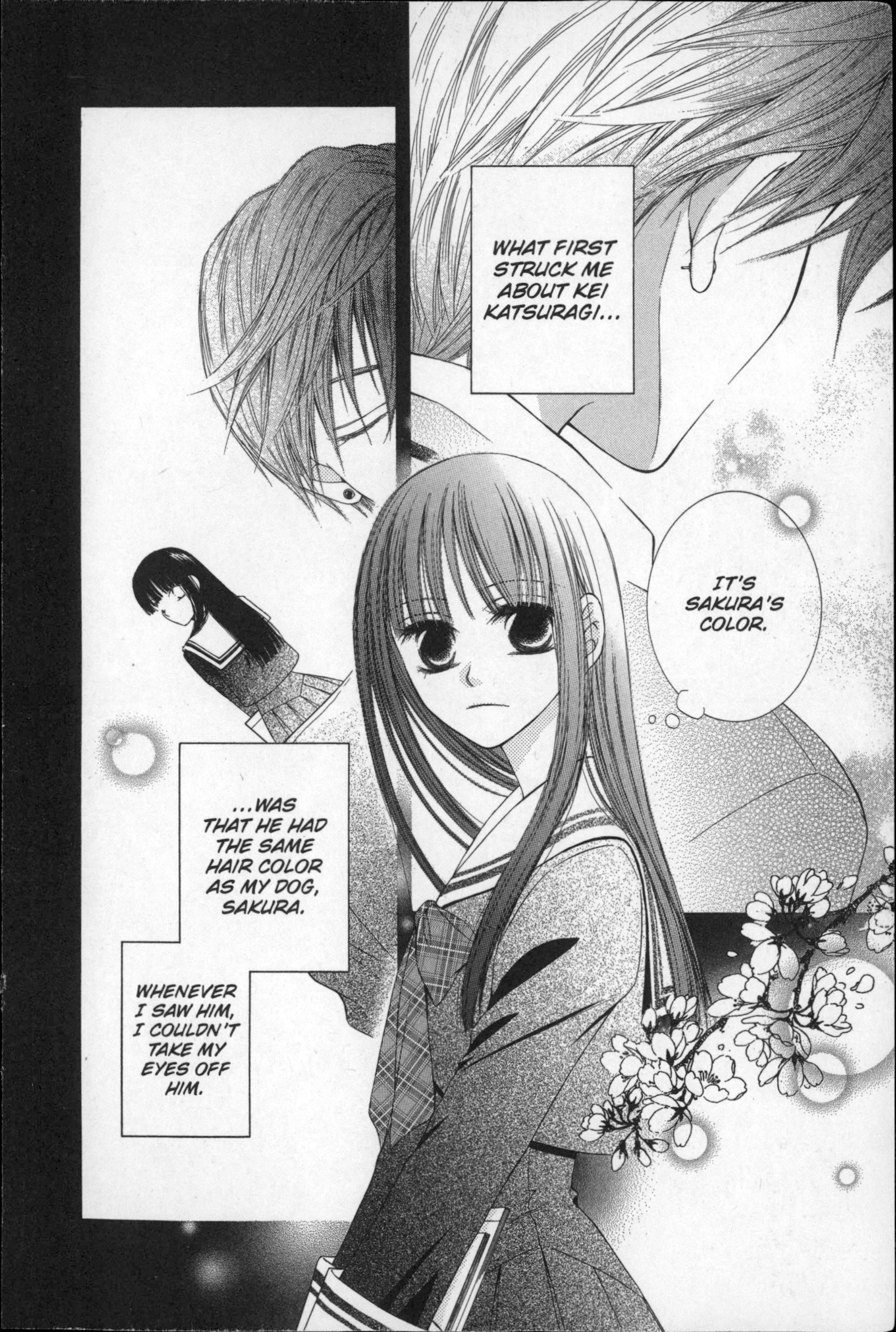
WHAT FIRST STRUCK ME ABOUT KEI KATSURAGI...
IT'S SAKURA'S COLOR.
...WAS THAT HE HAD THE SAME HAIR COLOR AS MY DOG, SAKURA.
WHENEVER I SAW HIM, I COULDN'T TAKE MY EYES OFF HIM.

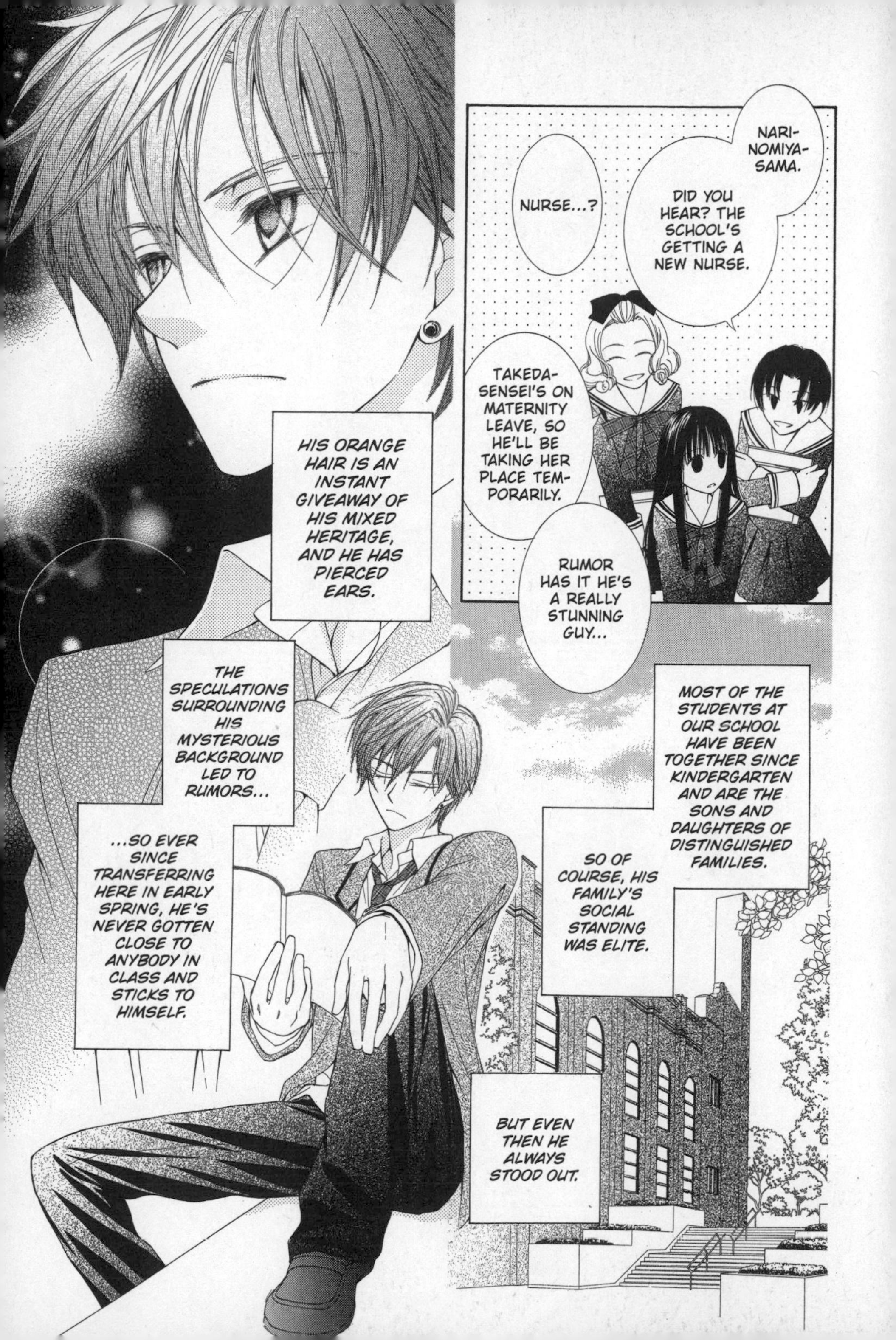
NARI-NOMIYA-SAMA.
DID YOU HEAR? THE SCHOOL'S GETTING A NEW NURSE.
NURSE...?
TAKEDA-SENSEI'S ON MATERNITY LEAVE, SO HE'LL BE TAKING HER PLACE TEM-PORARILY.
RUMOR HAS IT HE'S A REALLY STUNNING GUY...
MOST OF THE STUDENTS AT OUR SCHOOL HAVE BEEN TOGETHER SINCE KINDERGARTEN AND ARE THE SONS AND DAUGHTERS OF DISTINGUISHED FAMILIES.
SO OF COURSE, HIS FAMILY'S SOCIAL STANDING WAS ELITE.
BUT EVEN THEN HE ALWAYS STOOD OUT.
HIS ORANGE HAIR IS AN INSTANT GIVEAWAY OF HIS MIXED HERITAGE, AND HE HAS PIERCED EARS.
THE SPECULATIONS SURROUNDING HIS MYSTERIOUS BACKGROUND LED TO RUMORS...
...SO EVER SINCE TRANSFERRING HERE IN EARLY SPRING, HE'S NEVER GOTTEN CLOSE TO ANYBODY IN CLASS AND STICKS TO HIMSELF.

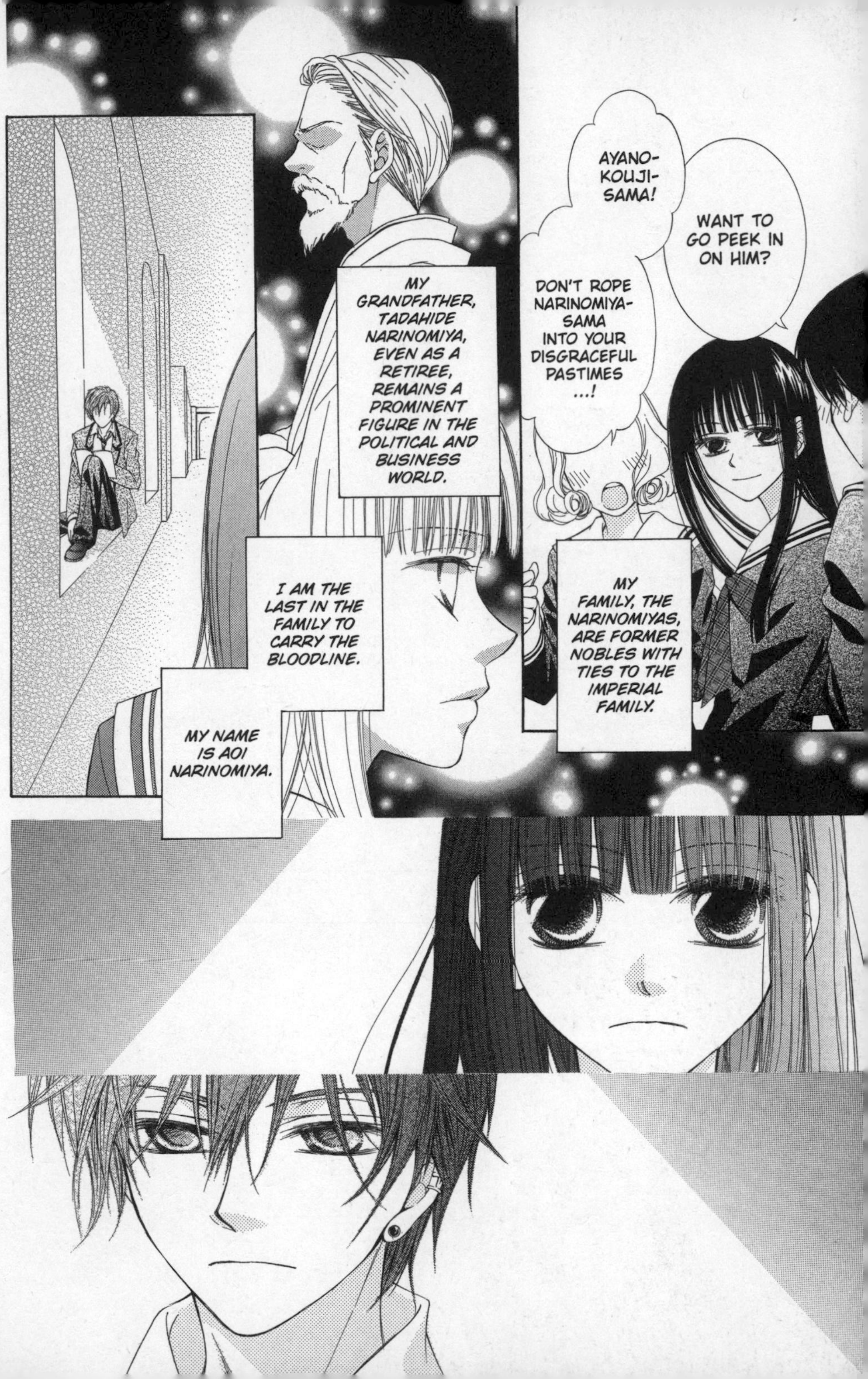
AYANO-KOUJI-SAMA!
WANT TO GO PEEK IN ON HIM?
DON'T ROPE NARINOMIYA-SAMA INTO YOUR DISGRACEFUL PASTIMES ...!
MY FAMILY, THE NARINOMIYAS, ARE FORMER NOBLES WITH TIES TO THE IMPERIAL FAMILY.
MY GRANDFATHER, TADAHIDE NARINOMIYA, EVEN AS A RETIREE, REMAINS A PROMINENT FIGURE IN THE POLITICAL AND BUSINESS WORLD.
I AM THE LAST IN THE FAMILY TO CARRY THE BLOODLINE.
MY NAME IS AOI NARINOMIYA.

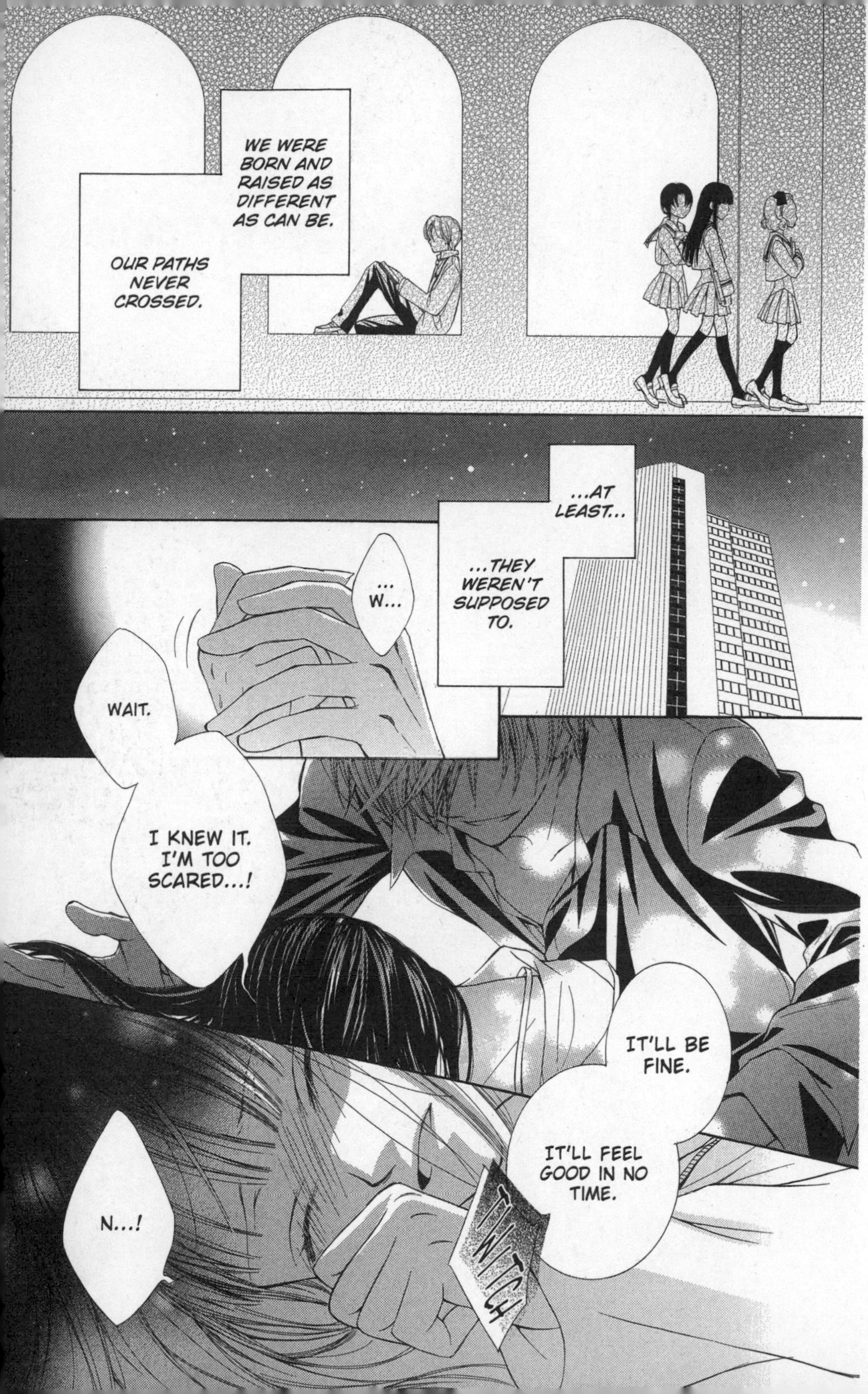
WE WERE BORN AND RAISED AS DIFFERENT AS CAN BE.
OUR PATHS NEVER CROSSED.
...AT LEAST...
...THEY WEREN'T SUPPOSED TO.
... W...
WAIT.
I KNEW IT. I'M TOO SCARED...!
IT'LL BE FINE.
IT'LL FEEL GOOD IN NO TIME.
TWITCH
N...!

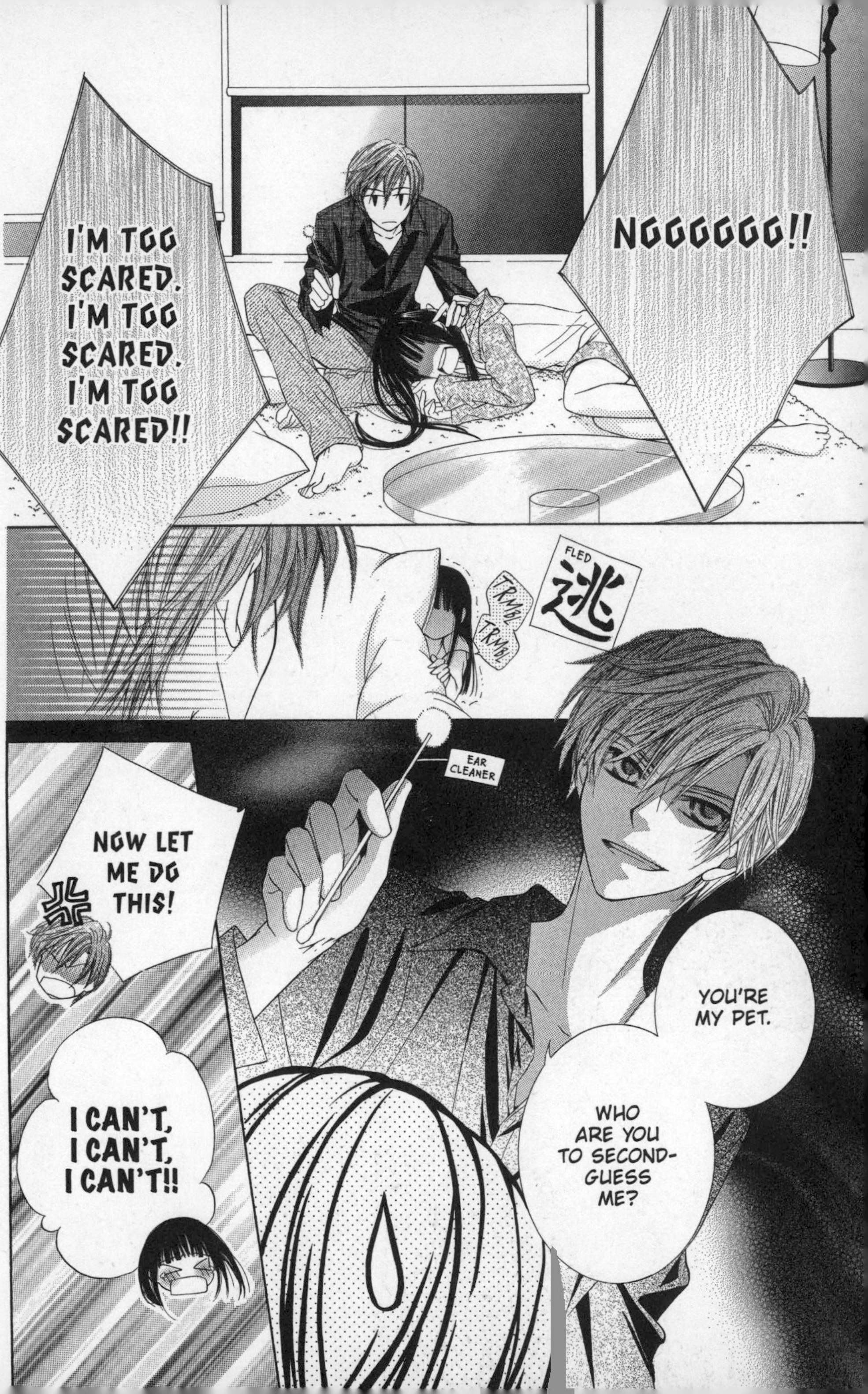

NOOOOOOO!!
I'M TOO SCARED. I'M TOO SCARED. I'M TOO SCARED!!
FLED 逃
TRMBL TRMBL
YOU'RE MY PET.
WHO ARE YOU TO SECOND-GUESS ME?
EAR CLEANER
NOW LET ME DO THIS!
I CAN'T, I CAN'T, I CAN'T!!

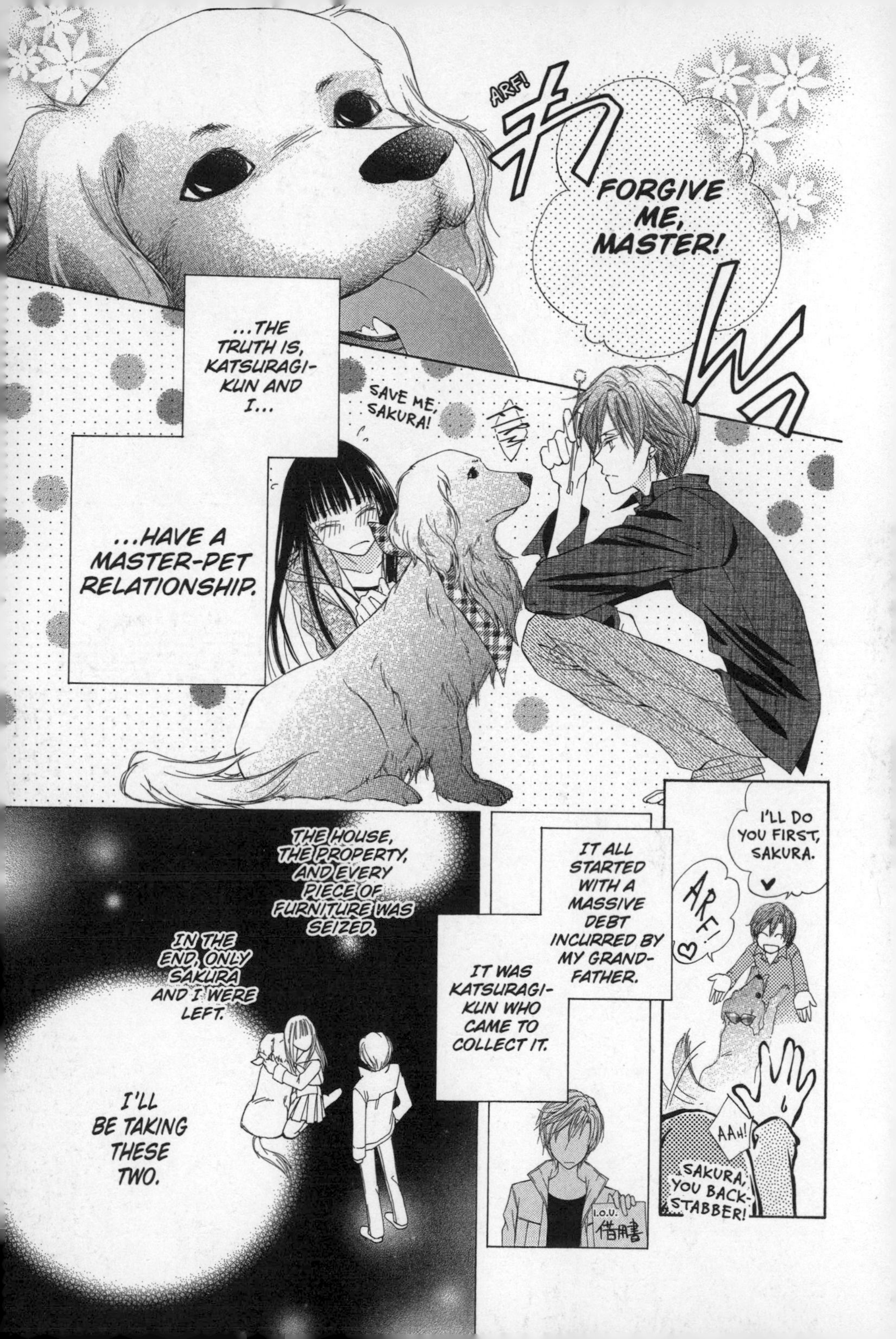
ARF!
FORGIVE ME, MASTER!
SAVE ME, SAKURA!
...THE TRUTH IS, KATSURAGI-KUN AND I...
...HAVE A MASTER-PET RELATIONSHIP.
I'LL DO YOU FIRST, SAKURA.
ARF!
AAH!
SAKURA, YOU BACK-STABBER!
IT ALL STARTED WITH A MASSIVE DEBT INCURRED BY MY GRAND-FATHER.
IT WAS KATSURAGI-KUN WHO CAME TO COLLECT IT.
I.O.U.
借用書
THE HOUSE, THE PROPERTY, AND EVERY PIECE OF FURNITURE WAS SEIZED.
IN THE END, ONLY SAKURA AND I WERE LEFT.
I'LL BE TAKING THESE TWO.

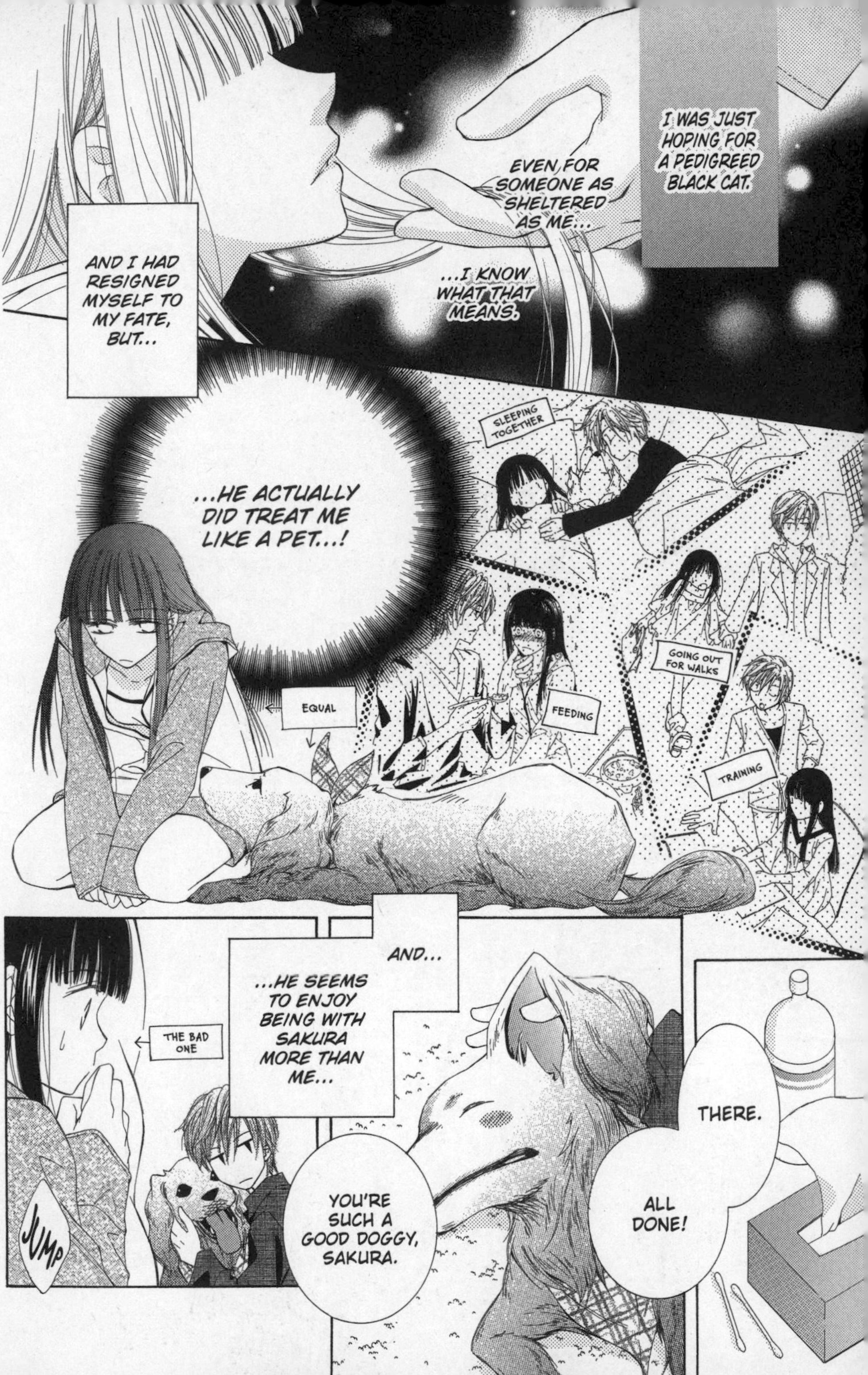

I WAS JUST HOPING FOR A PEDIGREED BLACK CAT.
EVEN FOR SOMEONE AS SHELTERED AS ME...
...I KNOW WHAT THAT MEANS.
AND I HAD RESIGNED MYSELF TO MY FATE, BUT...
SLEEPING TOGETHER
...HE ACTUALLY DID TREAT ME LIKE A PET...!
GOING OUT FOR WALKS
FEEDING
TRAINING
EQUAL
THERE.
ALL DONE!
YOU'RE SUCH A GOOD DOGGY, SAKURA.
AND...
...HE SEEMS TO ENJOY BEING WITH SAKURA MORE THAN ME...
THE BAD ONE
JUMP

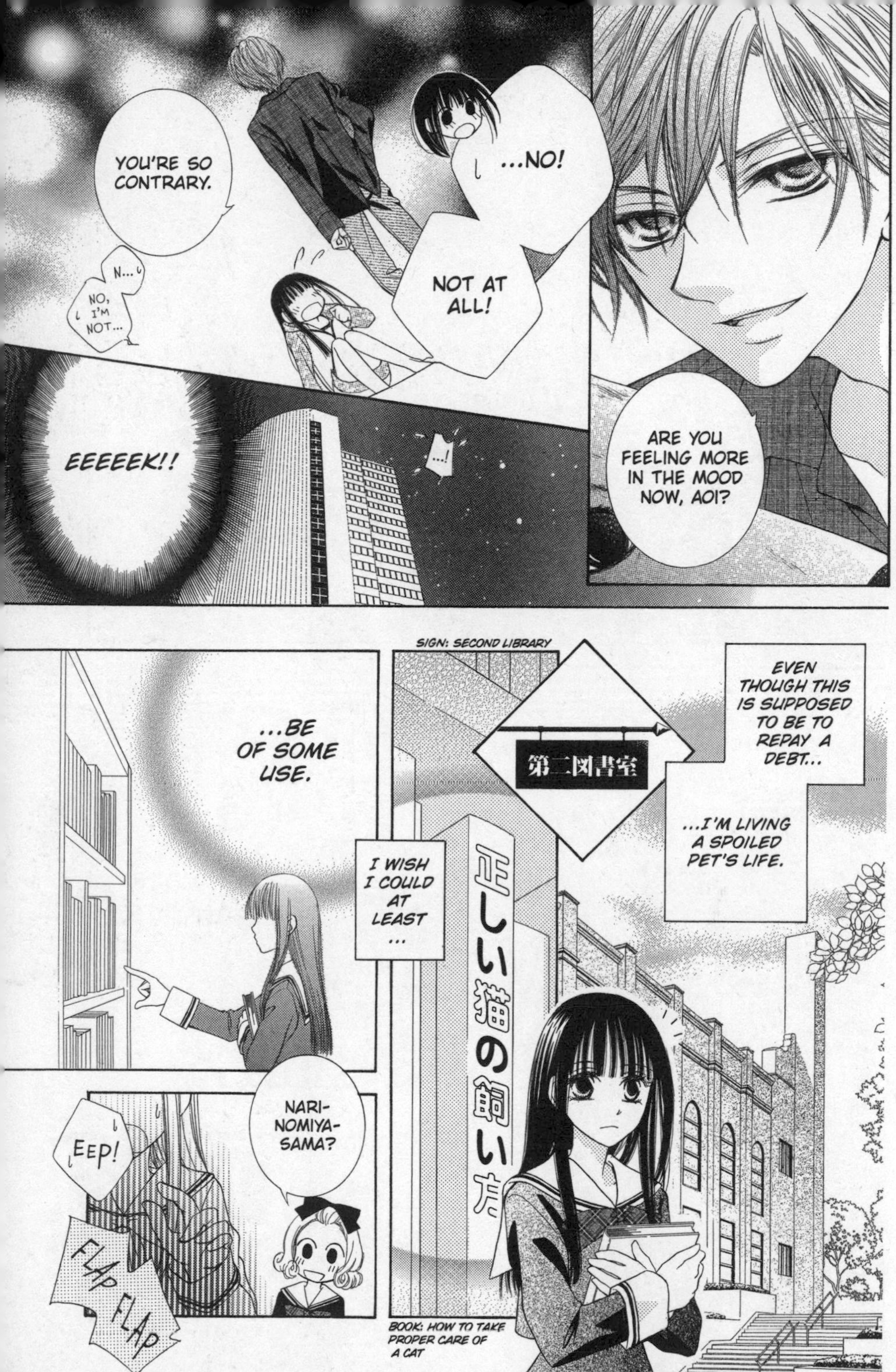

ARE YOU FEELING MORE IN THE MOOD NOW, AOI?
...NO!
NOT AT ALL!
YOU'RE SO CONTRARY.
N...
NO, I'M NOT...
...!
EEEEEK!!
SIGN: SECOND LIBRARY
第二図書室
EVEN THOUGH THIS IS SUPPOSED TO BE TO REPAY A DEBT...
...I'M LIVING A SPOILED PET'S LIFE.
I WISH I COULD AT LEAST ...
正しい猫の飼い
BOOK: HOW TO TAKE PROPER CARE OF A CAT
...BE OF SOME USE.
NARI-NOMIYA-SAMA?
EEP!
FLAP FLAP

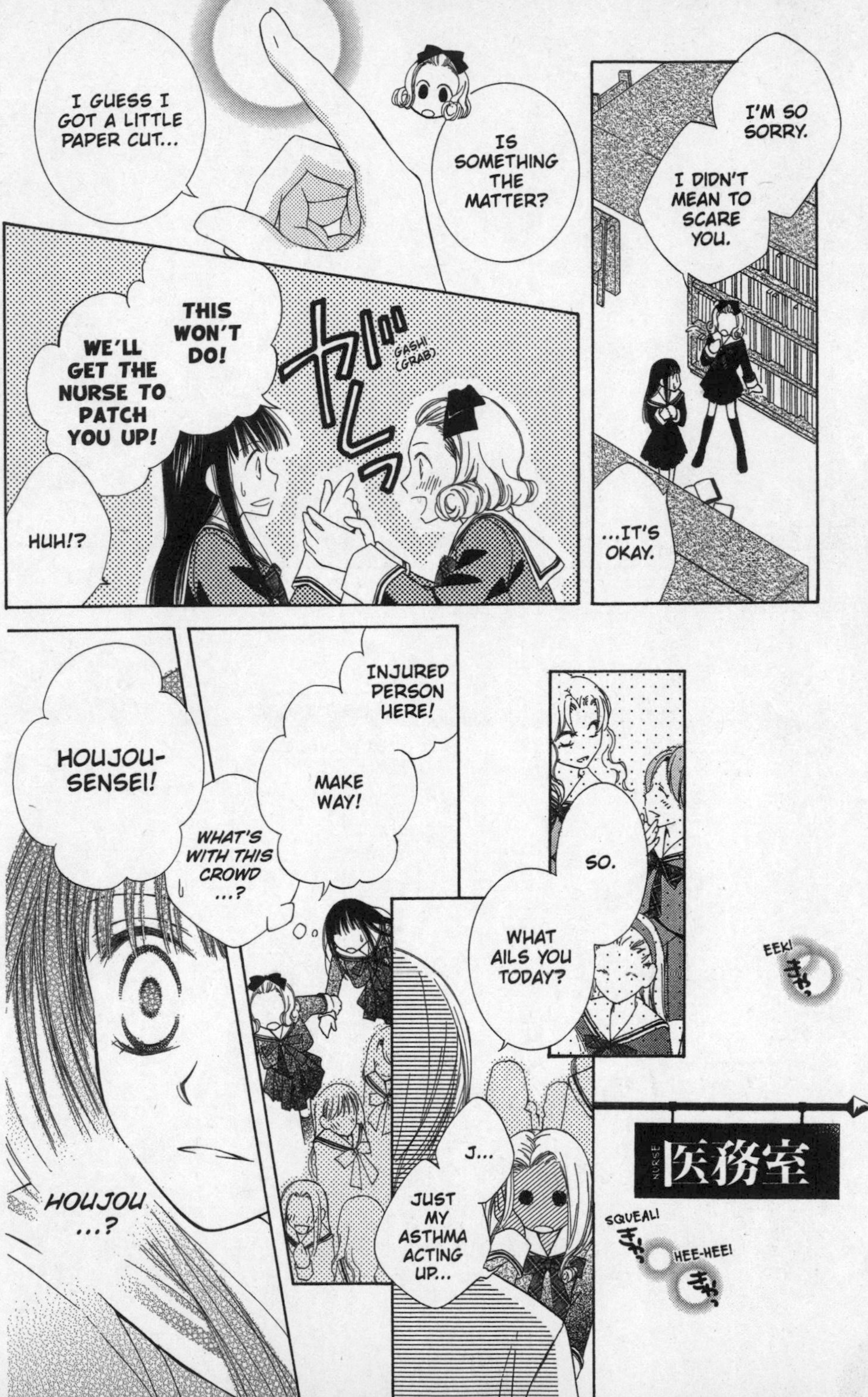
I'M SO SORRY.
I DIDN'T MEAN TO SCARE YOU.
...IT'S OKAY.
IS SOMETHING THE MATTER?
I GUESS I GOT A LITTLE PAPER CUT...
THIS WON'T DO!
WE'LL GET THE NURSE TO PATCH YOU UP!
GASHI (GRAB)
HUH!?
NURSE 医務室
EEK!
SQUEAL!
HEE-HEE!
SO.
WHAT AILS YOU TODAY?
J...
JUST MY ASTHMA ACTING UP...
INJURED PERSON HERE!
MAKE WAY!
HOUJOU-SENSEI!
WHAT'S WITH THIS CROWD ...?
HOUJOU ...?

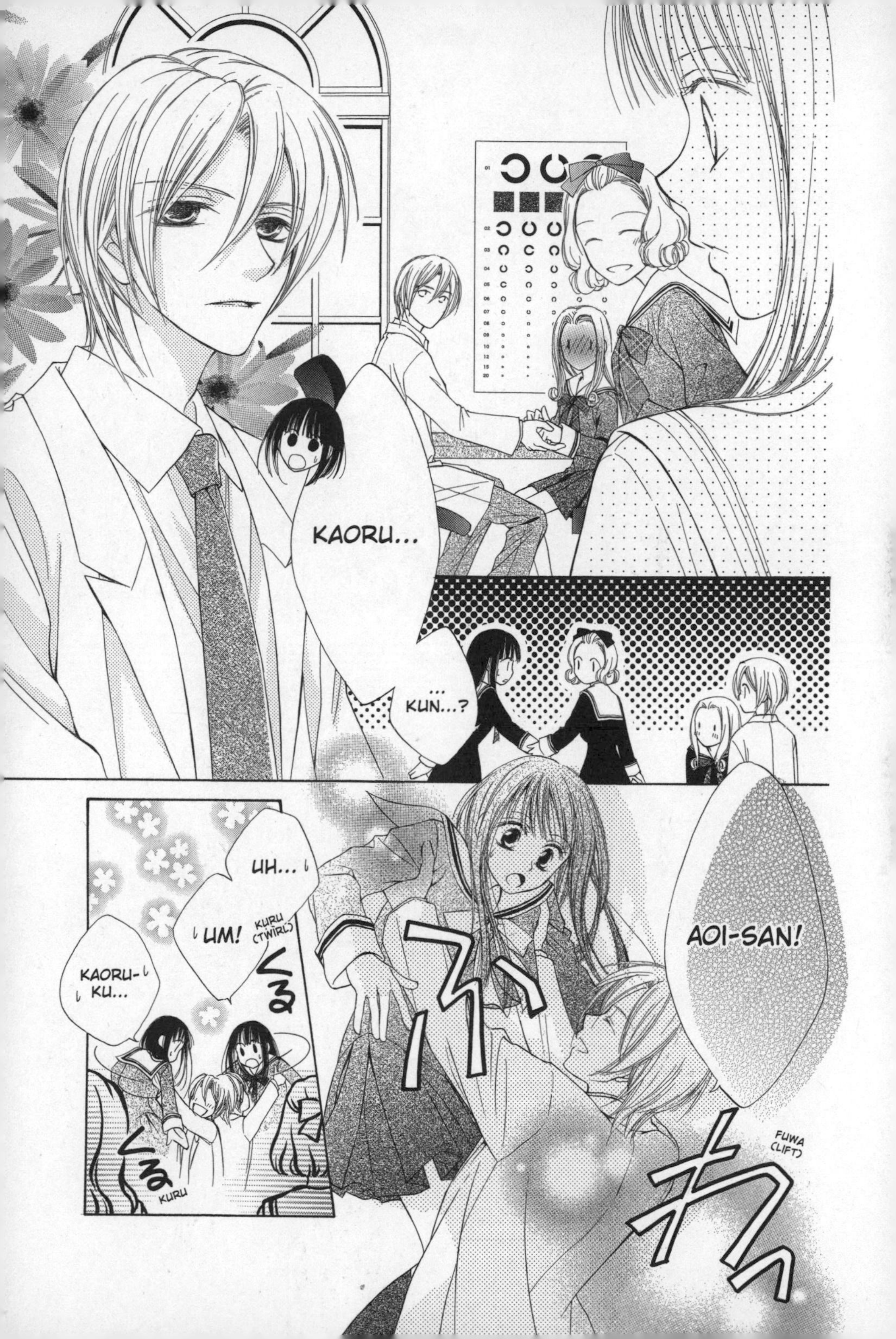
KAORU...
... KUN...?
AOI-SAN!
FUWA (LIFT)
UH...
UM!
KURU (TWIRL)
KAORU-KU...
KURU

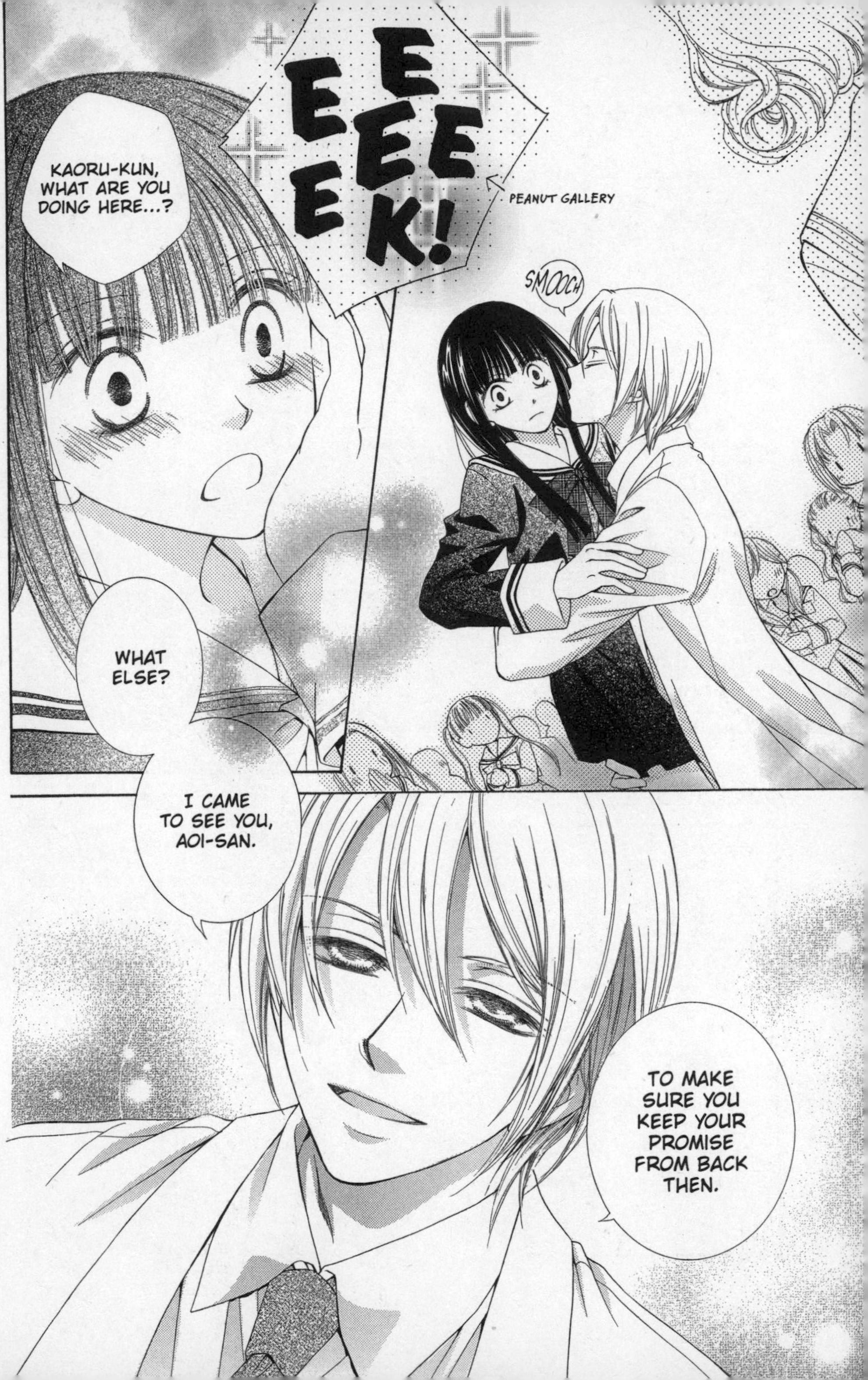
EEEEEK!
PEANUT GALLERY
SMOOCH
KAORU-KUN, WHAT ARE YOU DOING HERE...?
WHAT ELSE?
I CAME TO SEE YOU, AOI-SAN.
TO MAKE SURE YOU KEEP YOUR PROMISE FROM BACK THEN.

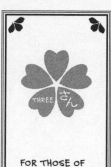

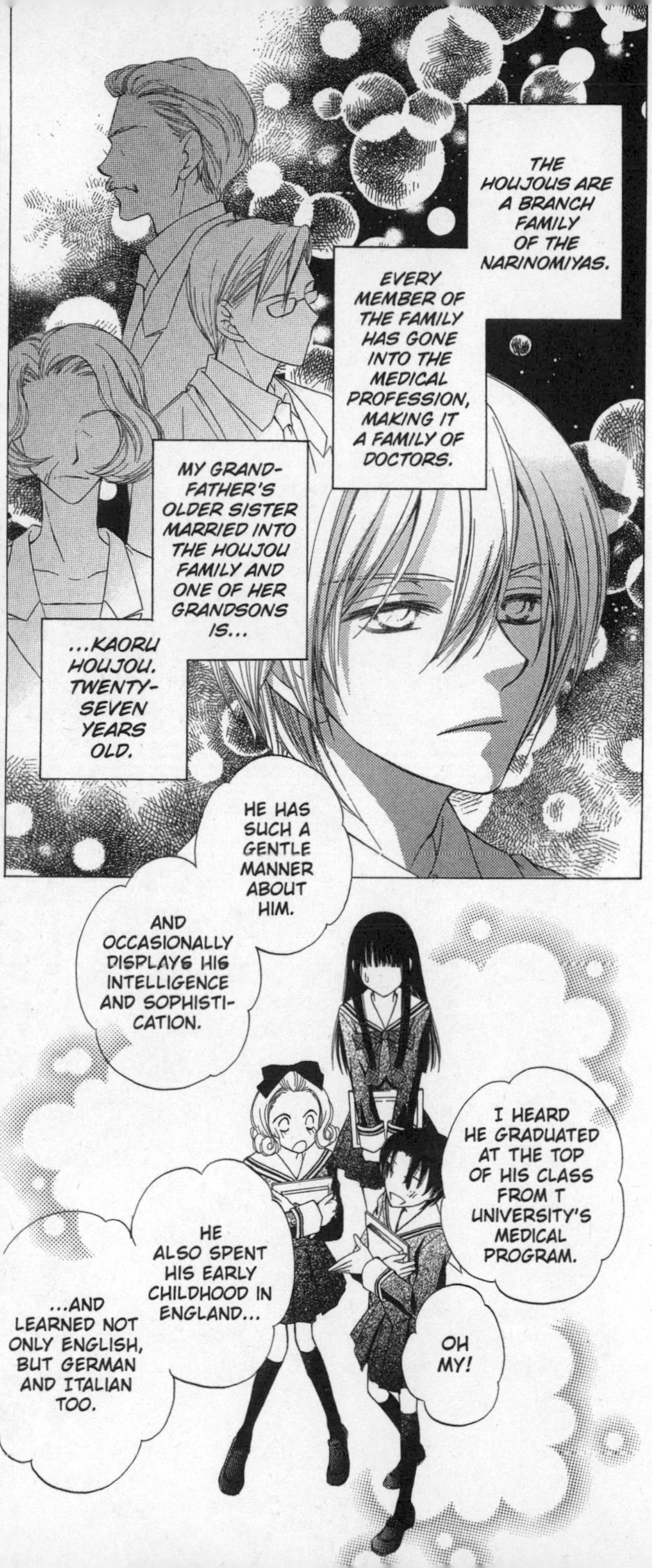
THE HOUJOUS ARE A BRANCH FAMILY OF THE NARINOMIYAS.
EVERY MEMBER OF THE FAMILY HAS GONE INTO THE MEDICAL PROFESSION, MAKING IT A FAMILY OF DOCTORS.
MY GRAND-FATHER'S OLDER SISTER MARRIED INTO THE HOUJOU FAMILY AND ONE OF HER GRANDSONS IS...
...KAORU HOUJOU. TWENTY-SEVEN YEARS OLD.
HE HAS SUCH A GENTLE MANNER ABOUT HIM.
AND OCCASIONALLY DISPLAYS HIS INTELLIGENCE AND SOPHISTI-CATION.
I HEARD HE GRADUATED AT THE TOP OF HIS CLASS FROM T UNIVERSITY'S MEDICAL PROGRAM.
HE ALSO SPENT HIS EARLY CHILDHOOD IN ENGLAND...
...AND LEARNED NOT ONLY ENGLISH, BUT GERMAN AND ITALIAN TOO.
OH MY!

THREE さん

FOR THOSE OF YOU FAMILIAR WITH MY OTHER WORKS, I'M SURE YOU'VE ALREADY PICKED UP ON THIS, BUT THE SIDE COLUMNS I'M DOING IN THIS VOLUME ARE DIFFERENT FROM MY USUAL STUFF.
IT'S ALL HANDWRITTEN!! AS YOU CAN SEE, I DON'T HAVE THE PRETTIEST HANDWRITING, SO I'VE ALWAYS AVOIDED IT IN THE PAST. I'VE CONSIDERED TAKING SOME CALLIGRAPHY CLASSES TO HELP ME IMPROVE, BUT NOTHING'S COME OF IT. IT REMAINS A PIPE DREAM.

I'D ALWAYS BELIEVED THAT IT'D NATURALLY IMPROVE THE OLDER I GOT...

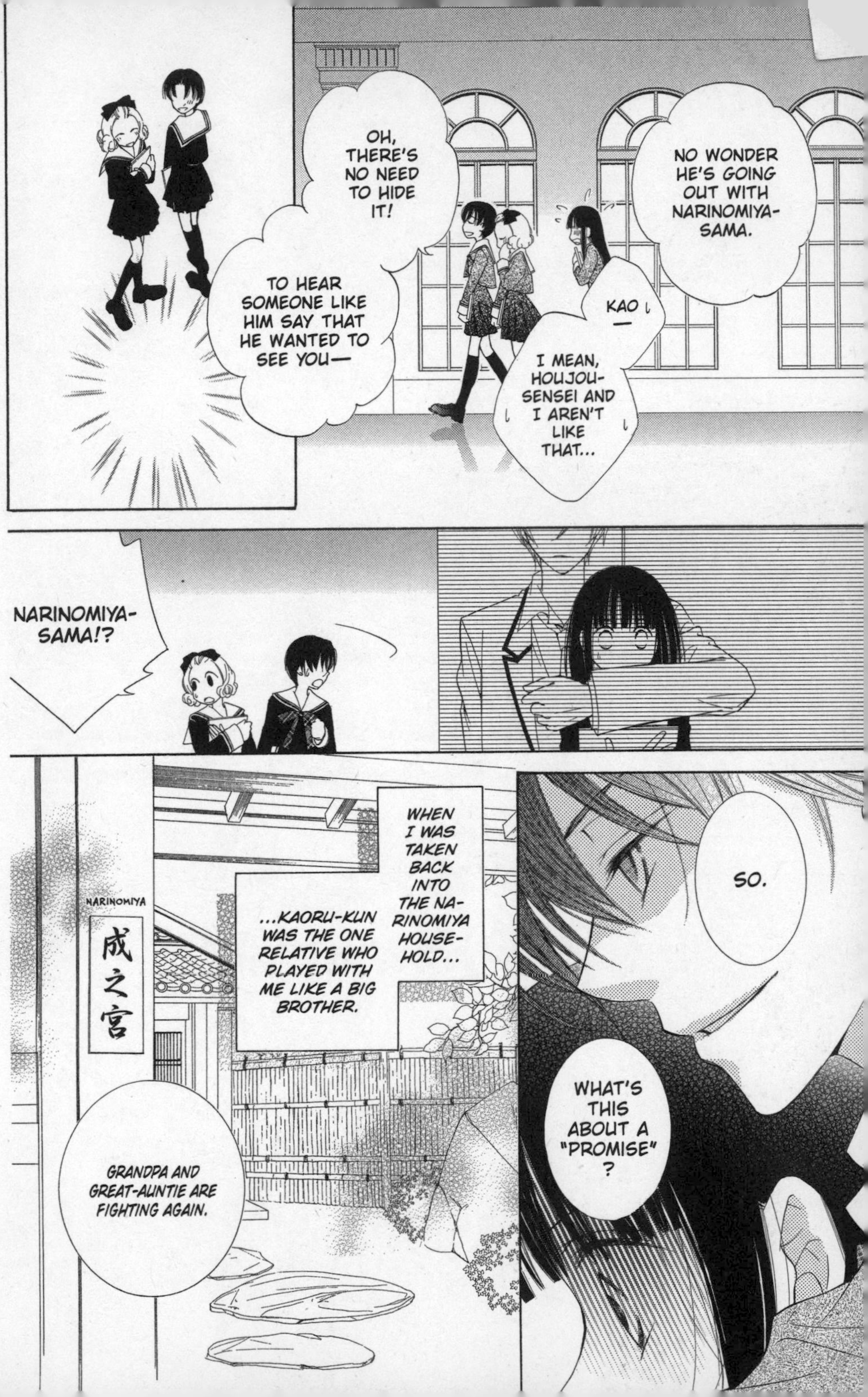
NO WONDER HE'S GOING OUT WITH NARINOMIYA-SAMA.
KAO—
I MEAN, HOUJOU-SENSEI AND I AREN'T LIKE THAT...
OH, THERE'S NO NEED TO HIDE IT!
TO HEAR SOMEONE LIKE HIM SAY THAT HE WANTED TO SEE YOU—
NARINOMIYA-SAMA!?
SO.
WHAT'S THIS ABOUT A "PROMISE"?
WHEN I WAS TAKEN BACK INTO THE NARINOMIYA HOUSEHOLD...
...KAORU-KUN WAS THE ONE RELATIVE WHO PLAYED WITH ME LIKE A BIG BROTHER.
NARINOMIYA
成之宮
GRANDPA AND GREAT-AUNTIE ARE FIGHTING AGAIN.

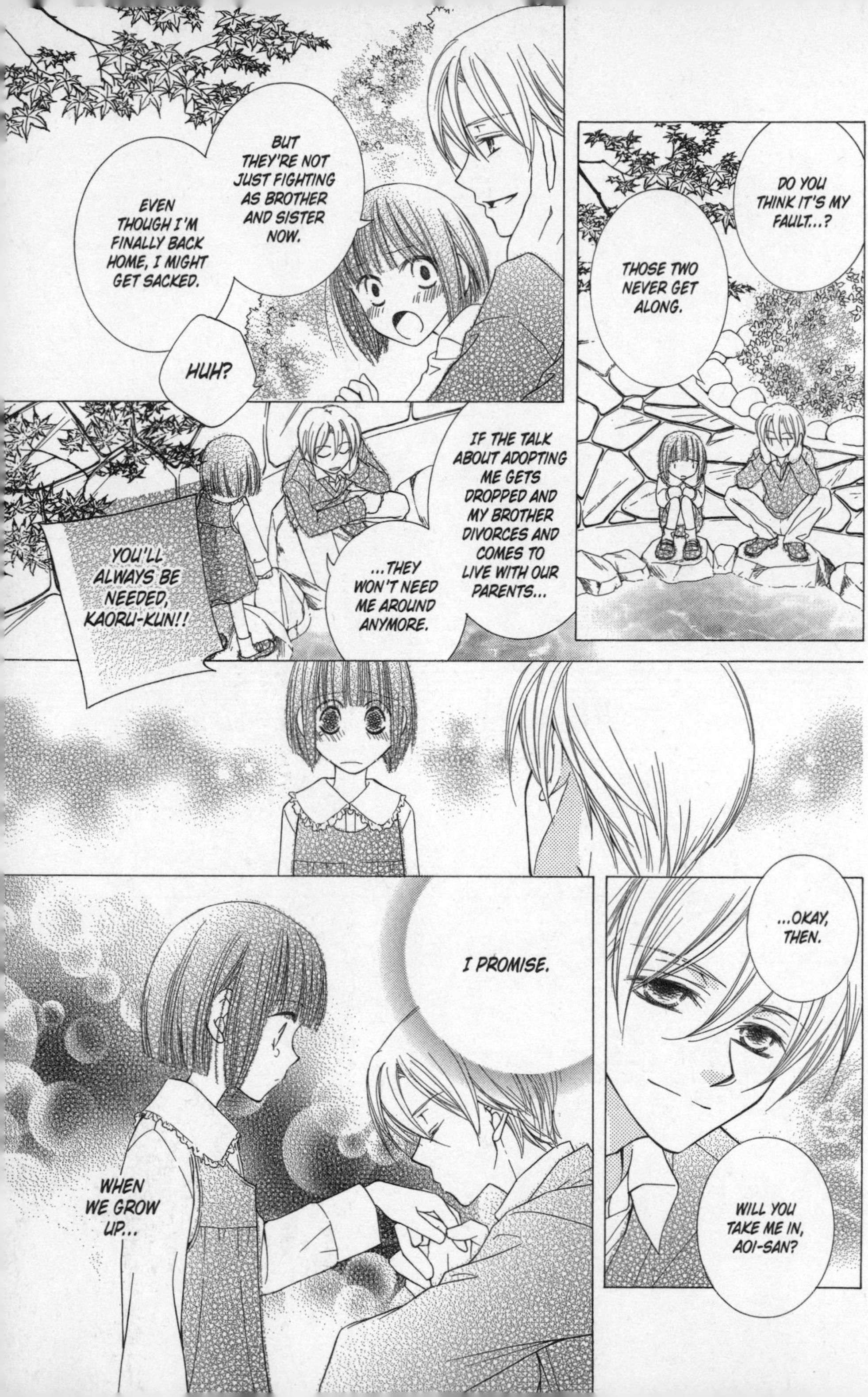
DO YOU THINK IT'S MY FAULT...?
THOSE TWO NEVER GET ALONG.
BUT THEY'RE NOT JUST FIGHTING AS BROTHER AND SISTER NOW.
EVEN THOUGH I'M FINALLY BACK HOME, I MIGHT GET SACKED.
HUH?
IF THE TALK ABOUT ADOPTING ME GETS DROPPED AND MY BROTHER DIVORCES AND COMES TO LIVE WITH OUR PARENTS...
...THEY WON'T NEED ME AROUND ANYMORE.
YOU'LL ALWAYS BE NEEDED, KAORU-KUN!!
...OKAY, THEN.
WILL YOU TAKE ME IN, AOI-SAN?
I PROMISE.
WHEN WE GROW UP...

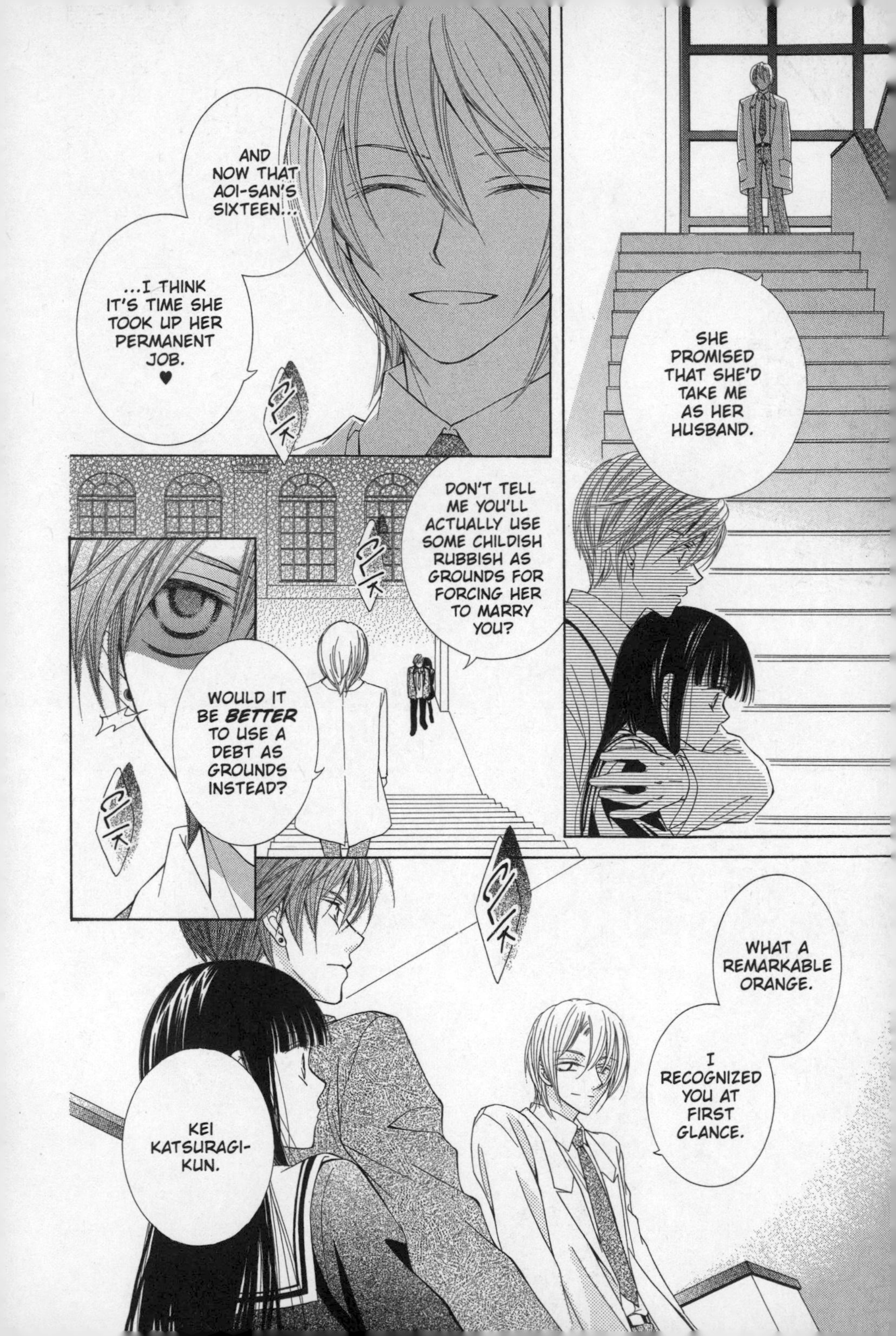
SHE PROMISED THAT SHE'D TAKE ME AS HER HUSBAND.
AND NOW THAT AOI-SAN'S SIXTEEN...
...I THINK IT'S TIME SHE TOOK UP HER PERMANENT JOB. ♥
CLIK
DON'T TELL ME YOU'LL ACTUALLY USE SOME CHILDISH RUBBISH AS GROUNDS FOR FORCING HER TO MARRY YOU?
CLIK
WOULD IT BE *BETTER* TO USE A DEBT AS GROUNDS INSTEAD?
CLIK
CLIK
WHAT A REMARKABLE ORANGE.
I RECOGNIZED YOU AT FIRST GLANCE.
KEI KATSURAGI-KUN.

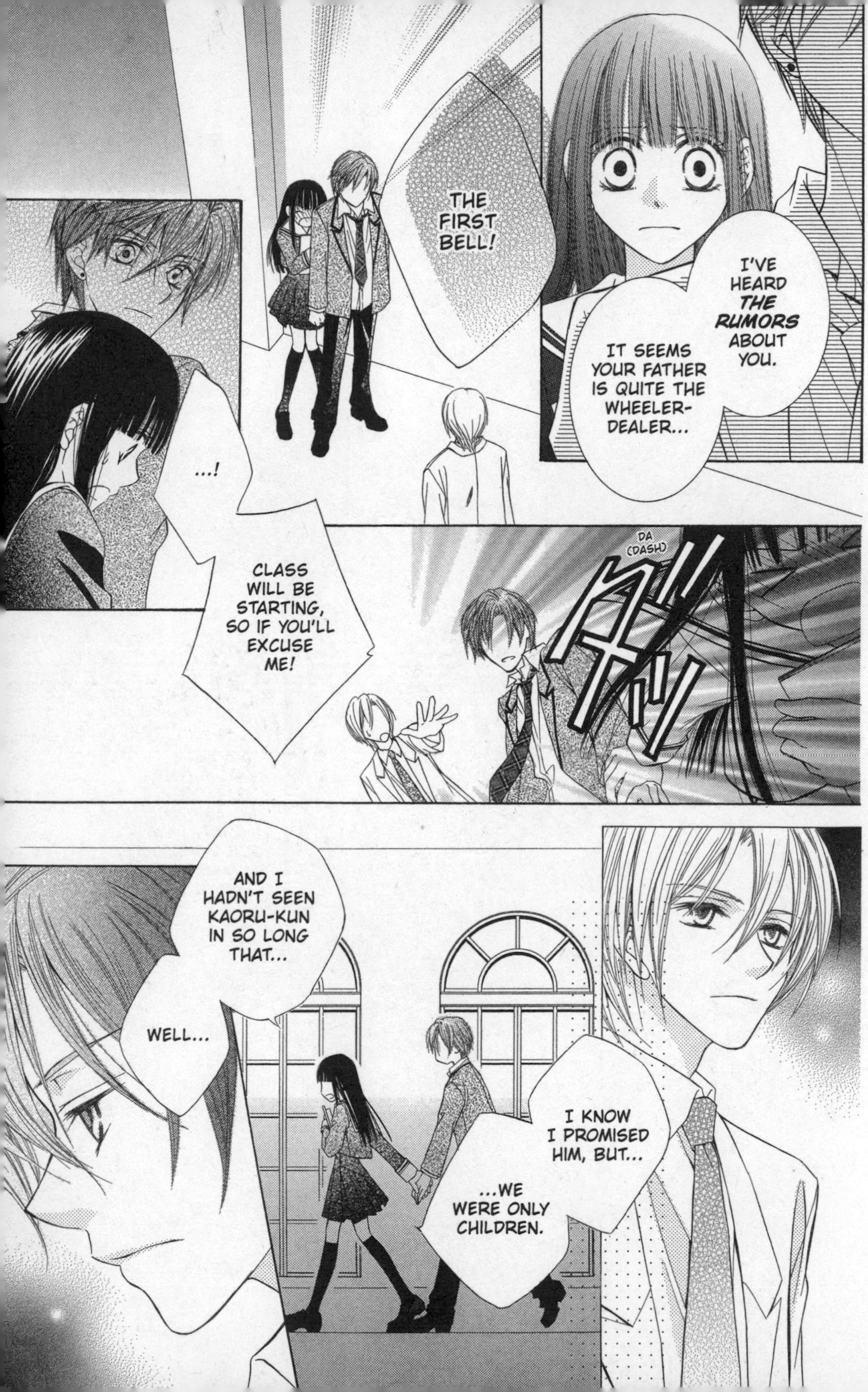
I'VE HEARD ***THE RUMORS*** ABOUT YOU.
IT SEEMS YOUR FATHER IS QUITE THE WHEELER-DEALER...
THE FIRST BELL!
...!
CLASS WILL BE STARTING, SO IF YOU'LL EXCUSE ME!
DA (DASH)
I KNOW I PROMISED HIM, BUT...
...WE WERE ONLY CHILDREN.
AND I HADN'T SEEN KAORU-KUN IN SO LONG THAT...
WELL...

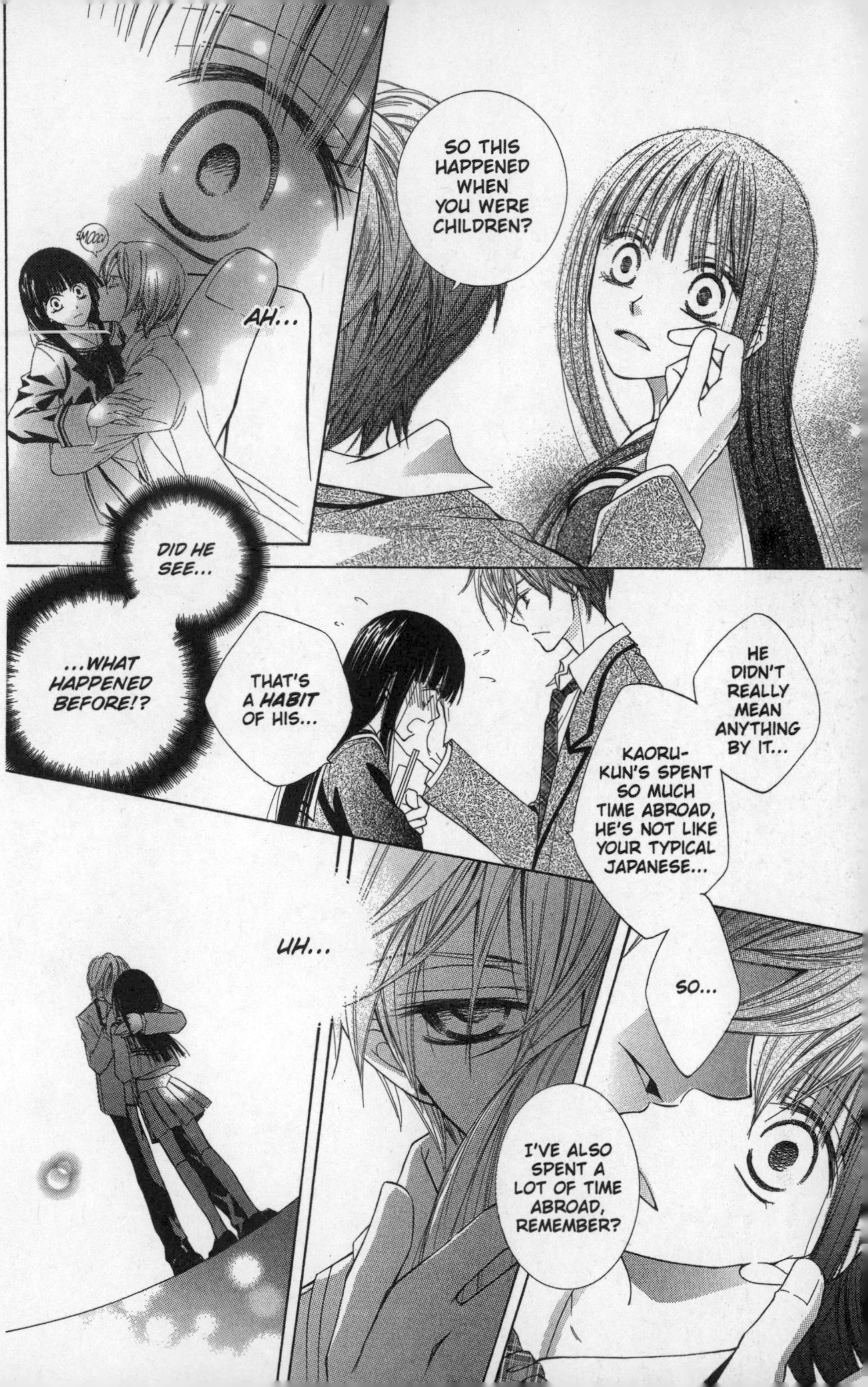
SO THIS HAPPENED WHEN YOU WERE CHILDREN?
AH...
DID HE SEE...
...WHAT HAPPENED BEFORE!?
THAT'S A *HABIT* OF HIS...
HE DIDN'T REALLY MEAN ANYTHING BY IT...
KAORU-KUN'S SPENT SO MUCH TIME ABROAD, HE'S NOT LIKE YOUR TYPICAL JAPANESE...
SO...
I'VE ALSO SPENT A LOT OF TIME ABROAD, REMEMBER?
UH...

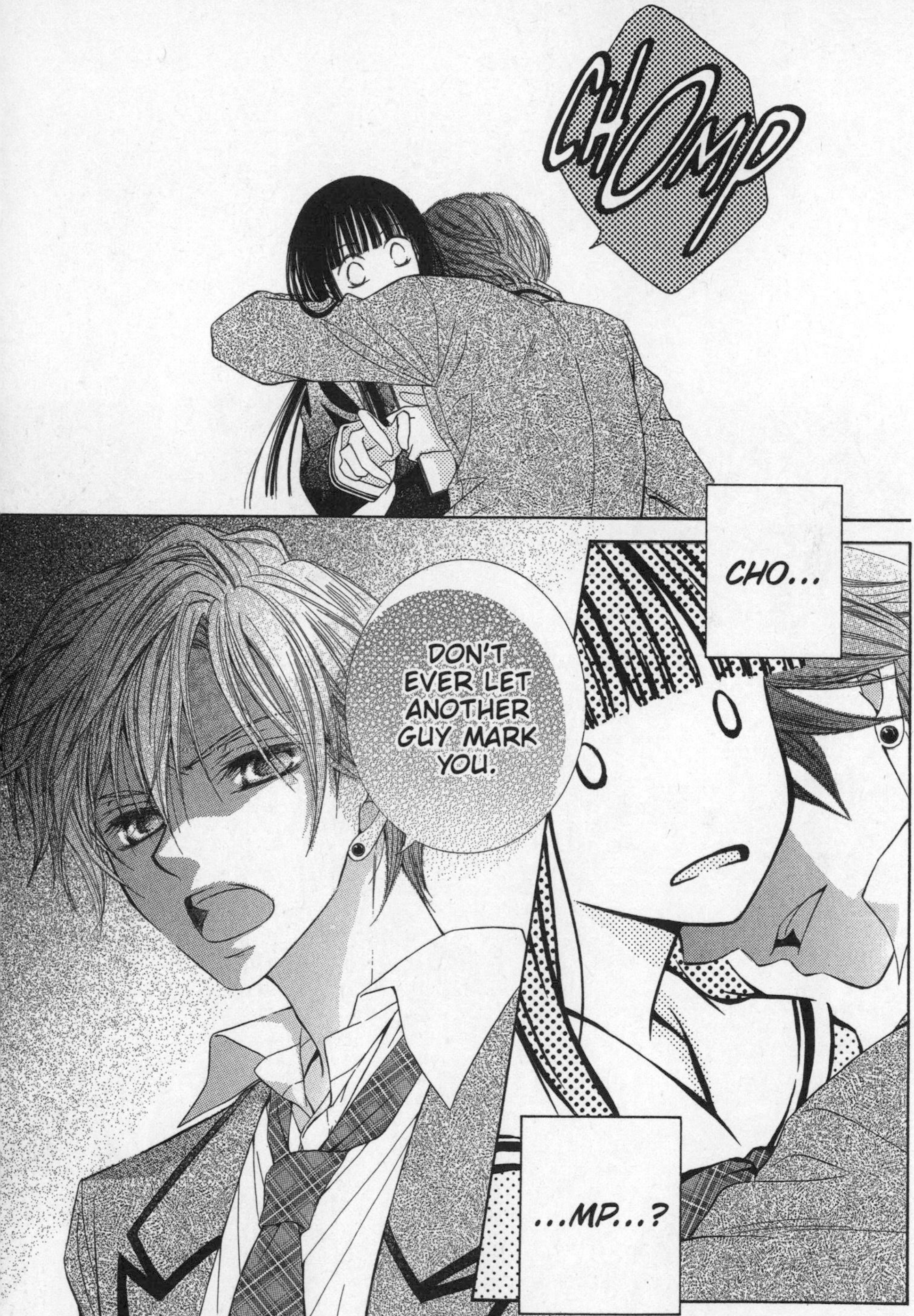
CHOMP
CHO...
DON'T EVER LET ANOTHER GUY MARK YOU.
...MP...?

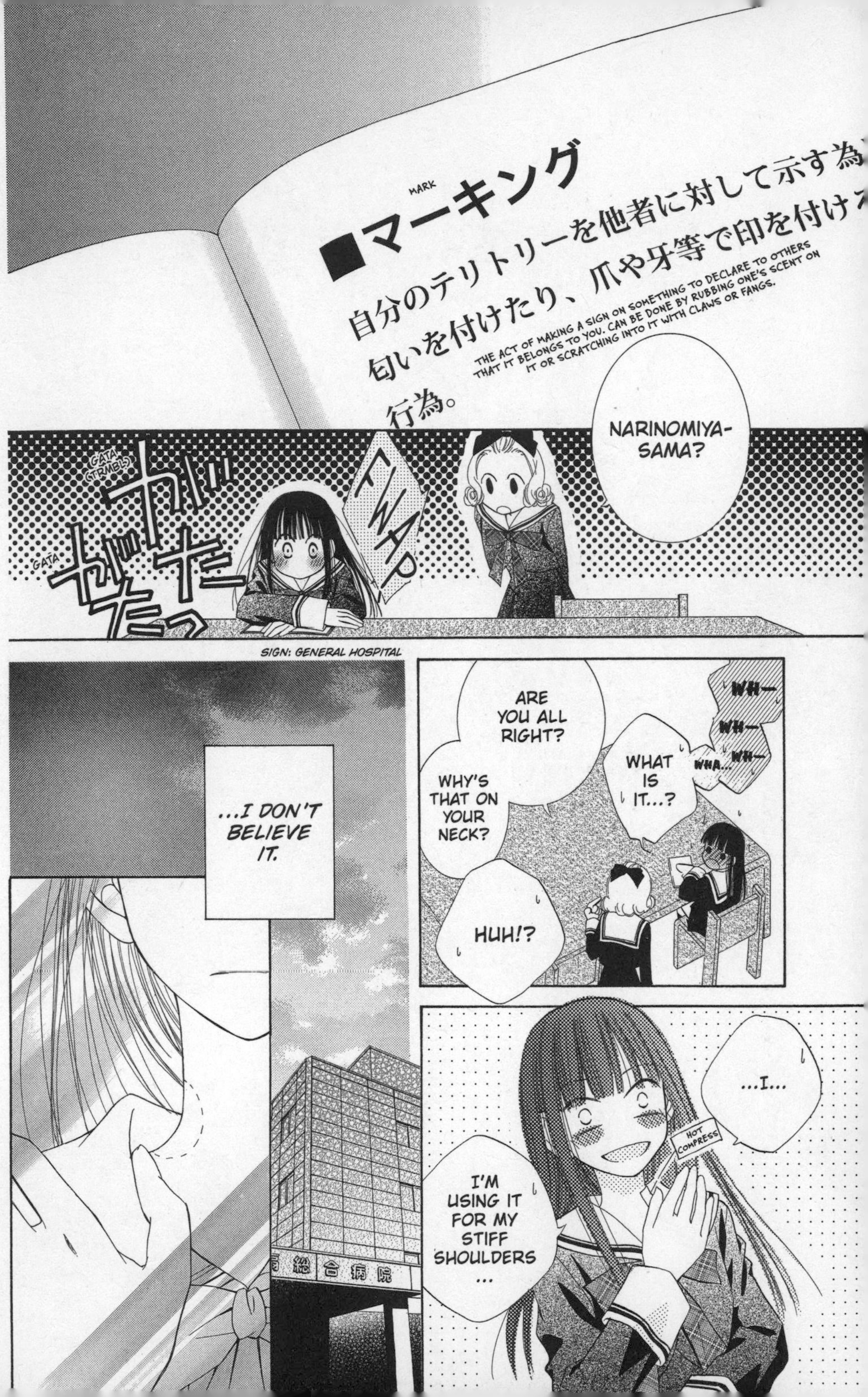
MARK
■マーキング
自分のテリトリーを他者に対して示す為
匂いを付けたり、爪や牙等で印を付け
行為。
THE ACT OF MAKING A SIGN ON SOMETHING TO DECLARE TO OTHERS THAT IT BELONGS TO YOU. CAN BE DONE BY RUBBING ONE'S SCENT ON IT OR SCRATCHING INTO IT WITH CLAWS OR FANGS.
NARINOMIYA-SAMA?
FWAP
GATA (TRMBL)
GATA
SIGN: GENERAL HOSPITAL
WH— WH— WH— WHA...
WHAT IS IT...?
ARE YOU ALL RIGHT?
WHY'S THAT ON YOUR NECK?
HUH!?
...I...
HOT COMPRESS
I'M USING IT FOR MY STIFF SHOULDERS ...
...I DON'T BELIEVE IT.
総合病院

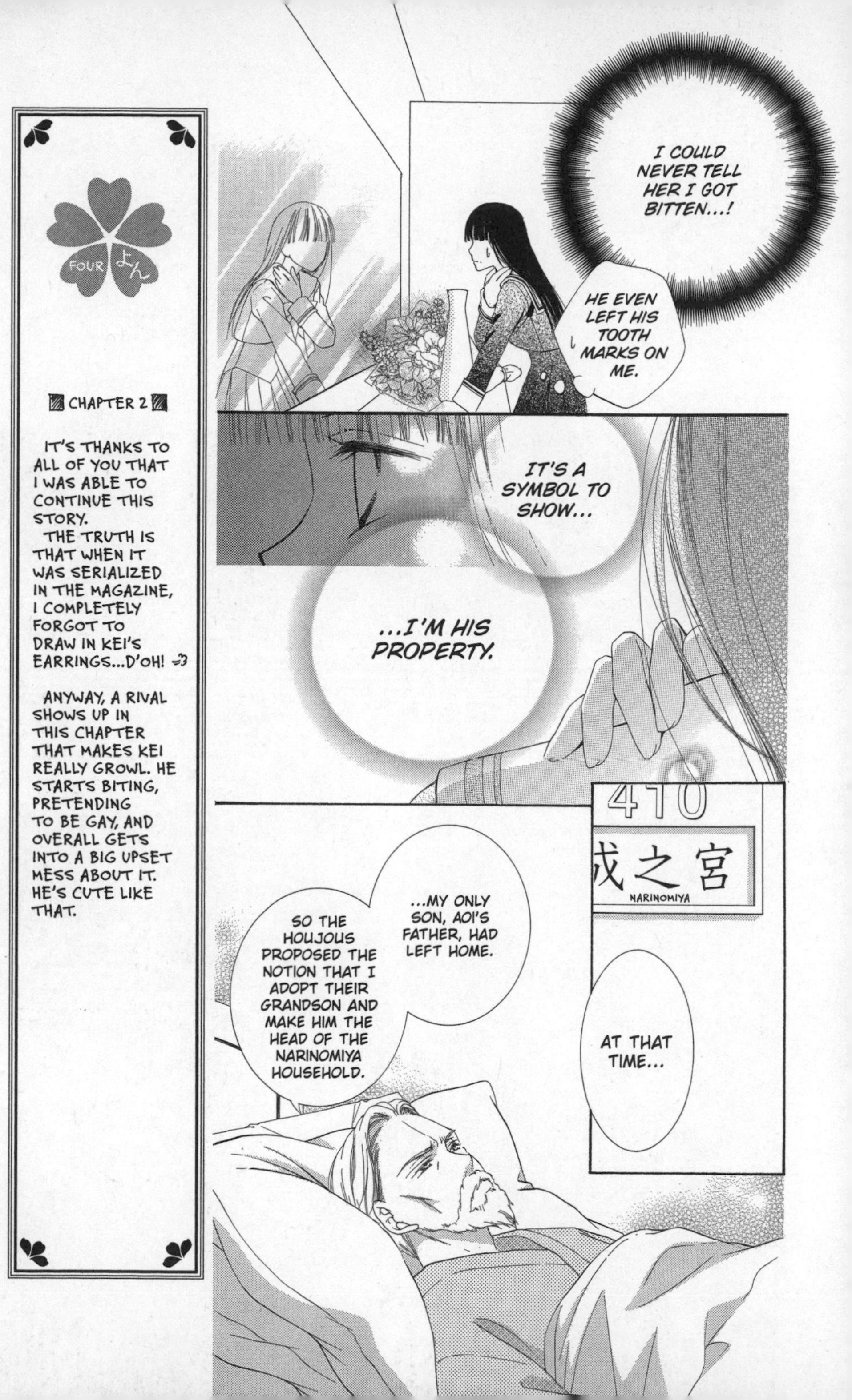

I COULD NEVER TELL HER I GOT BITTEN...!
HE EVEN LEFT HIS TOOTH MARKS ON ME.
IT'S A SYMBOL TO SHOW...
...I'M HIS PROPERTY.
410
成之宮
NARINOMIYA
AT THAT TIME...
...MY ONLY SON, AOI'S FATHER, HAD LEFT HOME.
SO THE HOUJOUS PROPOSED THE NOTION THAT I ADOPT THEIR GRANDSON AND MAKE HIM THE HEAD OF THE NARINOMIYA HOUSEHOLD.

FOUR よん

CHAPTER 2

IT'S THANKS TO ALL OF YOU THAT I WAS ABLE TO CONTINUE THIS STORY.

THE TRUTH IS THAT WHEN IT WAS SERIALIZED IN THE MAGAZINE, I COMPLETELY FORGOT TO DRAW IN KEI'S EARRINGS...D'OH!

ANYWAY, A RIVAL SHOWS UP IN THIS CHAPTER THAT MAKES KEI REALLY GROWL. HE STARTS BITING, PRETENDING TO BE GAY, AND OVERALL GETS INTO A BIG UPSET MESS ABOUT IT. HE'S CUTE LIKE THAT.

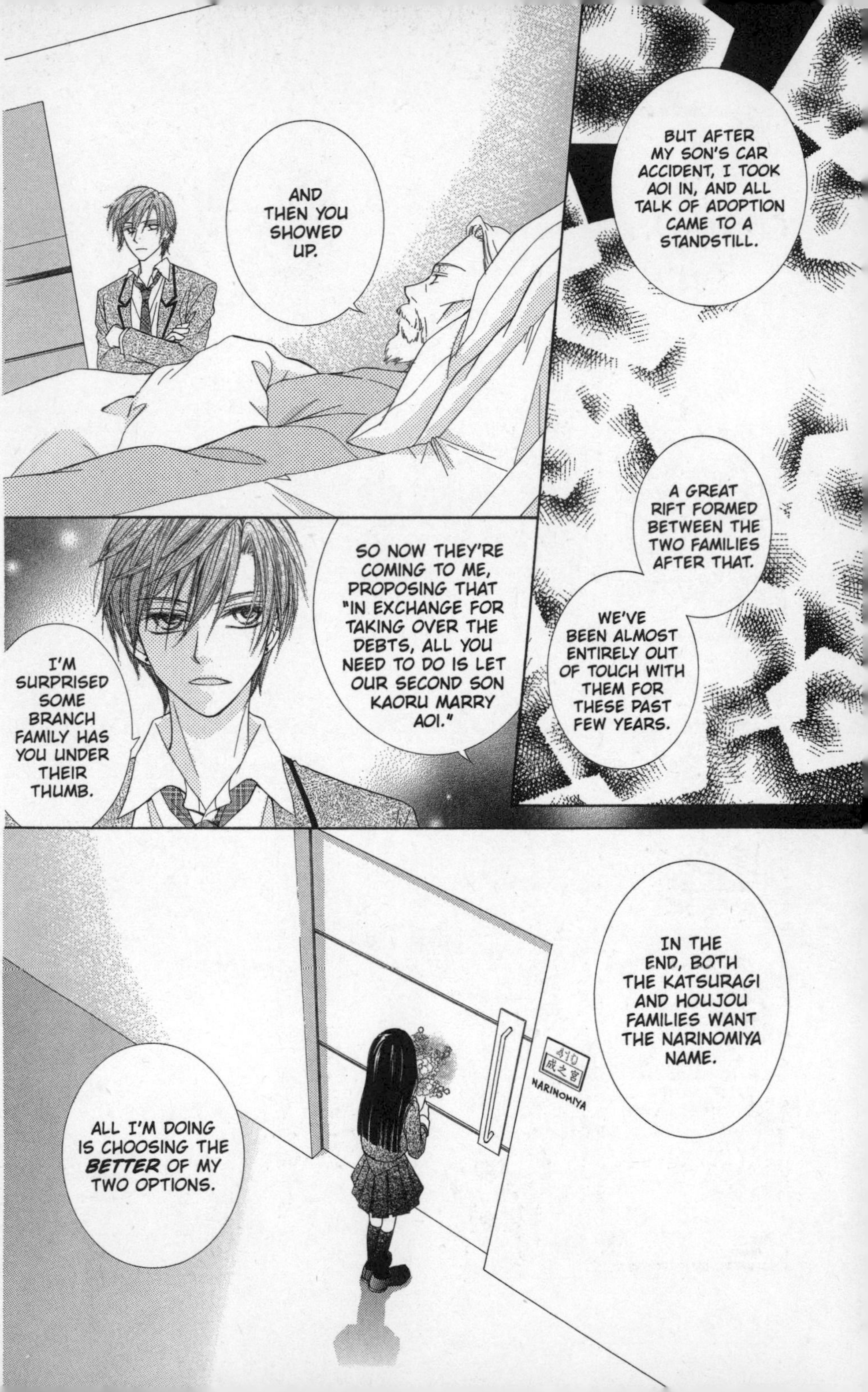
BUT AFTER MY SON'S CAR ACCIDENT, I TOOK AOI IN, AND ALL TALK OF ADOPTION CAME TO A STANDSTILL.
A GREAT RIFT FORMED BETWEEN THE TWO FAMILIES AFTER THAT.
WE'VE BEEN ALMOST ENTIRELY OUT OF TOUCH WITH THEM FOR THESE PAST FEW YEARS.
AND THEN YOU SHOWED UP.
SO NOW THEY'RE COMING TO ME, PROPOSING THAT "IN EXCHANGE FOR TAKING OVER THE DEBTS, ALL YOU NEED TO DO IS LET OUR SECOND SON KAORU MARRY AOI."
I'M SURPRISED SOME BRANCH FAMILY HAS YOU UNDER THEIR THUMB.
IN THE END, BOTH THE KATSURAGI AND HOUJOU FAMILIES WANT THE NARINOMIYA NAME.
410
成之宮
NARINOMIYA
ALL I'M DOING IS CHOOSING THE ***BETTER*** OF MY TWO OPTIONS.

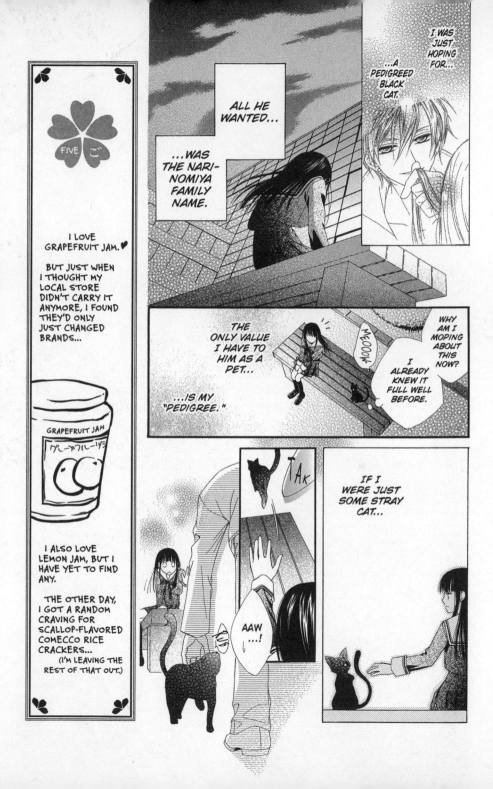

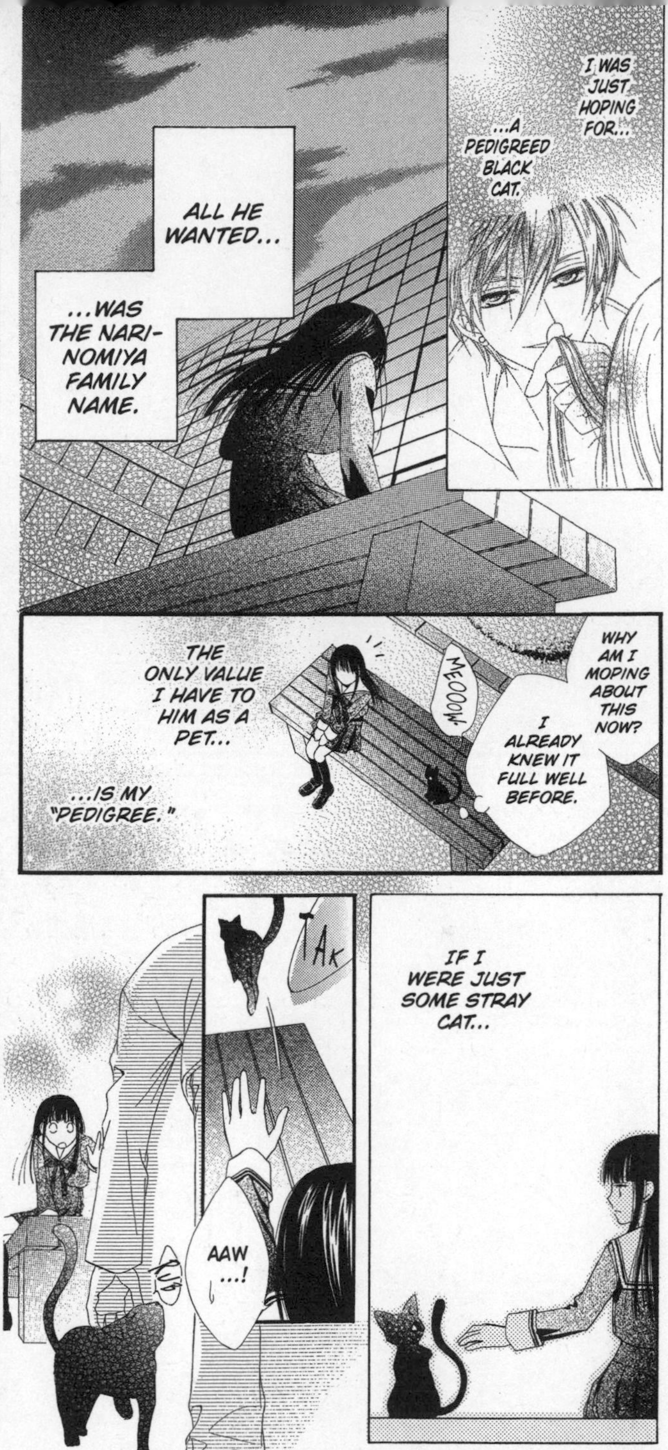
I WAS JUST HOPING FOR...
...A PEDIGREED BLACK CAT.
ALL HE WANTED...
...WAS THE NARI-NOMIYA FAMILY NAME.
WHY AM I MOPING ABOUT THIS NOW?
I ALREADY KNEW IT FULL WELL BEFORE.
MEOOOW
THE ONLY VALUE I HAVE TO HIM AS A PET...
...IS MY "PEDIGREE."
IF I WERE JUST SOME STRAY CAT...
TAK
AAW ...!
RUB

FIVE ご

I LOVE GRAPEFRUIT JAM.♥

BUT JUST WHEN I THOUGHT MY LOCAL STORE DIDN'T CARRY IT ANYMORE, I FOUND THEY'D ONLY JUST CHANGED BRANDS...

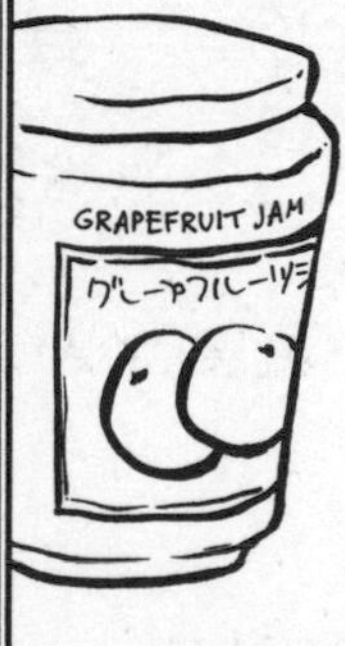
GRAPEFRUIT JAM
グレープフルーツジャ

I ALSO LOVE LEMON JAM, BUT I HAVE YET TO FIND ANY.

THE OTHER DAY, I GOT A RANDOM CRAVING FOR SCALLOP-FLAVORED COMECCO RICE CRACKERS...
(I'M LEAVING THE REST OF THAT OUT.)

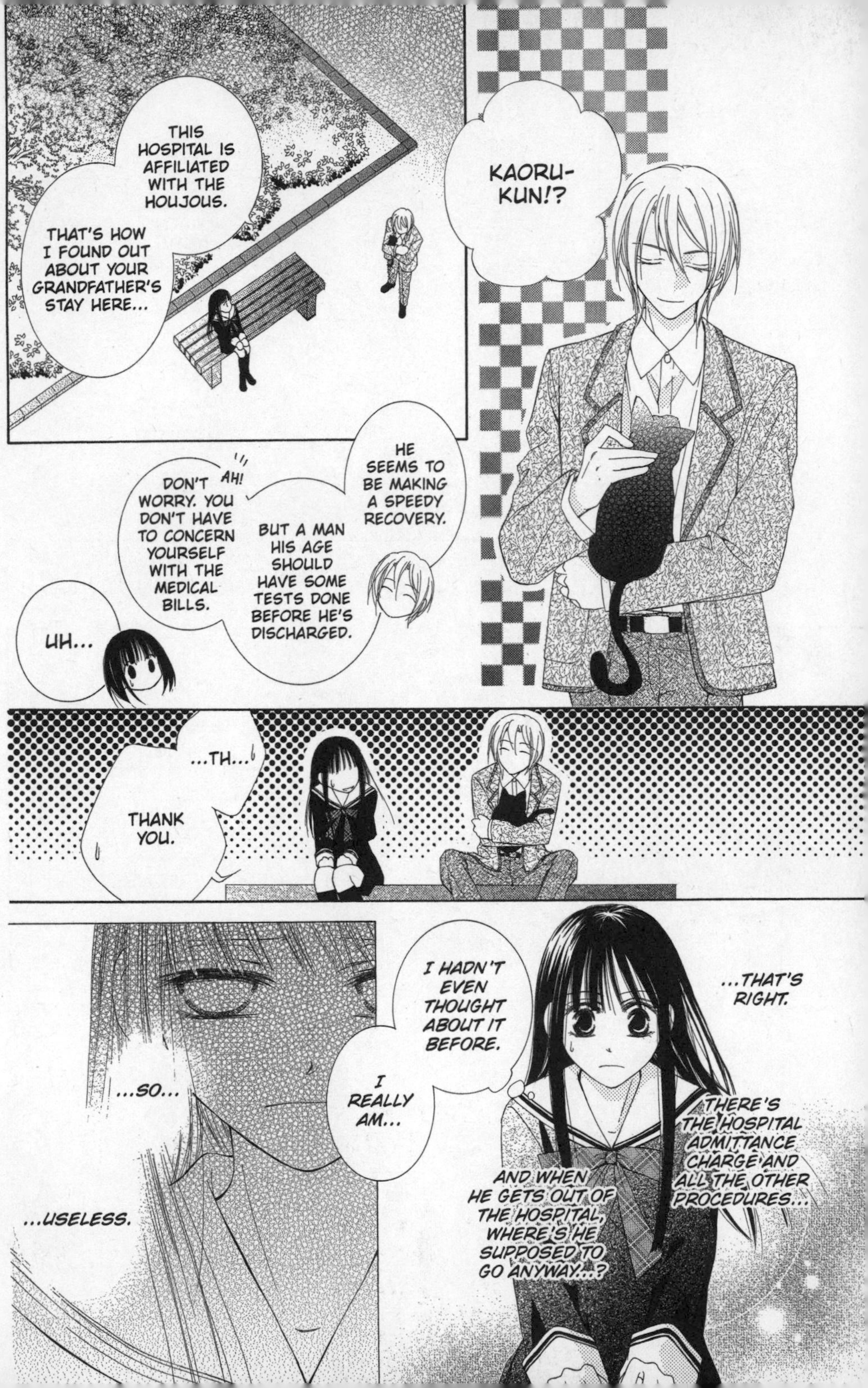
KAORU-KUN!?
THIS HOSPITAL IS AFFILIATED WITH THE HOUJOUS.
THAT'S HOW I FOUND OUT ABOUT YOUR GRANDFATHER'S STAY HERE...
HE SEEMS TO BE MAKING A SPEEDY RECOVERY.
BUT A MAN HIS AGE SHOULD HAVE SOME TESTS DONE BEFORE HE'S DISCHARGED.
AH!
DON'T WORRY. YOU DON'T HAVE TO CONCERN YOURSELF WITH THE MEDICAL BILLS.
UH...
...TH...
THANK YOU.
...THAT'S RIGHT.
THERE'S THE HOSPITAL ADMITTANCE CHARGE AND ALL THE OTHER PROCEDURES...
AND WHEN HE GETS OUT OF THE HOSPITAL, WHERE'S HE SUPPOSED TO GO ANYWAY...?
I HADN'T EVEN THOUGHT ABOUT IT BEFORE.
I REALLY AM...
...SO...
...USELESS.

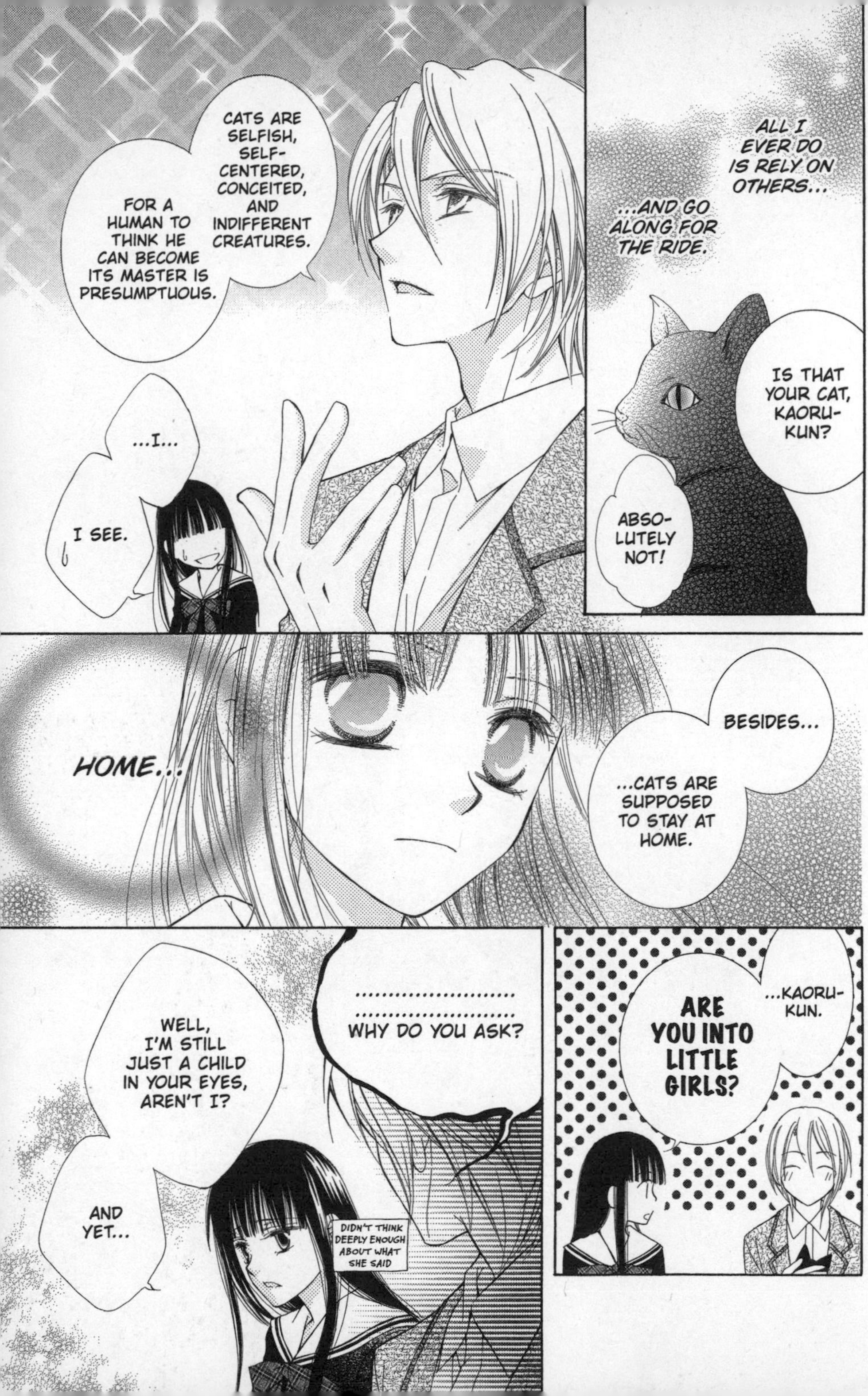
ALL I EVER DO IS RELY ON OTHERS...
...AND GO ALONG FOR THE RIDE.
IS THAT YOUR CAT, KAORU-KUN?
ABSOLUTELY NOT!
CATS ARE SELFISH, SELF-CENTERED, CONCEITED, AND INDIFFERENT CREATURES.
FOR A HUMAN TO THINK HE CAN BECOME ITS MASTER IS PRESUMPTUOUS.
...I...
I SEE.
BESIDES...
...CATS ARE SUPPOSED TO STAY AT HOME.
HOME...
...KAORU-KUN.
ARE YOU INTO LITTLE GIRLS?
....
....
WHY DO YOU ASK?
WELL, I'M STILL JUST A CHILD IN YOUR EYES, AREN'T I?
AND YET...
DIDN'T THINK DEEPLY ENOUGH ABOUT WHAT SHE SAID

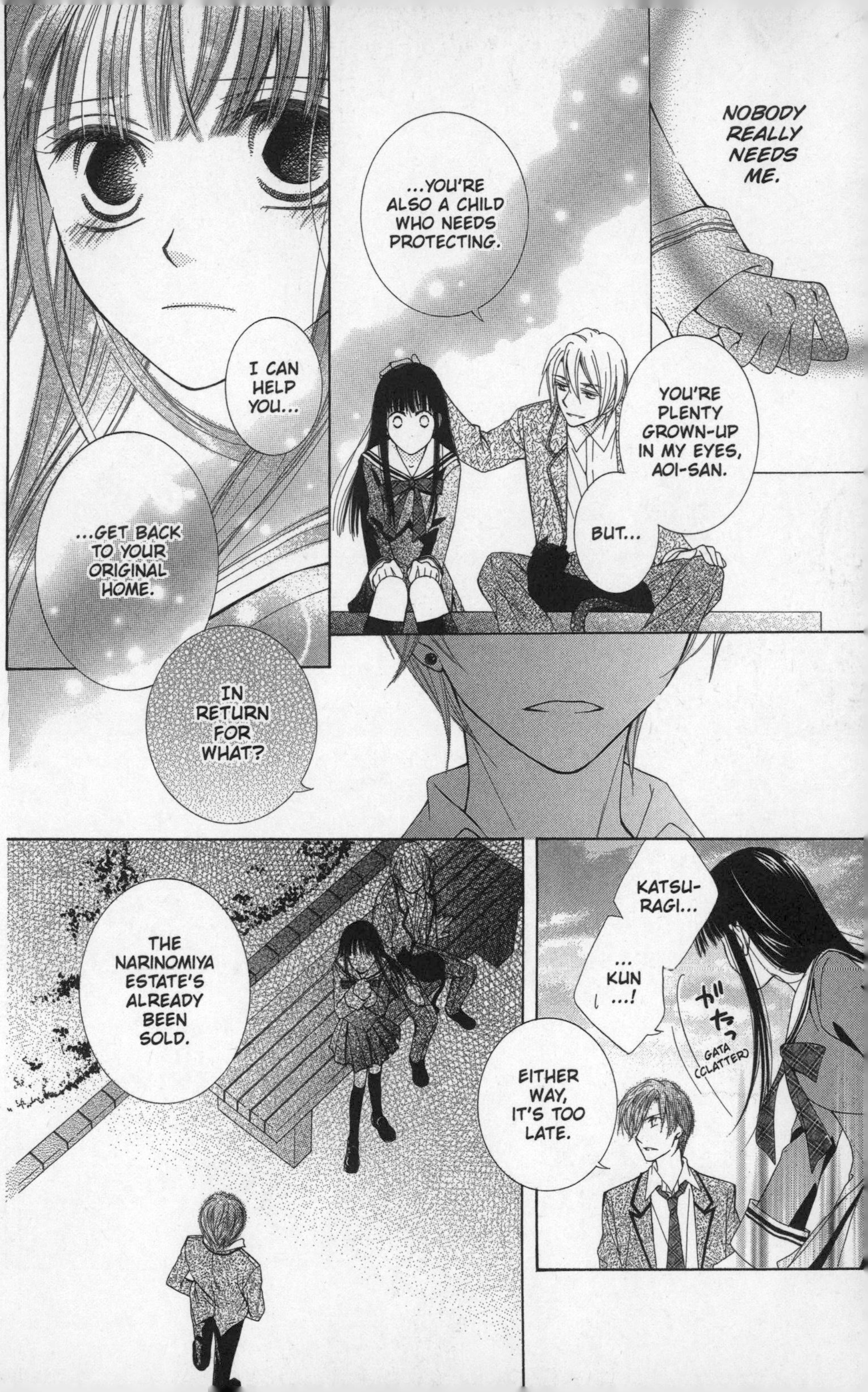
NOBODY REALLY NEEDS ME.
YOU'RE PLENTY GROWN-UP IN MY EYES, AOI-SAN.
BUT...
...YOU'RE ALSO A CHILD WHO NEEDS PROTECTING.
I CAN HELP YOU...
...GET BACK TO YOUR ORIGINAL HOME.
IN RETURN FOR WHAT?
KATSU-RAGI...
...KUN ...!
ガたっ
GATA (CLATTER)
EITHER WAY, IT'S TOO LATE.
THE NARINOMIYA ESTATE'S ALREADY BEEN SOLD.

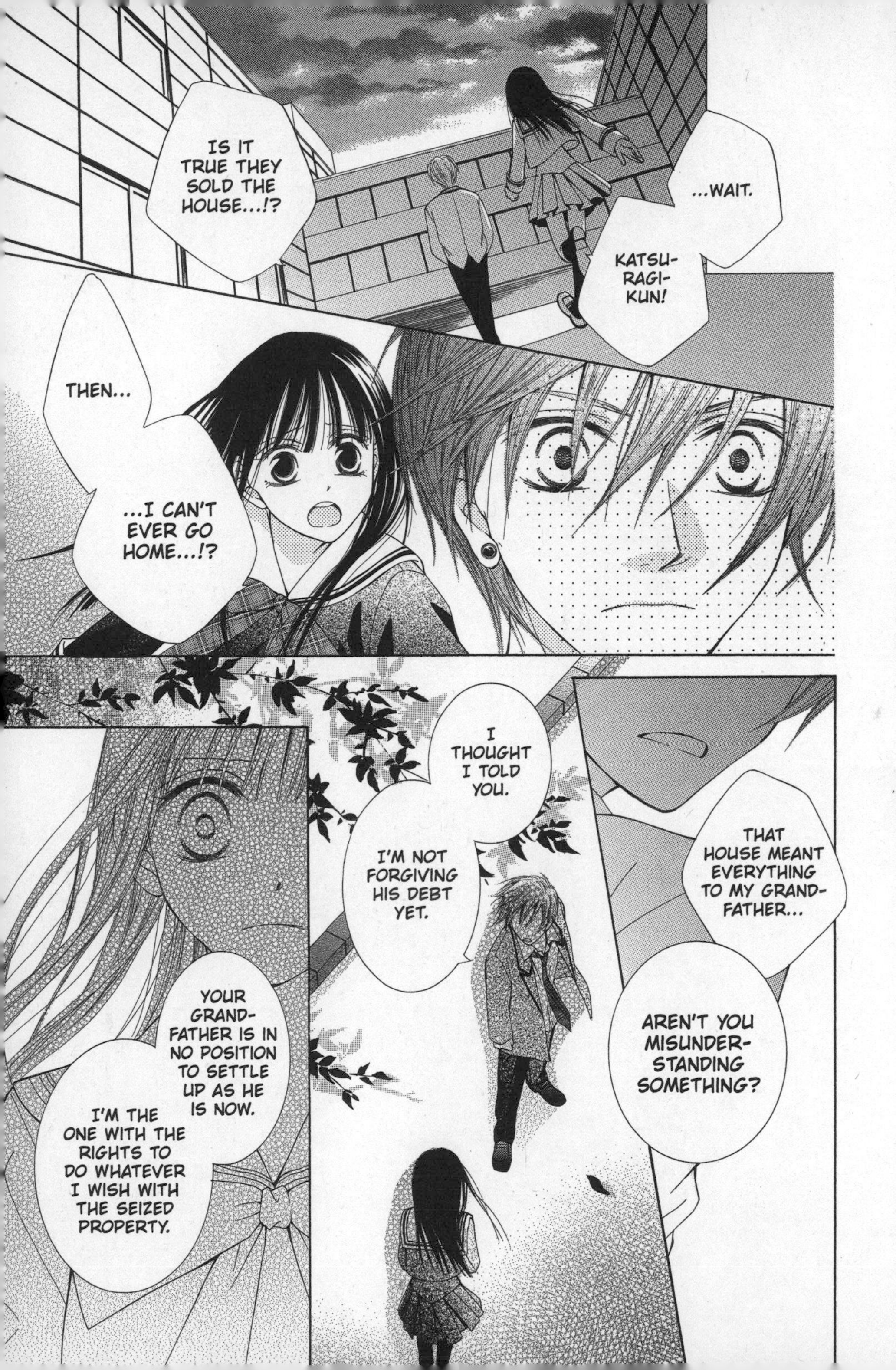
...WAIT.
KATSURAGI-KUN!
IS IT TRUE THEY SOLD THE HOUSE...!?
THEN...
...I CAN'T EVER GO HOME...!?
THAT HOUSE MEANT EVERYTHING TO MY GRANDFATHER...
AREN'T YOU MISUNDERSTANDING SOMETHING?
I THOUGHT I TOLD YOU.
I'M NOT FORGIVING HIS DEBT YET.
YOUR GRANDFATHER IS IN NO POSITION TO SETTLE UP AS HE IS NOW.
I'M THE ONE WITH THE RIGHTS TO DO WHATEVER I WISH WITH THE SEIZED PROPERTY.

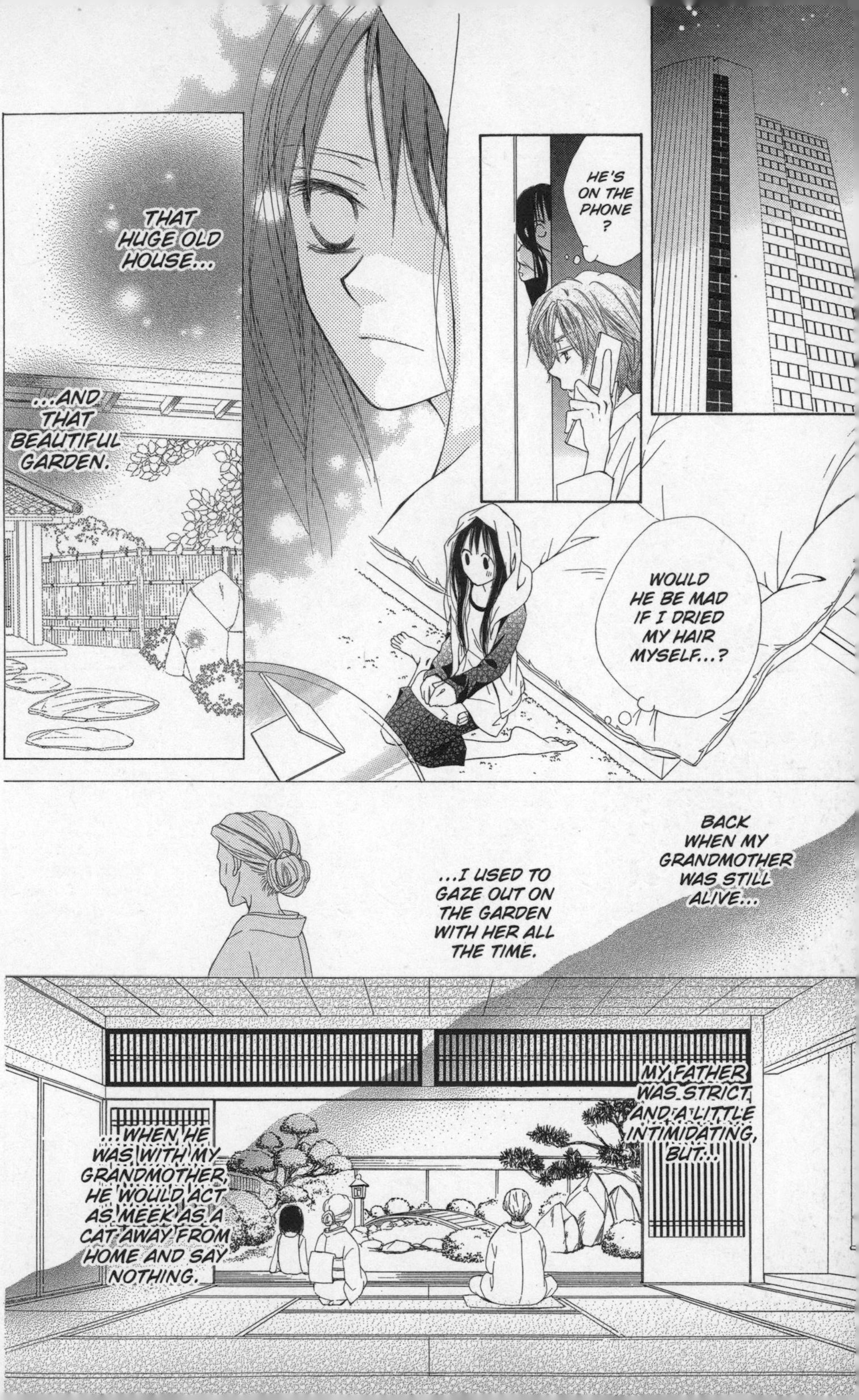
HE'S ON THE PHONE ?
WOULD HE BE MAD IF I DRIED MY HAIR MYSELF...?
THAT HUGE OLD HOUSE...
...AND THAT BEAUTIFUL GARDEN.
BACK WHEN MY GRANDMOTHER WAS STILL ALIVE...
...I USED TO GAZE OUT ON THE GARDEN WITH HER ALL THE TIME.
MY FATHER WAS STRICT AND A LITTLE INTIMIDATING, BUT...
...WHEN HE WAS WITH MY GRANDMOTHER, HE WOULD ACT AS MEEK AS A CAT AWAY FROM HOME AND SAY NOTHING.

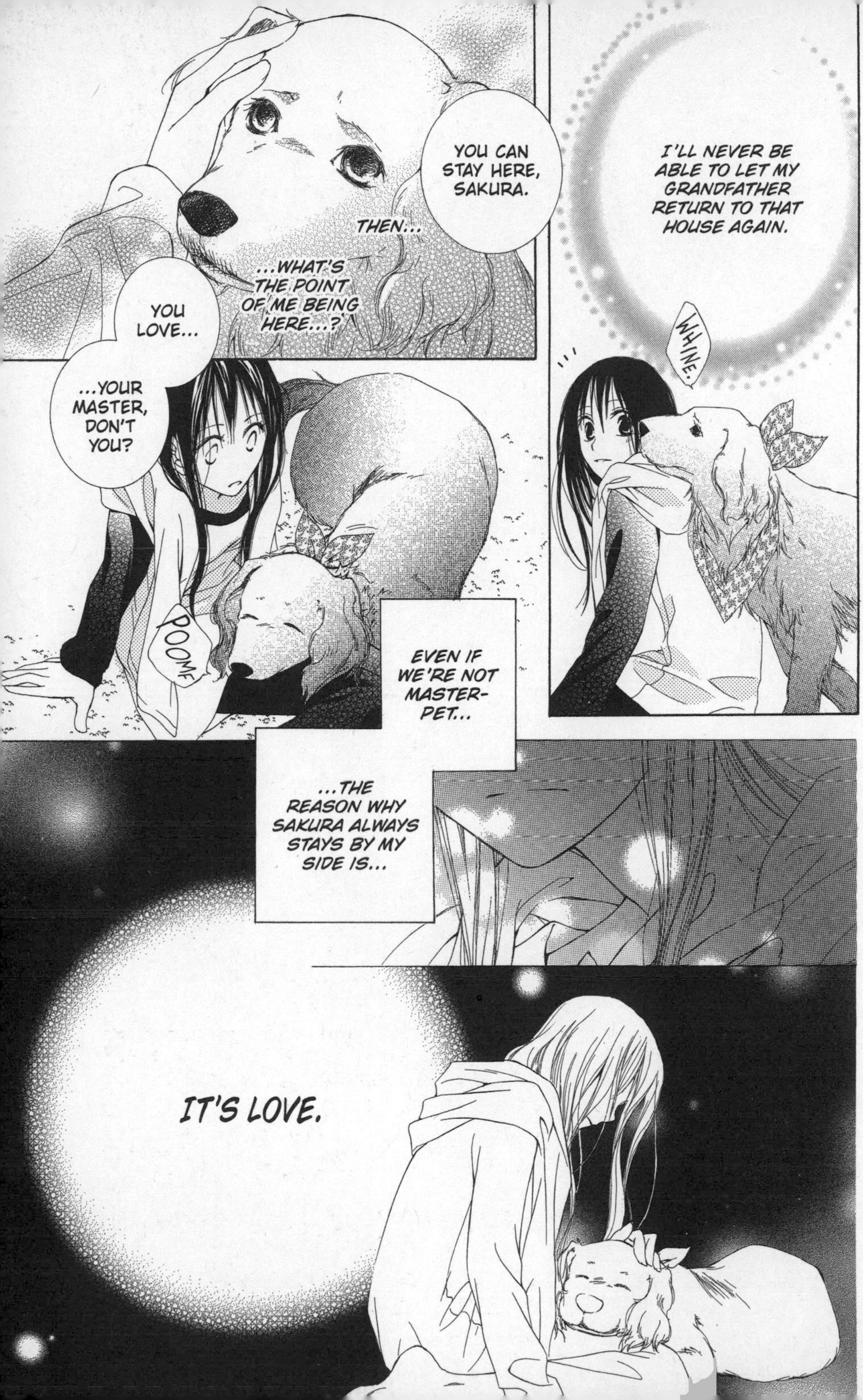
I'LL NEVER BE ABLE TO LET MY GRANDFATHER RETURN TO THAT HOUSE AGAIN.
WHINE.
YOU CAN STAY HERE, SAKURA.
THEN...
...WHAT'S THE POINT OF ME BEING HERE...?
YOU LOVE...
...YOUR MASTER, DON'T YOU?
POOMF
EVEN IF WE'RE NOT MASTER-PET...
...THE REASON WHY SAKURA ALWAYS STAYS BY MY SIDE IS...
IT'S LOVE.

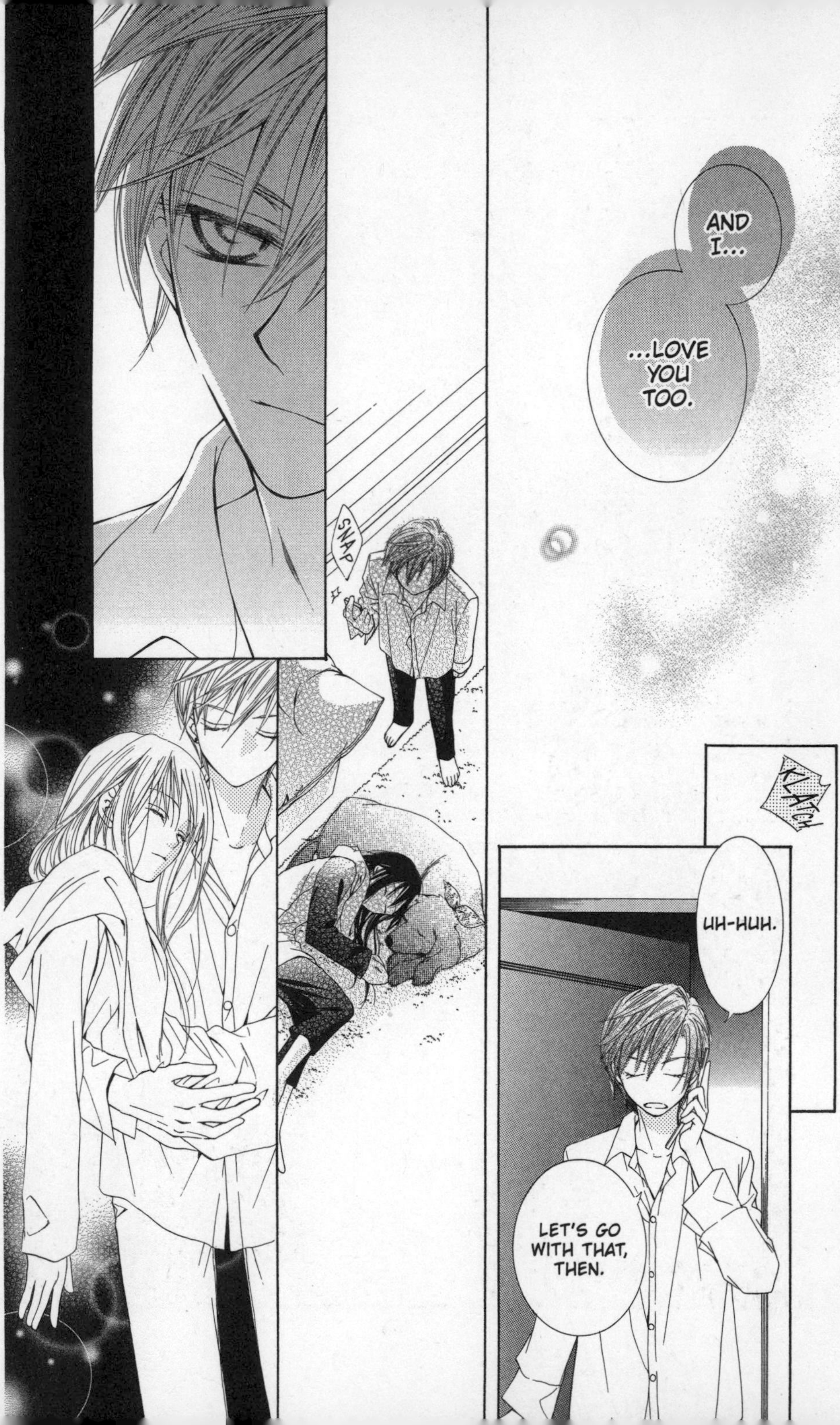
AND I...
...LOVE YOU TOO.
KLATCH
UH-HUH.
LET'S GO WITH THAT, THEN.
SNAP

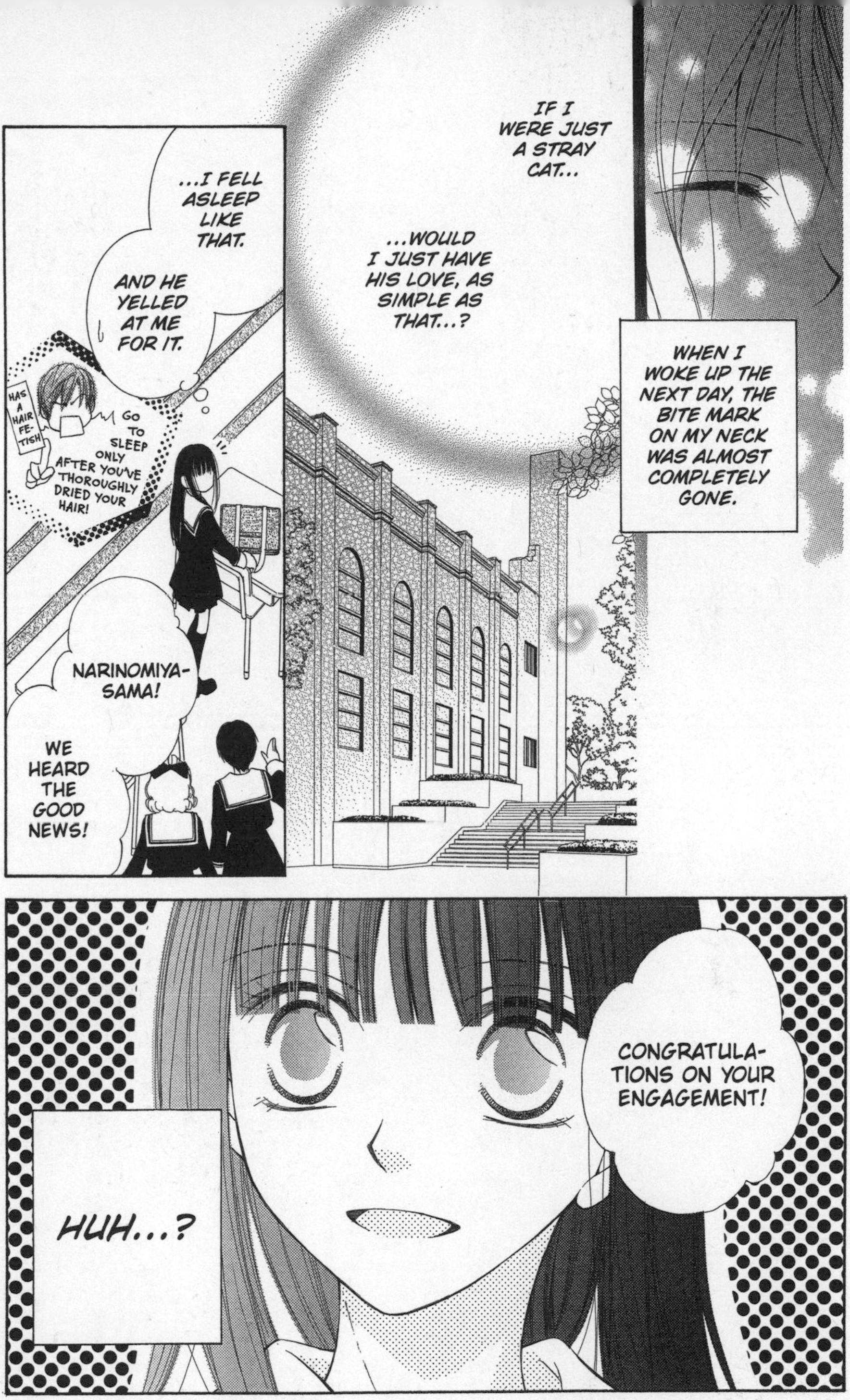
IF I WERE JUST A STRAY CAT...
...WOULD I JUST HAVE HIS LOVE, AS SIMPLE AS THAT...?
WHEN I WOKE UP THE NEXT DAY, THE BITE MARK ON MY NECK WAS ALMOST COMPLETELY GONE.
...I FELL ASLEEP LIKE THAT.
AND HE YELLED AT ME FOR IT.
HAS A HAIR FETISH
GO TO SLEEP ONLY AFTER YOU'VE THOROUGHLY DRIED YOUR HAIR!
NARINOMIYA-SAMA!
WE HEARD THE GOOD NEWS!
CONGRATULA-TIONS ON YOUR ENGAGEMENT!
HUH...?

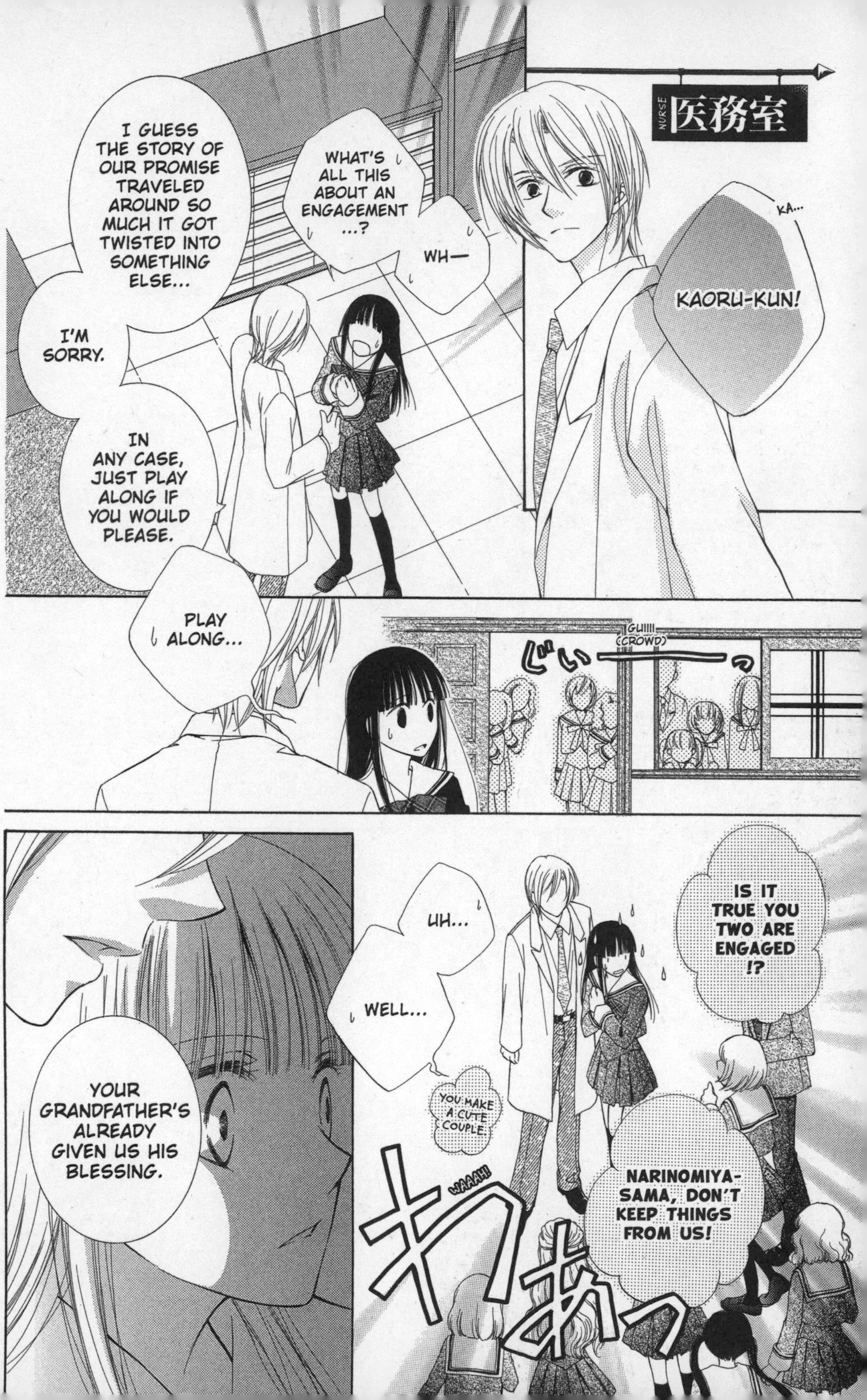
NURSE 医務室
KA...
KAORU-KUN!
WH—
WHAT'S ALL THIS ABOUT AN ENGAGEMENT ...?
I GUESS THE STORY OF OUR PROMISE TRAVELED AROUND SO MUCH IT GOT TWISTED INTO SOMETHING ELSE...
I'M SORRY.
IN ANY CASE, JUST PLAY ALONG IF YOU WOULD PLEASE.
GUIIII (CROWD)
じぃーーーっ
PLAY ALONG...
IS IT TRUE YOU TWO ARE ENGAGED !?
UH...
WELL...
YOU MAKE A CUTE COUPLE.
NARINOMIYA-SAMA, DON'T KEEP THINGS FROM US!
WAAAH!
キャあっ
YOUR GRANDFATHER'S ALREADY GIVEN US HIS BLESSING.

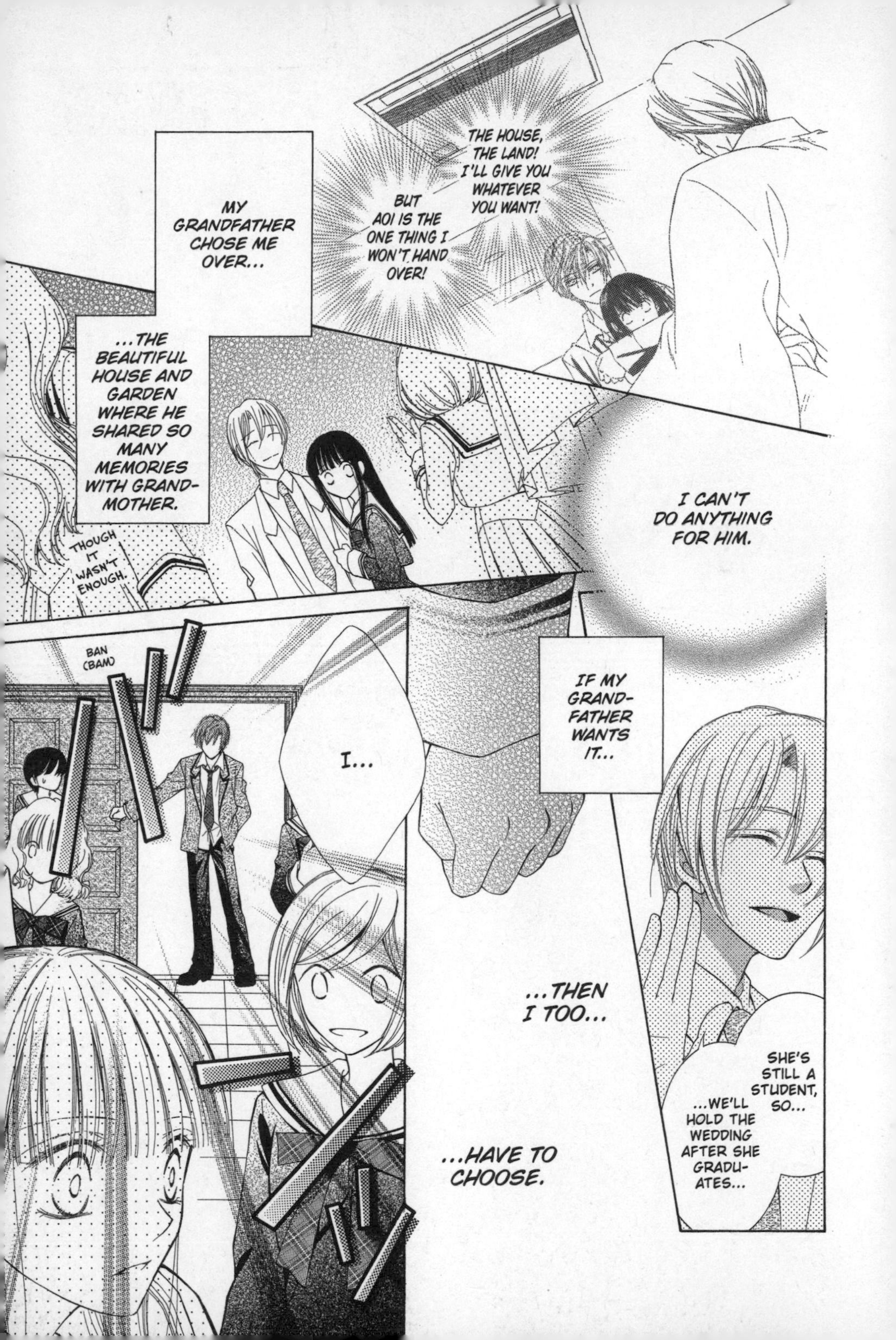
THE HOUSE, THE LAND! I'LL GIVE YOU WHATEVER YOU WANT!
BUT AOI IS THE ONE THING I WON'T HAND OVER!
MY GRANDFATHER CHOSE ME OVER...
...THE BEAUTIFUL HOUSE AND GARDEN WHERE HE SHARED SO MANY MEMORIES WITH GRAND-MOTHER.
THOUGH IT WASN'T ENOUGH.
I CAN'T DO ANYTHING FOR HIM.
IF MY GRAND-FATHER WANTS IT...
SHE'S STILL A STUDENT, SO...
...WE'LL HOLD THE WEDDING AFTER SHE GRADU-ATES...
...THEN I TOO...
...HAVE TO CHOOSE.
I...
BAN (BAM)

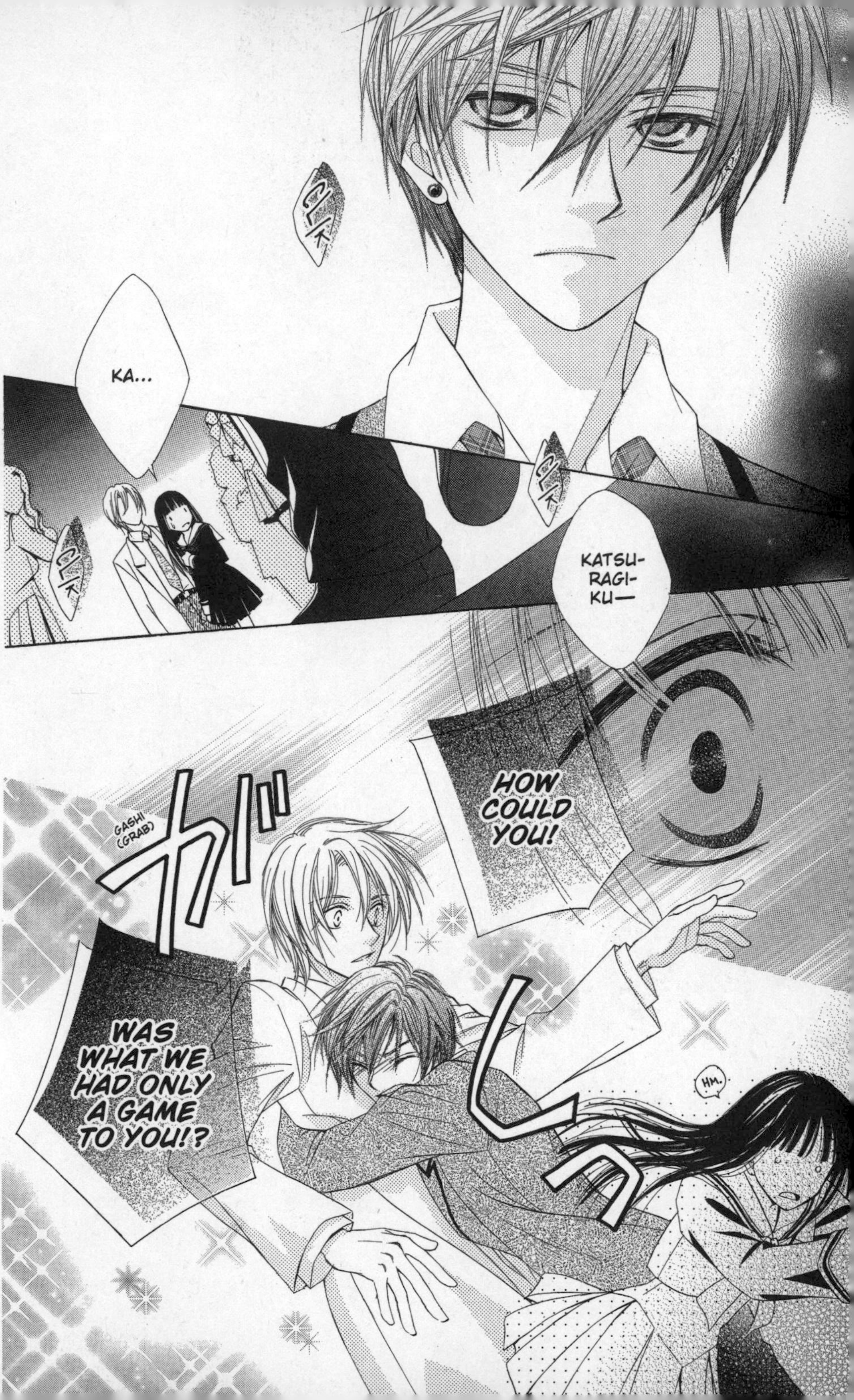
CLIK
KA...
CLIK
CLIK
KATSU-RAGI-KU—
HOW COULD YOU!
GASHI (GRAB)
WAS WHAT WE HAD ONLY A GAME TO YOU!?
HM.

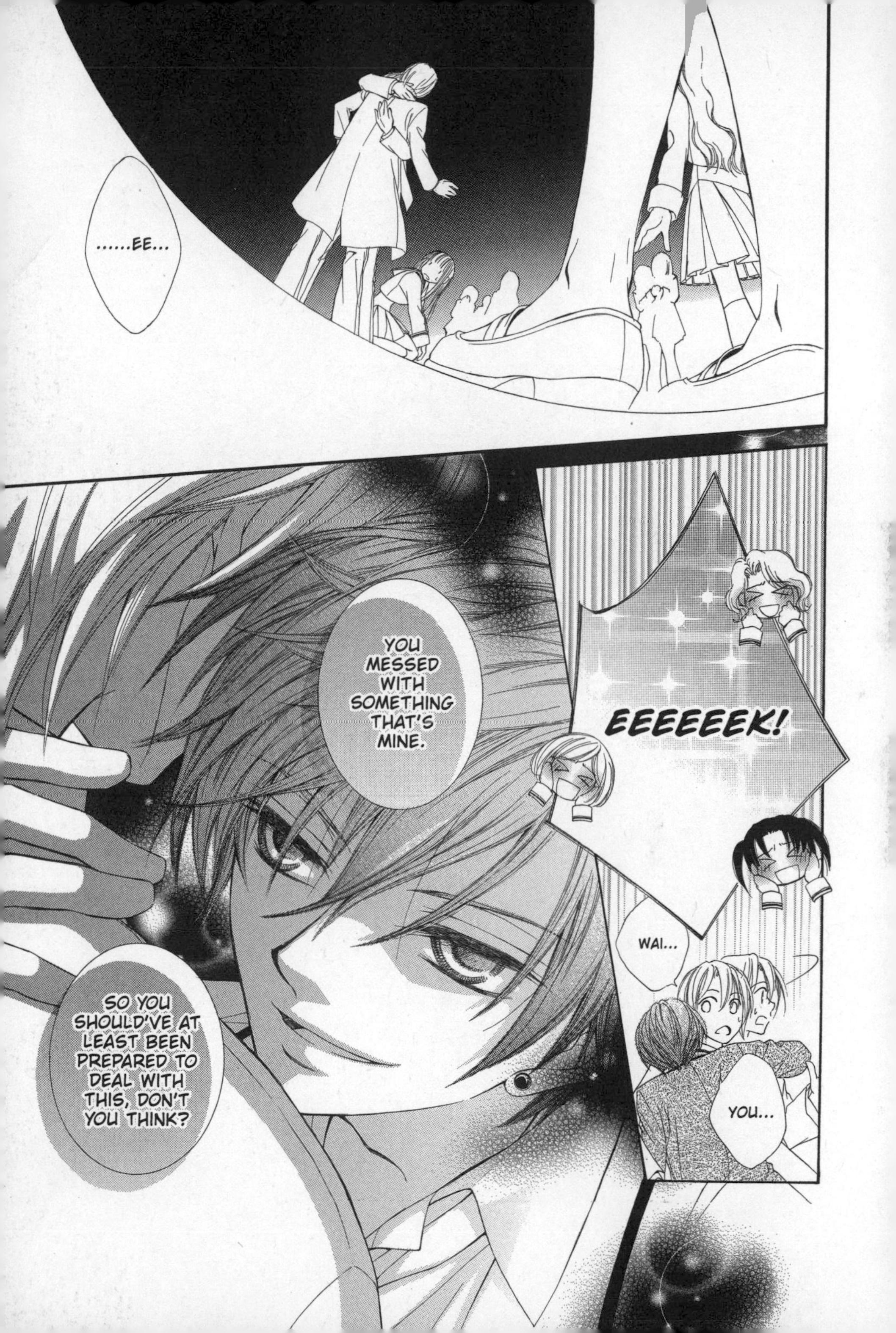
......EE...
EEEEEEK!
YOU MESSED WITH SOMETHING THAT'S MINE.
SO YOU SHOULD'VE AT LEAST BEEN PREPARED TO DEAL WITH THIS, DON'T YOU THINK?
WAI...
YOU...

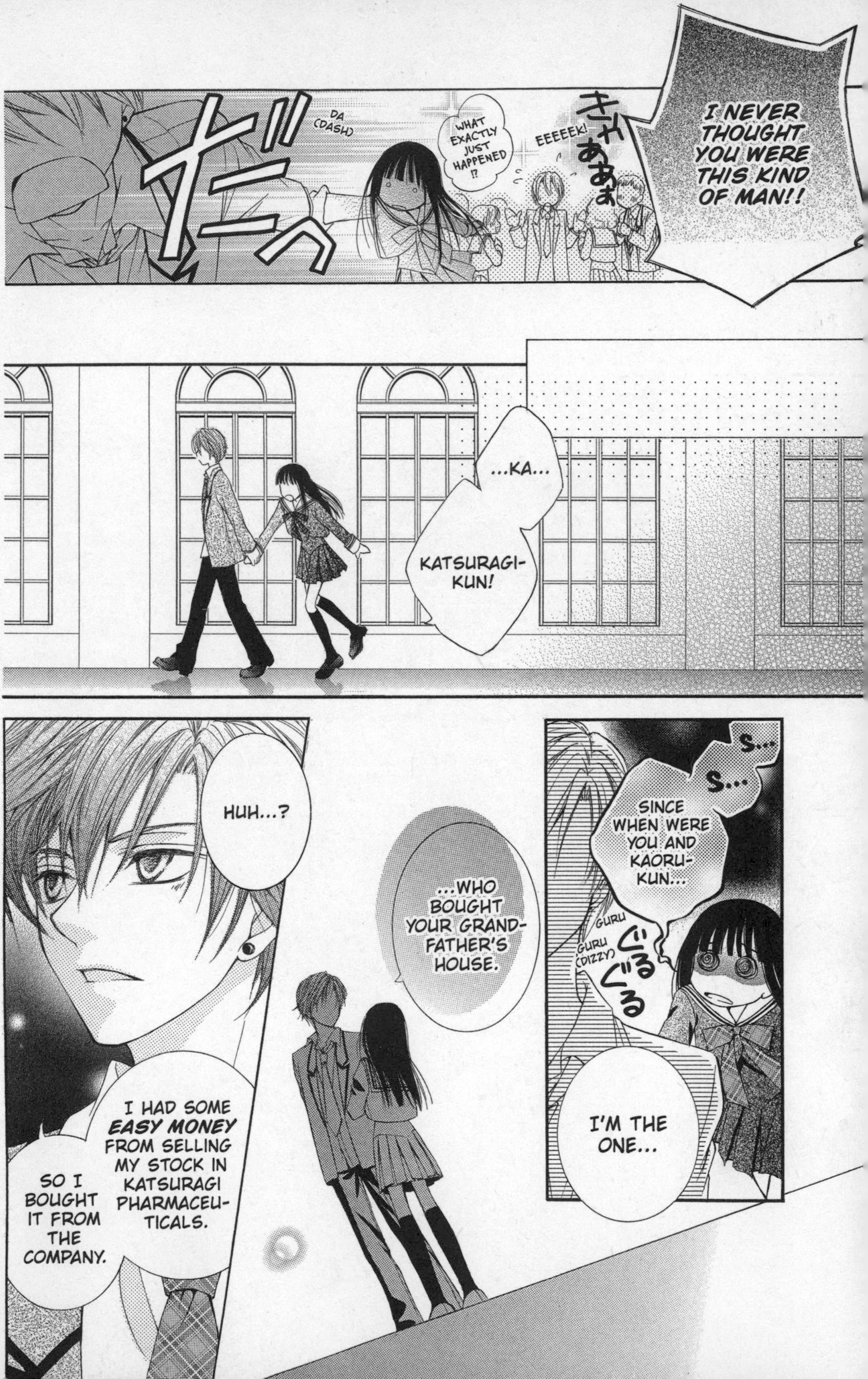

I NEVER THOUGHT YOU WERE THIS KIND OF MAN!!
きゃあああ
EEEEEK!
WHAT EXACTLY JUST HAPPENED!?
DA (DASH)
ダーッ
...KA...
KATSURAGI-KUN!
S... S...
SINCE WHEN WERE YOU AND KAORU-KUN...
GURU GURU (DIZZY)
ぐるぐる
I'M THE ONE...
...WHO BOUGHT YOUR GRAND-FATHER'S HOUSE.
HUH...?
I HAD SOME **EASY MONEY** FROM SELLING MY STOCK IN KATSURAGI PHARMACEU-TICALS.
SO I BOUGHT IT FROM THE COMPANY.

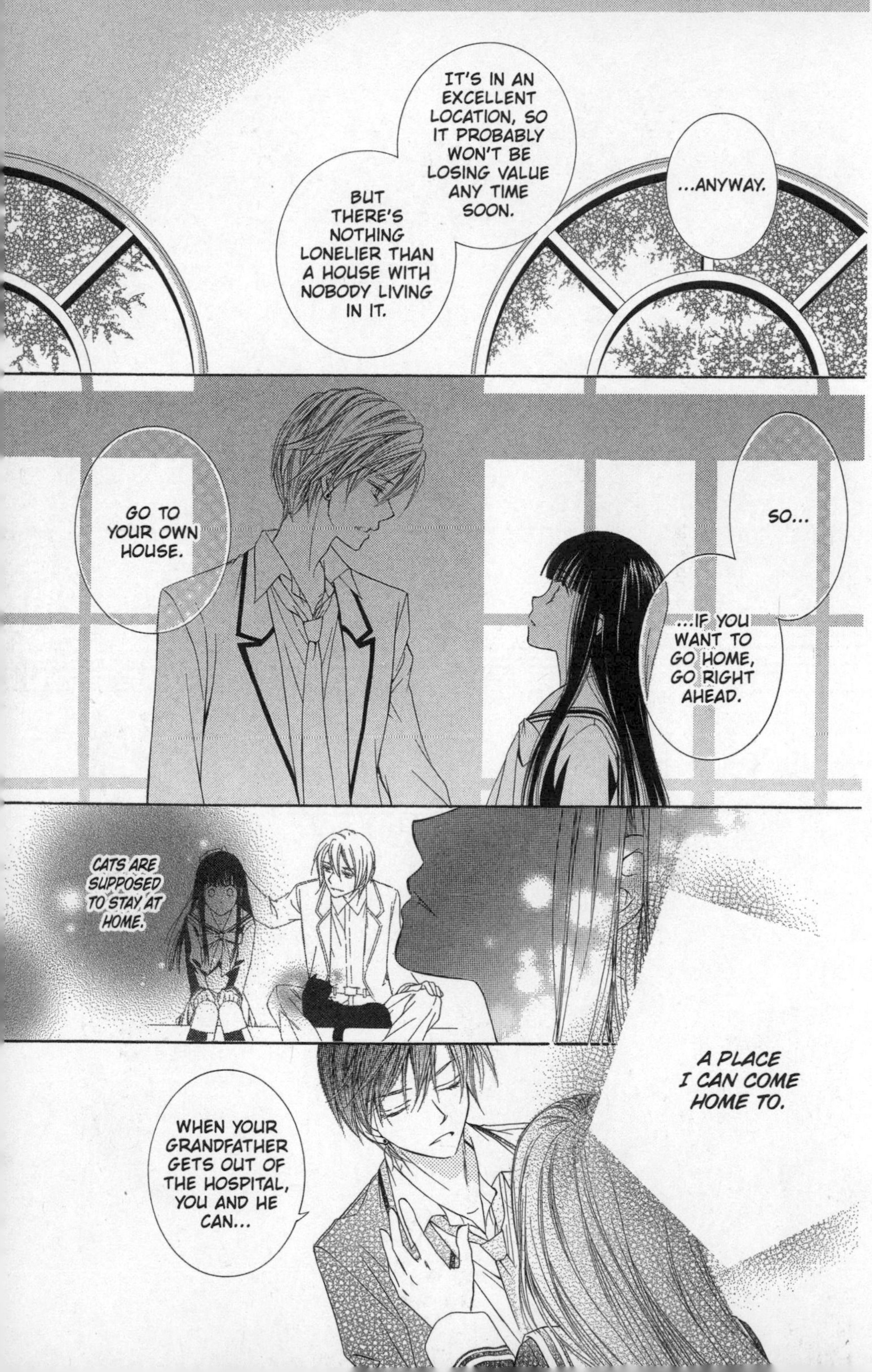
...ANYWAY.
IT'S IN AN EXCELLENT LOCATION, SO IT PROBABLY WON'T BE LOSING VALUE ANY TIME SOON.
BUT THERE'S NOTHING LONELIER THAN A HOUSE WITH NOBODY LIVING IN IT.
SO...
...IF YOU WANT TO GO HOME, GO RIGHT AHEAD.
GO TO YOUR OWN HOUSE.
CATS ARE SUPPOSED TO STAY AT HOME.
A PLACE I CAN COME HOME TO.
WHEN YOUR GRANDFATHER GETS OUT OF THE HOSPITAL, YOU AND HE CAN...

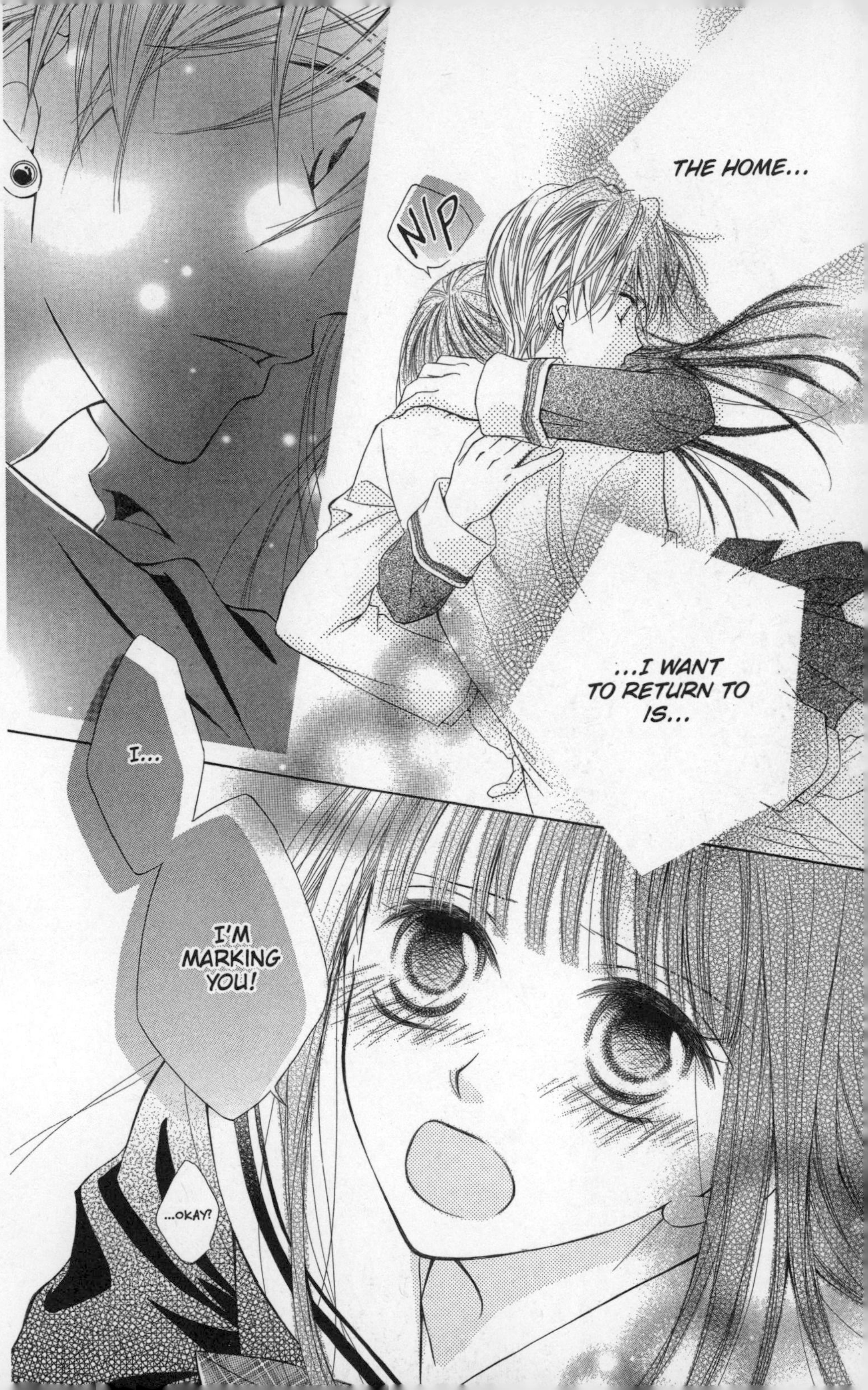
THE HOME...
NIP
...I WANT TO RETURN TO IS...
I...
I'M MARKING YOU!
...OKAY?

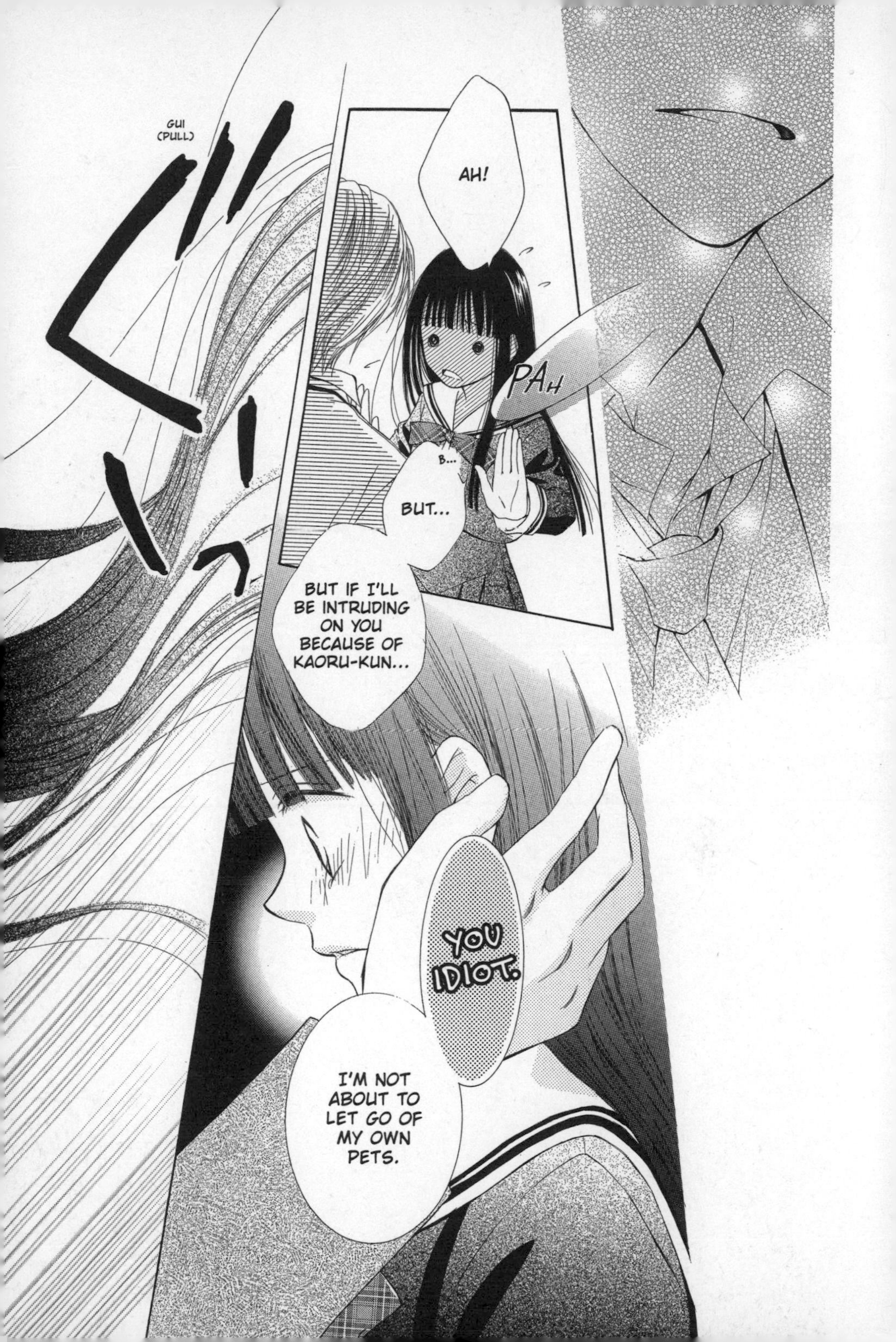
AH!
PAH
B...
BUT...
BUT IF I'LL BE INTRUDING ON YOU BECAUSE OF KAORU-KUN...
GUI (PULL)
YOU IDIOT.
I'M NOT ABOUT TO LET GO OF MY OWN PETS.

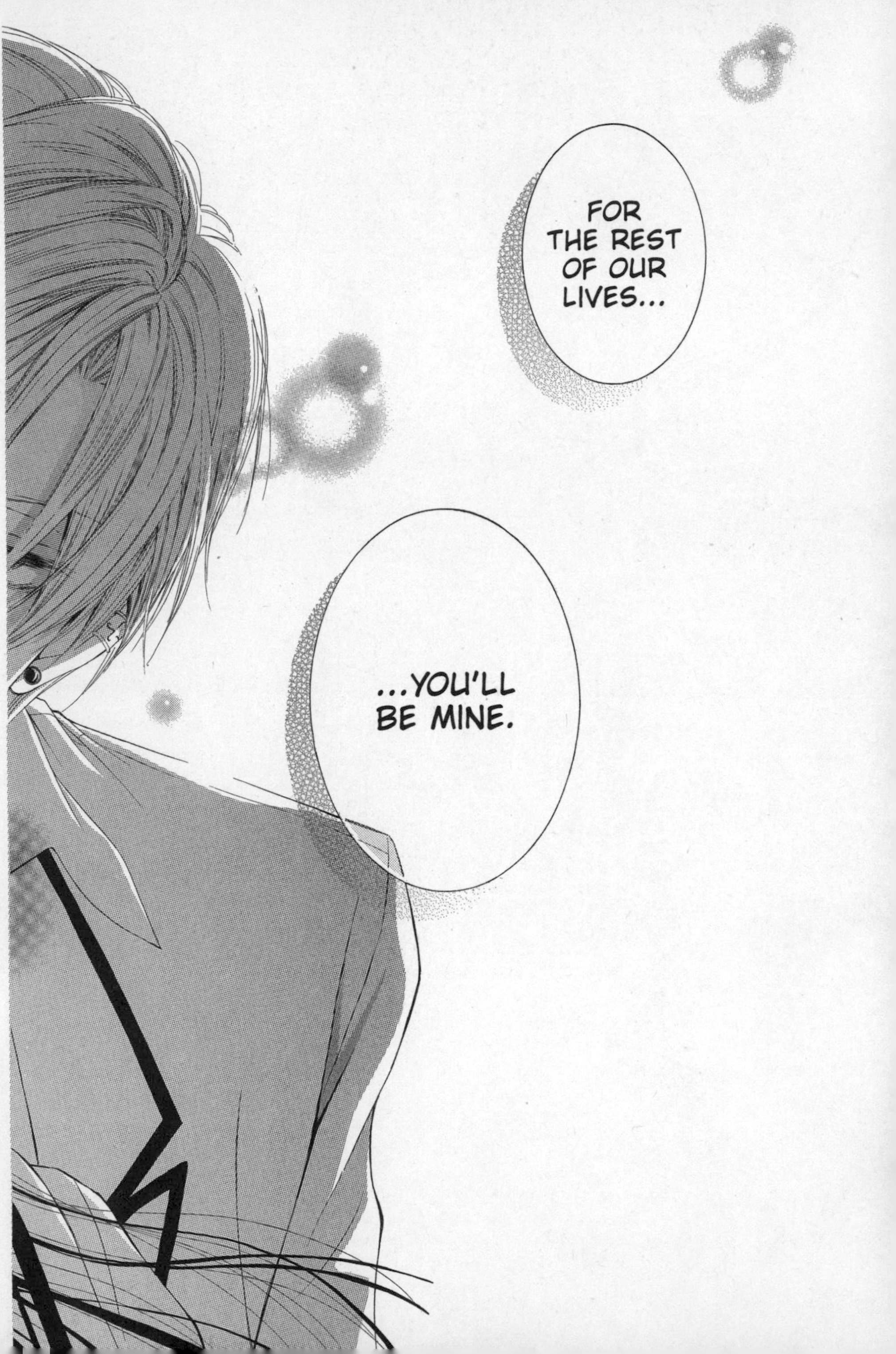
FOR THE REST OF OUR LIVES...
...YOU'LL BE MINE.

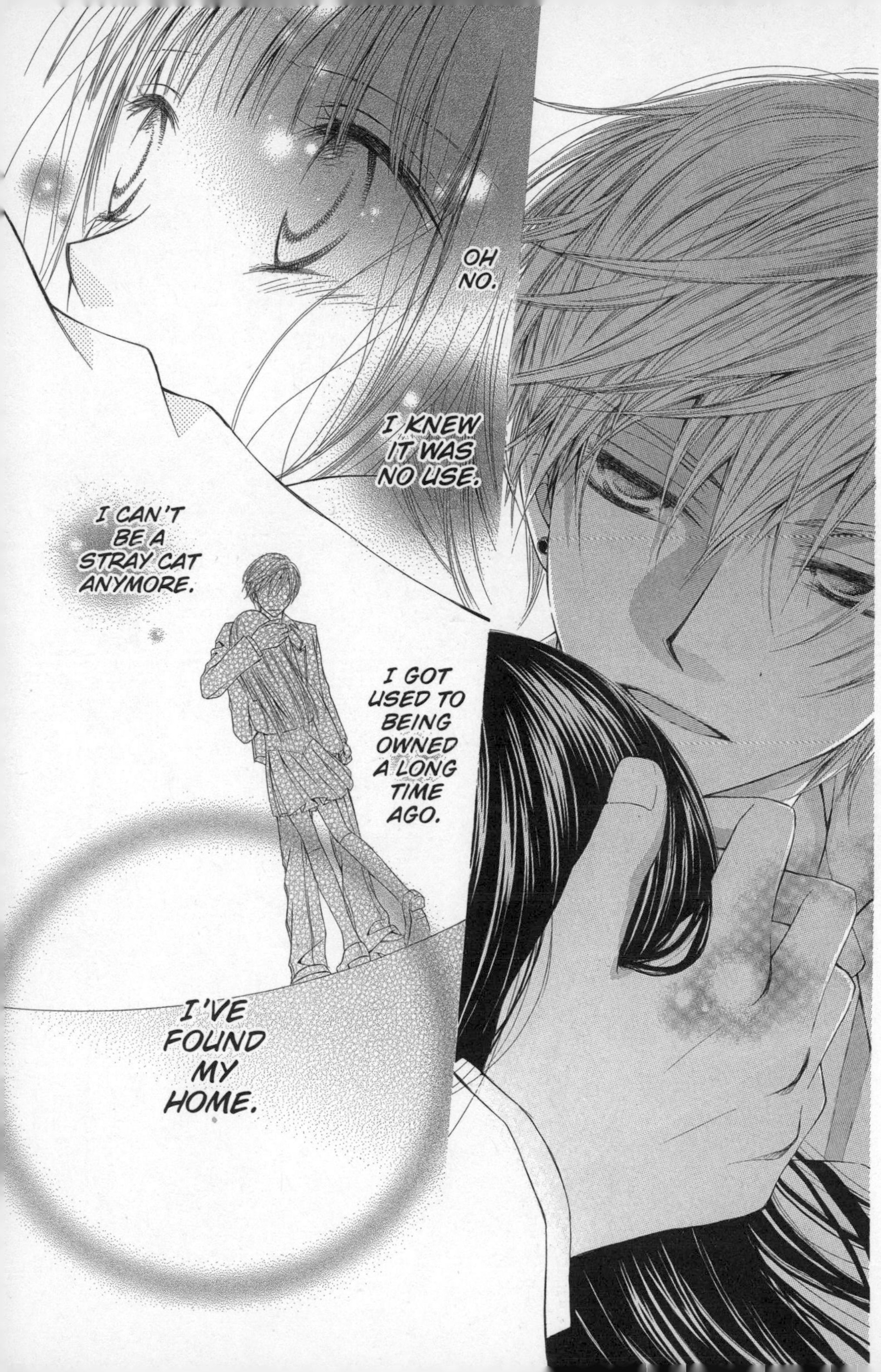
OH NO.
I KNEW IT WAS NO USE.
I CAN'T BE A STRAY CAT ANYMORE.
I GOT USED TO BEING OWNED A LONG TIME AGO.
I'VE FOUND MY HOME.

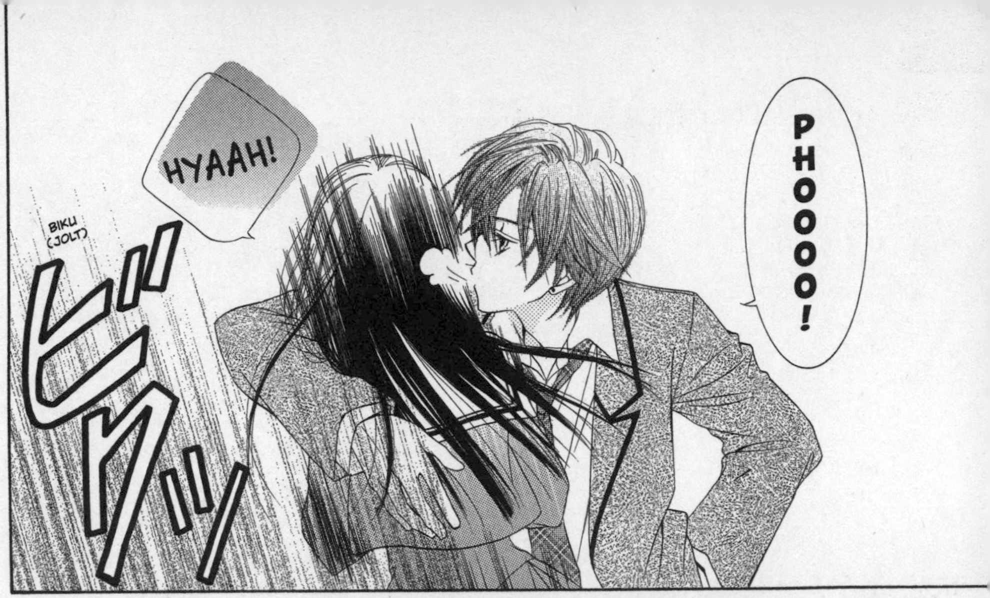
PHOOOO!
HYAAH!
BIKU (JOLT)

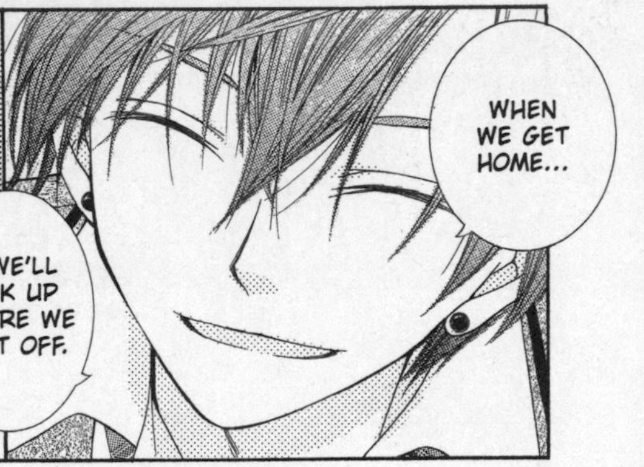
WHEN WE GET HOME...
...WE'LL PICK UP WHERE WE LEFT OFF.

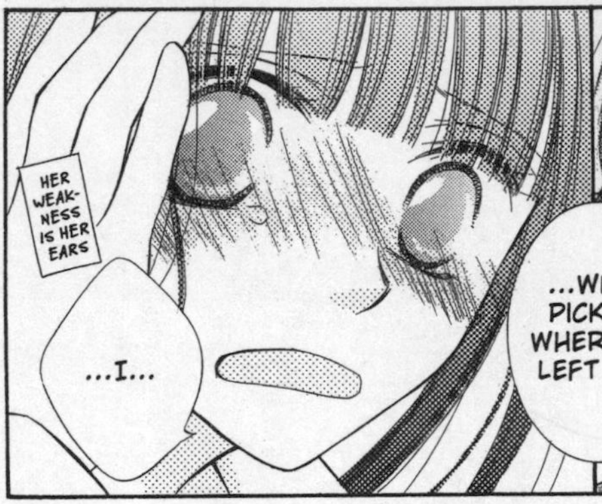
HER WEAKNESS IS HER EARS
...I...

ON SECOND THOUGHT, I DON'T WANT TO GO HOME...

...I DON'T THINK.

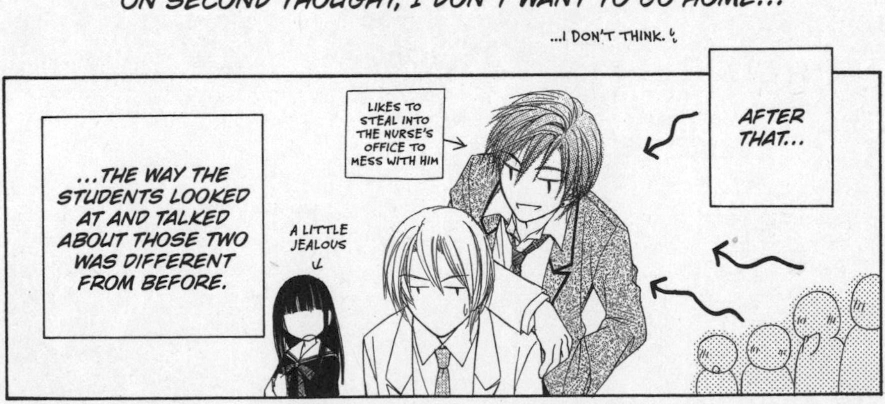
AFTER THAT...
LIKES TO STEAL INTO THE NURSE'S OFFICE TO MESS WITH HIM
...THE WAY THE STUDENTS LOOKED AT AND TALKED ABOUT THOSE TWO WAS DIFFERENT FROM BEFORE.
A LITTLE JEALOUS

scene.2 / *The End*

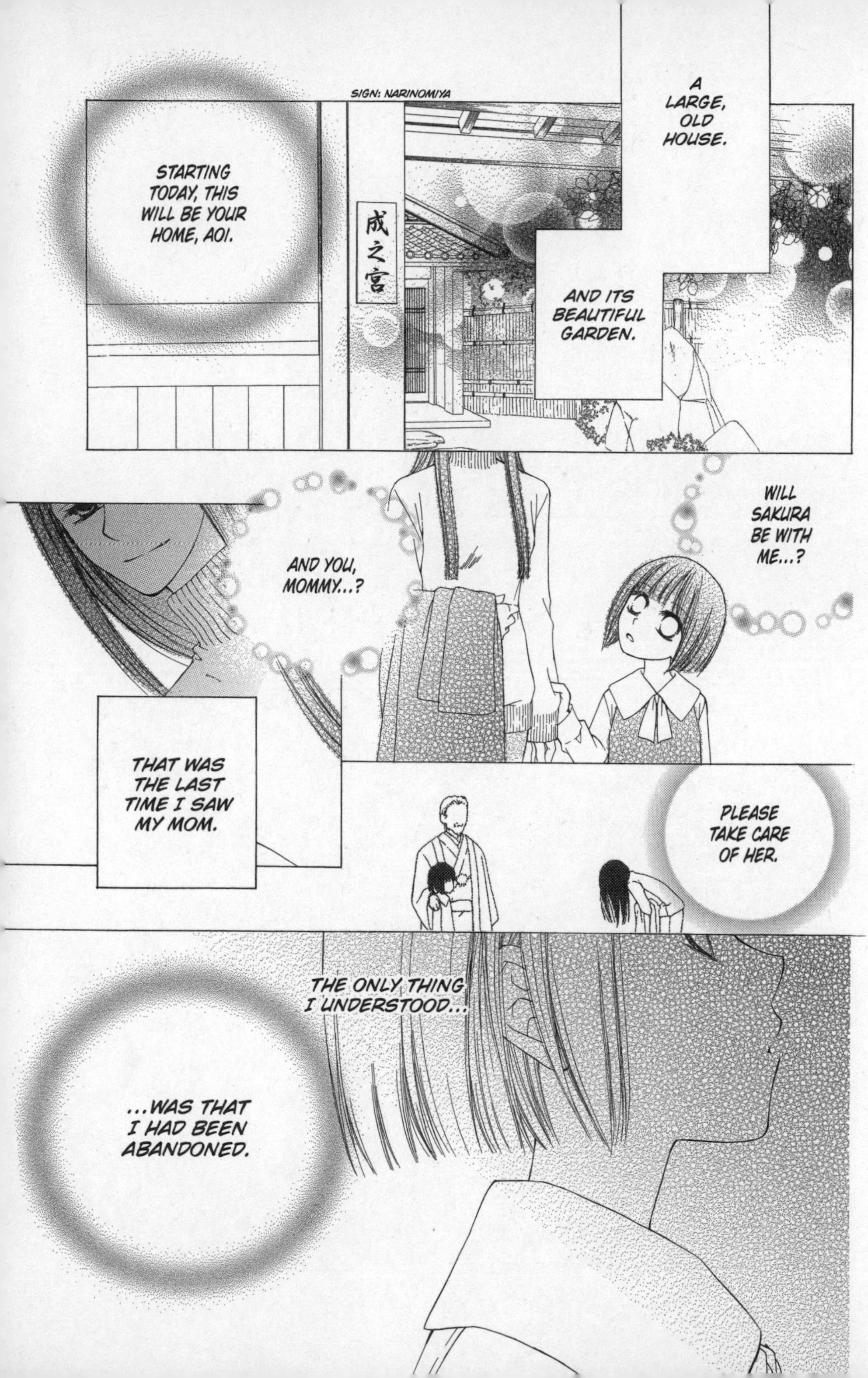
A LARGE, OLD HOUSE.
AND ITS BEAUTIFUL GARDEN.
SIGN: NARINOMIYA
成之宮
STARTING TODAY, THIS WILL BE YOUR HOME, AOI.
WILL SAKURA BE WITH ME...?
AND YOU, MOMMY...?
PLEASE TAKE CARE OF HER.
THAT WAS THE LAST TIME I SAW MY MOM.
THE ONLY THING I UNDERSTOOD...
...WAS THAT I HAD BEEN ABANDONED.

scene.3

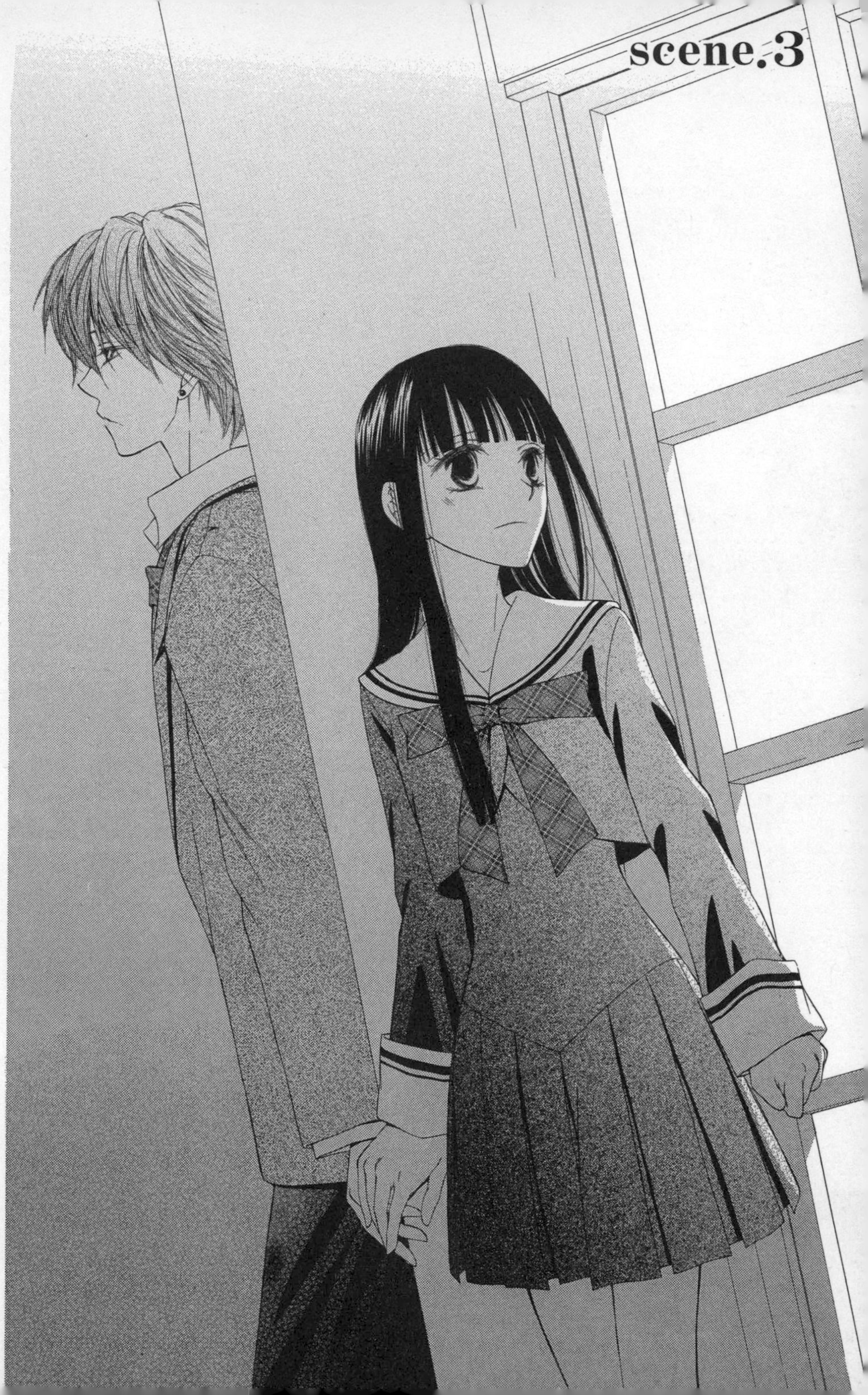

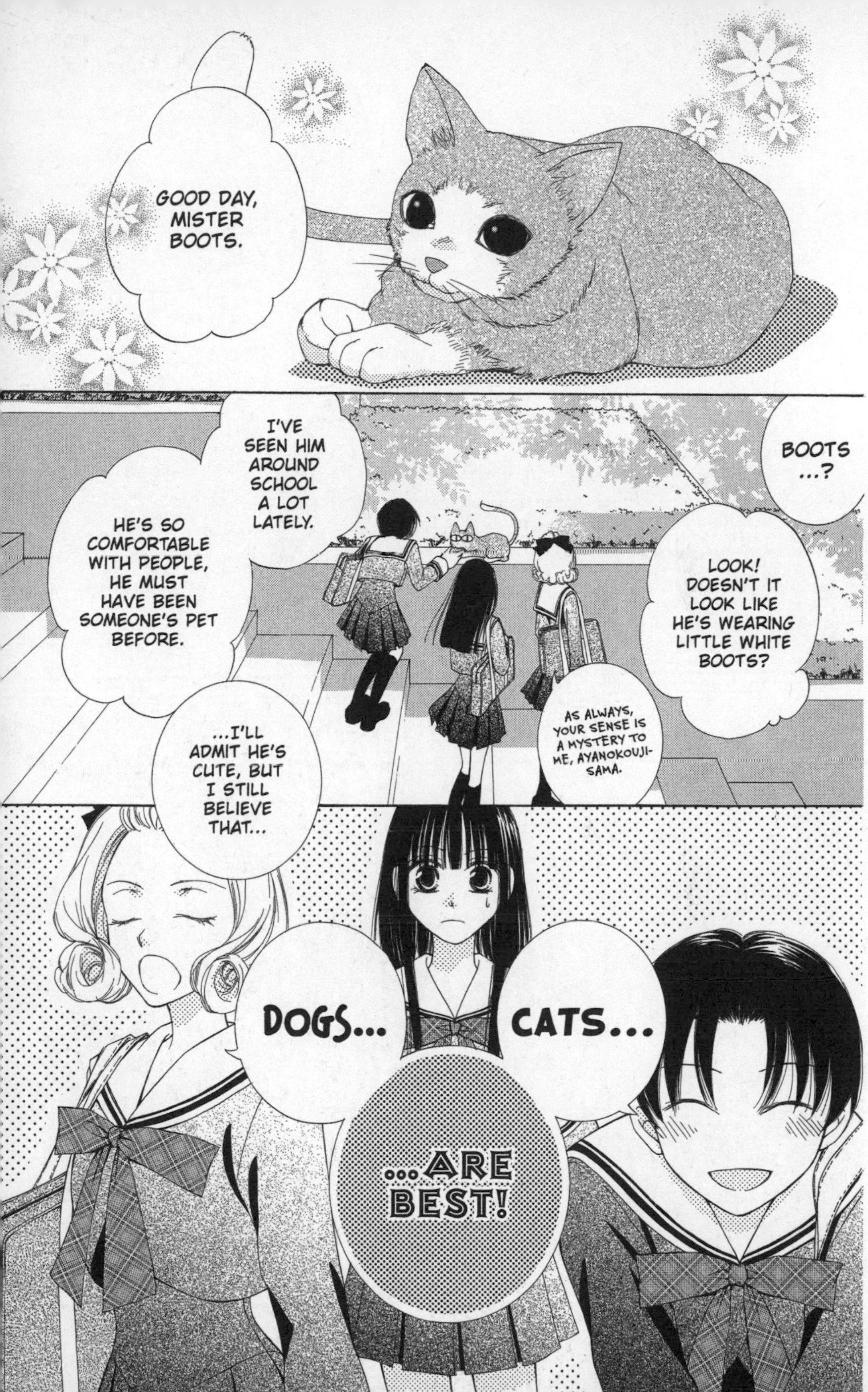
GOOD DAY, MISTER BOOTS.
BOOTS ...?
LOOK! DOESN'T IT LOOK LIKE HE'S WEARING LITTLE WHITE BOOTS?
I'VE SEEN HIM AROUND SCHOOL A LOT LATELY.
HE'S SO COMFORTABLE WITH PEOPLE, HE MUST HAVE BEEN SOMEONE'S PET BEFORE.
AS ALWAYS, YOUR SENSE IS A MYSTERY TO ME, AYANOKOUJI-SAMA.
...I'LL ADMIT HE'S CUTE, BUT I STILL BELIEVE THAT...
CATS...
DOGS...
...ARE BEST!

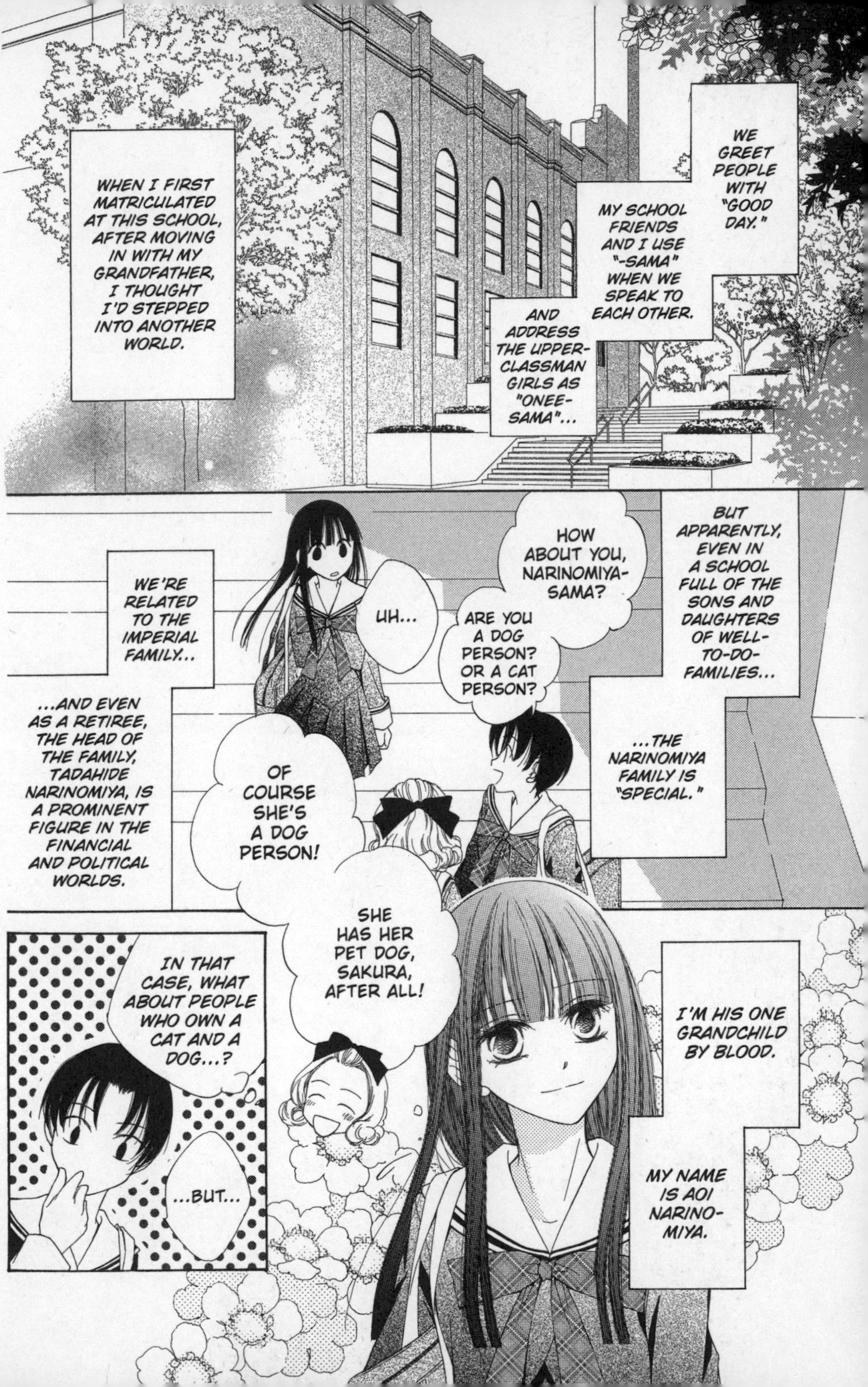
WE GREET PEOPLE WITH "GOOD DAY."
MY SCHOOL FRIENDS AND I USE "-SAMA" WHEN WE SPEAK TO EACH OTHER.
AND ADDRESS THE UPPER-CLASSMAN GIRLS AS "ONEE-SAMA"...
WHEN I FIRST MATRICULATED AT THIS SCHOOL, AFTER MOVING IN WITH MY GRANDFATHER, I THOUGHT I'D STEPPED INTO ANOTHER WORLD.
BUT APPARENTLY, EVEN IN A SCHOOL FULL OF THE SONS AND DAUGHTERS OF WELL-TO-DO-FAMILIES...
HOW ABOUT YOU, NARINOMIYA-SAMA?
ARE YOU A DOG PERSON? OR A CAT PERSON?
UH...
...THE NARINOMIYA FAMILY IS "SPECIAL."
OF COURSE SHE'S A DOG PERSON!
SHE HAS HER PET DOG, SAKURA, AFTER ALL!
WE'RE RELATED TO THE IMPERIAL FAMILY...
...AND EVEN AS A RETIREE, THE HEAD OF THE FAMILY, TADAHIDE NARINOMIYA, IS A PROMINENT FIGURE IN THE FINANCIAL AND POLITICAL WORLDS.
I'M HIS ONE GRANDCHILD BY BLOOD.
MY NAME IS AOI NARINO-MIYA.
IN THAT CASE, WHAT ABOUT PEOPLE WHO OWN A CAT AND A DOG...?
...BUT...

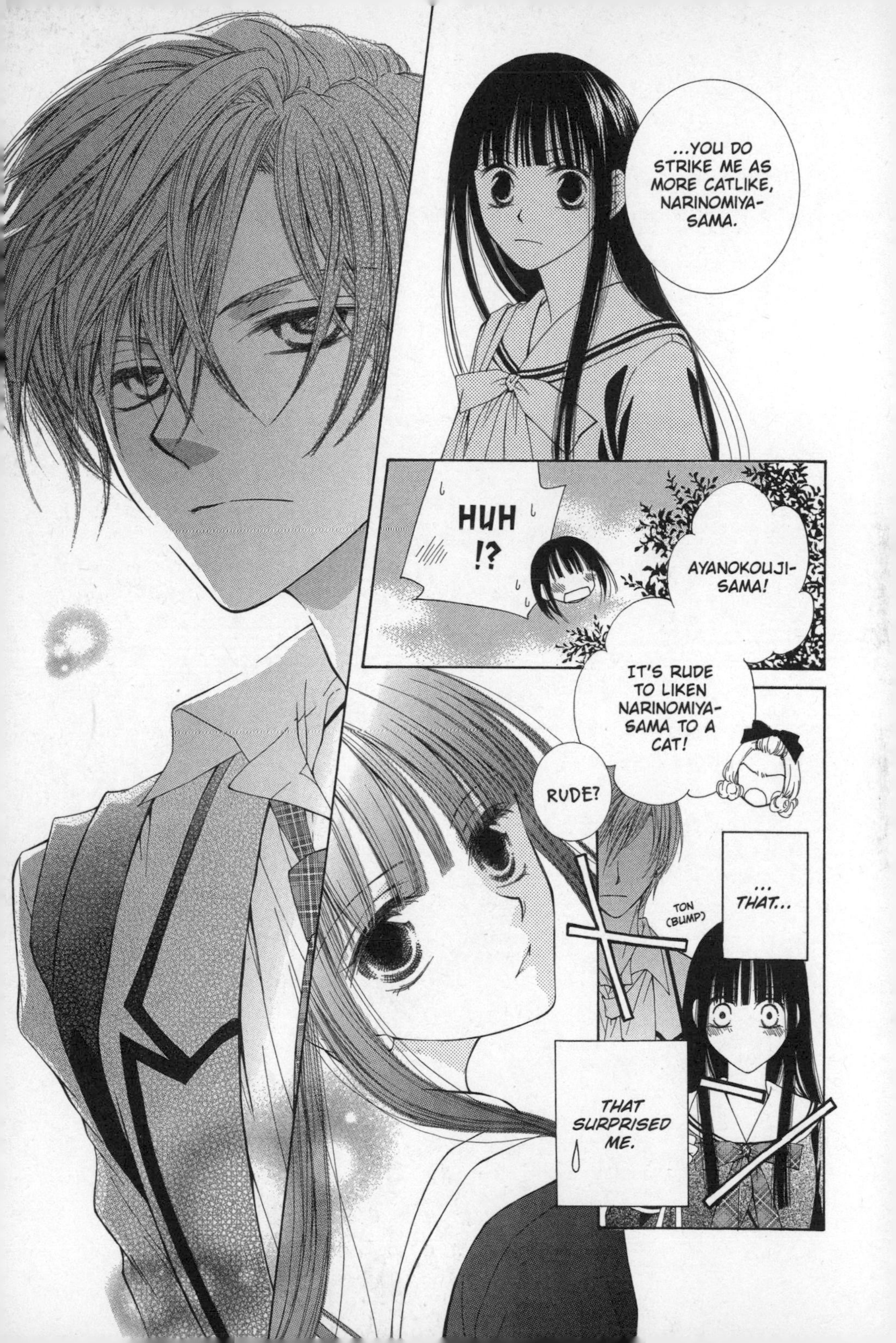
...YOU DO STRIKE ME AS MORE CATLIKE, NARINOMIYA-SAMA.
AYANOKOUJI-SAMA!
HUH !?
IT'S RUDE TO LIKEN NARINOMIYA-SAMA TO A CAT!
RUDE?
... THAT...
TON (BUMP)
THAT SURPRISED ME.

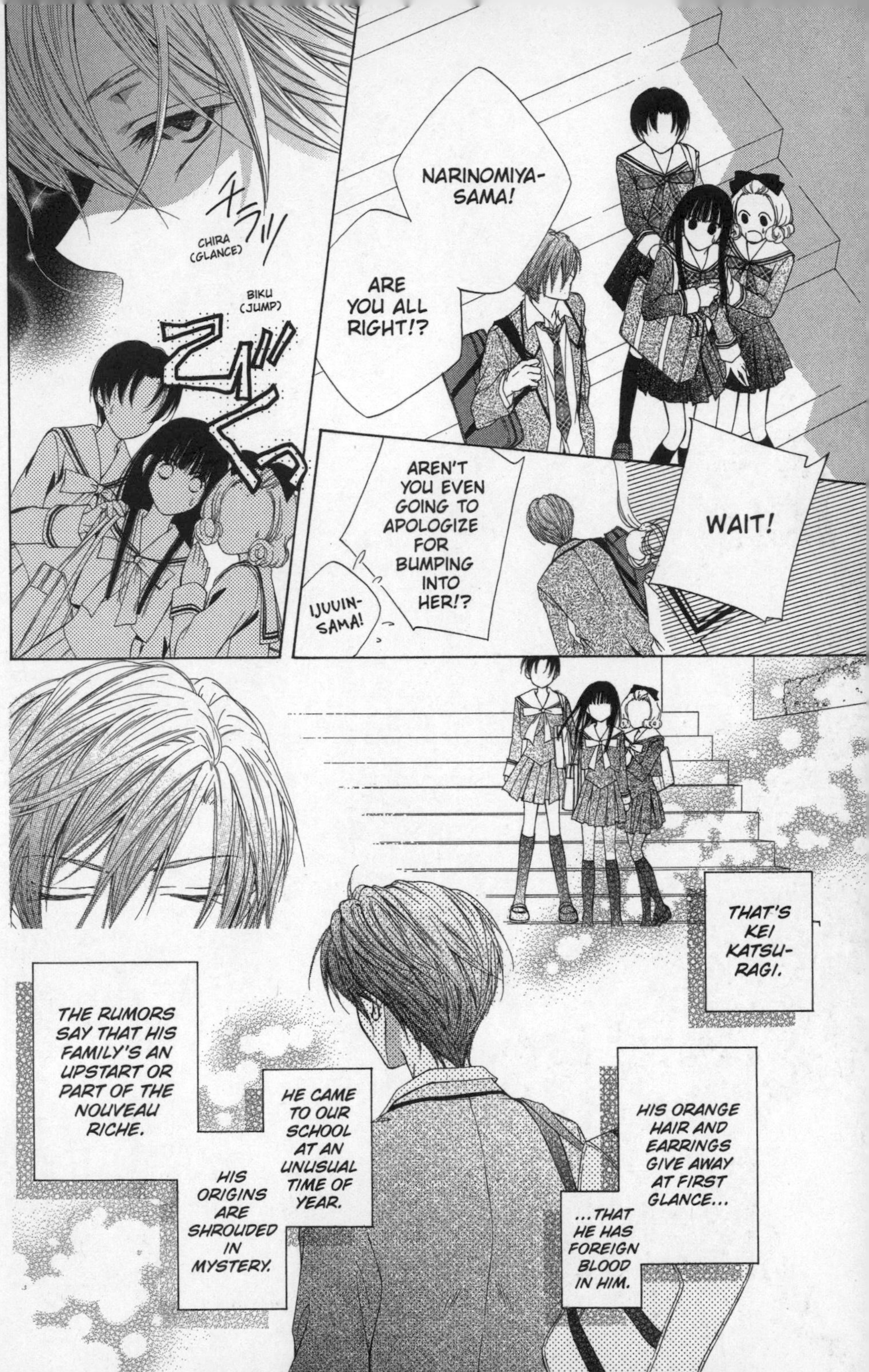
NARINOMIYA-SAMA!
ARE YOU ALL RIGHT!?
WAIT!
AREN'T YOU EVEN GOING TO APOLOGIZE FOR BUMPING INTO HER!?
IJUUIN-SAMA!
CHIRA (GLANCE)
BIKU (JUMP)
THAT'S KEI KATSURAGI.
HIS ORANGE HAIR AND EARRINGS GIVE AWAY AT FIRST GLANCE...
...THAT HE HAS FOREIGN BLOOD IN HIM.
HE CAME TO OUR SCHOOL AT AN UNUSUAL TIME OF YEAR.
HIS ORIGINS ARE SHROUDED IN MYSTERY.
THE RUMORS SAY THAT HIS FAMILY'S AN UPSTART OR PART OF THE NOUVEAU RICHE.

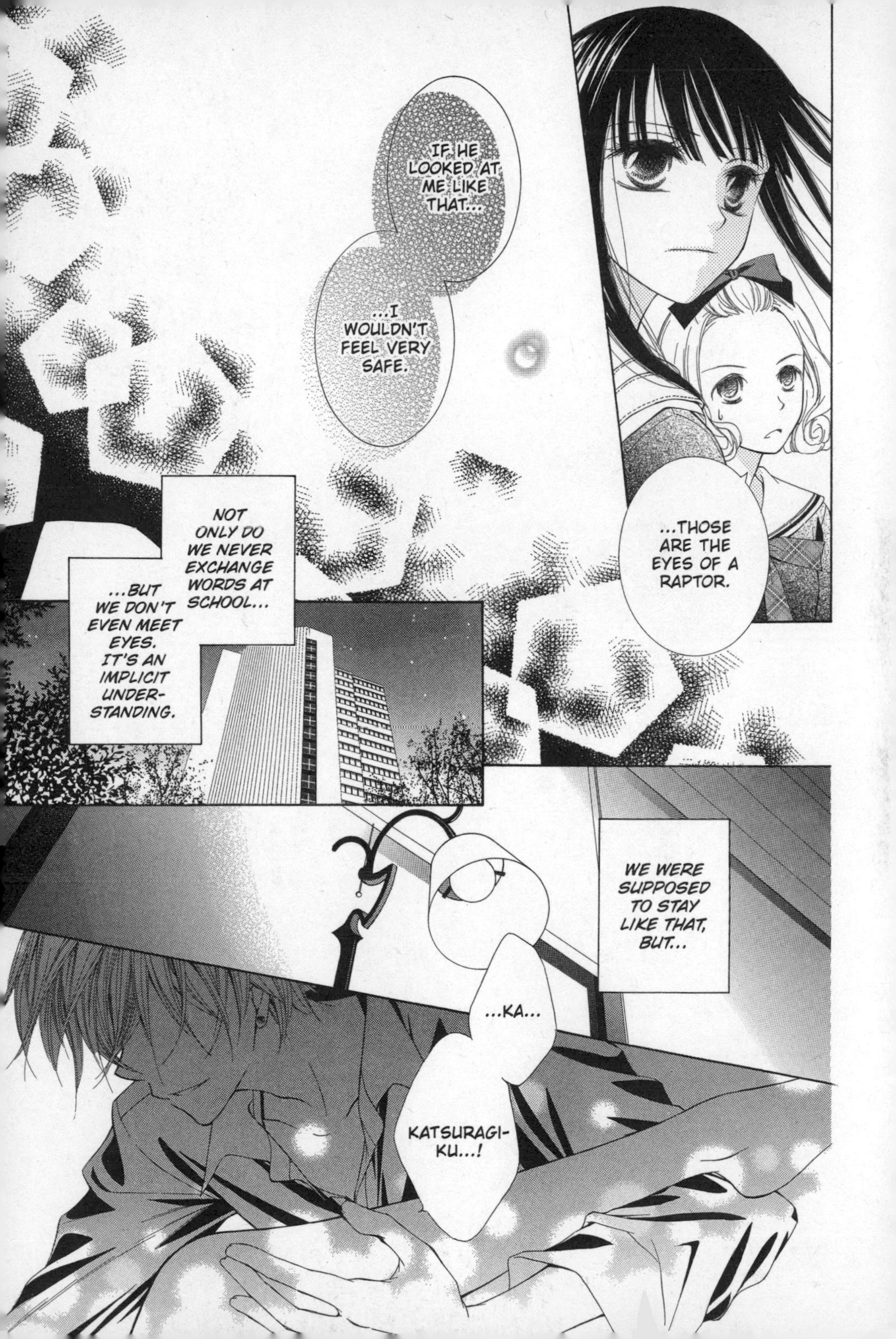
...THOSE ARE THE EYES OF A RAPTOR.
IF HE LOOKED AT ME LIKE THAT...
...I WOULDN'T FEEL VERY SAFE.
NOT ONLY DO WE NEVER EXCHANGE WORDS AT SCHOOL...
...BUT WE DON'T EVEN MEET EYES. IT'S AN IMPLICIT UNDER-STANDING.
WE WERE SUPPOSED TO STAY LIKE THAT, BUT...
...KA...
KATSURAGI-KU...!

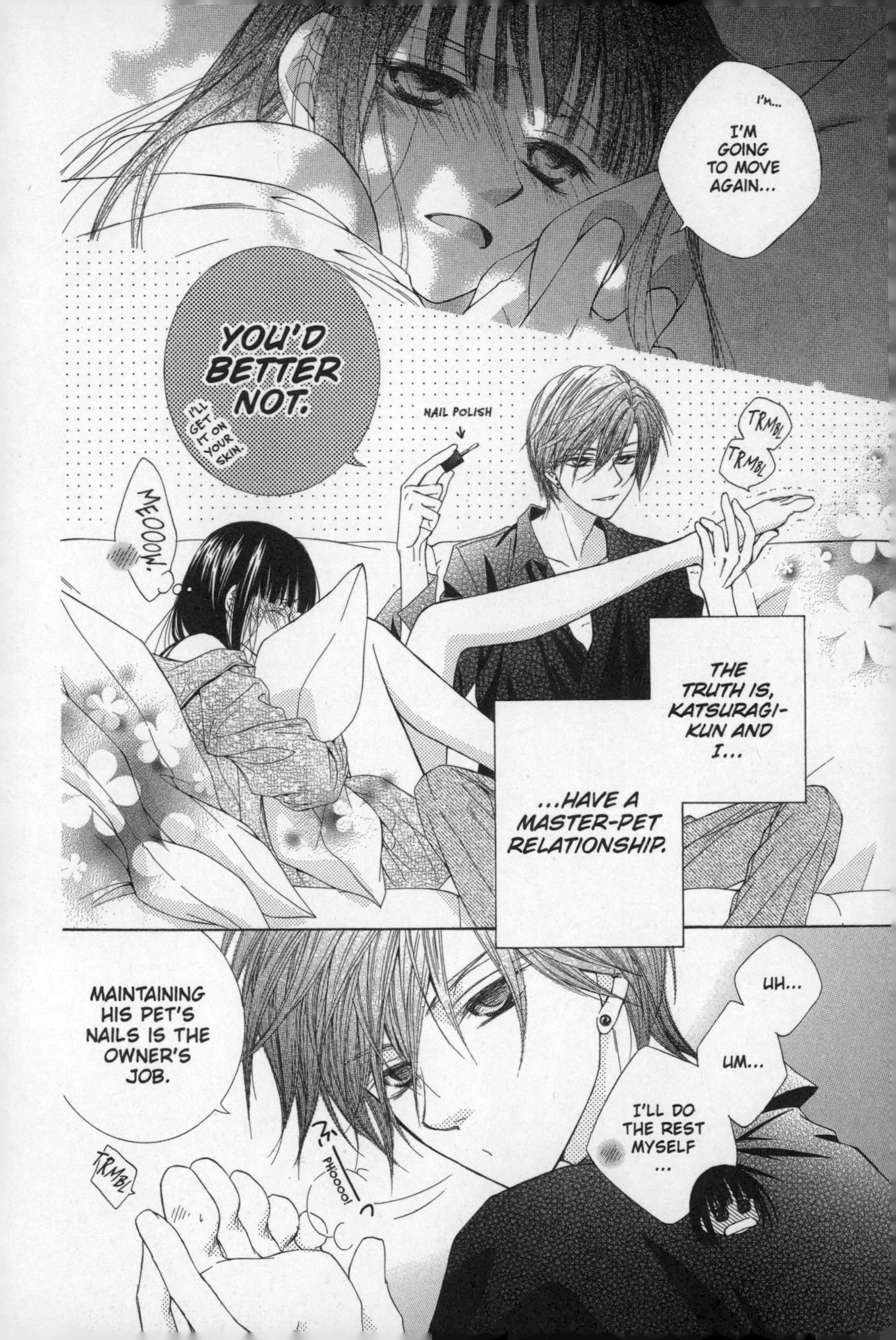
I'M...
I'M GOING TO MOVE AGAIN...
TRMBL
TRMBL
YOU'D BETTER NOT.
I'LL GET IT ON YOUR SKIN.
NAIL POLISH
MEOOOW.
THE TRUTH IS, KATSURAGI-KUN AND I...
...HAVE A MASTER-PET RELATIONSHIP.
UH...
UM...
I'LL DO THE REST MYSELF ...
MAINTAINING HIS PET'S NAILS IS THE OWNER'S JOB.
PHOOOO!
TRMBL

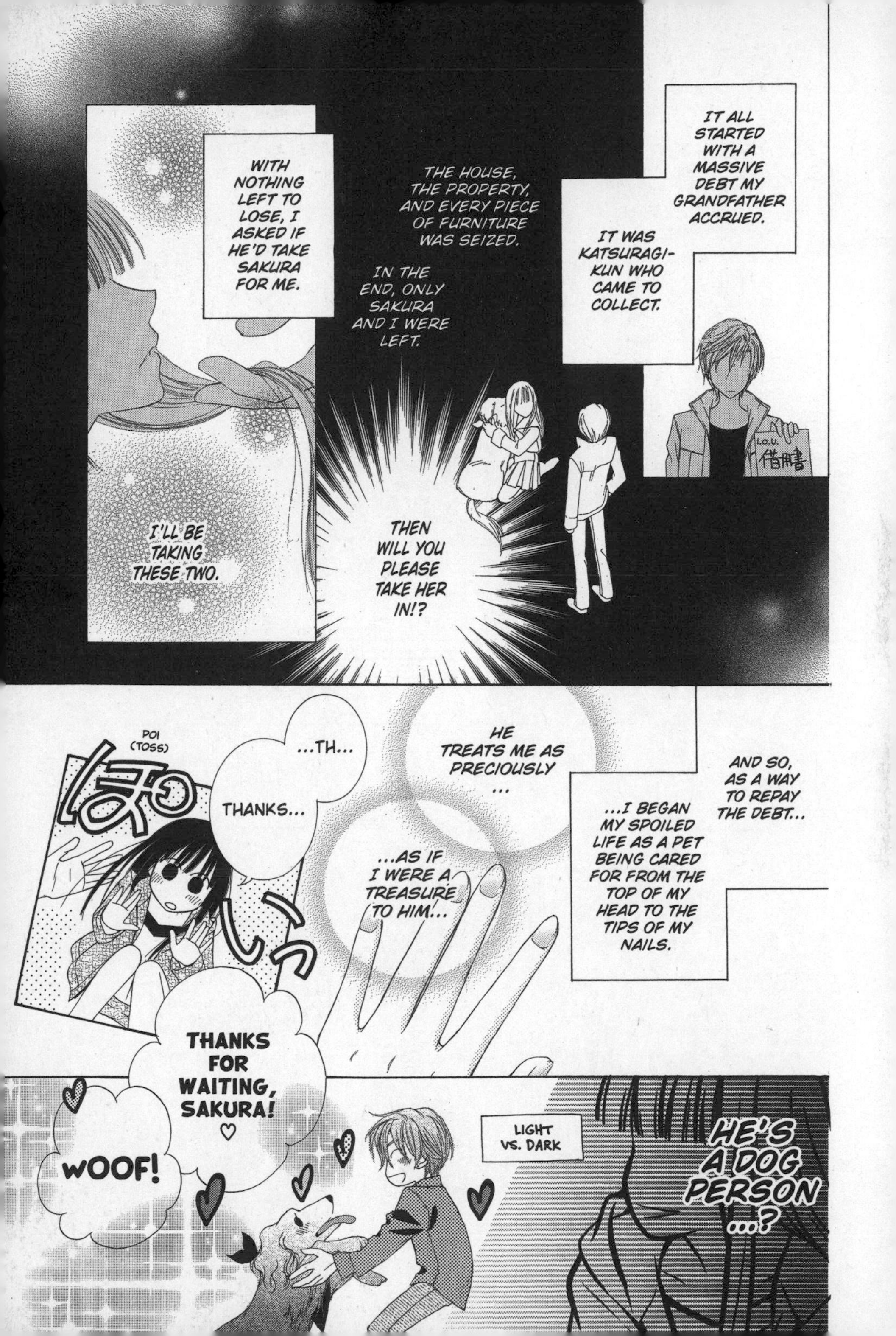
IT ALL STARTED WITH A MASSIVE DEBT MY GRANDFATHER ACCRUED.
IT WAS KATSURAGI-KUN WHO CAME TO COLLECT.
I.O.U.
借用書
THE HOUSE, THE PROPERTY, AND EVERY PIECE OF FURNITURE WAS SEIZED.
IN THE END, ONLY SAKURA AND I WERE LEFT.
THEN WILL YOU PLEASE TAKE HER IN!?
WITH NOTHING LEFT TO LOSE, I ASKED IF HE'D TAKE SAKURA FOR ME.
I'LL BE TAKING THESE TWO.
AND SO, AS A WAY TO REPAY THE DEBT...
...I BEGAN MY SPOILED LIFE AS A PET BEING CARED FOR FROM THE TOP OF MY HEAD TO THE TIPS OF MY NAILS.
HE TREATS ME AS PRECIOUSLY...
...AS IF I WERE A TREASURE TO HIM...
POI (TOSS)
...TH...
THANKS...
HE'S A DOG PERSON...?
LIGHT VS. DARK
THANKS FOR WAITING, SAKURA! ♡
WOOF!

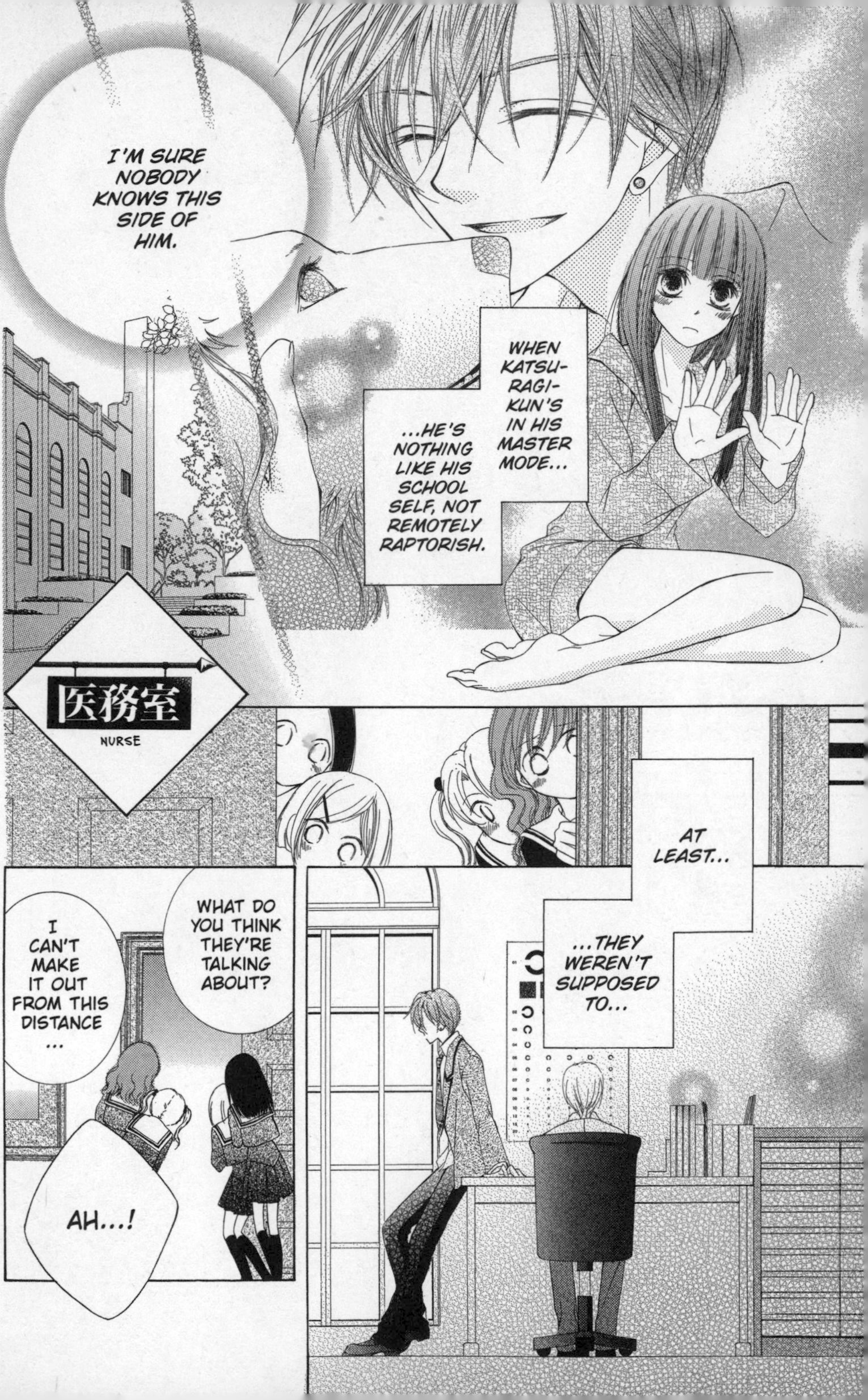
WHEN KATSURAGI-KUN'S IN HIS MASTER MODE...
...HE'S NOTHING LIKE HIS SCHOOL SELF, NOT REMOTELY RAPTORISH.
I'M SURE NOBODY KNOWS THIS SIDE OF HIM.
医務室
NURSE
AT LEAST...
...THEY WEREN'T SUPPOSED TO...
WHAT DO YOU THINK THEY'RE TALKING ABOUT?
I CAN'T MAKE IT OUT FROM THIS DISTANCE ...
AH...!

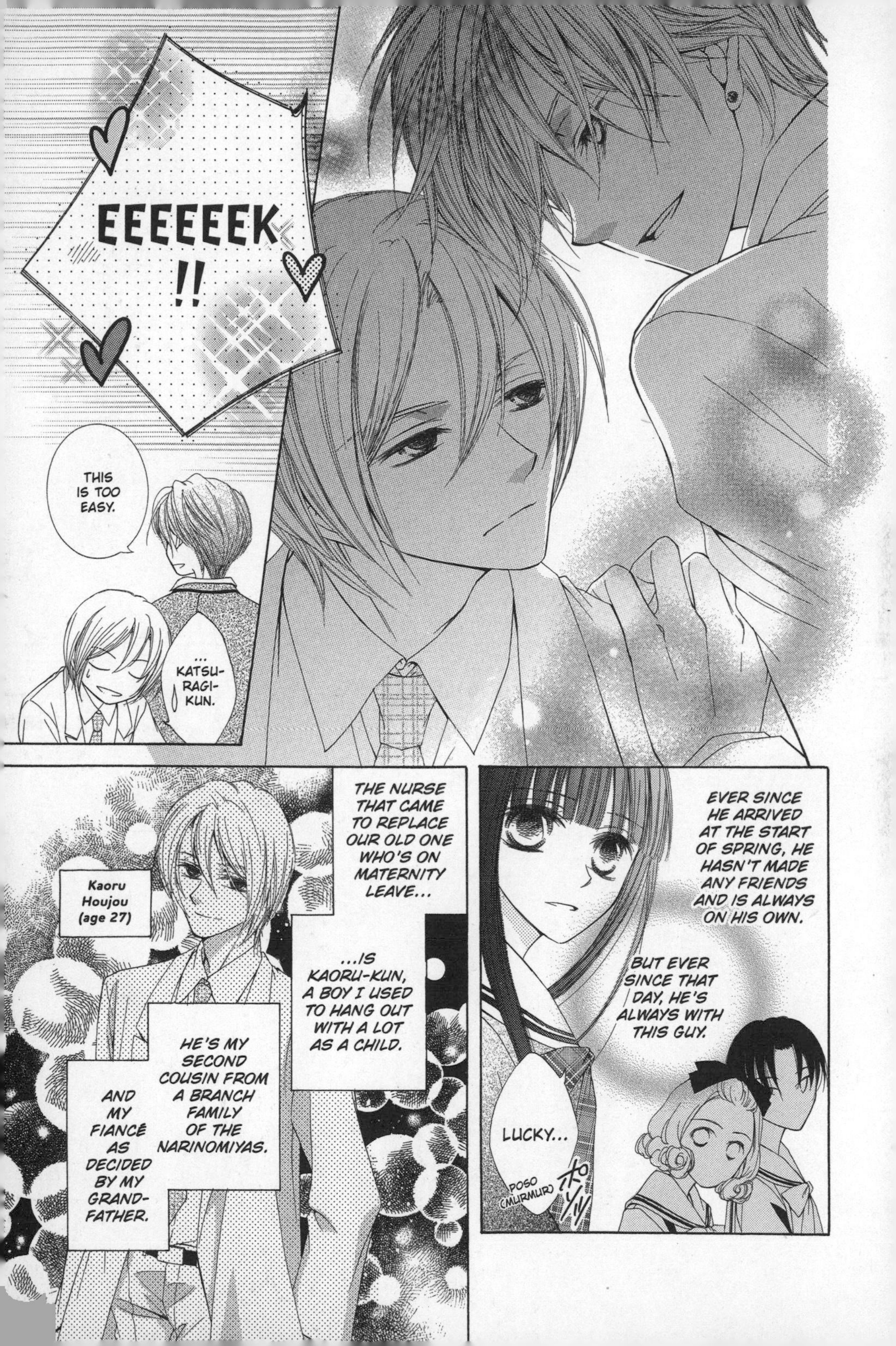
EEEEEEK!!
THIS IS TOO EASY.
...KATSURAGI-KUN.
EVER SINCE HE ARRIVED AT THE START OF SPRING, HE HASN'T MADE ANY FRIENDS AND IS ALWAYS ON HIS OWN.
BUT EVER SINCE THAT DAY, HE'S ALWAYS WITH THIS GUY.
LUCKY...
POSO (MURMUR)
THE NURSE THAT CAME TO REPLACE OUR OLD ONE WHO'S ON MATERNITY LEAVE...
...IS KAORU-KUN, A BOY I USED TO HANG OUT WITH A LOT AS A CHILD.
Kaoru Houjou (age 27)
HE'S MY SECOND COUSIN FROM A BRANCH FAMILY OF THE NARINOMIYAS.
AND MY FIANCÉ AS DECIDED BY MY GRANDFATHER.

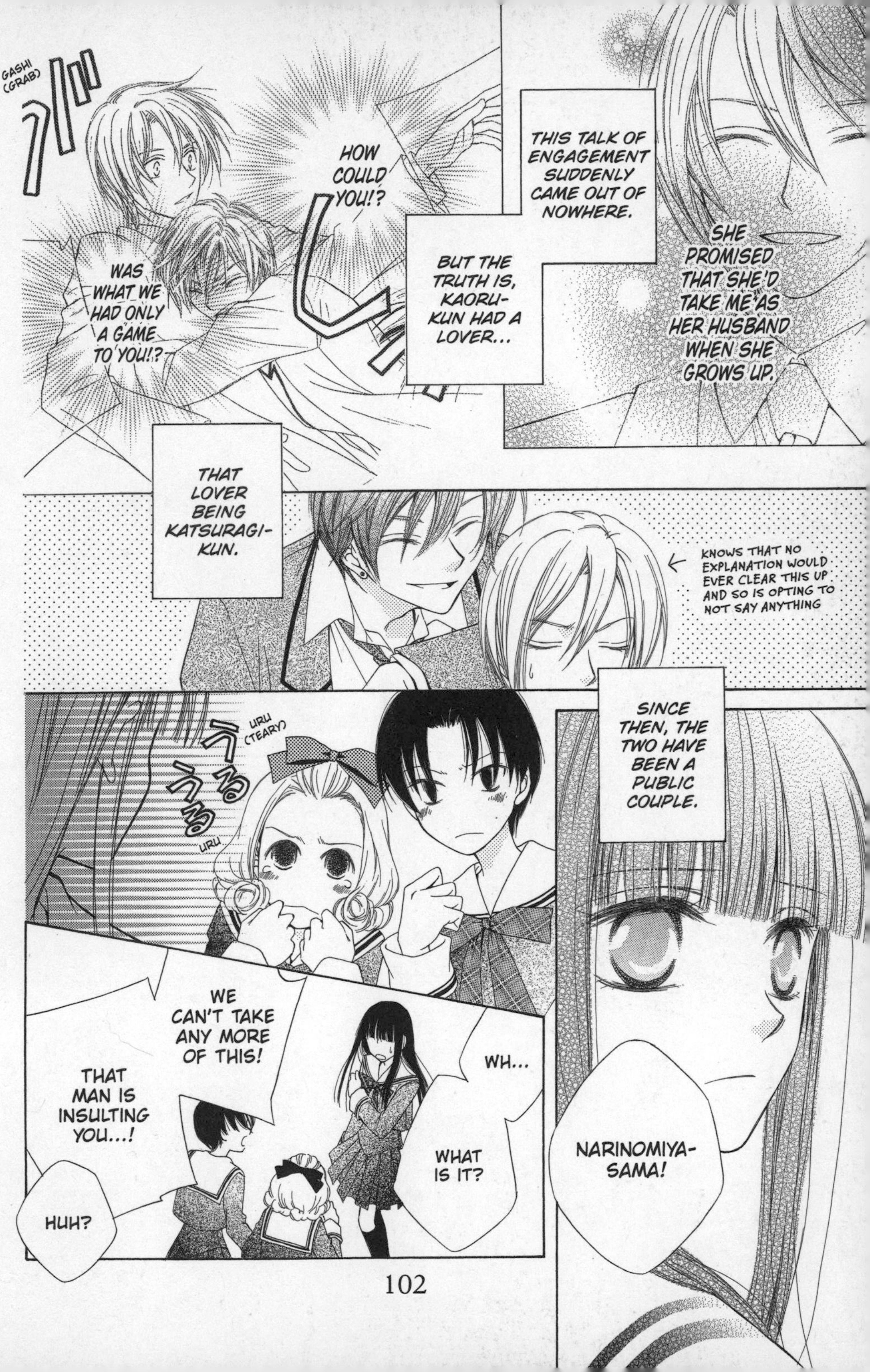
THIS TALK OF ENGAGEMENT SUDDENLY CAME OUT OF NOWHERE.
SHE PROMISED THAT SHE'D TAKE ME AS HER HUSBAND WHEN SHE GROWS UP.
BUT THE TRUTH IS, KAORU-KUN HAD A LOVER...
GASHI (GRAB)
HOW COULD YOU!?
WAS WHAT WE HAD ONLY A GAME TO YOU!?
THAT LOVER BEING KATSURAGI-KUN.
KNOWS THAT NO EXPLANATION WOULD EVER CLEAR THIS UP AND SO IS OPTING TO NOT SAY ANYTHING
SINCE THEN, THE TWO HAVE BEEN A PUBLIC COUPLE.
URU (TEARY)
URU
NARINOMIYA-SAMA!
WH...
WHAT IS IT?
WE CAN'T TAKE ANY MORE OF THIS!
THAT MAN IS INSULTING YOU...!
HUH?

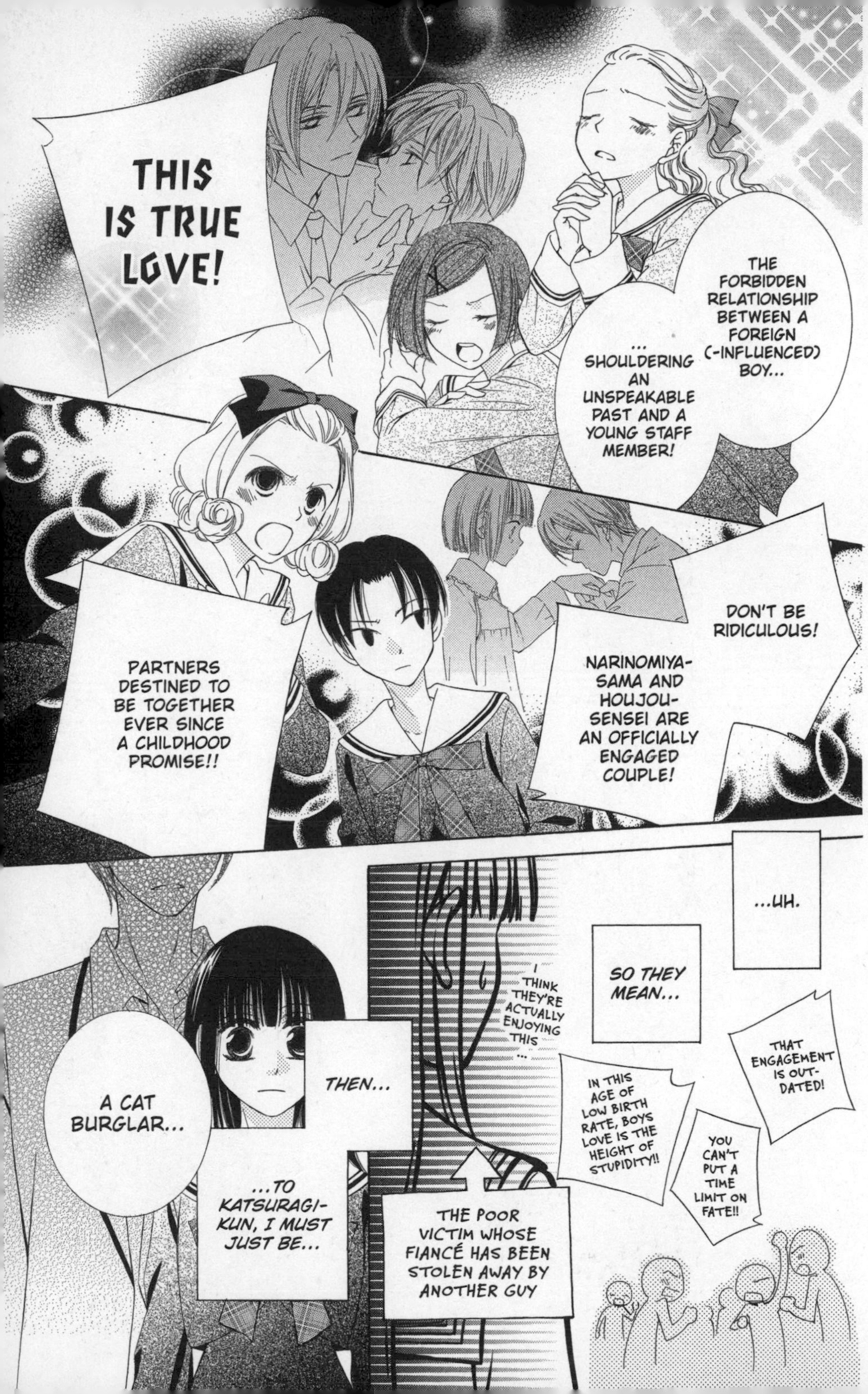
THE FORBIDDEN RELATIONSHIP BETWEEN A FOREIGN (-INFLUENCED) BOY...
...SHOULDERING AN UNSPEAKABLE PAST AND A YOUNG STAFF MEMBER!
THIS IS TRUE LOVE!
DON'T BE RIDICULOUS!
NARINOMIYA-SAMA AND HOUJOU-SENSEI ARE AN OFFICIALLY ENGAGED COUPLE!
PARTNERS DESTINED TO BE TOGETHER EVER SINCE A CHILDHOOD PROMISE!!
...UH.
SO THEY MEAN...
THAT ENGAGEMENT IS OUT-DATED!
YOU CAN'T PUT A TIME LIMIT ON FATE!!
IN THIS AGE OF LOW BIRTH RATE, BOYS LOVE IS THE HEIGHT OF STUPIDITY!!
I THINK THEY'RE ACTUALLY ENJOYING THIS...
THEN...
A CAT BURGLAR...
...TO KATSURAGI-KUN, I MUST JUST BE...
THE POOR VICTIM WHOSE FIANCÉ HAS BEEN STOLEN AWAY BY ANOTHER GUY

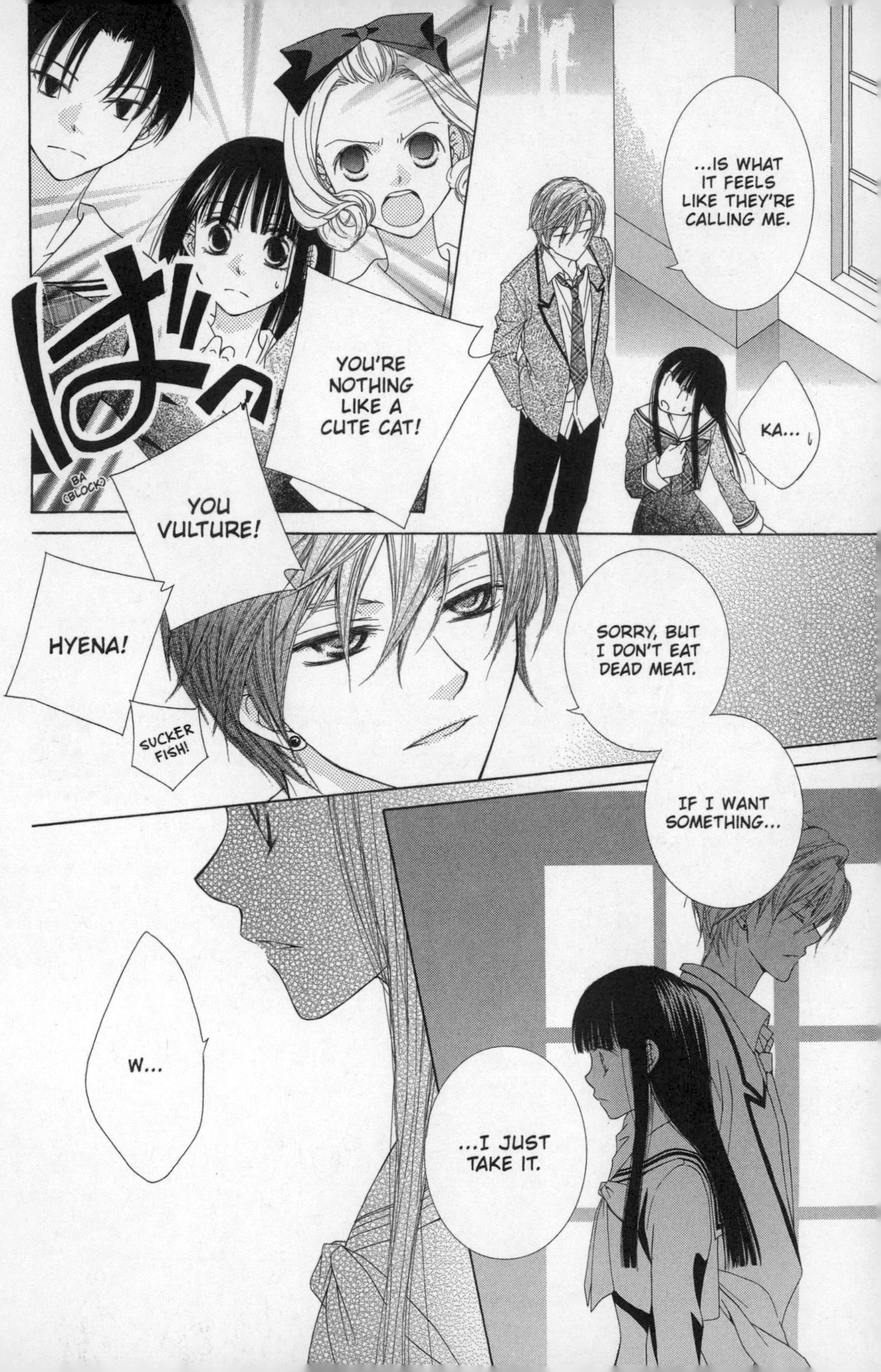
...IS WHAT IT FEELS LIKE THEY'RE CALLING ME.
KA...
YOU'RE NOTHING LIKE A CUTE CAT!
ばっ
BA (BLOCK)
YOU VULTURE!
SORRY, BUT I DON'T EAT DEAD MEAT.
HYENA!
SUCKER FISH!
IF I WANT SOMETHING...
...I JUST TAKE IT.
W...

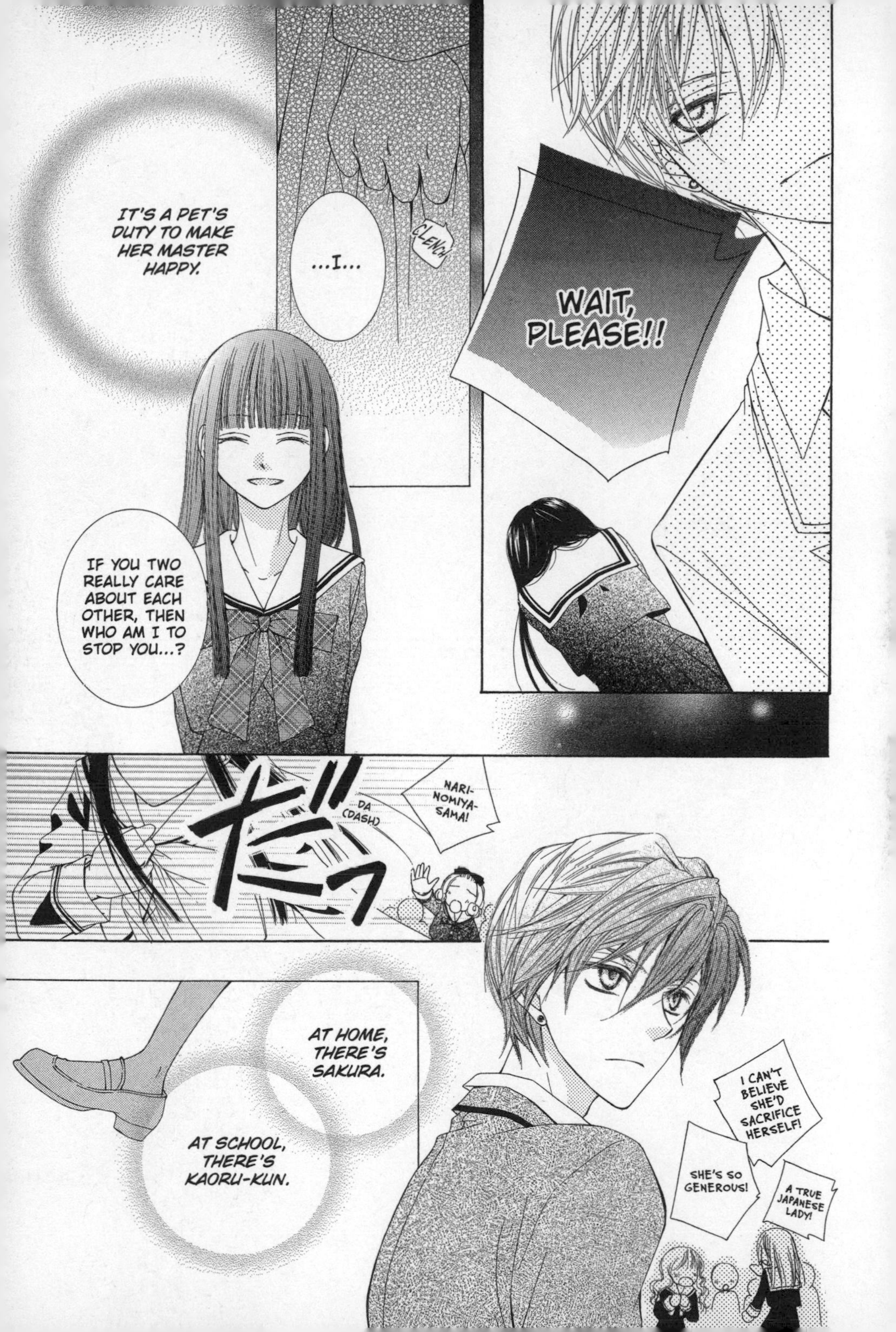
WAIT, PLEASE!!
...I...
CLENCH
IT'S A PET'S DUTY TO MAKE HER MASTER HAPPY.
IF YOU TWO REALLY CARE ABOUT EACH OTHER, THEN WHO AM I TO STOP YOU...?
NARI-NOMIYA-SAMA!
DA (DASH)
I CAN'T BELIEVE SHE'D SACRIFICE HERSELF!
A TRUE JAPANESE LADY!
SHE'S SO GENEROUS!
AT HOME, THERE'S SAKURA.
AT SCHOOL, THERE'S KAORU-KUN.

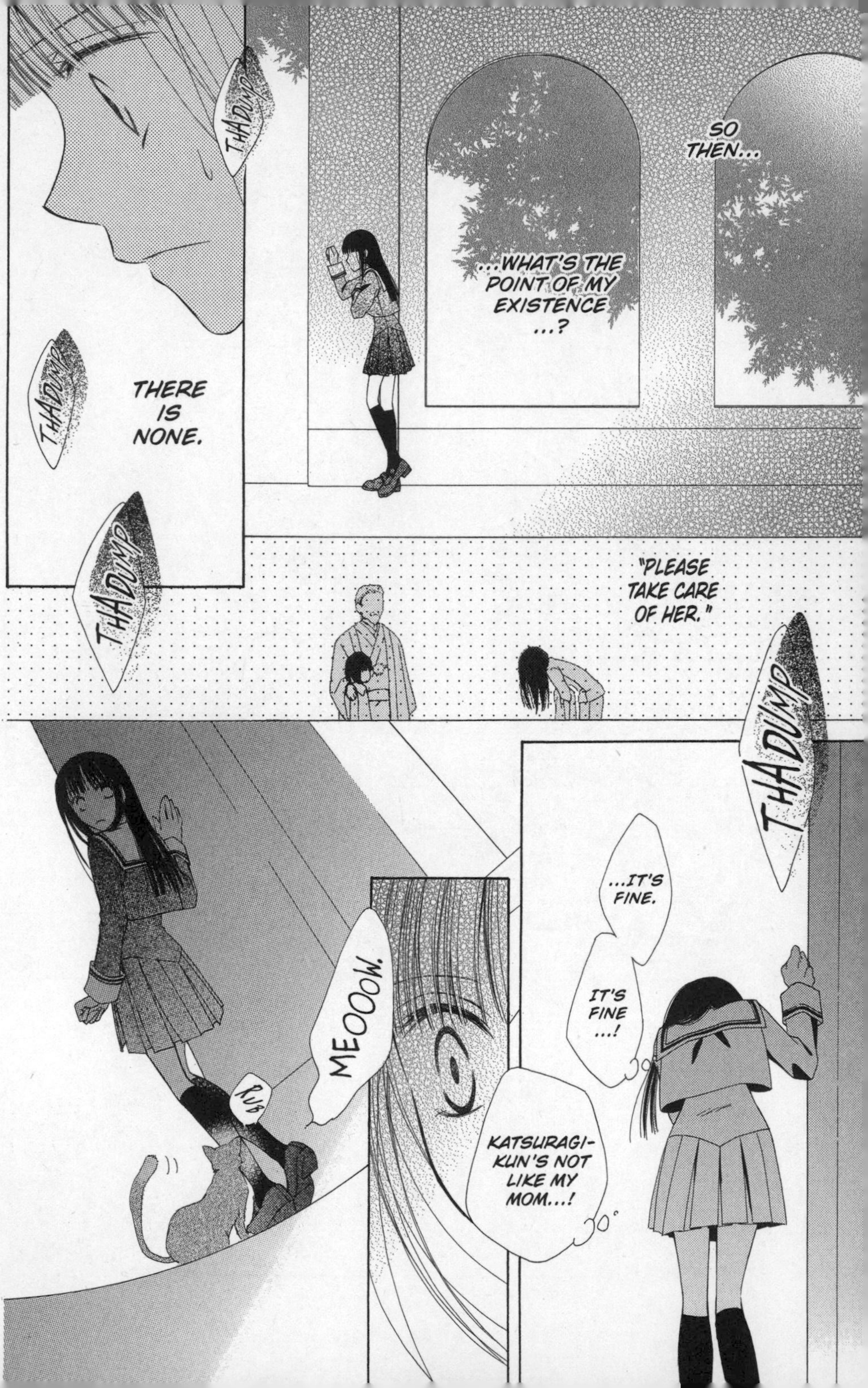
SO THEN...
...WHAT'S THE POINT OF MY EXISTENCE ...?
THADUMP
THADUMP
THERE IS NONE.
THADUMP
"PLEASE TAKE CARE OF HER."
THADUMP
...IT'S FINE.
IT'S FINE ...!
KATSURAGI-KUN'S NOT LIKE MY MOM...!
MEOOOW.
RUB

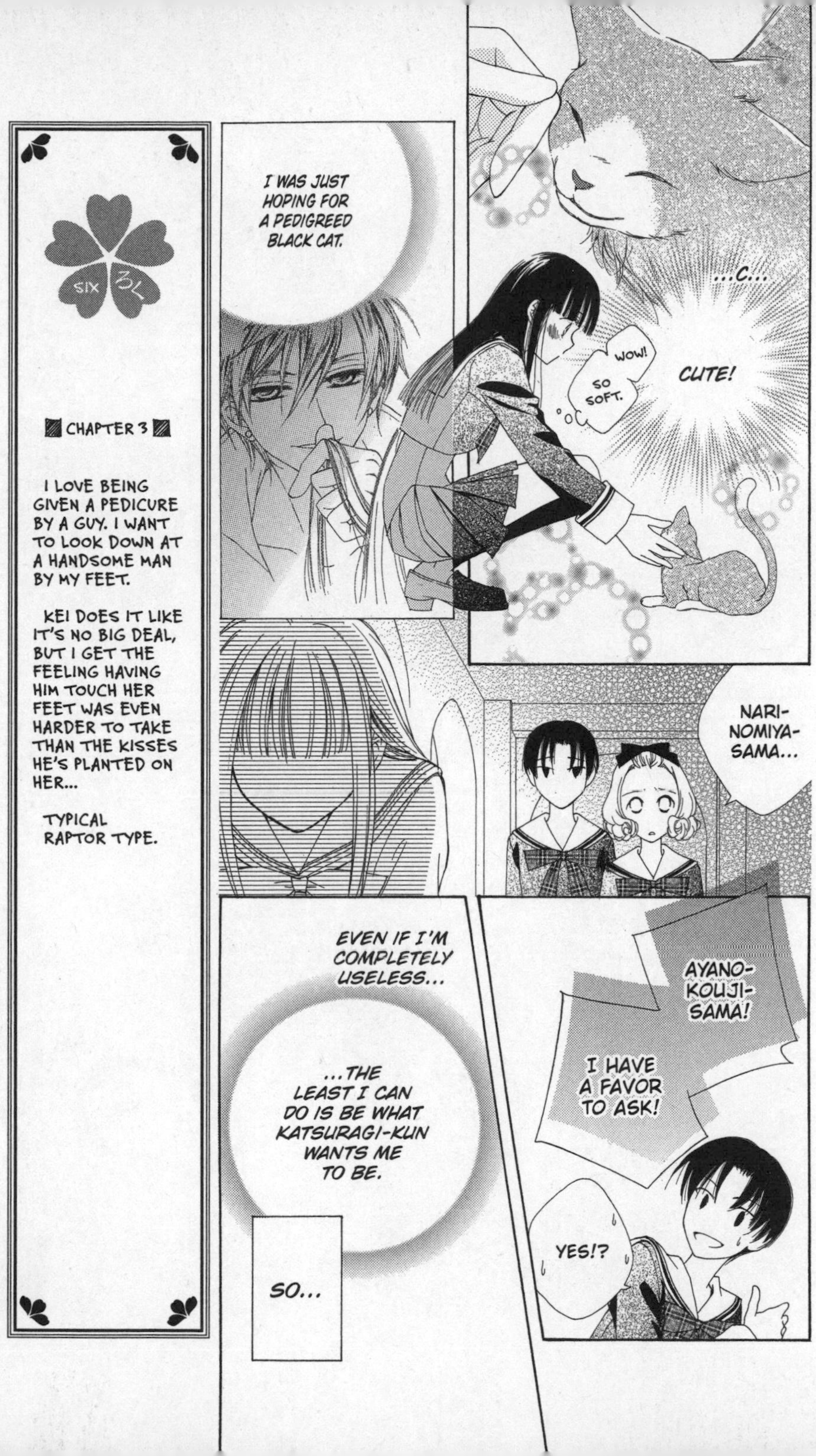
...C...
CUTE!
WOW!
SO SOFT.
I WAS JUST HOPING FOR A PEDIGREED BLACK CAT.
NARI-NOMIYA-SAMA...
AYANO-KOUJI-SAMA!
I HAVE A FAVOR TO ASK!
YES!?
EVEN IF I'M COMPLETELY USELESS...
...THE LEAST I CAN DO IS BE WHAT KATSURAGI-KUN WANTS ME TO BE.
SO...

SIX ろく

CHAPTER 3

I LOVE BEING GIVEN A PEDICURE BY A GUY. I WANT TO LOOK DOWN AT A HANDSOME MAN BY MY FEET.

KEI DOES IT LIKE IT'S NO BIG DEAL, BUT I GET THE FEELING HAVING HIM TOUCH HER FEET WAS EVEN HARDER TO TAKE THAN THE KISSES HE'S PLANTED ON HER...

TYPICAL RAPTOR TYPE.

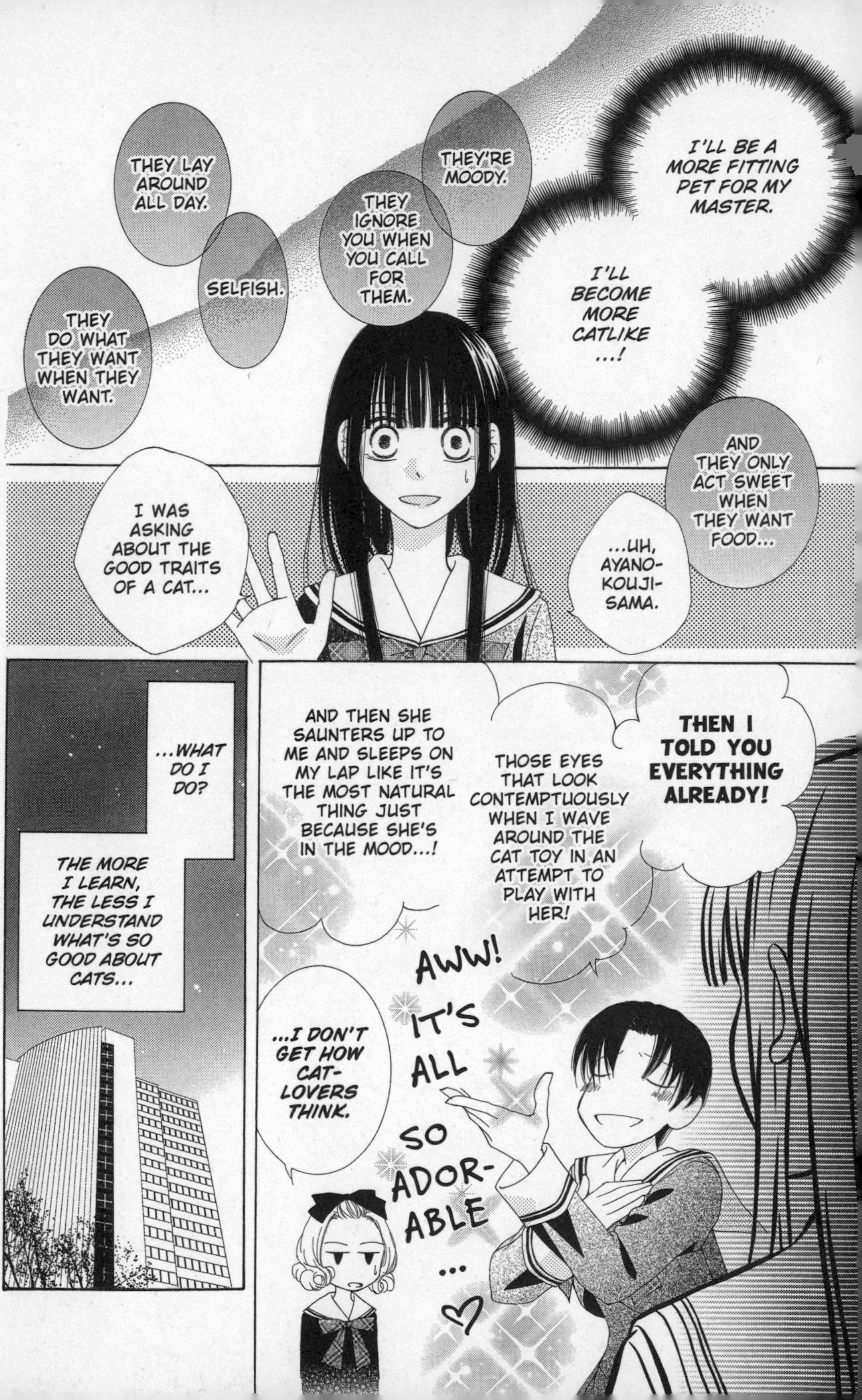
I'LL BE A MORE FITTING PET FOR MY MASTER.
I'LL BECOME MORE CATLIKE ...!
THEY'RE MOODY.
THEY IGNORE YOU WHEN YOU CALL FOR THEM.
THEY LAY AROUND ALL DAY.
SELFISH.
THEY DO WHAT THEY WANT WHEN THEY WANT.
AND THEY ONLY ACT SWEET WHEN THEY WANT FOOD...
...UH, AYANO-KOUJI-SAMA.
I WAS ASKING ABOUT THE GOOD TRAITS OF A CAT...
THEN I TOLD YOU EVERYTHING ALREADY!
THOSE EYES THAT LOOK CONTEMPTUOUSLY WHEN I WAVE AROUND THE CAT TOY IN AN ATTEMPT TO PLAY WITH HER!
AND THEN SHE SAUNTERS UP TO ME AND SLEEPS ON MY LAP LIKE IT'S THE MOST NATURAL THING JUST BECAUSE SHE'S IN THE MOOD...!
AWW! IT'S ALL SO ADOR-ABLE ...
...I DON'T GET HOW CAT-LOVERS THINK.
...WHAT DO I DO?
THE MORE I LEARN, THE LESS I UNDERSTAND WHAT'S SO GOOD ABOUT CATS...

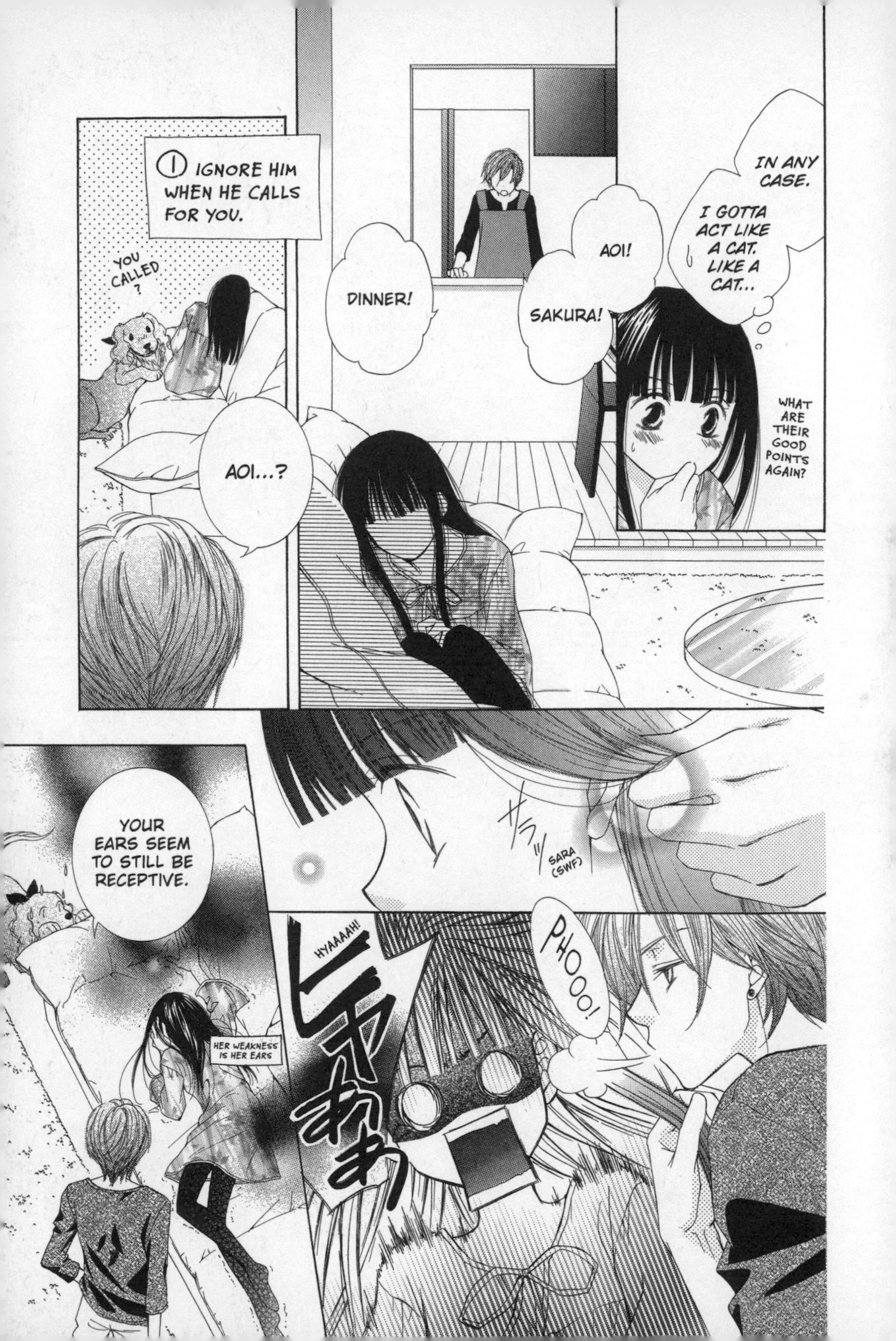
IN ANY CASE.
I GOTTA ACT LIKE A CAT. LIKE A CAT...
AOI!
SAKURA!
DINNER!
WHAT ARE THEIR GOOD POINTS AGAIN?
AOI...?
① IGNORE HIM WHEN HE CALLS FOR YOU.
YOU CALLED?
SARA (SWF)
PHOOO!
HYAAAAH!
HER WEAKNESS IS HER EARS
YOUR EARS SEEM TO STILL BE RECEPTIVE.

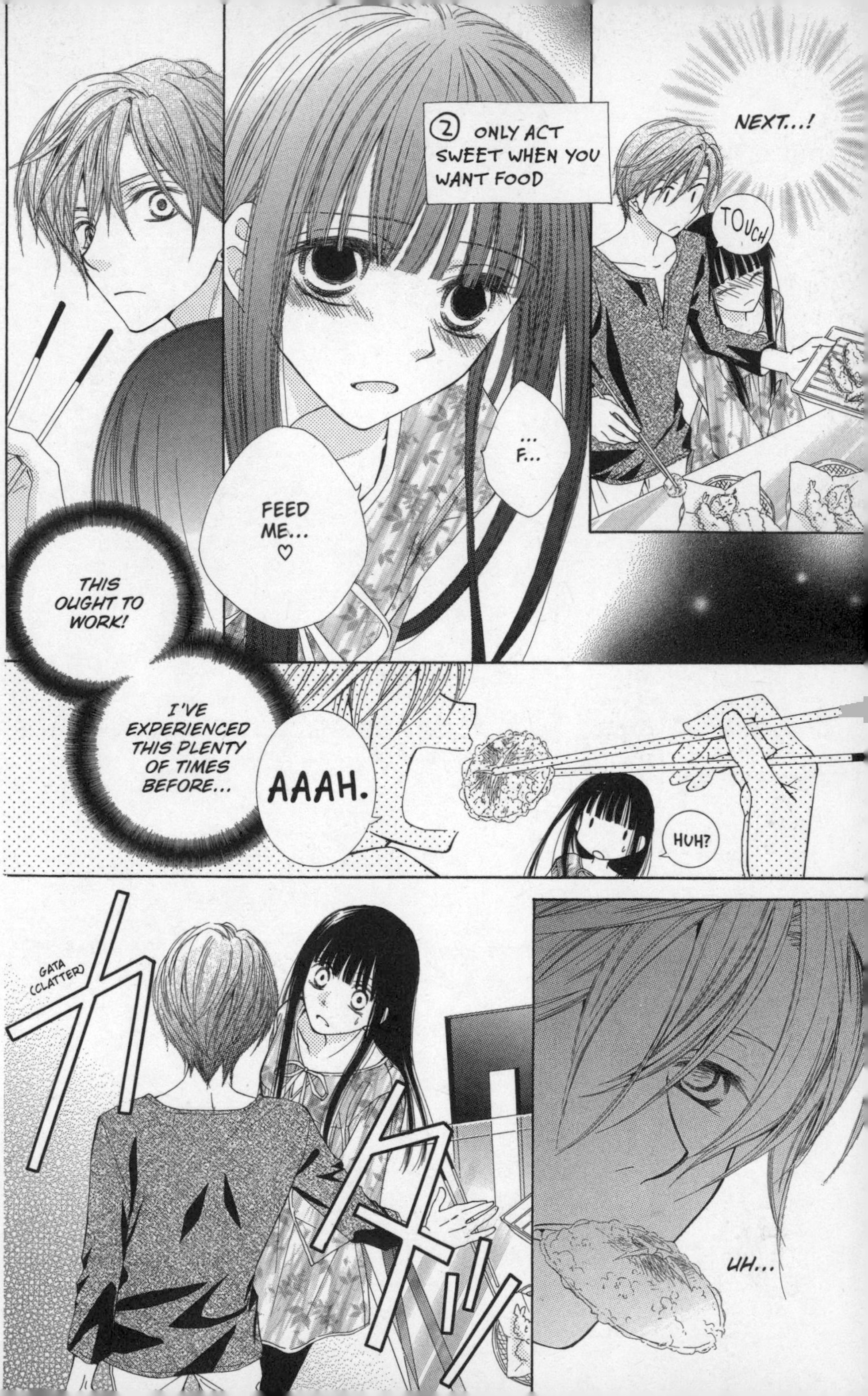
NEXT...!
② ONLY ACT SWEET WHEN YOU WANT FOOD
TOUCH
... F...
FEED ME... ♡
THIS OUGHT TO WORK!
HUH?
AAAH.
I'VE EXPERIENCED THIS PLENTY OF TIMES BEFORE...
UH...
GATA (CLATTER)

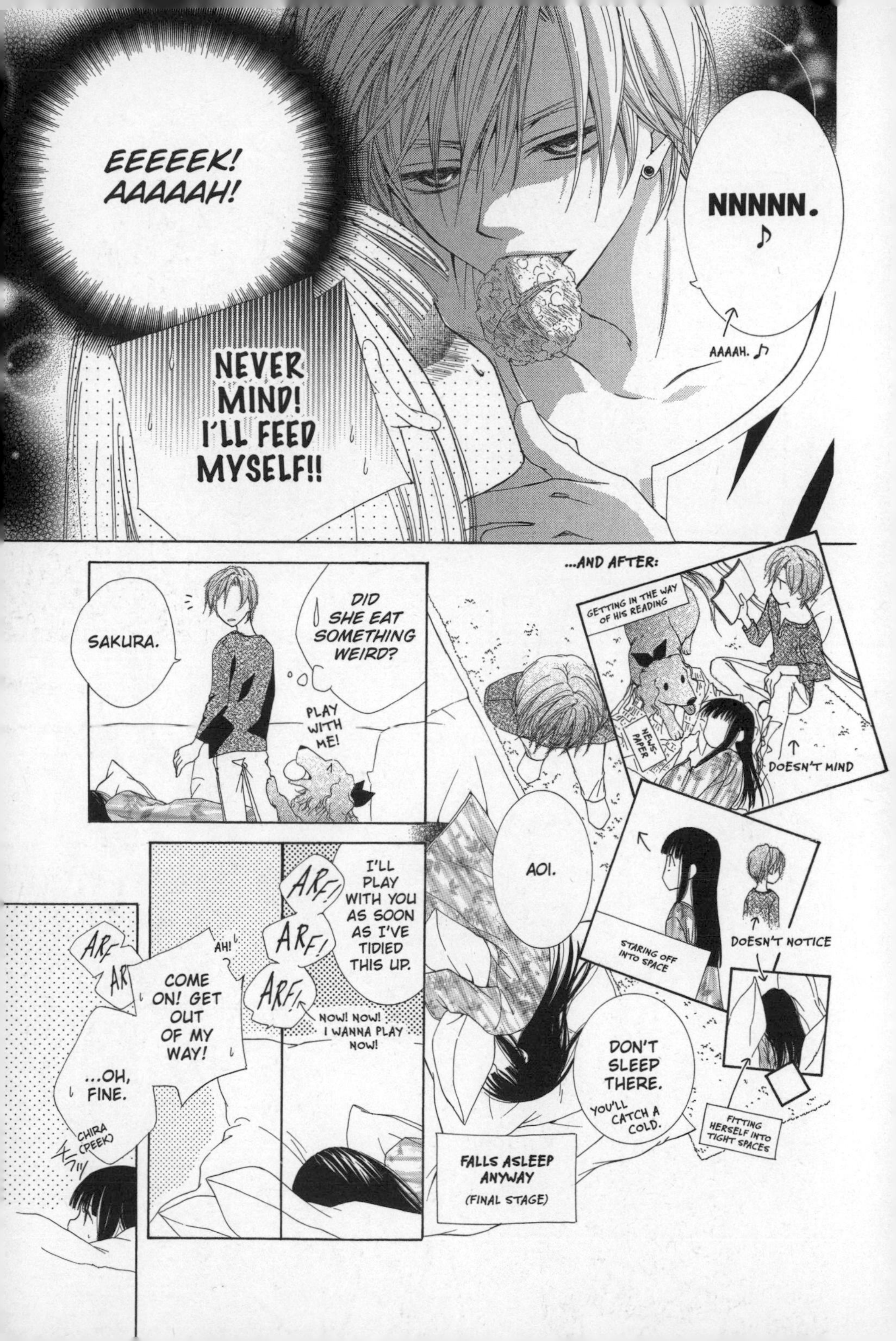
NNNNN. ♪
AAAAH. ♪
EEEEEK! AAAAAH!
NEVER MIND! I'LL FEED MYSELF!!
...AND AFTER:
GETTING IN THE WAY OF HIS READING
NEWS-PAPER
DOESN'T MIND
STARING OFF INTO SPACE
DOESN'T NOTICE
FITTING HERSELF INTO TIGHT SPACES
AOI.
DON'T SLEEP THERE.
YOU'LL CATCH A COLD.
FALLS ASLEEP ANYWAY
(FINAL STAGE)
DID SHE EAT SOMETHING WEIRD?
SAKURA.
PLAY WITH ME!
I'LL PLAY WITH YOU AS SOON AS I'VE TIDIED THIS UP.
ARF!
ARF!
ARF!
NOW! NOW! I WANNA PLAY NOW!
AH!
ARF
COME ON! GET OUT OF MY WAY!
...OH, FINE.
CHIRA (PEEK)

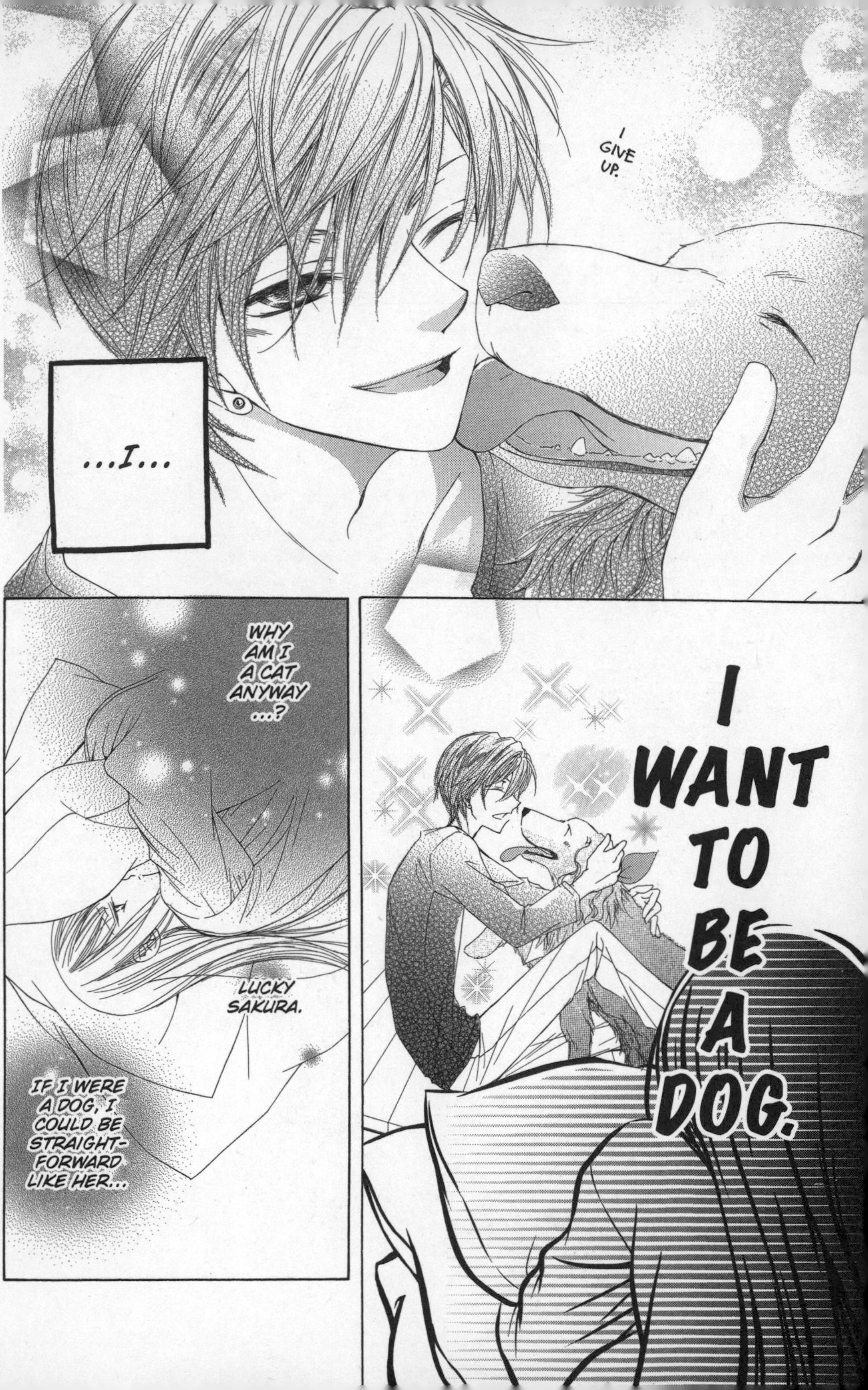
I GIVE UP.
...I...
I WANT TO BE A DOG.
WHY AM I A CAT ANYWAY ...?
LUCKY SAKURA.
IF I WERE A DOG, I COULD BE STRAIGHT-FORWARD LIKE HER...

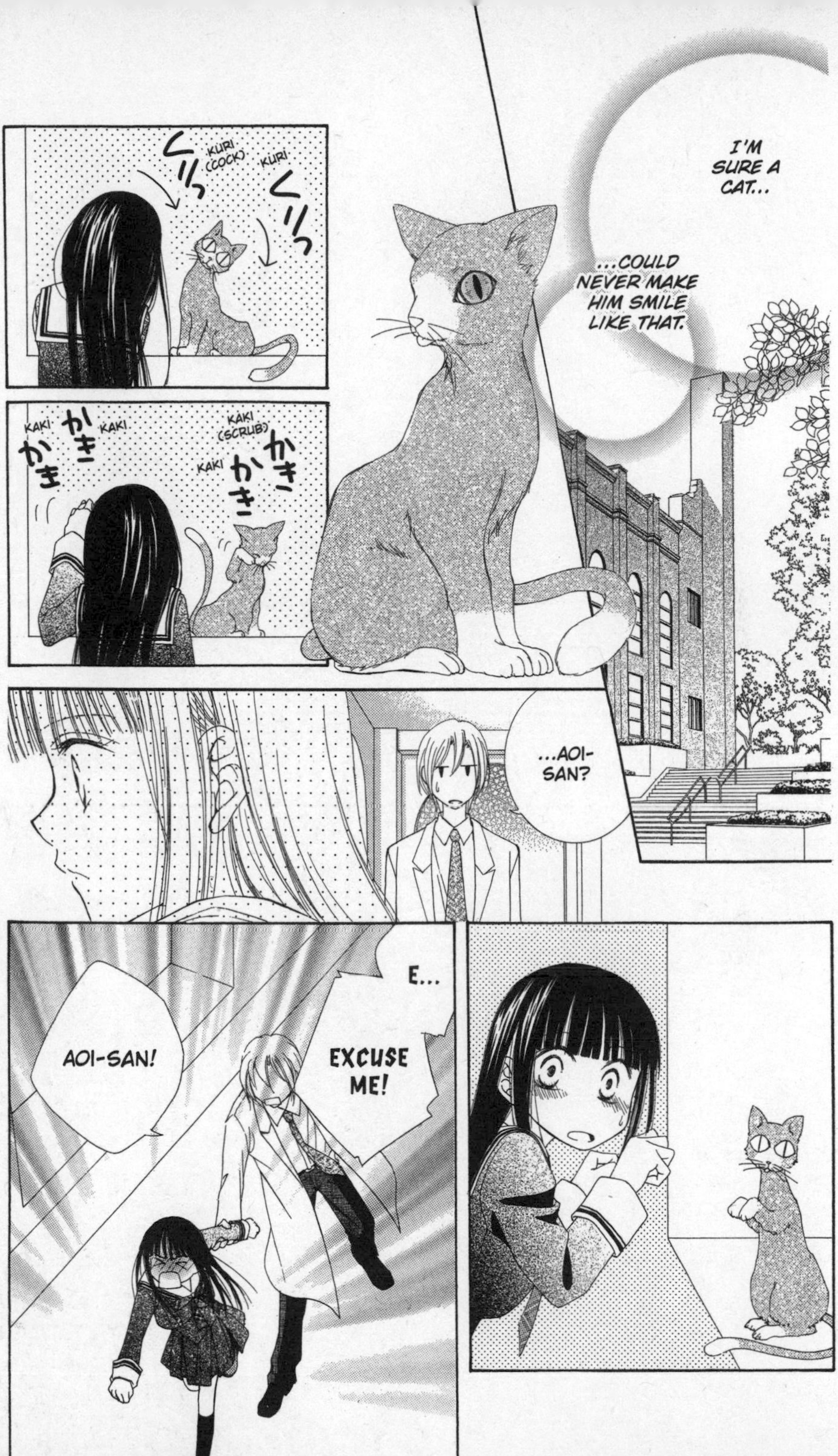
I'M SURE A CAT...
...COULD NEVER MAKE HIM SMILE LIKE THAT.
くりっ
KURI
くりっ
KURI (COCK)
かきかき
KAKI (SCRUB)
KAKI
かきかき
KAKI
KAKI
...AOI-SAN?
E...
EXCUSE ME!
AOI-SAN!

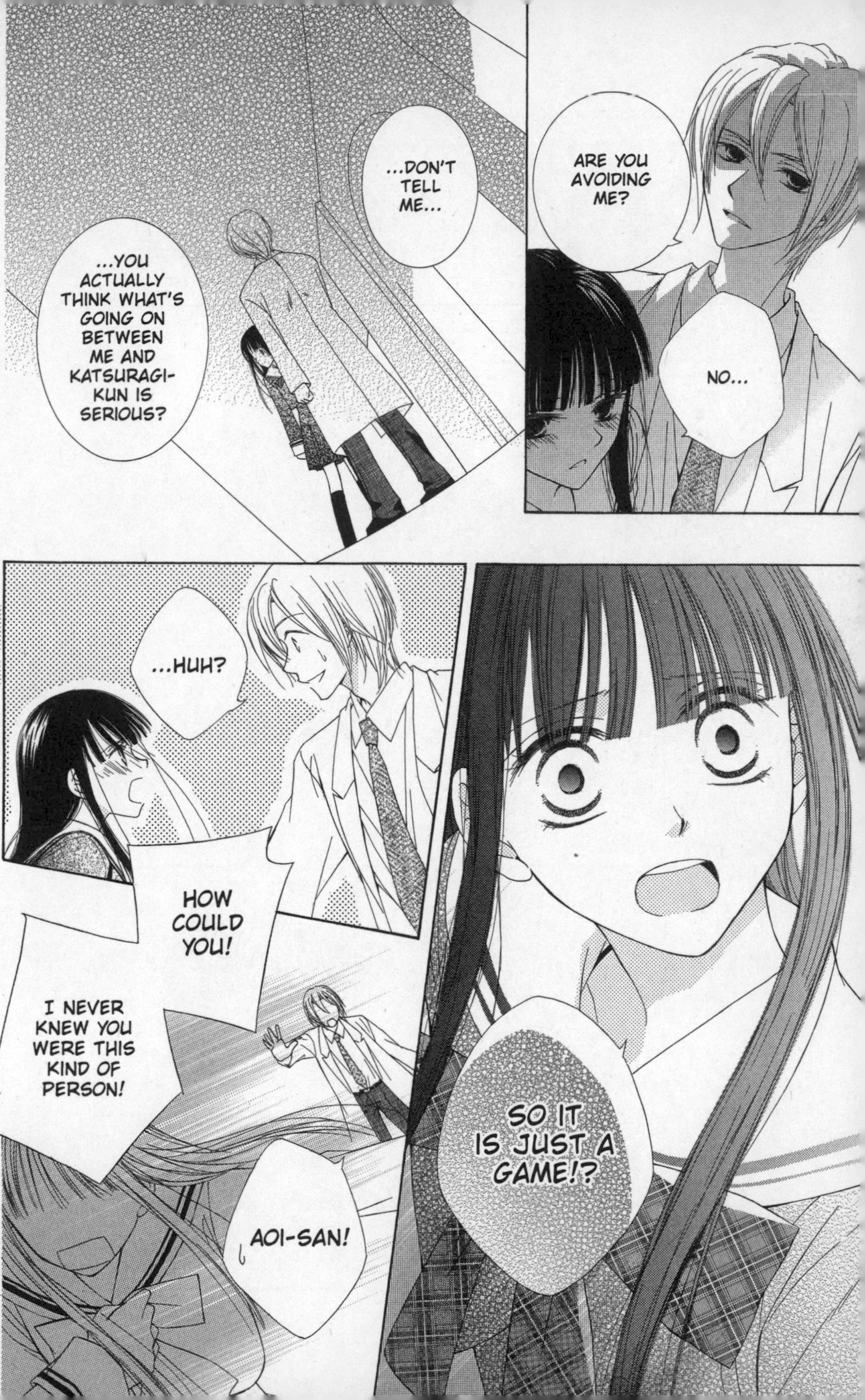
ARE YOU AVOIDING ME?
NO...
...DON'T TELL ME...
...YOU ACTUALLY THINK WHAT'S GOING ON BETWEEN ME AND KATSURAGI-KUN IS SERIOUS?
SO IT IS JUST A GAME!?
...HUH?
HOW COULD YOU!
I NEVER KNEW YOU WERE THIS KIND OF PERSON!
AOI-SAN!

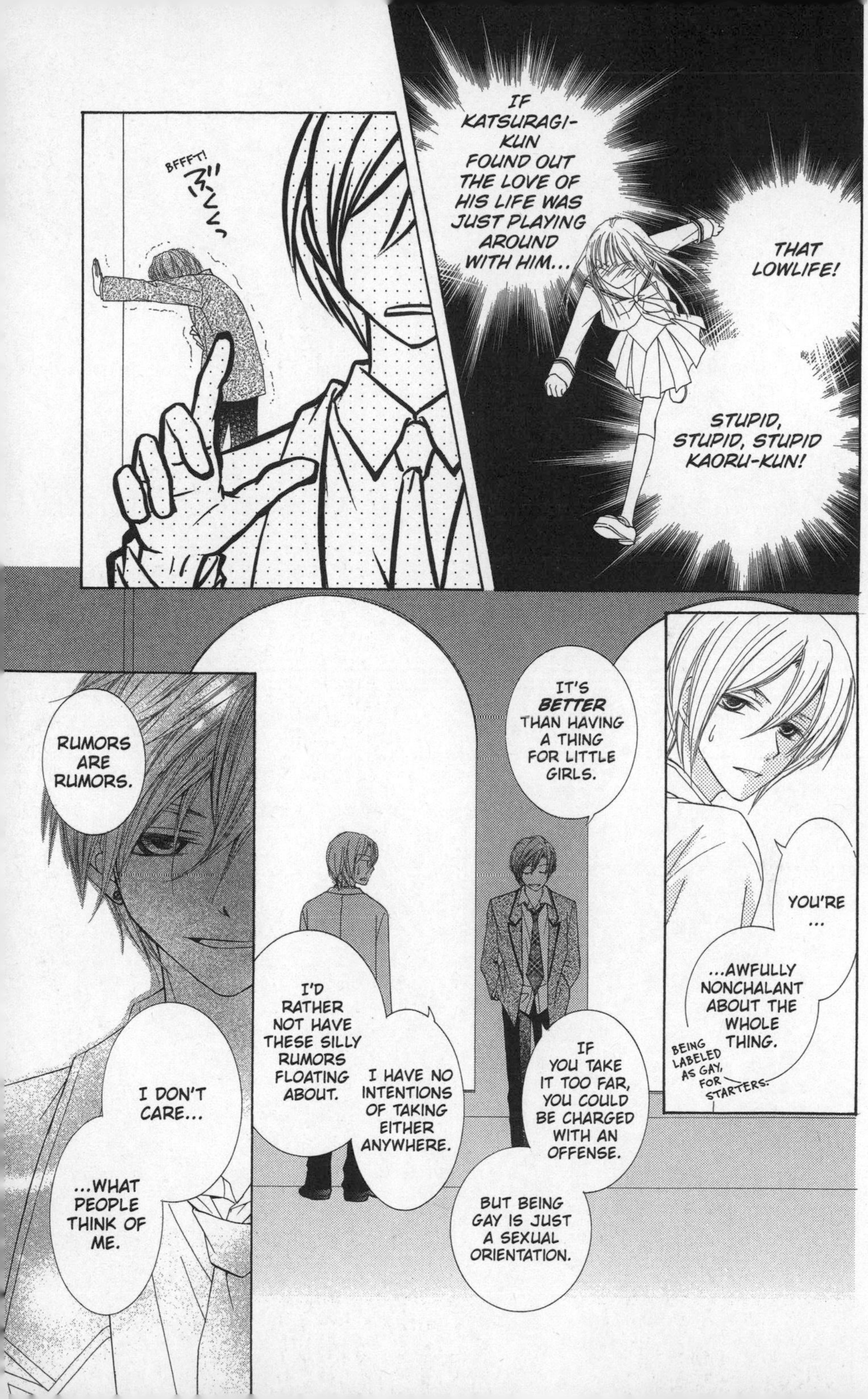
IF KATSURAGI-KUN FOUND OUT THE LOVE OF HIS LIFE WAS JUST PLAYING AROUND WITH HIM...
THAT LOWLIFE!
STUPID, STUPID, STUPID KAORU-KUN!
BFFFT!
ぶくく
YOU'RE ...
...AWFULLY NONCHALANT ABOUT THE WHOLE THING.
BEING LABELED AS GAY, FOR STARTERS.
IT'S BETTER THAN HAVING A THING FOR LITTLE GIRLS.
IF YOU TAKE IT TOO FAR, YOU COULD BE CHARGED WITH AN OFFENSE.
BUT BEING GAY IS JUST A SEXUAL ORIENTATION.
I'D RATHER NOT HAVE THESE SILLY RUMORS FLOATING ABOUT.
I HAVE NO INTENTIONS OF TAKING EITHER ANYWHERE.
RUMORS ARE RUMORS.
I DON'T CARE...
...WHAT PEOPLE THINK OF ME.

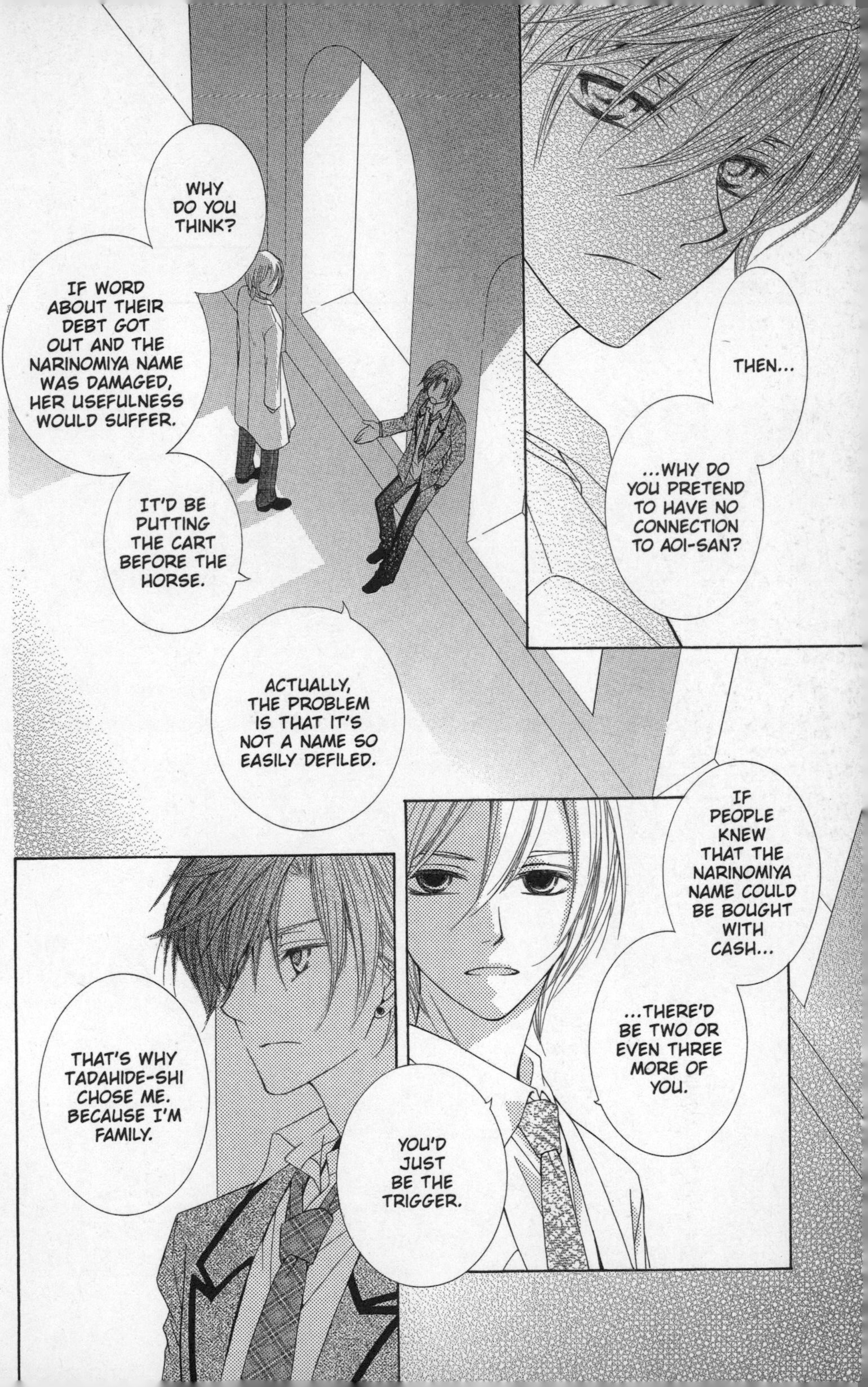
THEN...
...WHY DO YOU PRETEND TO HAVE NO CONNECTION TO AOI-SAN?
WHY DO YOU THINK?
IF WORD ABOUT THEIR DEBT GOT OUT AND THE NARINOMIYA NAME WAS DAMAGED, HER USEFULNESS WOULD SUFFER.
IT'D BE PUTTING THE CART BEFORE THE HORSE.
ACTUALLY, THE PROBLEM IS THAT IT'S NOT A NAME SO EASILY DEFILED.
IF PEOPLE KNEW THAT THE NARINOMIYA NAME COULD BE BOUGHT WITH CASH...
...THERE'D BE TWO OR EVEN THREE MORE OF YOU.
YOU'D JUST BE THE TRIGGER.
THAT'S WHY TADAHIDE-SHI CHOSE ME. BECAUSE I'M FAMILY.

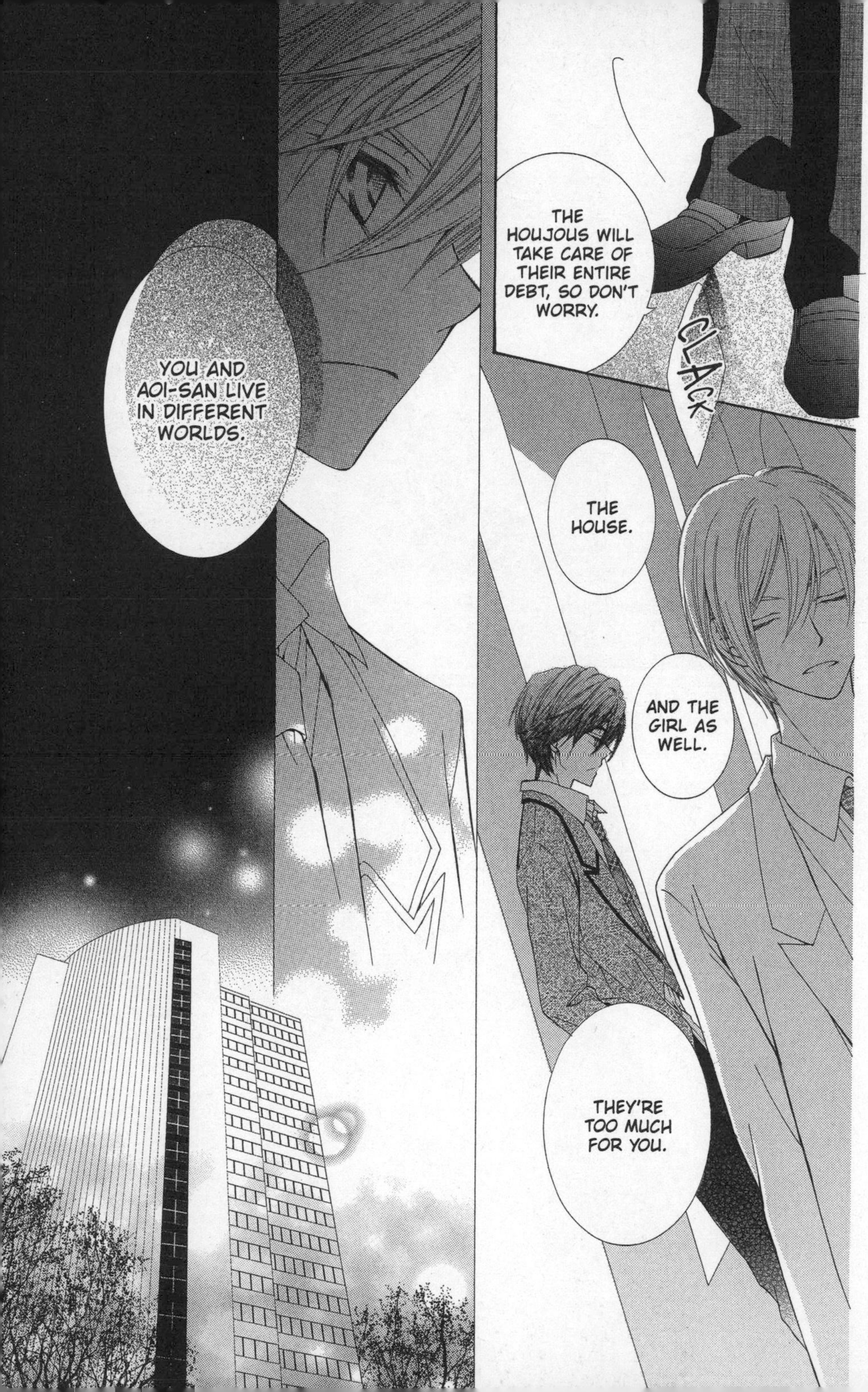
THE HOUJOUS WILL TAKE CARE OF THEIR ENTIRE DEBT, SO DON'T WORRY.
CLACK
THE HOUSE.
AND THE GIRL AS WELL.
THEY'RE TOO MUCH FOR YOU.
YOU AND AOI-SAN LIVE IN DIFFERENT WORLDS.

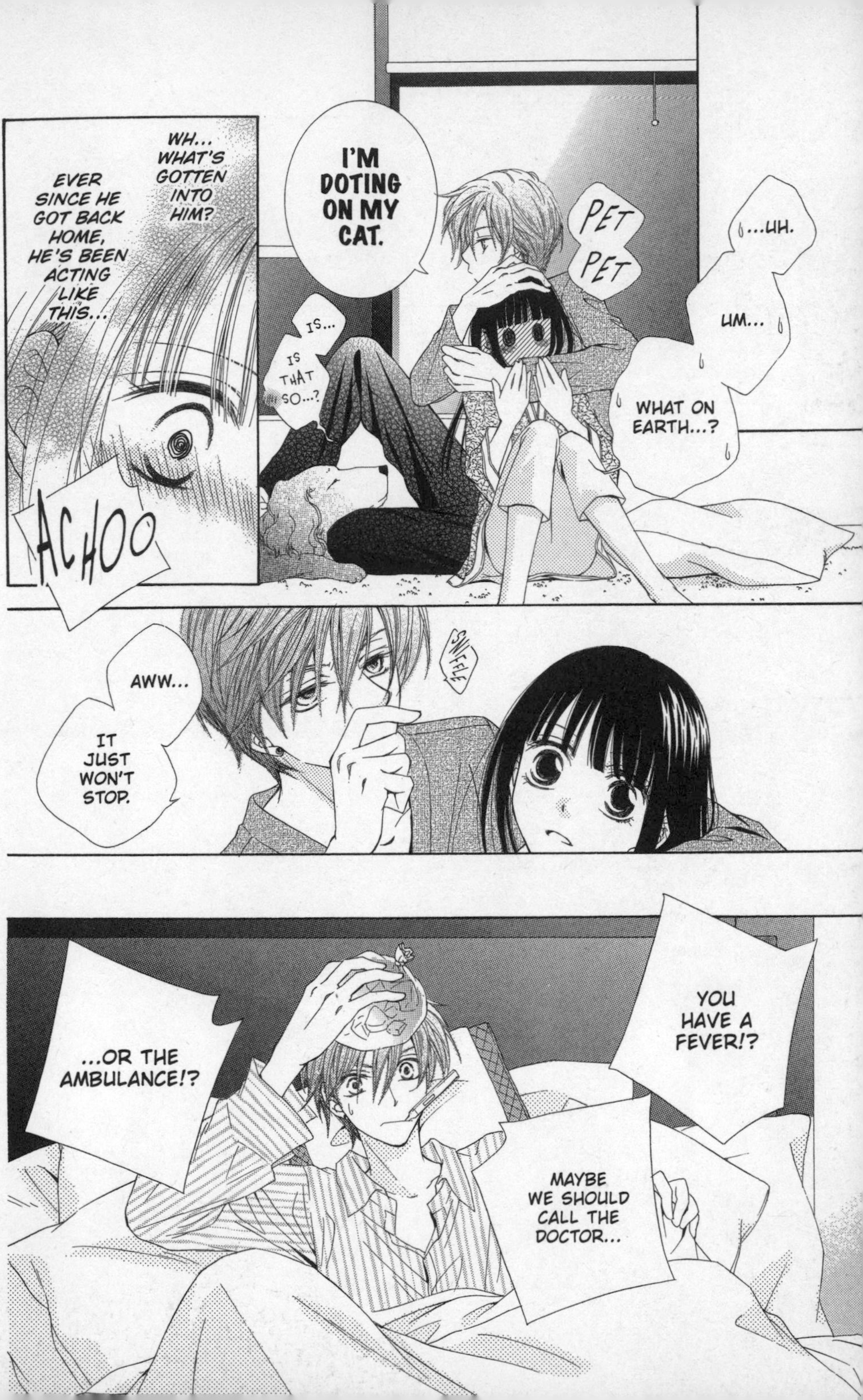
...UH.
UM...
PET PET
I'M DOTING ON MY CAT.
WHAT ON EARTH...?
IS... IS THAT SO...?
WH... WHAT'S GOTTEN INTO HIM?
EVER SINCE HE GOT BACK HOME, HE'S BEEN ACTING LIKE THIS...
ACHOO
SNIFFLE
AWW... IT JUST WON'T STOP.
YOU HAVE A FEVER!?
MAYBE WE SHOULD CALL THE DOCTOR...
...OR THE AMBULANCE!?

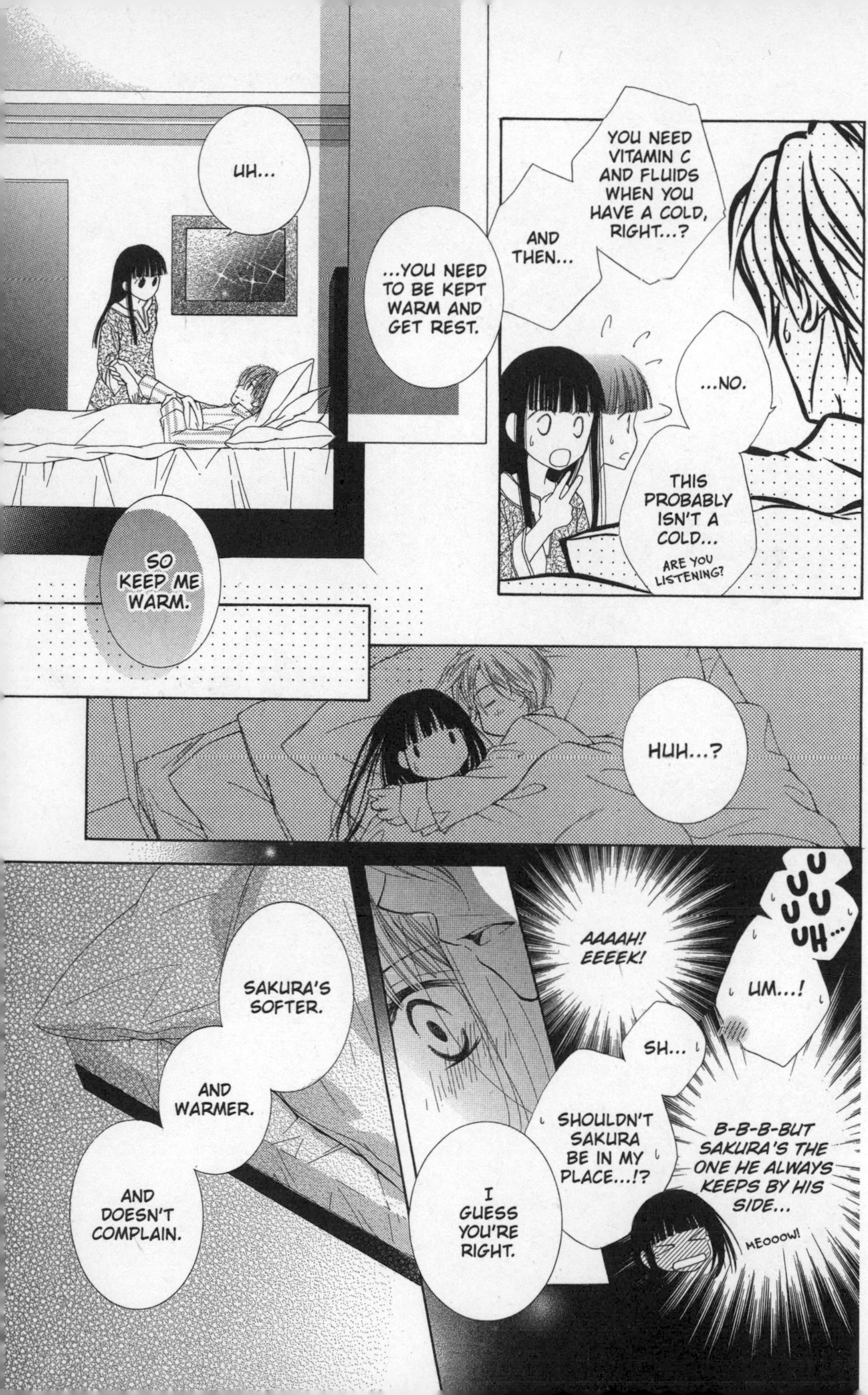
YOU NEED VITAMIN C AND FLUIDS WHEN YOU HAVE A COLD, RIGHT...?
AND THEN...
...YOU NEED TO BE KEPT WARM AND GET REST.
...NO.
THIS PROBABLY ISN'T A COLD...
ARE YOU LISTENING?
UH...
SO KEEP ME WARM.
HUH...?
UUUUUUH...
UM...!
AAAAH! EEEEK!
SH...
SHOULDN'T SAKURA BE IN MY PLACE...!?
B-B-B-BUT SAKURA'S THE ONE HE ALWAYS KEEPS BY HIS SIDE...
MEOOOW!
I GUESS YOU'RE RIGHT.
SAKURA'S SOFTER.
AND WARMER.
AND DOESN'T COMPLAIN.

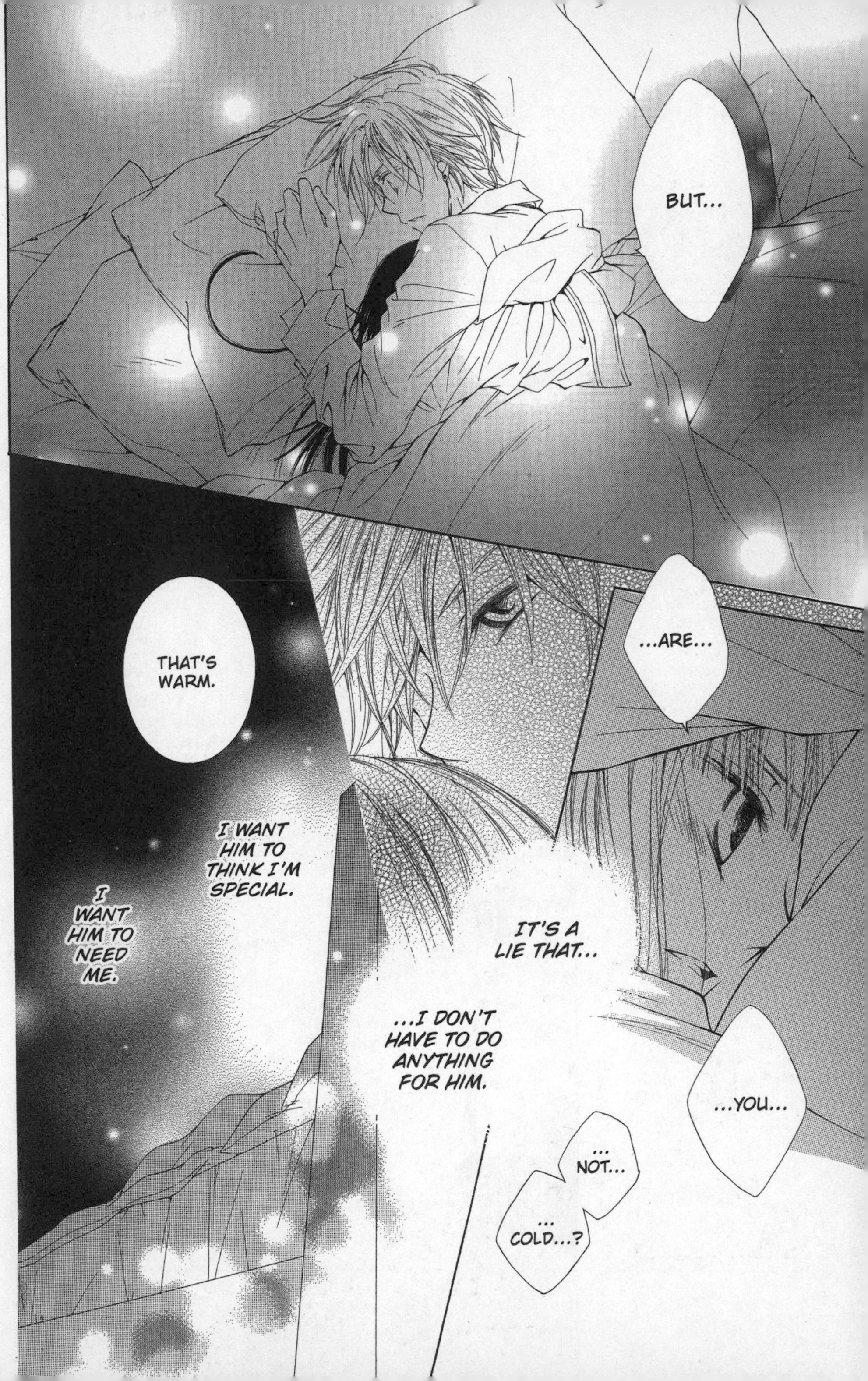
BUT...
...ARE...
...YOU...
...NOT...
...COLD...?
THAT'S WARM.
IT'S A LIE THAT...
...I DON'T HAVE TO DO ANYTHING FOR HIM.
I WANT HIM TO THINK I'M SPECIAL.
I WANT HIM TO NEED ME.

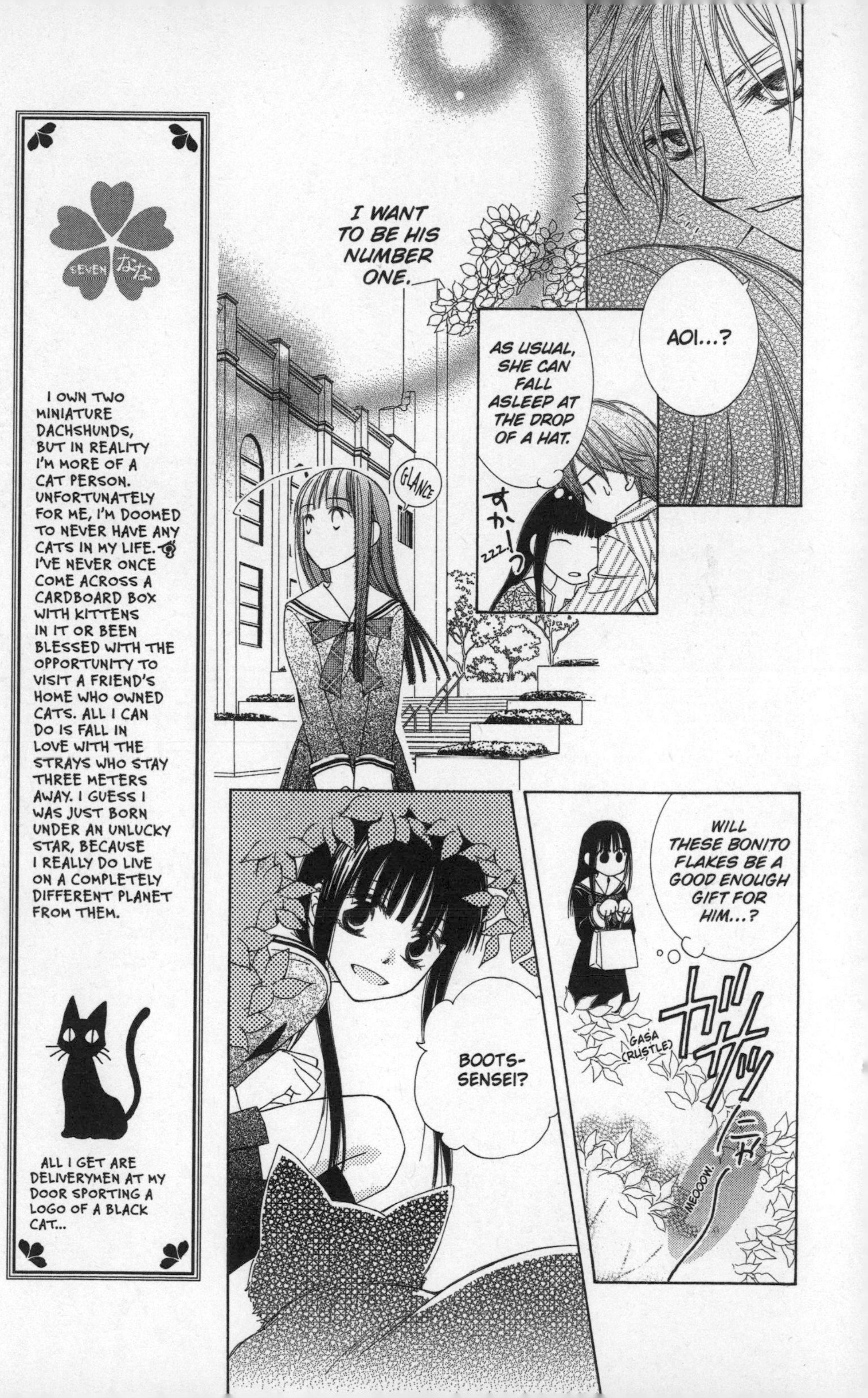
AOI...?
AS USUAL, SHE CAN FALL ASLEEP AT THE DROP OF A HAT.
すか～
ZZZ...
I WANT TO BE HIS NUMBER ONE.
GLANCE
WILL THESE BONITO FLAKES BE A GOOD ENOUGH GIFT FOR HIM...?
ガサッ
GASA (RUSTLE)
ニャー
MEOOOW.
BOOTS-SENSEI?

I OWN TWO MINIATURE DACHSHUNDS, BUT IN REALITY I'M MORE OF A CAT PERSON. UNFORTUNATELY FOR ME, I'M DOOMED TO NEVER HAVE ANY CATS IN MY LIFE. I'VE NEVER ONCE COME ACROSS A CARDBOARD BOX WITH KITTENS IN IT OR BEEN BLESSED WITH THE OPPORTUNITY TO VISIT A FRIEND'S HOME WHO OWNED CATS. ALL I CAN DO IS FALL IN LOVE WITH THE STRAYS WHO STAY THREE METERS AWAY. I GUESS I WAS JUST BORN UNDER AN UNLUCKY STAR, BECAUSE I REALLY DO LIVE ON A COMPLETELY DIFFERENT PLANET FROM THEM.

ALL I GET ARE DELIVERYMEN AT MY DOOR SPORTING A LOGO OF A BLACK CAT...

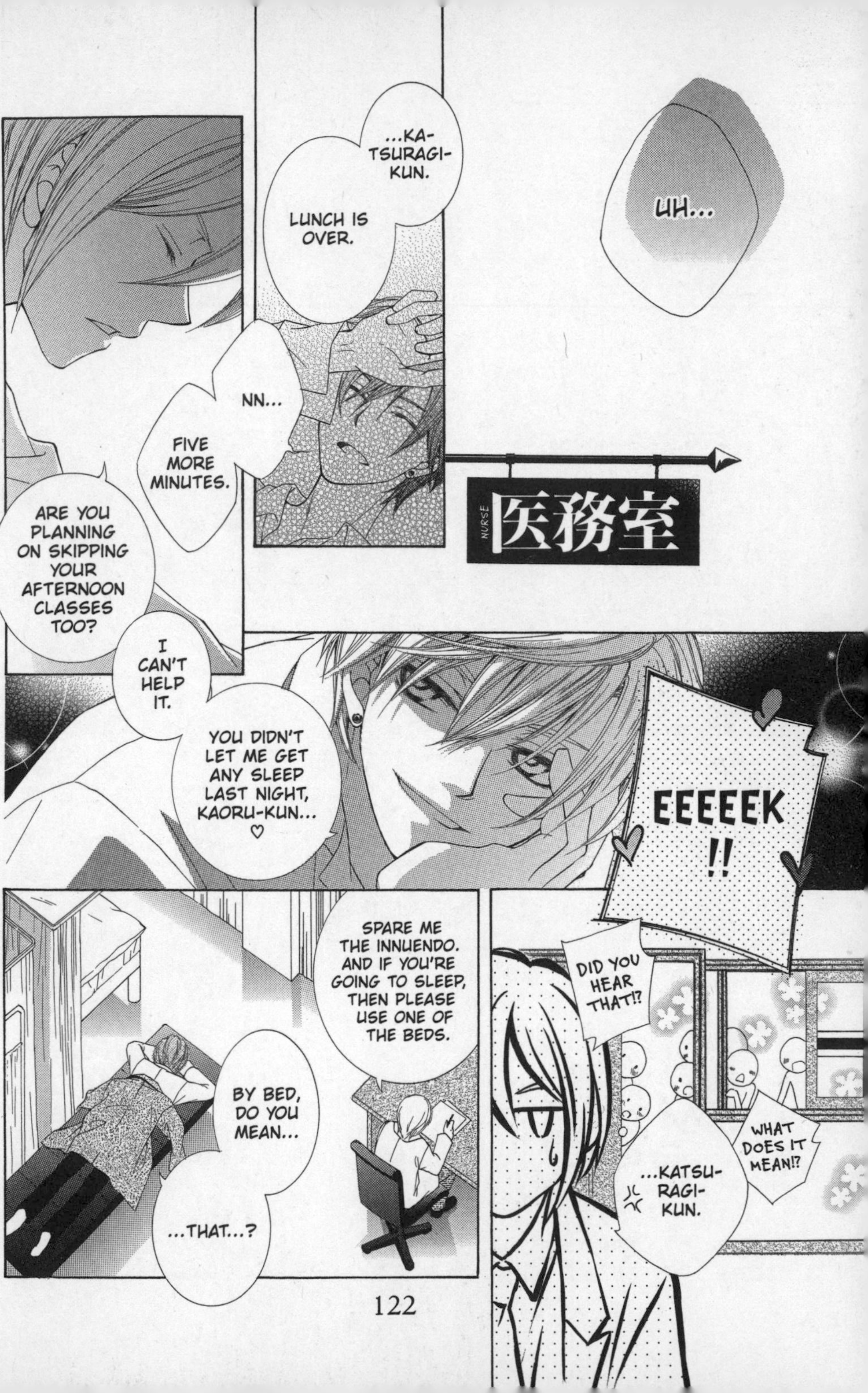
UH...
NURSE 医務室
...KA-TSURAGI-KUN.
LUNCH IS OVER.
NN...
FIVE MORE MINUTES.
ARE YOU PLANNING ON SKIPPING YOUR AFTERNOON CLASSES TOO?
I CAN'T HELP IT.
YOU DIDN'T LET ME GET ANY SLEEP LAST NIGHT, KAORU-KUN...♡
EEEEEK!!
DID YOU HEAR THAT!?
WHAT DOES IT MEAN!?
...KATSU-RAGI-KUN.
SPARE ME THE INNUENDO. AND IF YOU'RE GOING TO SLEEP, THEN PLEASE USE ONE OF THE BEDS.
BY BED, DO YOU MEAN...
...THAT...?

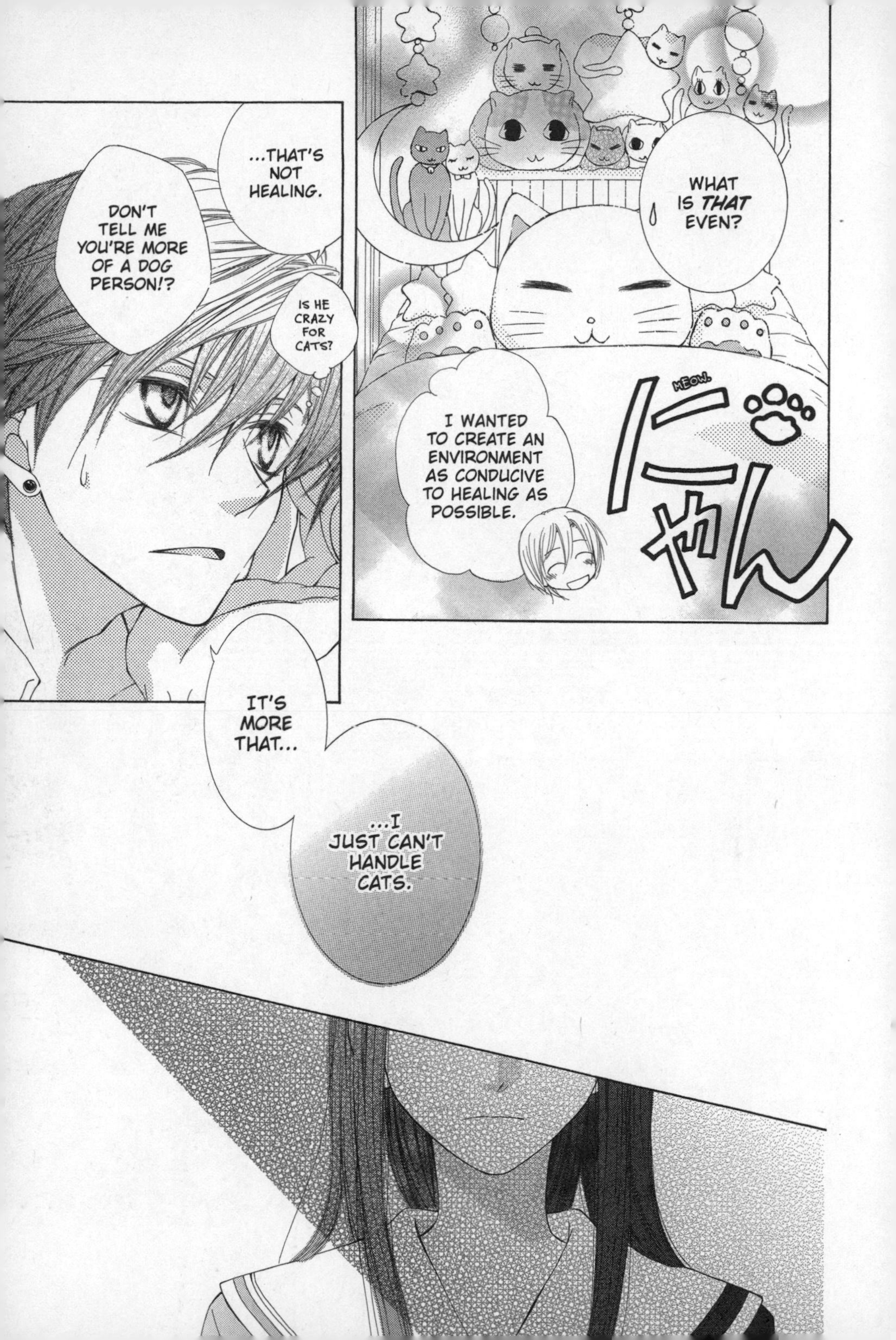
WHAT IS THAT EVEN?
I WANTED TO CREATE AN ENVIRONMENT AS CONDUCIVE TO HEALING AS POSSIBLE.
MEOW.
にゃーん
...THAT'S NOT HEALING.
DON'T TELL ME YOU'RE MORE OF A DOG PERSON!?
IS HE CRAZY FOR CATS?
IT'S MORE THAT...
...I JUST CAN'T HANDLE CATS.

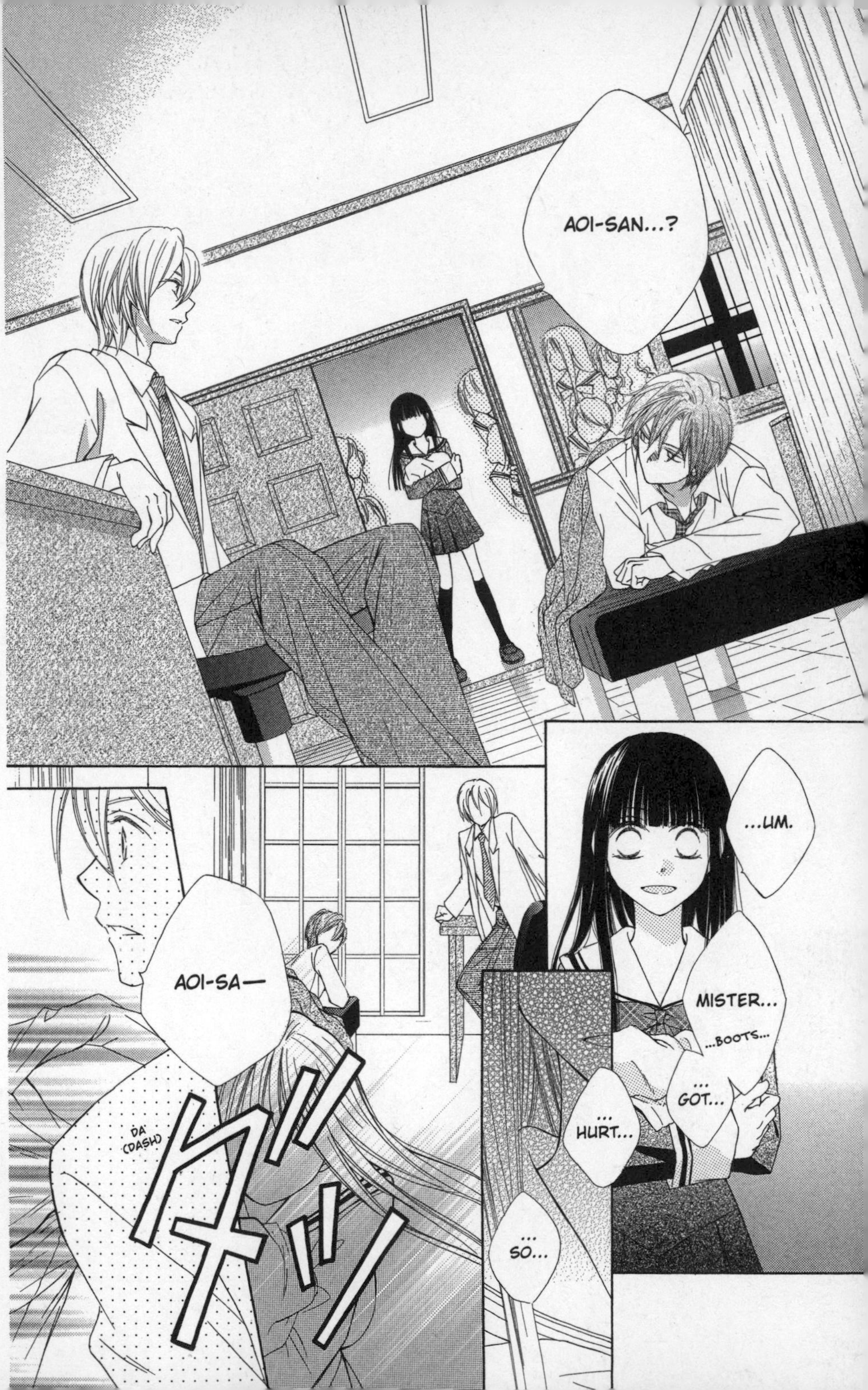
AOI-SAN...?
...UM.
MISTER...
...BOOTS...
...GOT...
...HURT...
...SO...
AOI-SA—
DA (DASH)

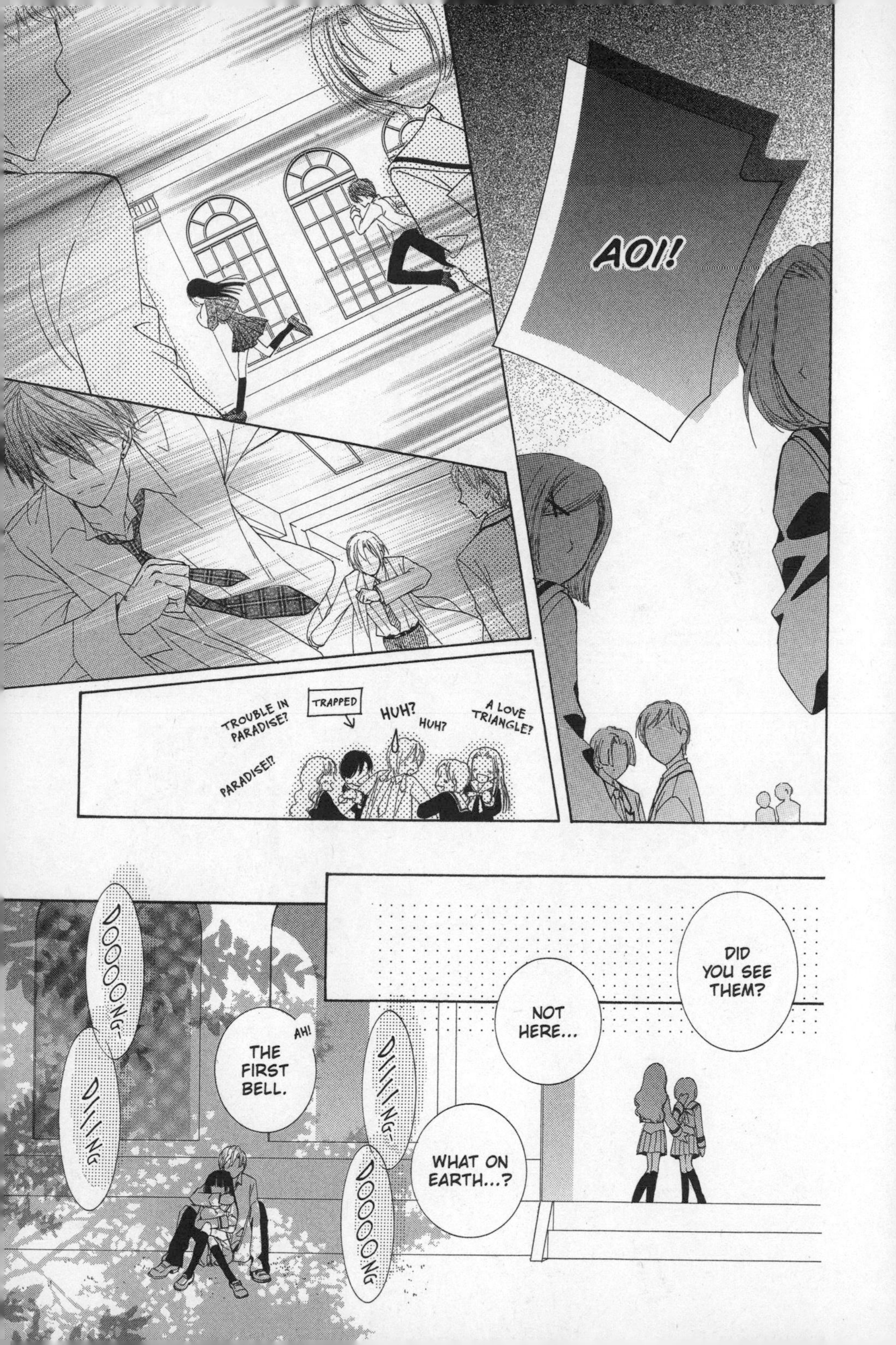
AOI!
A LOVE TRIANGLE?
HUH?
HUH?
TRAPPED
TROUBLE IN PARADISE?
PARADISE!?
DID YOU SEE THEM?
NOT HERE...
WHAT ON EARTH...?
DIIING-
DOOOONG
AH!
THE FIRST BELL.
DOOOONG-
DIIING

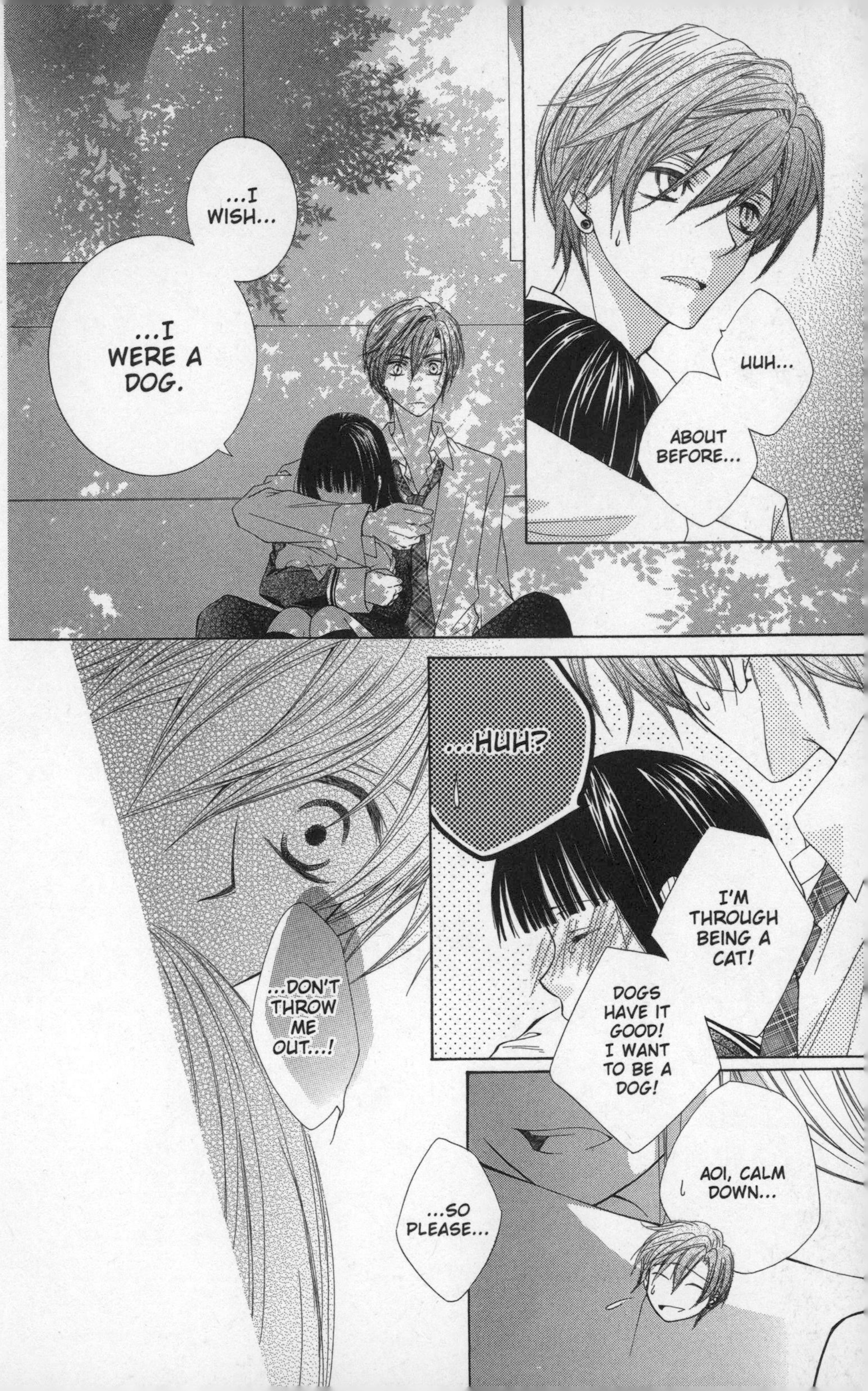
UUH...
ABOUT BEFORE...
...I WISH...
...I WERE A DOG.
...HUH?
I'M THROUGH BEING A CAT!
DOGS HAVE IT GOOD! I WANT TO BE A DOG!
AOI, CALM DOWN...
...DON'T THROW ME OUT...!
...SO PLEASE...

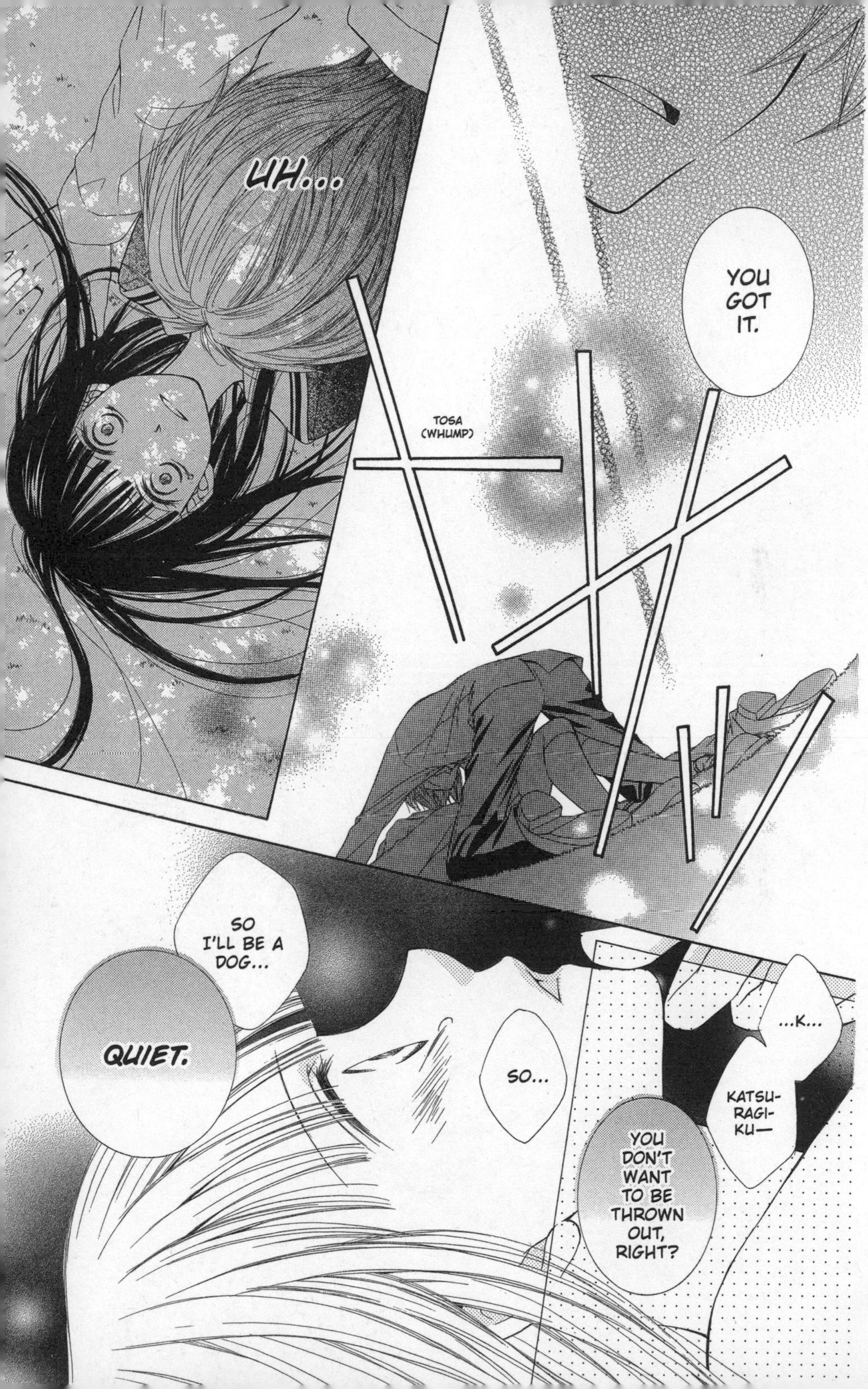
YOU GOT IT.
TOSA (WHUMP)
UH...
...K...
KATSU-RAGI-KU—
YOU DON'T WANT TO BE THROWN OUT, RIGHT?
SO...
SO I'LL BE A DOG...
QUIET.

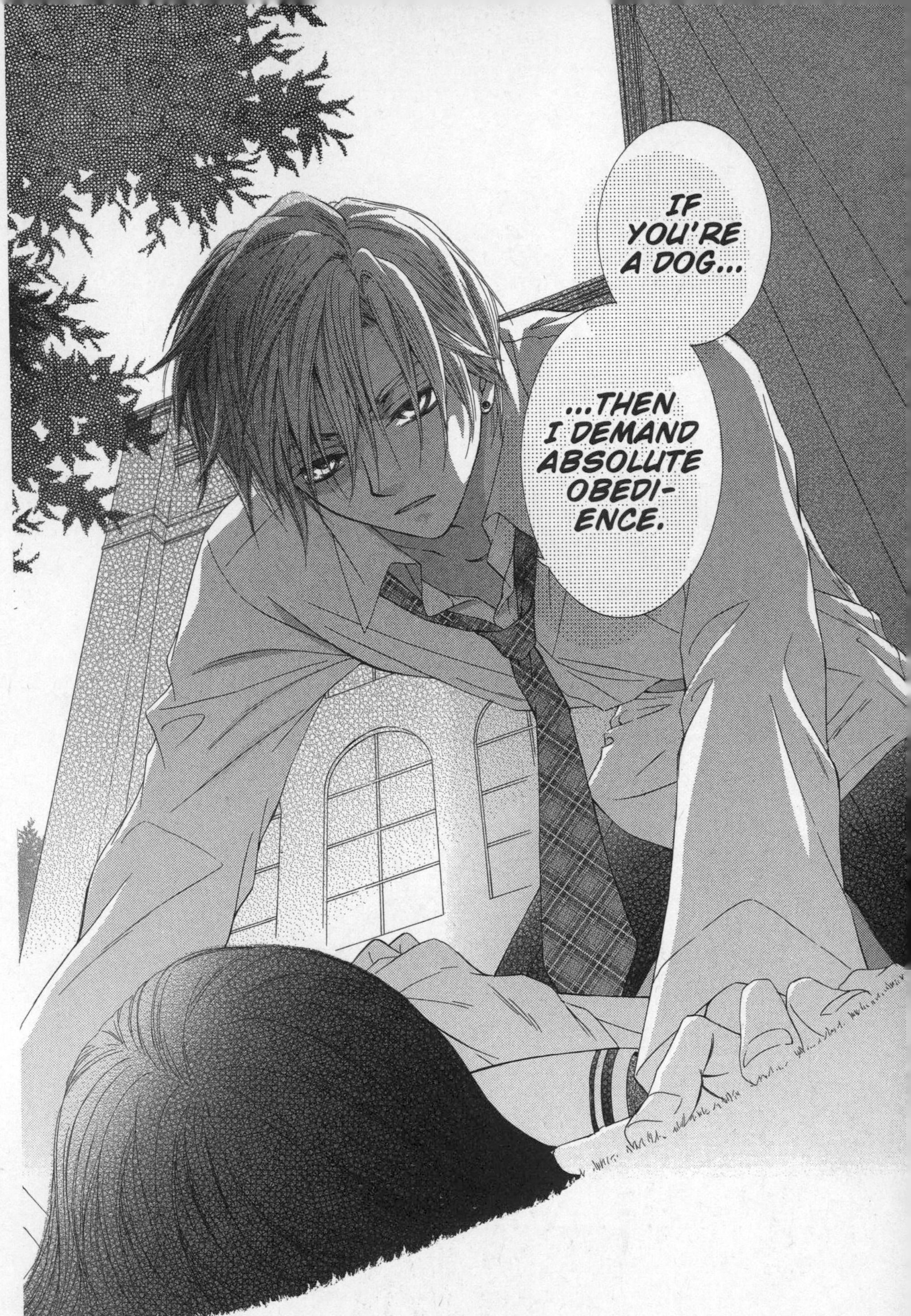
IF YOU'RE A DOG...
...THEN I DEMAND ABSOLUTE OBEDI- ENCE.

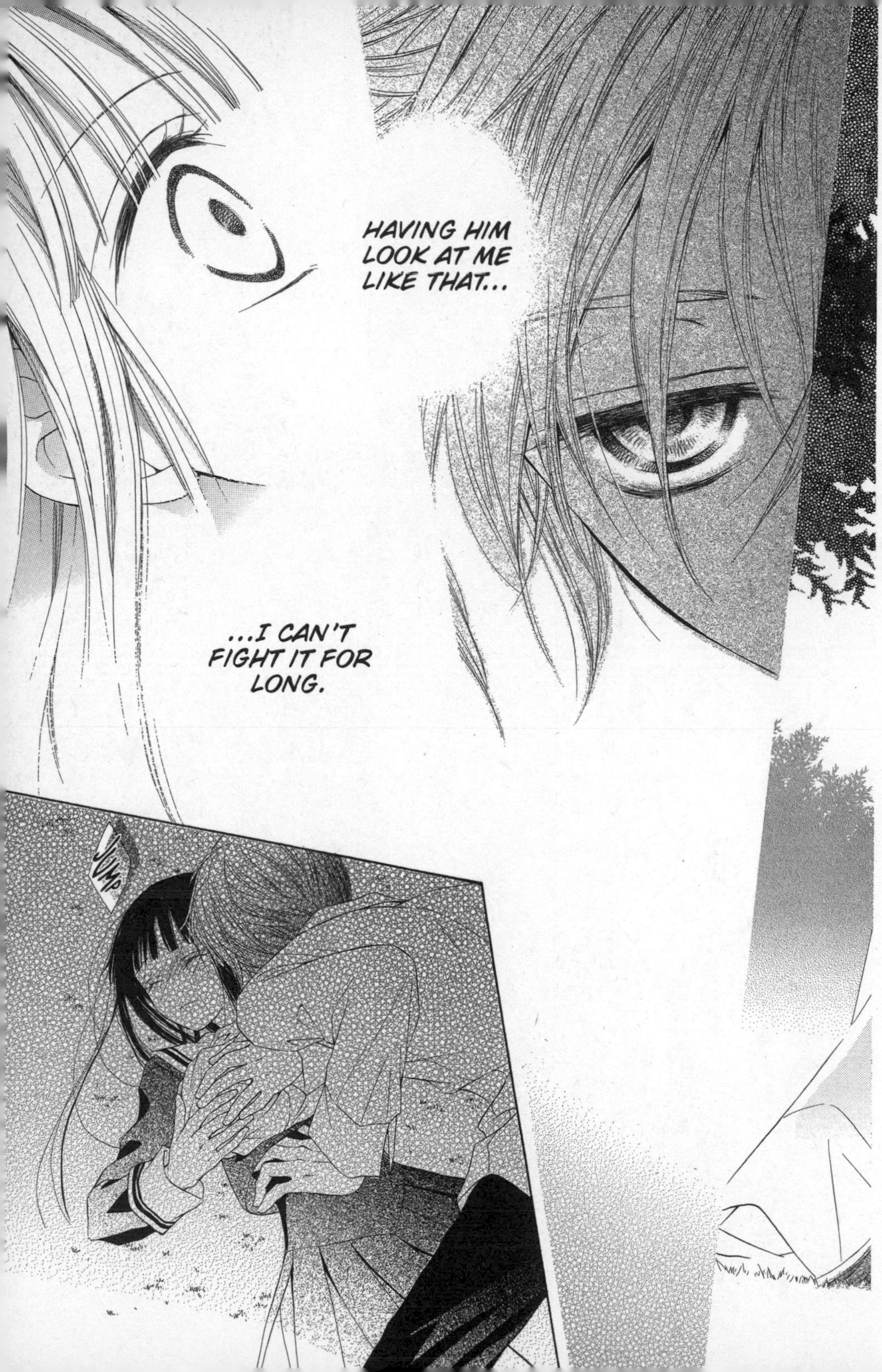
HAVING HIM LOOK AT ME LIKE THAT...
...I CAN'T FIGHT IT FOR LONG.
JUMP

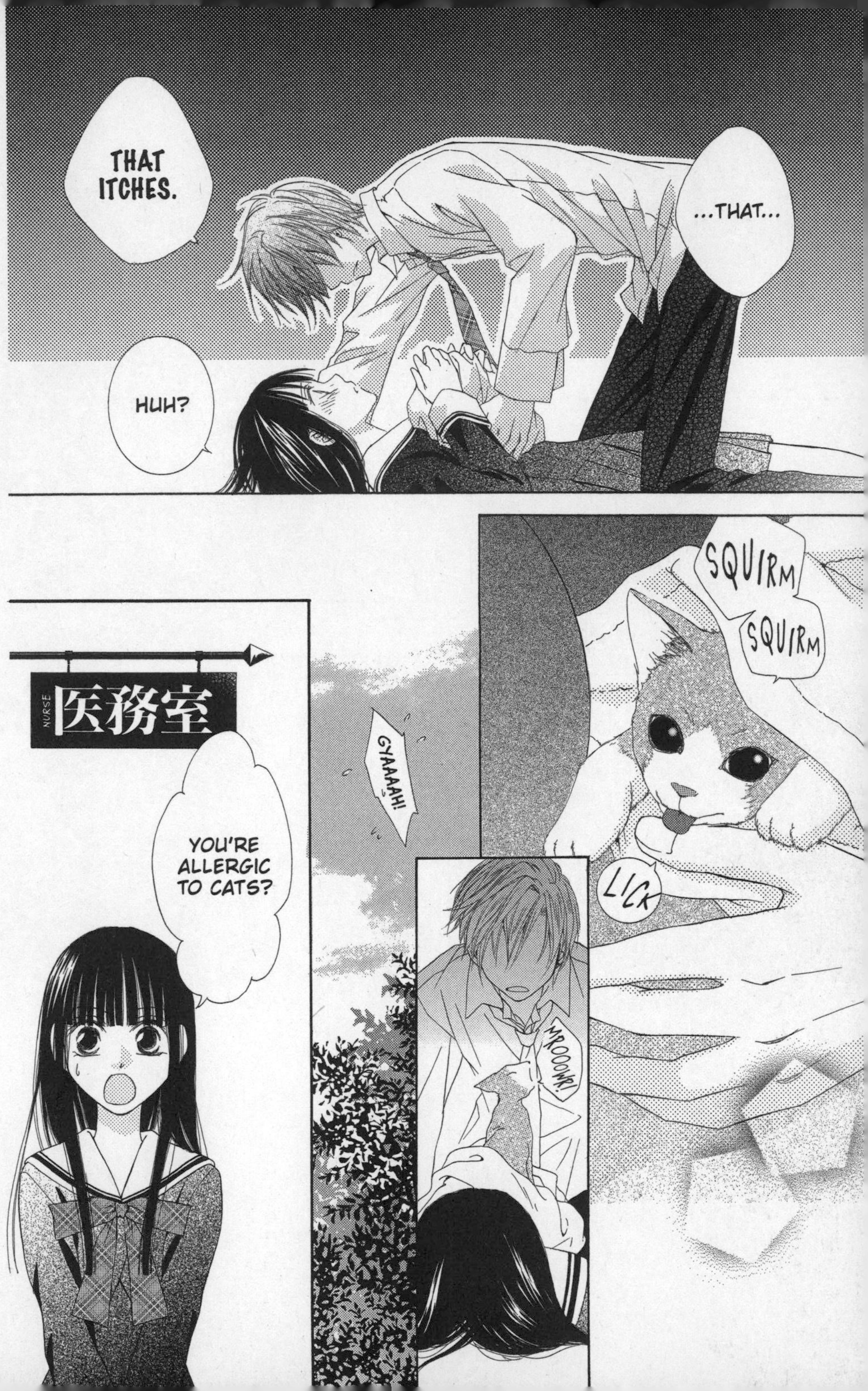

...THAT...
THAT ITCHES.
HUH?
SQUIRM
SQUIRM
LICK
MROOOWR!
GYAAAAH!
NURSE
医務室
YOU'RE ALLERGIC TO CATS?

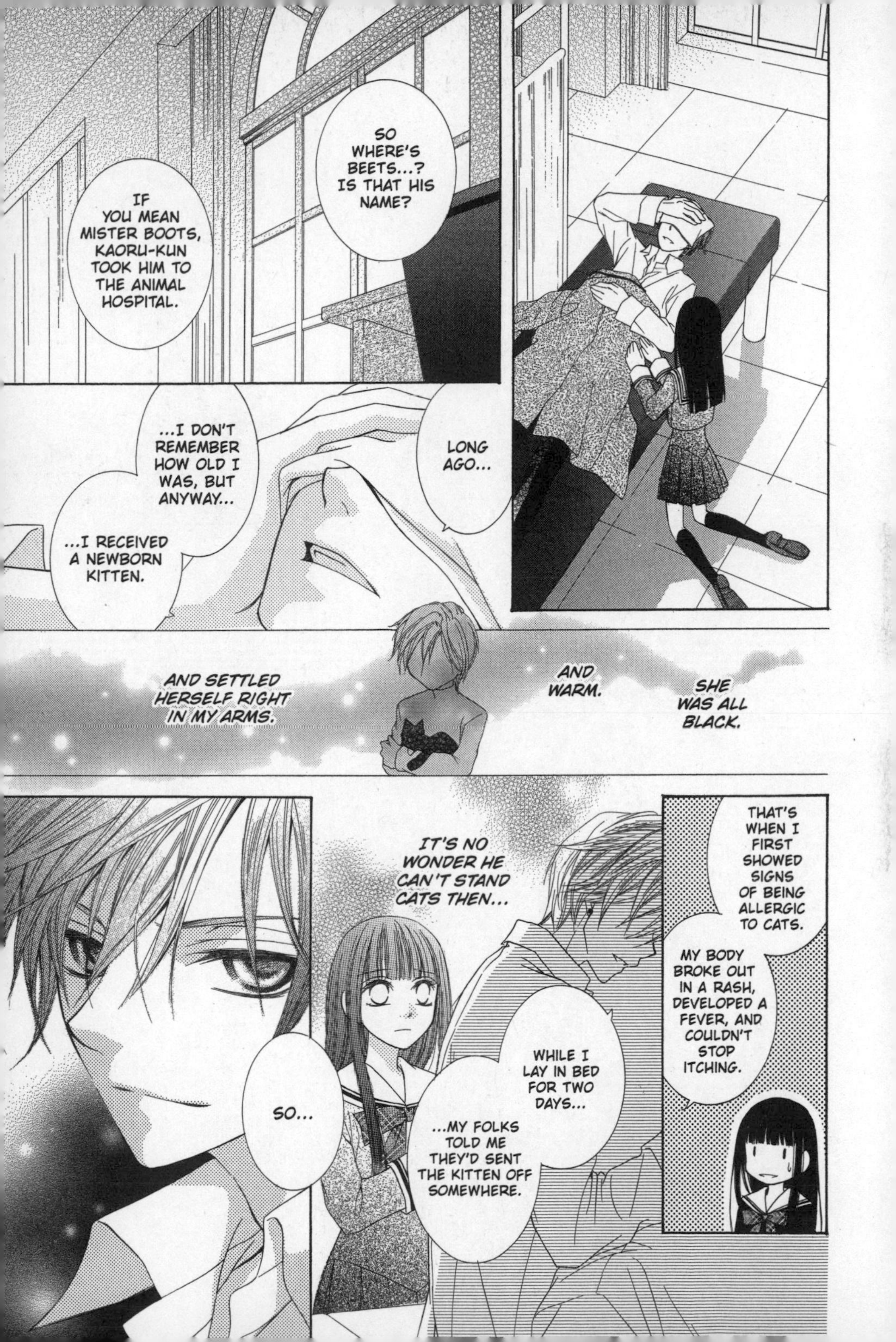
SO WHERE'S BEETS...? IS THAT HIS NAME?
IF YOU MEAN MISTER BOOTS, KAORU-KUN TOOK HIM TO THE ANIMAL HOSPITAL.
LONG AGO...
...I DON'T REMEMBER HOW OLD I WAS, BUT ANYWAY...
...I RECEIVED A NEWBORN KITTEN.
SHE WAS ALL BLACK.
AND WARM.
AND SETTLED HERSELF RIGHT IN MY ARMS.
THAT'S WHEN I FIRST SHOWED SIGNS OF BEING ALLERGIC TO CATS.
MY BODY BROKE OUT IN A RASH, DEVELOPED A FEVER, AND COULDN'T STOP ITCHING.
IT'S NO WONDER HE CAN'T STAND CATS THEN...
WHILE I LAY IN BED FOR TWO DAYS...
...MY FOLKS TOLD ME THEY'D SENT THE KITTEN OFF SOMEWHERE.
SO...

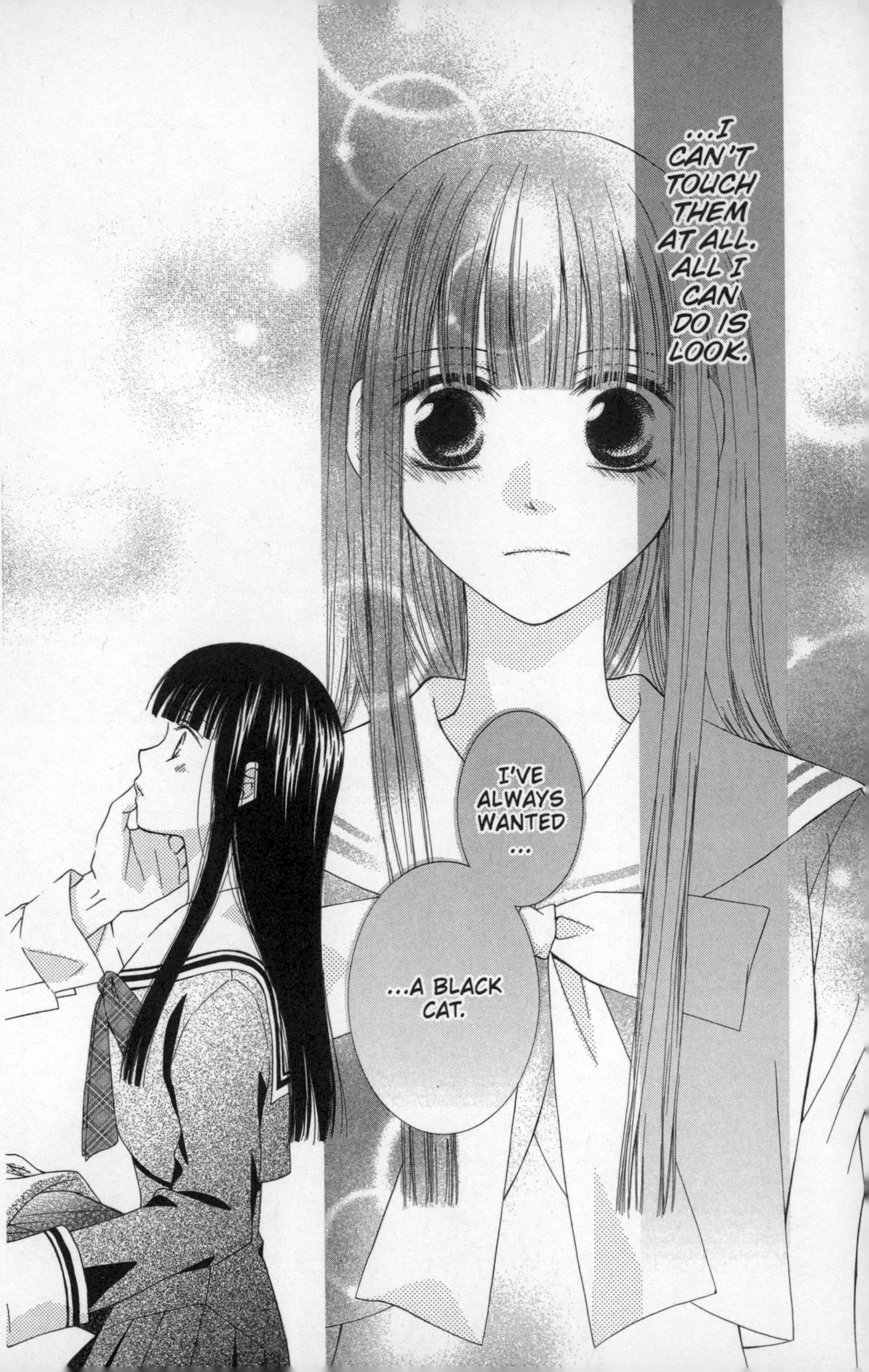
...I CAN'T TOUCH THEM AT ALL. ALL I CAN DO IS LOOK.
I'VE ALWAYS WANTED ...
...A BLACK CAT.

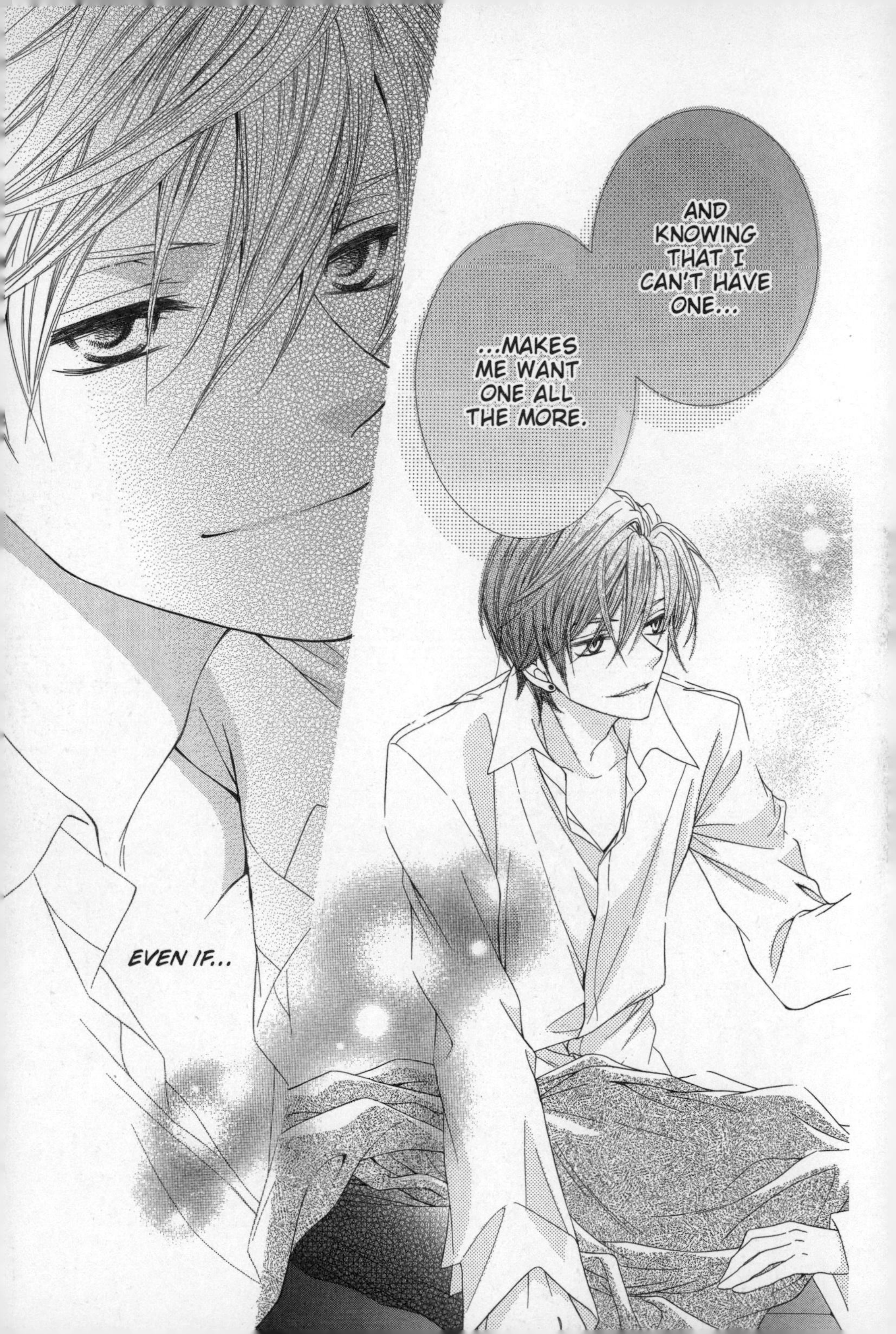
AND KNOWING THAT I CAN'T HAVE ONE...
...MAKES ME WANT ONE ALL THE MORE.
EVEN IF...

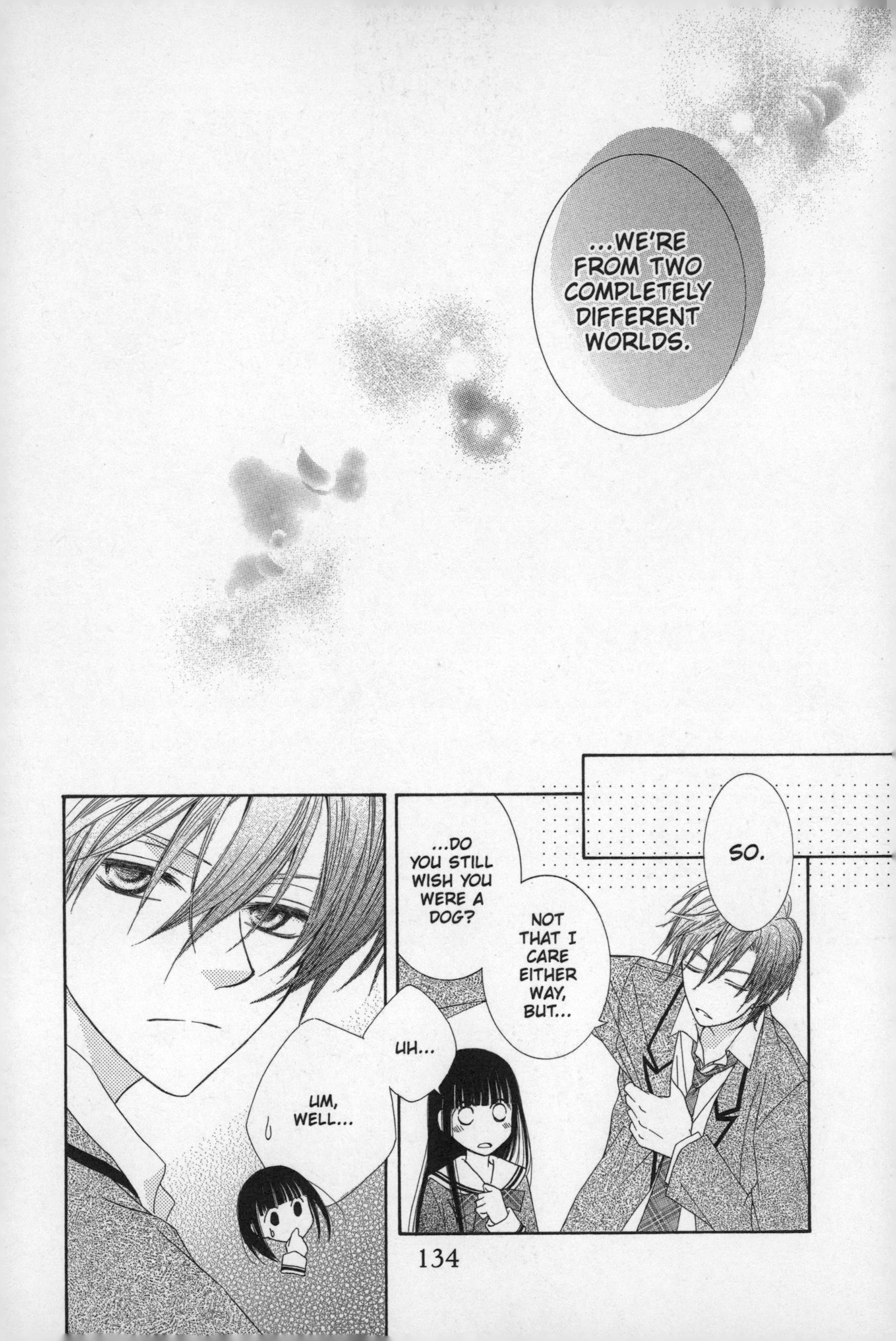
...WE'RE FROM TWO COMPLETELY DIFFERENT WORLDS.
SO.
...DO YOU STILL WISH YOU WERE A DOG?
NOT THAT I CARE EITHER WAY, BUT...
UH...
UM, WELL...

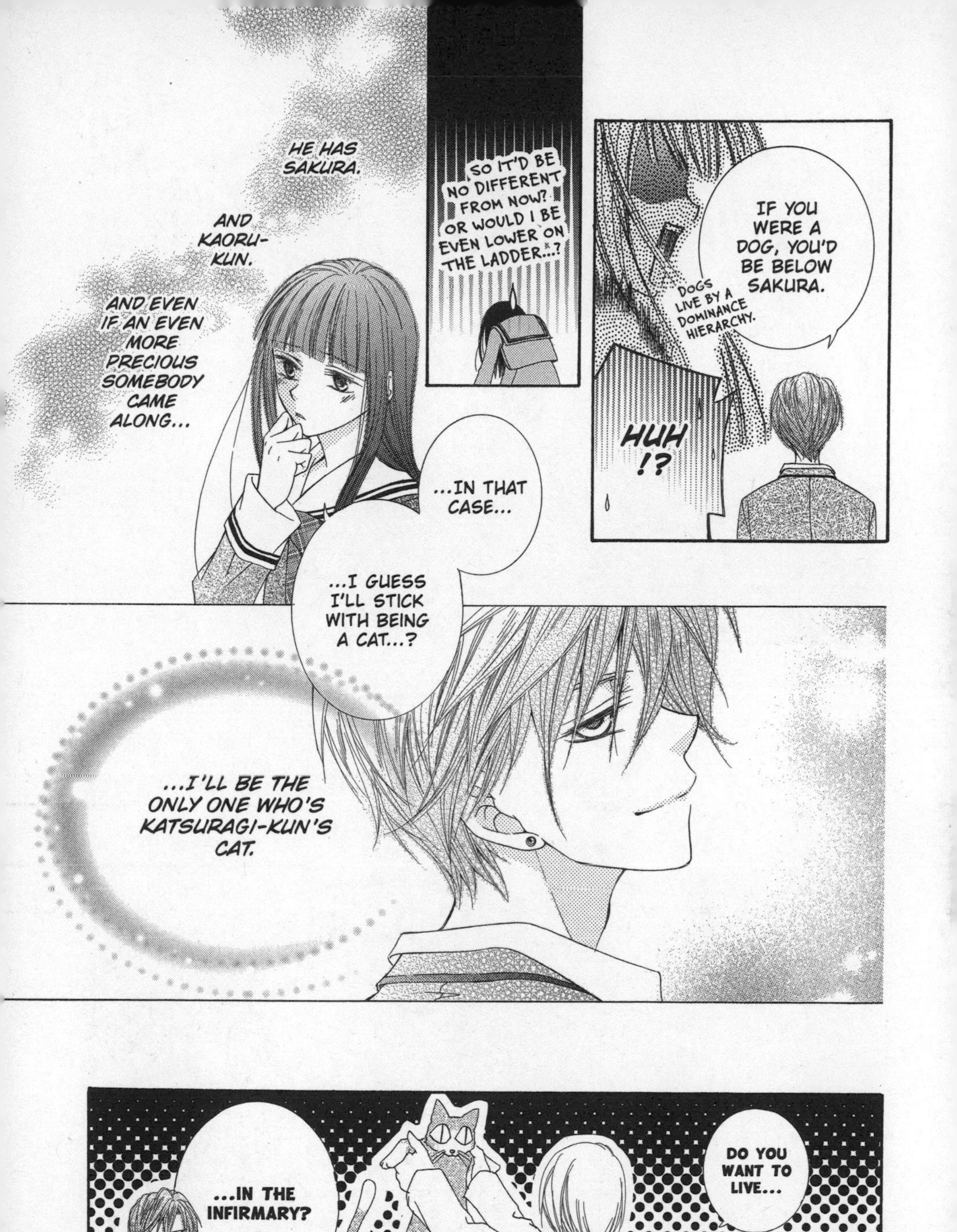
IF YOU WERE A DOG, YOU'D BE BELOW SAKURA.
DOGS LIVE BY A DOMINANCE HIERARCHY.
HUH!?
SO IT'D BE NO DIFFERENT FROM NOW? OR WOULD I BE EVEN LOWER ON THE LADDER...?
HE HAS SAKURA.
AND KAORU-KUN.
AND EVEN IF AN EVEN MORE PRECIOUS SOMEBODY CAME ALONG...
...IN THAT CASE...
...I GUESS I'LL STICK WITH BEING A CAT...?
...I'LL BE THE ONLY ONE WHO'S KATSURAGI-KUN'S CAT.
DO YOU WANT TO LIVE...
...IN THE INFIRMARY?
TO KEEP HIM AWAY.

scene.3 / *The End*

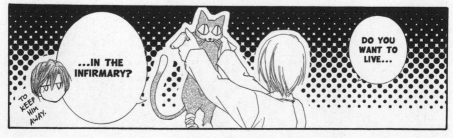

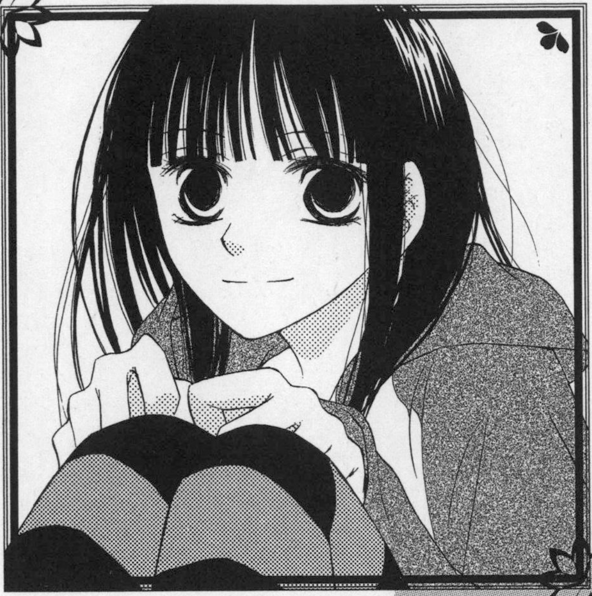

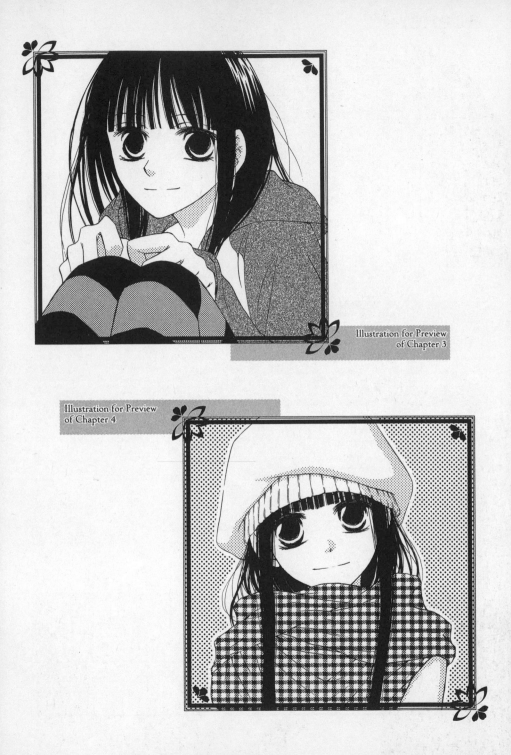

Illustration for Preview of Chapter 3

Illustration for Preview of Chapter 4

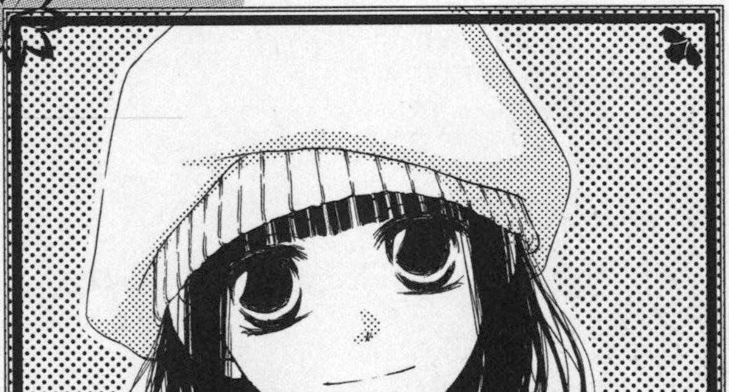

scene. 4

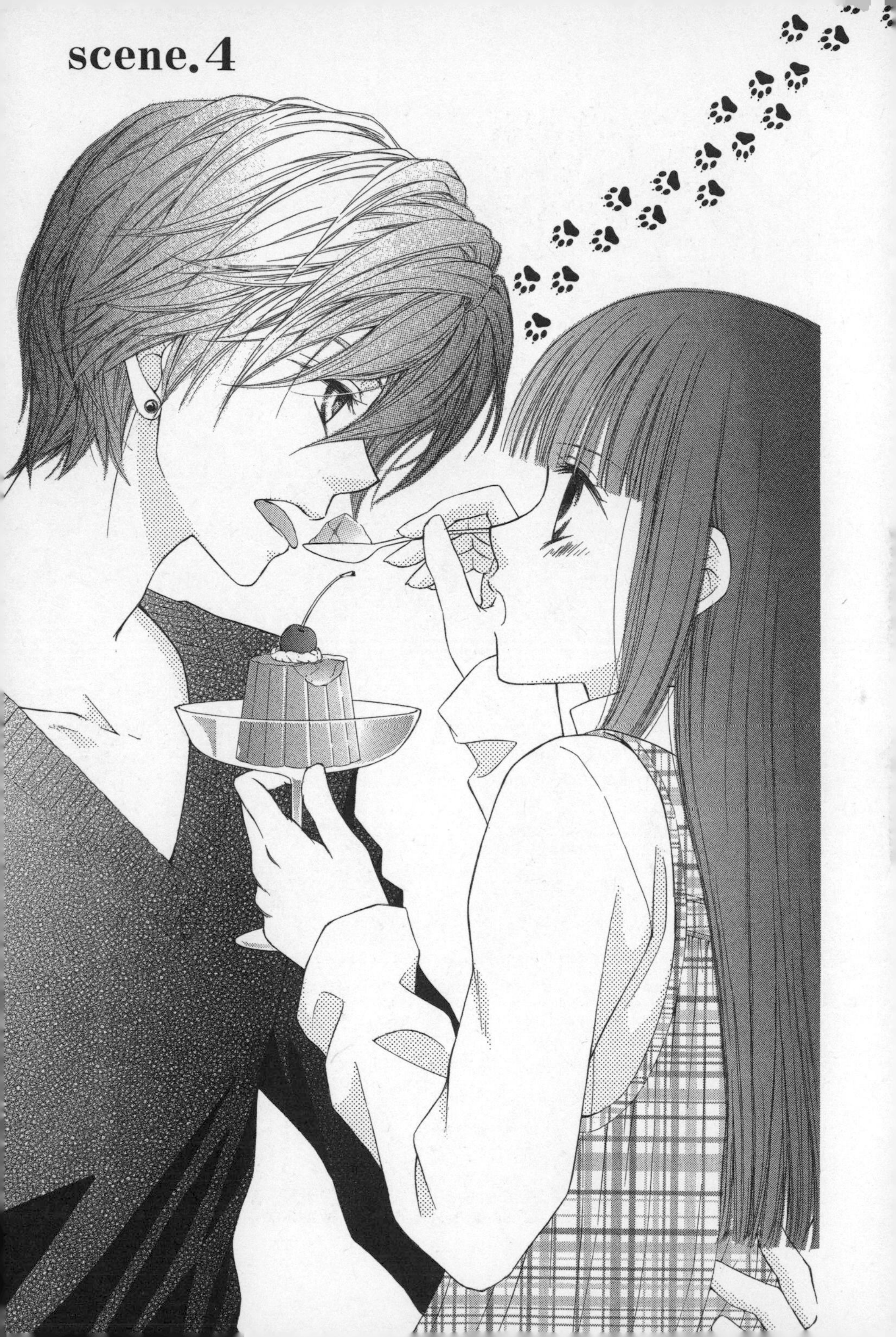

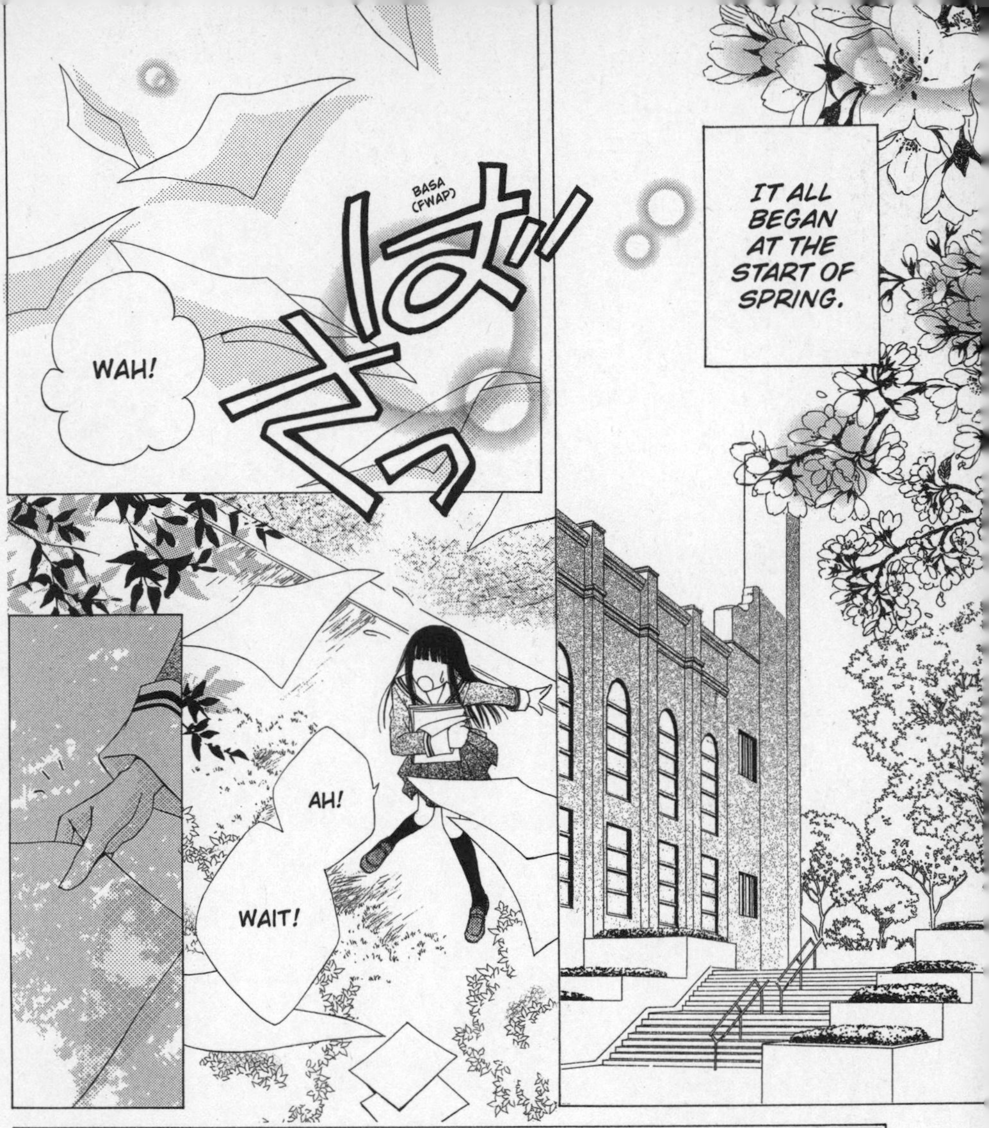
IT ALL BEGAN AT THE START OF SPRING.
BASA (FWAP)
WAH!
AH!
WAIT!

犬のいる生活

LIFE WITH A DOG

THE OTHER DAY, MY WASHLETTE BROKE DOWN, SO I HAD A REPAIRMAN COME OVER TO FIX IT. WHEN THE REPAIRMAN OPENED THE LID OF THE TOILET, THERE WAS A POOP FROM MY DOG IN THERE THAT I HAD FORGOTTEN TO FLUSH...

"I-IT'S NOT WHAT YOU THINK! THAT'S THE DOG'S...!"

OF COURSE IF I SAID THAT, IT'D SOUND LIKE THE MOST PATHETIC EXCUSE EVER.

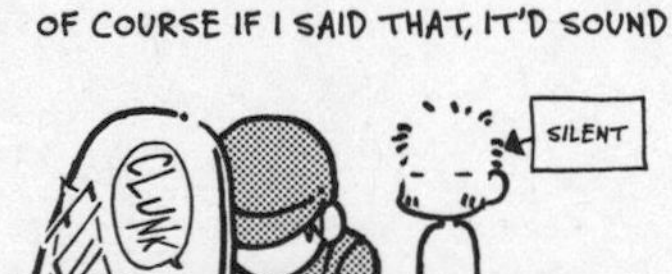
SILENT
CLUNK
FLUSSSH
FLUSHES IT DOWN SILENTLY

...I ONLY PRAY I NEVER MEET HIM AGAIN.

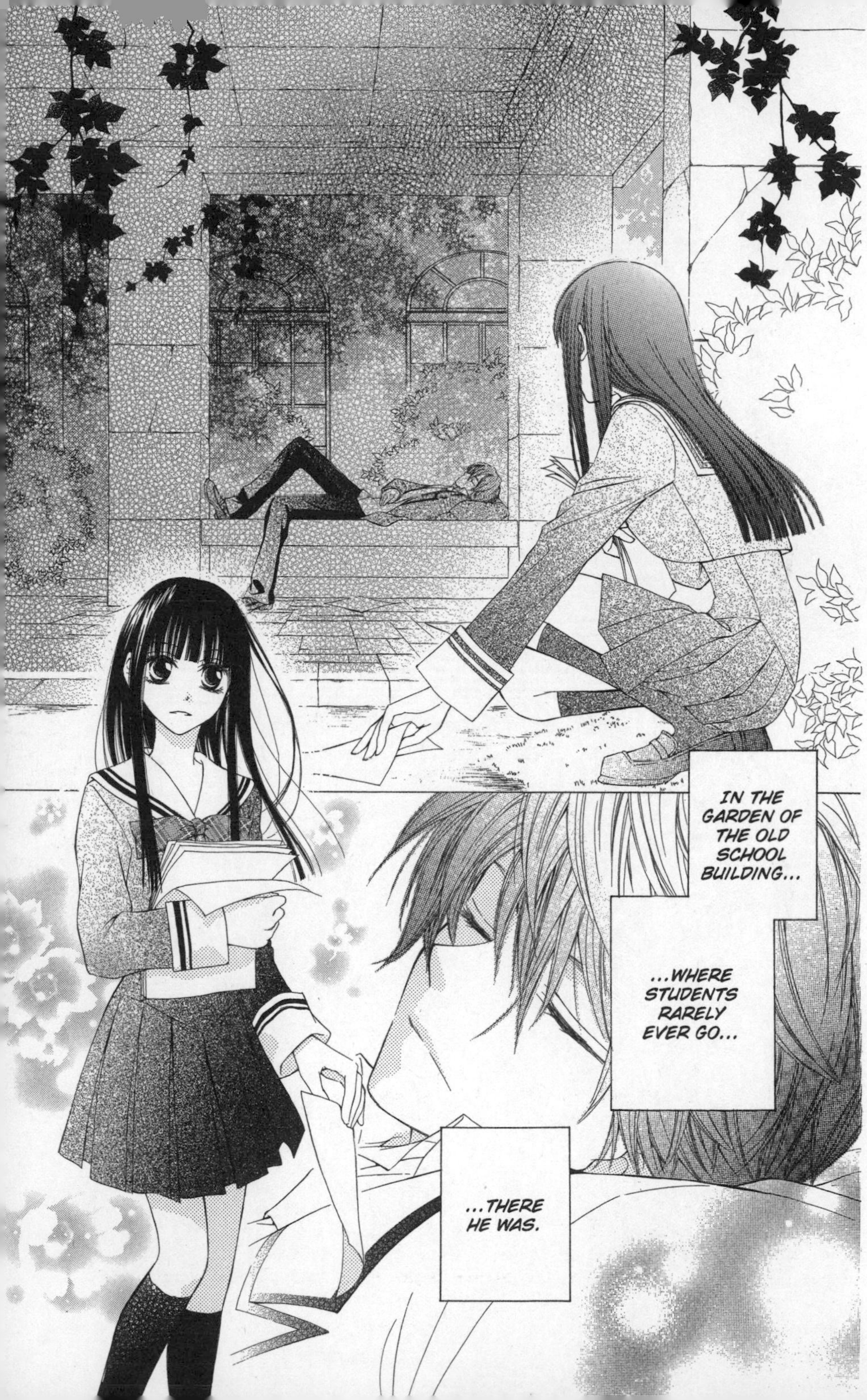
IN THE GARDEN OF THE OLD SCHOOL BUILDING...
...WHERE STUDENTS RARELY EVER GO...
...THERE HE WAS.

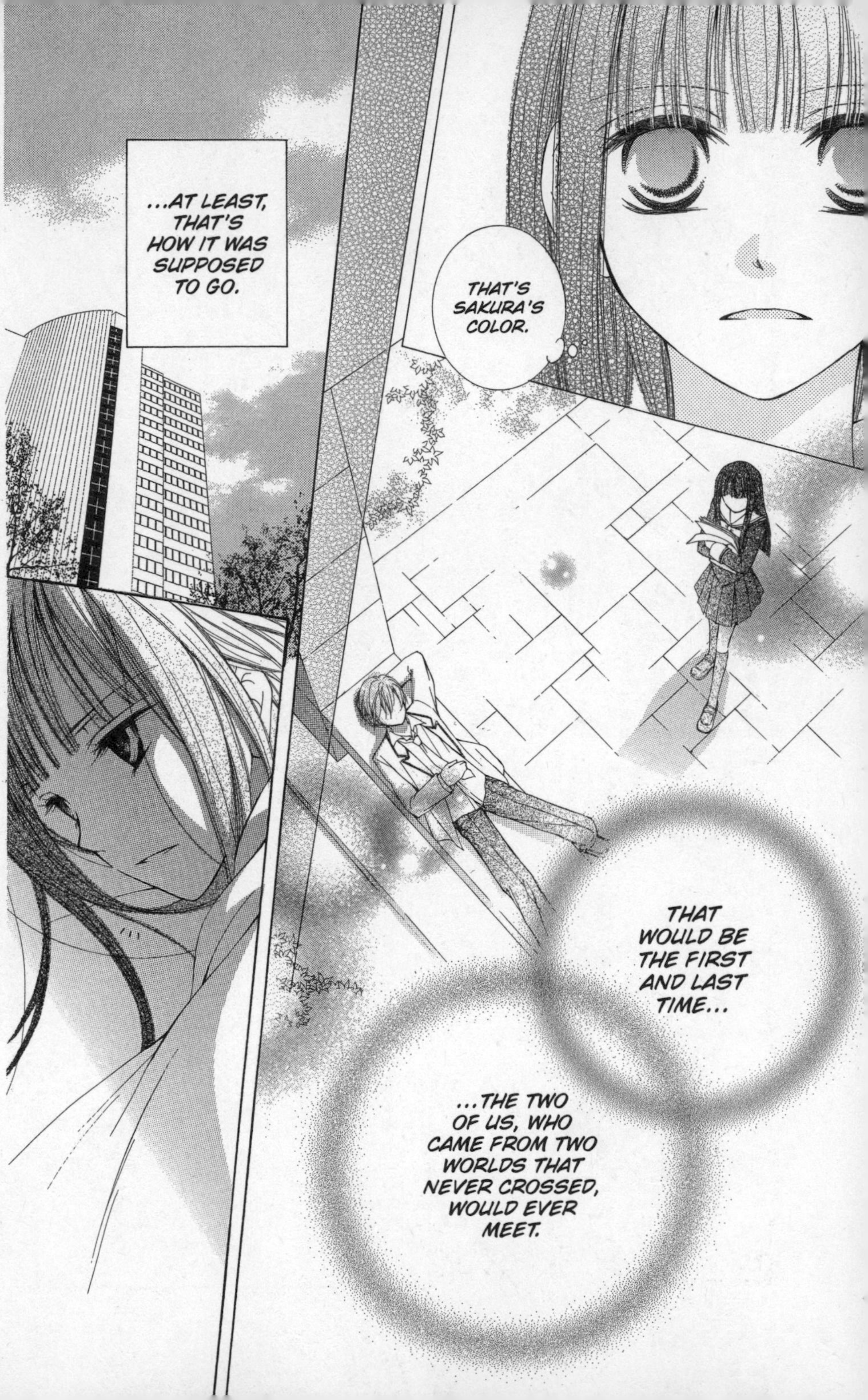
THAT'S SAKURA'S COLOR.
THAT WOULD BE THE FIRST AND LAST TIME...
...THE TWO OF US, WHO CAME FROM TWO WORLDS THAT NEVER CROSSED, WOULD EVER MEET.
...AT LEAST, THAT'S HOW IT WAS SUPPOSED TO GO.

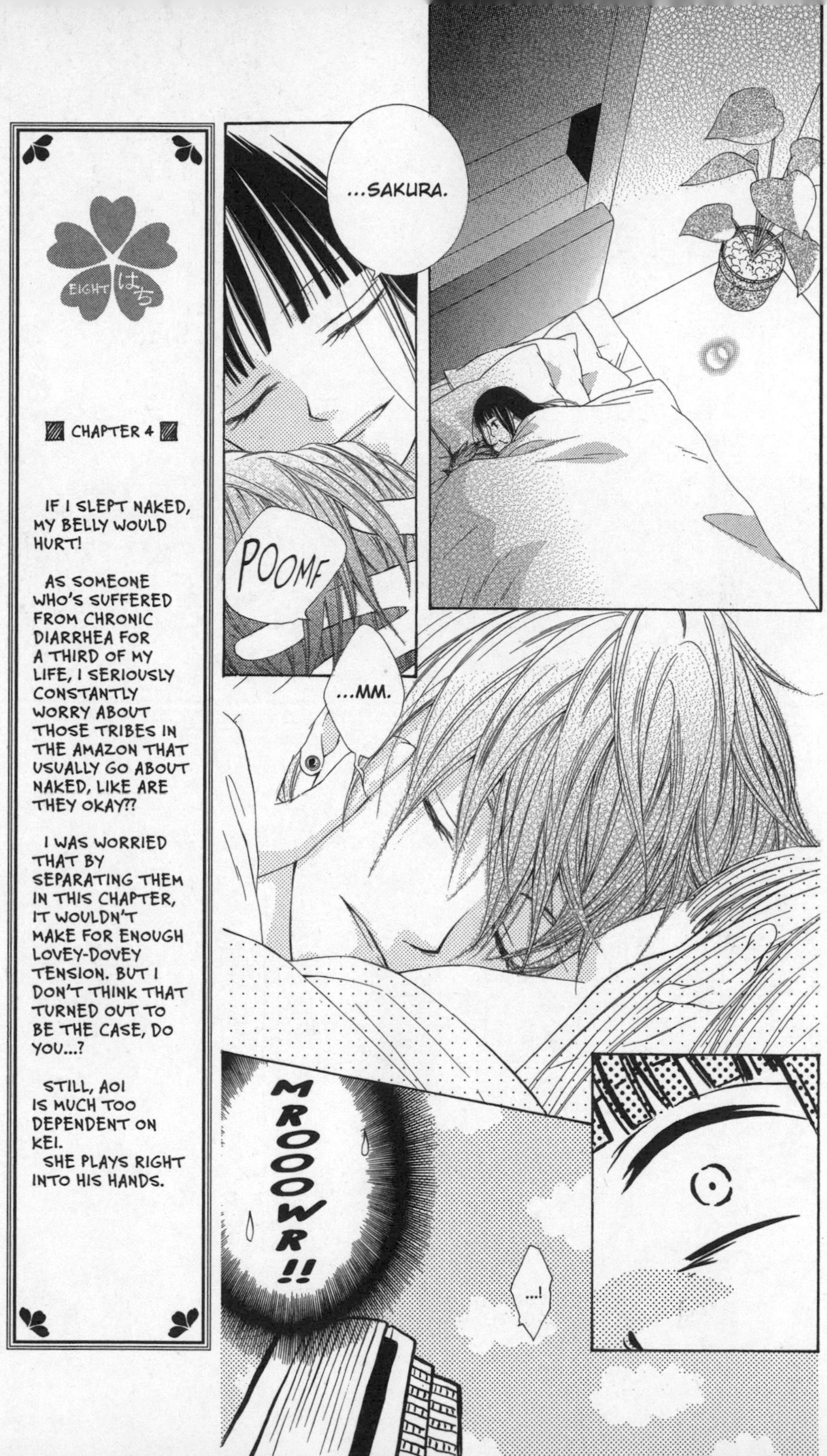
...SAKURA.
POOMF
...MM.
MROOOOWR!!
...!

EIGHT はち

CHAPTER 4

IF I SLEPT NAKED, MY BELLY WOULD HURT!

AS SOMEONE WHO'S SUFFERED FROM CHRONIC DIARRHEA FOR A THIRD OF MY LIFE, I SERIOUSLY CONSTANTLY WORRY ABOUT THOSE TRIBES IN THE AMAZON THAT USUALLY GO ABOUT NAKED, LIKE ARE THEY OKAY??

I WAS WORRIED THAT BY SEPARATING THEM IN THIS CHAPTER, IT WOULDN'T MAKE FOR ENOUGH LOVEY-DOVEY TENSION. BUT I DON'T THINK THAT TURNED OUT TO BE THE CASE, DO YOU...?

STILL, AOI IS MUCH TOO DEPENDENT ON KEI.
SHE PLAYS RIGHT INTO HIS HANDS.

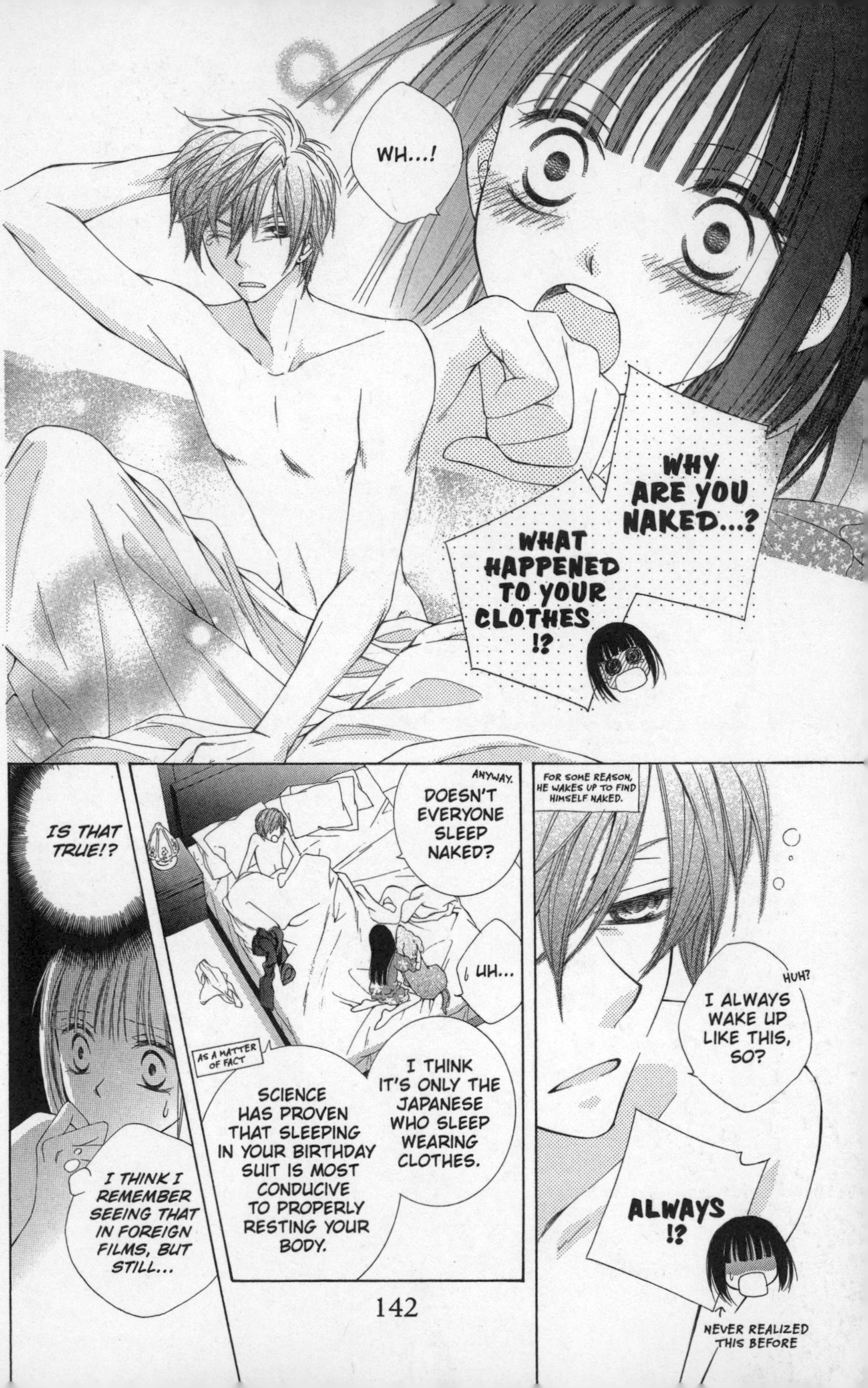
WH...!
WHY ARE YOU NAKED...?
WHAT HAPPENED TO YOUR CLOTHES!?
FOR SOME REASON, HE WAKES UP TO FIND HIMSELF NAKED.
HUH?
I ALWAYS WAKE UP LIKE THIS, SO?
ALWAYS!?
NEVER REALIZED THIS BEFORE
ANYWAY.
DOESN'T EVERYONE SLEEP NAKED?
UH...
I THINK IT'S ONLY THE JAPANESE WHO SLEEP WEARING CLOTHES.
AS A MATTER OF FACT
SCIENCE HAS PROVEN THAT SLEEPING IN YOUR BIRTHDAY SUIT IS MOST CONDUCIVE TO PROPERLY RESTING YOUR BODY.
IS THAT TRUE!?
I THINK I REMEMBER SEEING THAT IN FOREIGN FILMS, BUT STILL...

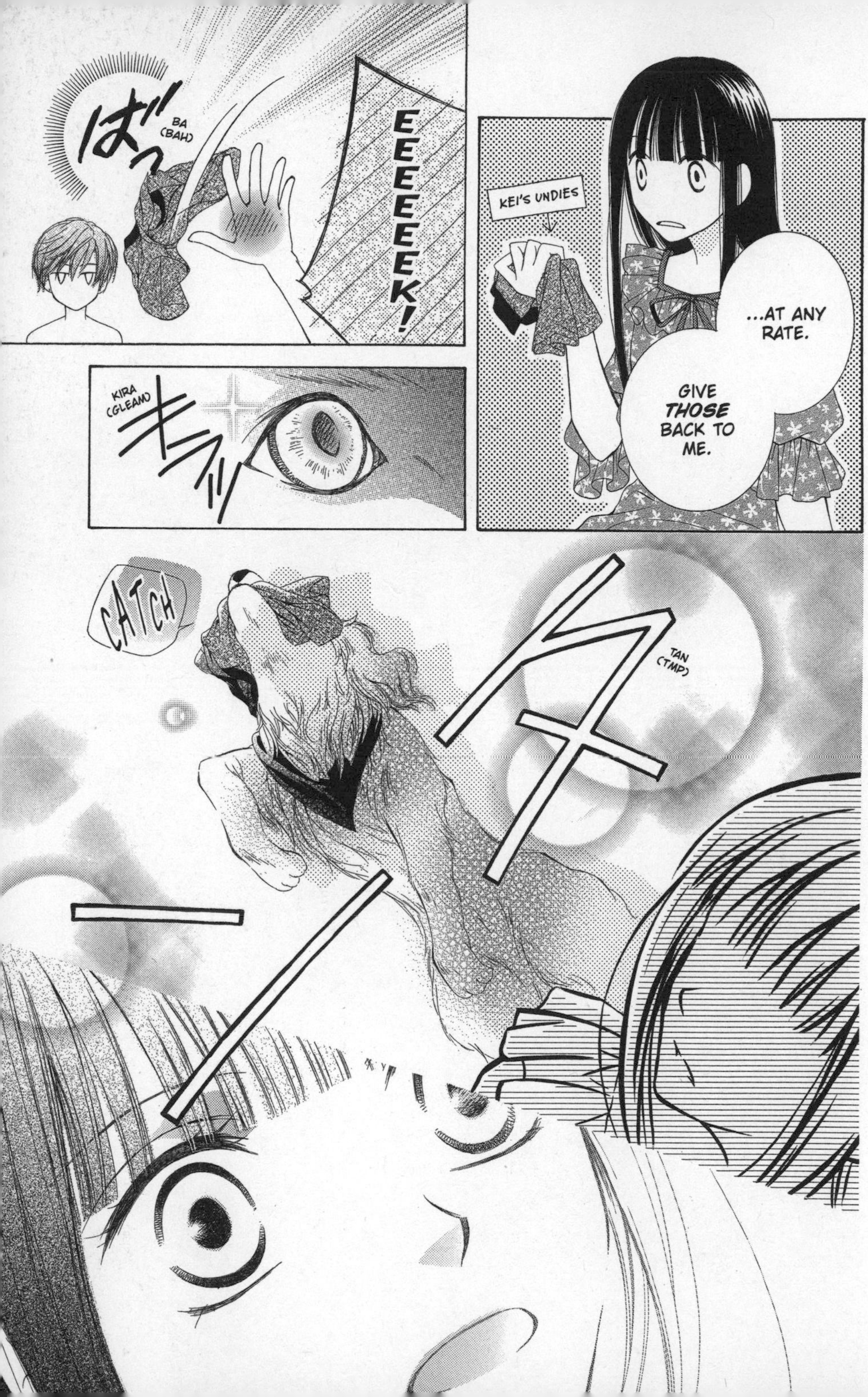
...AT ANY RATE.
GIVE THOSE BACK TO ME.
KEI'S UNDIES
EEEEEEEK!
ばっ
BA (BAH)
KIRA (GLEAM)
TAN (TMP)
CATCH

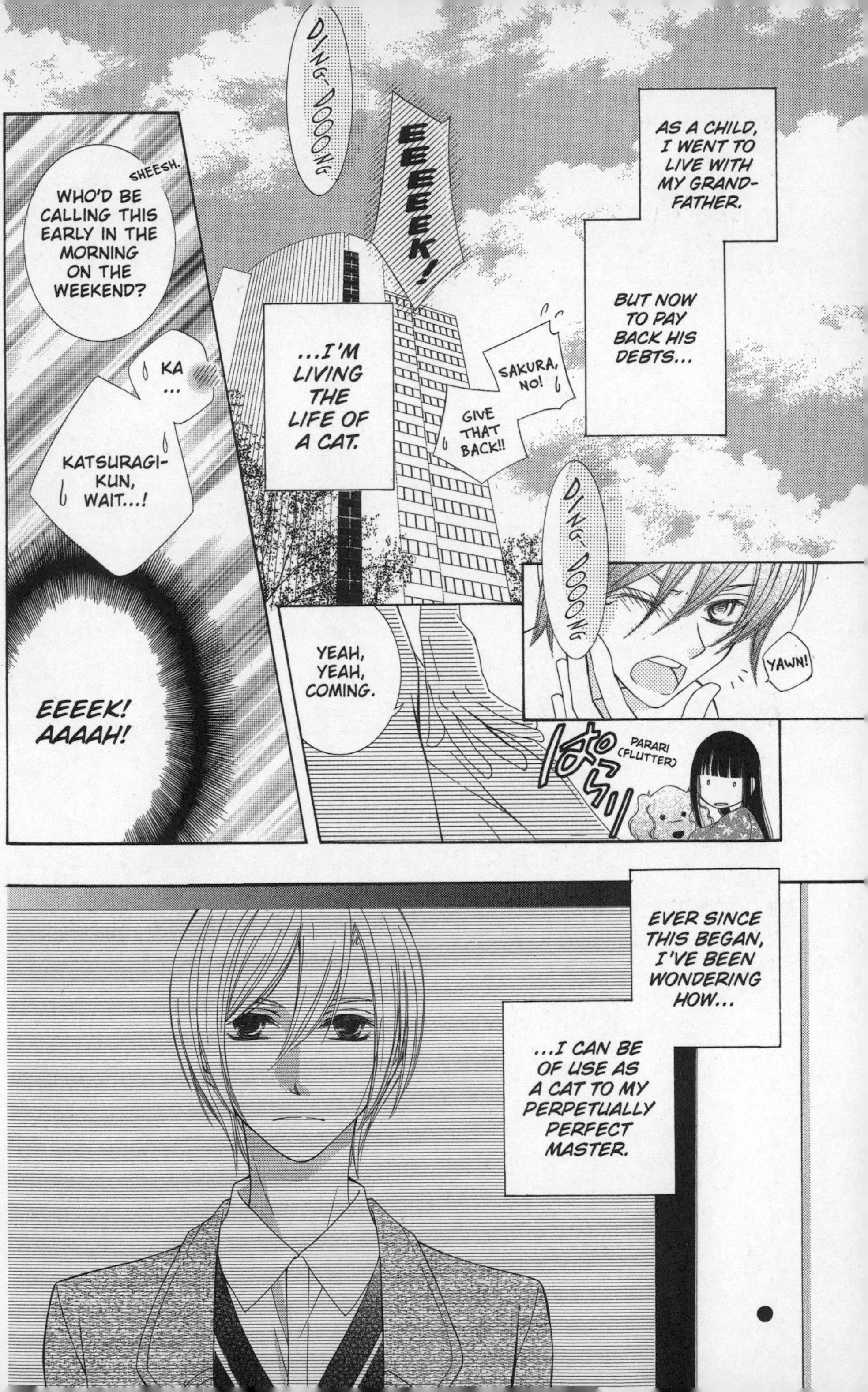
AS A CHILD, I WENT TO LIVE WITH MY GRAND-FATHER.
BUT NOW TO PAY BACK HIS DEBTS...
DING-DOOOONG
EEEEEK!
...I'M LIVING THE LIFE OF A CAT.
SAKURA, NO!
GIVE THAT BACK!!
DING-DOOOONG
YAWN!
YEAH, YEAH, COMING.
PARARI (FLUTTER)
SHEESH.
WHO'D BE CALLING THIS EARLY IN THE MORNING ON THE WEEKEND?
KA...
KATSURAGI-KUN, WAIT...!
EEEEK! AAAAH!
EVER SINCE THIS BEGAN, I'VE BEEN WONDERING HOW...
...I CAN BE OF USE AS A CAT TO MY PERPETUALLY PERFECT MASTER.

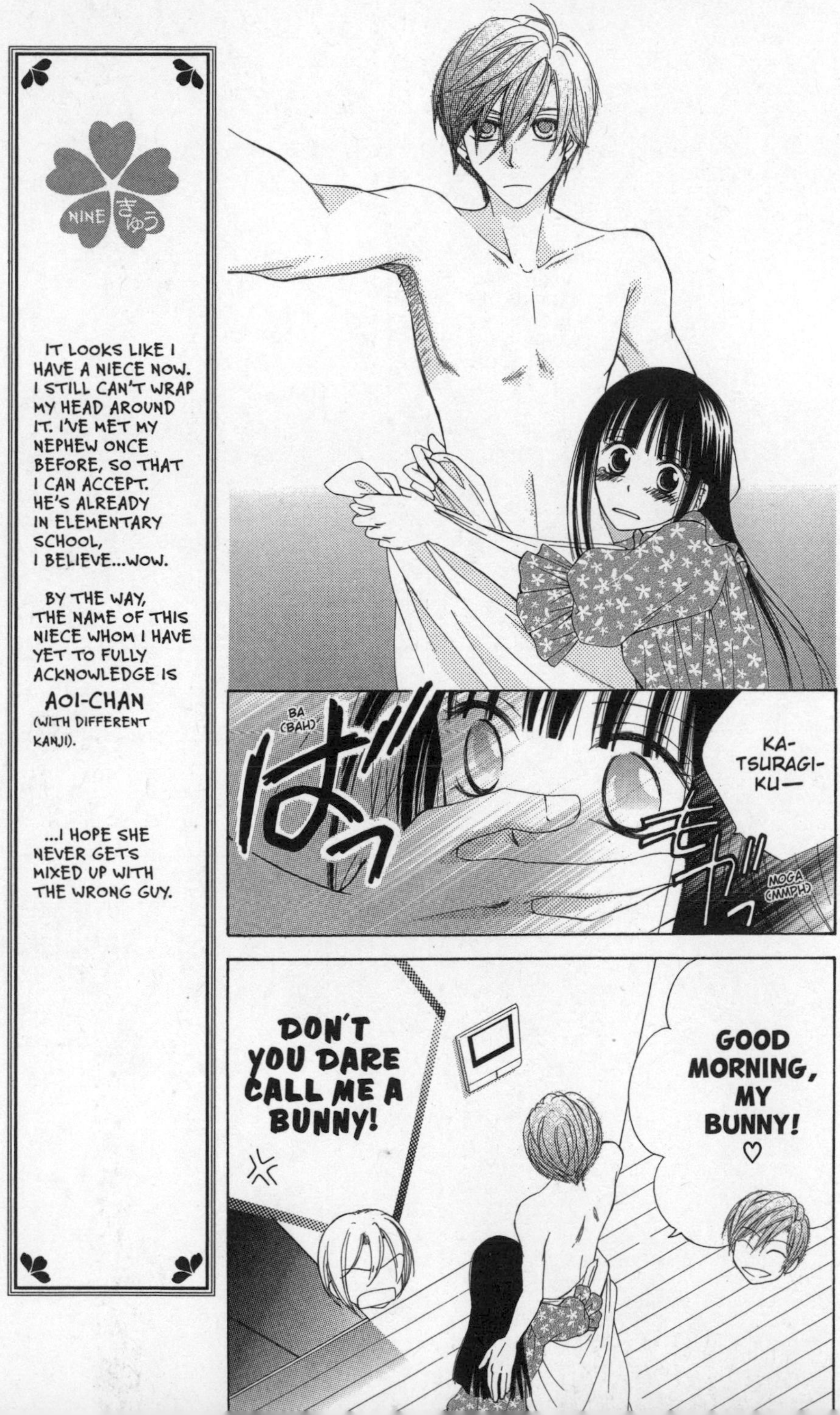
KA-TSURAGI-KU—
MOGA (MMPH)
BA (BAH)
GOOD MORNING, MY BUNNY! ♡
DON'T YOU DARE CALL ME A BUNNY!

NINE きゅう

IT LOOKS LIKE I HAVE A NIECE NOW. I STILL CAN'T WRAP MY HEAD AROUND IT. I'VE MET MY NEPHEW ONCE BEFORE, SO THAT I CAN ACCEPT. HE'S ALREADY IN ELEMENTARY SCHOOL, I BELIEVE...WOW.

BY THE WAY, THE NAME OF THIS NIECE WHOM I HAVE YET TO FULLY ACKNOWLEDGE IS

AOI-CHAN

(WITH DIFFERENT KANJI).

...I HOPE SHE NEVER GETS MIXED UP WITH THE WRONG GUY.

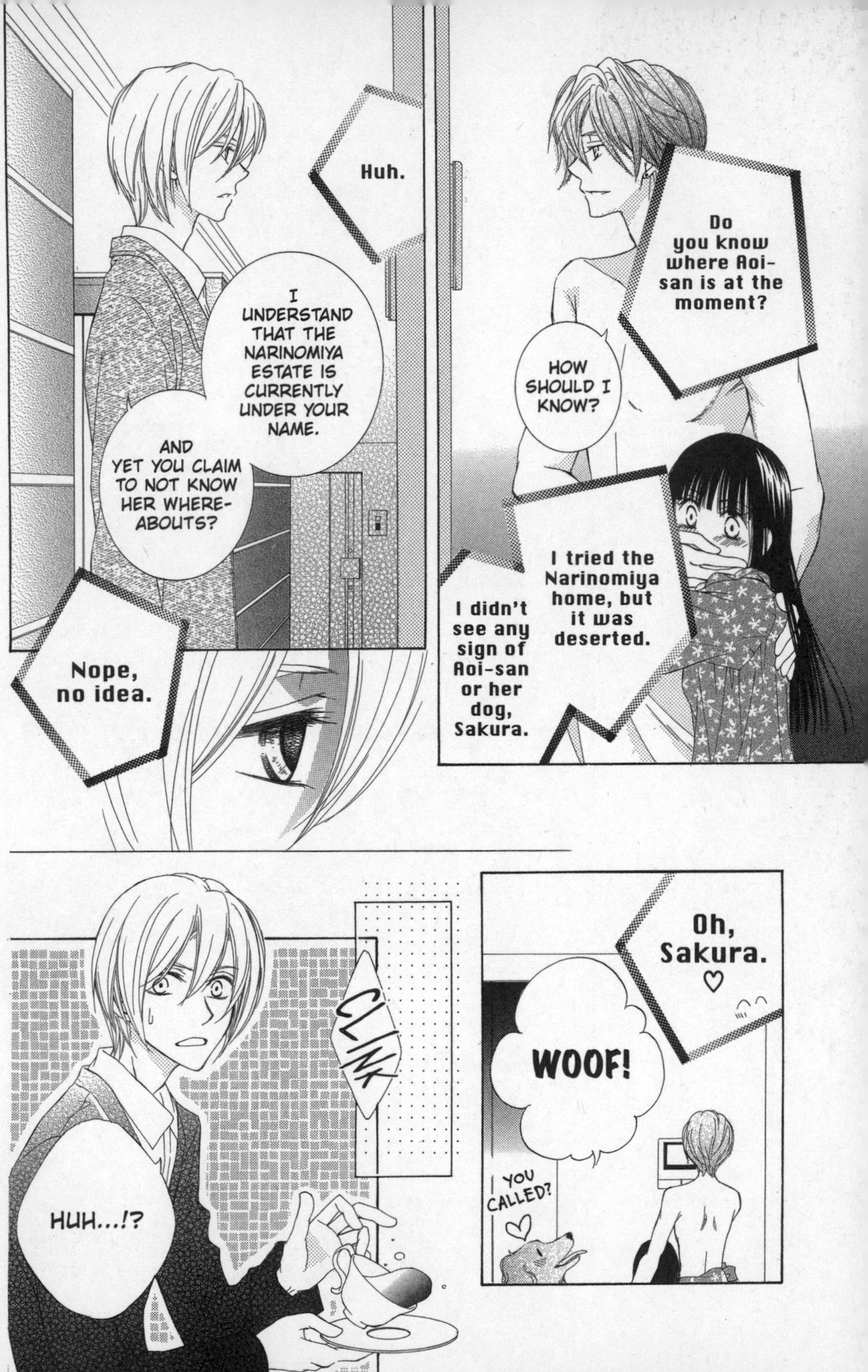
Do you know where Aoi-san is at the moment?
HOW SHOULD I KNOW?
I tried the Narinomiya home, but it was deserted.
I didn't see any sign of Aoi-san or her dog, Sakura.
Huh.
I UNDERSTAND THAT THE NARINOMIYA ESTATE IS CURRENTLY UNDER YOUR NAME.
AND YET YOU CLAIM TO NOT KNOW HER WHERE-ABOUTS?
Nope, no idea.
Oh, Sakura. ♡
WOOF!
YOU CALLED? ♡
CLINK
HUH...!?

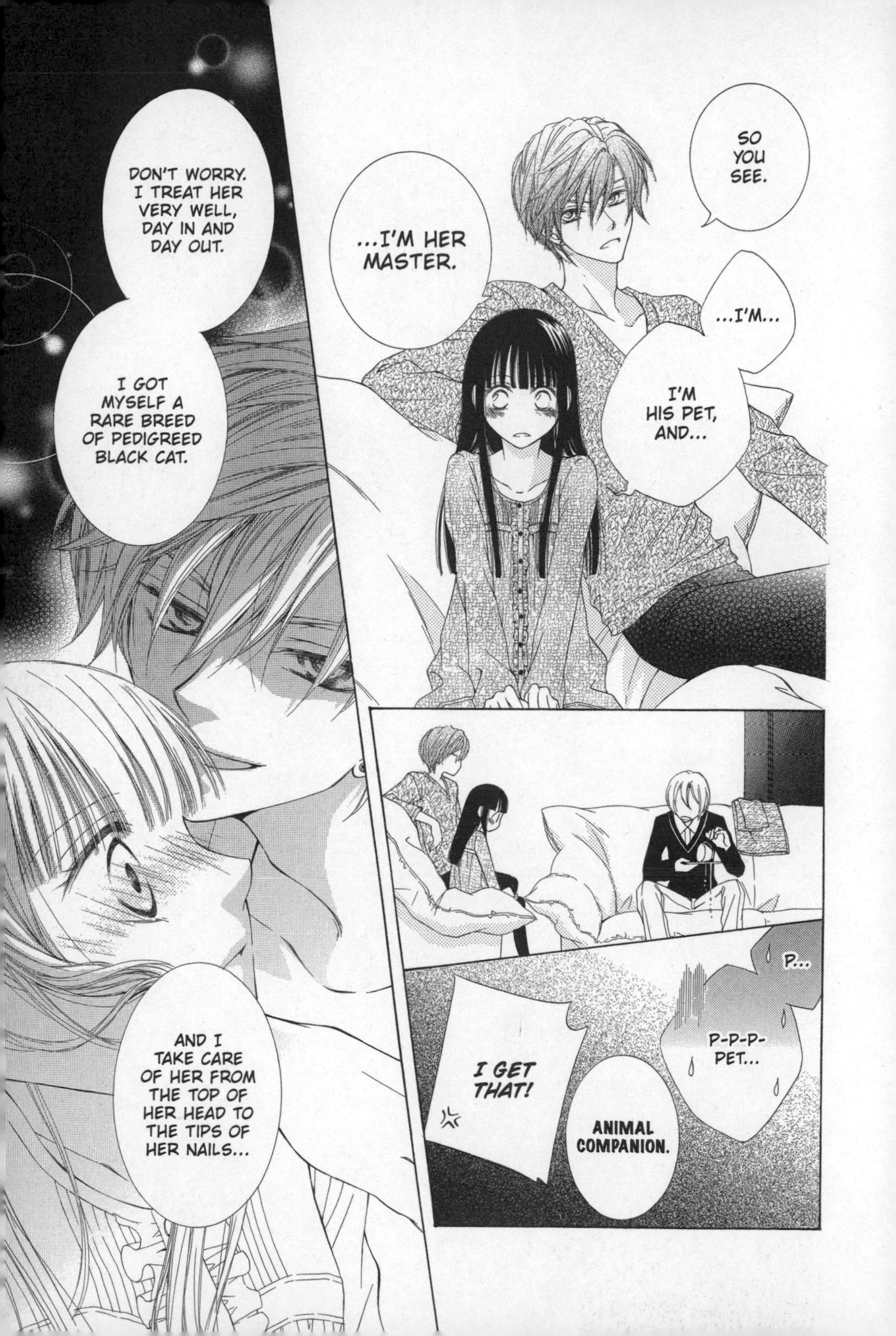
SO YOU SEE.
...I'M HER MASTER.
...I'M...
I'M HIS PET, AND...
P...
P-P-P-PET...
ANIMAL COMPANION.
I GET THAT!
DON'T WORRY. I TREAT HER VERY WELL, DAY IN AND DAY OUT.
I GOT MYSELF A RARE BREED OF PEDIGREED BLACK CAT.
AND I TAKE CARE OF HER FROM THE TOP OF HER HEAD TO THE TIPS OF HER NAILS...

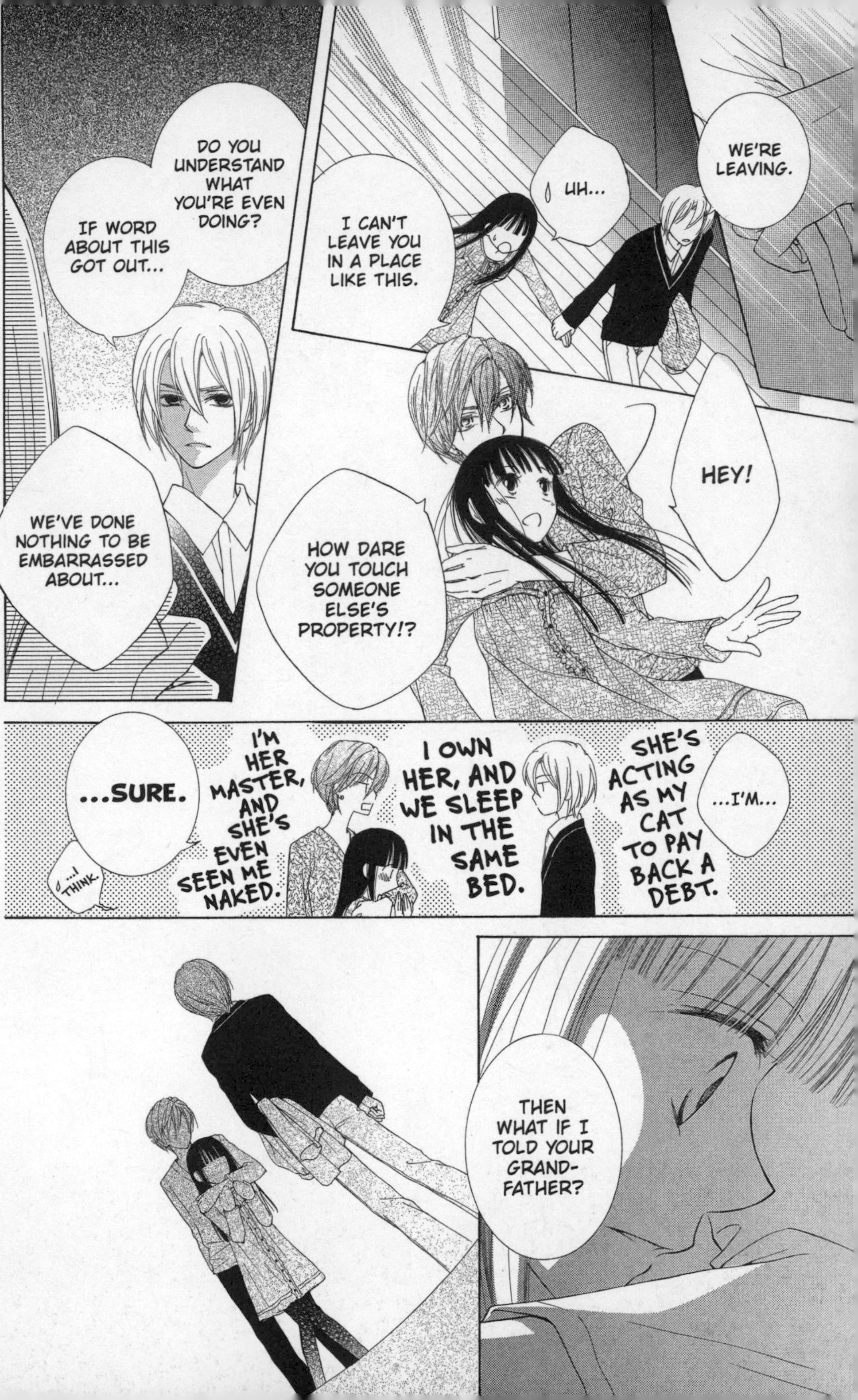
WE'RE LEAVING.
UH...
I CAN'T LEAVE YOU IN A PLACE LIKE THIS.
HEY!
HOW DARE YOU TOUCH SOMEONE ELSE'S PROPERTY!?
DO YOU UNDERSTAND WHAT YOU'RE EVEN DOING?
IF WORD ABOUT THIS GOT OUT...
WE'VE DONE NOTHING TO BE EMBARRASSED ABOUT...
...I'M...
SHE'S ACTING AS MY CAT TO PAY BACK A DEBT.
I OWN HER, AND WE SLEEP IN THE SAME BED.
I'M HER MASTER, AND SHE'S EVEN SEEN ME NAKED.
...SURE.
...I THINK.
THEN WHAT IF I TOLD YOUR GRAND-FATHER?

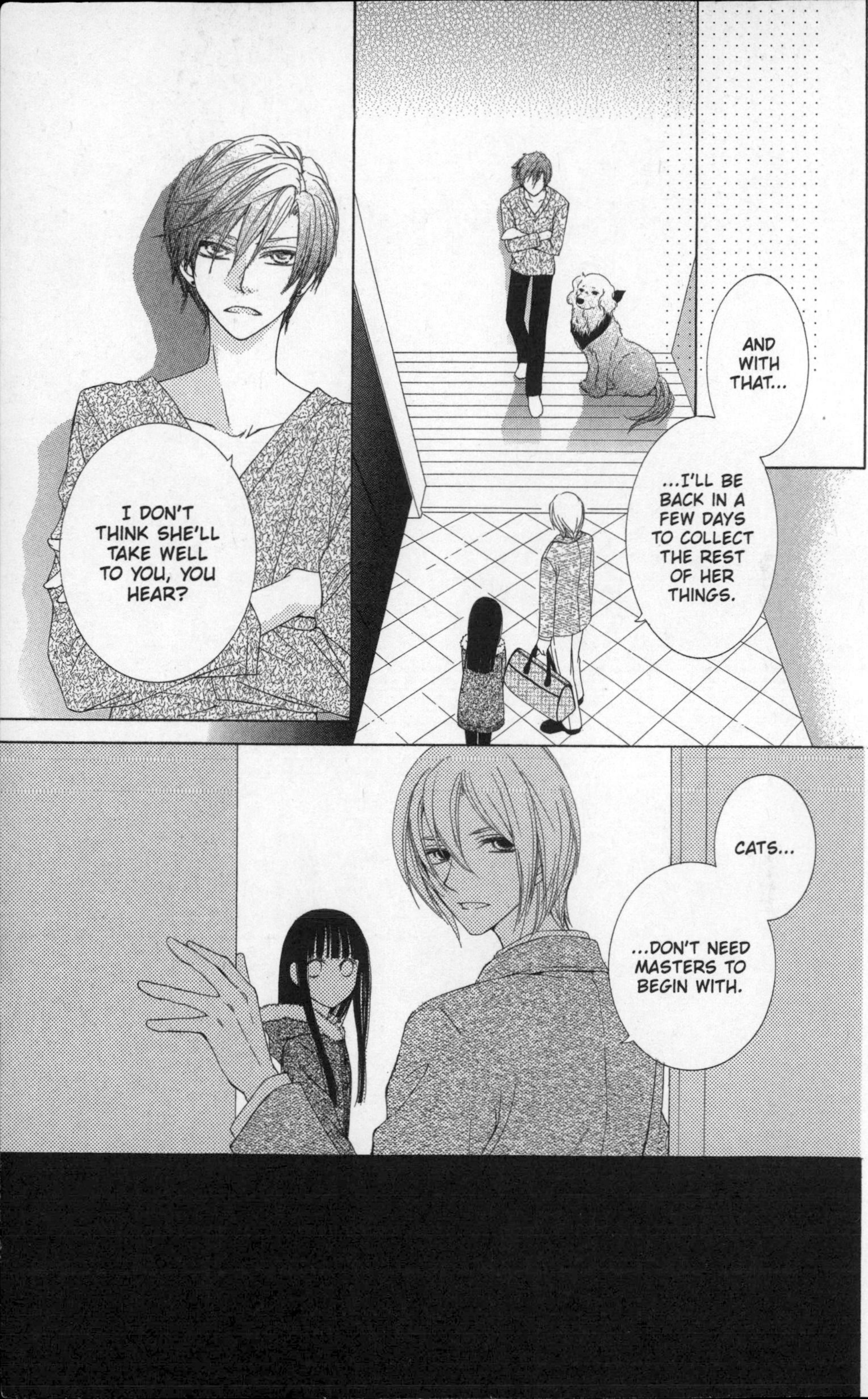
AND WITH THAT...
...I'LL BE BACK IN A FEW DAYS TO COLLECT THE REST OF HER THINGS.
I DON'T THINK SHE'LL TAKE WELL TO YOU, YOU HEAR?
CATS...
...DON'T NEED MASTERS TO BEGIN WITH.

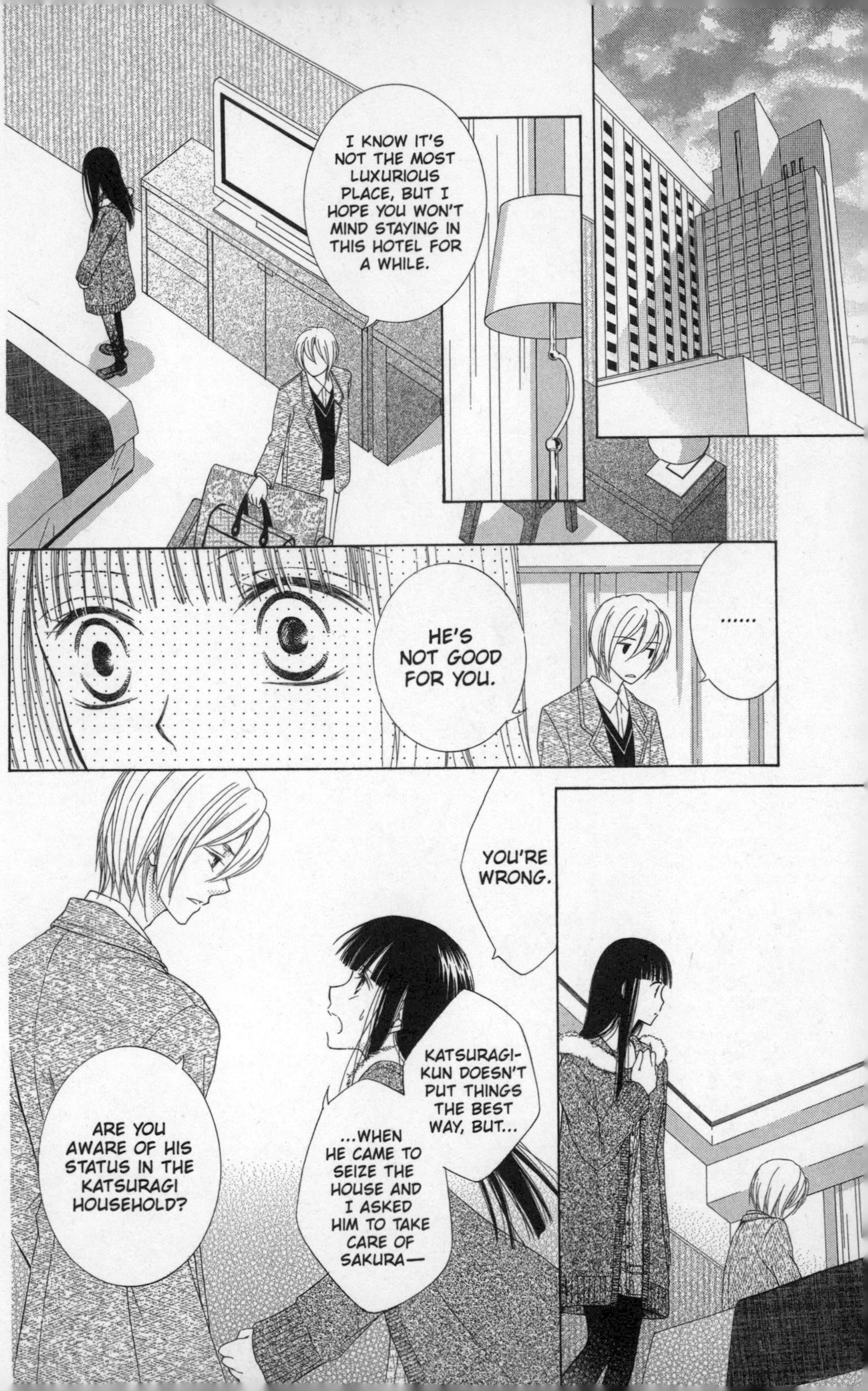
I KNOW IT'S NOT THE MOST LUXURIOUS PLACE, BUT I HOPE YOU WON'T MIND STAYING IN THIS HOTEL FOR A WHILE.
......
HE'S NOT GOOD FOR YOU.
YOU'RE WRONG.
KATSURAGI-KUN DOESN'T PUT THINGS THE BEST WAY, BUT...
...WHEN HE CAME TO SEIZE THE HOUSE AND I ASKED HIM TO TAKE CARE OF SAKURA—
ARE YOU AWARE OF HIS STATUS IN THE KATSURAGI HOUSEHOLD?

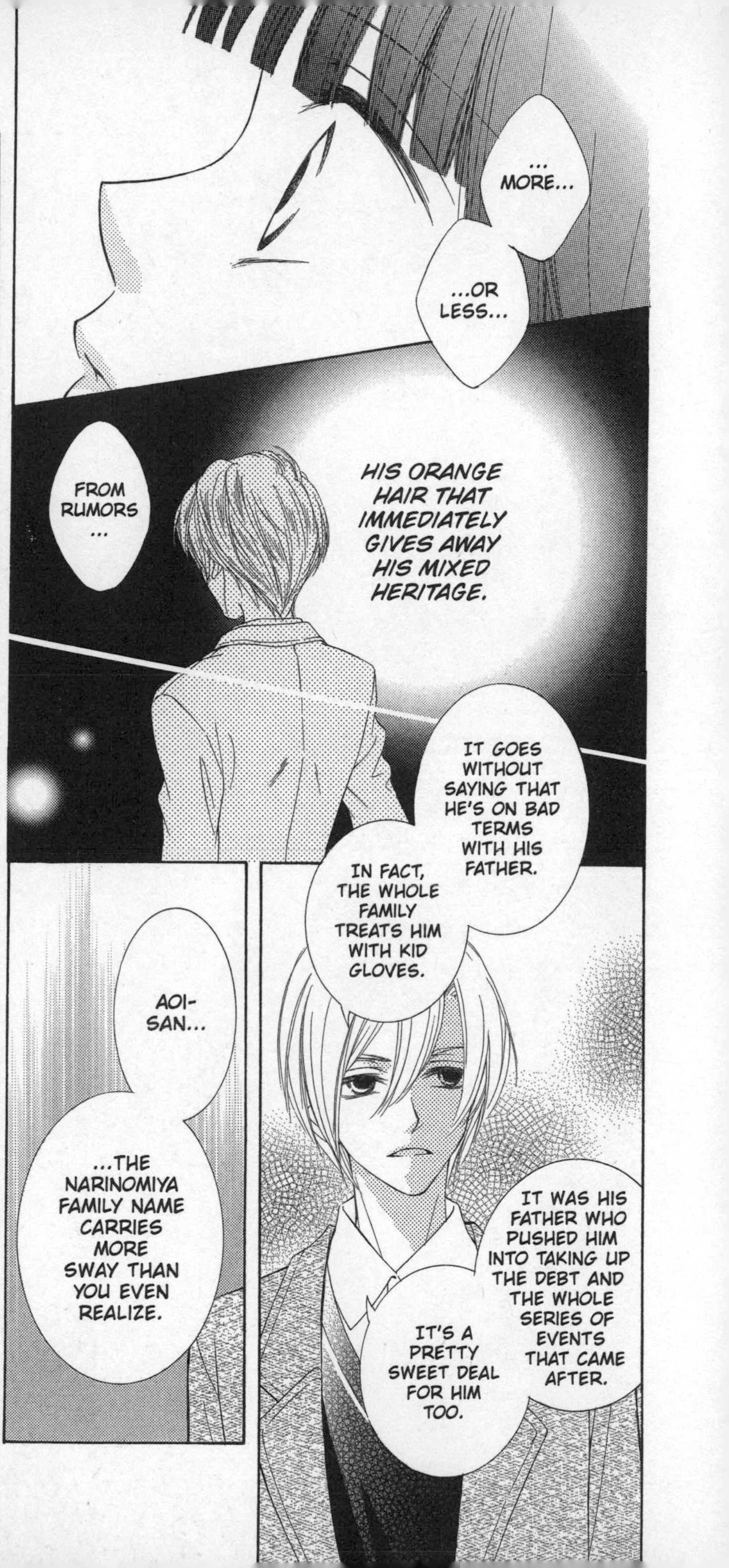

... MORE...
...OR LESS...
HIS ORANGE HAIR THAT IMMEDIATELY GIVES AWAY HIS MIXED HERITAGE.
FROM RUMORS ...
IT GOES WITHOUT SAYING THAT HE'S ON BAD TERMS WITH HIS FATHER.
IN FACT, THE WHOLE FAMILY TREATS HIM WITH KID GLOVES.
IT WAS HIS FATHER WHO PUSHED HIM INTO TAKING UP THE DEBT AND THE WHOLE SERIES OF EVENTS THAT CAME AFTER.
IT'S A PRETTY SWEET DEAL FOR HIM TOO.
AOI-SAN...
...THE NARINOMIYA FAMILY NAME CARRIES MORE SWAY THAN YOU EVEN REALIZE.

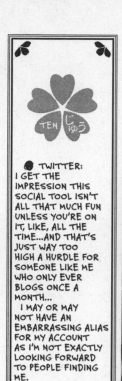

TEN じゅう

TWITTER:
I GET THE IMPRESSION THIS SOCIAL TOOL ISN'T ALL THAT MUCH FUN UNLESS YOU'RE ON IT, LIKE, ALL THE TIME...AND THAT'S JUST WAY TOO HIGH A HURDLE FOR SOMEONE LIKE ME WHO ONLY EVER BLOGS ONCE A MONTH...

I MAY OR MAY NOT HAVE AN EMBARRASSING ALIAS FOR MY ACCOUNT AS I'M NOT EXACTLY LOOKING FORWARD TO PEOPLE FINDING ME.

FACEBOOK:
I'M A LITTLE SCARED ABOUT USING MY REAL NAME...LEAVE ME ALONE. DON'T FIND ME. DON'T ASK ME WHAT I'M UP TO.

THOUGH I DO ADMIT THAT THE ONE TIME I ACCIDENTALLY LOGGED INTO MY FRIEND'S ACCOUNT, IT WAS PRETTY FUN.

I WANT TO BE CONNECTED, AND YET I DON'T WANT TO BE CONNECTED.

I'M RATHER AMBIVALENT ABOUT IT.

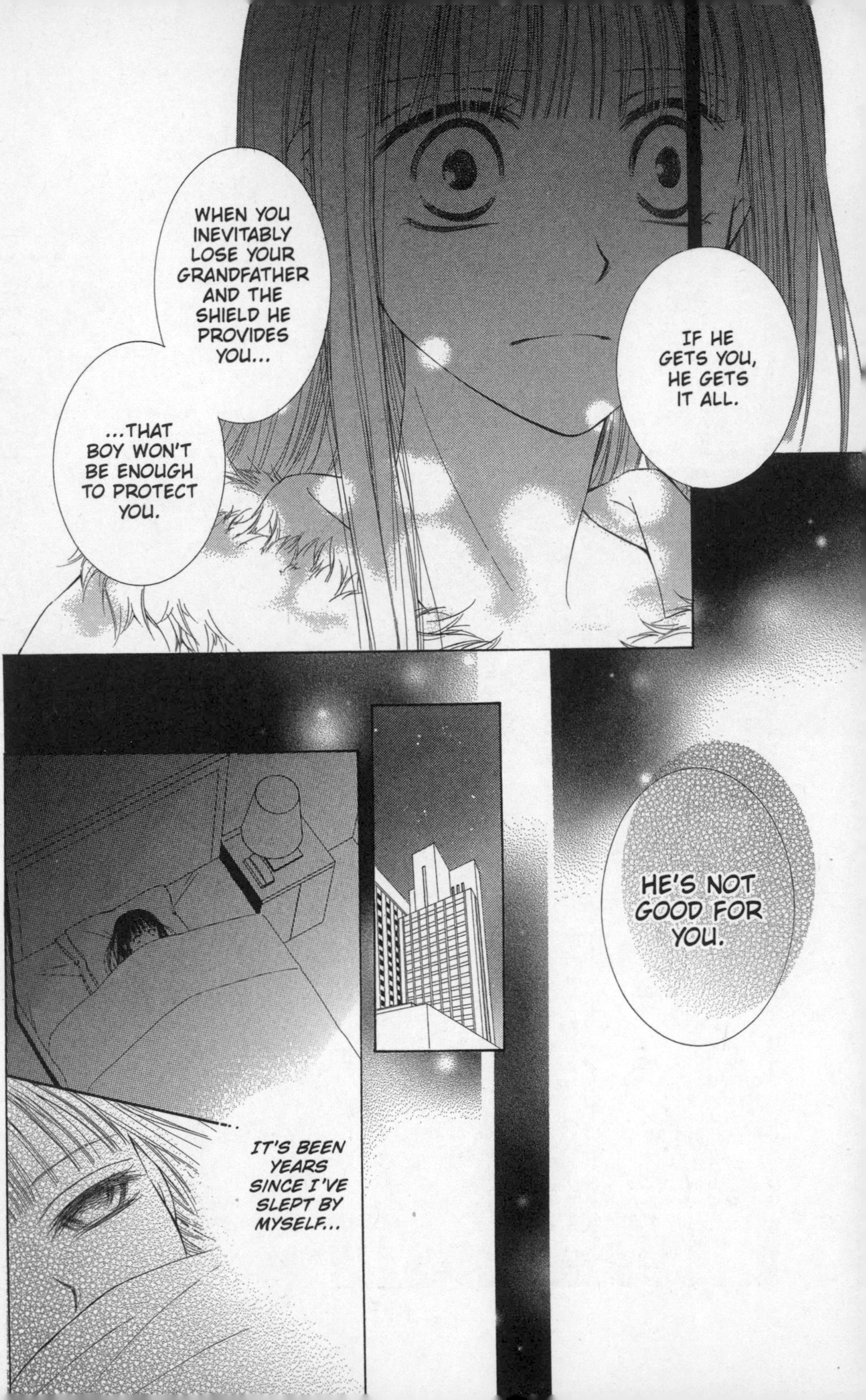
IF HE GETS YOU, HE GETS IT ALL.
WHEN YOU INEVITABLY LOSE YOUR GRANDFATHER AND THE SHIELD HE PROVIDES YOU...
...THAT BOY WON'T BE ENOUGH TO PROTECT YOU.
HE'S NOT GOOD FOR YOU.
...
IT'S BEEN YEARS SINCE I'VE SLEPT BY MYSELF...

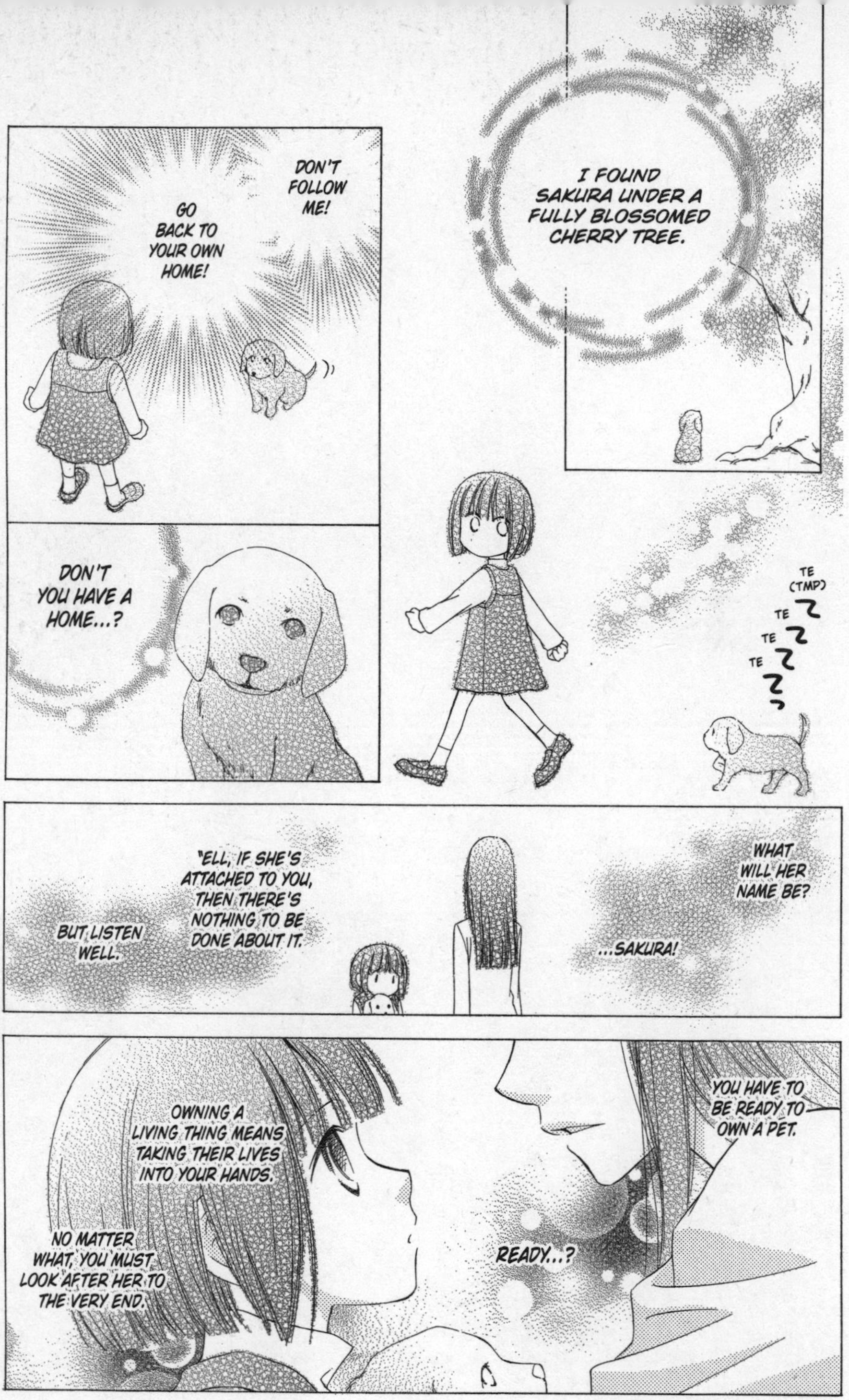
I FOUND SAKURA UNDER A FULLY BLOSSOMED CHERRY TREE.
TE TE TE TE (TMP)
DON'T FOLLOW ME!
GO BACK TO YOUR OWN HOME!
DON'T YOU HAVE A HOME...?
WHAT WILL HER NAME BE?
...SAKURA!
"ELL, IF SHE'S ATTACHED TO YOU, THEN THERE'S NOTHING TO BE DONE ABOUT IT.
BUT LISTEN WELL.
YOU HAVE TO BE READY TO OWN A PET.
READY...?
OWNING A LIVING THING MEANS TAKING THEIR LIVES INTO YOUR HANDS.
NO MATTER WHAT, YOU MUST LOOK AFTER HER TO THE VERY END.

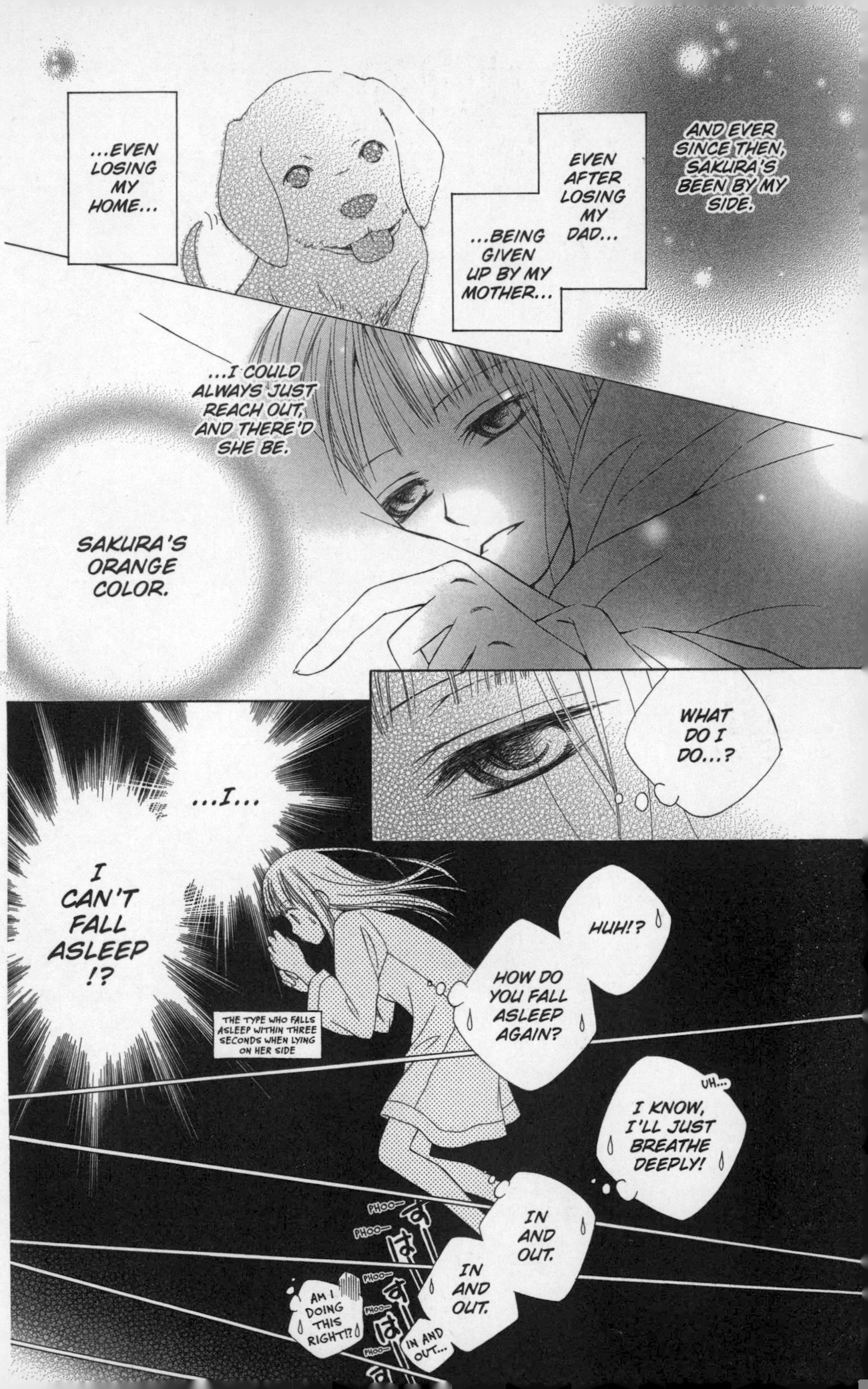
AND EVER SINCE THEN, SAKURA'S BEEN BY MY SIDE.
EVEN AFTER LOSING MY DAD...
...BEING GIVEN UP BY MY MOTHER...
...EVEN LOSING MY HOME...
...I COULD ALWAYS JUST REACH OUT, AND THERE'D SHE BE.
SAKURA'S ORANGE COLOR.
WHAT DO I DO...?
...I...
I CAN'T FALL ASLEEP!?
HUH!?
HOW DO YOU FALL ASLEEP AGAIN?
THE TYPE WHO FALLS ASLEEP WITHIN THREE SECONDS WHEN LYING ON HER SIDE
UH...
I KNOW, I'LL JUST BREATHE DEEPLY!
IN AND OUT.
IN AND OUT.
PHOO—
PHOO—
PHOO—
PHOO—
PHOO—
IN AND OUT...
AM I DOING THIS RIGHT!?

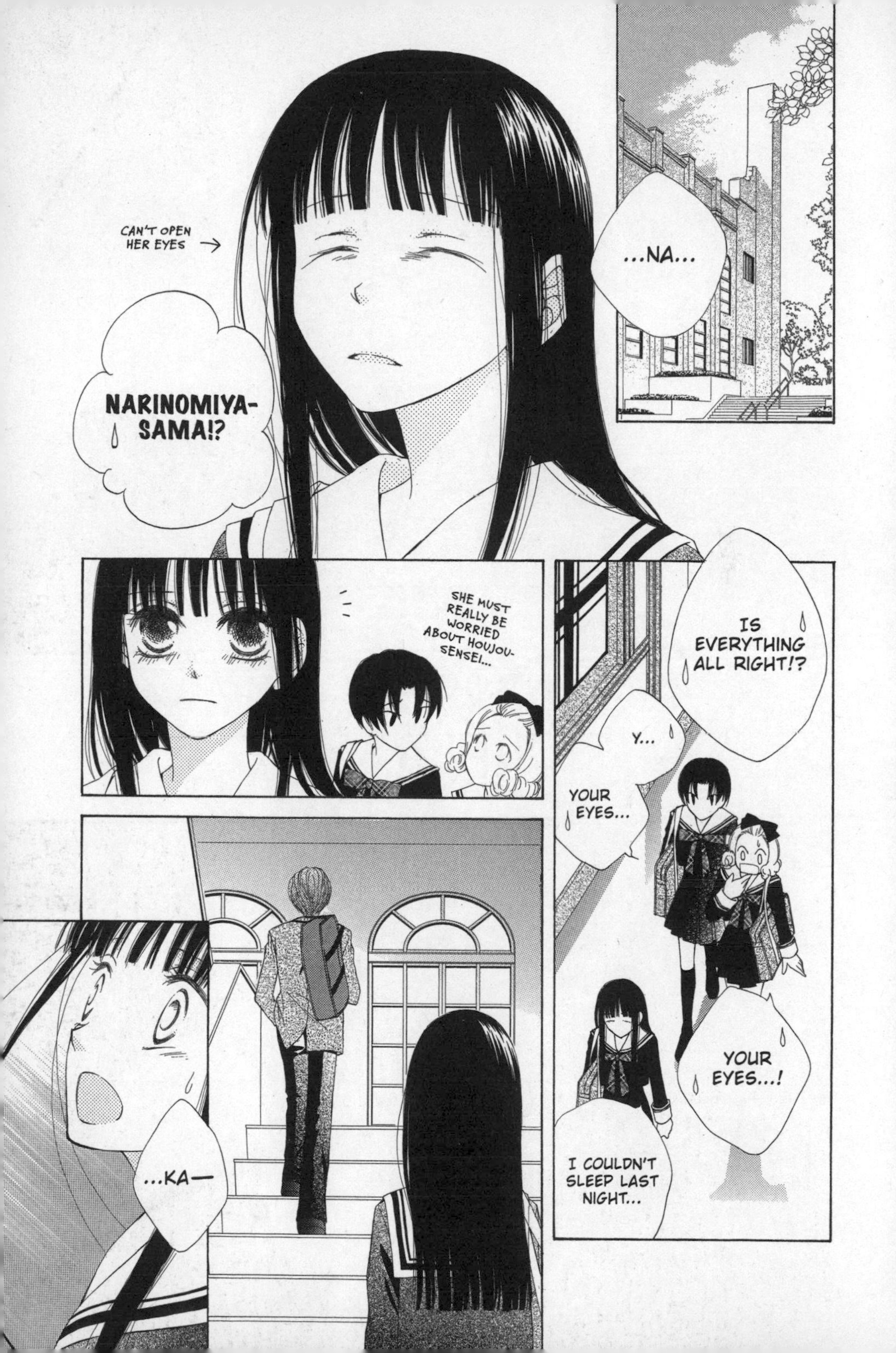
...NA...
CAN'T OPEN HER EYES
NARINOMIYA-SAMA!?
IS EVERYTHING ALL RIGHT!?
Y...
YOUR EYES...
YOUR EYES...!
I COULDN'T SLEEP LAST NIGHT...
SHE MUST REALLY BE WORRIED ABOUT HOUJOU-SENSEI...
...KA—

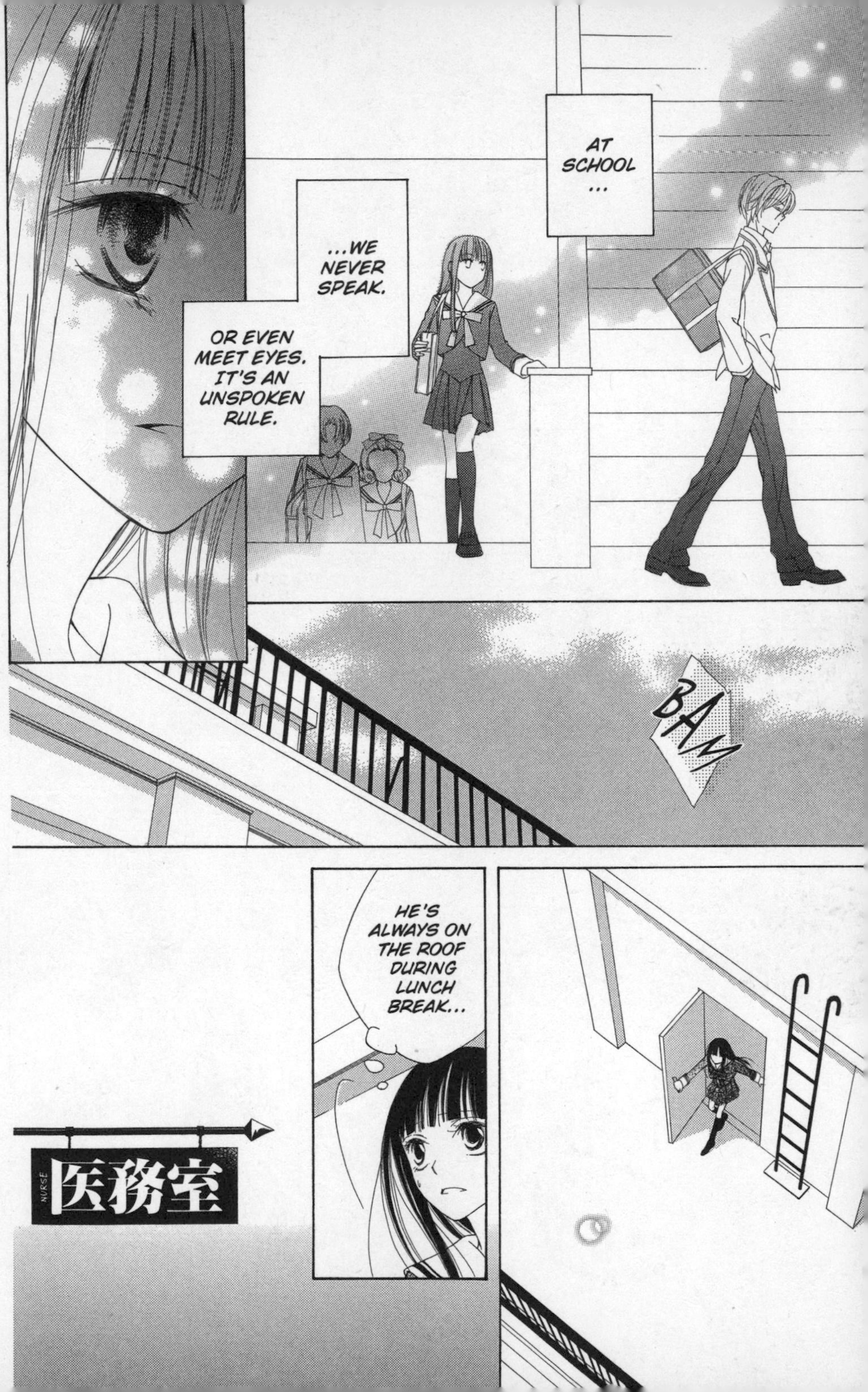
AT SCHOOL ...
...WE NEVER SPEAK.
OR EVEN MEET EYES. IT'S AN UNSPOKEN RULE.
BAM
HE'S ALWAYS ON THE ROOF DURING LUNCH BREAK...
NURSE
医務室

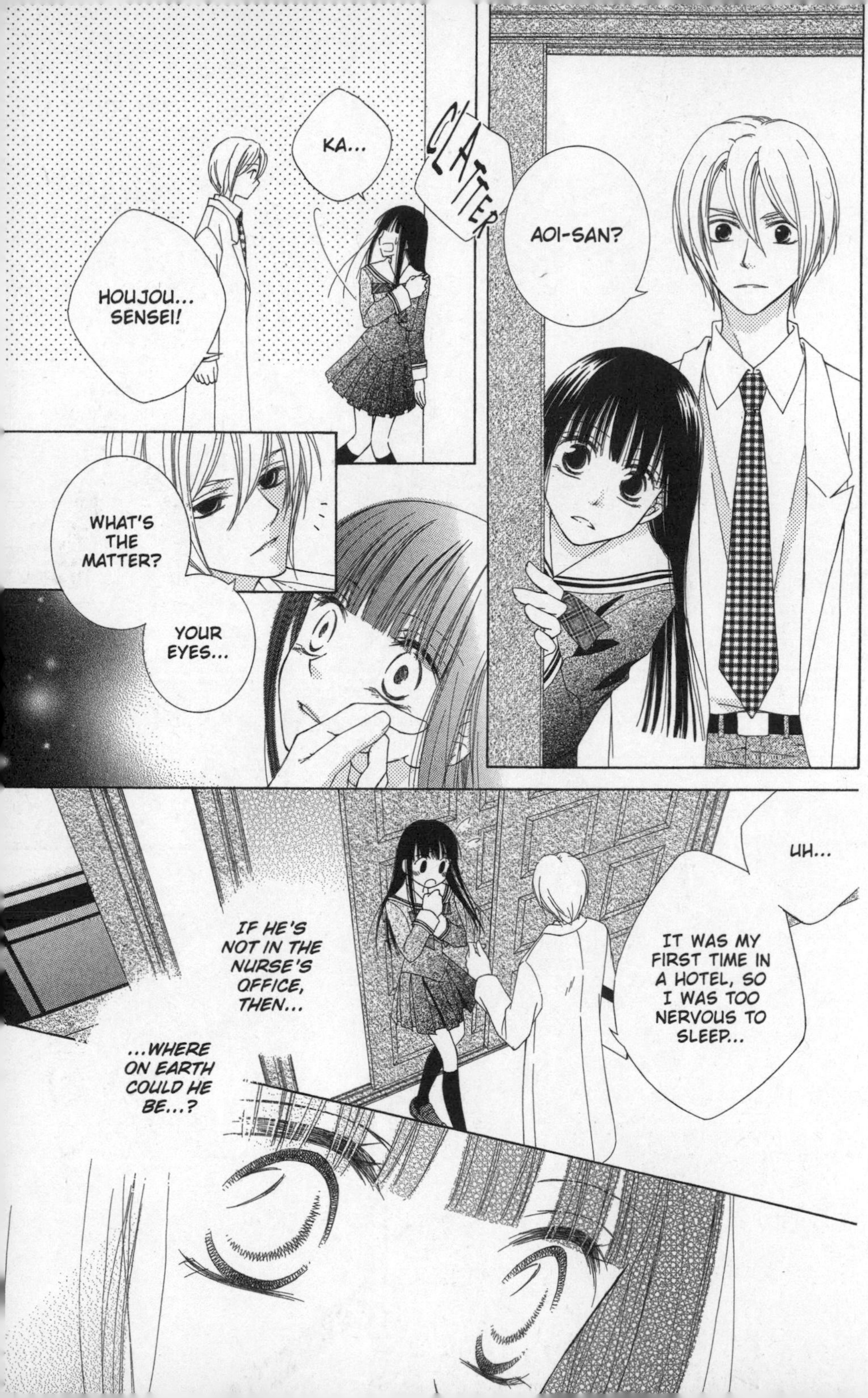
CLATTER
AOI-SAN?
KA...
HOUJOU... SENSEI!
WHAT'S THE MATTER?
YOUR EYES...
UH...
IT WAS MY FIRST TIME IN A HOTEL, SO I WAS TOO NERVOUS TO SLEEP...
IF HE'S NOT IN THE NURSE'S OFFICE, THEN...
...WHERE ON EARTH COULD HE BE...?

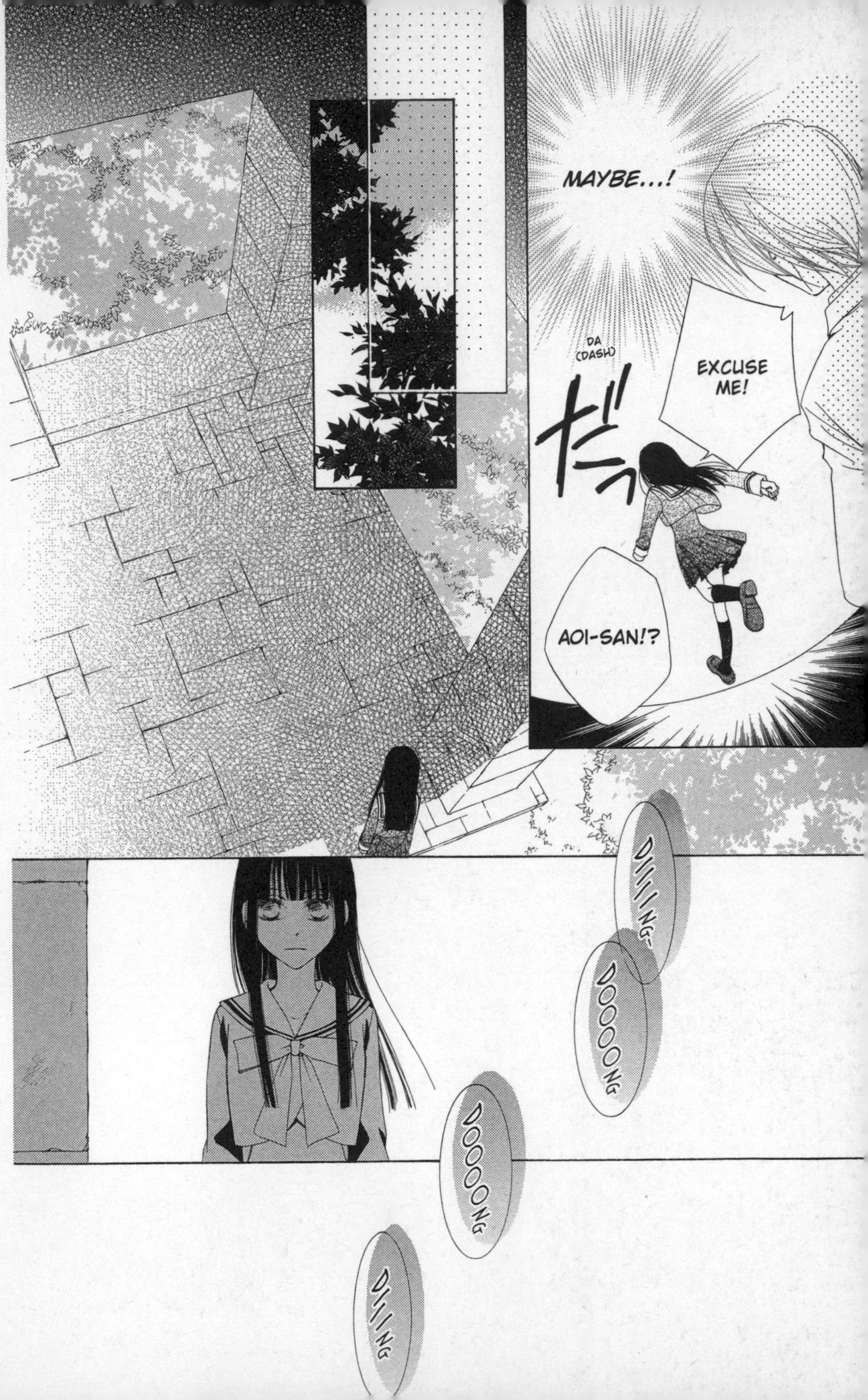
MAYBE...!
EXCUSE ME!
DA (DASH)
AOI-SAN!?
DIIIING-
DOOOONG
DOOOONG
DIIING

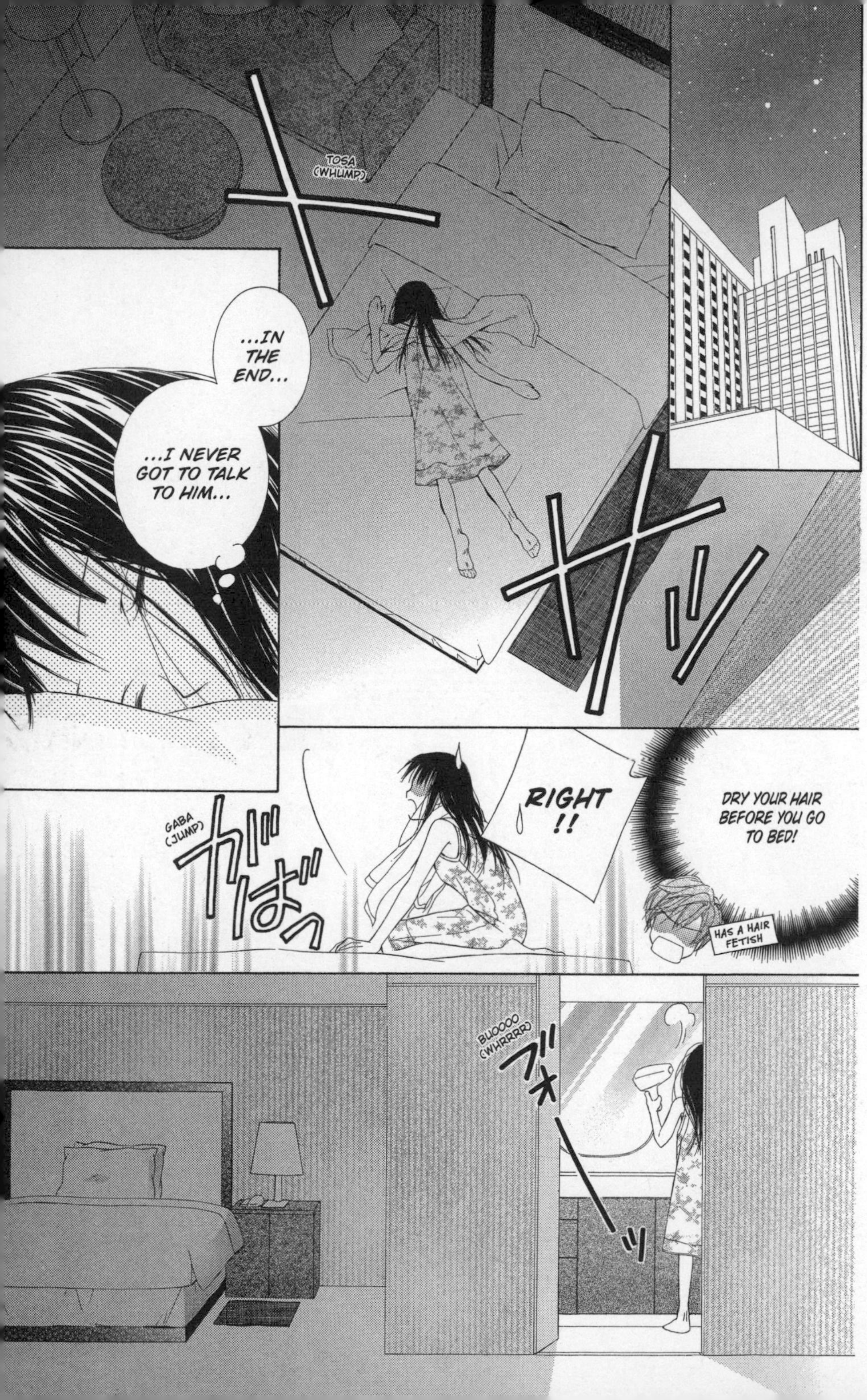
TOSA (WHUMP)
...IN THE END...
...I NEVER GOT TO TALK TO HIM...
DRY YOUR HAIR BEFORE YOU GO TO BED!
HAS A HAIR FETISH
RIGHT!!
GABA (JUMP)
BUOOOO (WHRRRR)

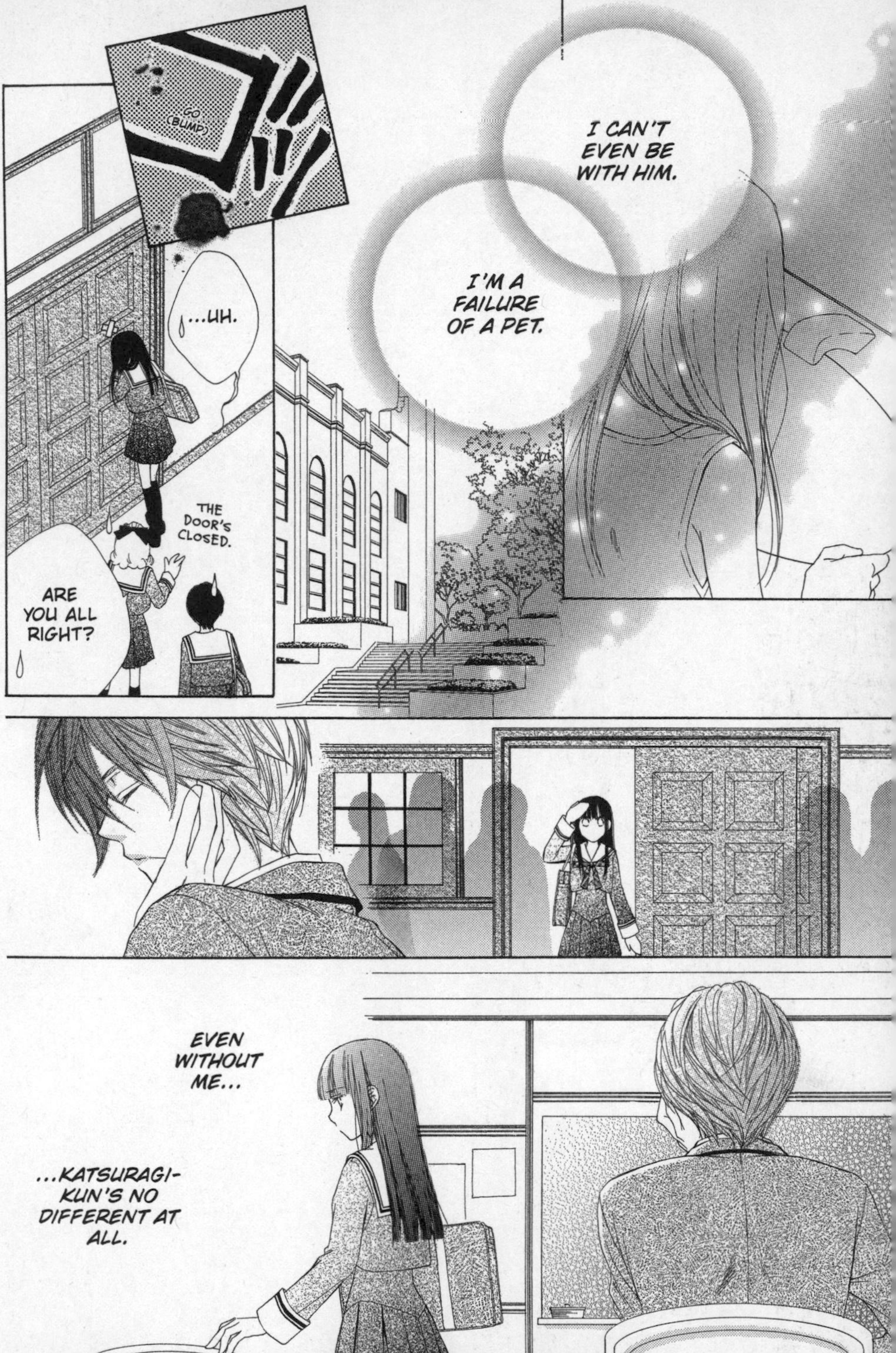
I CAN'T EVEN BE WITH HIM.
I'M A FAILURE OF A PET.
GO (BUMP)
...UH.
THE DOOR'S CLOSED.
ARE YOU ALL RIGHT?
EVEN WITHOUT ME...
...KATSURAGI-KUN'S NO DIFFERENT AT ALL.

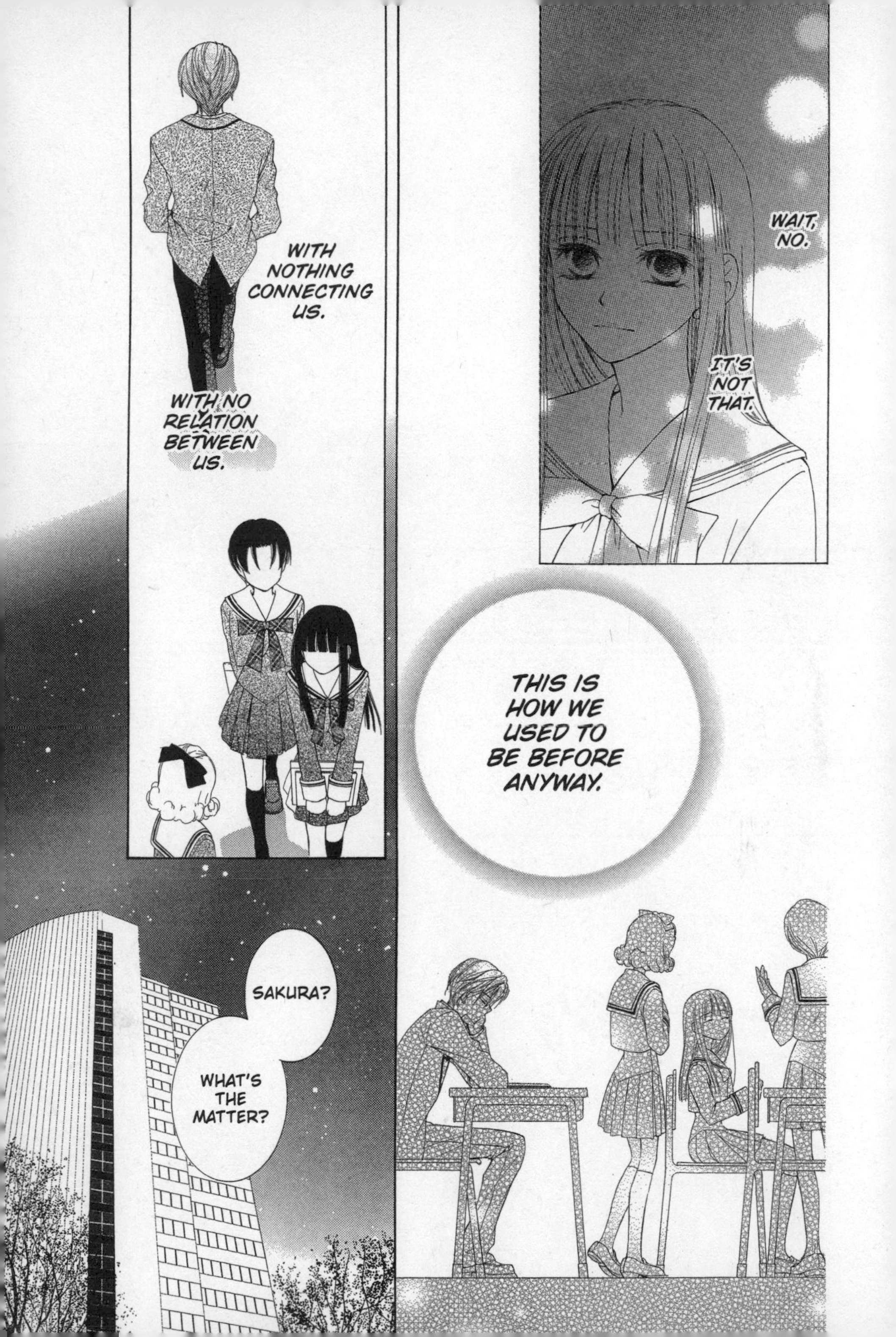
WAIT, NO.
IT'S NOT THAT.
WITH NOTHING CONNECTING US.
WITH NO RELATION BETWEEN US.
THIS IS HOW WE USED TO BE BEFORE ANYWAY.
SAKURA?
WHAT'S THE MATTER?

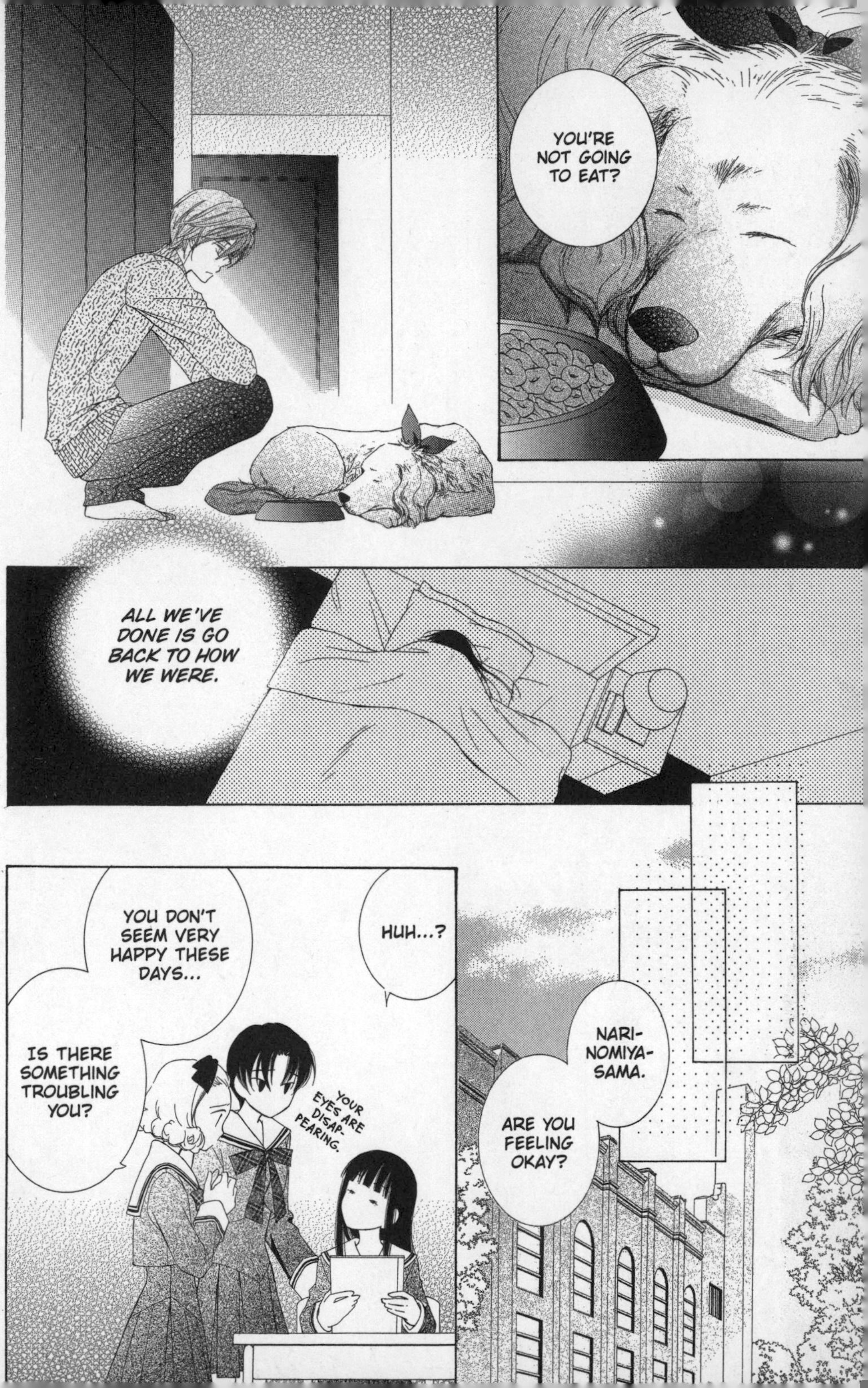
YOU'RE NOT GOING TO EAT?
ALL WE'VE DONE IS GO BACK TO HOW WE WERE.
NARI-NOMIYA-SAMA.
ARE YOU FEELING OKAY?
HUH...?
YOU DON'T SEEM VERY HAPPY THESE DAYS...
IS THERE SOMETHING TROUBLING YOU?
YOUR EYES ARE DISAP-PEARING.

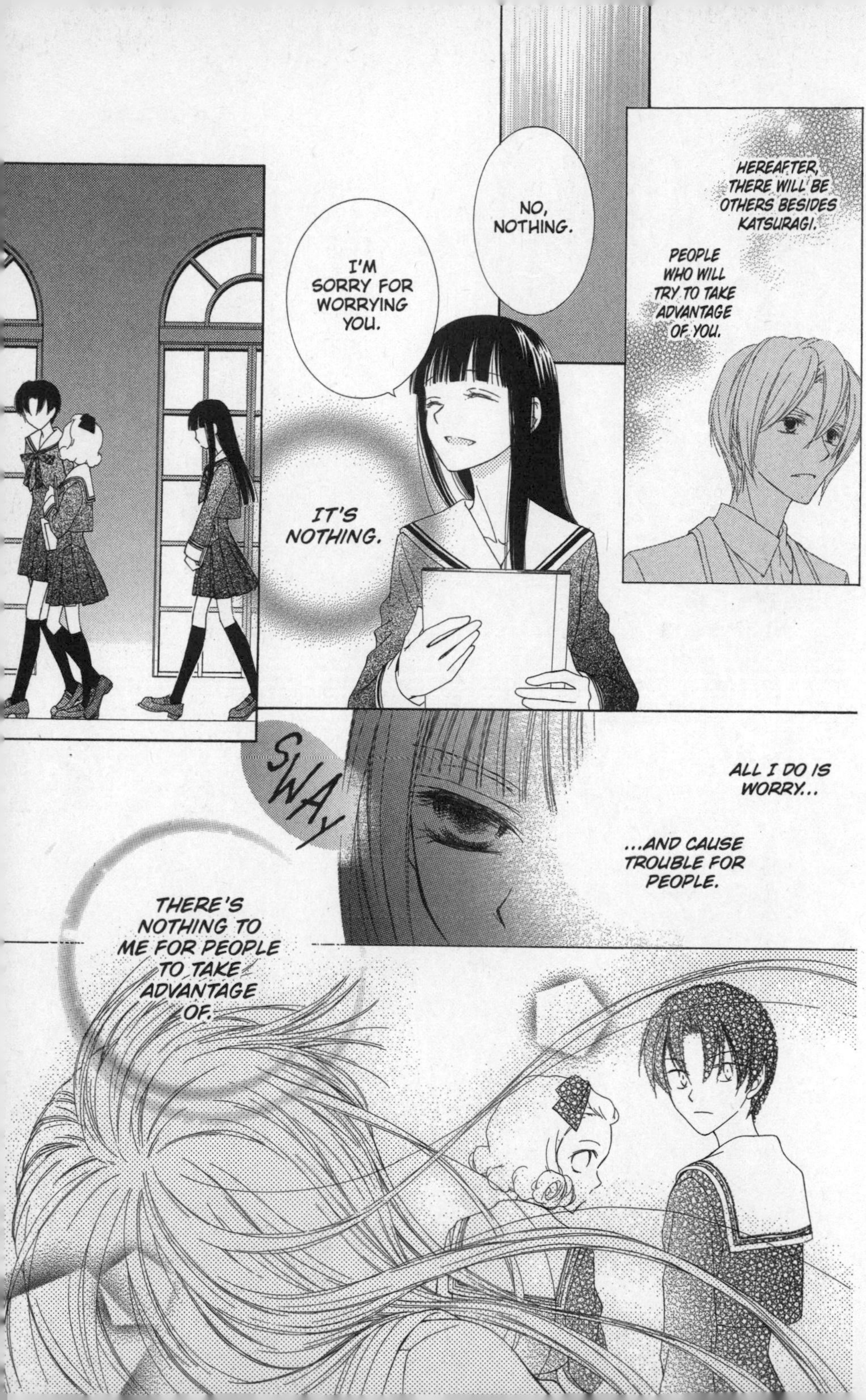
HEREAFTER, THERE WILL BE OTHERS BESIDES KATSURAGI.
PEOPLE WHO WILL TRY TO TAKE ADVANTAGE OF YOU.
NO, NOTHING.
I'M SORRY FOR WORRYING YOU.
IT'S NOTHING.
ALL I DO IS WORRY...
SWAY
...AND CAUSE TROUBLE FOR PEOPLE.
THERE'S NOTHING TO ME FOR PEOPLE TO TAKE ADVANTAGE OF.

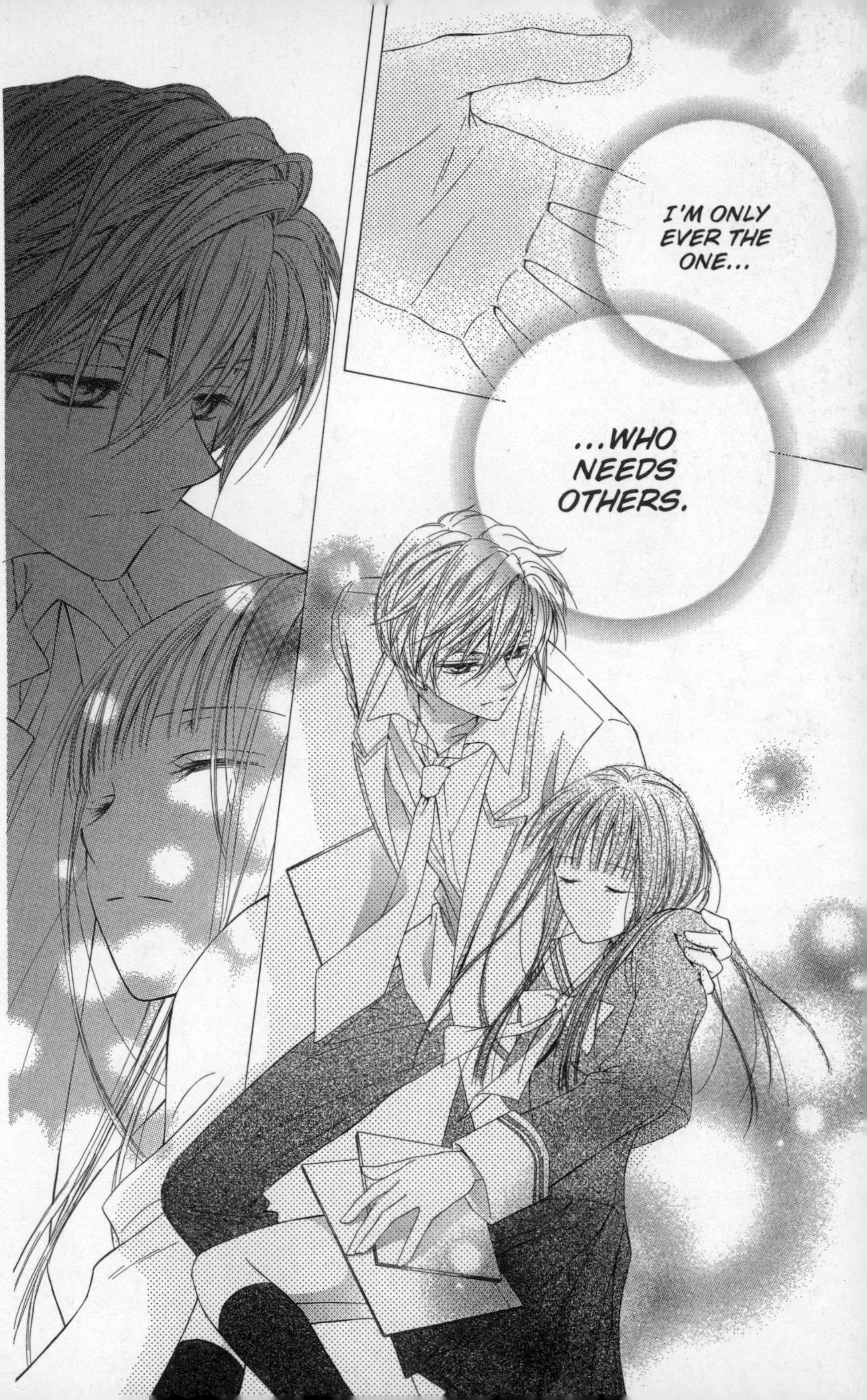
I'M ONLY EVER THE ONE...
...WHO NEEDS OTHERS.

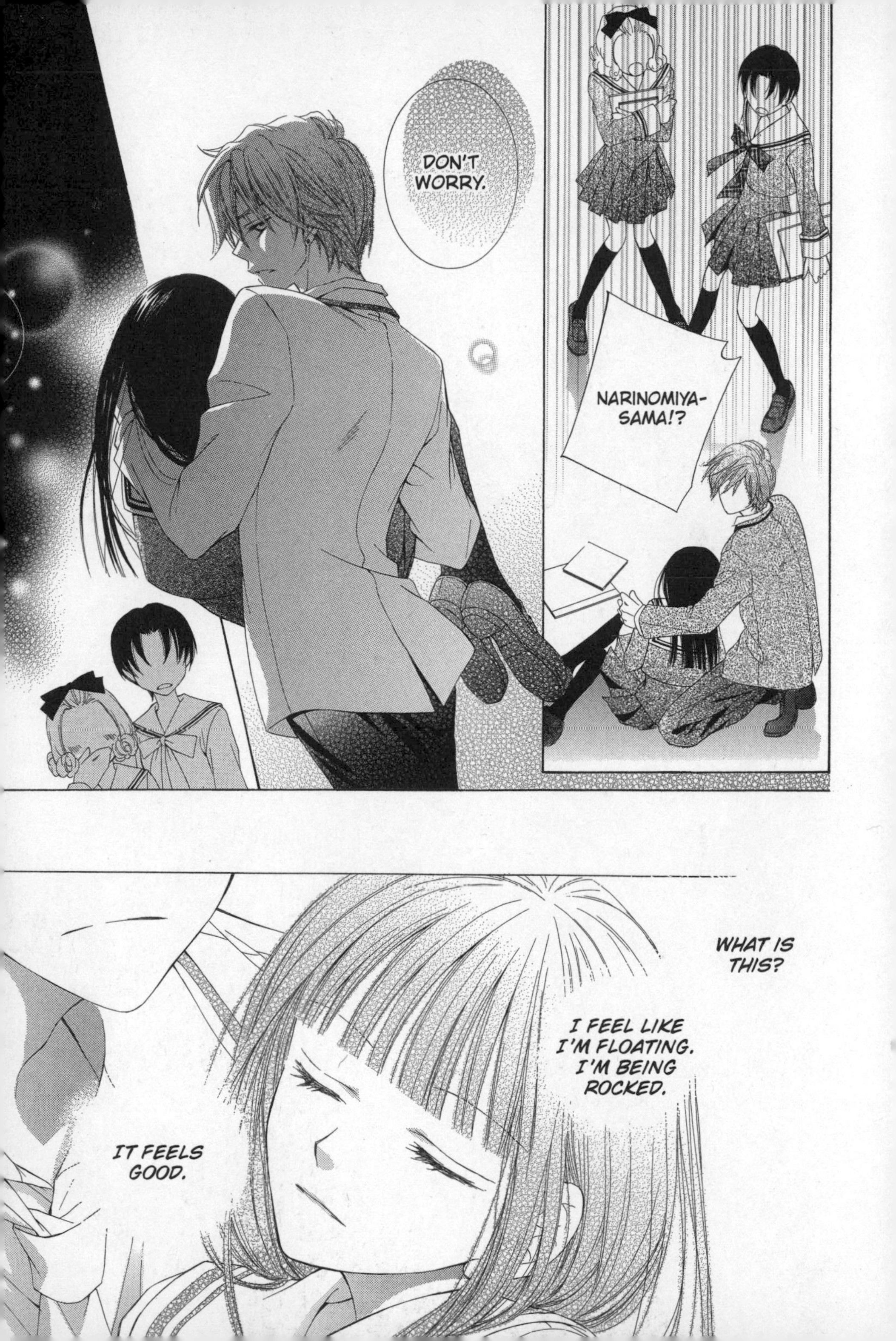
NARINOMIYA-SAMA!?
DON'T WORRY.
WHAT IS THIS?
I FEEL LIKE I'M FLOATING. I'M BEING ROCKED.
IT FEELS GOOD.

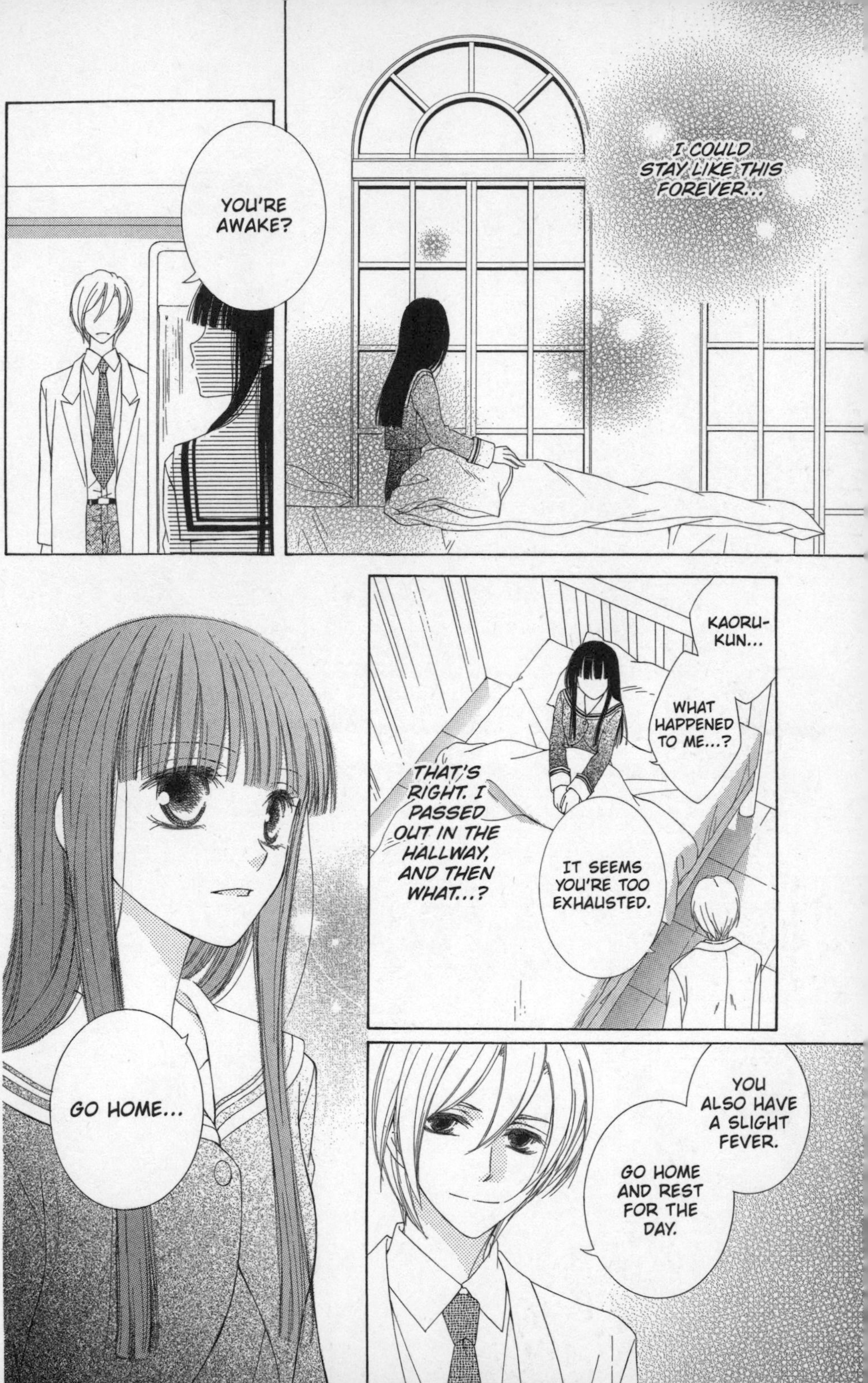
I COULD STAY LIKE THIS FOREVER...
YOU'RE AWAKE?
KAORU-KUN...
WHAT HAPPENED TO ME...?
THAT'S RIGHT. I PASSED OUT IN THE HALLWAY, AND THEN WHAT...?
IT SEEMS YOU'RE TOO EXHAUSTED.
YOU ALSO HAVE A SLIGHT FEVER.
GO HOME AND REST FOR THE DAY.
GO HOME...

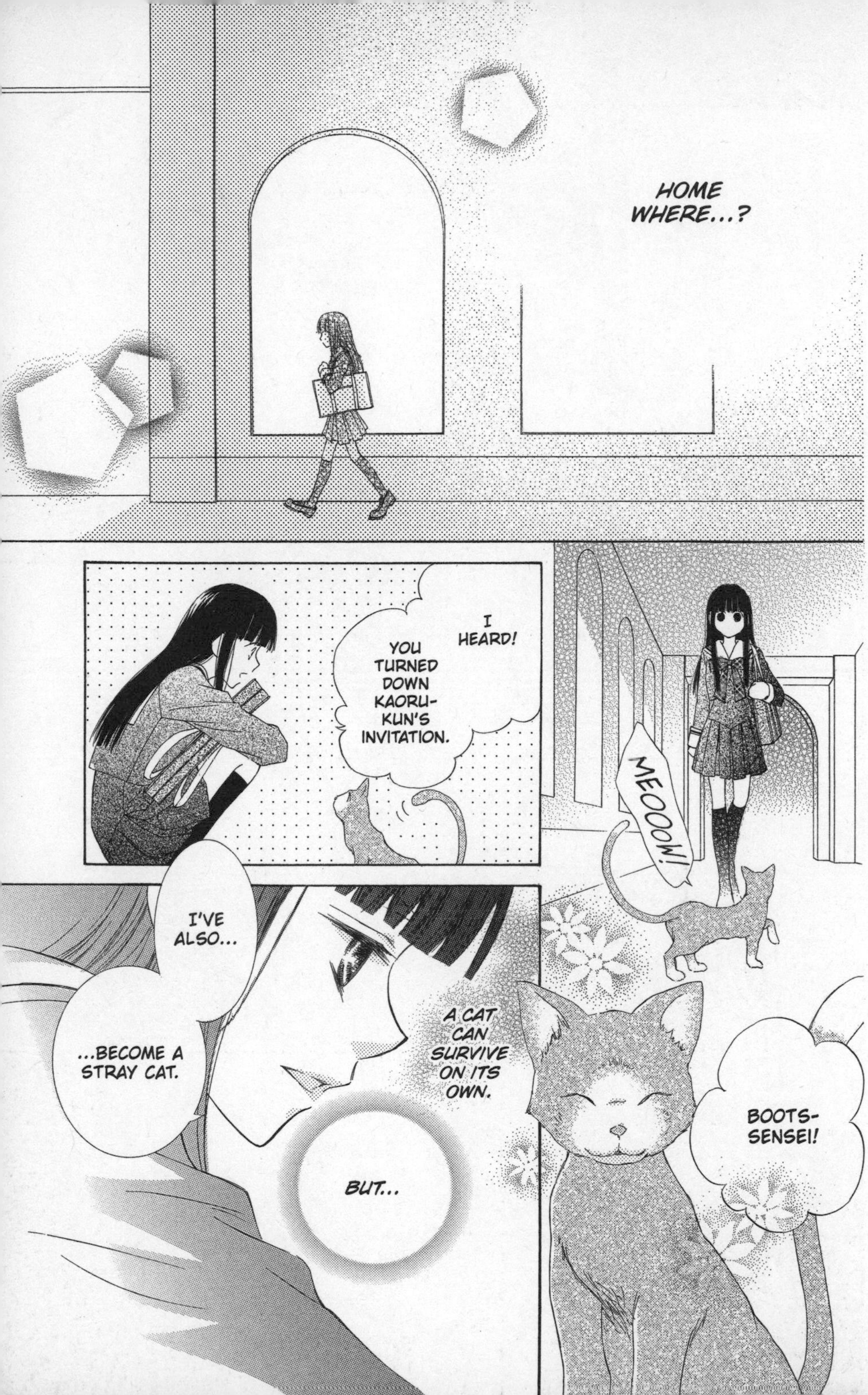
HOME WHERE...?
MEOOOW!
I HEARD!
YOU TURNED DOWN KAORU-KUN'S INVITATION.
BOOTS-SENSEI!
A CAT CAN SURVIVE ON ITS OWN.
I'VE ALSO...
...BECOME A STRAY CAT.
BUT...

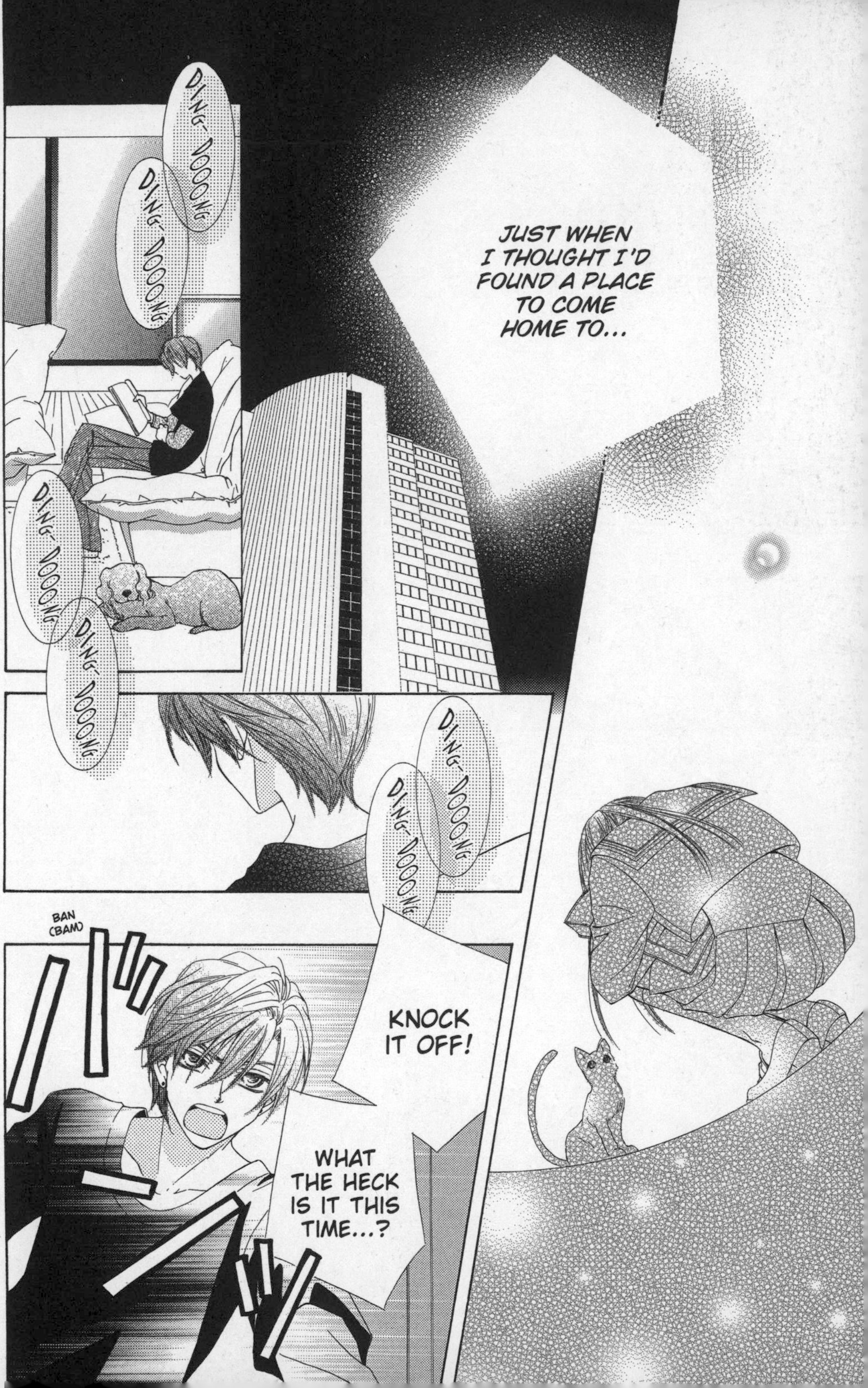
JUST WHEN I THOUGHT I'D FOUND A PLACE TO COME HOME TO...
DING-DOOONG
DING-DOOONG
DING-DOOONG
DING-DOOONG
DING-DOOONG
DING-DOOONG
BAN (BAM)
KNOCK IT OFF!
WHAT THE HECK IS IT THIS TIME...?

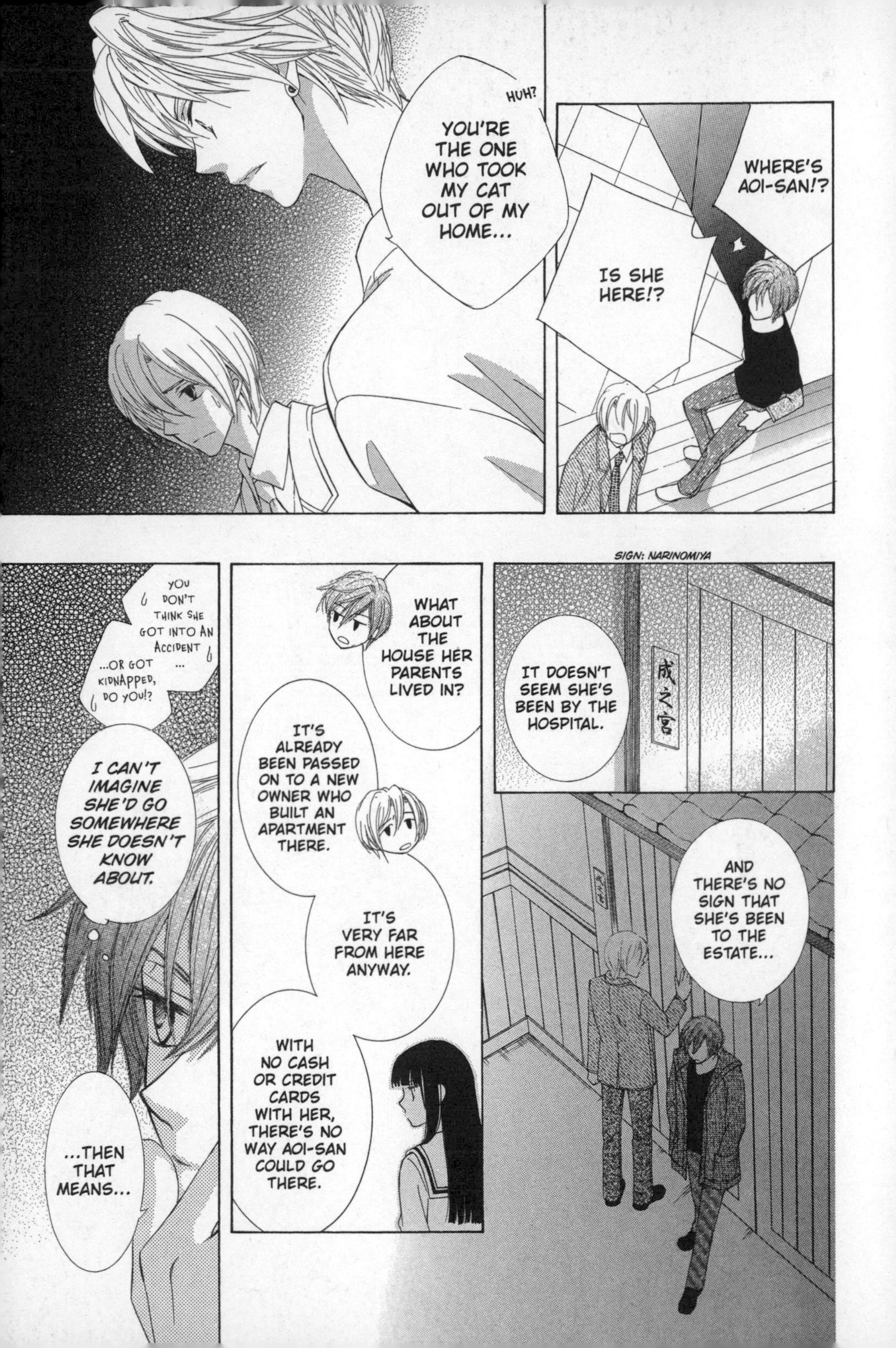
WHERE'S AOI-SAN!?
IS SHE HERE!?
HUH?
YOU'RE THE ONE WHO TOOK MY CAT OUT OF MY HOME...
SIGN: NARINOMIYA
成之宮
IT DOESN'T SEEM SHE'S BEEN BY THE HOSPITAL.
AND THERE'S NO SIGN THAT SHE'S BEEN TO THE ESTATE...
WHAT ABOUT THE HOUSE HER PARENTS LIVED IN?
IT'S ALREADY BEEN PASSED ON TO A NEW OWNER WHO BUILT AN APARTMENT THERE.
IT'S VERY FAR FROM HERE ANYWAY.
WITH NO CASH OR CREDIT CARDS WITH HER, THERE'S NO WAY AOI-SAN COULD GO THERE.
YOU DON'T THINK SHE GOT INTO AN ACCIDENT ...
...OR GOT KIDNAPPED, DO YOU!?
I CAN'T IMAGINE SHE'D GO SOMEWHERE SHE DOESN'T KNOW ABOUT.
...THEN THAT MEANS...

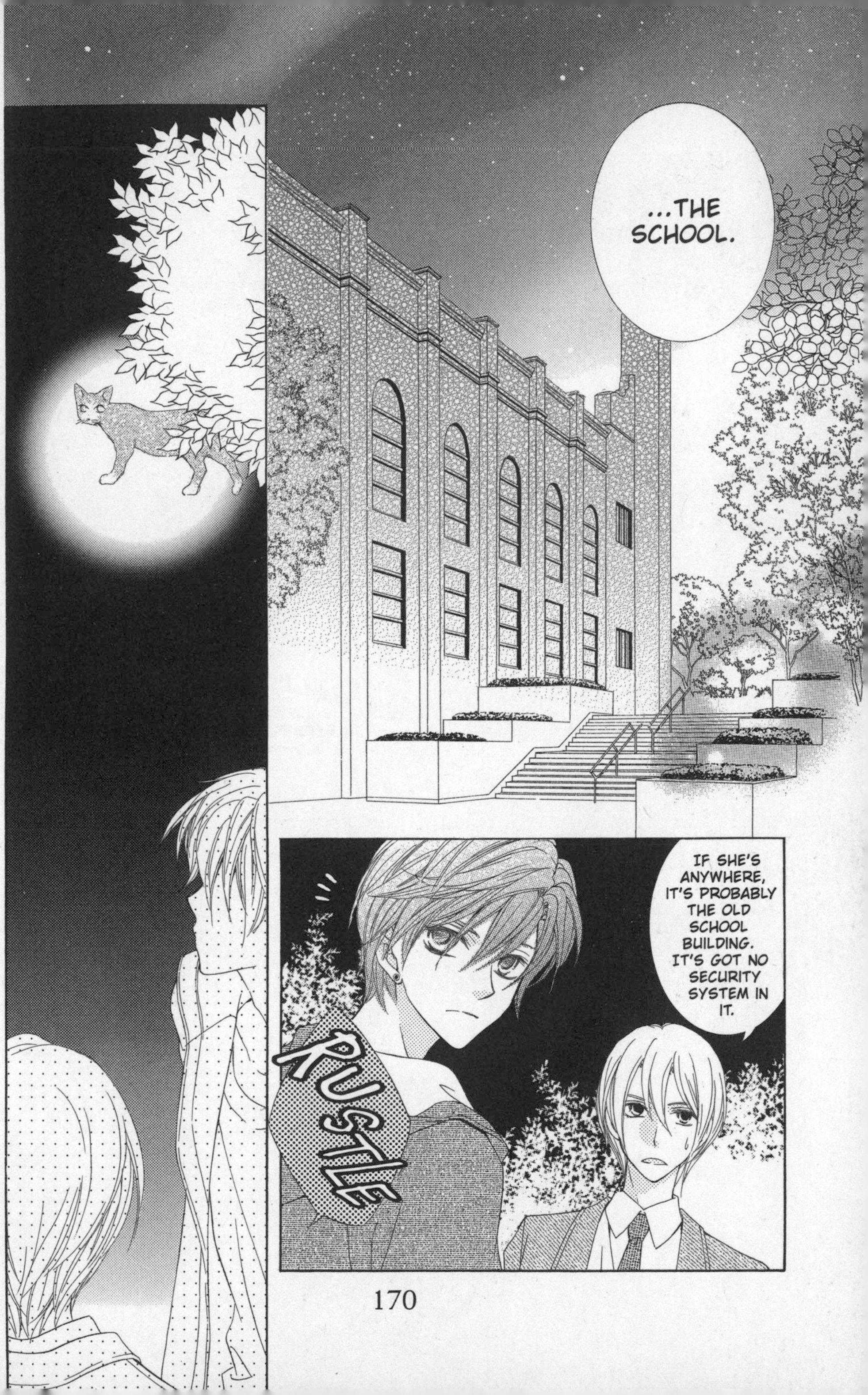
...THE SCHOOL.
IF SHE'S ANYWHERE, IT'S PROBABLY THE OLD SCHOOL BUILDING. IT'S GOT NO SECURITY SYSTEM IN IT.
RUSTLE

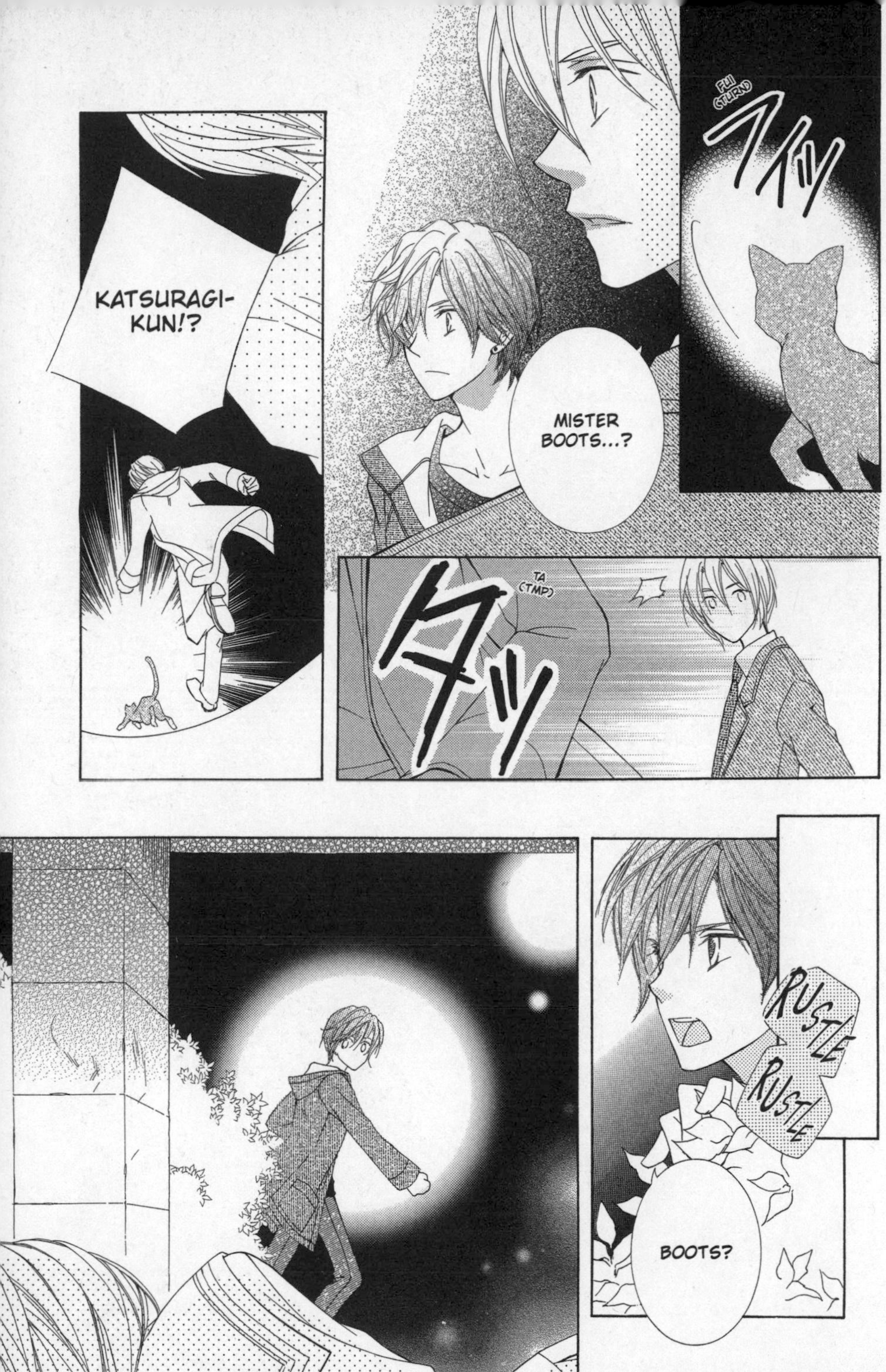
FUI (TURN)
MISTER BOOTS...?
TA (TMP)
KATSURAGI-KUN!?
RUSTLE RUSTLE
BOOTS?

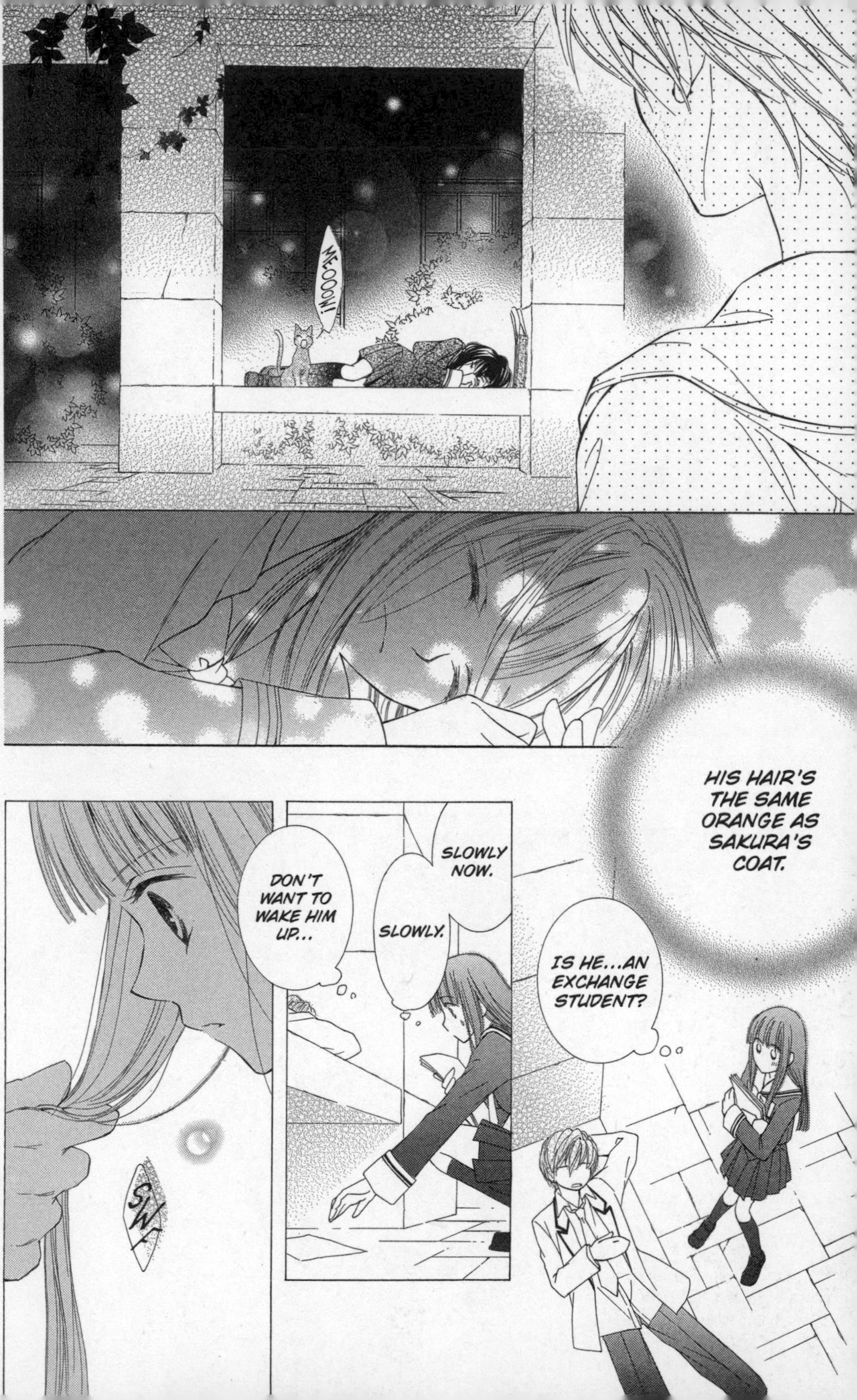
MEOOOW!
HIS HAIR'S THE SAME ORANGE AS SAKURA'S COAT.
IS HE...AN EXCHANGE STUDENT?
SLOWLY NOW.
SLOWLY.
DON'T WANT TO WAKE HIM UP...
SWF

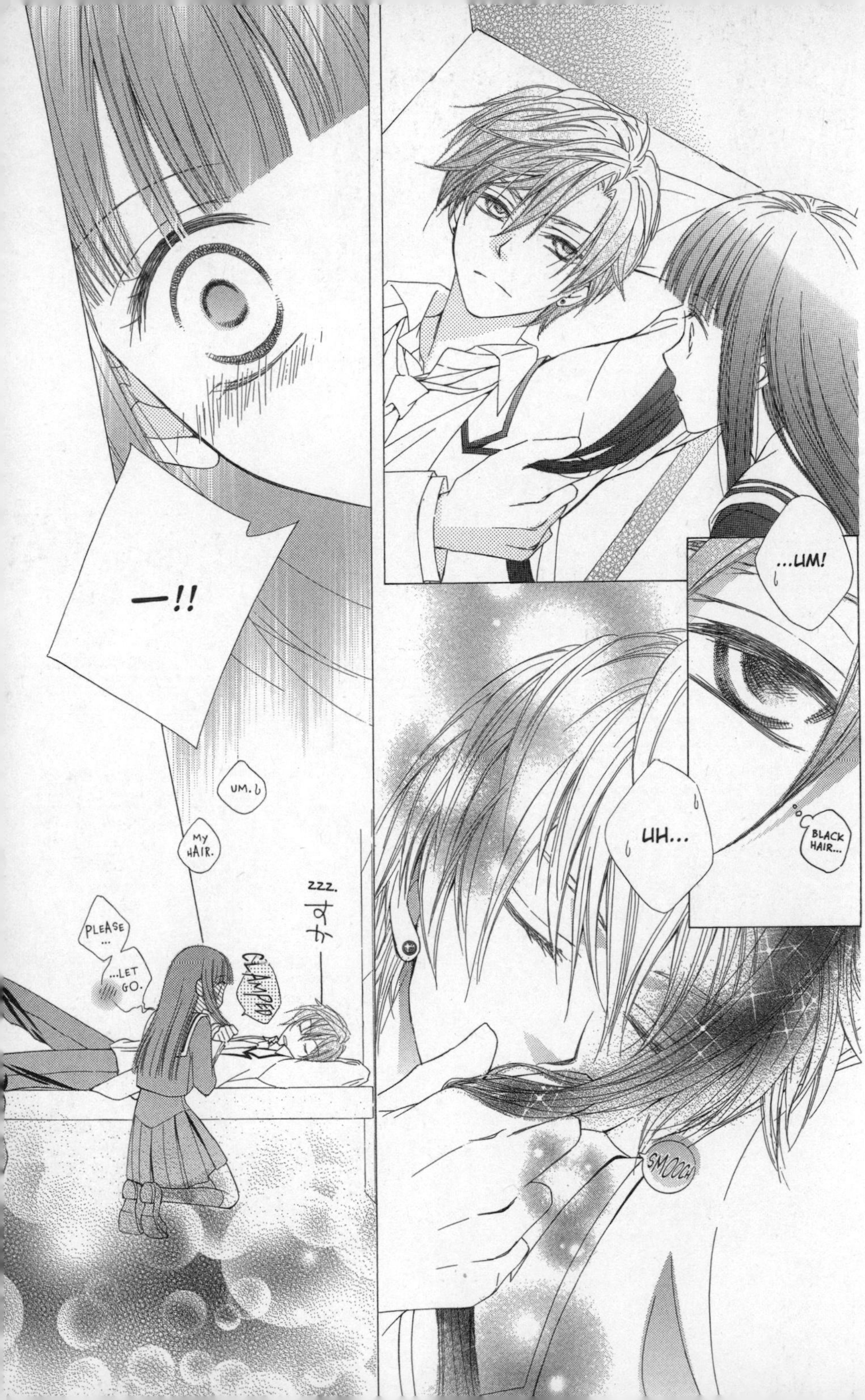
...UM!
BLACK HAIR...
UH...
SMOOCH
—!!
UM.
MY HAIR.
ZZZ.
PLEASE...
...LET GO.
CLAMPED

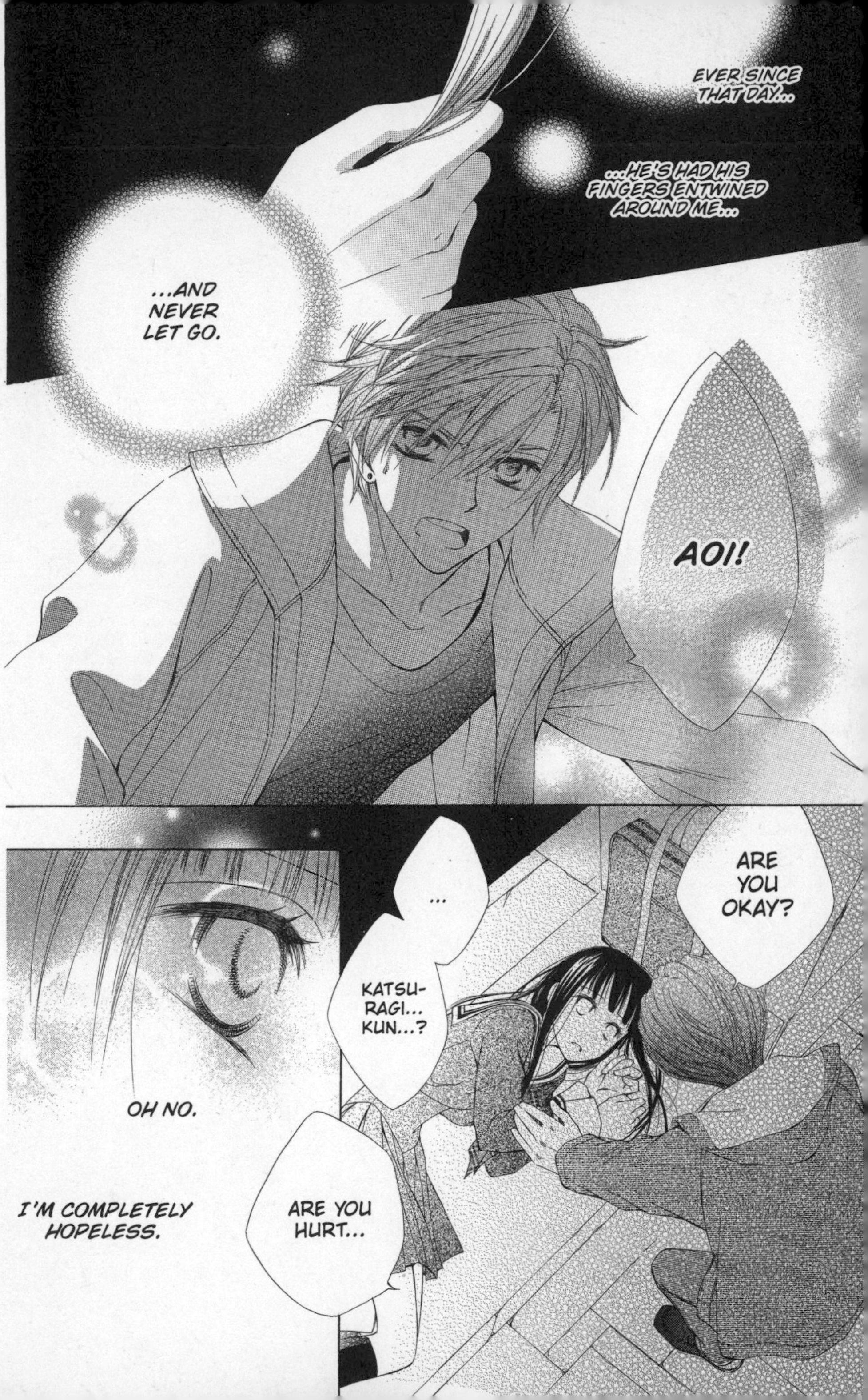
EVER SINCE THAT DAY...
...HE'S HAD HIS FINGERS ENTWINED AROUND ME...
...AND NEVER LET GO.
AOI!
ARE YOU OKAY?
...
KATSURAGI... KUN...?
ARE YOU HURT...
OH NO.
I'M COMPLETELY HOPELESS.

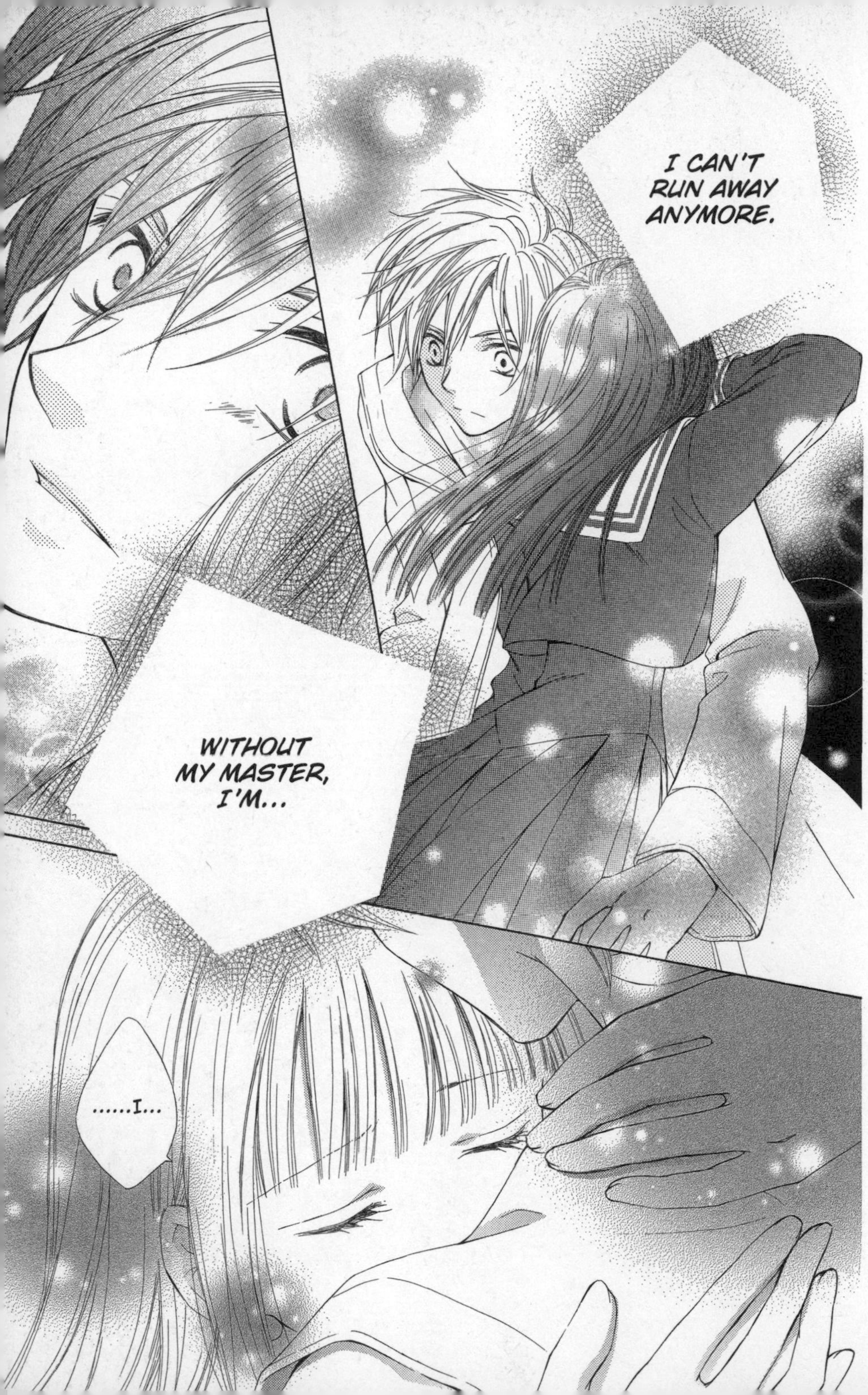
I CAN'T RUN AWAY ANYMORE.
WITHOUT MY MASTER, I'M...
......I...

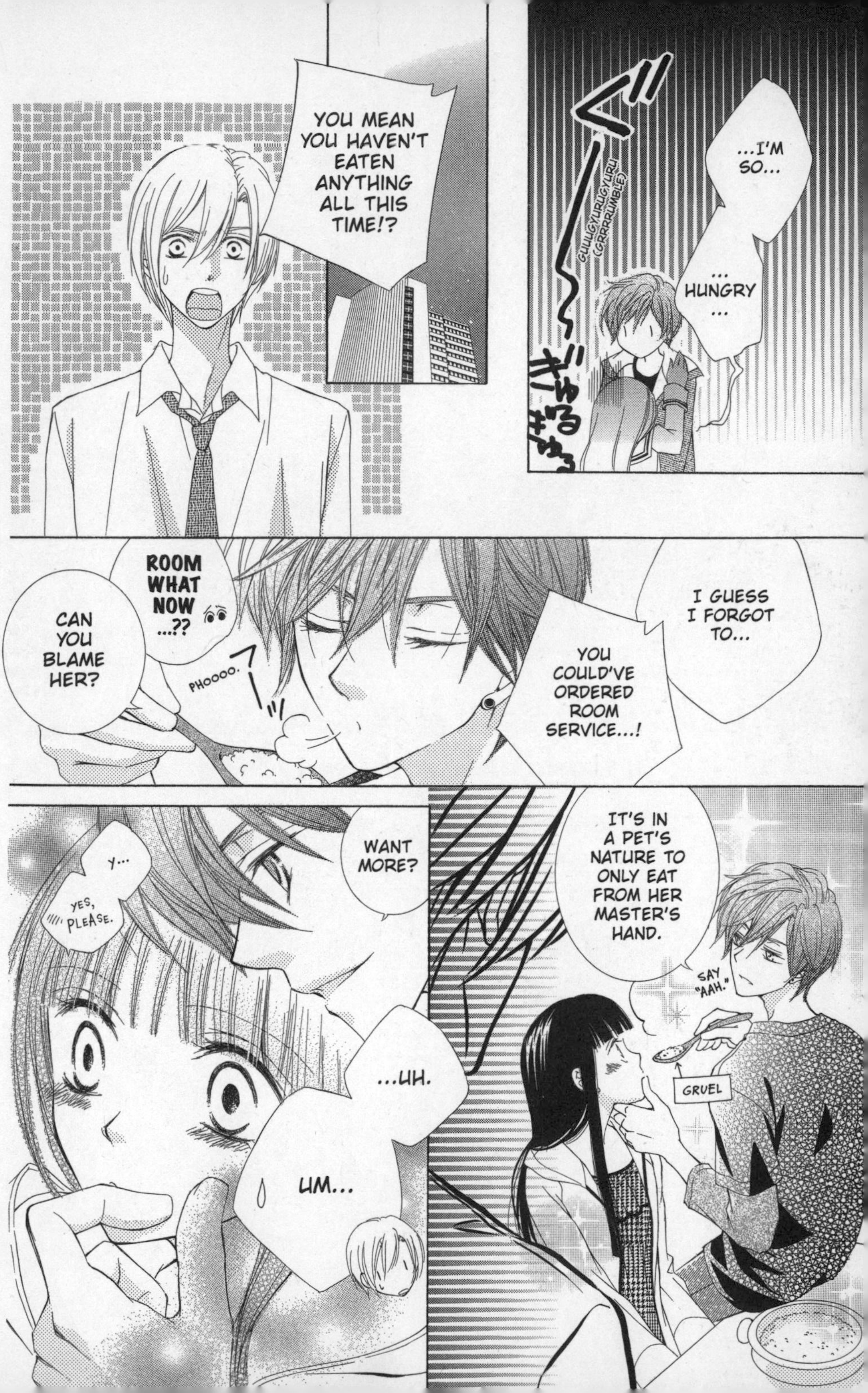
...I'M SO...
... HUNGRY ...
GUUUGYURUGYURU (GRRRRUMBLE)
YOU MEAN YOU HAVEN'T EATEN ANYTHING ALL THIS TIME!?
I GUESS I FORGOT TO...
YOU COULD'VE ORDERED ROOM SERVICE...!
ROOM WHAT NOW ...??
PHOOOO.
CAN YOU BLAME HER?
IT'S IN A PET'S NATURE TO ONLY EAT FROM HER MASTER'S HAND.
SAY "AAH."
GRUEL
WANT MORE?
Y...
YES, PLEASE.
...UH.
UM...

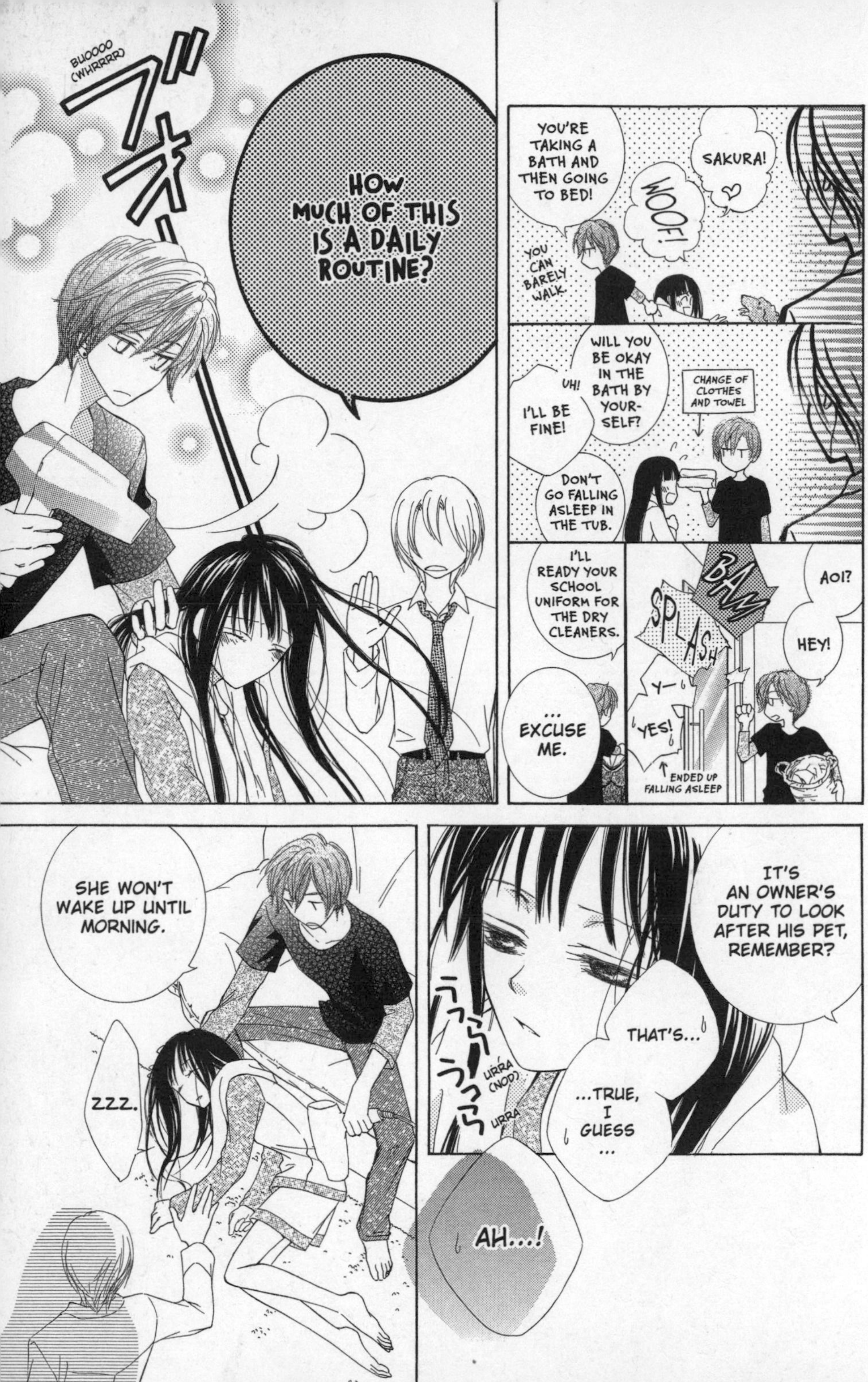
SAKURA! ♡
WOOF!
YOU'RE TAKING A BATH AND THEN GOING TO BED!
YOU CAN BARELY WALK.
CHANGE OF CLOTHES AND TOWEL
WILL YOU BE OKAY IN THE BATH BY YOUR-SELF?
UH!
I'LL BE FINE!
DON'T GO FALLING ASLEEP IN THE TUB.
AOI?
HEY!
BAM
SPLASH
Y-
YES!
ENDED UP FALLING ASLEEP
I'LL READY YOUR SCHOOL UNIFORM FOR THE DRY CLEANERS.
...EXCUSE ME.
BUOOOO (WHRRRR)
HOW MUCH OF THIS IS A DAILY ROUTINE?
IT'S AN OWNER'S DUTY TO LOOK AFTER HIS PET, REMEMBER?
THAT'S...
URRA (NOD)
URRA
...TRUE, I GUESS...
AH...!
SHE WON'T WAKE UP UNTIL MORNING.
ZZZ.

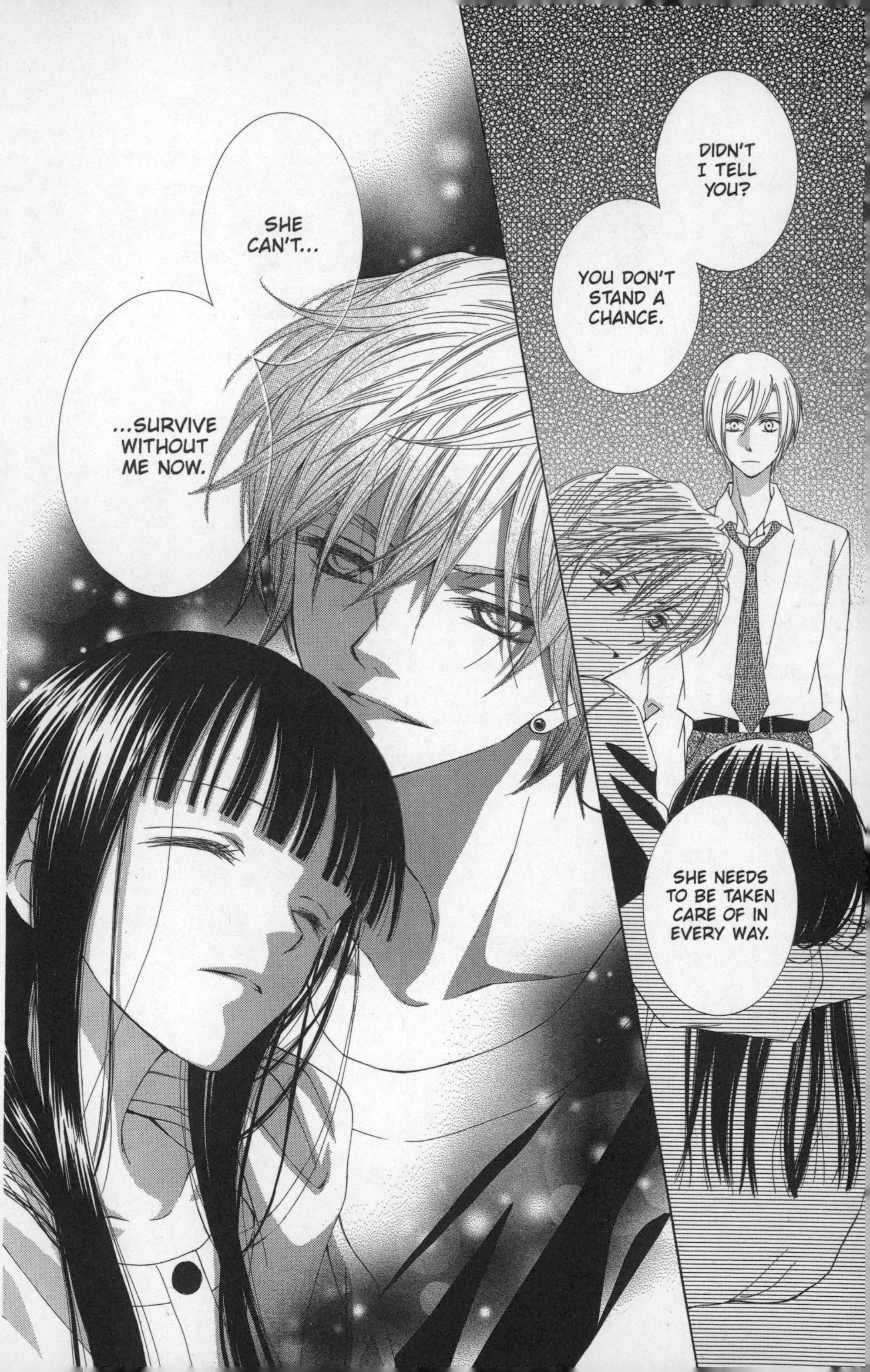
DIDN'T I TELL YOU?
YOU DON'T STAND A CHANCE.
SHE NEEDS TO BE TAKEN CARE OF IN EVERY WAY.
SHE CAN'T...
...SURVIVE WITHOUT ME NOW.

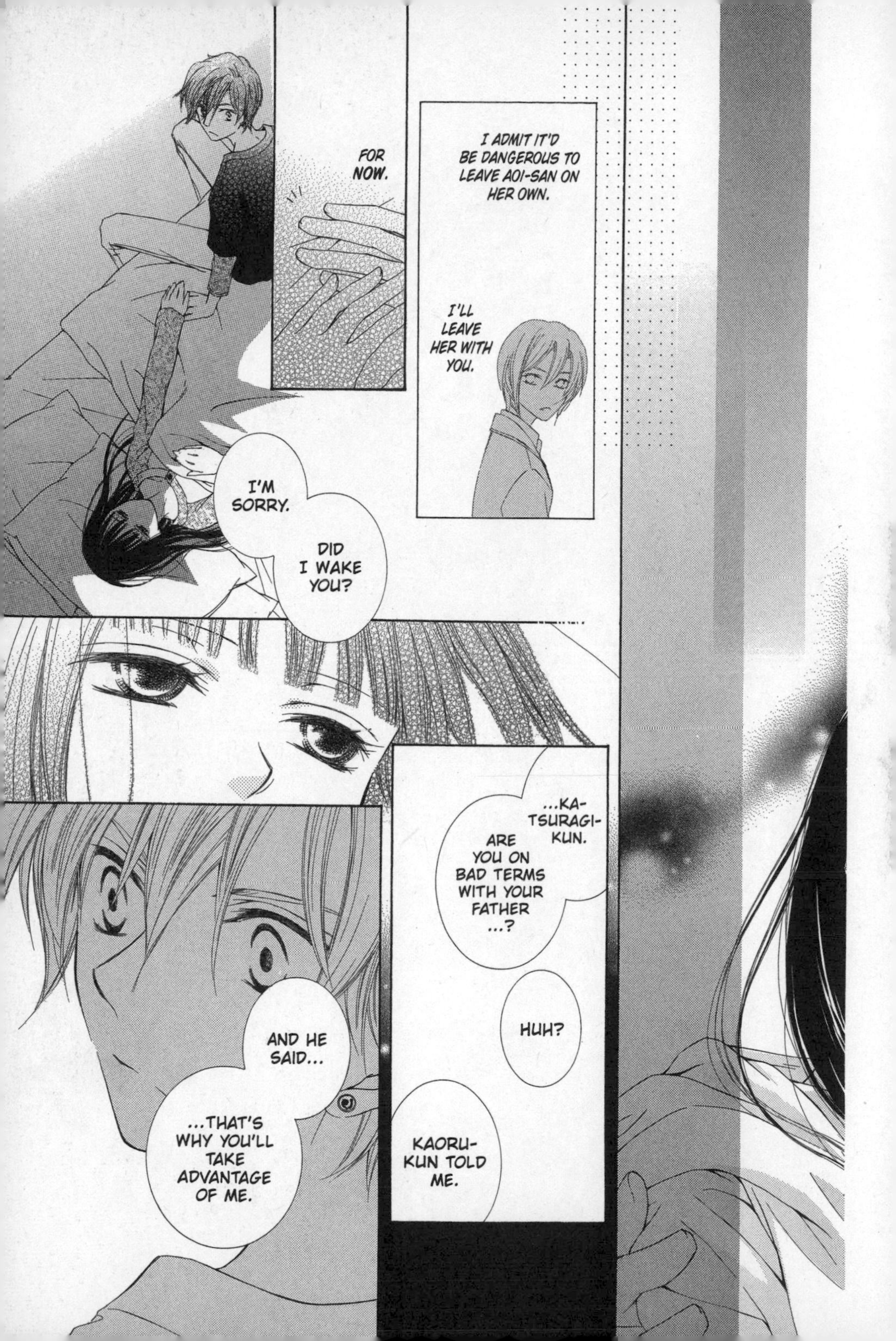
I ADMIT IT'D BE DANGEROUS TO LEAVE AOI-SAN ON HER OWN.
I'LL LEAVE HER WITH YOU.
FOR NOW.
I'M SORRY.
DID I WAKE YOU?
...KATSURAGI-KUN.
ARE YOU ON BAD TERMS WITH YOUR FATHER ...?
HUH?
KAORU-KUN TOLD ME.
AND HE SAID...
...THAT'S WHY YOU'LL TAKE ADVANTAGE OF ME.

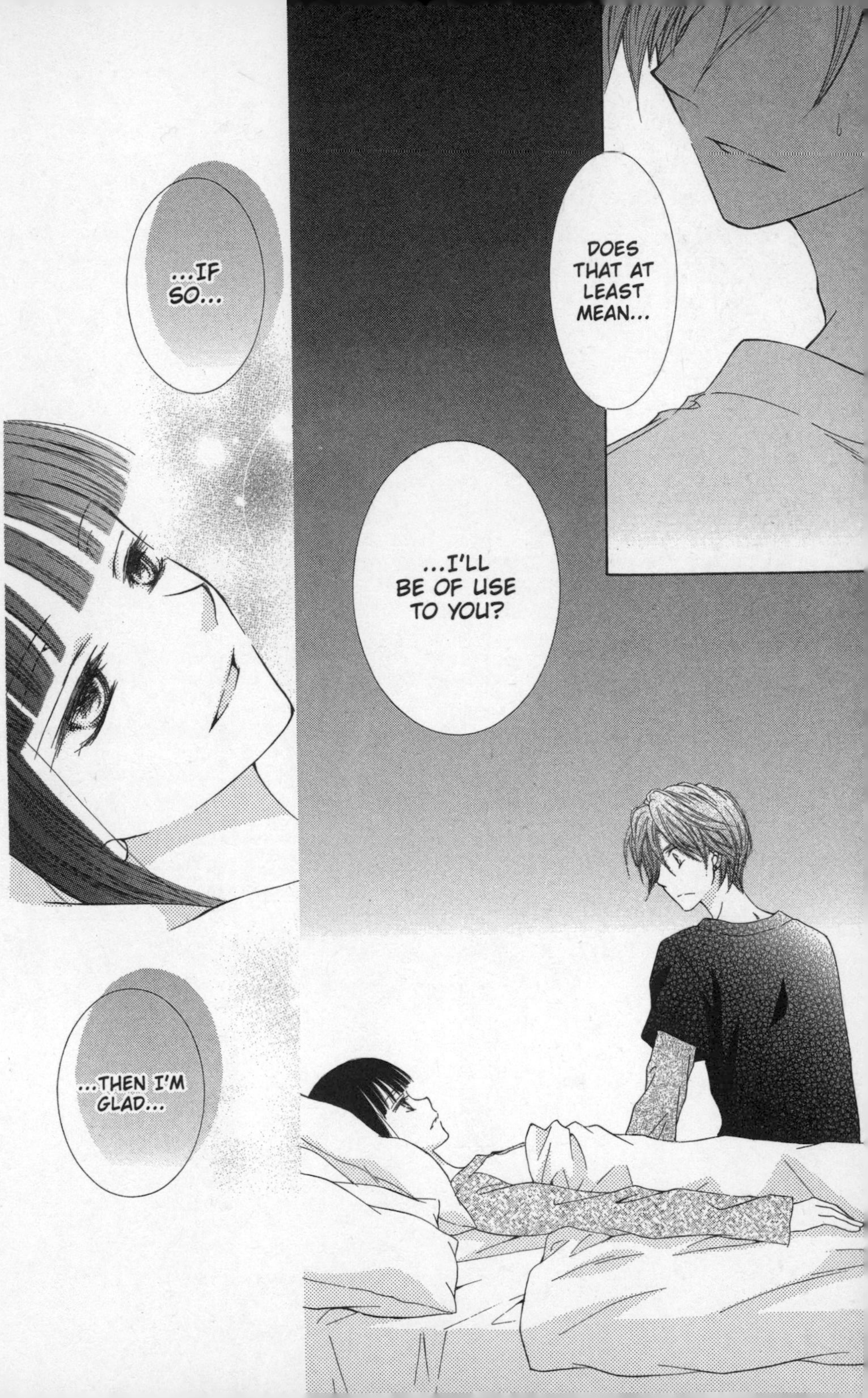
DOES THAT AT LEAST MEAN...
...I'LL BE OF USE TO YOU?
...IF SO...
...THEN I'M GLAD...

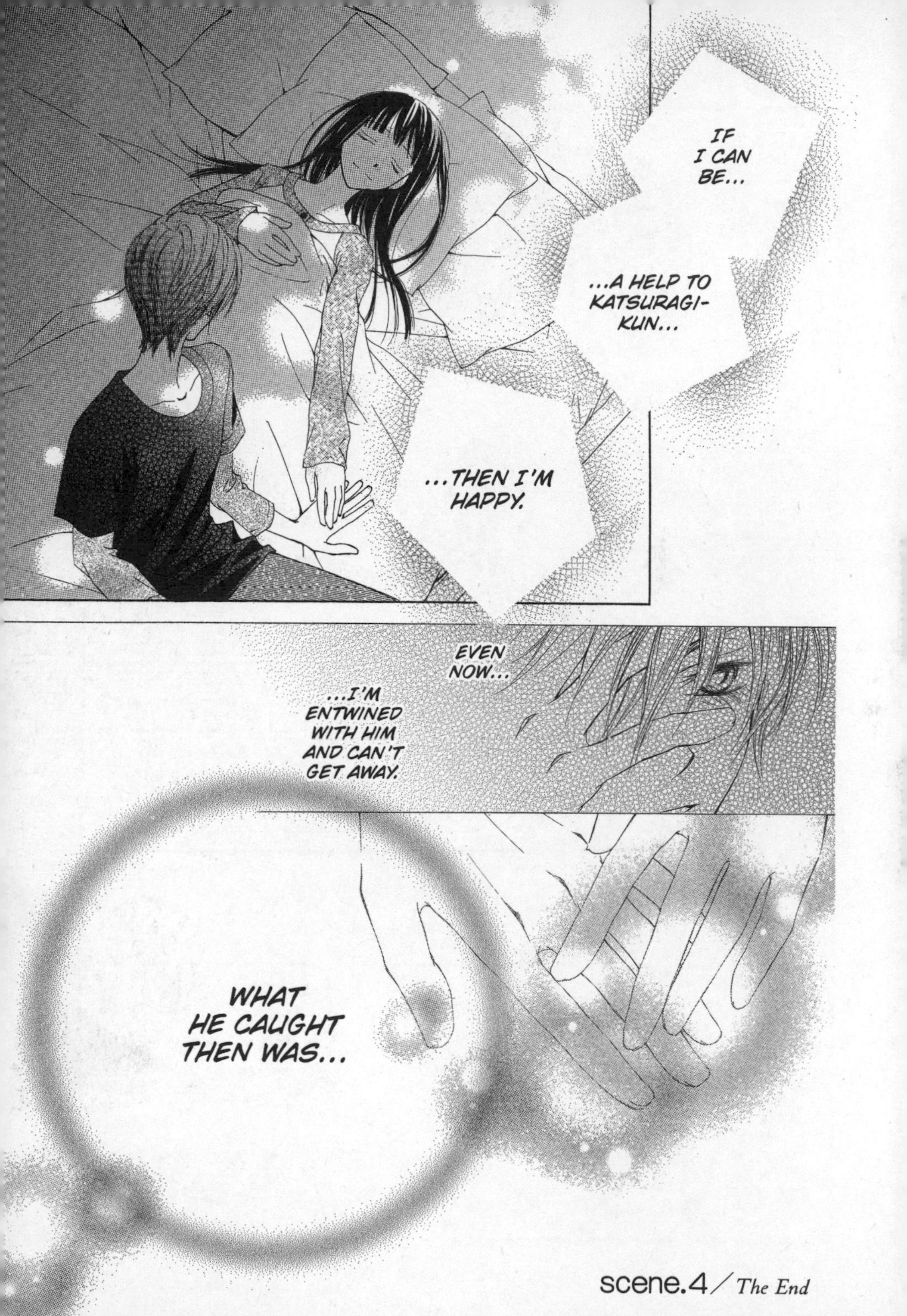
IF I CAN BE...
...A HELP TO KATSURAGI-KUN...
...THEN I'M HAPPY.
EVEN NOW...
...I'M ENTWINED WITH HIM AND CAN'T GET AWAY.
WHAT HE CAUGHT THEN WAS...

scene.4 / The End

BONUS
END OF VOLUME
CONTENT

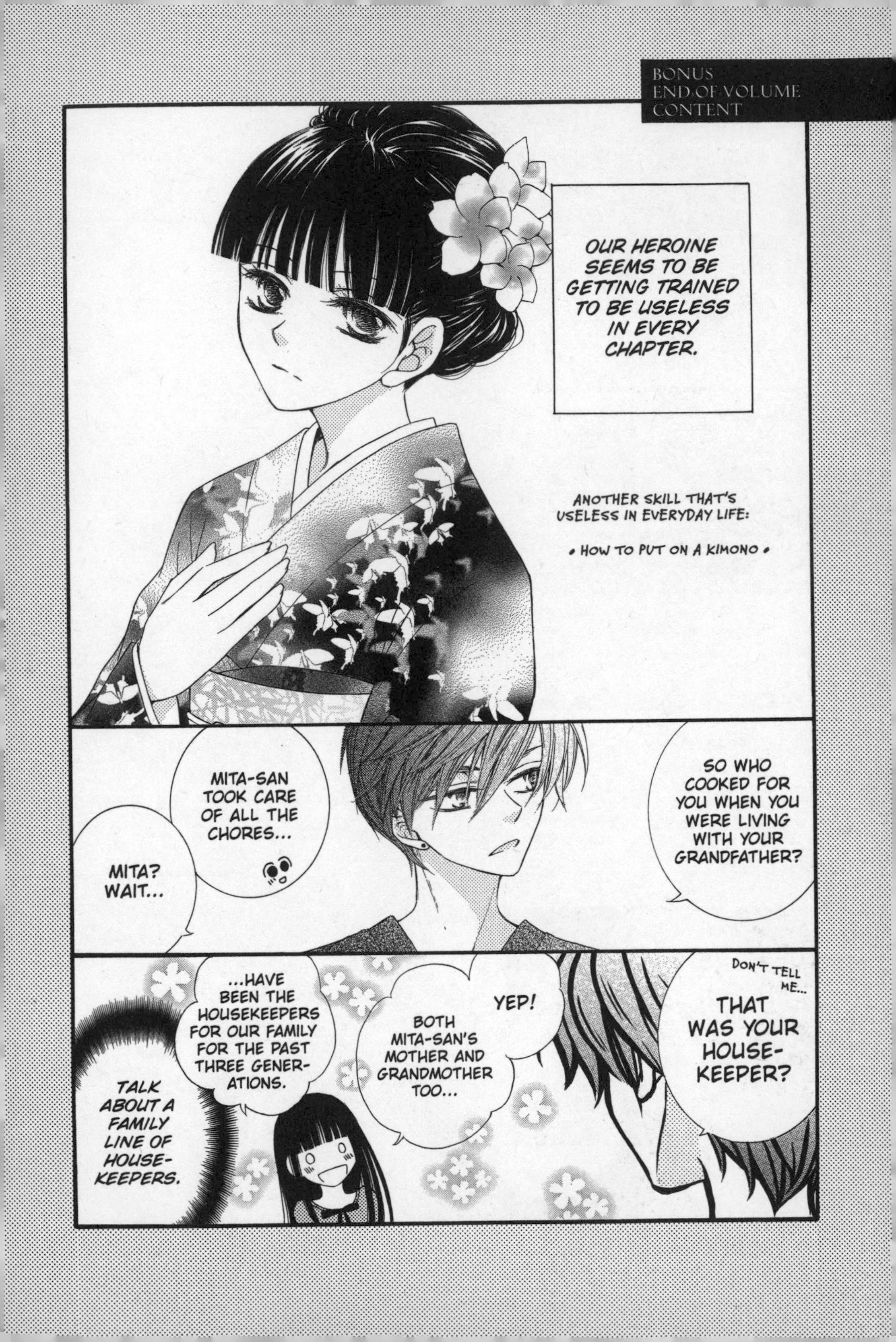
OUR HEROINE SEEMS TO BE GETTING TRAINED TO BE USELESS IN EVERY CHAPTER.
ANOTHER SKILL THAT'S USELESS IN EVERYDAY LIFE:
• HOW TO PUT ON A KIMONO •
SO WHO COOKED FOR YOU WHEN YOU WERE LIVING WITH YOUR GRANDFATHER?
MITA-SAN TOOK CARE OF ALL THE CHORES...
MITA? WAIT...
DON'T TELL ME...
THAT WAS YOUR HOUSE-KEEPER?
YEP!
BOTH MITA-SAN'S MOTHER AND GRANDMOTHER TOO...
...HAVE BEEN THE HOUSEKEEPERS FOR OUR FAMILY FOR THE PAST THREE GENER-ATIONS.
TALK ABOUT A FAMILY LINE OF HOUSE-KEEPERS.

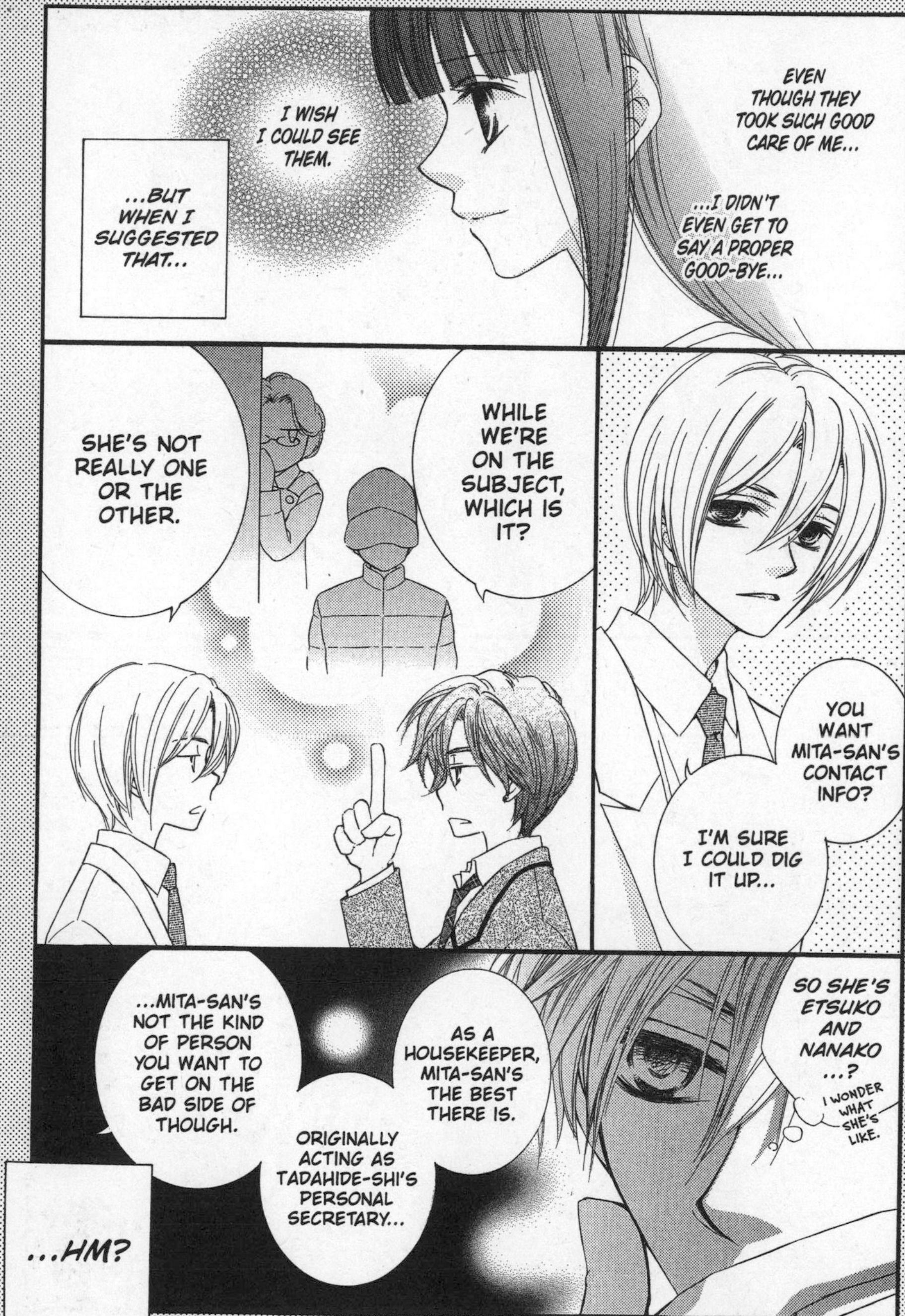
EVEN THOUGH THEY TOOK SUCH GOOD CARE OF ME...
...I DIDN'T EVEN GET TO SAY A PROPER GOOD-BYE...
I WISH I COULD SEE THEM.
...BUT WHEN I SUGGESTED THAT...
YOU WANT MITA-SAN'S CONTACT INFO?
I'M SURE I COULD DIG IT UP...
WHILE WE'RE ON THE SUBJECT, WHICH IS IT?
SHE'S NOT REALLY ONE OR THE OTHER.
SO SHE'S ETSUKO AND NANAKO ...?
I WONDER WHAT SHE'S LIKE.
AS A HOUSEKEEPER, MITA-SAN'S THE BEST THERE IS.
ORIGINALLY ACTING AS TADAHIDE-SHI'S PERSONAL SECRETARY...
...MITA-SAN'S NOT THE KIND OF PERSON YOU WANT TO GET ON THE BAD SIDE OF THOUGH.
...HM?

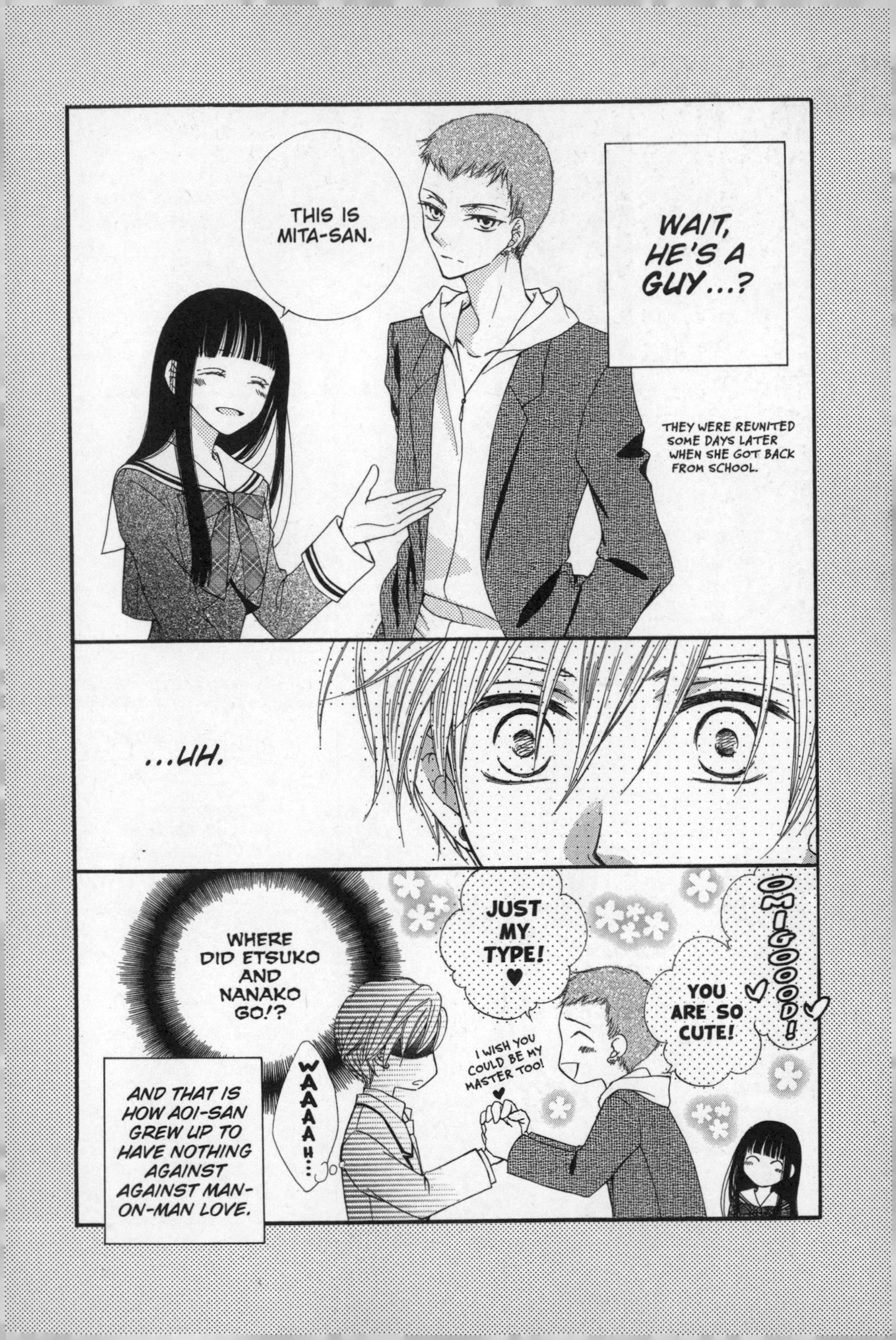
WAIT, HE'S A GUY...?
THIS IS MITA-SAN.
THEY WERE REUNITED SOME DAYS LATER WHEN SHE GOT BACK FROM SCHOOL.
...UH.
OMIGOOOD!
JUST MY TYPE! ♥
YOU ARE SO CUTE!
I WISH YOU COULD BE MY MASTER TOO! ♥
WHERE DID ETSUKO AND NANAKO GO!?
WAAAAAH...
AND THAT IS HOW AOI-SAN GREW UP TO HAVE NOTHING AGAINST AGAINST MAN-ON-MAN LOVE.

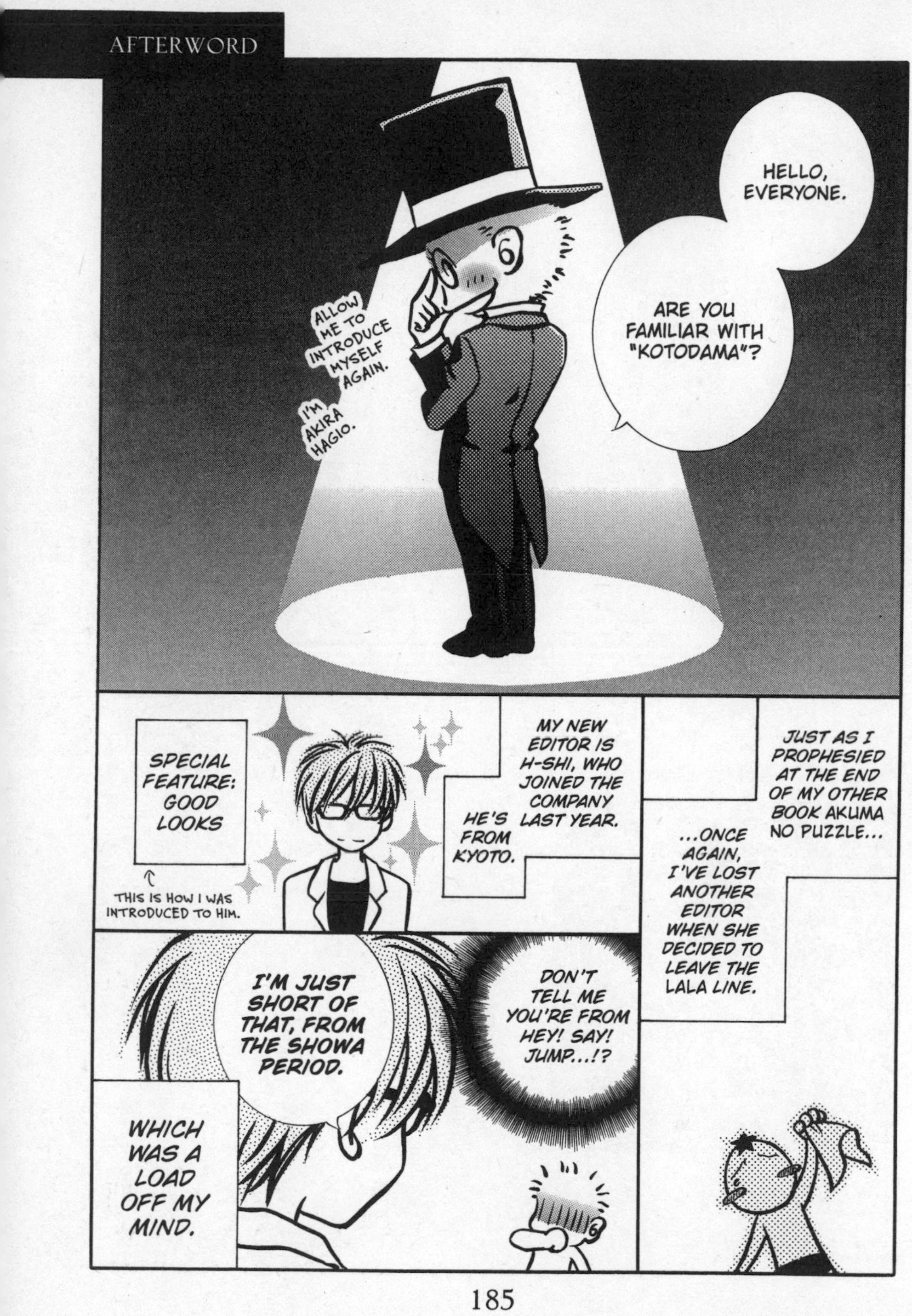
HELLO, EVERYONE.
ARE YOU FAMILIAR WITH "KOTODAMA"?
ALLOW ME TO INTRODUCE MYSELF AGAIN.
I'M AKIRA HAGIO.
JUST AS I PROPHESIED AT THE END OF MY OTHER BOOK AKUMA NO PUZZLE...
...ONCE AGAIN, I'VE LOST ANOTHER EDITOR WHEN SHE DECIDED TO LEAVE THE LALA LINE.
MY NEW EDITOR IS H-SHI, WHO JOINED THE COMPANY LAST YEAR.
HE'S FROM KYOTO.
SPECIAL FEATURE: GOOD LOOKS
↑ THIS IS HOW I WAS INTRODUCED TO HIM.
DON'T TELL ME YOU'RE FROM HEY! SAY! JUMP...!?
I'M JUST SHORT OF THAT, FROM THE SHOWA PERIOD.
WHICH WAS A LOAD OFF MY MIND.

Special Thanks!

KANAME HIRAMA-SAMA,
GARO-SAMA,
MOMO HACHIYA-SAMA,
SUGAWARA-SAMA,
MY SISTER, TOMO-CHAN,
HII-SAN, ALL MY EDITORS,
EVERYONE FROM THE EDITORIAL
DEPARTMENT, EVERYONE
INVOLVED IN THE PRINTING
AND MARKETING OF THIS BOOK,
AND YOU, FOR PICKING IT UP.
THANK YOU EVERYONE FOR
SUPPORTING ME!

The Secret Sakura Shares

The Secret Sakura Shares

The Secret Sakura Shares

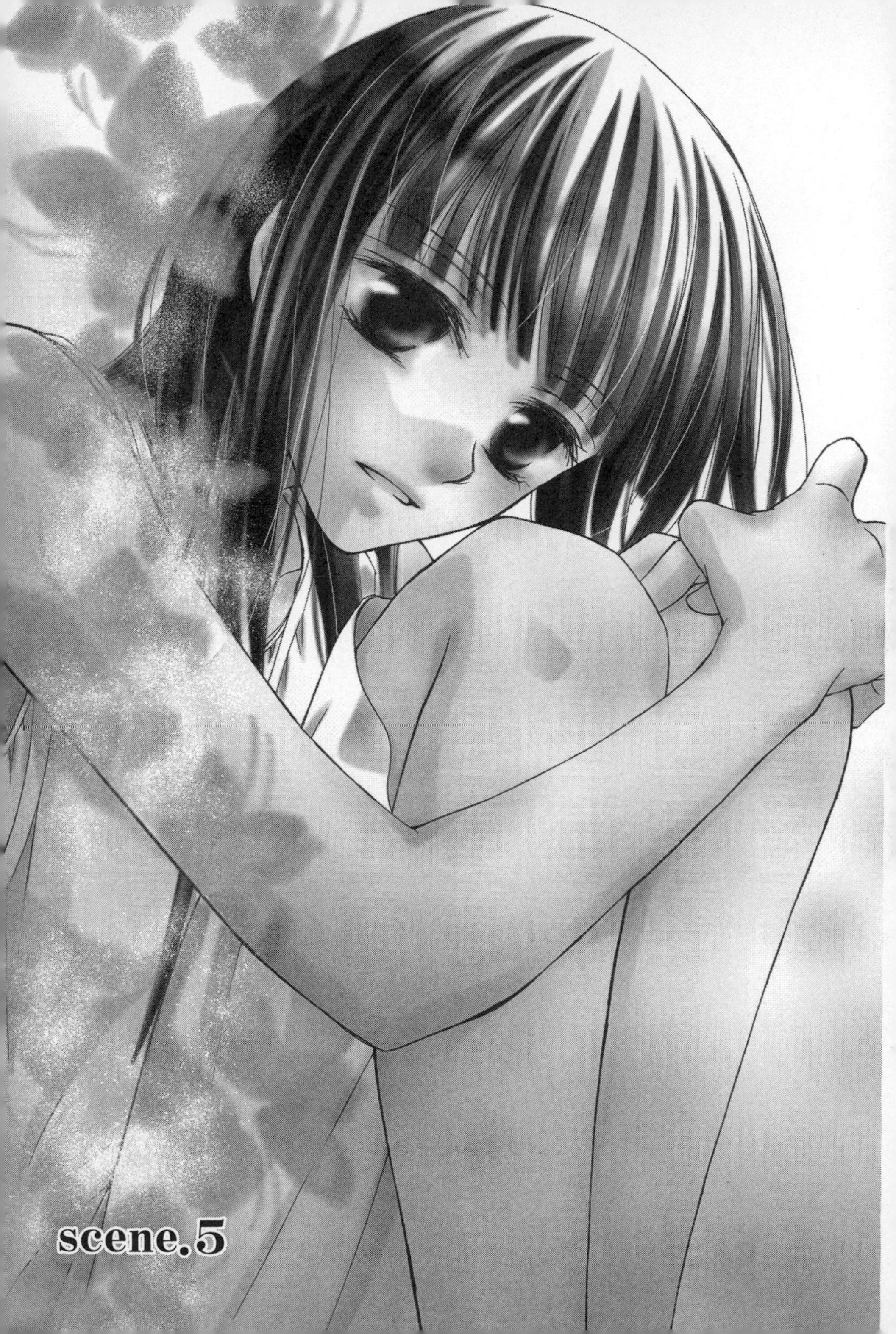
scene.5

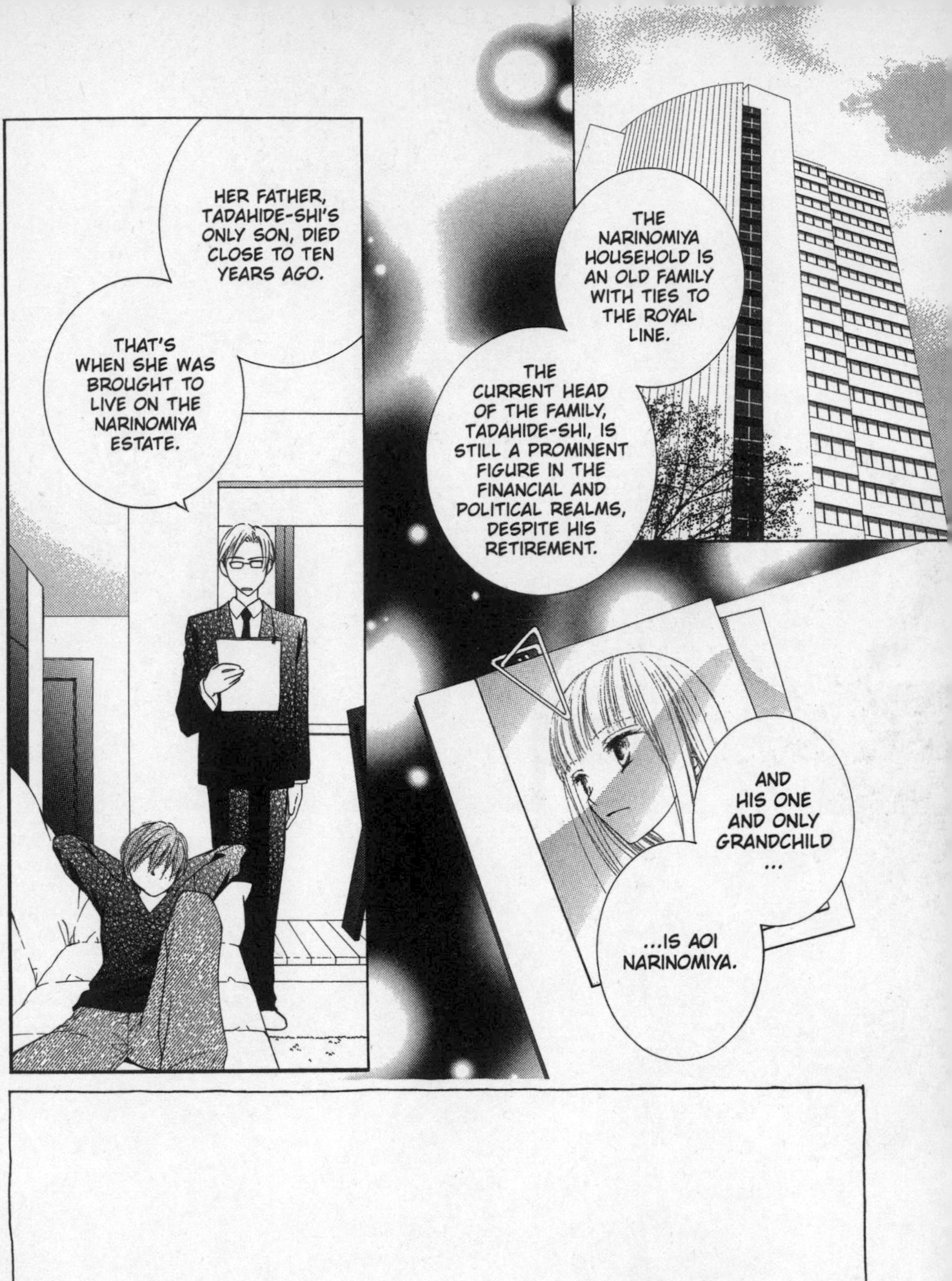
THE NARINOMIYA HOUSEHOLD IS AN OLD FAMILY WITH TIES TO THE ROYAL LINE.
THE CURRENT HEAD OF THE FAMILY, TADAHIDE-SHI, IS STILL A PROMINENT FIGURE IN THE FINANCIAL AND POLITICAL REALMS, DESPITE HIS RETIREMENT.
AND HIS ONE AND ONLY GRANDCHILD ...
...IS AOI NARINOMIYA.
HER FATHER, TADAHIDE-SHI'S ONLY SON, DIED CLOSE TO TEN YEARS AGO.
THAT'S WHEN SHE WAS BROUGHT TO LIVE ON THE NARINOMIYA ESTATE.

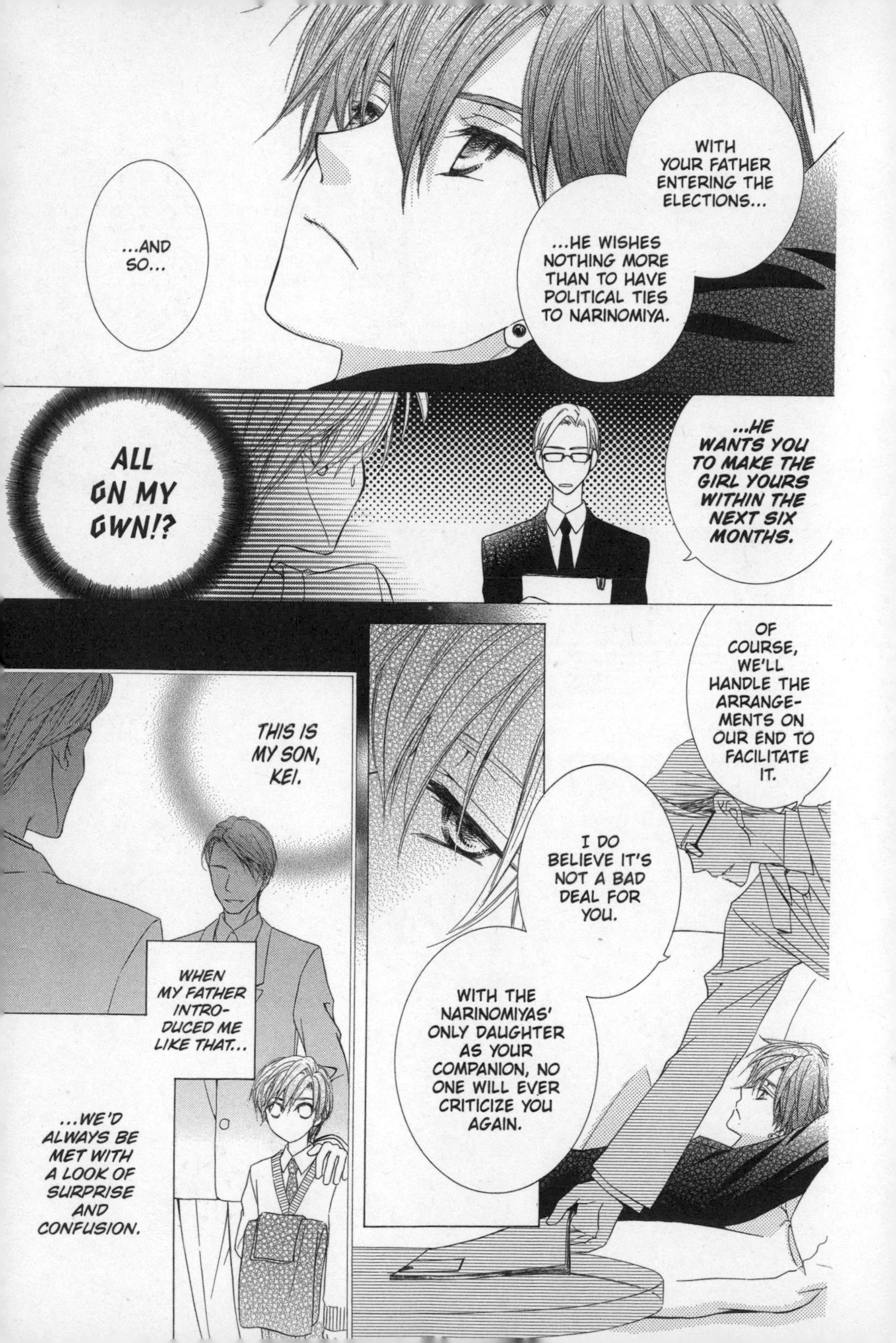
WITH YOUR FATHER ENTERING THE ELECTIONS...
...HE WISHES NOTHING MORE THAN TO HAVE POLITICAL TIES TO NARINOMIYA.
...AND SO...
...HE WANTS YOU TO MAKE THE GIRL YOURS WITHIN THE NEXT SIX MONTHS.
ALL ON MY OWN!?
OF COURSE, WE'LL HANDLE THE ARRANGE-MENTS ON OUR END TO FACILITATE IT.
I DO BELIEVE IT'S NOT A BAD DEAL FOR YOU.
WITH THE NARINOMIYAS' ONLY DAUGHTER AS YOUR COMPANION, NO ONE WILL EVER CRITICIZE YOU AGAIN.
THIS IS MY SON, KEI.
WHEN MY FATHER INTRO-DUCED ME LIKE THAT...
...WE'D ALWAYS BE MET WITH A LOOK OF SURPRISE AND CONFUSION.

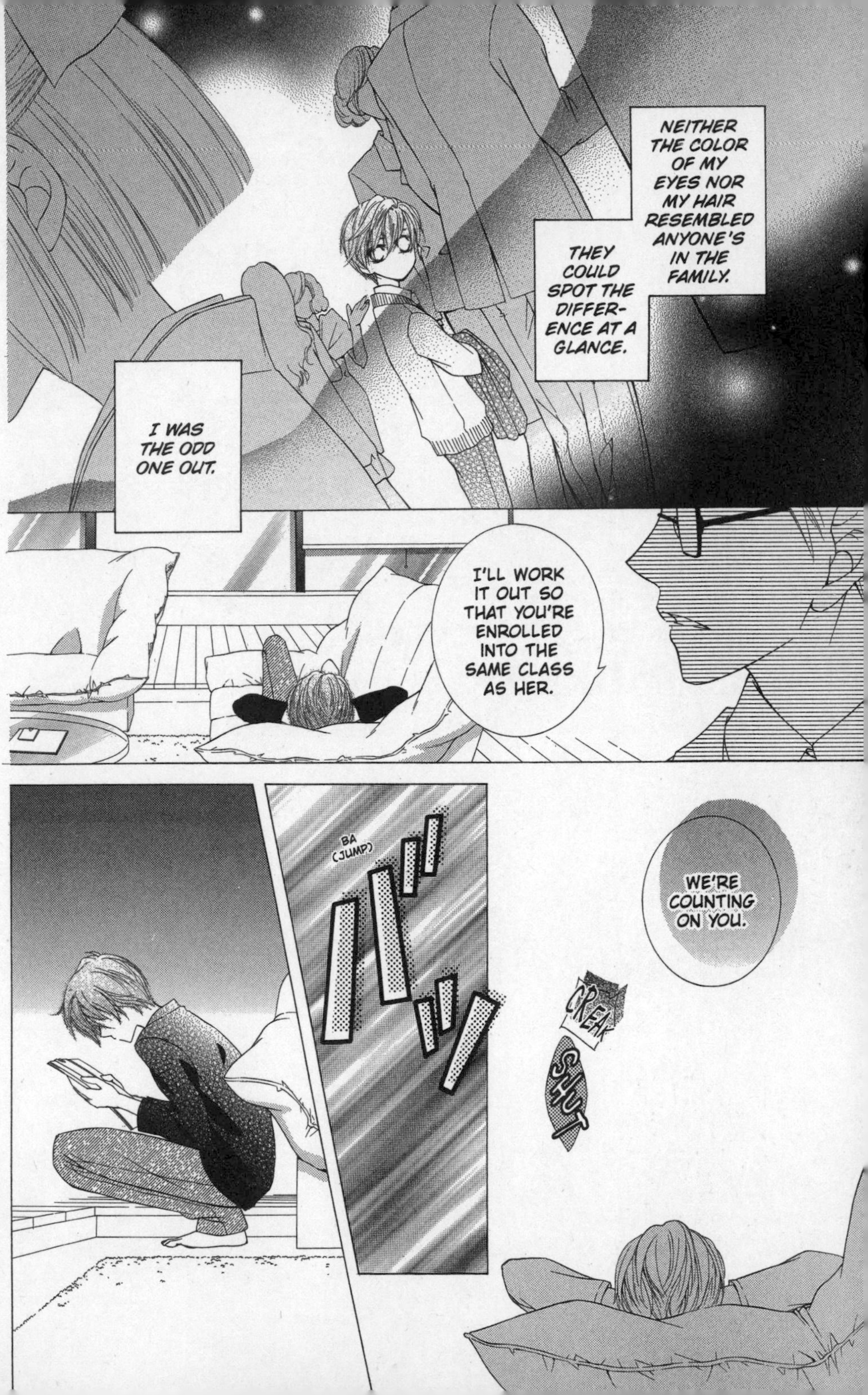
NEITHER THE COLOR OF MY EYES NOR MY HAIR RESEMBLED ANYONE'S IN THE FAMILY.
THEY COULD SPOT THE DIFFER-ENCE AT A GLANCE.
I WAS THE ODD ONE OUT.
I'LL WORK IT OUT SO THAT YOU'RE ENROLLED INTO THE SAME CLASS AS HER.
WE'RE COUNTING ON YOU.
CREAK
SHUT
BA (JUMP)

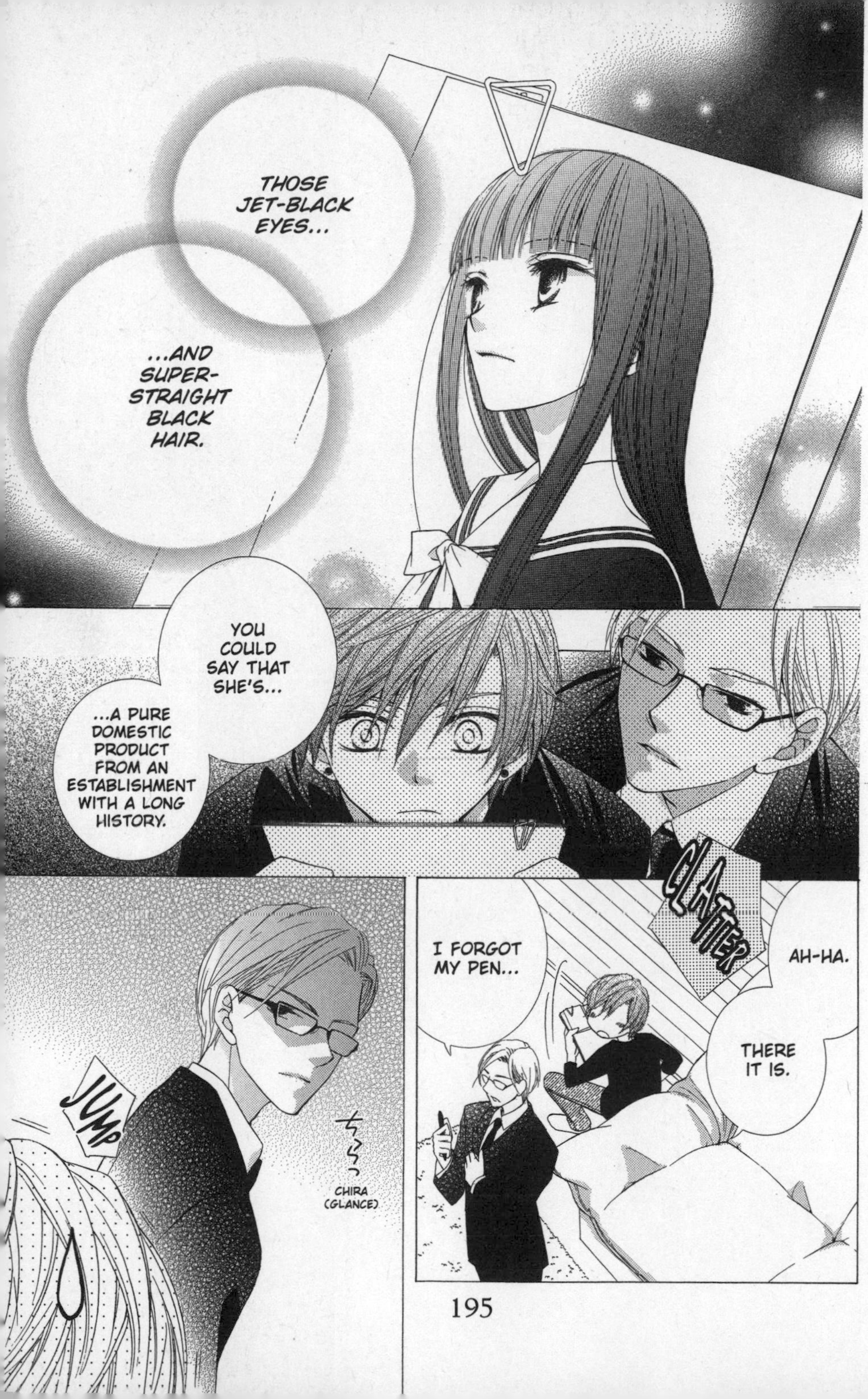
THOSE JET-BLACK EYES...
...AND SUPER-STRAIGHT BLACK HAIR.
YOU COULD SAY THAT SHE'S...
...A PURE DOMESTIC PRODUCT FROM AN ESTABLISHMENT WITH A LONG HISTORY.
CLATTER
I FORGOT MY PEN...
AH-HA.
THERE IT IS.
JUMP
CHIRA (GLANCE)

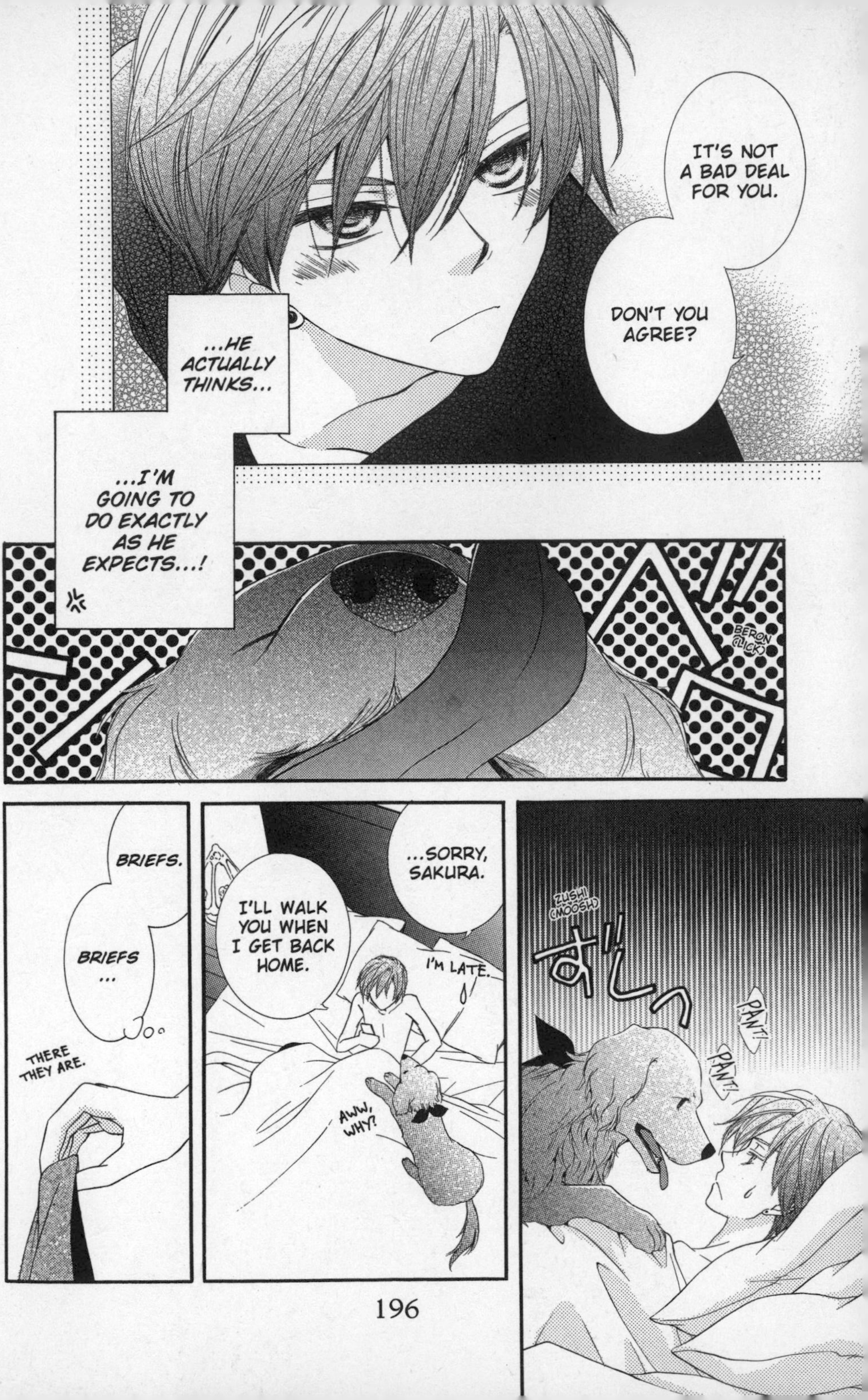
IT'S NOT A BAD DEAL FOR YOU.
DON'T YOU AGREE?
...HE ACTUALLY THINKS...
...I'M GOING TO DO EXACTLY AS HE EXPECTS...!
BERON (LICK)
ZUSH! (MOOSH)
PANT! PANT!
...SORRY, SAKURA.
I'LL WALK YOU WHEN I GET BACK HOME.
I'M LATE.
AWW, WHY?
BRIEFS.
BRIEFS...
THERE THEY ARE.

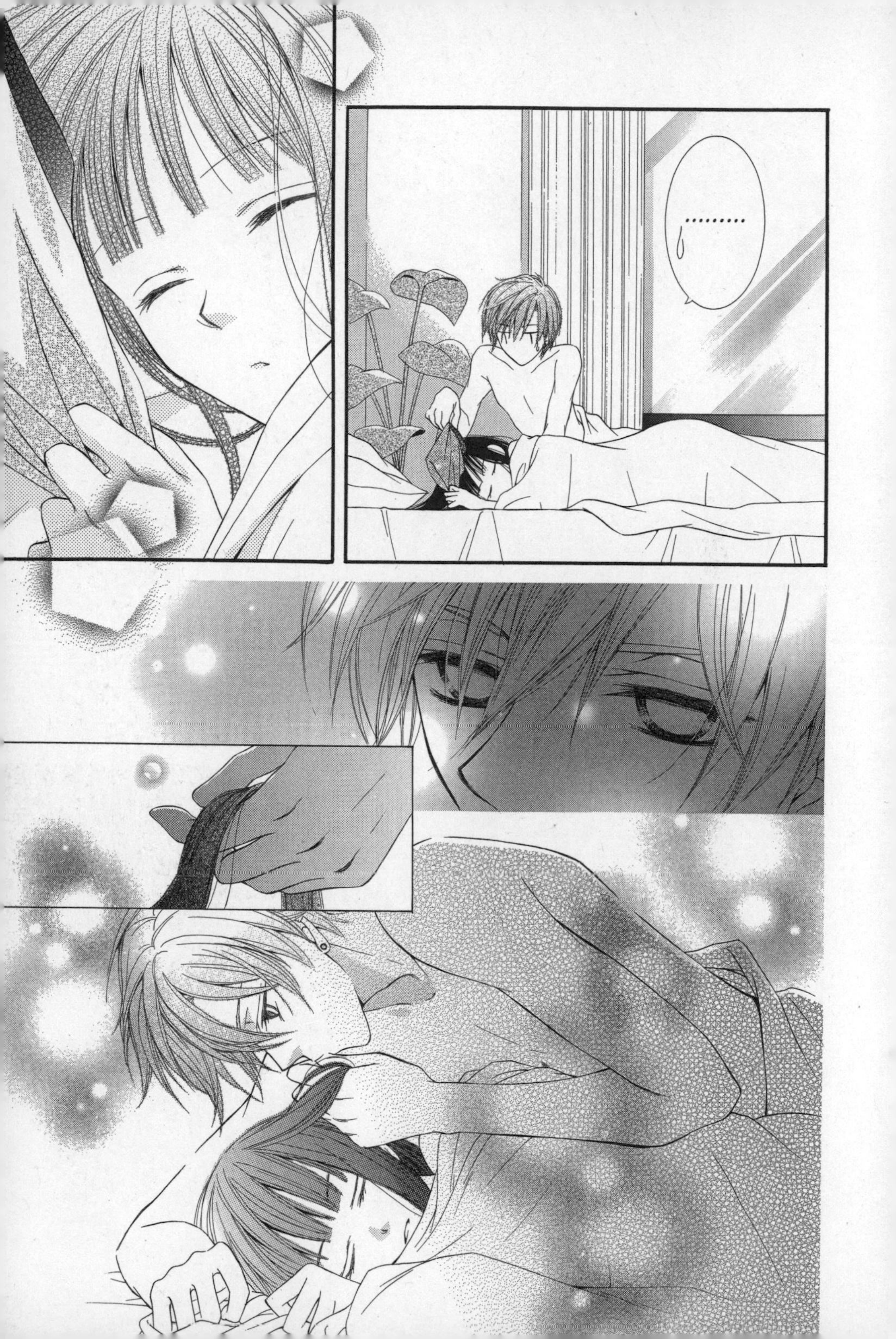
....

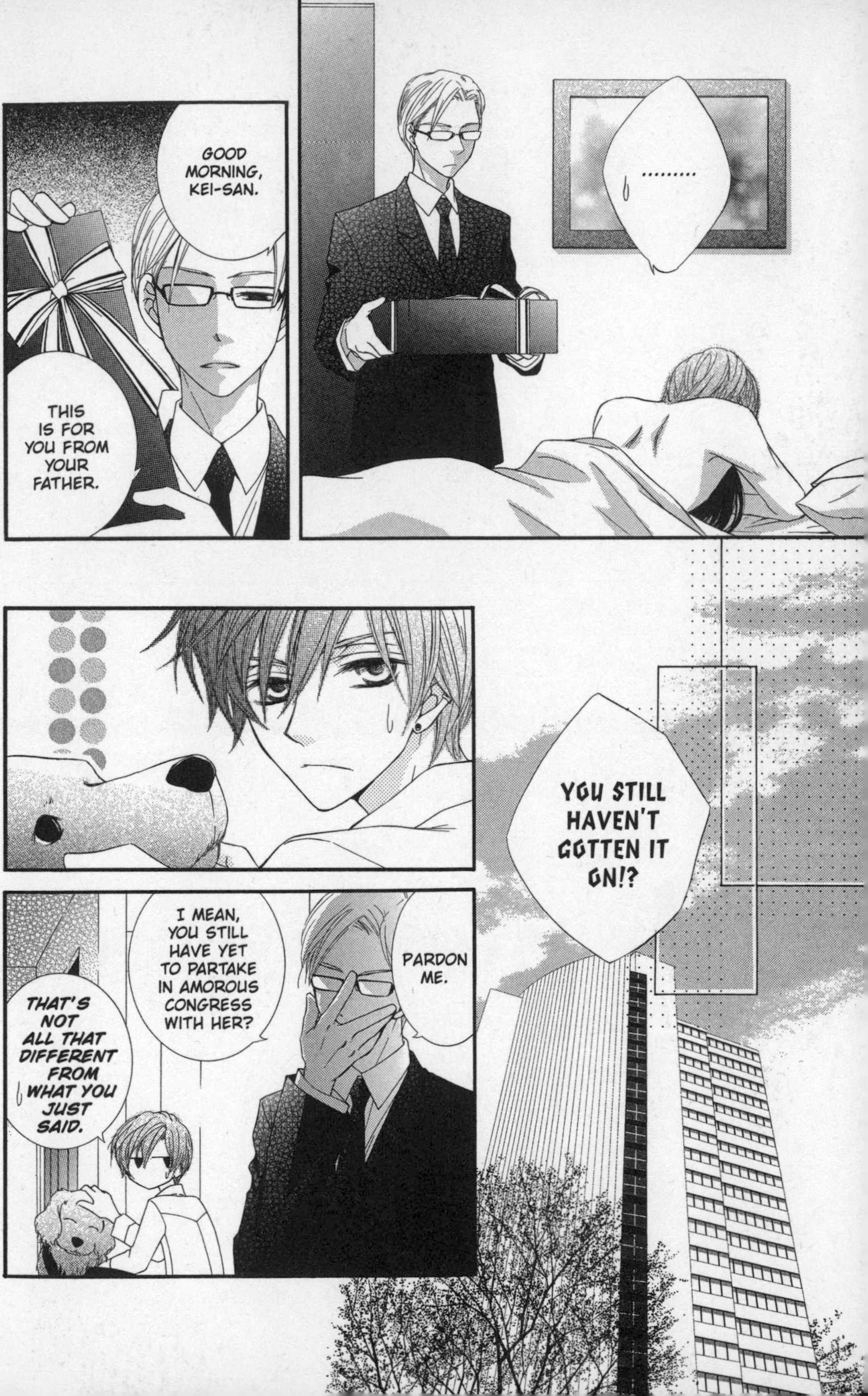
....
GOOD MORNING, KEI-SAN.
THIS IS FOR YOU FROM YOUR FATHER.
YOU STILL HAVEN'T GOTTEN IT ON!?
PARDON ME.
I MEAN, YOU STILL HAVE YET TO PARTAKE IN AMOROUS CONGRESS WITH HER?
THAT'S NOT ALL THAT DIFFERENT FROM WHAT YOU JUST SAID.

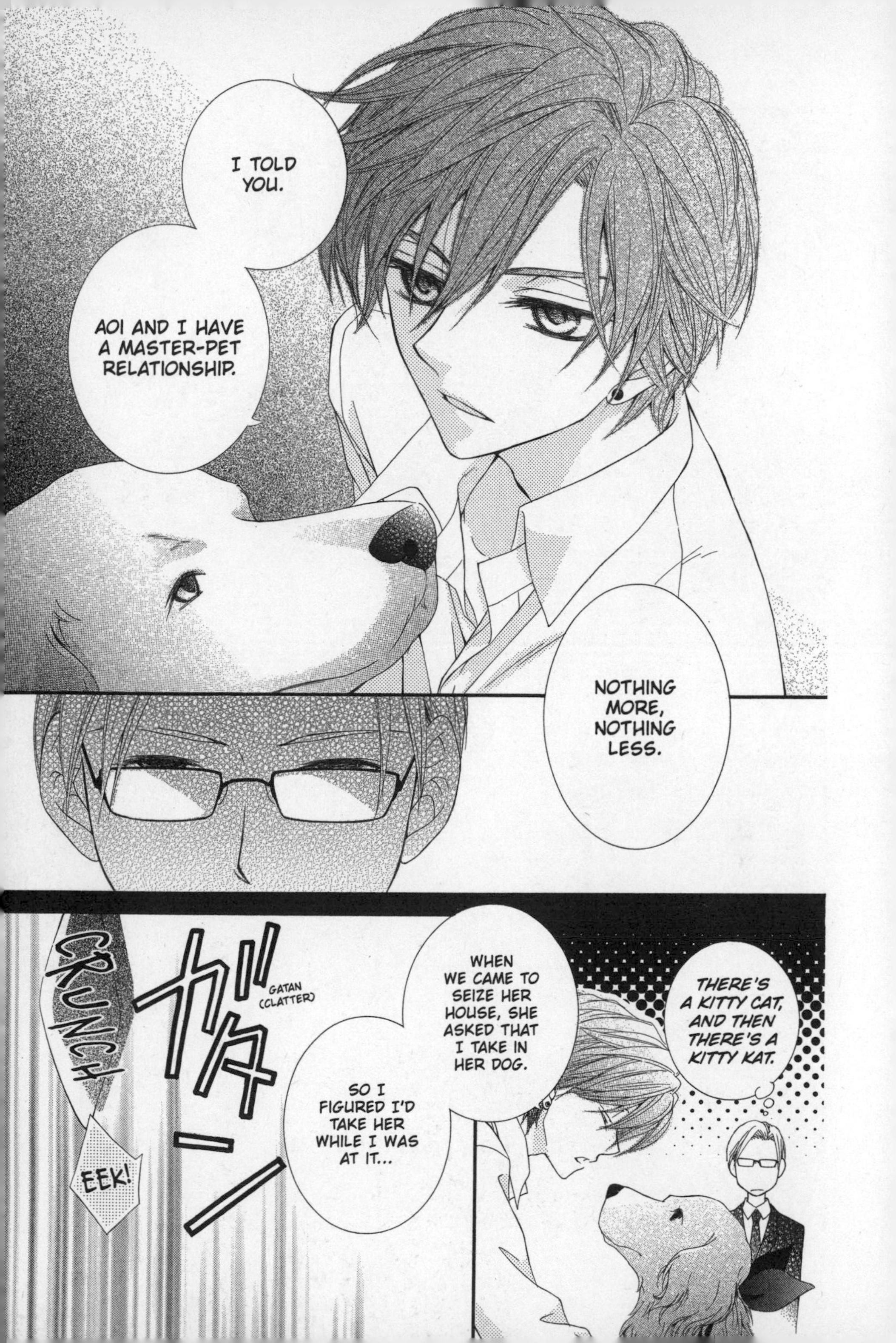
I TOLD YOU.
AOI AND I HAVE A MASTER-PET RELATIONSHIP.
NOTHING MORE, NOTHING LESS.
THERE'S A KITTY CAT, AND THEN THERE'S A KITTY KAT.
WHEN WE CAME TO SEIZE HER HOUSE, SHE ASKED THAT I TAKE IN HER DOG.
SO I FIGURED I'D TAKE HER WHILE I WAS AT IT...
GATAN (CLATTER)
CRUNCH
EEK!

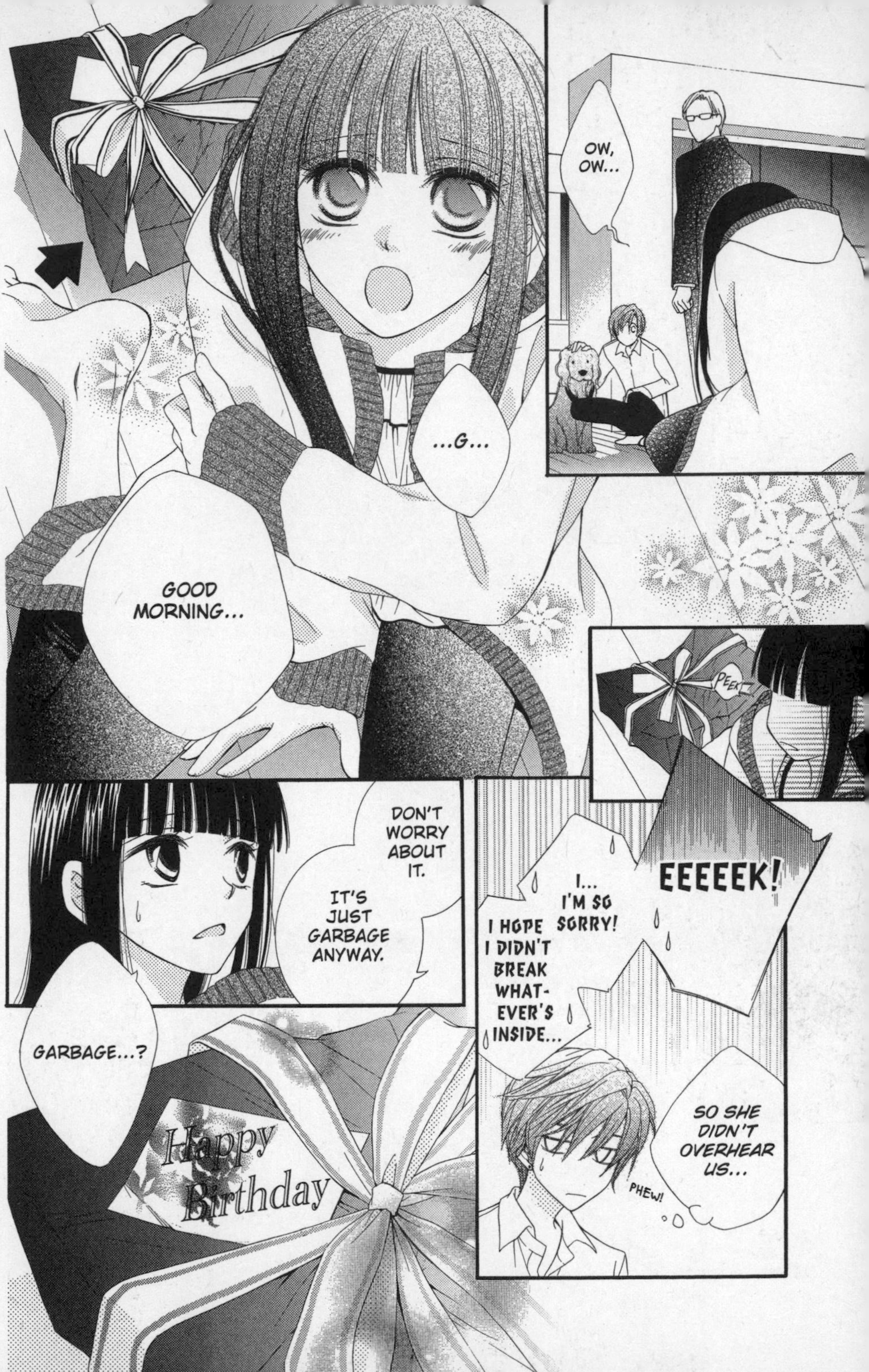
OW, OW...
PEEK
...G...
GOOD MORNING...
EEEEEK!
I... I'M SO SORRY!
I HOPE I DIDN'T BREAK WHATEVER'S INSIDE...
SO SHE DIDN'T OVERHEAR US...
PHEW!
DON'T WORRY ABOUT IT.
IT'S JUST GARBAGE ANYWAY.
GARBAGE...?
Happy Birthday

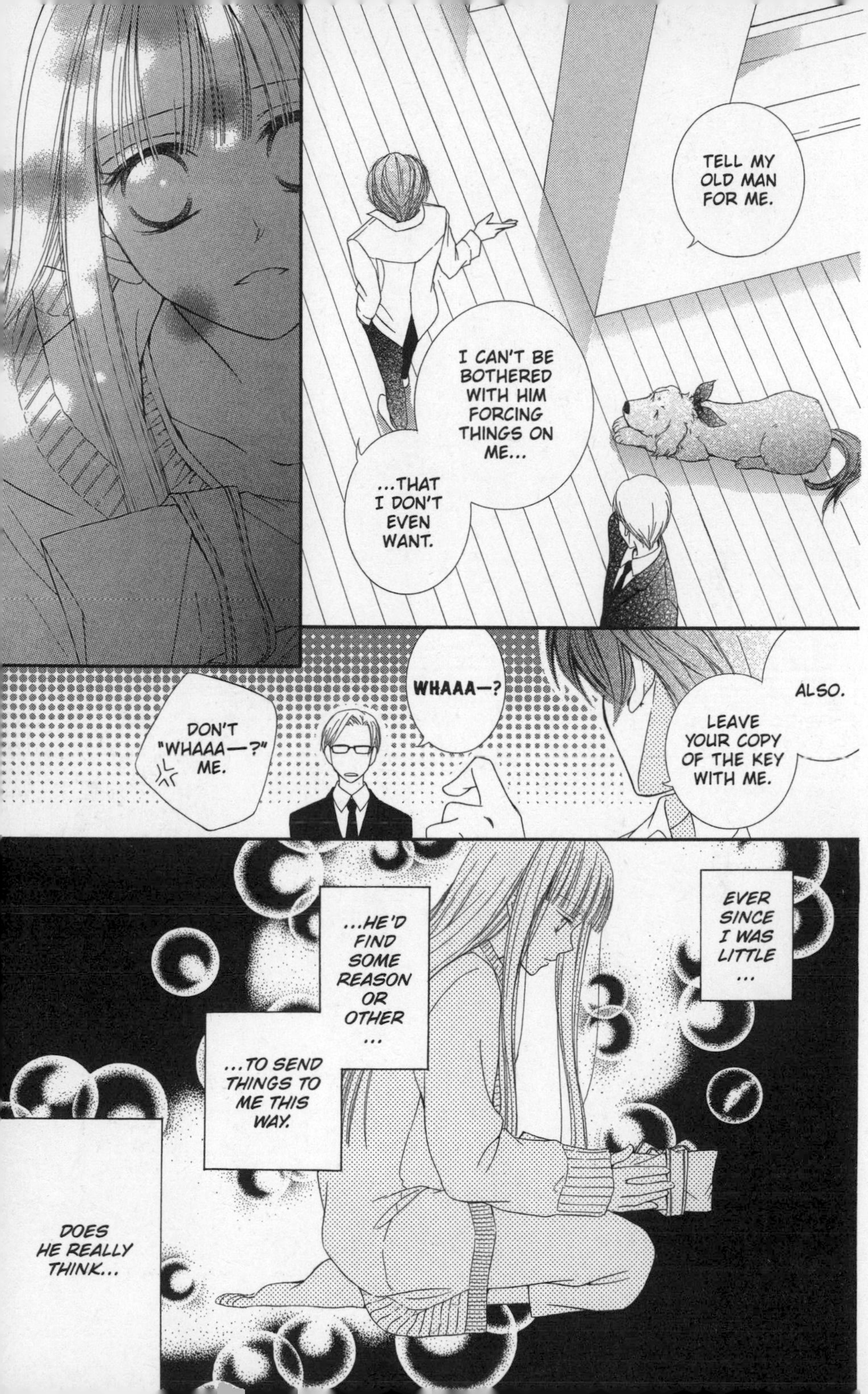
TELL MY OLD MAN FOR ME.
I CAN'T BE BOTHERED WITH HIM FORCING THINGS ON ME...
...THAT I DON'T EVEN WANT.
ALSO.
LEAVE YOUR COPY OF THE KEY WITH ME.
WHAAA—?
DON'T "WHAAA—?" ME.
EVER SINCE I WAS LITTLE...
...HE'D FIND SOME REASON OR OTHER...
...TO SEND THINGS TO ME THIS WAY.
DOES HE REALLY THINK...

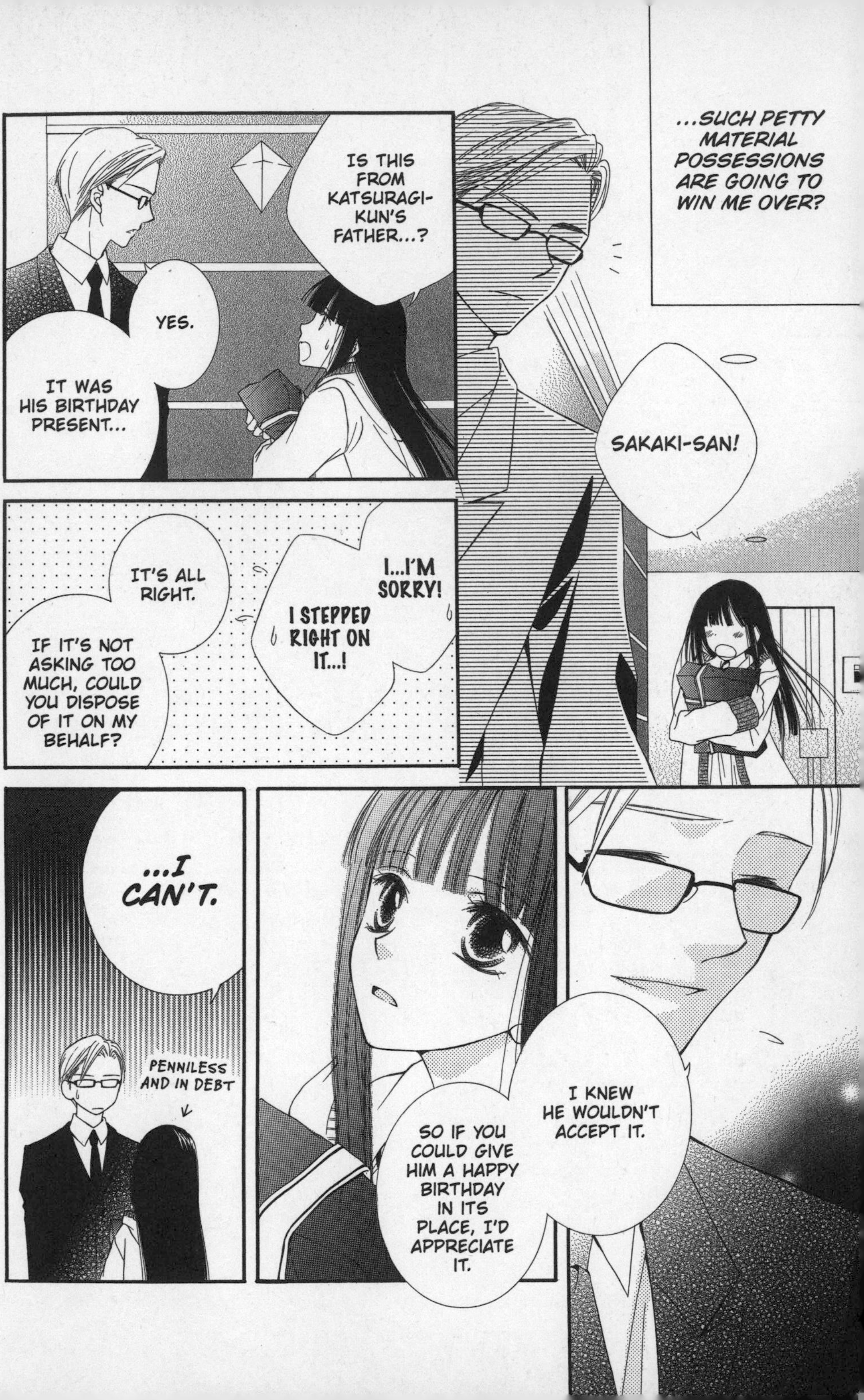
...SUCH PETTY MATERIAL POSSESSIONS ARE GOING TO WIN ME OVER?
SAKAKI-SAN!
IS THIS FROM KATSURAGI-KUN'S FATHER...?
YES.
IT WAS HIS BIRTHDAY PRESENT...
I...I'M SORRY!
I STEPPED RIGHT ON IT...!
IT'S ALL RIGHT.
IF IT'S NOT ASKING TOO MUCH, COULD YOU DISPOSE OF IT ON MY BEHALF?
I KNEW HE WOULDN'T ACCEPT IT.
SO IF YOU COULD GIVE HIM A HAPPY BIRTHDAY IN ITS PLACE, I'D APPRECIATE IT.
...I CAN'T.
PENNILESS AND IN DEBT

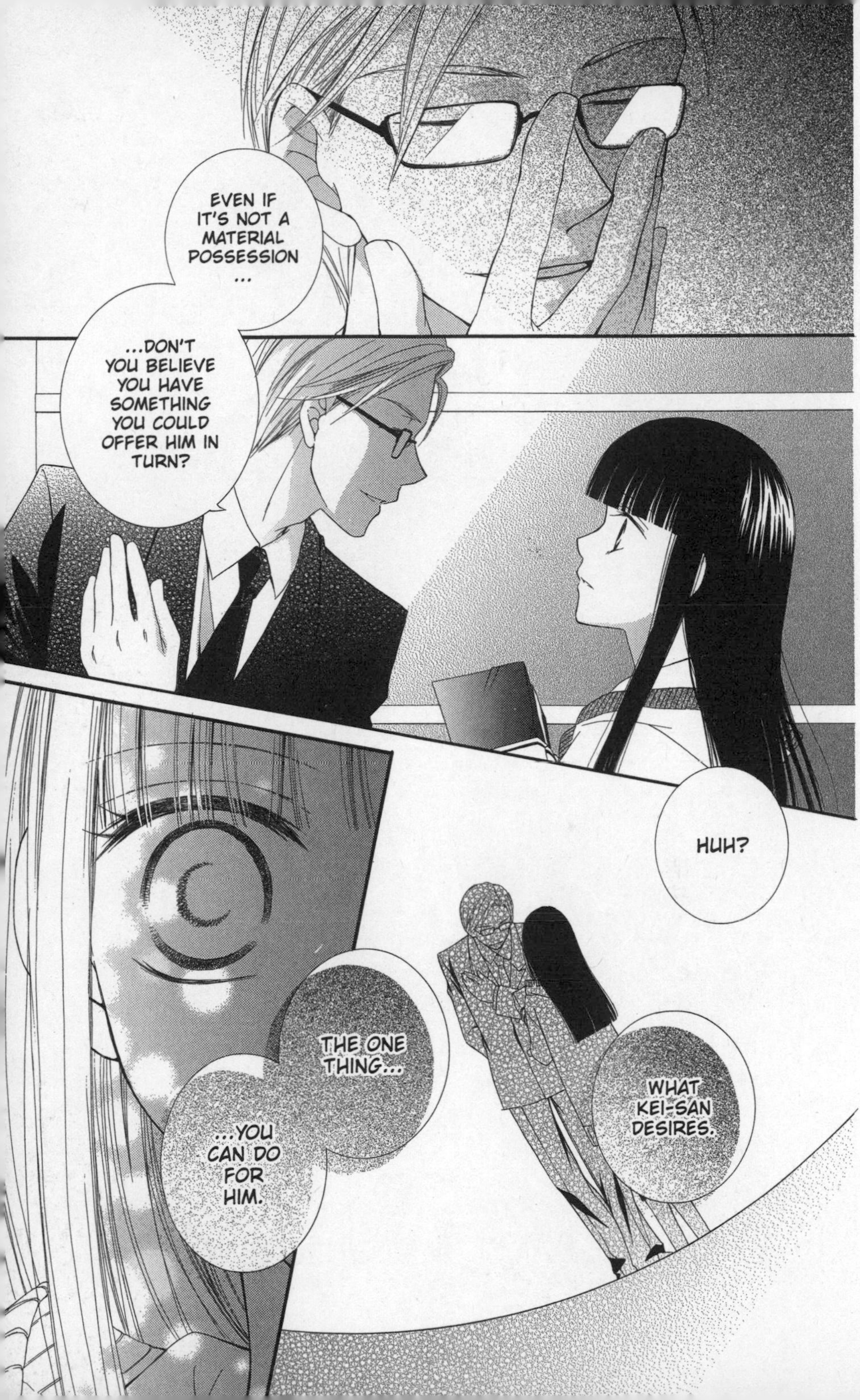
EVEN IF IT'S NOT A MATERIAL POSSESSION ...
...DON'T YOU BELIEVE YOU HAVE SOMETHING YOU COULD OFFER HIM IN TURN?
HUH?
THE ONE THING...
WHAT KEI-SAN DESIRES.
...YOU CAN DO FOR HIM.

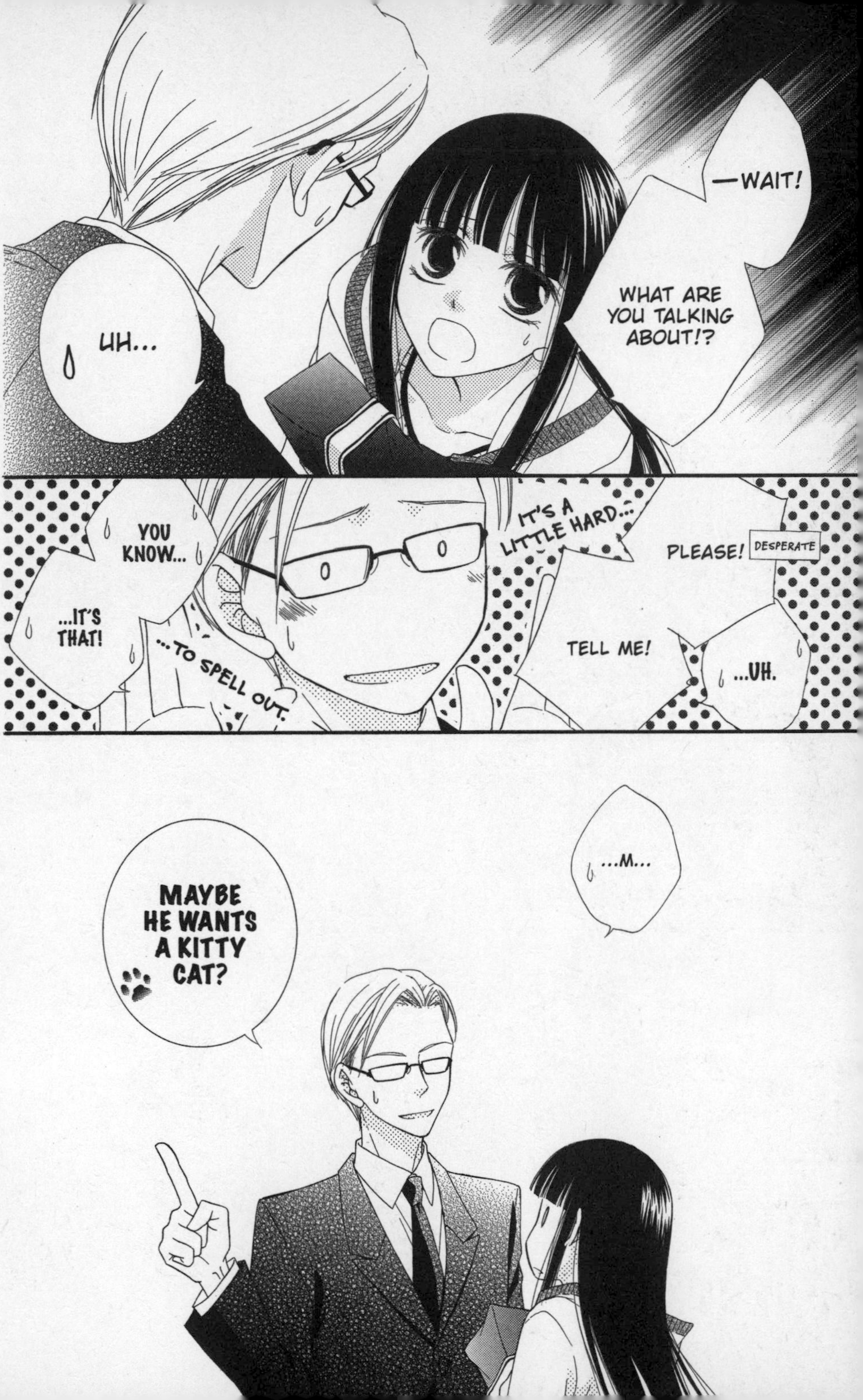
—WAIT!
WHAT ARE YOU TALKING ABOUT!?
UH...
PLEASE!
DESPERATE
TELL ME!
...UH.
IT'S A LITTLE HARD...
...TO SPELL OUT.
YOU KNOW...
...IT'S THAT!
...M...
MAYBE HE WANTS A KITTY CAT?

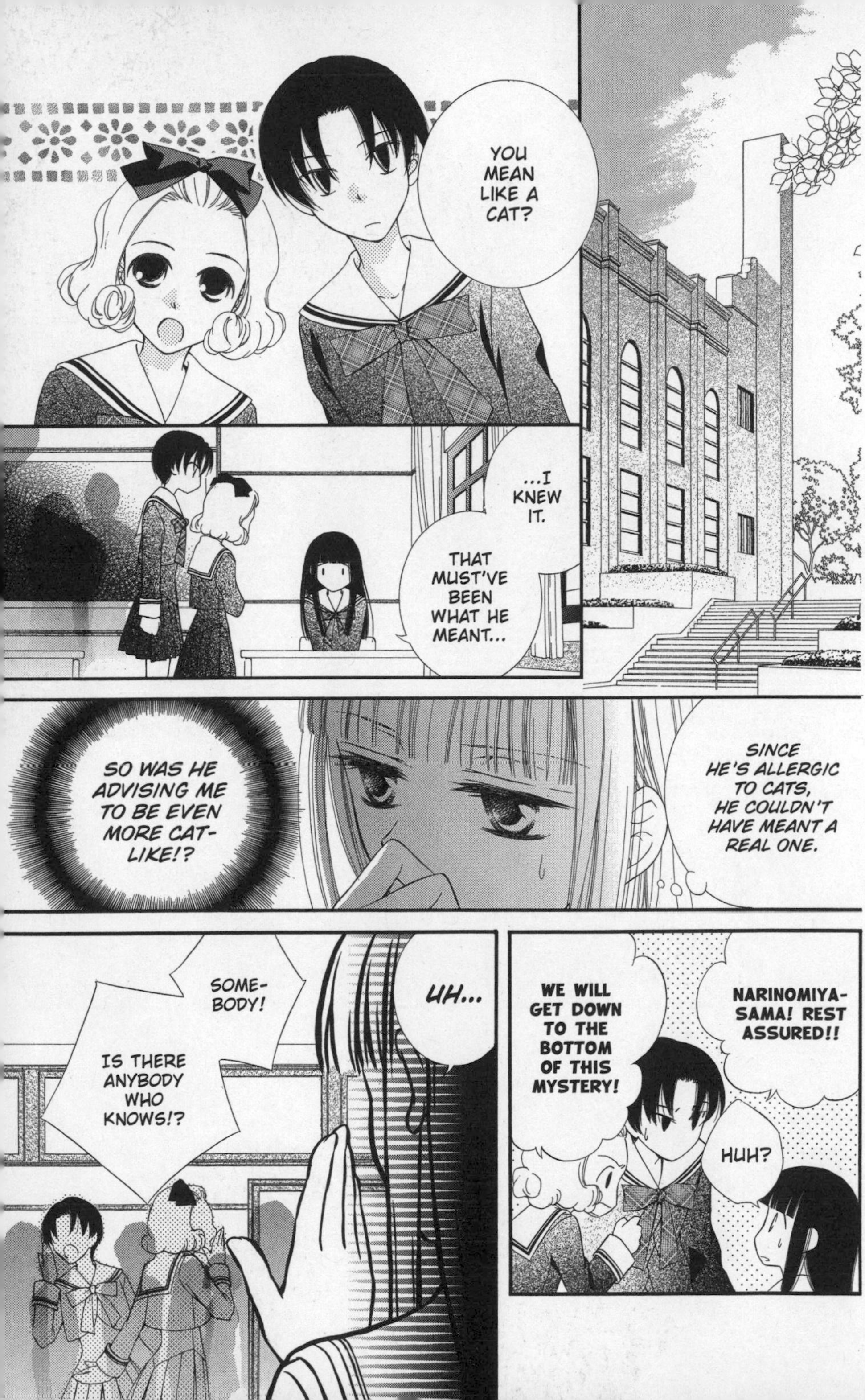
YOU MEAN LIKE A CAT?
...I KNEW IT.
THAT MUST'VE BEEN WHAT HE MEANT...
SINCE HE'S ALLERGIC TO CATS, HE COULDN'T HAVE MEANT A REAL ONE.
SO WAS HE ADVISING ME TO BE EVEN MORE CAT-LIKE!?
NARINOMIYA-SAMA! REST ASSURED!!
WE WILL GET DOWN TO THE BOTTOM OF THIS MYSTERY!
HUH?
UH...
SOME-BODY!
IS THERE ANYBODY WHO KNOWS!?

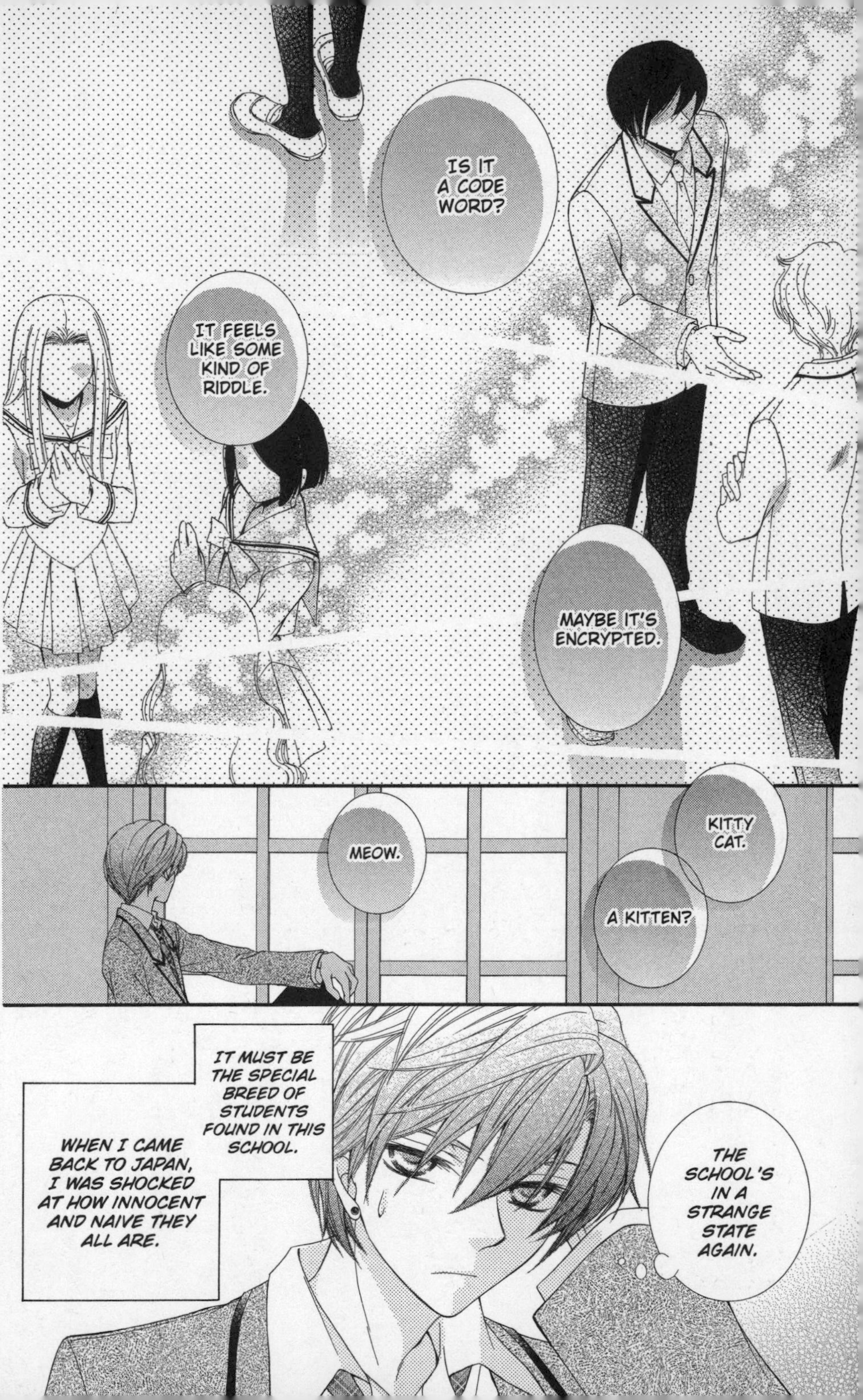
IS IT A CODE WORD?
IT FEELS LIKE SOME KIND OF RIDDLE.
MAYBE IT'S ENCRYPTED.
KITTY CAT.
A KITTEN?
MEOW.
THE SCHOOL'S IN A STRANGE STATE AGAIN.
IT MUST BE THE SPECIAL BREED OF STUDENTS FOUND IN THIS SCHOOL.
WHEN I CAME BACK TO JAPAN, I WAS SHOCKED AT HOW INNOCENT AND NAIVE THEY ALL ARE.

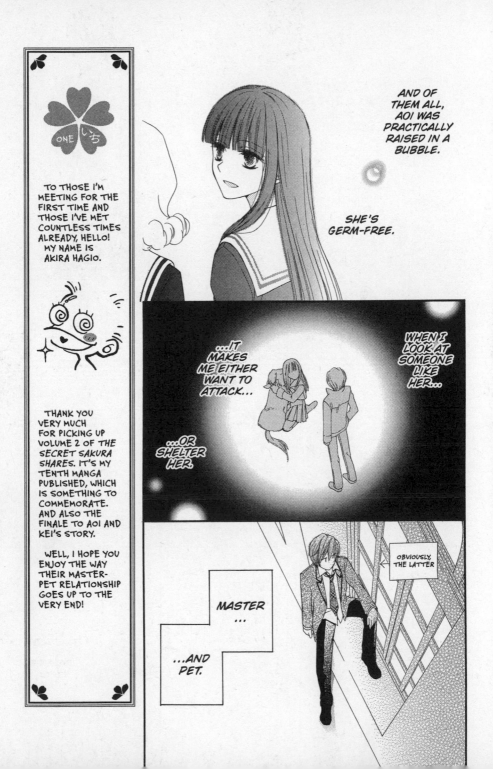

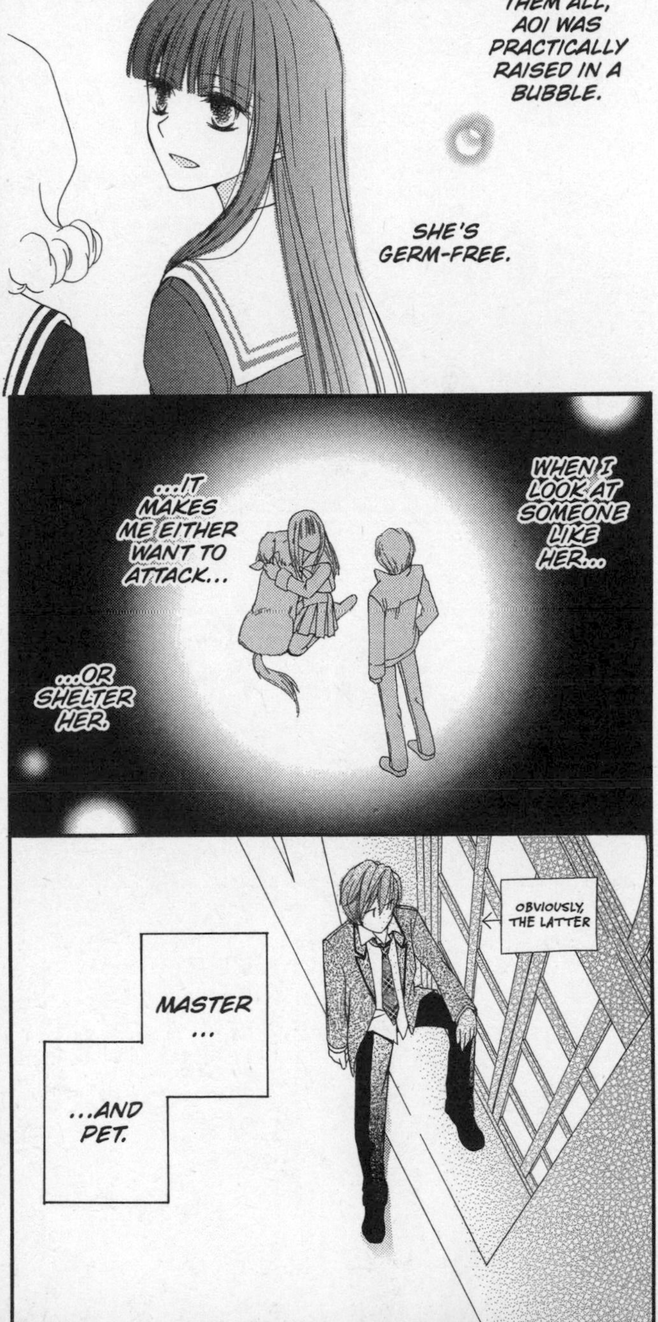
AND OF THEM ALL, AOI WAS PRACTICALLY RAISED IN A BUBBLE.
SHE'S GERM-FREE.
WHEN I LOOK AT SOMEONE LIKE HER...
...IT MAKES ME EITHER WANT TO ATTACK...
...OR SHELTER HER.
OBVIOUSLY, THE LATTER
MASTER...
...AND PET.

ONE いち

TO THOSE I'M MEETING FOR THE FIRST TIME AND THOSE I'VE MET COUNTLESS TIMES ALREADY, HELLO! MY NAME IS AKIRA HAGIO.

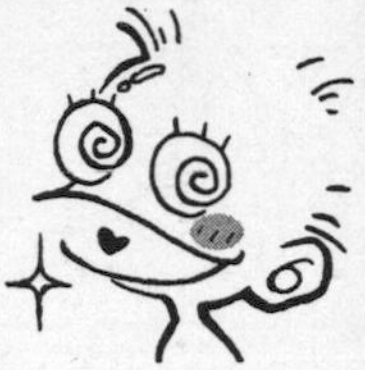

THANK YOU VERY MUCH FOR PICKING UP VOLUME 2 OF THE SECRET SAKURA SHARES. IT'S MY TENTH MANGA PUBLISHED, WHICH IS SOMETHING TO COMMEMORATE. AND ALSO THE FINALE TO AOI AND KEI'S STORY.

WELL, I HOPE YOU ENJOY THE WAY THEIR MASTER-PET RELATIONSHIP GOES UP TO THE VERY END!

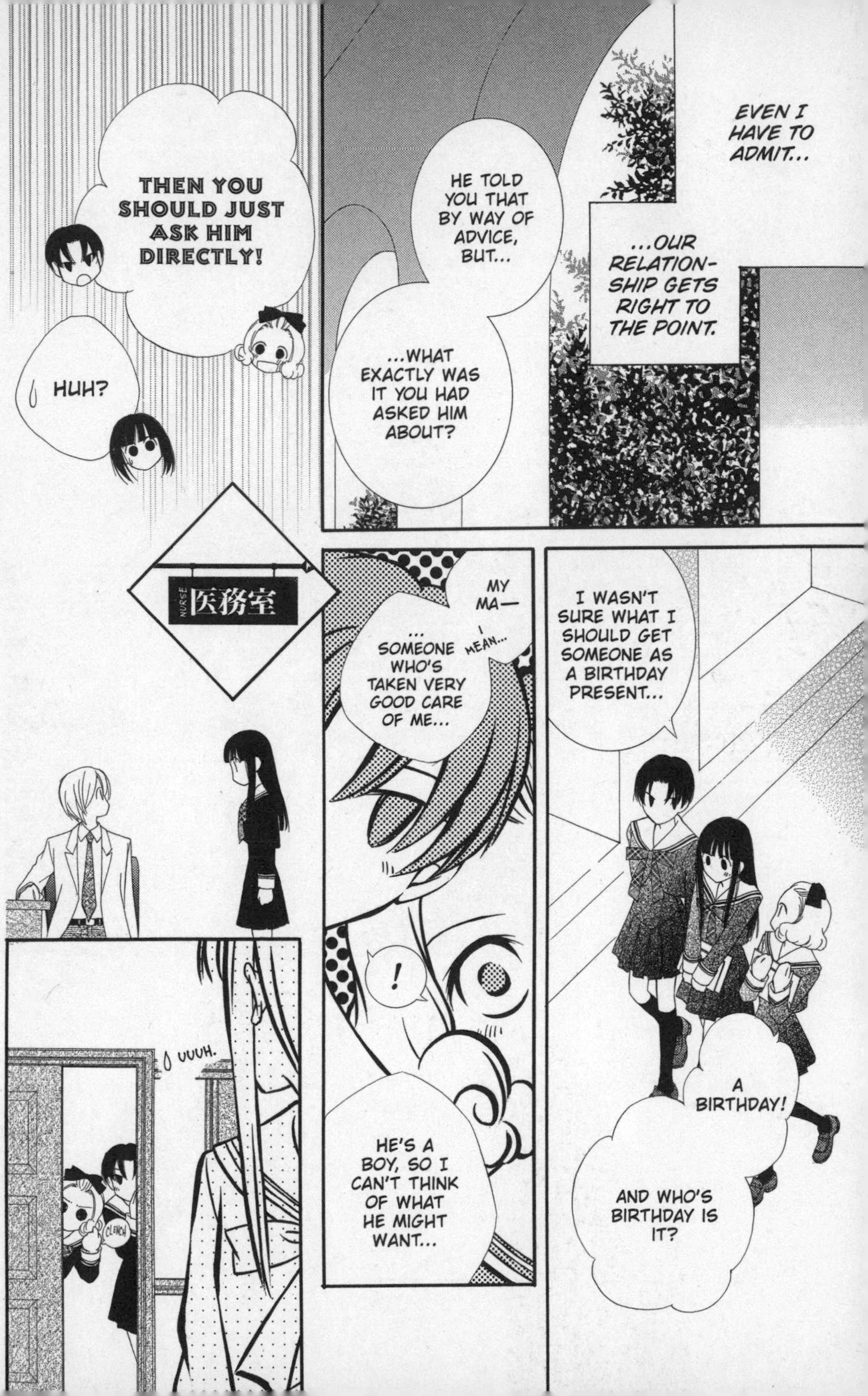
EVEN I HAVE TO ADMIT...
...OUR RELATIONSHIP GETS RIGHT TO THE POINT.
HE TOLD YOU THAT BY WAY OF ADVICE, BUT...
...WHAT EXACTLY WAS IT YOU HAD ASKED HIM ABOUT?
THEN YOU SHOULD JUST ASK HIM DIRECTLY!
HUH?
I WASN'T SURE WHAT I SHOULD GET SOMEONE AS A BIRTHDAY PRESENT...
A BIRTHDAY!
AND WHO'S BIRTHDAY IS IT?
MY MA—
I MEAN...
...SOMEONE WHO'S TAKEN VERY GOOD CARE OF ME...
!
HE'S A BOY, SO I CAN'T THINK OF WHAT HE MIGHT WANT...
NURSE 医務室
UUUH.
CLENCH

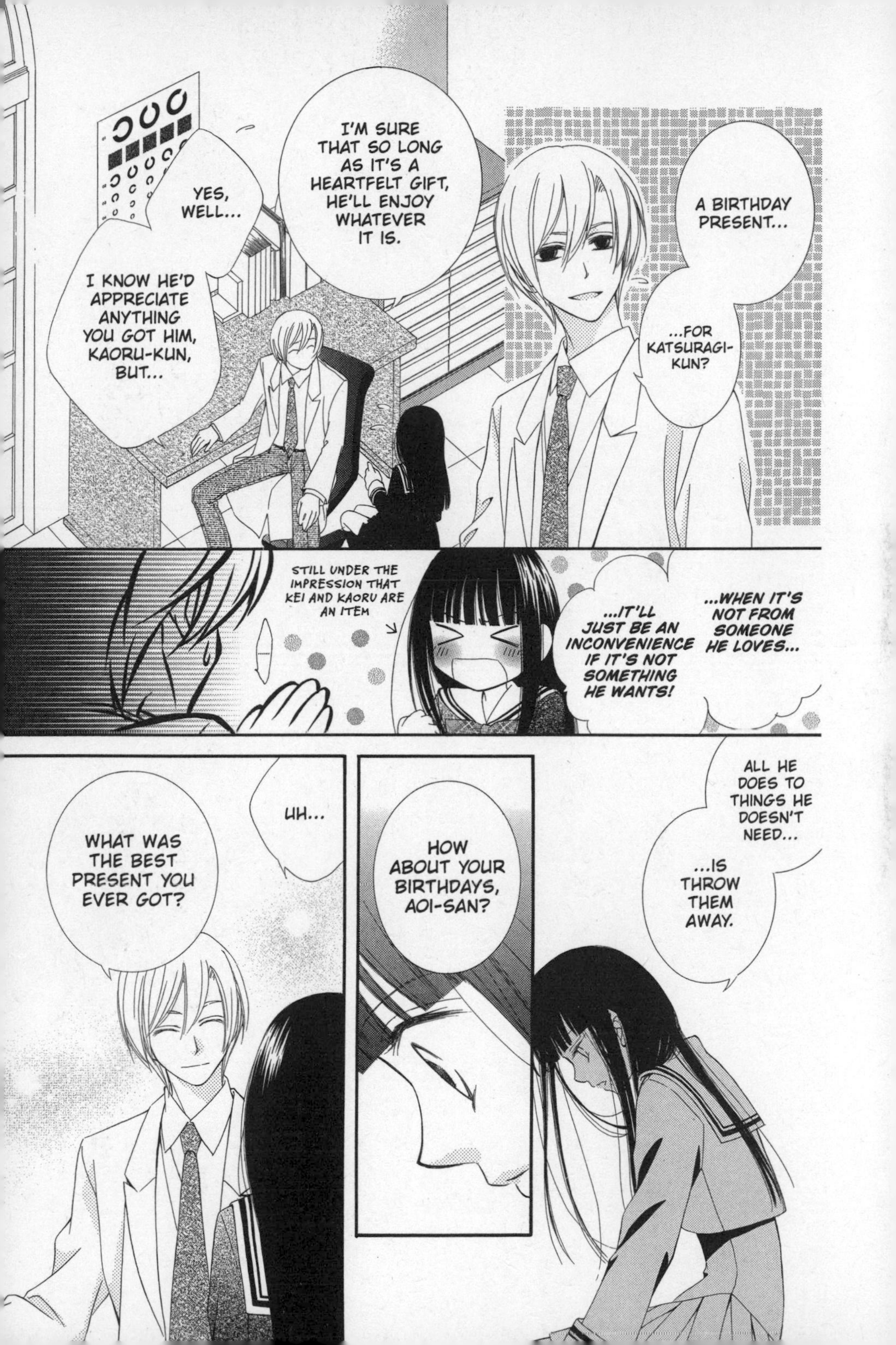
A BIRTHDAY PRESENT...
...FOR KATSURAGI-KUN?
I'M SURE THAT SO LONG AS IT'S A HEARTFELT GIFT, HE'LL ENJOY WHATEVER IT IS.
YES, WELL...
I KNOW HE'D APPRECIATE ANYTHING YOU GOT HIM, KAORU-KUN, BUT...
...WHEN IT'S NOT FROM SOMEONE HE LOVES...
...IT'LL JUST BE AN INCONVENIENCE IF IT'S NOT SOMETHING HE WANTS!
STILL UNDER THE IMPRESSION THAT KEI AND KAORU ARE AN ITEM
ALL HE DOES TO THINGS HE DOESN'T NEED...
...IS THROW THEM AWAY.
HOW ABOUT YOUR BIRTHDAYS, AOI-SAN?
UH...
WHAT WAS THE BEST PRESENT YOU EVER GOT?

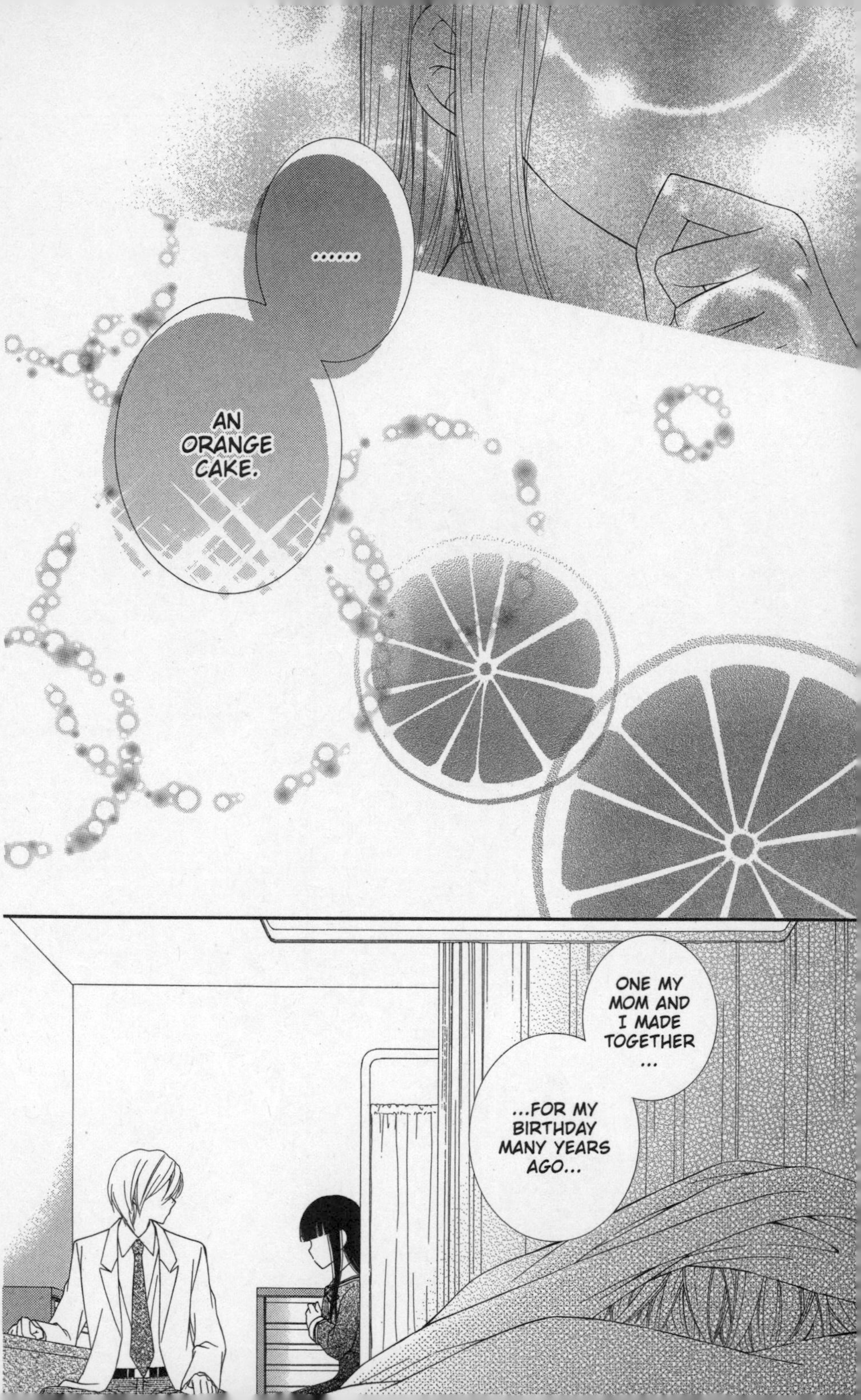
......
AN ORANGE CAKE.
ONE MY MOM AND I MADE TOGETHER ...
...FOR MY BIRTHDAY MANY YEARS AGO...

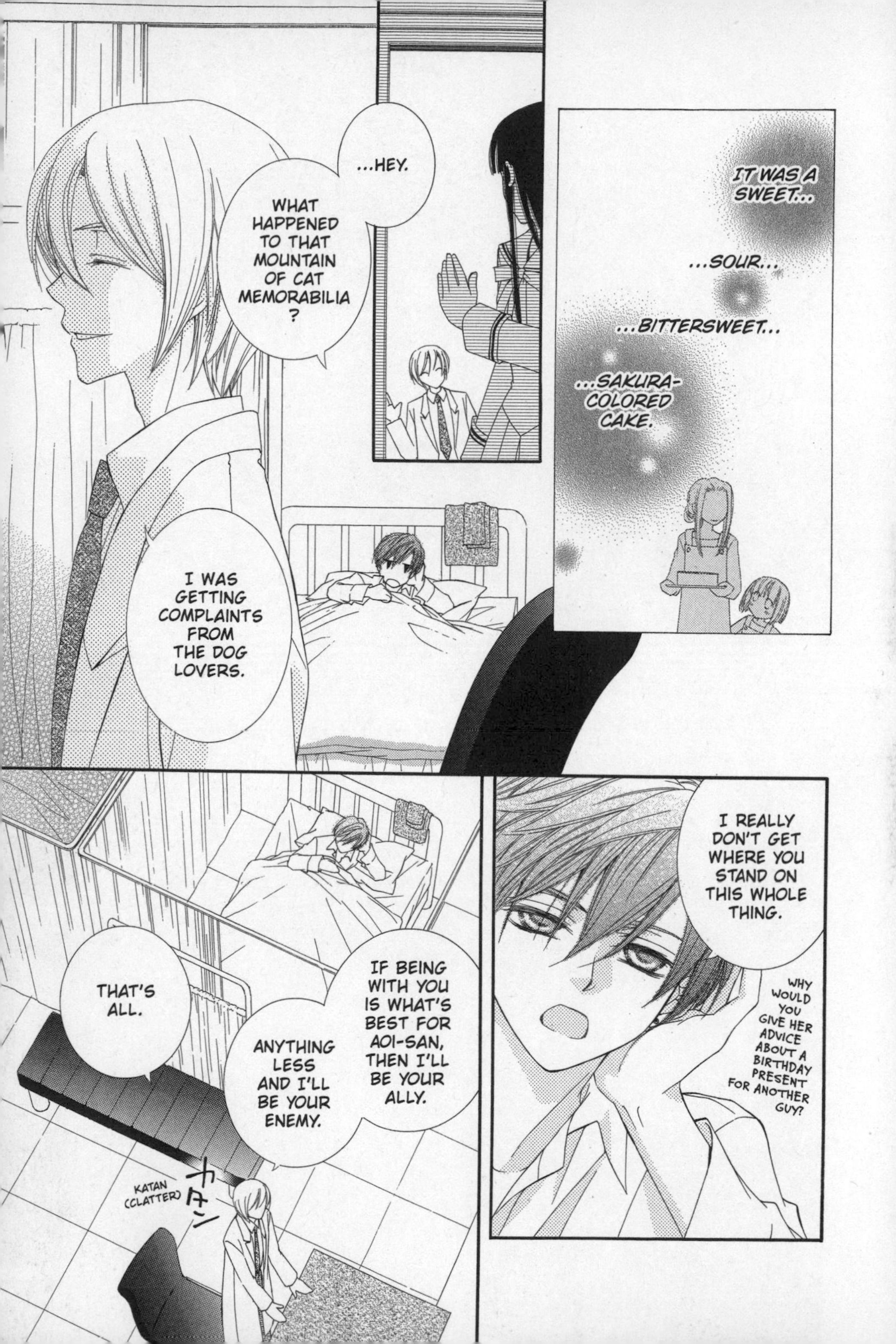
IT WAS A SWEET...
...SOUR...
...BITTERSWEET...
...SAKURA-COLORED CAKE.
...HEY.
WHAT HAPPENED TO THAT MOUNTAIN OF CAT MEMORABILIA ?
I WAS GETTING COMPLAINTS FROM THE DOG LOVERS.
I REALLY DON'T GET WHERE YOU STAND ON THIS WHOLE THING.
WHY WOULD YOU GIVE HER ADVICE ABOUT A BIRTHDAY PRESENT FOR ANOTHER GUY?
IF BEING WITH YOU IS WHAT'S BEST FOR AOI-SAN, THEN I'LL BE YOUR ALLY.
ANYTHING LESS AND I'LL BE YOUR ENEMY.
THAT'S ALL.
KATAN (CLATTER)

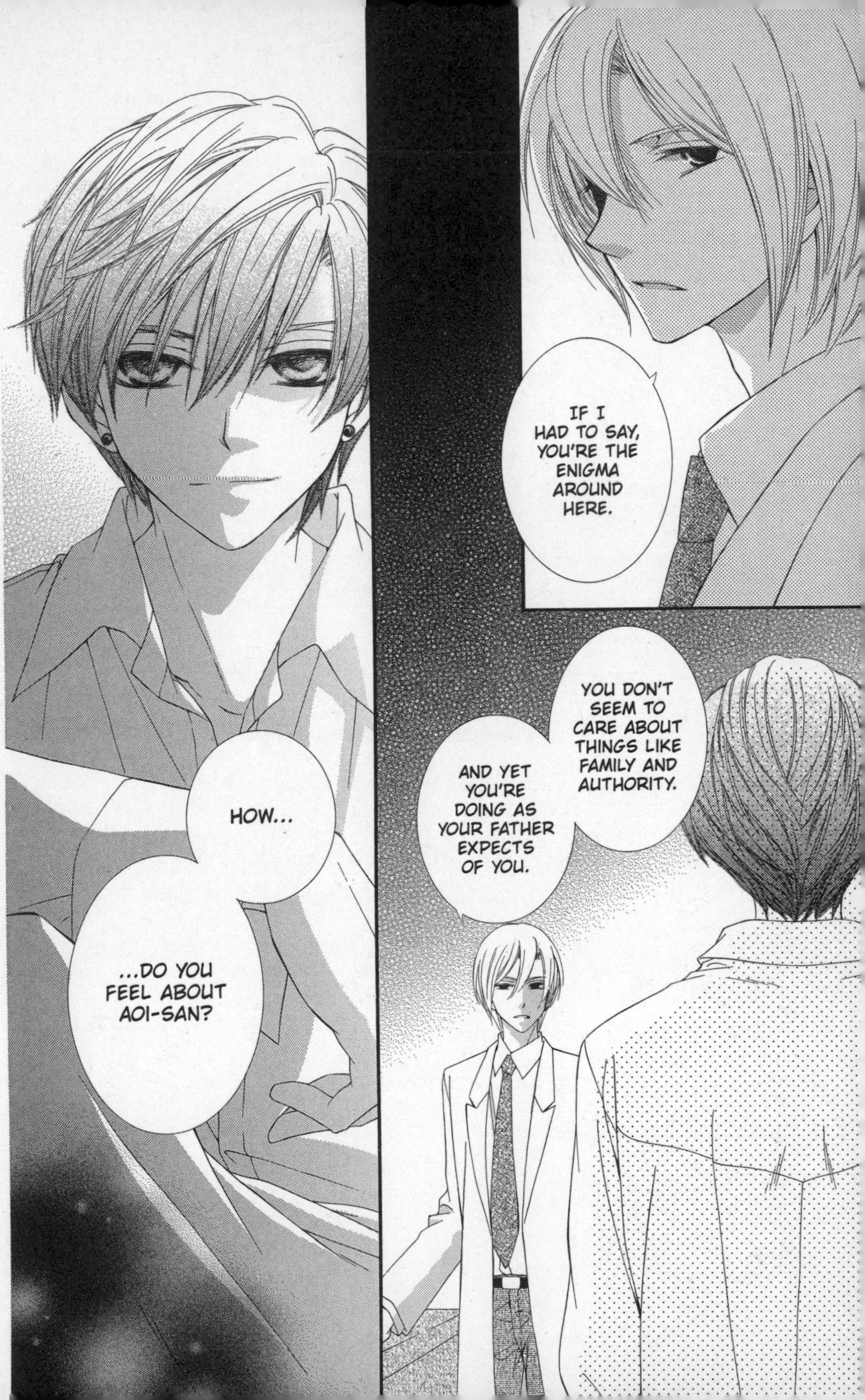
IF I HAD TO SAY, YOU'RE THE ENIGMA AROUND HERE.
YOU DON'T SEEM TO CARE ABOUT THINGS LIKE FAMILY AND AUTHORITY.
AND YET YOU'RE DOING AS YOUR FATHER EXPECTS OF YOU.
HOW...
...DO YOU FEEL ABOUT AOI-SAN?

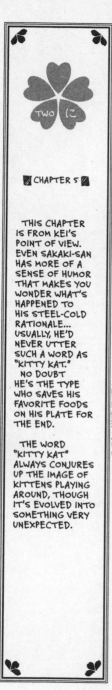

TWO に

CHAPTER 5

THIS CHAPTER IS FROM KEI'S POINT OF VIEW. EVEN SAKAKI-SAN HAS MORE OF A SENSE OF HUMOR THAT MAKES YOU WONDER WHAT'S HAPPENED TO HIS STEEL-COLD RATIONALE... USUALLY, HE'D NEVER UTTER SUCH A WORD AS "KITTY KAT."

NO DOUBT HE'S THE TYPE WHO SAVES HIS FAVORITE FOODS ON HIS PLATE FOR THE END.

THE WORD "KITTY KAT" ALWAYS CONJURES UP THE IMAGE OF KITTENS PLAYING AROUND, THOUGH IT'S EVOLVED INTO SOMETHING VERY UNEXPECTED.

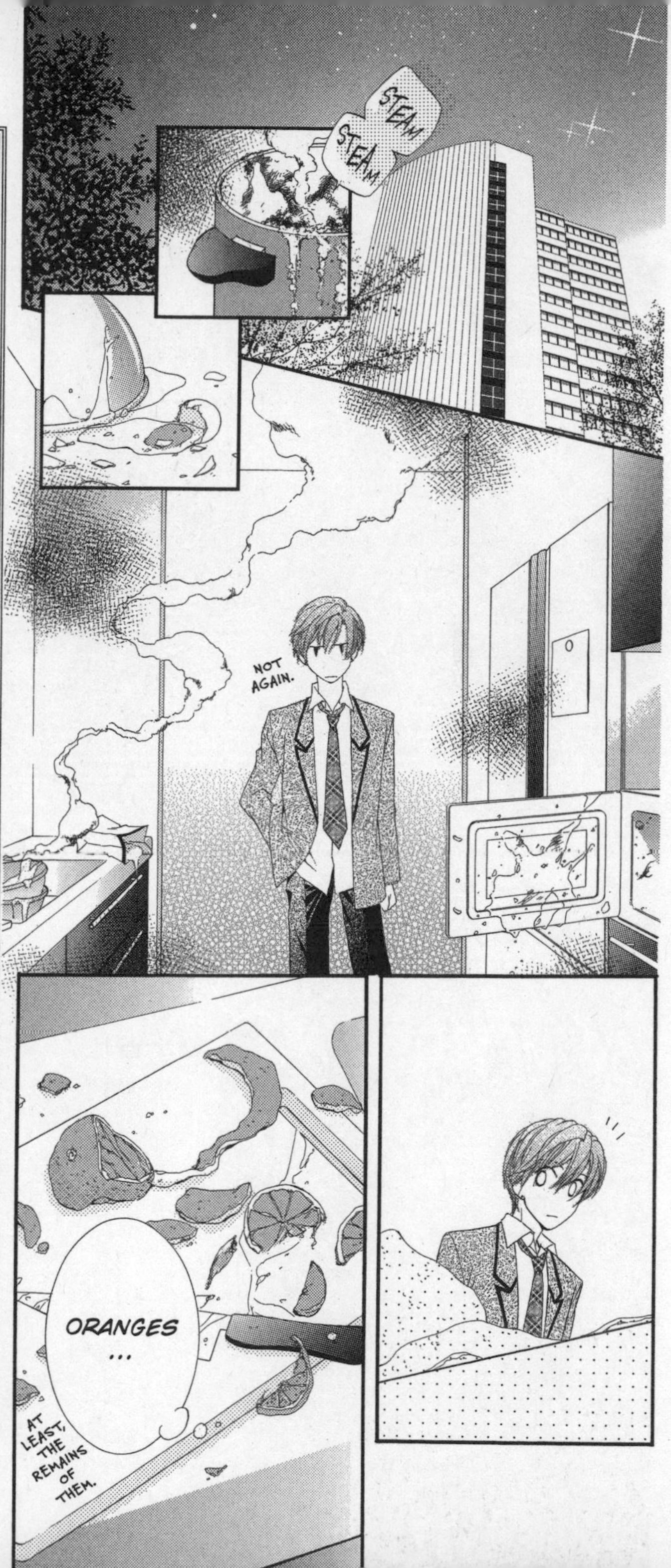
STEAM
STEAM
NOT AGAIN.
ORANGES ...
AT LEAST, THE REMAINS OF THEM.

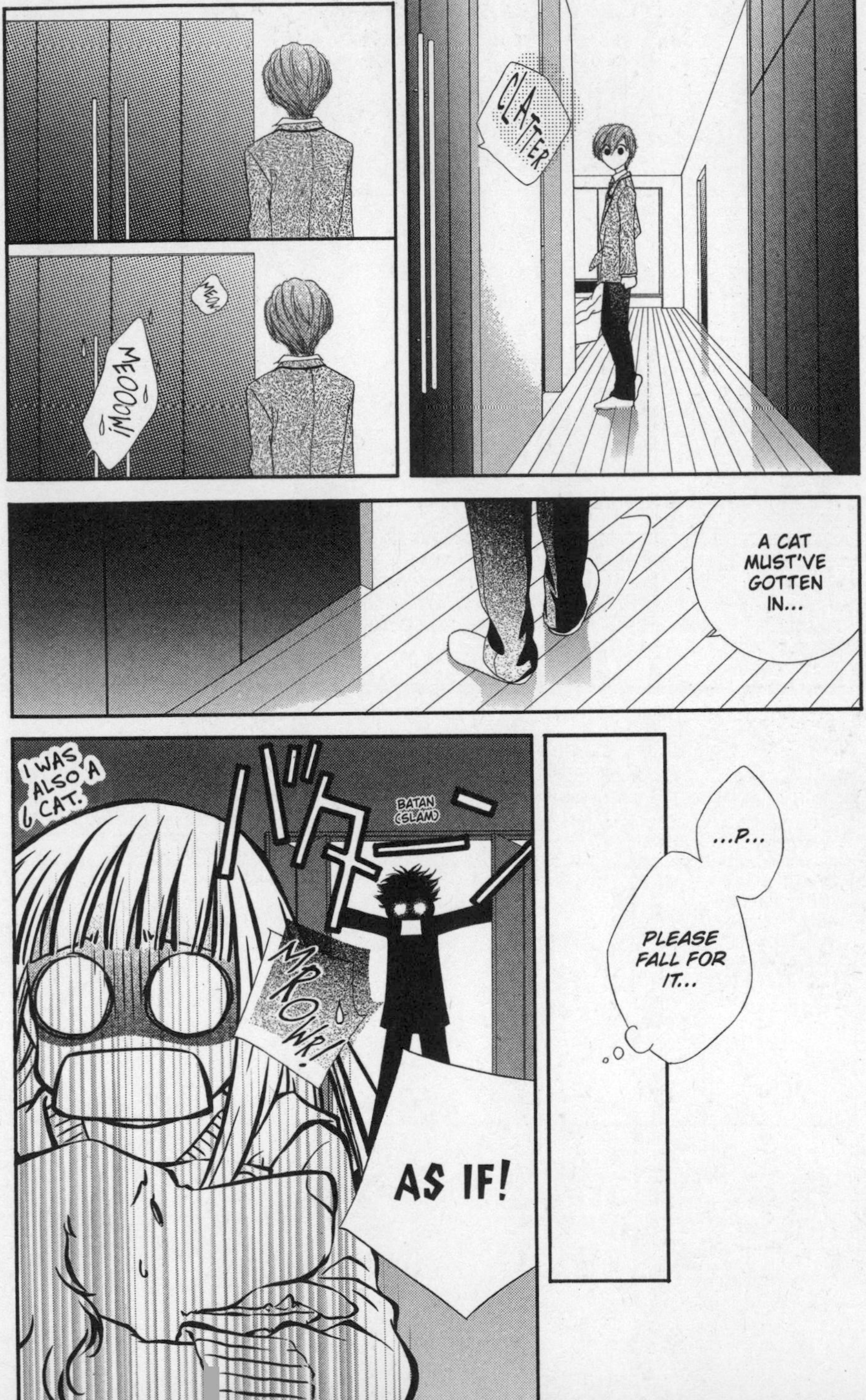
CLATTER
MEOW
MEOOW!
A CAT MUST'VE GOTTEN IN...
...P...
PLEASE FALL FOR IT...
I WAS ALSO A CAT.
BATAN (SLAM)
MROWR!
AS IF!

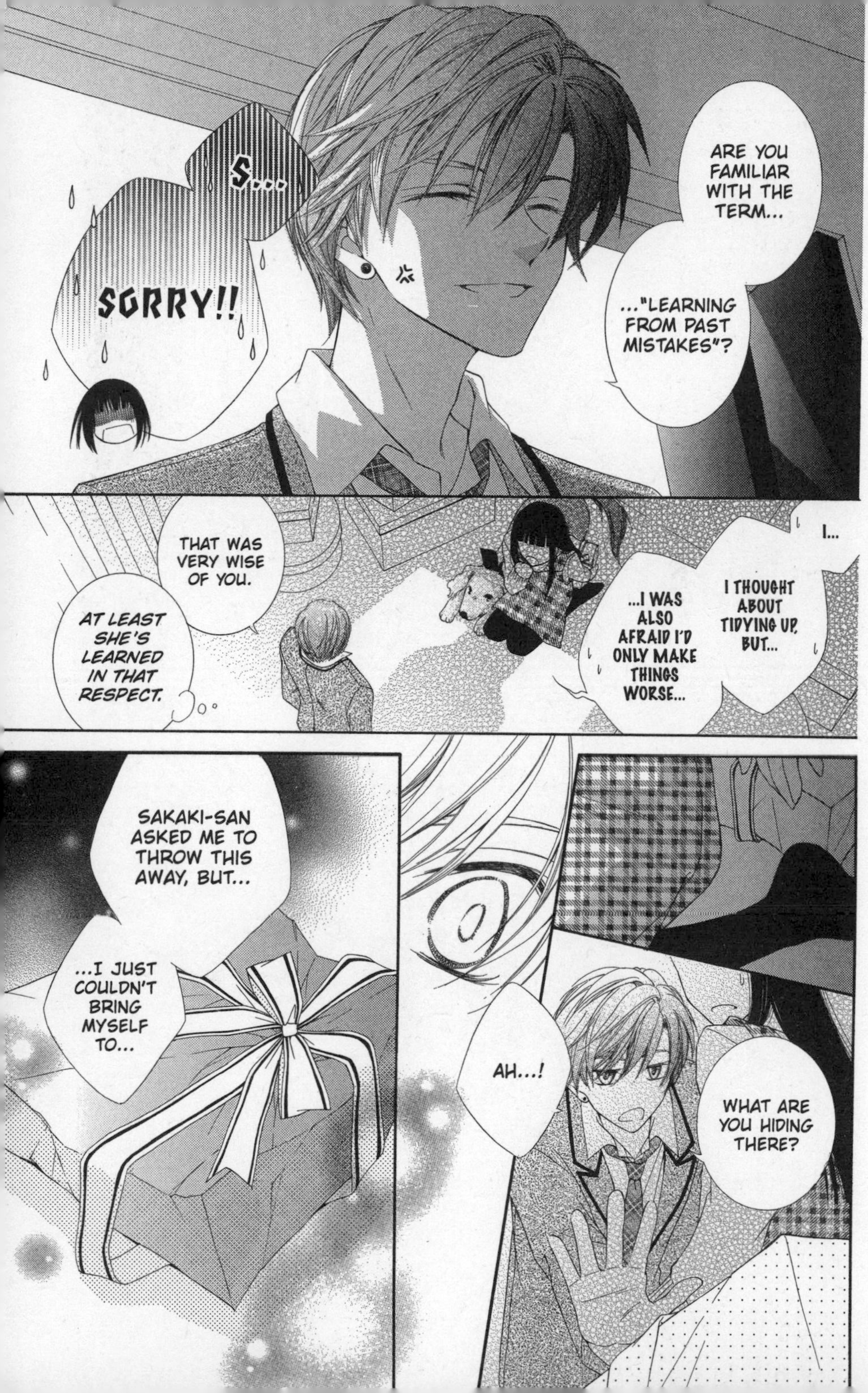
ARE YOU FAMILIAR WITH THE TERM...
..."LEARNING FROM PAST MISTAKES"?
S...
SORRY!!
I...
I THOUGHT ABOUT TIDYING UP, BUT...
...I WAS ALSO AFRAID I'D ONLY MAKE THINGS WORSE...
THAT WAS VERY WISE OF YOU.
AT LEAST SHE'S LEARNED IN THAT RESPECT.
WHAT ARE YOU HIDING THERE?
AH...!
SAKAKI-SAN ASKED ME TO THROW THIS AWAY, BUT...
...I JUST COULDN'T BRING MYSELF TO...

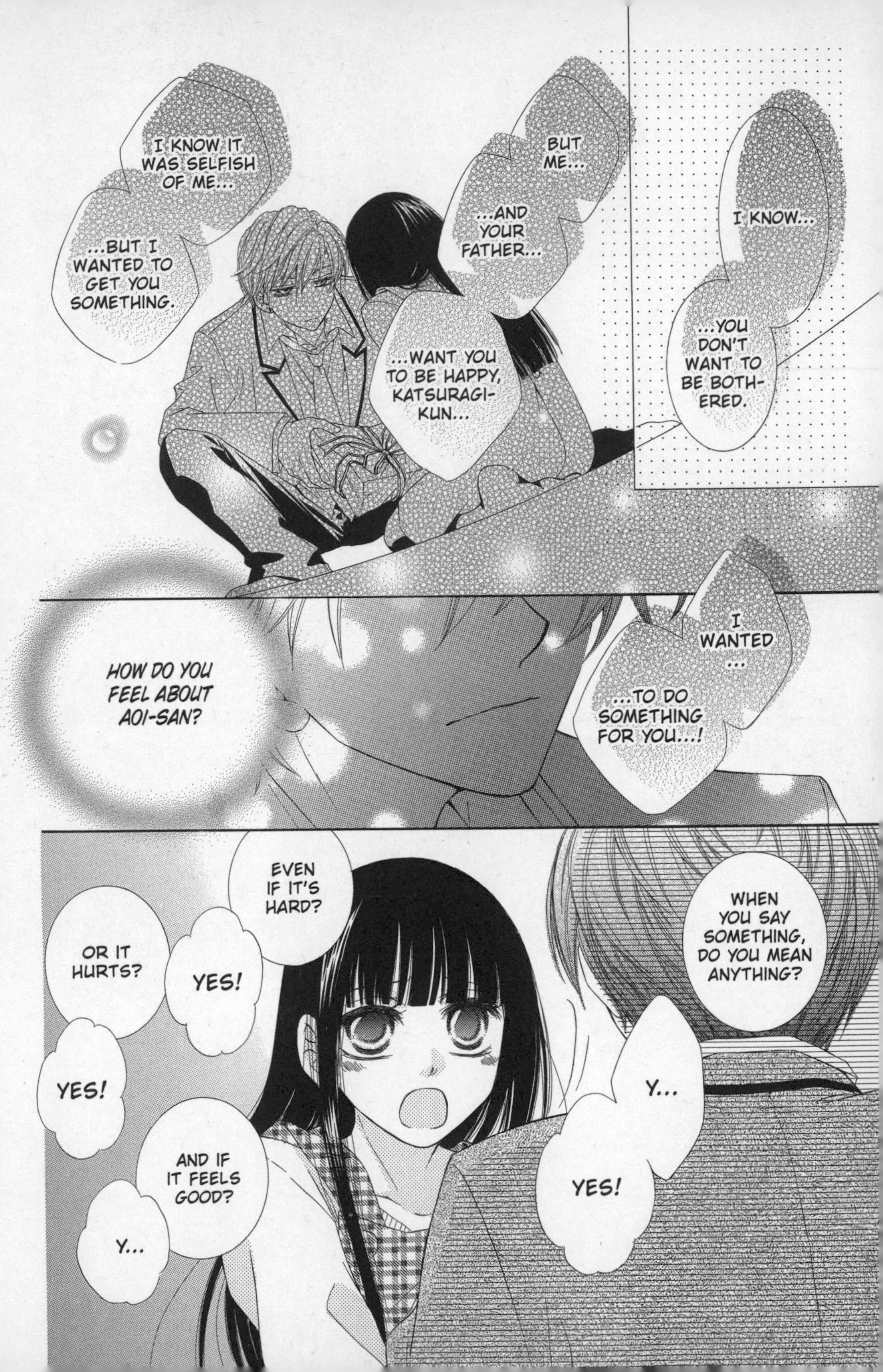
I KNOW...
...YOU DON'T WANT TO BE BOTH-ERED.
BUT ME...
...AND YOUR FATHER...
...WANT YOU TO BE HAPPY, KATSURAGI-KUN...
I KNOW IT WAS SELFISH OF ME...
...BUT I WANTED TO GET YOU SOMETHING.
I WANTED ...
...TO DO SOMETHING FOR YOU...!
HOW DO YOU FEEL ABOUT AOI-SAN?
WHEN YOU SAY SOMETHING, DO YOU MEAN ANYTHING?
Y...
YES!
EVEN IF IT'S HARD?
YES!
OR IT HURTS?
YES!
AND IF IT FEELS GOOD?
Y...

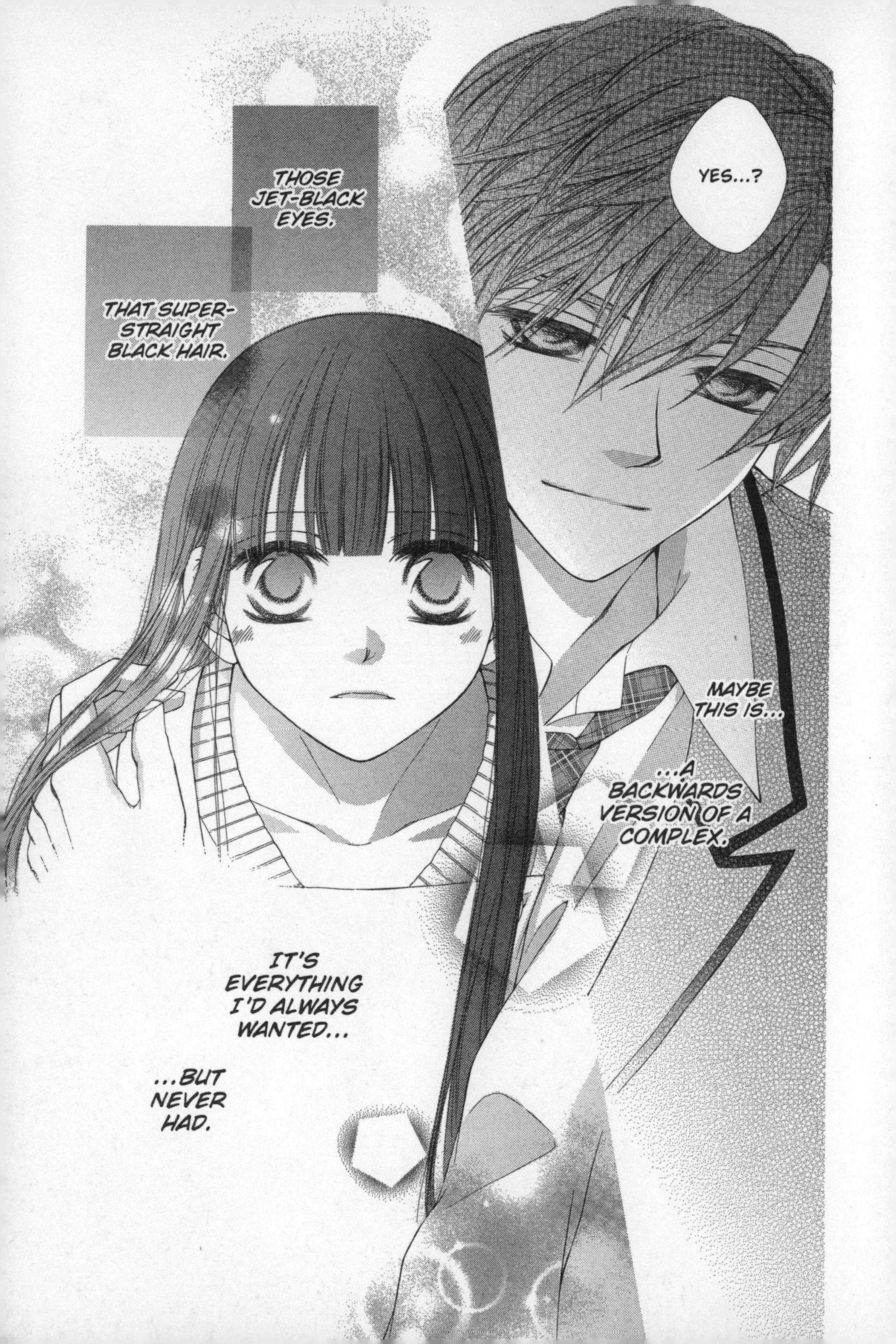
YES...?
THOSE JET-BLACK EYES.
THAT SUPER-STRAIGHT BLACK HAIR.
MAYBE THIS IS...
...A BACKWARDS VERSION OF A COMPLEX.
IT'S EVERYTHING I'D ALWAYS WANTED...
...BUT NEVER HAD.

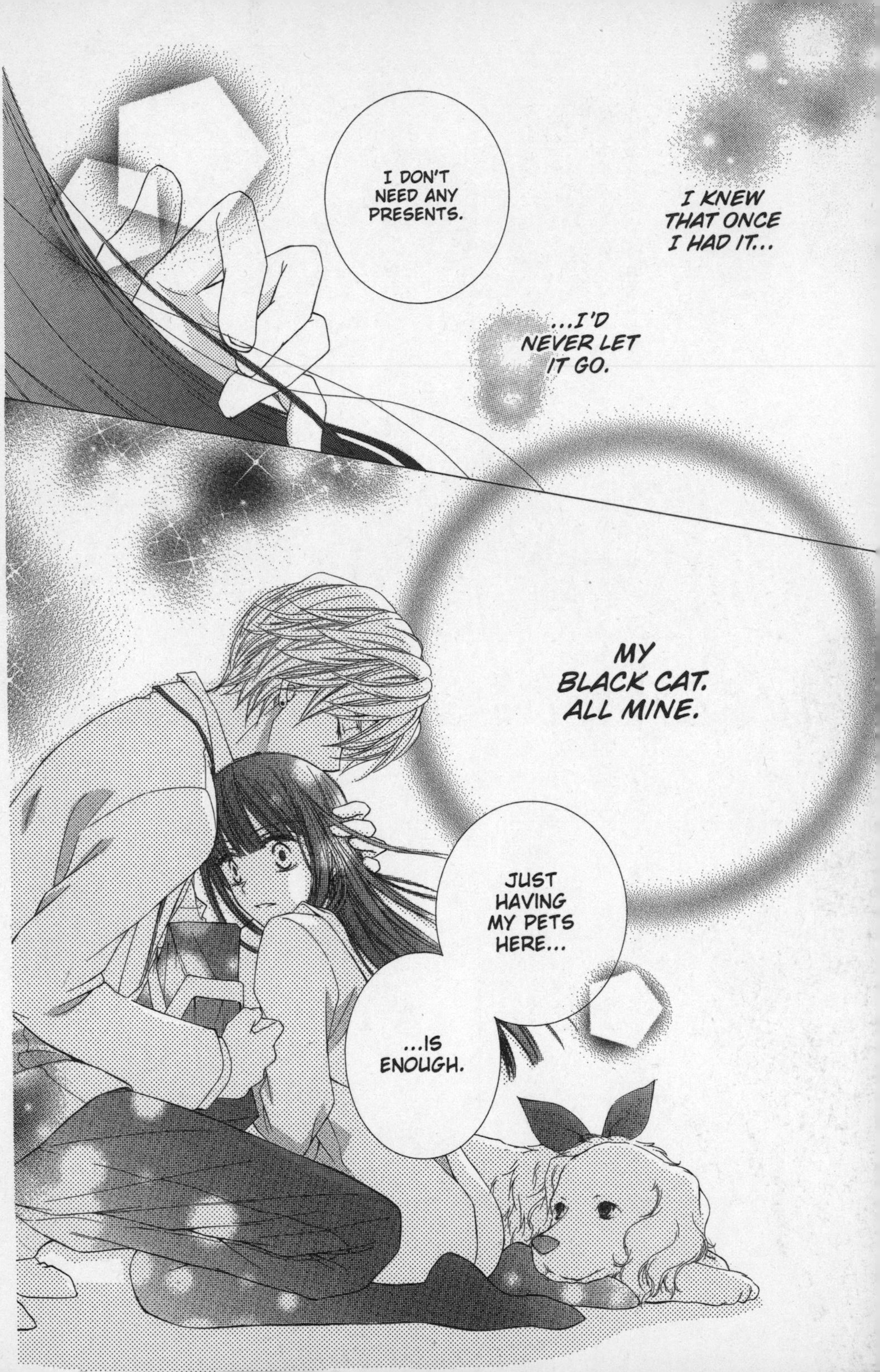
I KNEW THAT ONCE I HAD IT...
I DON'T NEED ANY PRESENTS.
...I'D NEVER LET IT GO.
MY BLACK CAT. ALL MINE.
JUST HAVING MY PETS HERE...
...IS ENOUGH.

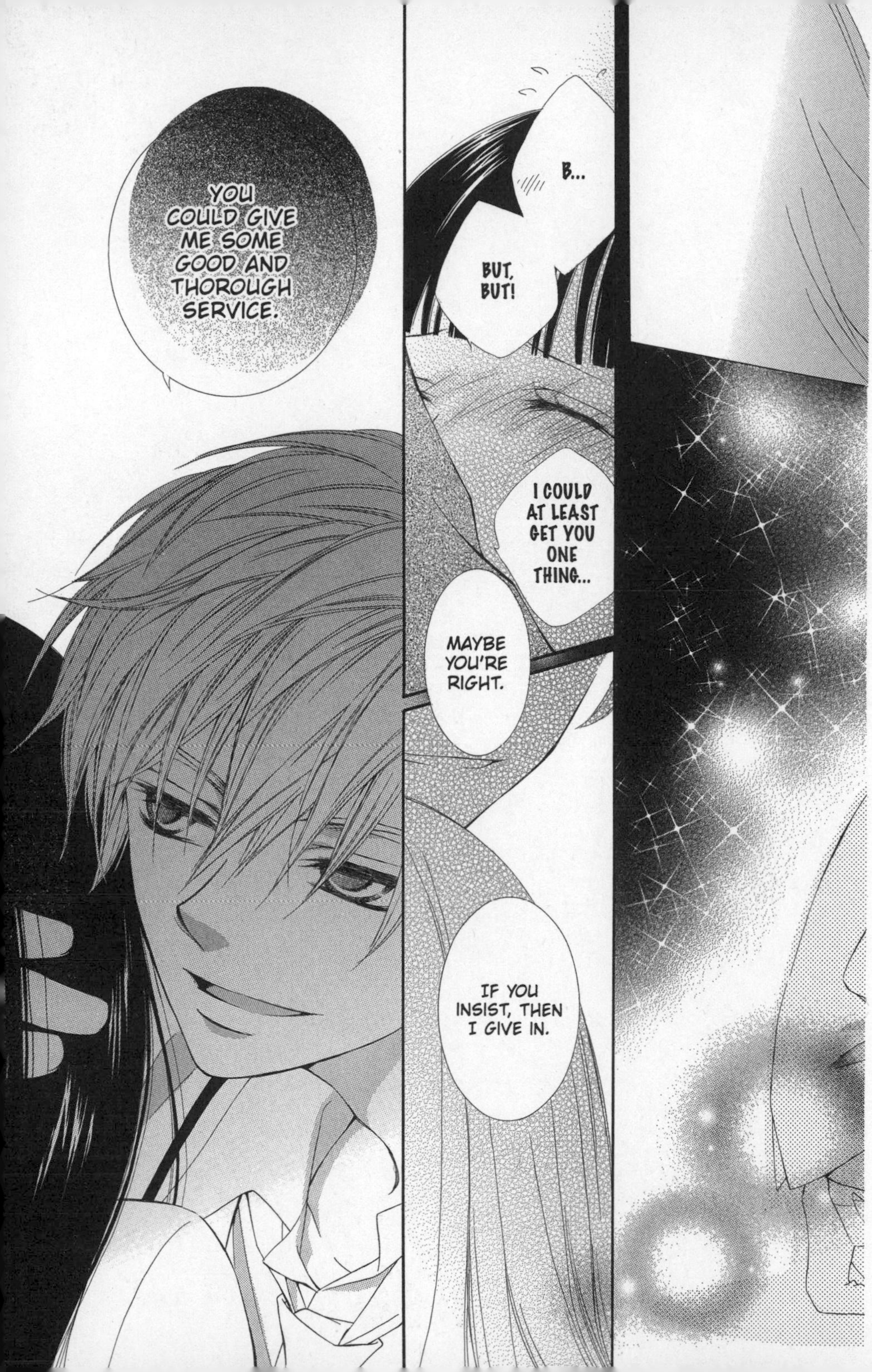
B...
BUT, BUT!
I COULD AT LEAST GET YOU ONE THING...
MAYBE YOU'RE RIGHT.
IF YOU INSIST, THEN I GIVE IN.
YOU COULD GIVE ME SOME GOOD AND THOROUGH SERVICE.

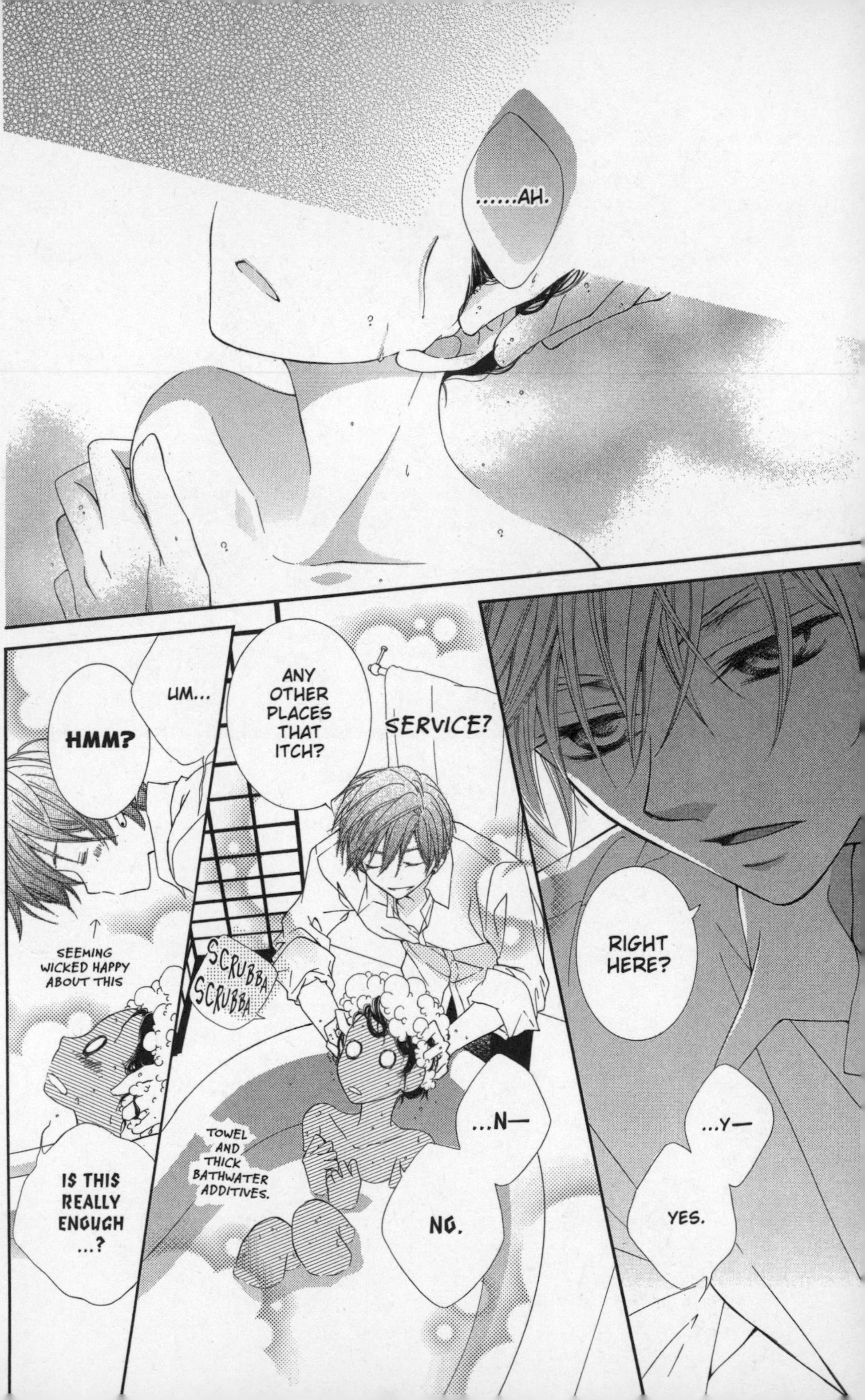
......AH.
RIGHT HERE?
...Y— YES.
ANY OTHER PLACES THAT ITCH?
SERVICE?
SCRUBBA SCRUBBA
...N— NG.
TOWEL AND THICK BATHWATER ADDITIVES.
UM...
HMM?
SEEMING WICKED HAPPY ABOUT THIS
IS THIS REALLY ENOUGH ...?

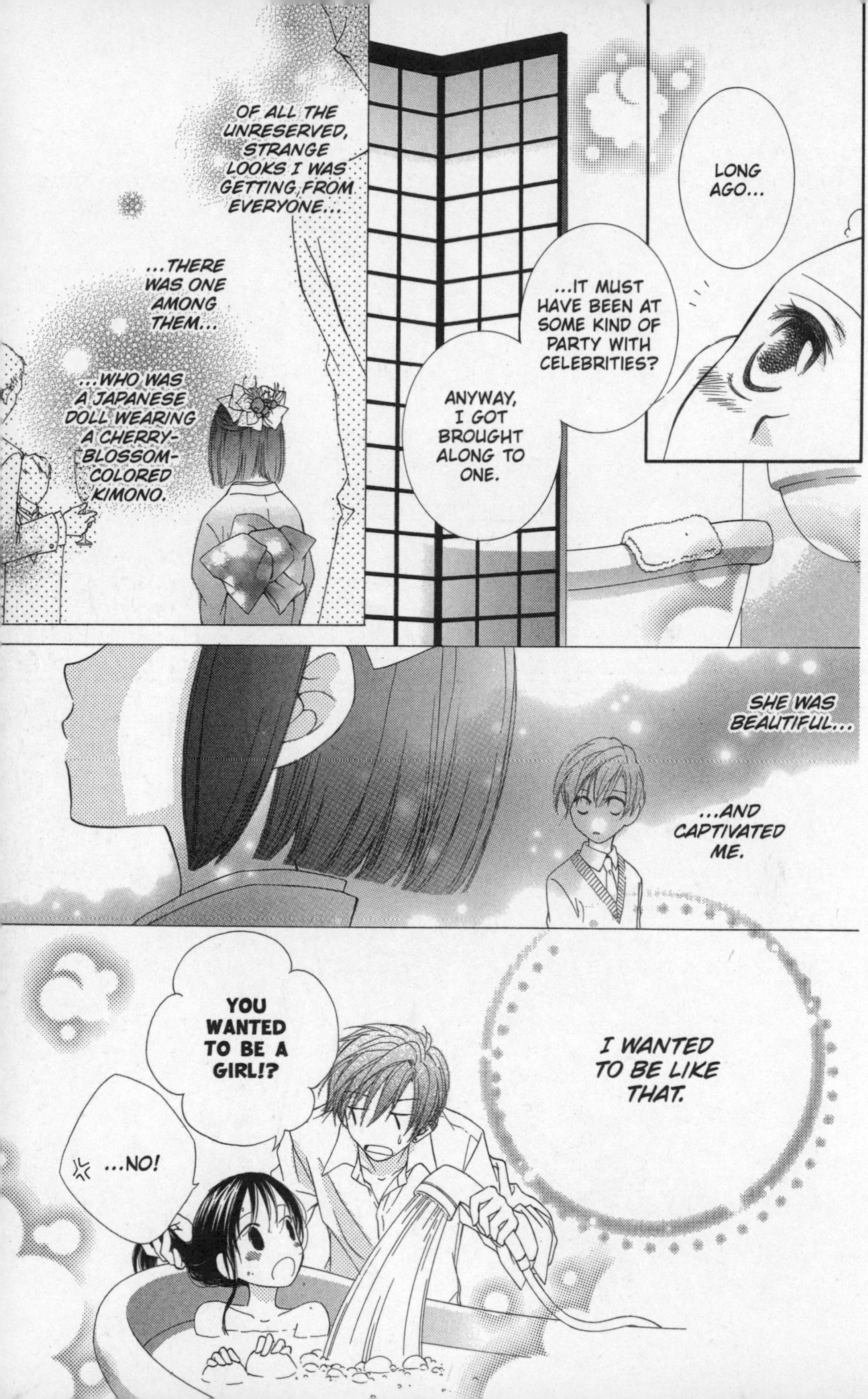
LONG AGO...
...IT MUST HAVE BEEN AT SOME KIND OF PARTY WITH CELEBRITIES?
ANYWAY, I GOT BROUGHT ALONG TO ONE.
OF ALL THE UNRESERVED, STRANGE LOOKS I WAS GETTING FROM EVERYONE...
...THERE WAS ONE AMONG THEM...
...WHO WAS A JAPANESE DOLL WEARING A CHERRY-BLOSSOM-COLORED KIMONO.
SHE WAS BEAUTIFUL...
...AND CAPTIVATED ME.
I WANTED TO BE LIKE THAT.
YOU WANTED TO BE A GIRL!?
...NO!

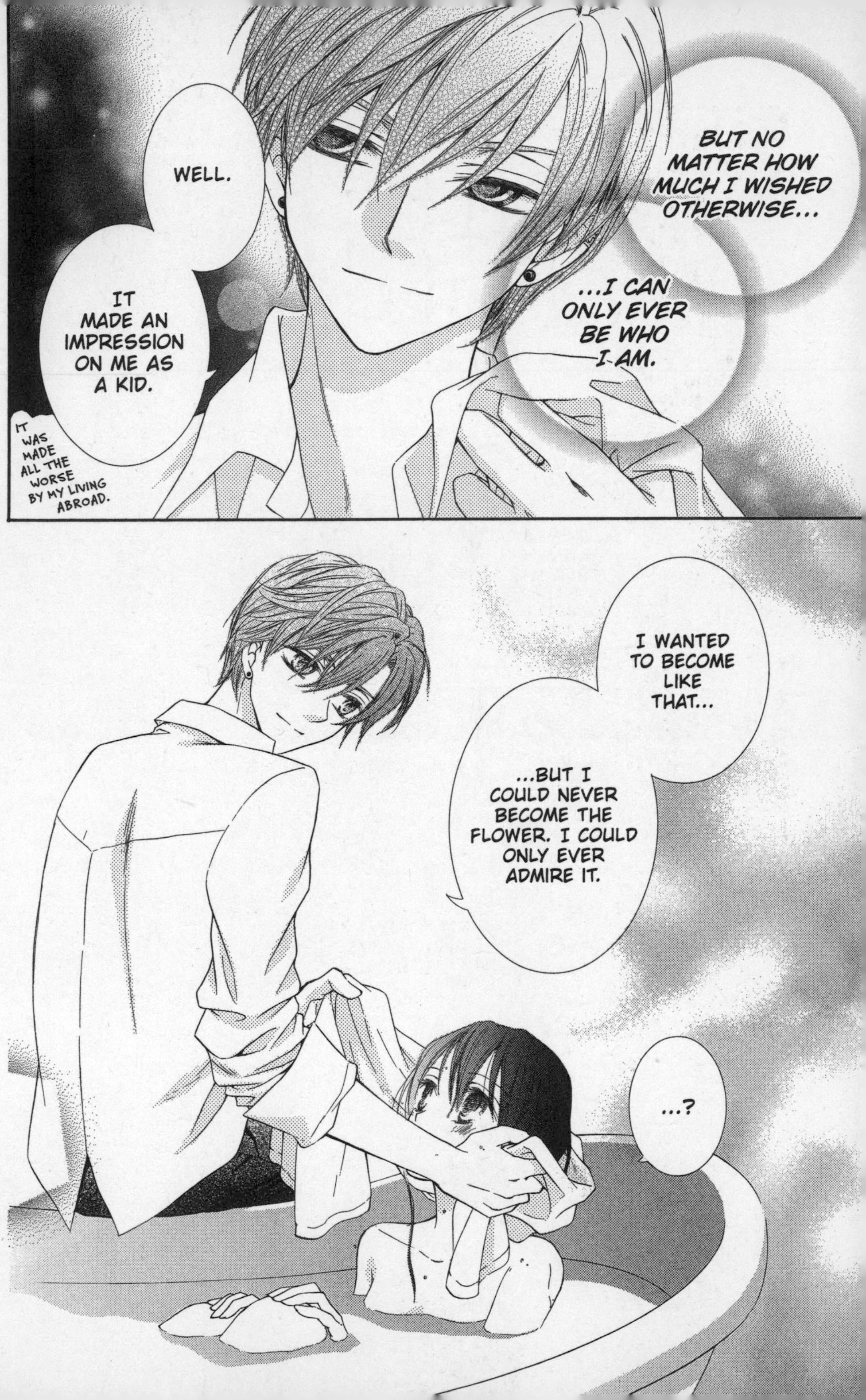
BUT NO MATTER HOW MUCH I WISHED OTHERWISE...
...I CAN ONLY EVER BE WHO I AM.
WELL.
IT MADE AN IMPRESSION ON ME AS A KID.
IT WAS MADE ALL THE WORSE BY MY LIVING ABROAD.
I WANTED TO BECOME LIKE THAT...
...BUT I COULD NEVER BECOME THE FLOWER. I COULD ONLY EVER ADMIRE IT.
...?

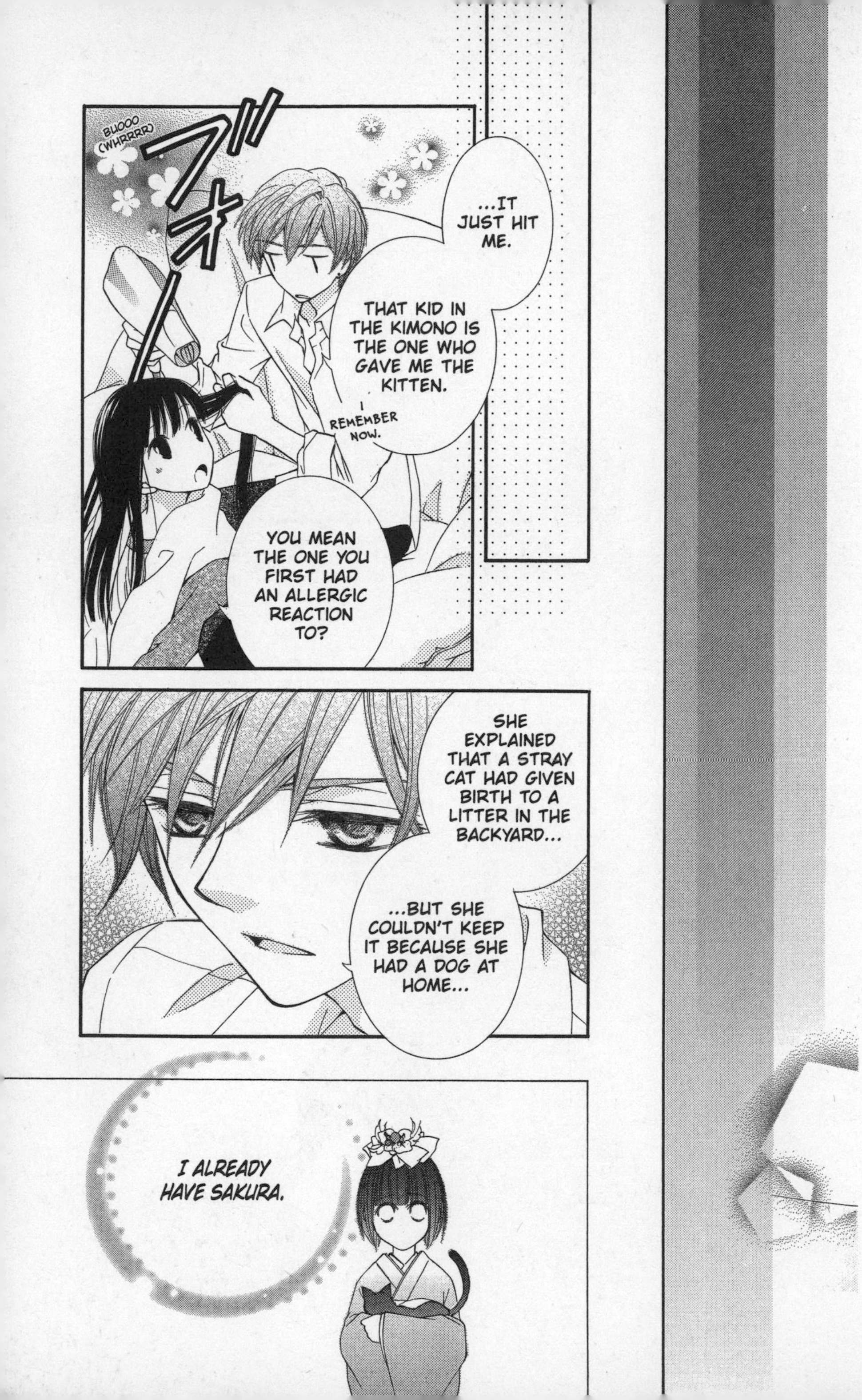
...IT JUST HIT ME.
BUOOO (WHRRRR)
THAT KID IN THE KIMONO IS THE ONE WHO GAVE ME THE KITTEN.
I REMEMBER NOW.
YOU MEAN THE ONE YOU FIRST HAD AN ALLERGIC REACTION TO?
SHE EXPLAINED THAT A STRAY CAT HAD GIVEN BIRTH TO A LITTER IN THE BACKYARD...
...BUT SHE COULDN'T KEEP IT BECAUSE SHE HAD A DOG AT HOME...
I ALREADY HAVE SAKURA.

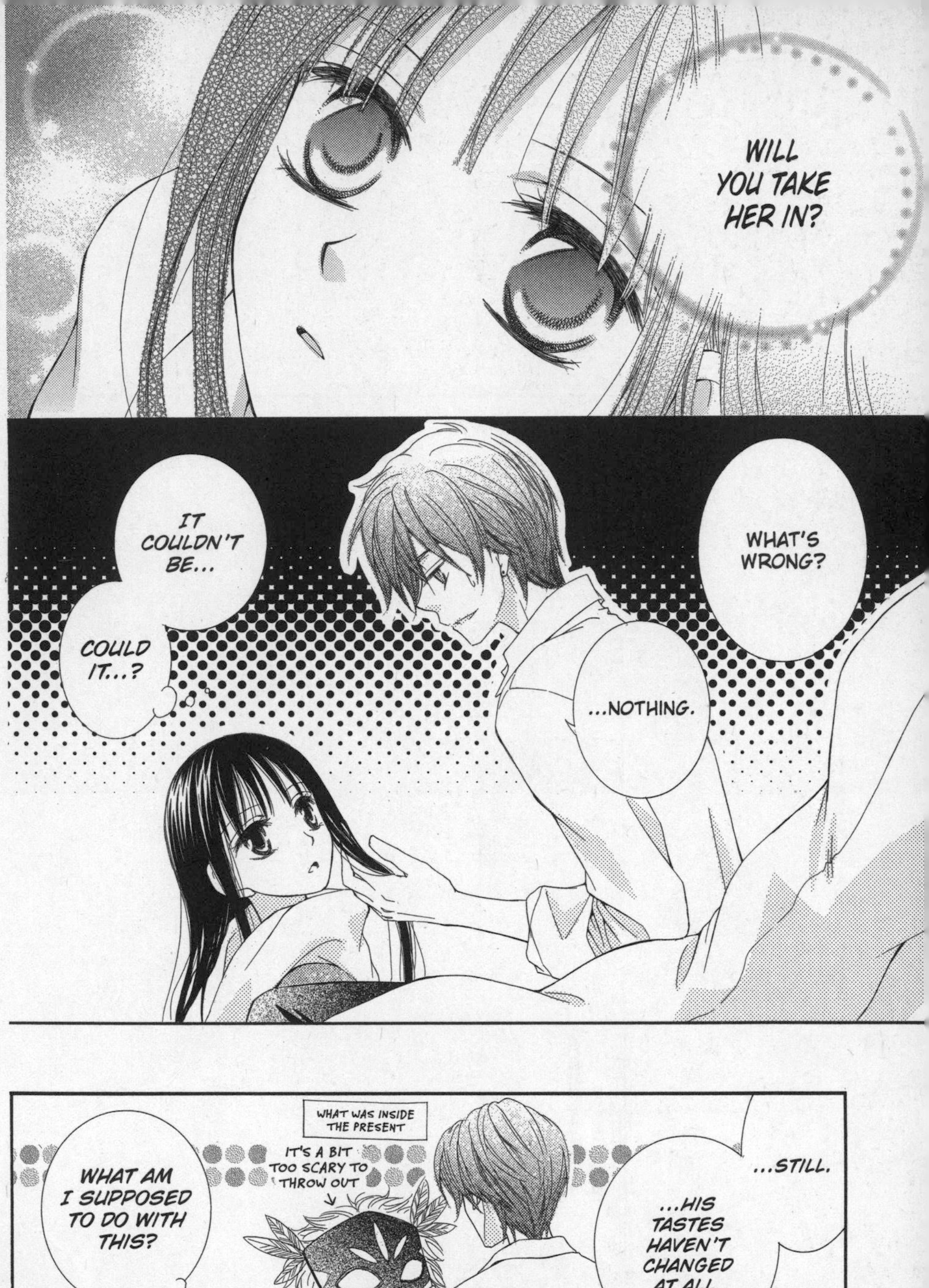
WILL YOU TAKE HER IN?
WHAT'S WRONG?
...NOTHING.
IT COULDN'T BE...
COULD IT...?
...STILL.
...HIS TASTES HAVEN'T CHANGED AT ALL.
WHAT WAS INSIDE THE PRESENT
IT'S A BIT TOO SCARY TO THROW OUT
WHAT AM I SUPPOSED TO DO WITH THIS?
IS THIS HARASSMENT?

scene.5 / *The End*

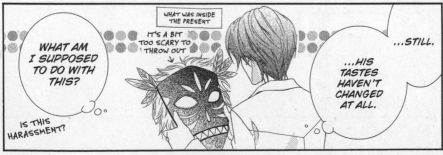

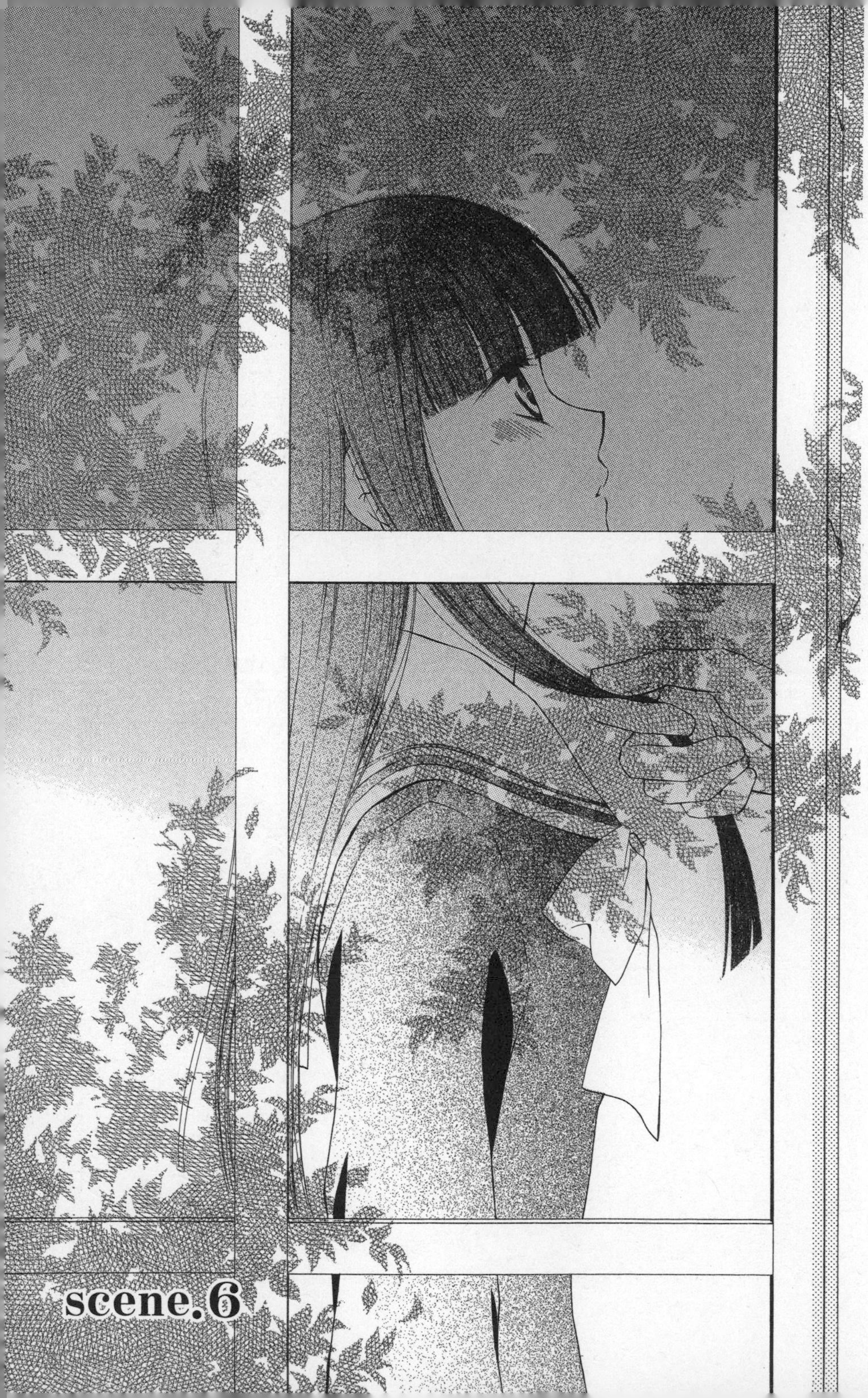
scene.6

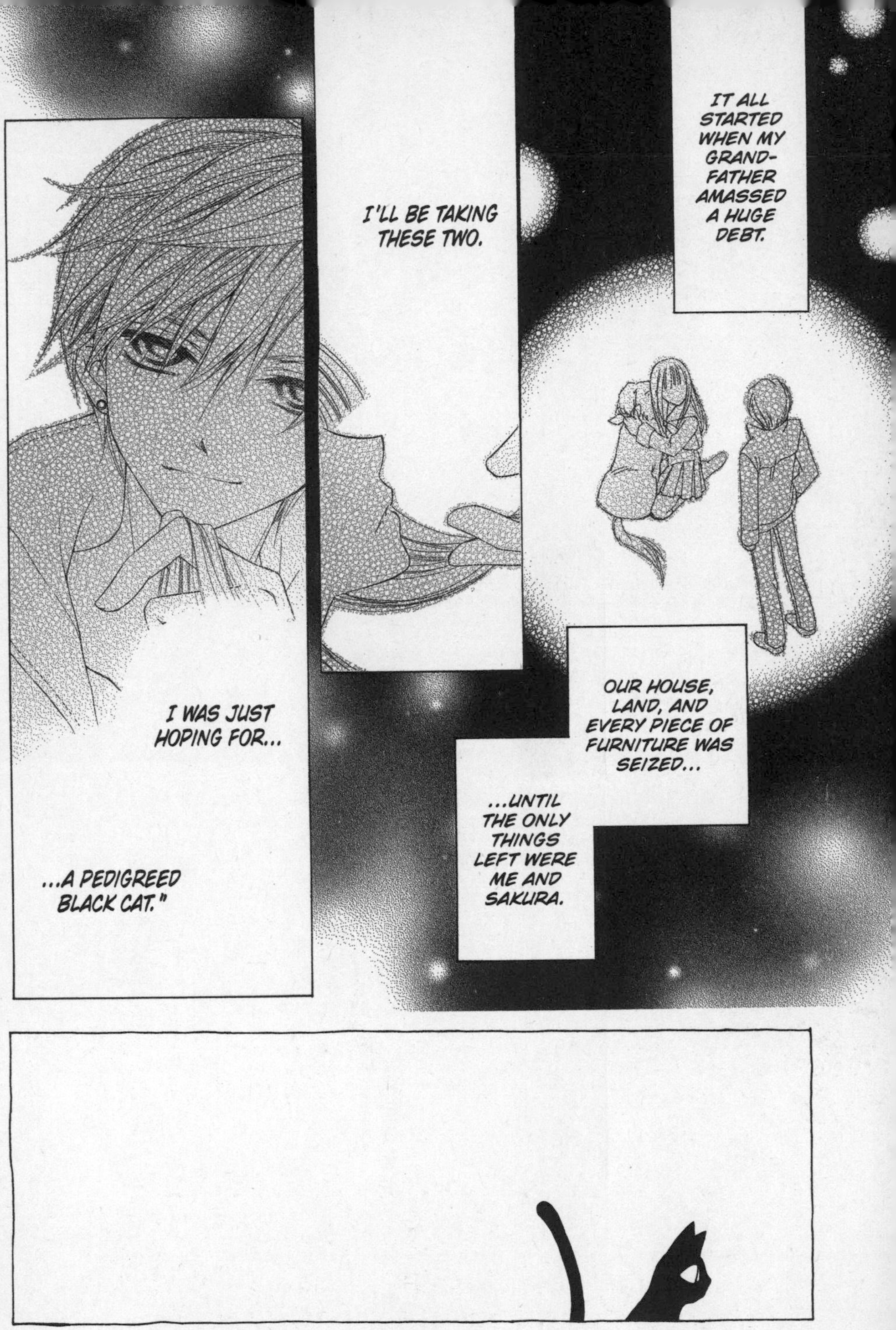
IT ALL STARTED WHEN MY GRAND-FATHER AMASSED A HUGE DEBT.
OUR HOUSE, LAND, AND EVERY PIECE OF FURNITURE WAS SEIZED...
...UNTIL THE ONLY THINGS LEFT WERE ME AND SAKURA.
I'LL BE TAKING THESE TWO.
I WAS JUST HOPING FOR...
...A PEDIGREED BLACK CAT."

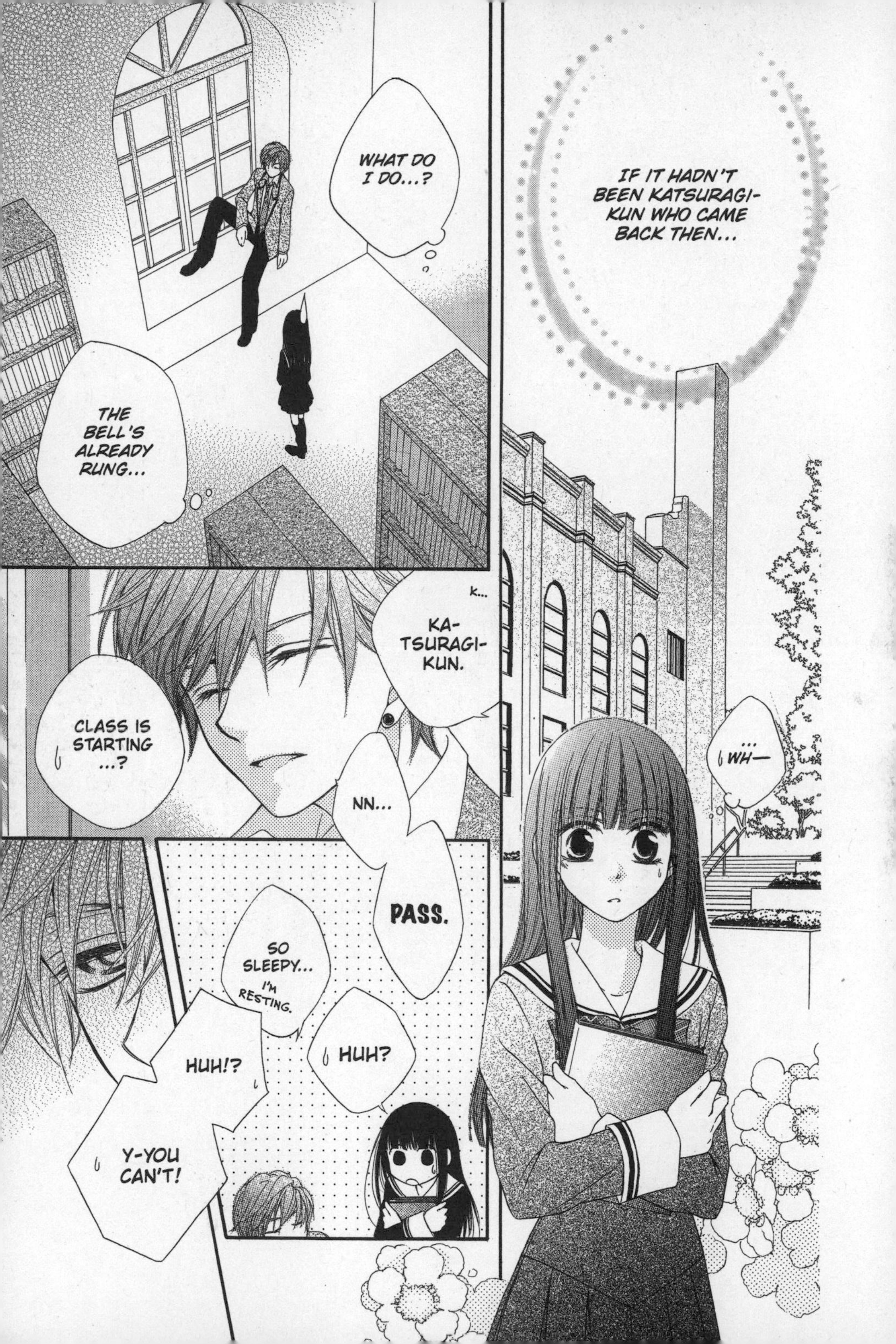
IF IT HADN'T BEEN KATSURAGI-KUN WHO CAME BACK THEN...
... WH—
WHAT DO I DO...?
THE BELL'S ALREADY RUNG...
K...
KA-TSURAGI-KUN.
CLASS IS STARTING ...?
NN...
PASS.
SO SLEEPY...
I'M RESTING.
HUH?
HUH!?
Y-YOU CAN'T!

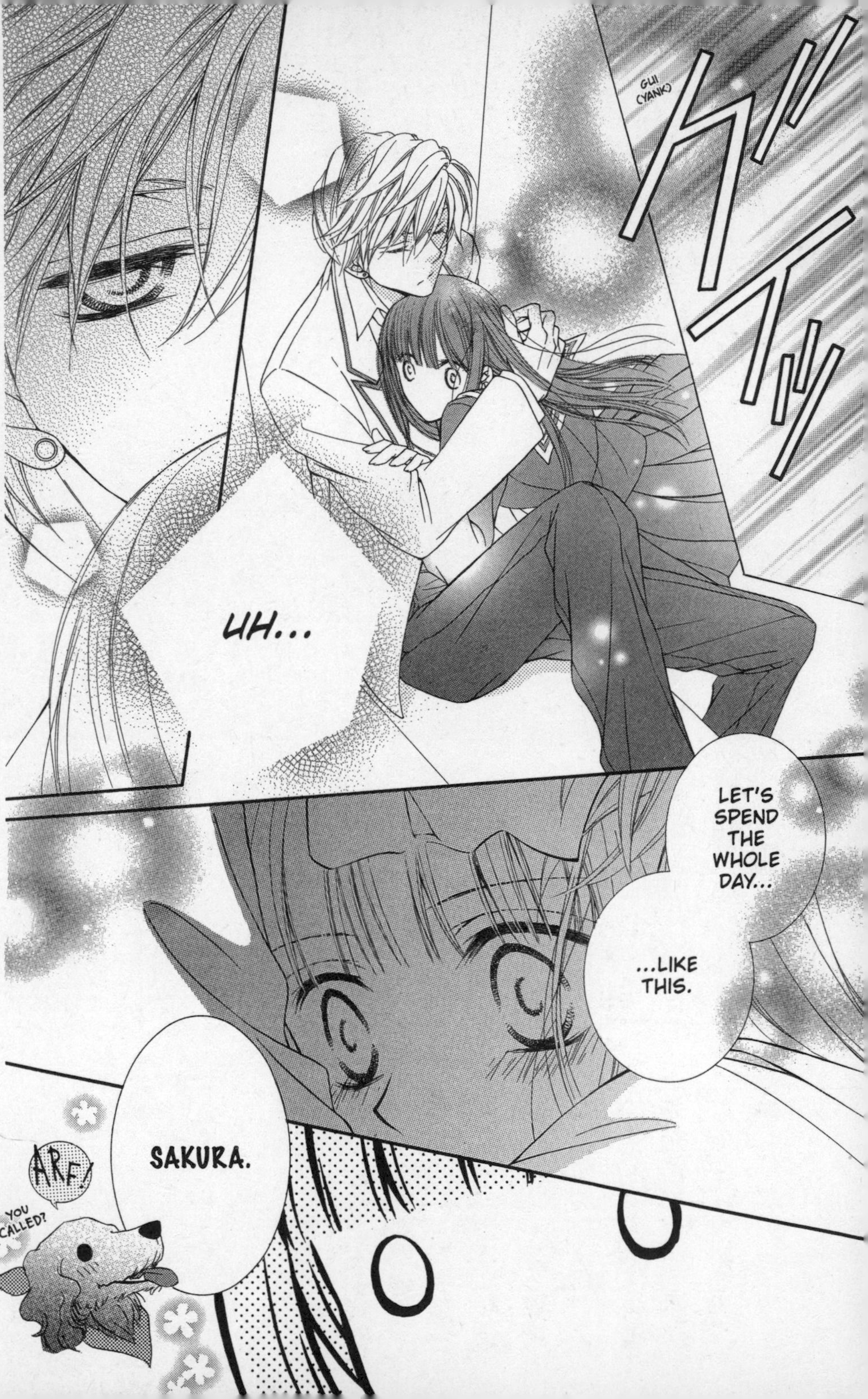
GUI (YANK)
UH...
LET'S SPEND THE WHOLE DAY...
...LIKE THIS.
SAKURA.
ARF!
YOU CALLED?

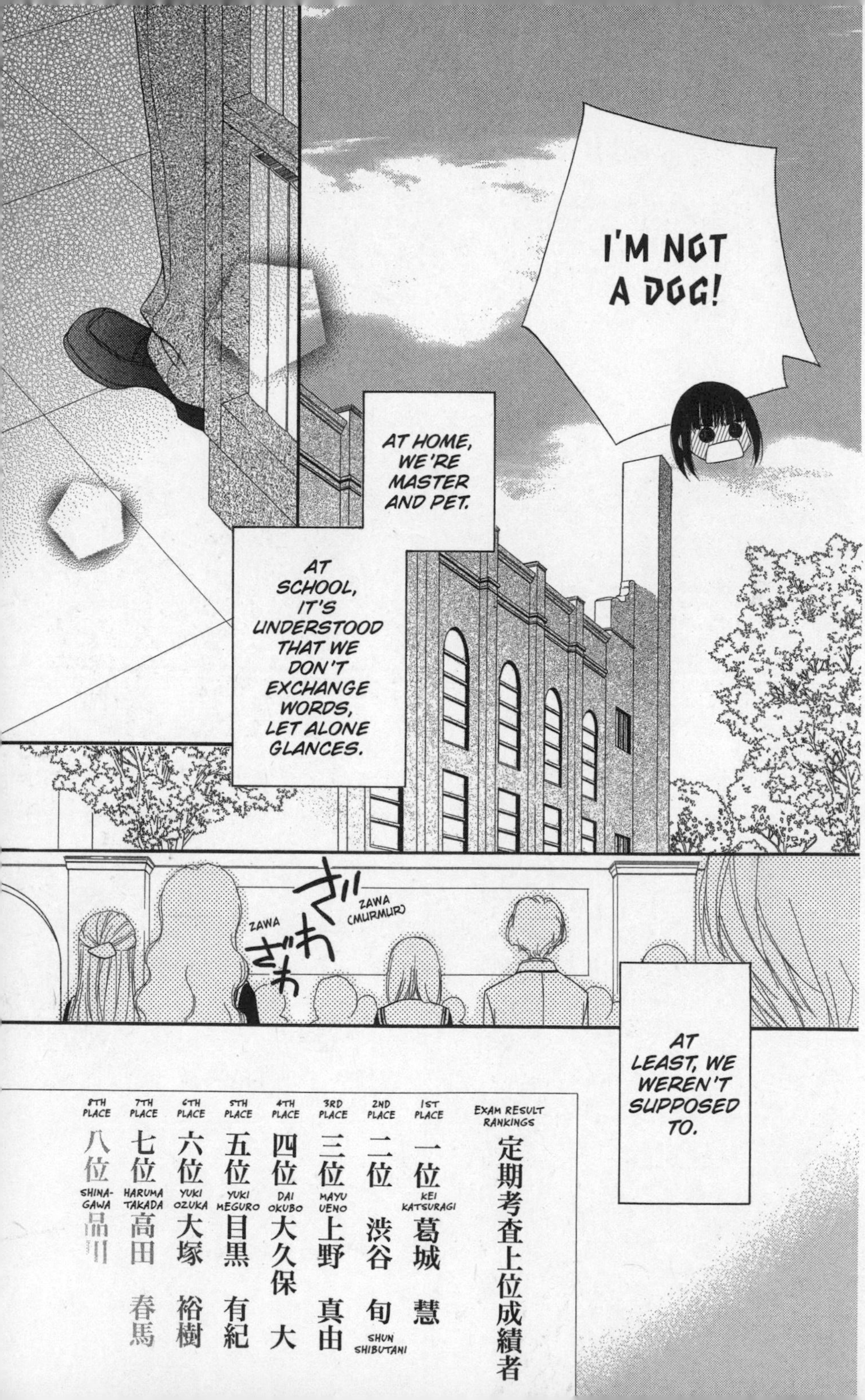
I'M NOT A DOG!
AT HOME, WE'RE MASTER AND PET.
AT SCHOOL, IT'S UNDERSTOOD THAT WE DON'T EXCHANGE WORDS, LET ALONE GLANCES.
ざわ ZAWA (MURMUR)
ざわ ZAWA
AT LEAST, WE WEREN'T SUPPOSED TO.
定期考査上位成績者 EXAM RESULT RANKINGS
一位 葛城 慧 1ST PLACE KEI KATSURAGI
二位 渋谷 旬 2ND PLACE SHUN SHIBUTANI
三位 上野 真由 3RD PLACE MAYU UENO
四位 大久保 大 4TH PLACE DAI OKUBO
五位 目黒 有紀 5TH PLACE YUKI MEGURO
六位 大塚 裕樹 6TH PLACE YUKI OZUKA
七位 高田 春馬 7TH PLACE HARUMA TAKADA
八位 品川 8TH PLACE SHINA-GAWA

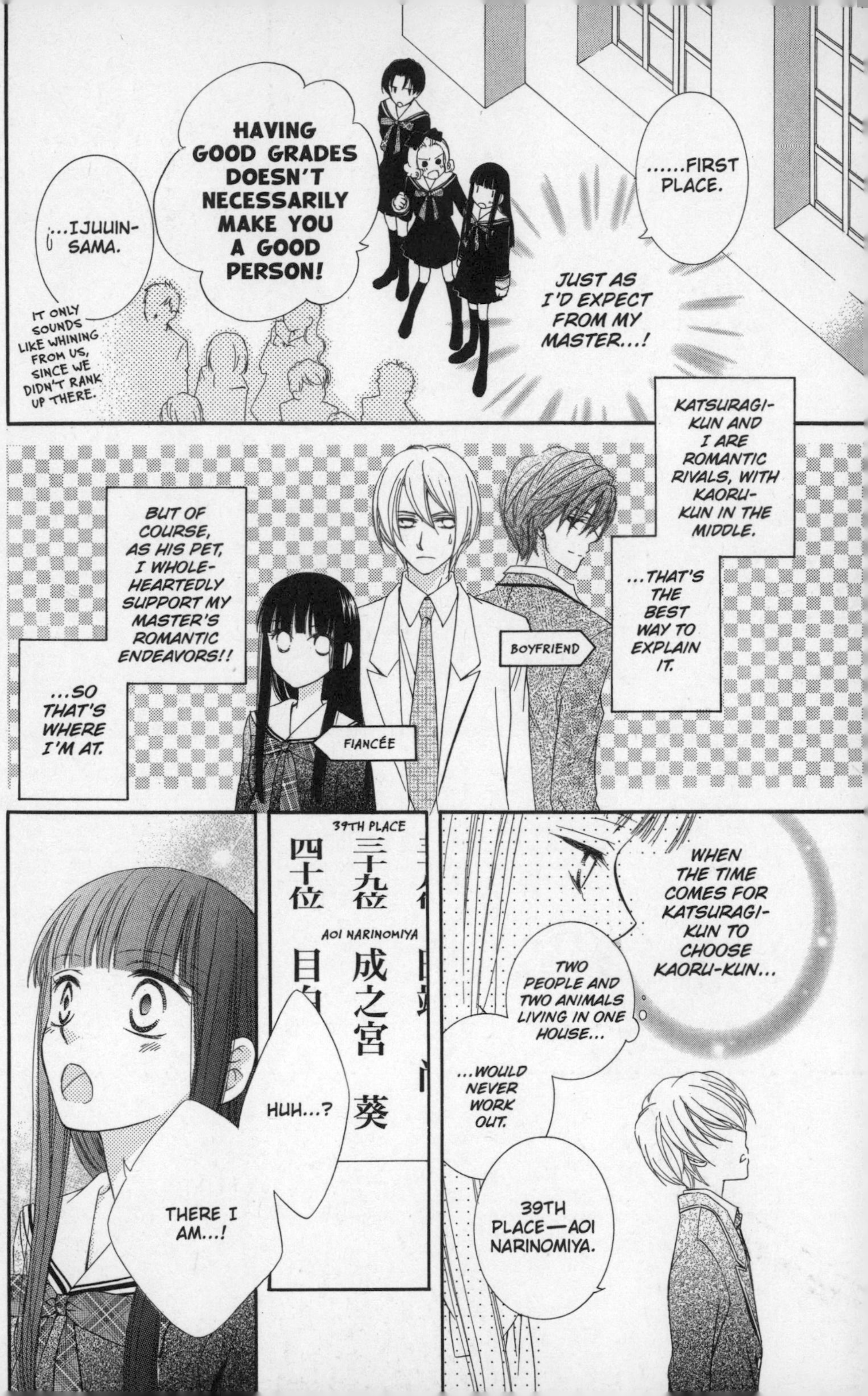
......FIRST PLACE.
JUST AS I'D EXPECT FROM MY MASTER...!
HAVING GOOD GRADES DOESN'T NECESSARILY MAKE YOU A GOOD PERSON!
...IJUUIN-SAMA.
IT ONLY SOUNDS LIKE WHINING FROM US, SINCE WE DIDN'T RANK UP THERE.
KATSURAGI-KUN AND I ARE ROMANTIC RIVALS, WITH KAORU-KUN IN THE MIDDLE.
...THAT'S THE BEST WAY TO EXPLAIN IT.
BOYFRIEND
BUT OF COURSE, AS HIS PET, I WHOLE-HEARTEDLY SUPPORT MY MASTER'S ROMANTIC ENDEAVORS!!
...SO THAT'S WHERE I'M AT.
FIANCÉE
WHEN THE TIME COMES FOR KATSURAGI-KUN TO CHOOSE KAORU-KUN...
TWO PEOPLE AND TWO ANIMALS LIVING IN ONE HOUSE...
...WOULD NEVER WORK OUT.
39TH PLACE—AOI NARINOMIYA.
39TH PLACE
三十九位
AOI NARINOMIYA
成之宮 葵
四十位
HUH...?
THERE I AM...!

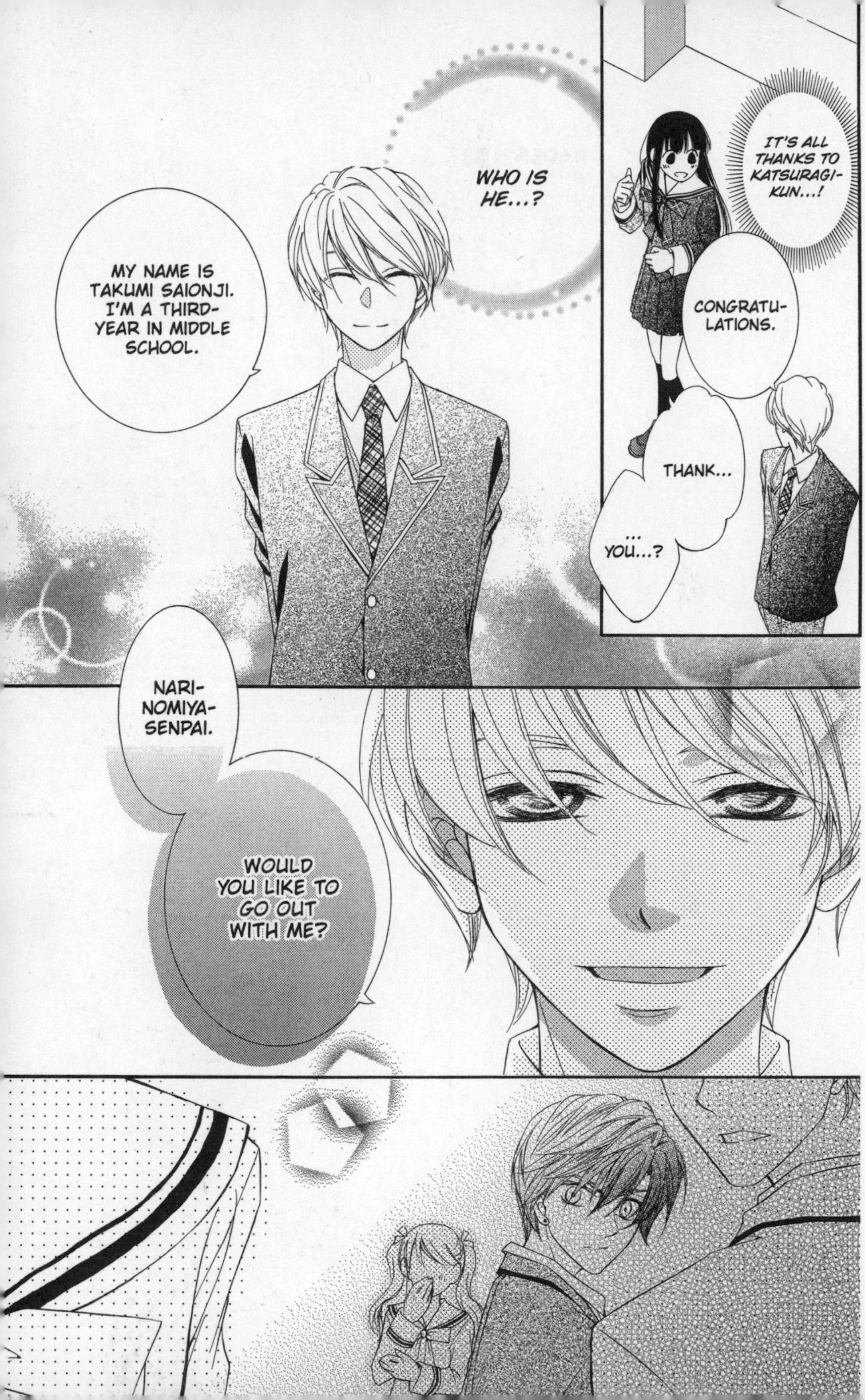
IT'S ALL THANKS TO KATSURAGI-KUN...!
CONGRATULATIONS.
THANK...
... YOU...?
WHO IS HE...?
MY NAME IS TAKUMI SAIONJI. I'M A THIRD-YEAR IN MIDDLE SCHOOL.
NARI-NOMIYA-SENPAI.
WOULD YOU LIKE TO GO OUT WITH ME?

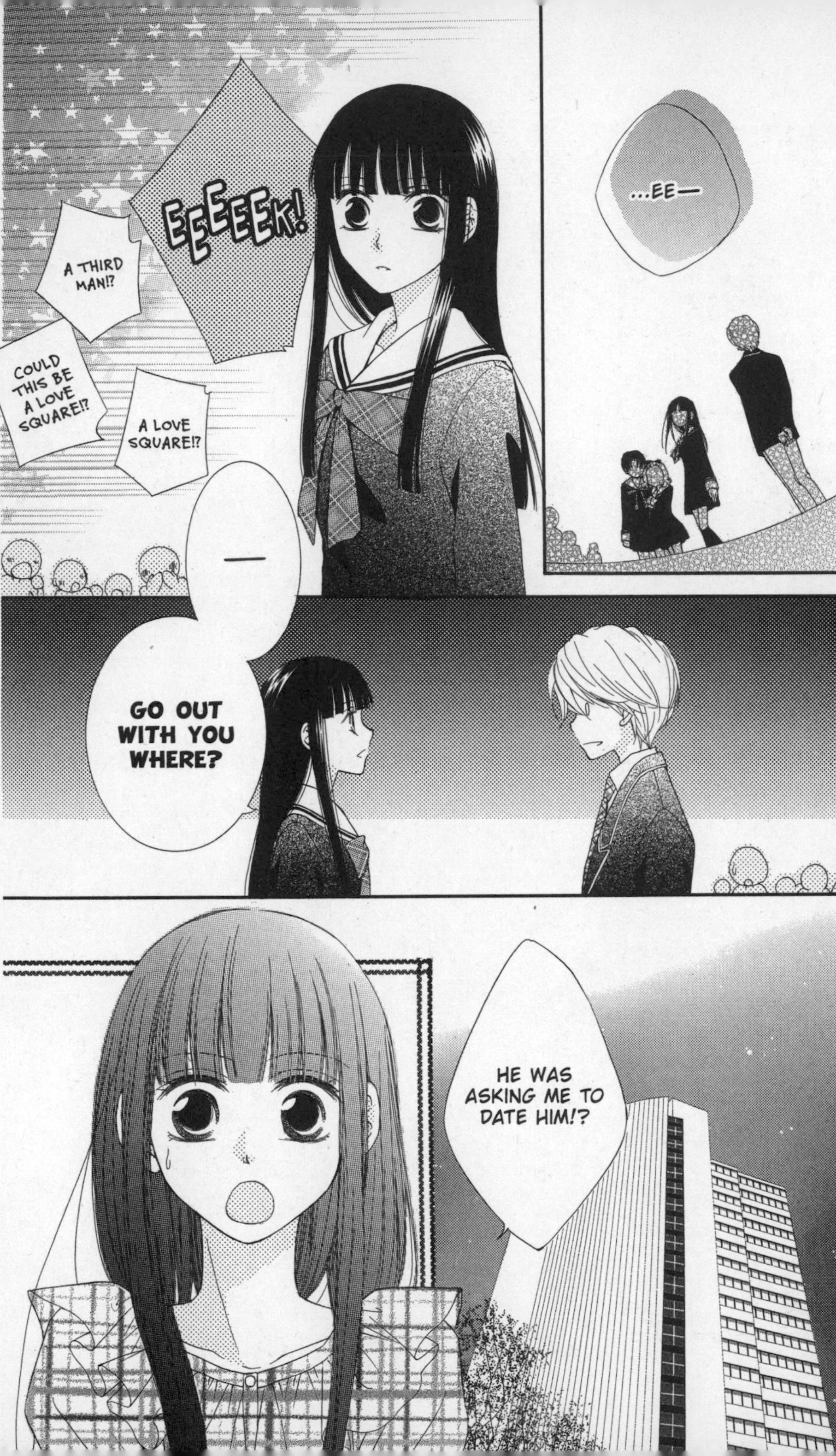
...EE—
EEEEEK!
A THIRD MAN!?
COULD THIS BE A LOVE SQUARE!?
A LOVE SQUARE!?
—
GO OUT WITH YOU WHERE?
HE WAS ASKING ME TO DATE HIM!?

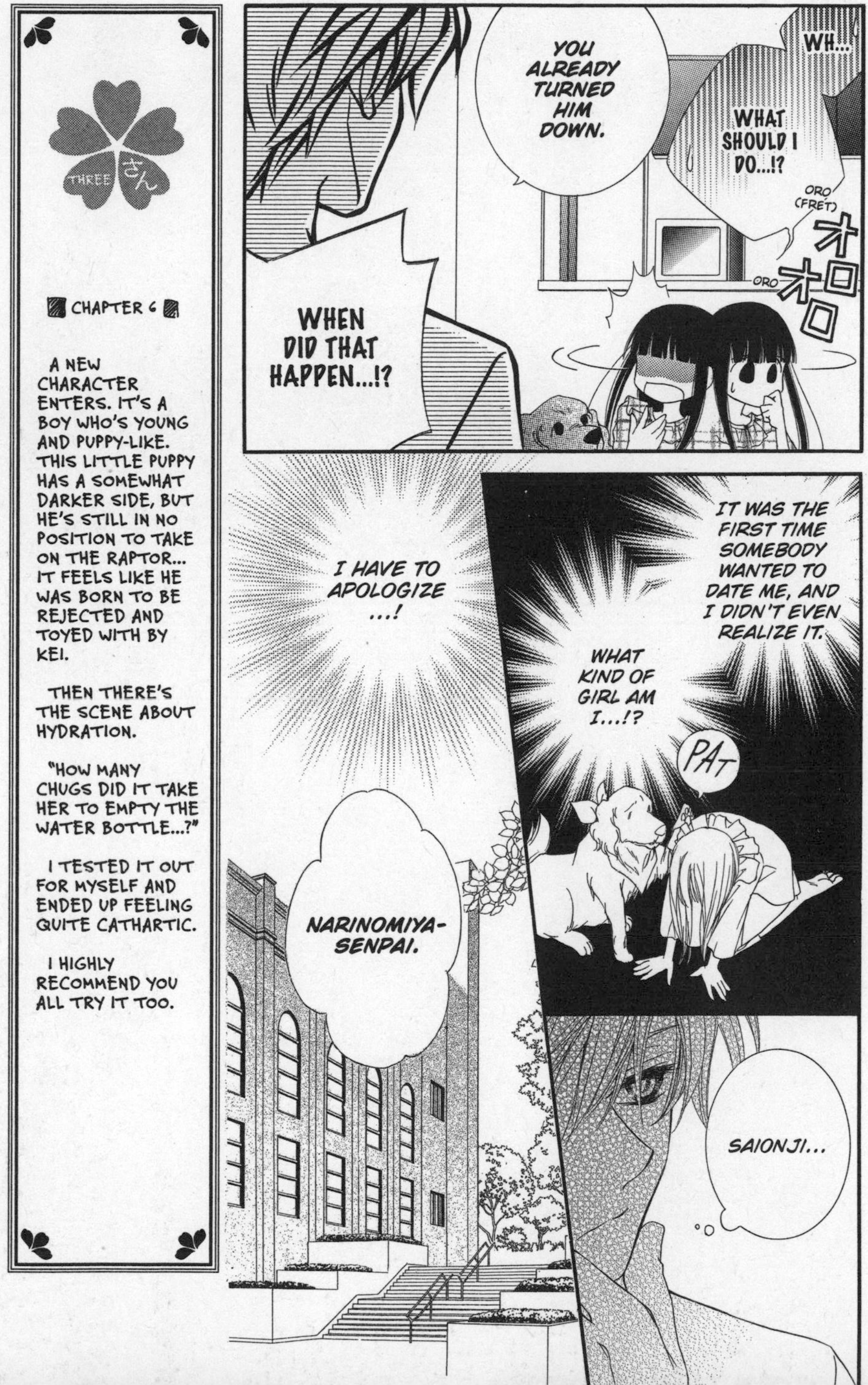
WH...
YOU ALREADY TURNED HIM DOWN.
WHAT SHOULD I DO...!?
ORO (FRET)
ORO
WHEN DID THAT HAPPEN...!?
IT WAS THE FIRST TIME SOMEBODY WANTED TO DATE ME, AND I DIDN'T EVEN REALIZE IT.
WHAT KIND OF GIRL AM I...!?
PAT
SAIONJI...
I HAVE TO APOLOGIZE ...!
NARINOMIYA-SENPAI.

THREE さん

CHAPTER 6

A NEW CHARACTER ENTERS. IT'S A BOY WHO'S YOUNG AND PUPPY-LIKE. THIS LITTLE PUPPY HAS A SOMEWHAT DARKER SIDE, BUT HE'S STILL IN NO POSITION TO TAKE ON THE RAPTOR... IT FEELS LIKE HE WAS BORN TO BE REJECTED AND TOYED WITH BY KEI.

THEN THERE'S THE SCENE ABOUT HYDRATION.

"HOW MANY CHUGS DID IT TAKE HER TO EMPTY THE WATER BOTTLE...?"

I TESTED IT OUT FOR MYSELF AND ENDED UP FEELING QUITE CATHARTIC.

I HIGHLY RECOMMEND YOU ALL TRY IT TOO.

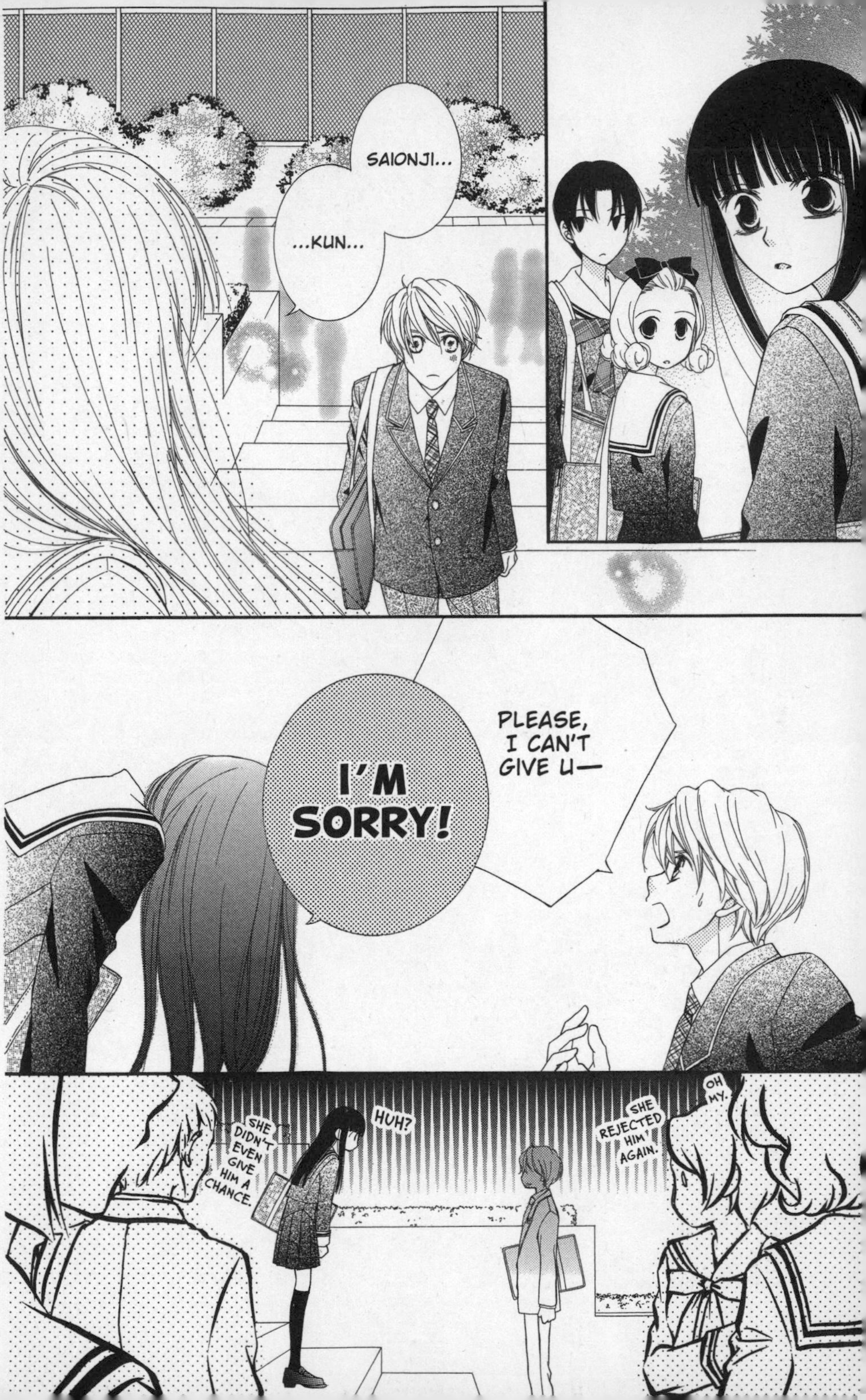
SAIONJI...
...KUN...
PLEASE, I CAN'T GIVE U—
I'M SORRY!
OH MY.
SHE REJECTED HIM AGAIN.
HUH?
SHE DIDN'T EVEN GIVE HIM A CHANCE.

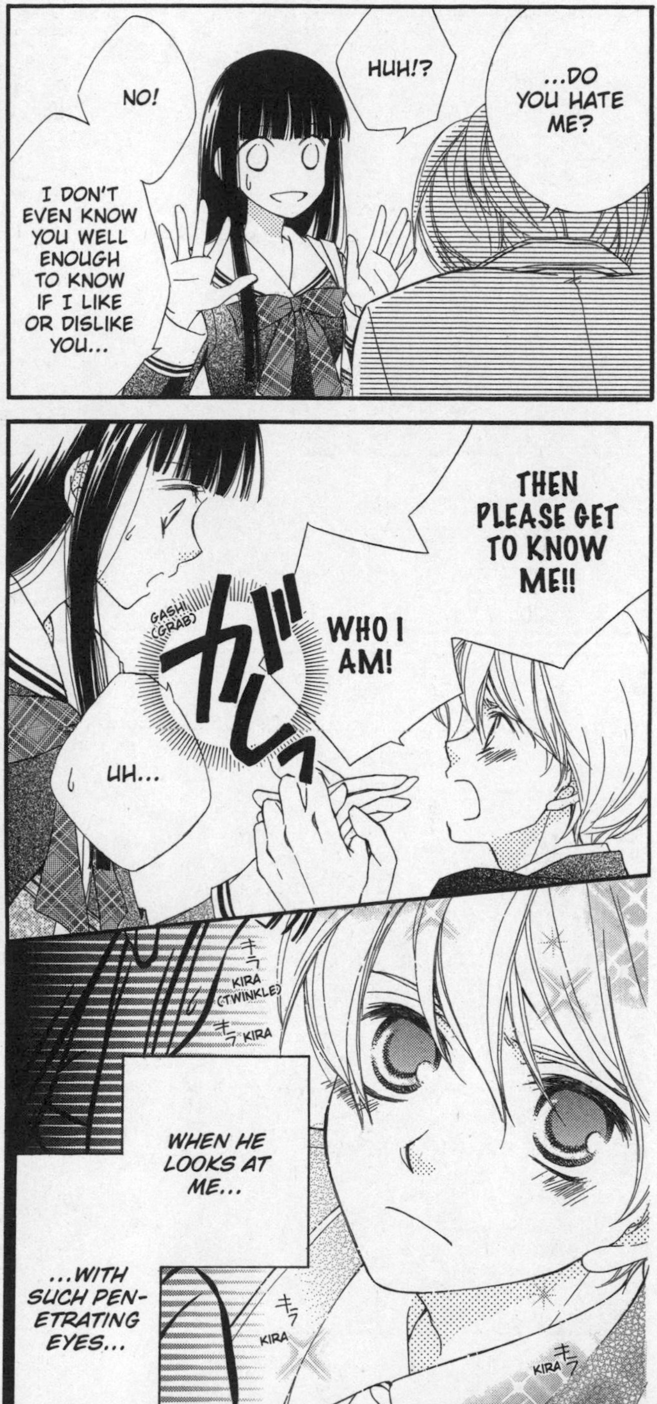
...DO YOU HATE ME?
HUH!?
NO!
I DON'T EVEN KNOW YOU WELL ENOUGH TO KNOW IF I LIKE OR DISLIKE YOU...
THEN PLEASE GET TO KNOW ME!!
WHO I AM!
GASHI (GRAB)
UH...
KIRA (TWINKLE)
KIRA
WHEN HE LOOKS AT ME...
...WITH SUCH PEN-ETRATING EYES...
KIRA
KIRA

FOUR よん

THE NEWEST ADDITION TO MY HOUSE IS A COCKATIEL NAMED MARI-CHAN (♂).

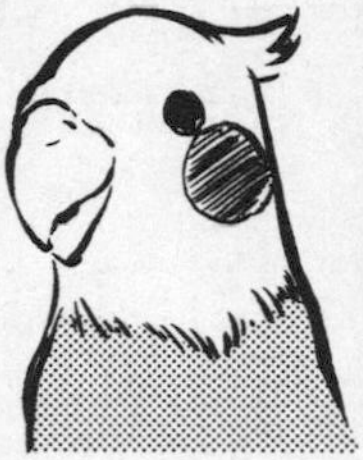

EVERY TIME I WENT TO THE PET SHOP, THE LADY THERE WOULD ALWAYS TELL ME, "...I JUST CAN'T SEEM TO SELL HIM," AND ON THE SECOND OR THIRD TIME, JUST AS I WAS TELLING MYSELF NOT TO BRING HIM HOME, THAT'S ACTUALLY EXACTLY WHAT HAPPENED. RECENTLY, HE'S EVEN LEARNED TO SAY MY NAME. EVERY DAY AND WIIIICKED LOUD AND HAPPILY.

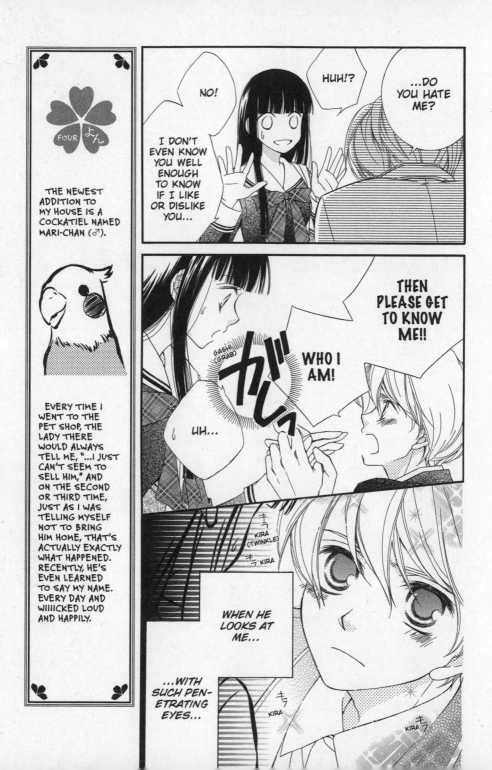

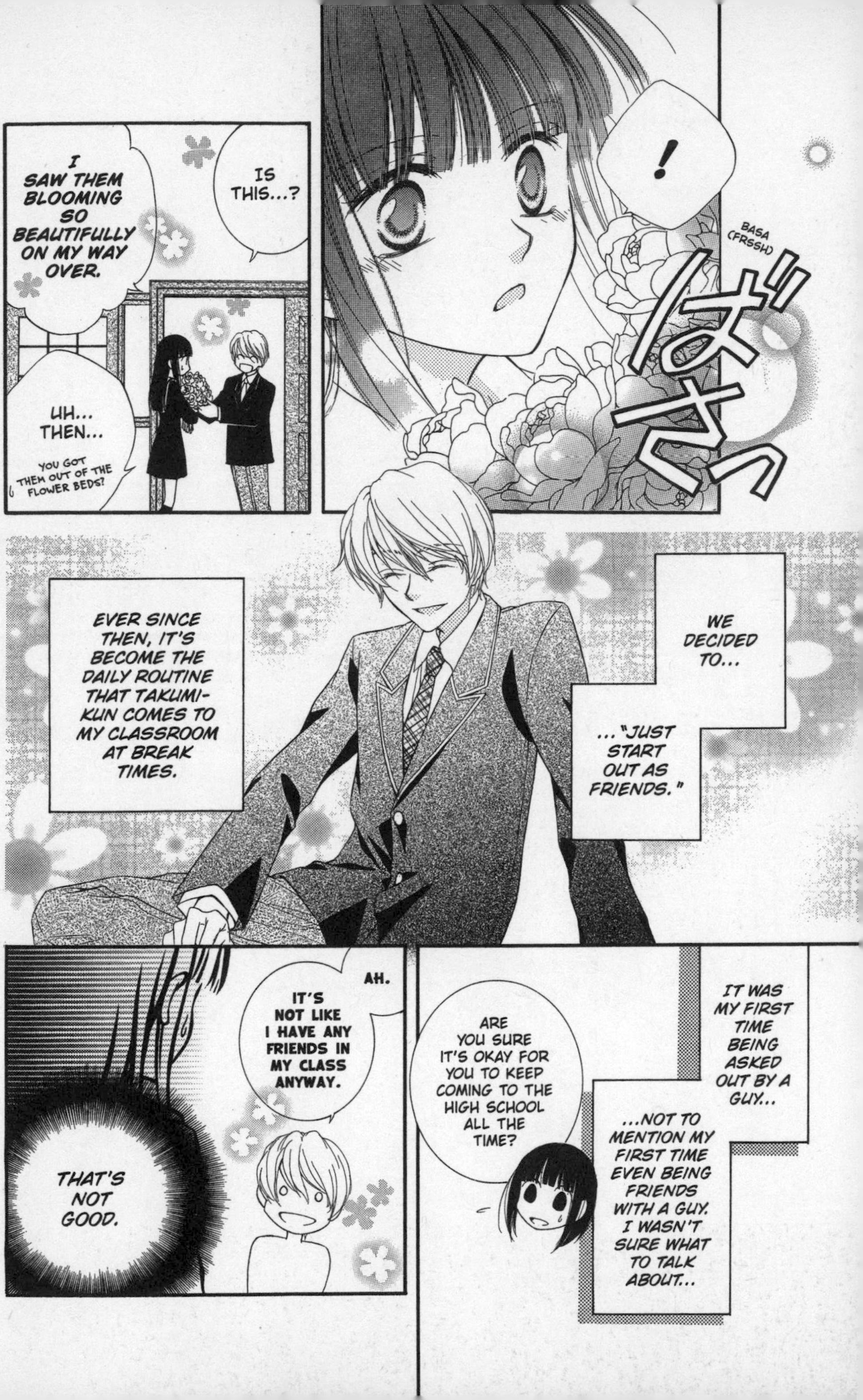
!
BASA (FRSSH)
ばさっ
IS THIS...?
I SAW THEM BLOOMING SO BEAUTIFULLY ON MY WAY OVER.
UH... THEN...
YOU GOT THEM OUT OF THE FLOWER BEDS?
WE DECIDED TO...
..."JUST START OUT AS FRIENDS."
EVER SINCE THEN, IT'S BECOME THE DAILY ROUTINE THAT TAKUMI-KUN COMES TO MY CLASSROOM AT BREAK TIMES.
IT WAS MY FIRST TIME BEING ASKED OUT BY A GUY...
...NOT TO MENTION MY FIRST TIME EVEN BEING FRIENDS WITH A GUY. I WASN'T SURE WHAT TO TALK ABOUT...
ARE YOU SURE IT'S OKAY FOR YOU TO KEEP COMING TO THE HIGH SCHOOL ALL THE TIME?
AH.
IT'S NOT LIKE I HAVE ANY FRIENDS IN MY CLASS ANYWAY.
THAT'S NOT GOOD.

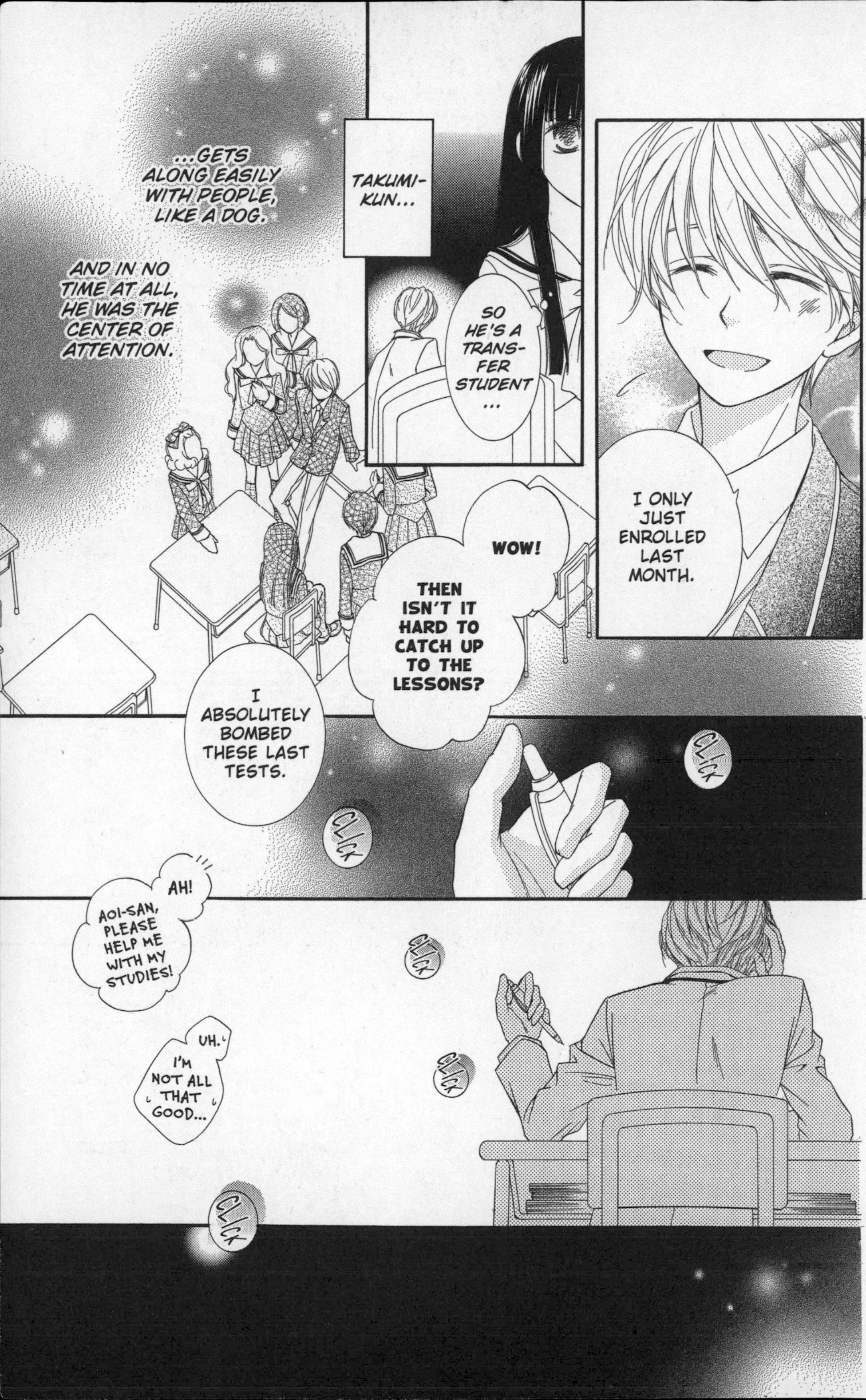
I ONLY JUST ENROLLED LAST MONTH.
TAKUMI-KUN...
SO HE'S A TRANS-FER STUDENT...
...GETS ALONG EASILY WITH PEOPLE, LIKE A DOG.
AND IN NO TIME AT ALL, HE WAS THE CENTER OF ATTENTION.
WOW!
THEN ISN'T IT HARD TO CATCH UP TO THE LESSONS?
I ABSOLUTELY BOMBED THESE LAST TESTS.
CLICK
CLICK
AH!
AOI-SAN, PLEASE HELP ME WITH MY STUDIES!
CLICK
UH.
I'M NOT ALL THAT GOOD...
CLICK
CLICK

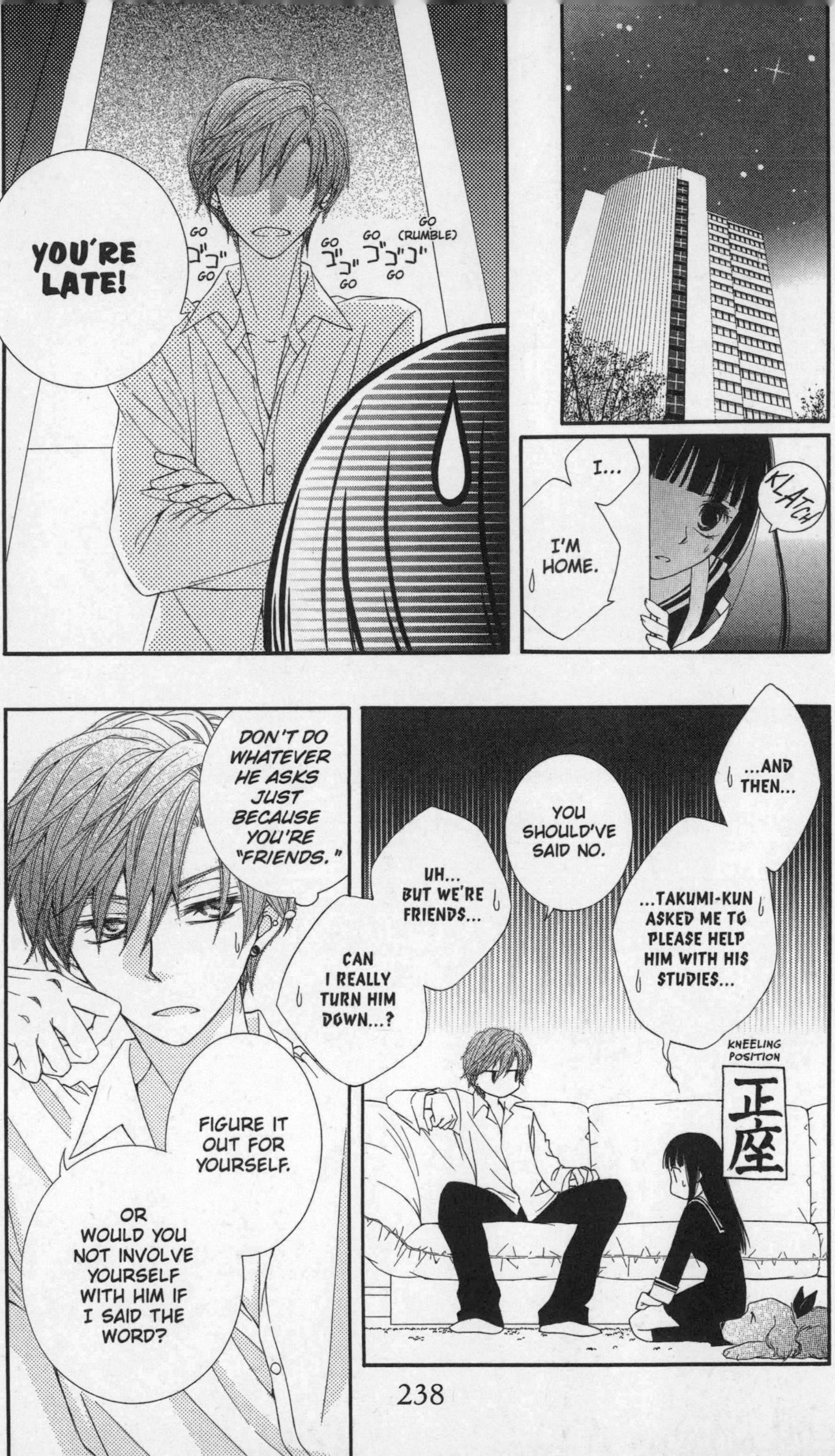
I...
I'M HOME.
KLATCH
YOU'RE LATE!
GO ゴゴ GO
GO ゴ" GO
GO ゴ"ゴ" GO
GO (RUMBLE)
...AND THEN...
...TAKUMI-KUN ASKED ME TO PLEASE HELP HIM WITH HIS STUDIES...
YOU SHOULD'VE SAID NO.
UH... BUT WE'RE FRIENDS...
CAN I REALLY TURN HIM DOWN...?
KNEELING POSITION
正座
DON'T DO WHATEVER HE ASKS JUST BECAUSE YOU'RE "FRIENDS."
FIGURE IT OUT FOR YOURSELF.
OR WOULD YOU NOT INVOLVE YOURSELF WITH HIM IF I SAID THE WORD?

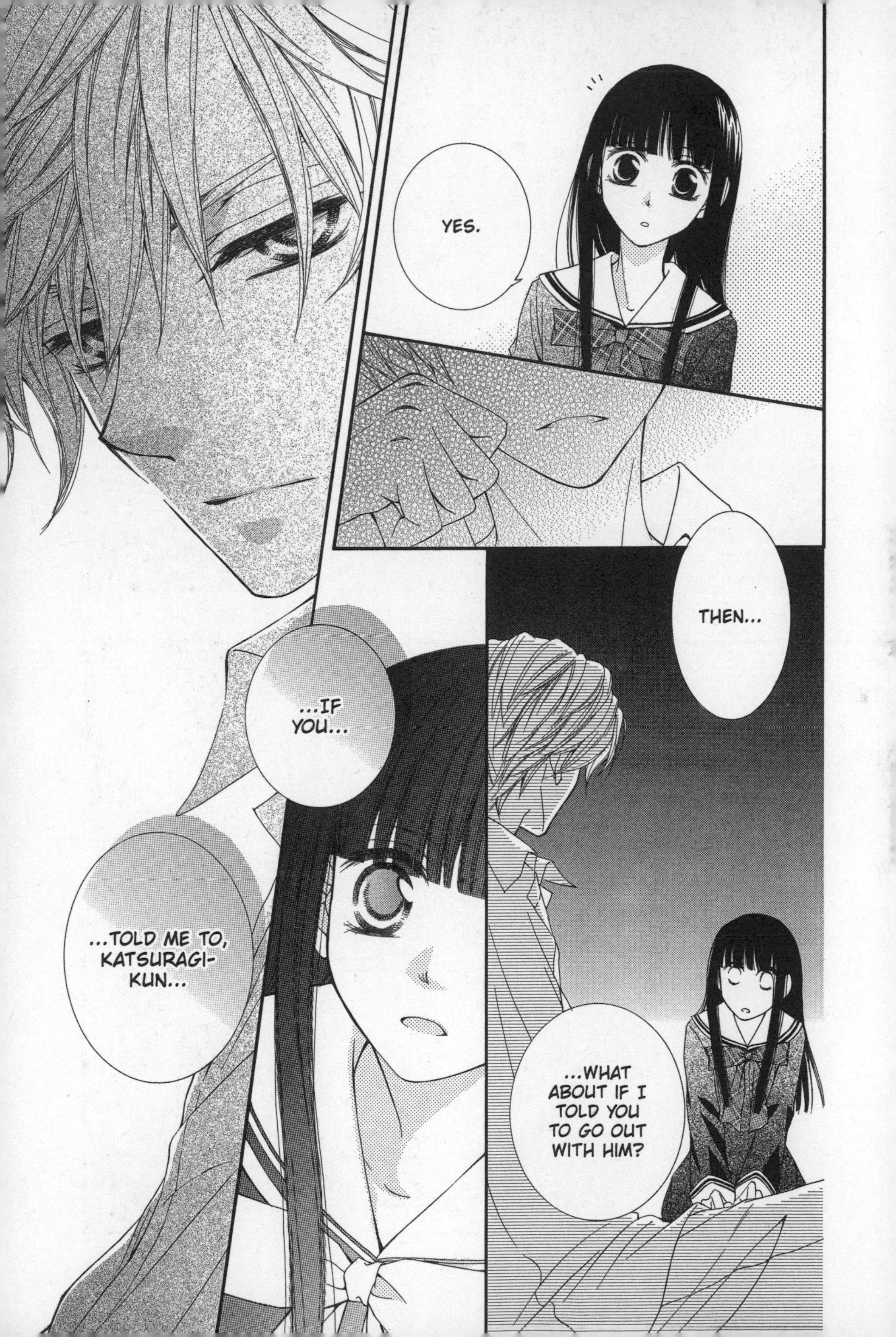
YES.
THEN...
...WHAT ABOUT IF I TOLD YOU TO GO OUT WITH HIM?
...IF YOU...
...TOLD ME TO, KATSURAGI-KUN...

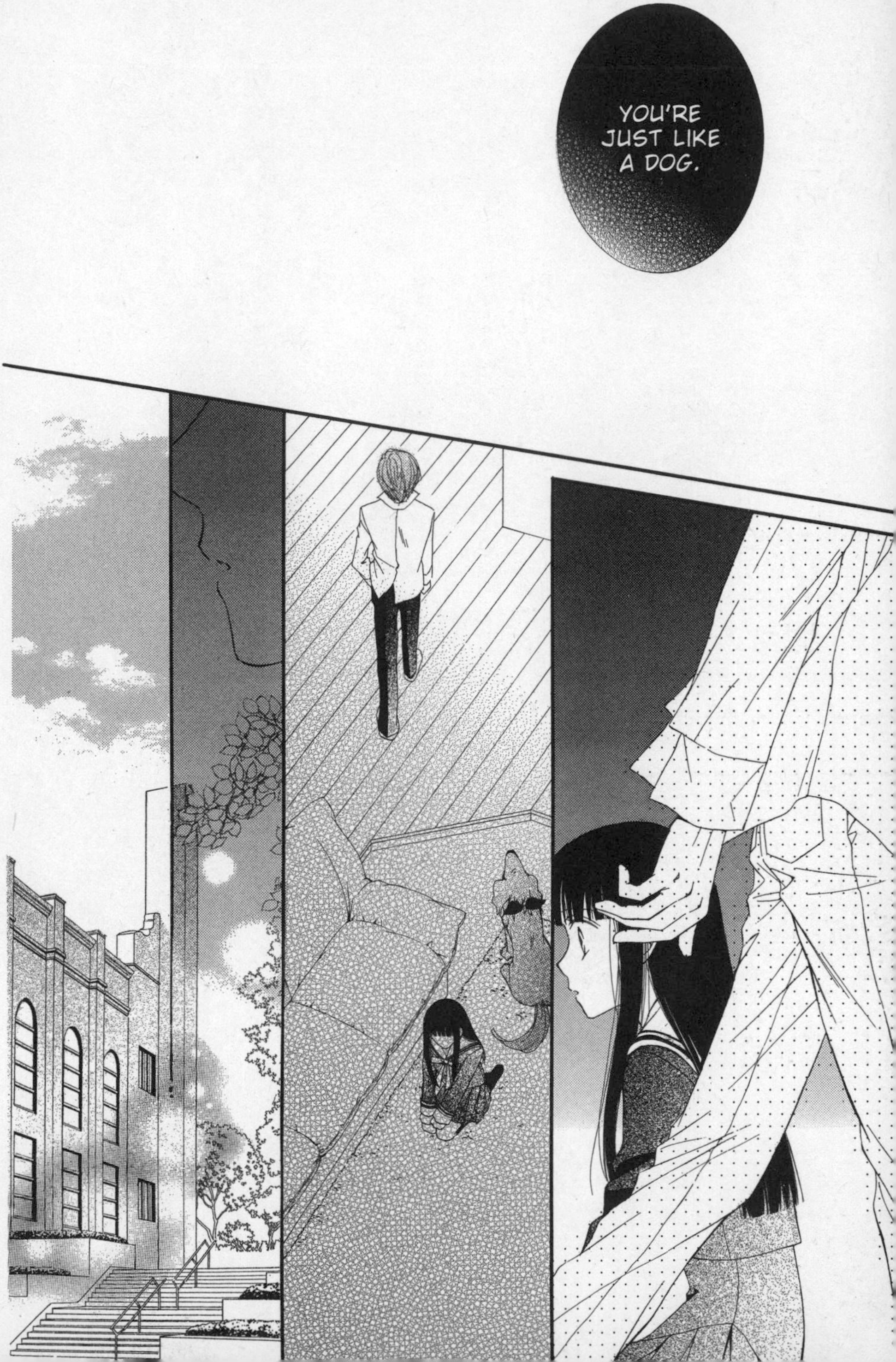
YOU'RE JUST LIKE A DOG.

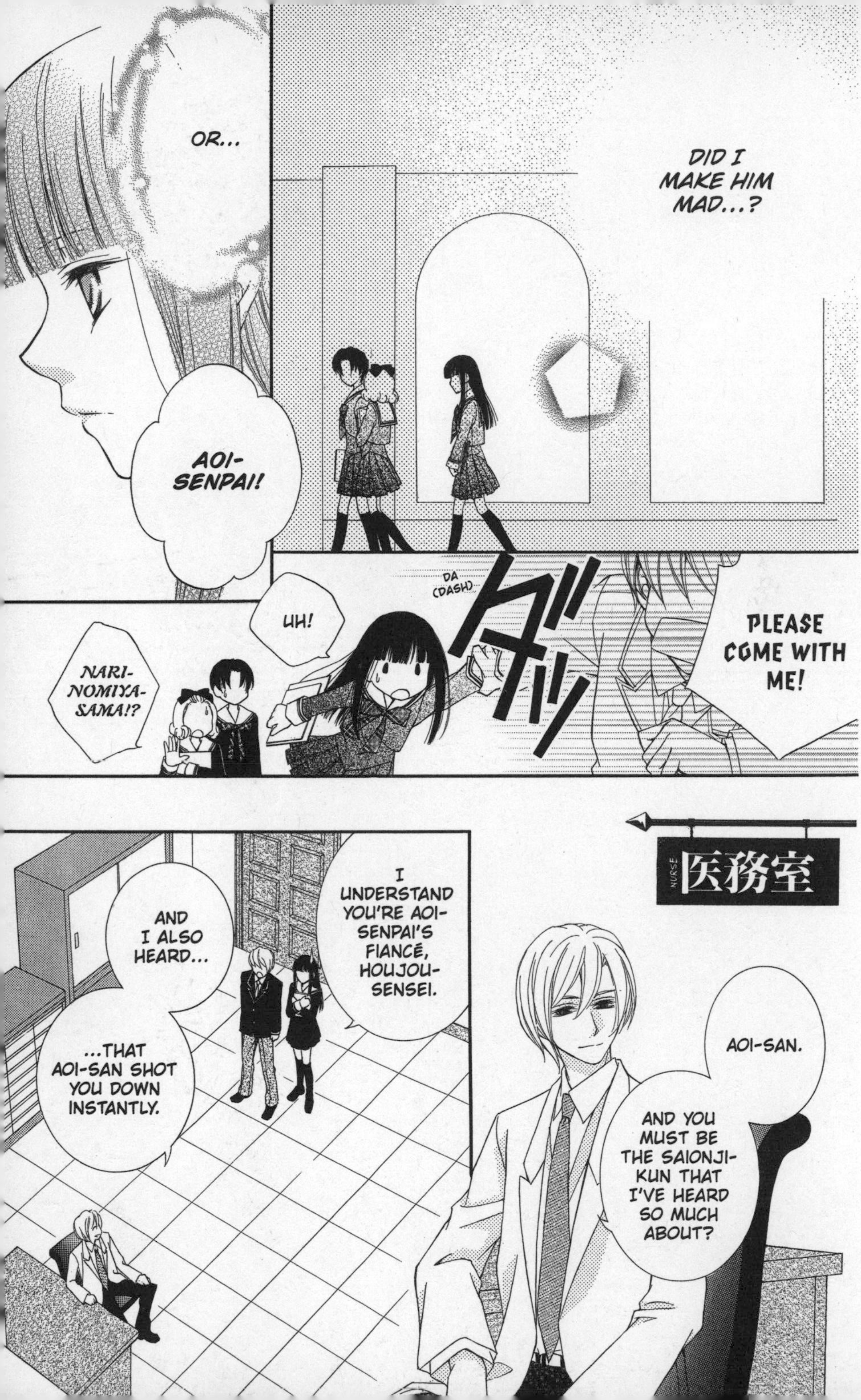
DID I MAKE HIM MAD...?
OR...
AOI-SENPAI!
PLEASE COME WITH ME!
DA (DASH)
UH!
NARI-NOMIYA-SAMA!?
NURSE 医務室
AOI-SAN.
AND YOU MUST BE THE SAIONJI-KUN THAT I'VE HEARD SO MUCH ABOUT?
I UNDERSTAND YOU'RE AOI-SENPAI'S FIANCÉ, HOUJOU-SENSEI.
AND I ALSO HEARD...
...THAT AOI-SAN SHOT YOU DOWN INSTANTLY.

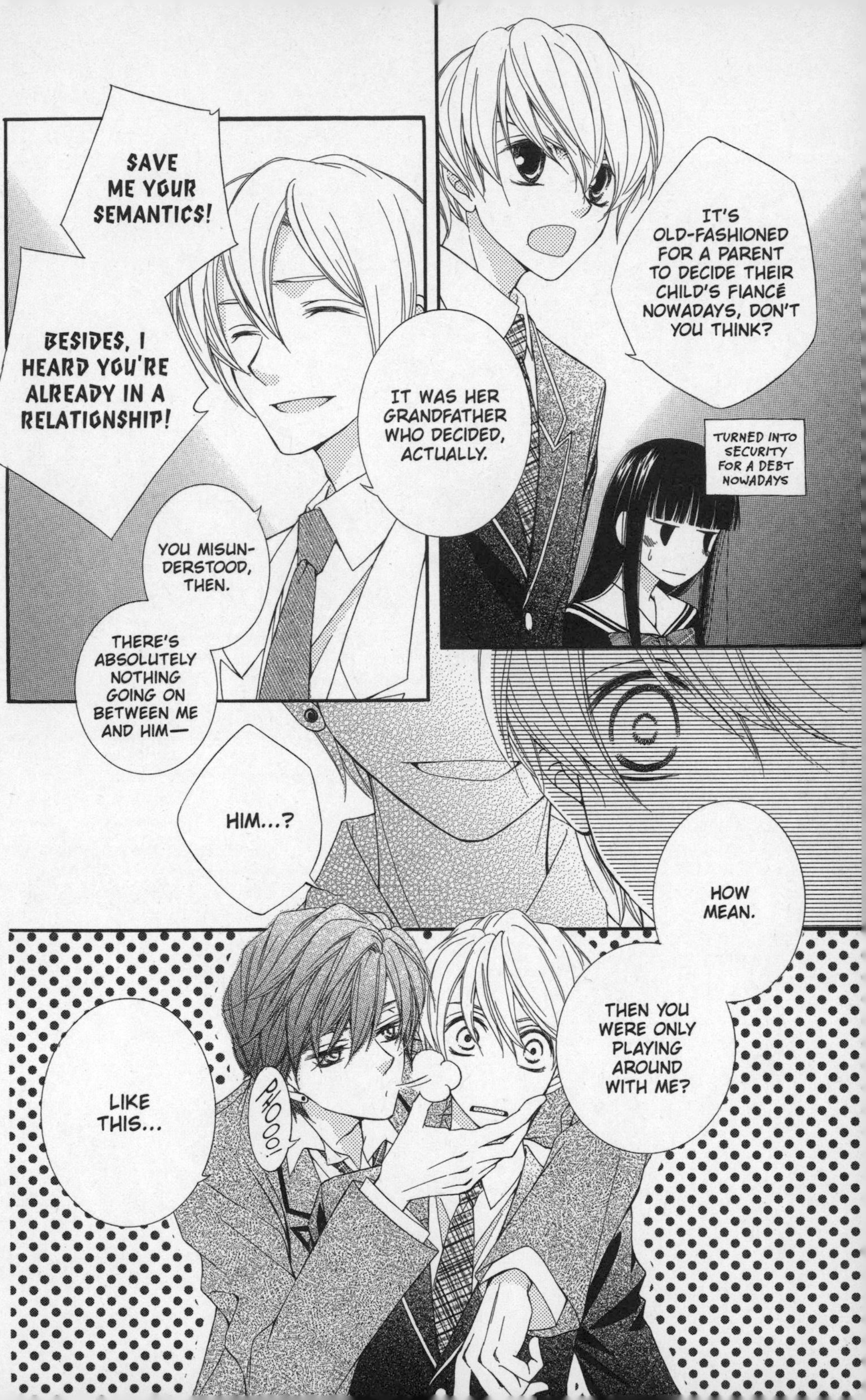
IT'S OLD-FASHIONED FOR A PARENT TO DECIDE THEIR CHILD'S FIANCÉ NOWADAYS, DON'T YOU THINK?
TURNED INTO SECURITY FOR A DEBT NOWADAYS
IT WAS HER GRANDFATHER WHO DECIDED, ACTUALLY.
SAVE ME YOUR SEMANTICS!
BESIDES, I HEARD YOU'RE ALREADY IN A RELATIONSHIP!
YOU MISUNDERSTOOD, THEN.
THERE'S ABSOLUTELY NOTHING GOING ON BETWEEN ME AND HIM—
HIM...?
HOW MEAN.
THEN YOU WERE ONLY PLAYING AROUND WITH ME?
PHOOO!
LIKE THIS...

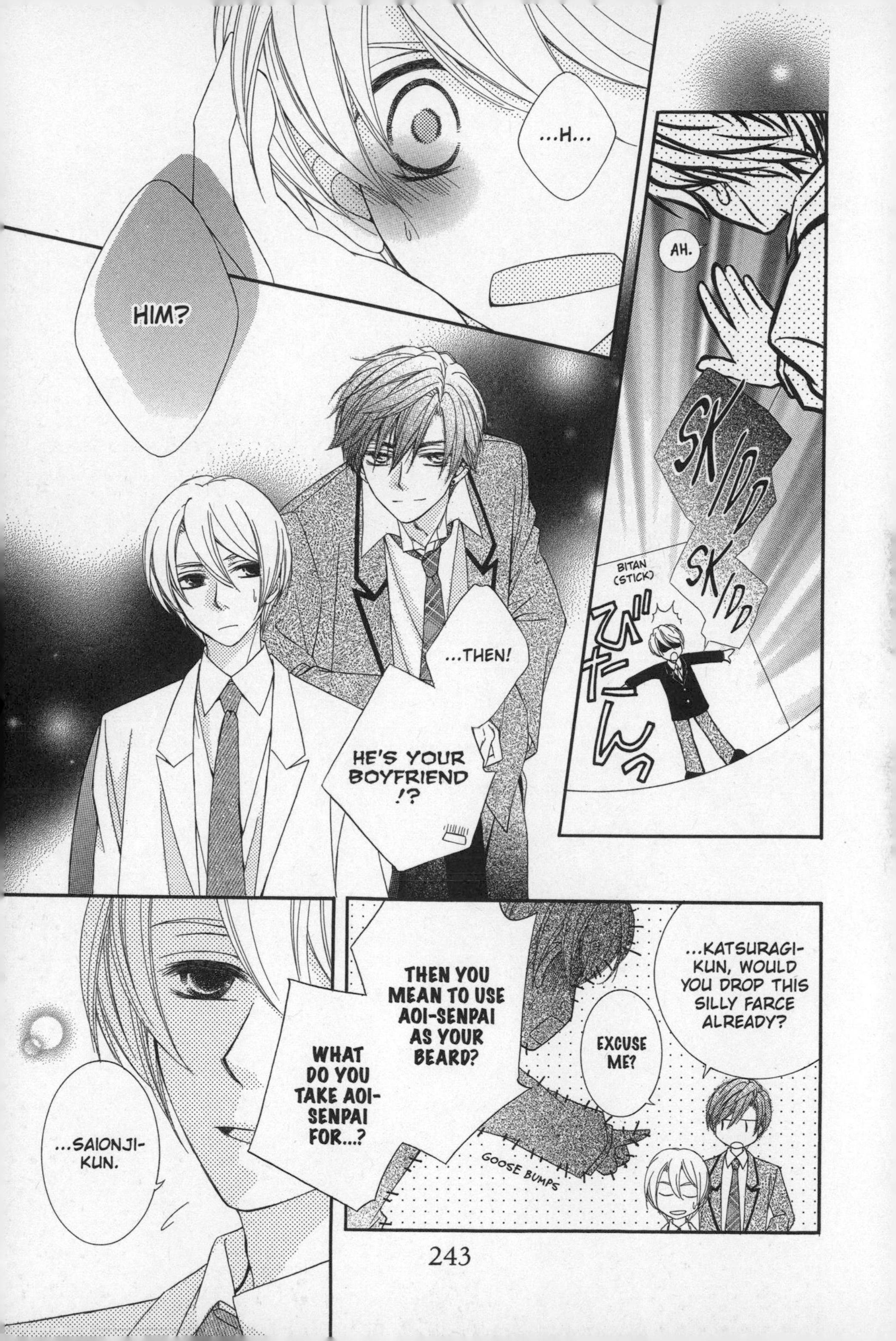
...H...
HIM?
AH.
SKIDD
SKIDD
BITAN (STICK)
びたーんっ
...THEN!
HE'S YOUR BOYFRIEND!?
...KATSURAGI-KUN, WOULD YOU DROP THIS SILLY FARCE ALREADY?
EXCUSE ME?
GOOSE BUMPS
THEN YOU MEAN TO USE AOI-SENPAI AS YOUR BEARD?
WHAT DO YOU TAKE AOI-SENPAI FOR...?
...SAIONJI-KUN.

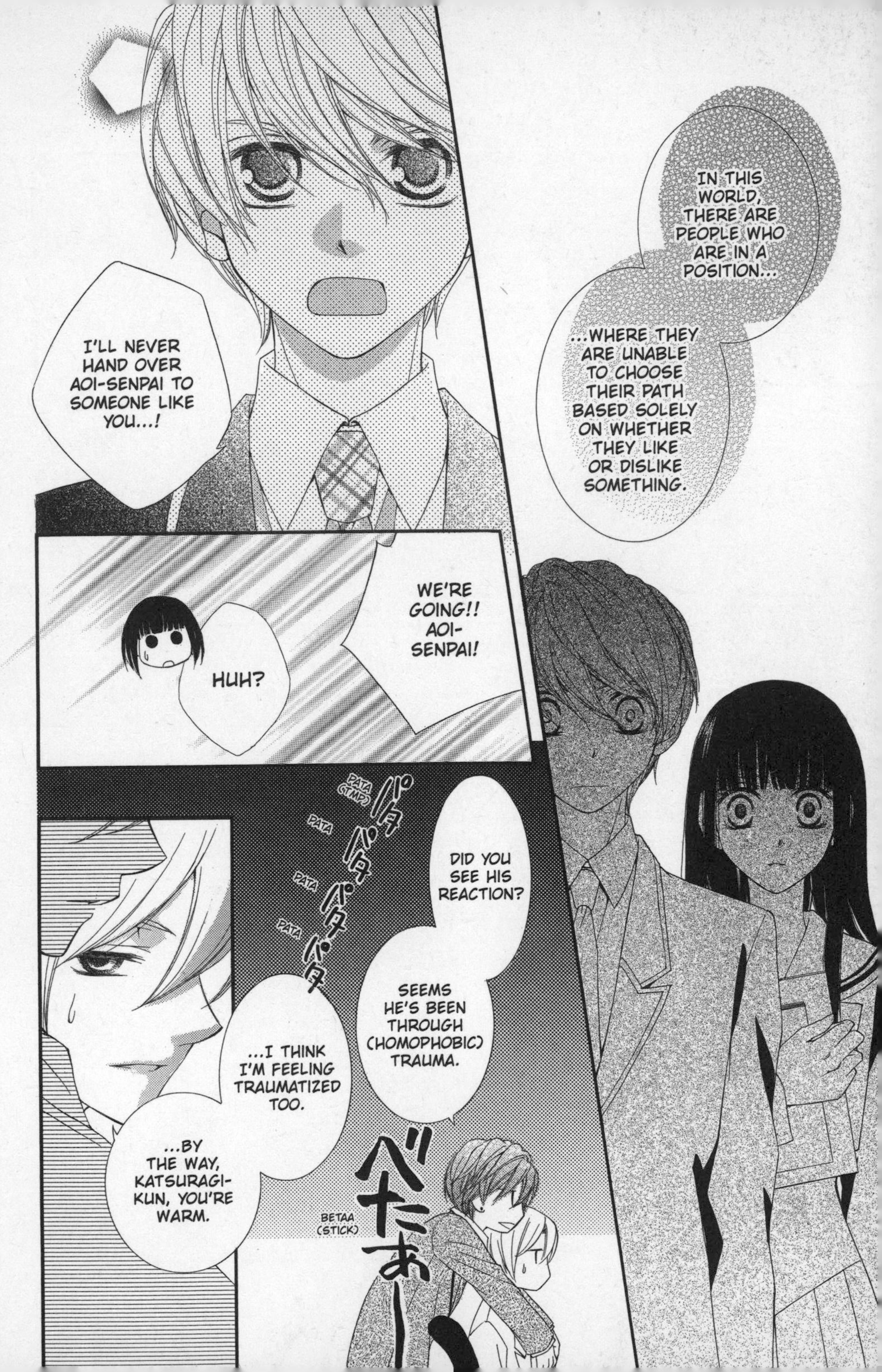
IN THIS WORLD, THERE ARE PEOPLE WHO ARE IN A POSITION...
...WHERE THEY ARE UNABLE TO CHOOSE THEIR PATH BASED SOLELY ON WHETHER THEY LIKE OR DISLIKE SOMETHING.
I'LL NEVER HAND OVER AOI-SENPAI TO SOMEONE LIKE YOU...!
WE'RE GOING!! AOI-SENPAI!
HUH?
PATA (TMP)
PATA
PATA
PATA
DID YOU SEE HIS REACTION?
SEEMS HE'S BEEN THROUGH (HOMOPHOBIC) TRAUMA.
...I THINK I'M FEELING TRAUMATIZED TOO.
...BY THE WAY, KATSURAGI-KUN, YOU'RE WARM.
BETAA (STICK)

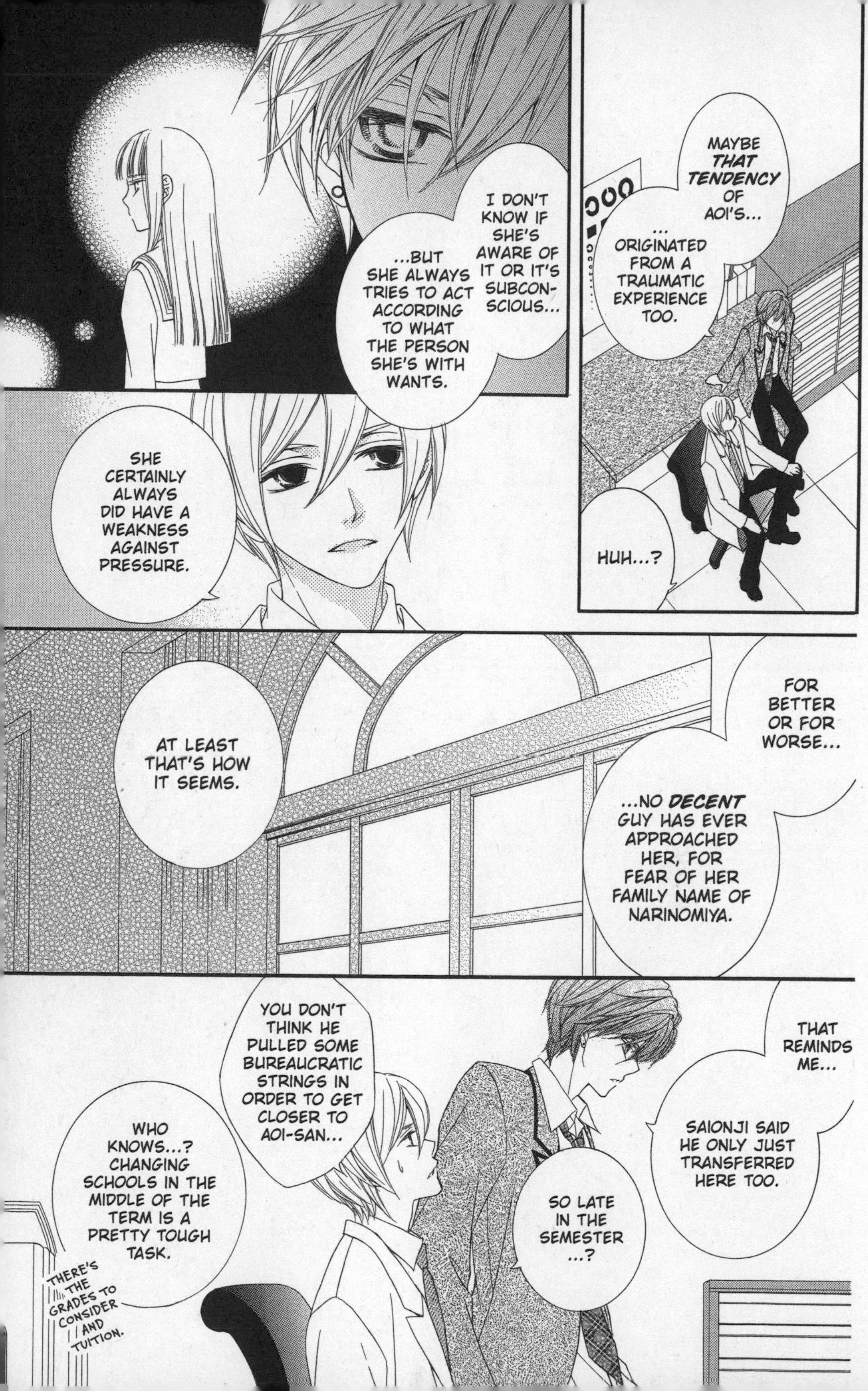
MAYBE *THAT TENDENCY* OF AOI'S...
...ORIGINATED FROM A TRAUMATIC EXPERIENCE TOO.
HUH...?
I DON'T KNOW IF SHE'S AWARE OF IT OR IT'S SUBCONSCIOUS...
...BUT SHE ALWAYS TRIES TO ACT ACCORDING TO WHAT THE PERSON SHE'S WITH WANTS.
SHE CERTAINLY ALWAYS DID HAVE A WEAKNESS AGAINST PRESSURE.
FOR BETTER OR FOR WORSE...
...NO *DECENT* GUY HAS EVER APPROACHED HER, FOR FEAR OF HER FAMILY NAME OF NARINOMIYA.
AT LEAST THAT'S HOW IT SEEMS.
THAT REMINDS ME...
SAIONJI SAID HE ONLY JUST TRANSFERRED HERE TOO.
SO LATE IN THE SEMESTER...?
YOU DON'T THINK HE PULLED SOME BUREAUCRATIC STRINGS IN ORDER TO GET CLOSER TO AOI-SAN...
WHO KNOWS...? CHANGING SCHOOLS IN THE MIDDLE OF THE TERM IS A PRETTY TOUGH TASK.
THERE'S THE GRADES TO CONSIDER AND TUITION.

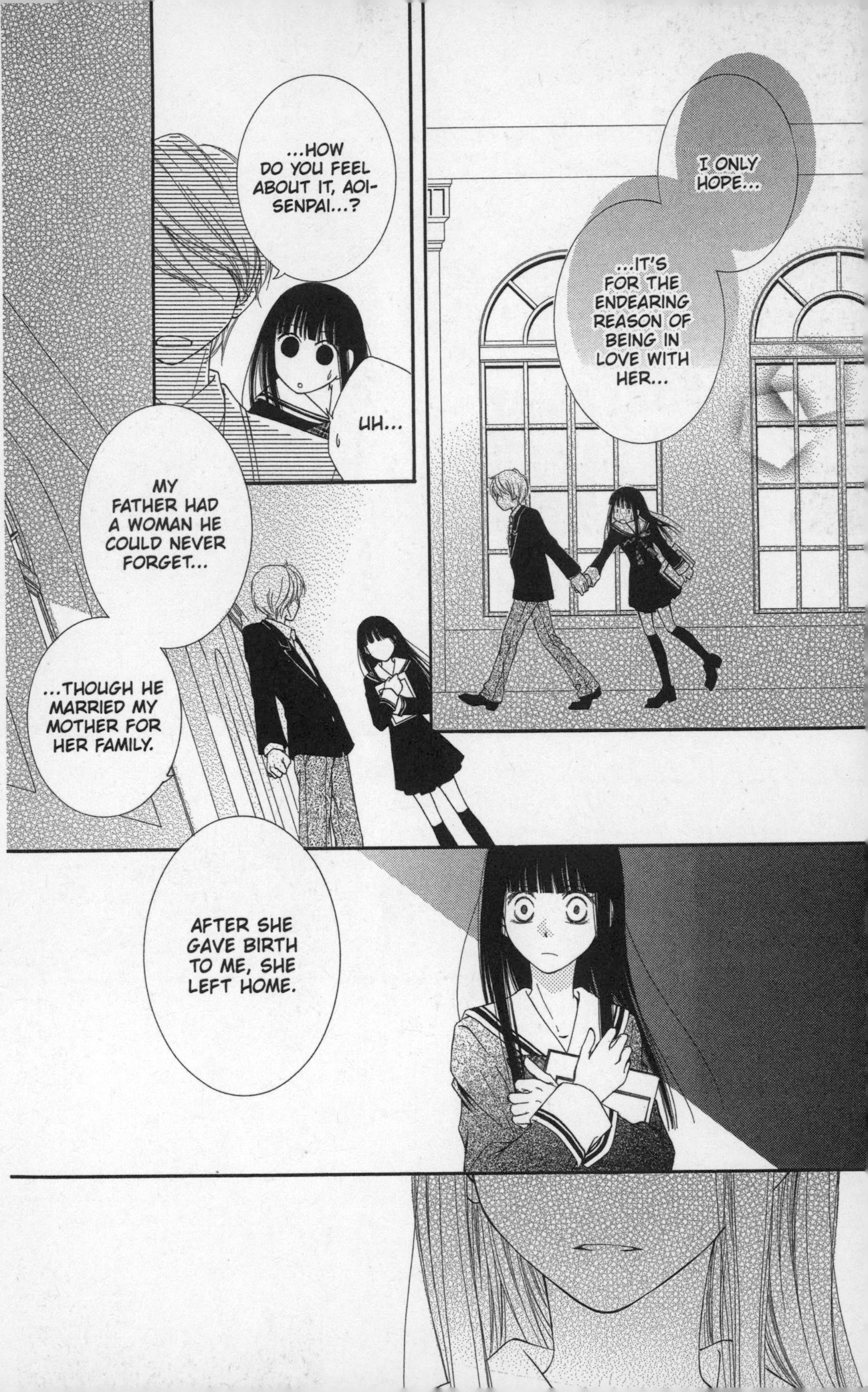
I ONLY HOPE...
...IT'S FOR THE ENDEARING REASON OF BEING IN LOVE WITH HER...
...HOW DO YOU FEEL ABOUT IT, AOI-SENPAI...?
UH...
MY FATHER HAD A WOMAN HE COULD NEVER FORGET...
...THOUGH HE MARRIED MY MOTHER FOR HER FAMILY.
AFTER SHE GAVE BIRTH TO ME, SHE LEFT HOME.

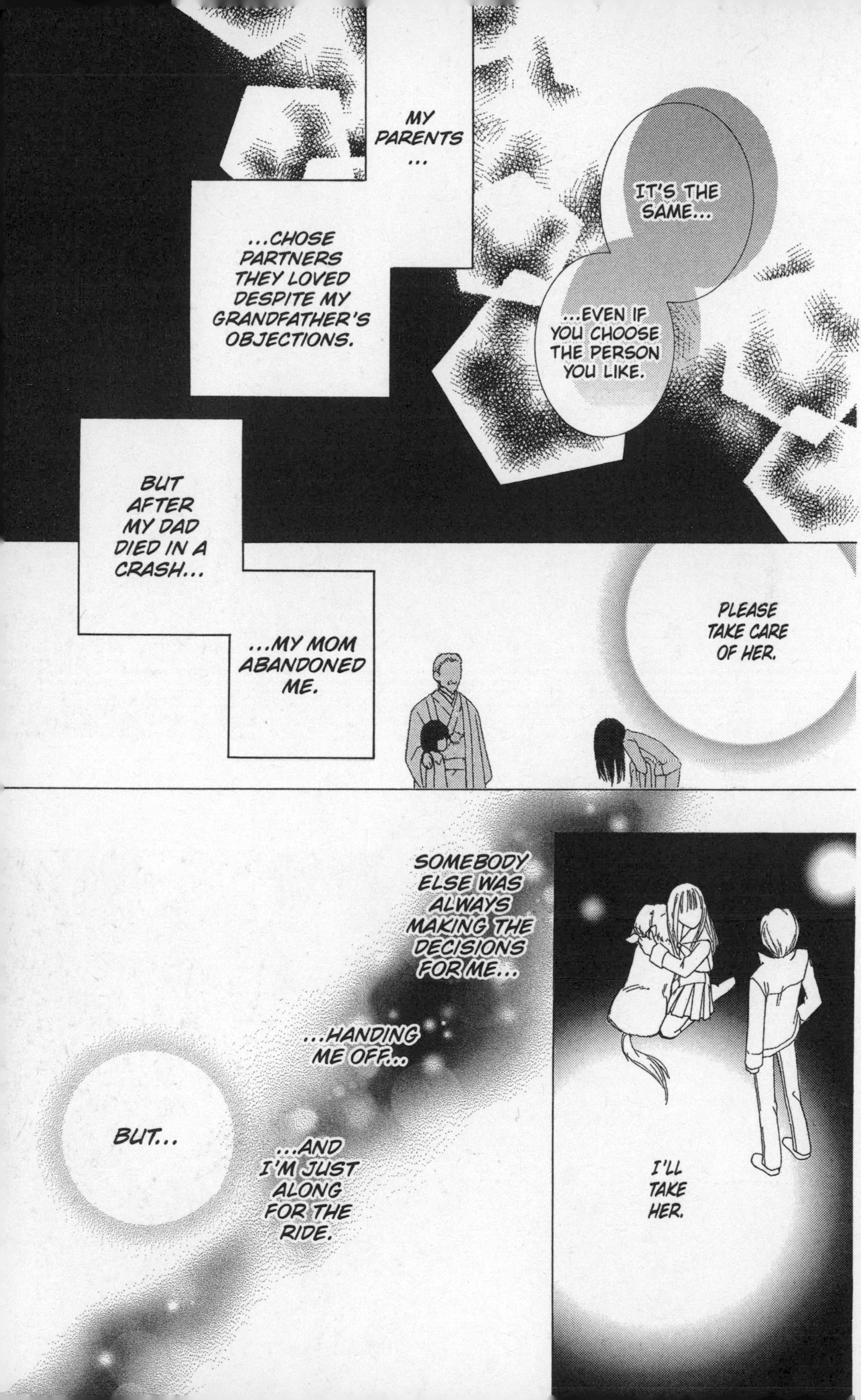
IT'S THE SAME...
...EVEN IF YOU CHOOSE THE PERSON YOU LIKE.
MY PARENTS...
...CHOSE PARTNERS THEY LOVED DESPITE MY GRANDFATHER'S OBJECTIONS.
BUT AFTER MY DAD DIED IN A CRASH...
...MY MOM ABANDONED ME.
PLEASE TAKE CARE OF HER.
SOMEBODY ELSE WAS ALWAYS MAKING THE DECISIONS FOR ME...
I'LL TAKE HER.
...HANDING ME OFF...
...AND I'M JUST ALONG FOR THE RIDE.
BUT...

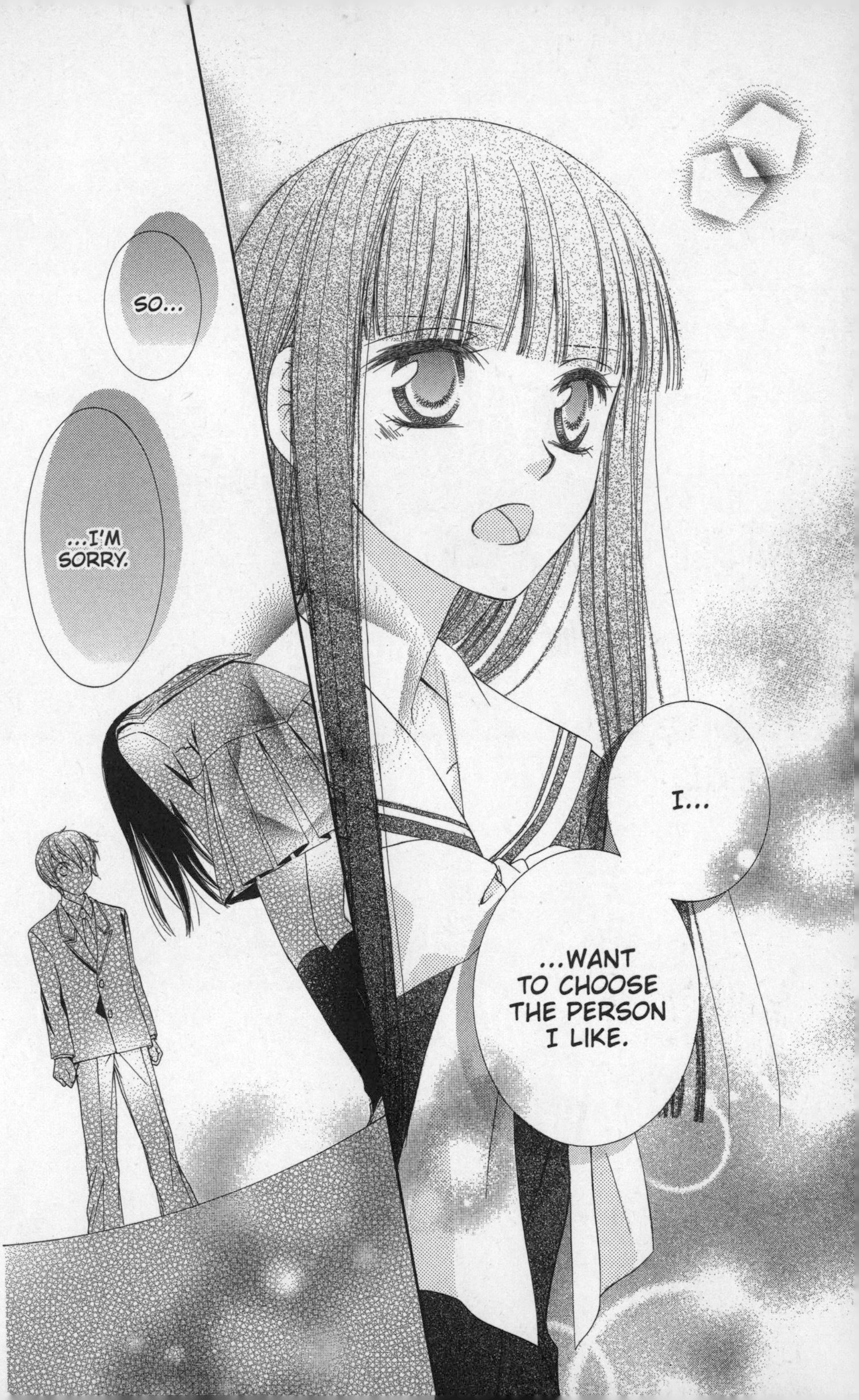
I...
...WANT TO CHOOSE THE PERSON I LIKE.
SO...
...I'M SORRY.

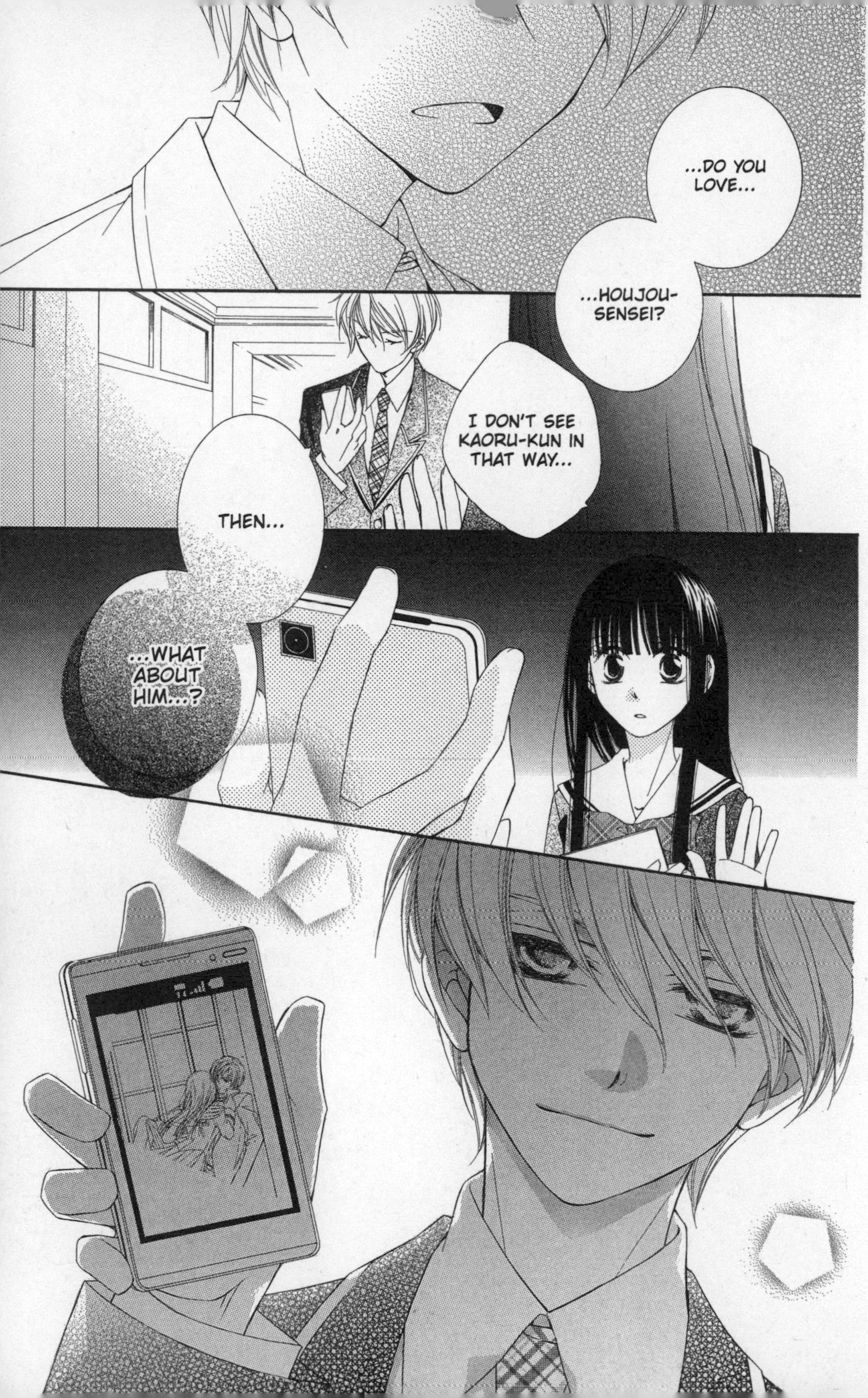
...DO YOU LOVE...
...HOUJOU-SENSEI?
I DON'T SEE KAORU-KUN IN THAT WAY...
THEN...
...WHAT ABOUT HIM...?

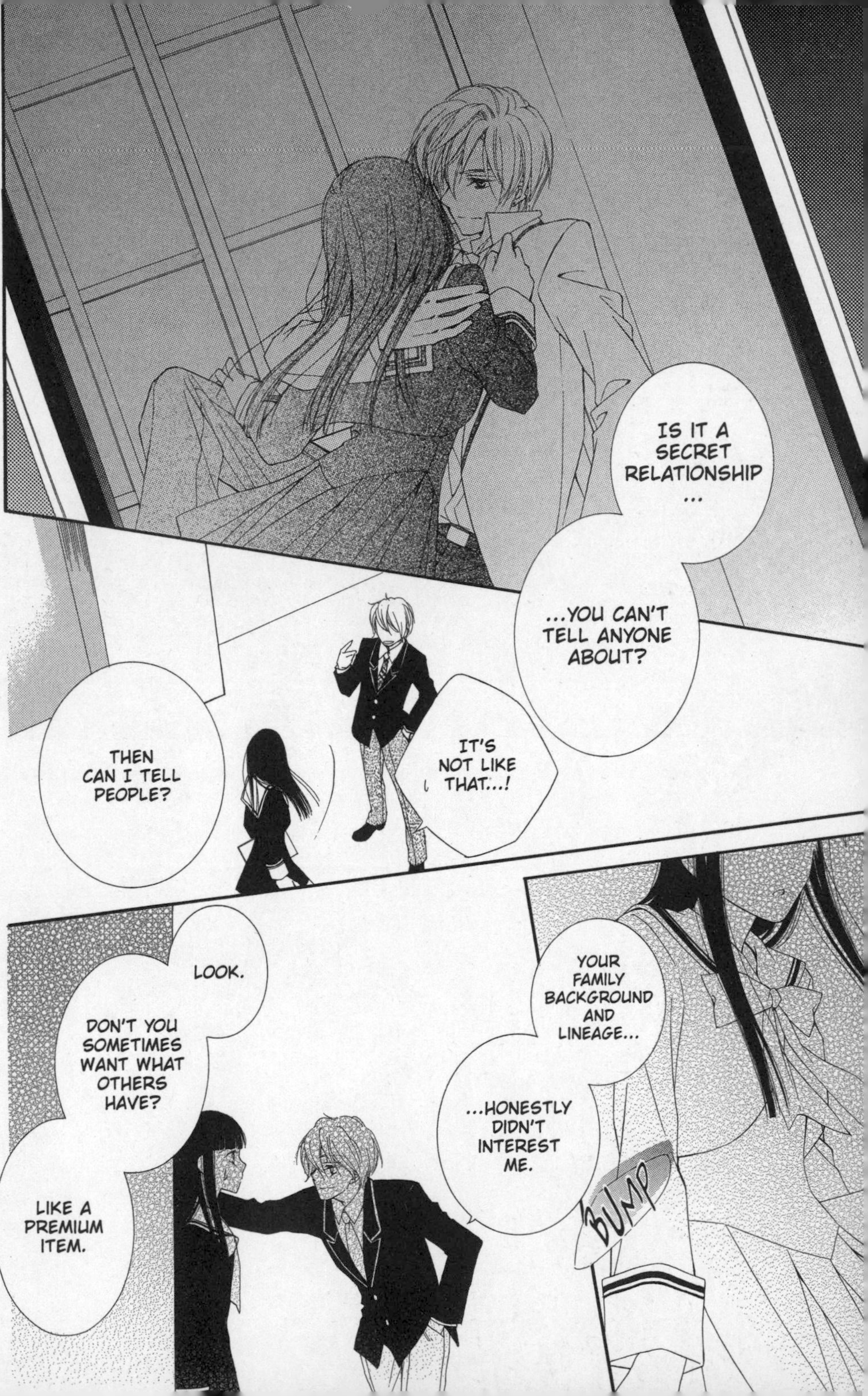
IS IT A SECRET RELATIONSHIP...
...YOU CAN'T TELL ANYONE ABOUT?
IT'S NOT LIKE THAT...!
THEN CAN I TELL PEOPLE?
YOUR FAMILY BACKGROUND AND LINEAGE...
...HONESTLY DIDN'T INTEREST ME.
BUMP
LOOK.
DON'T YOU SOMETIMES WANT WHAT OTHERS HAVE?
LIKE A PREMIUM ITEM.

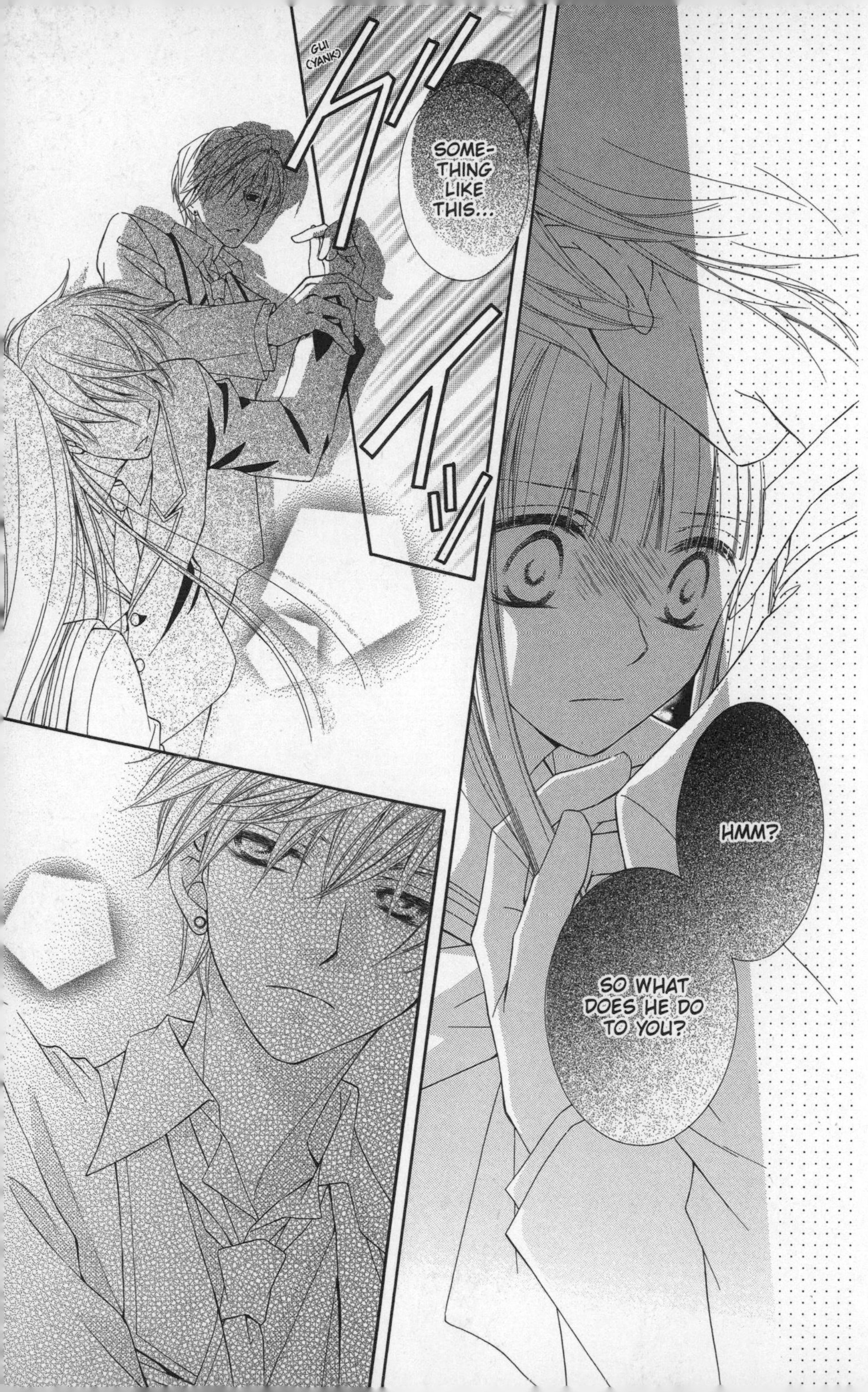
HMM?
SO WHAT DOES HE DO TO YOU?
GUI (YANK)
SOME-THING LIKE THIS...

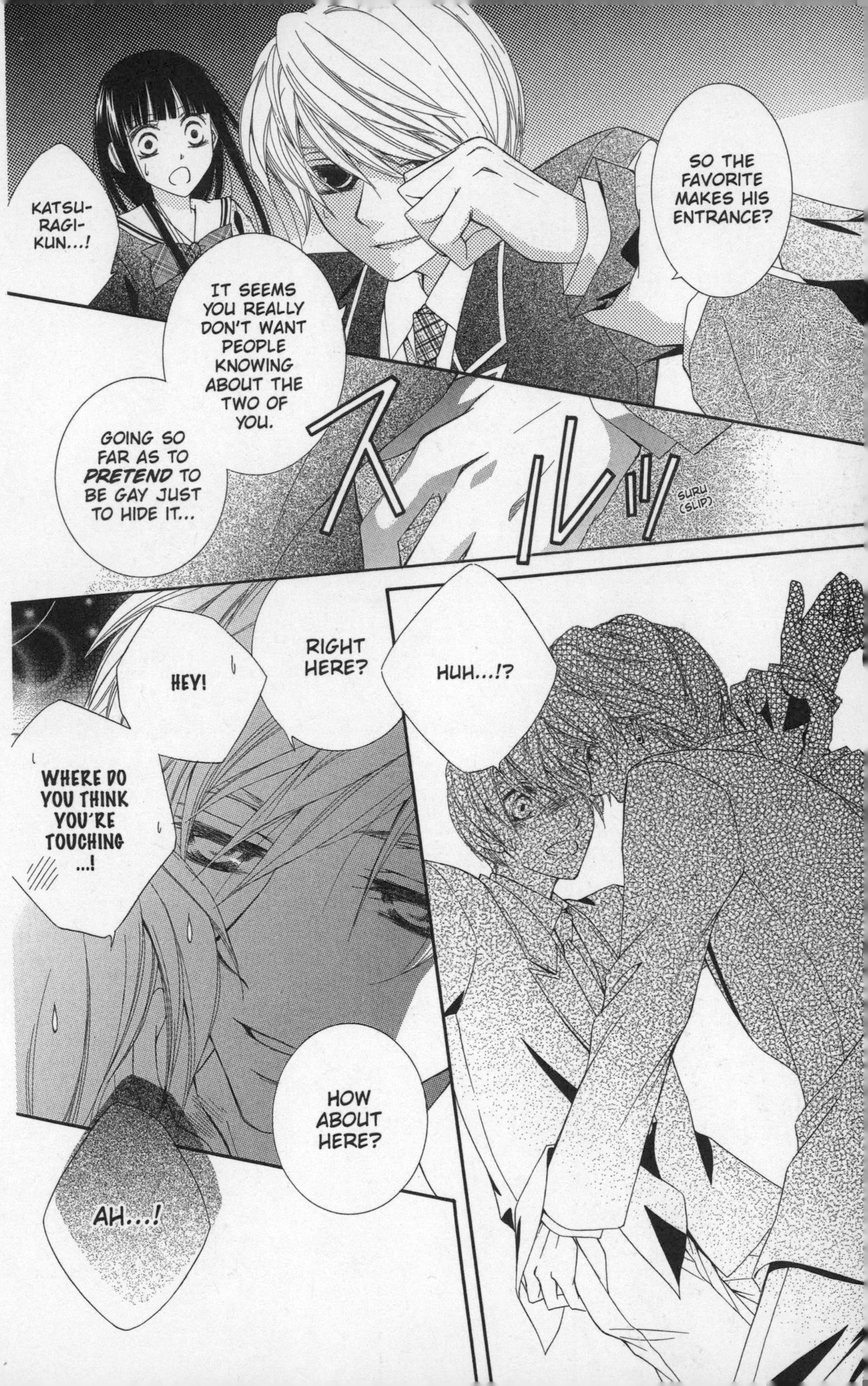
SO THE FAVORITE MAKES HIS ENTRANCE?
KATSU-RAGI-KUN...!
IT SEEMS YOU REALLY DON'T WANT PEOPLE KNOWING ABOUT THE TWO OF YOU.
GOING SO FAR AS TO *PRETEND* TO BE GAY JUST TO HIDE IT...
スルッ
SURU (SLIP)
HUH...!?
RIGHT HERE?
HEY!
WHERE DO YOU THINK YOU'RE TOUCHING...!
HOW ABOUT HERE?
AH...!

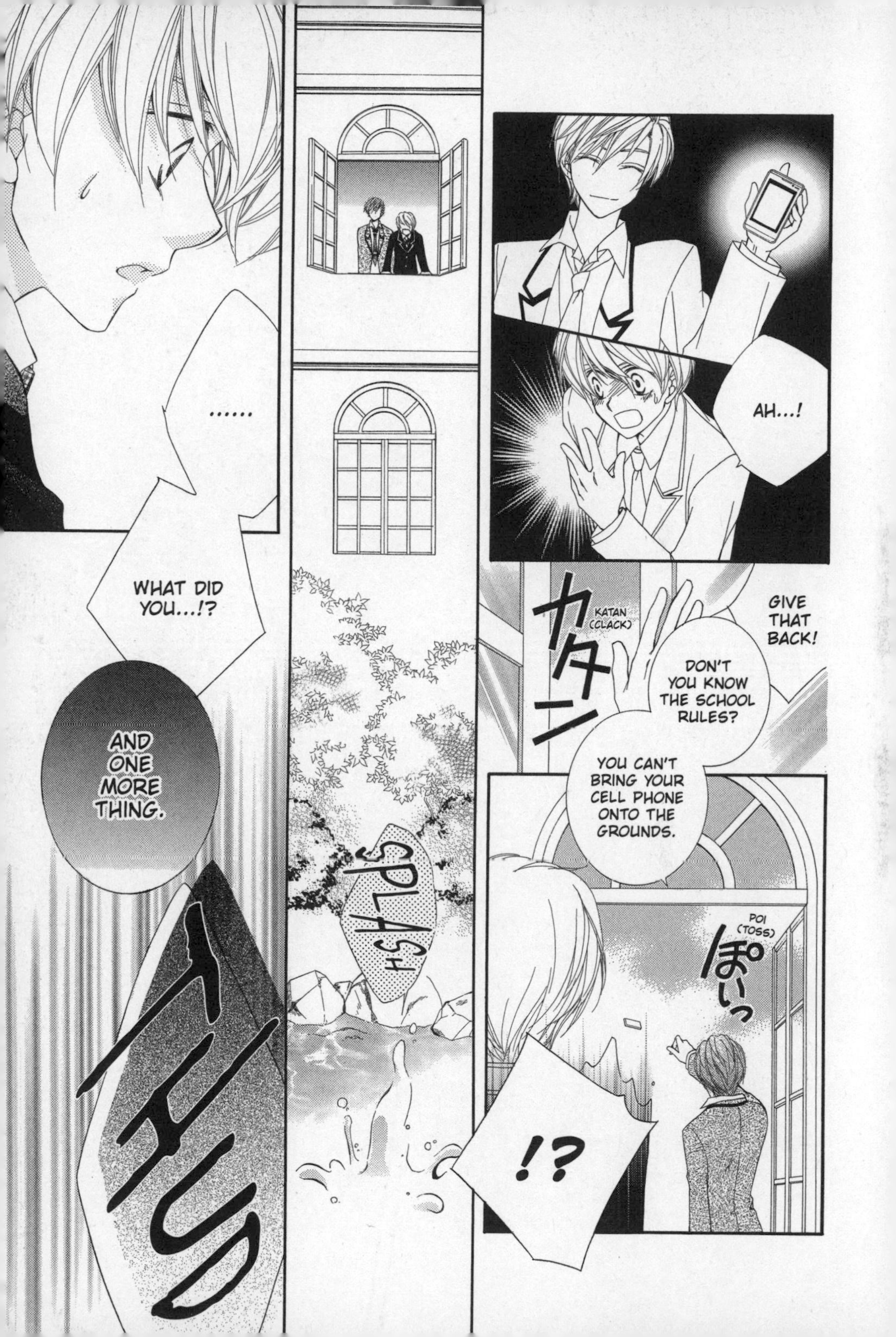
AH...!
カタン
KATAN (CLACK)
GIVE THAT BACK!
DON'T YOU KNOW THE SCHOOL RULES?
YOU CAN'T BRING YOUR CELL PHONE ONTO THE GROUNDS.
ぽいっ
POI (TOSS)
!?
SPLASH
......
WHAT DID YOU...!?
AND ONE MORE THING.
THUD

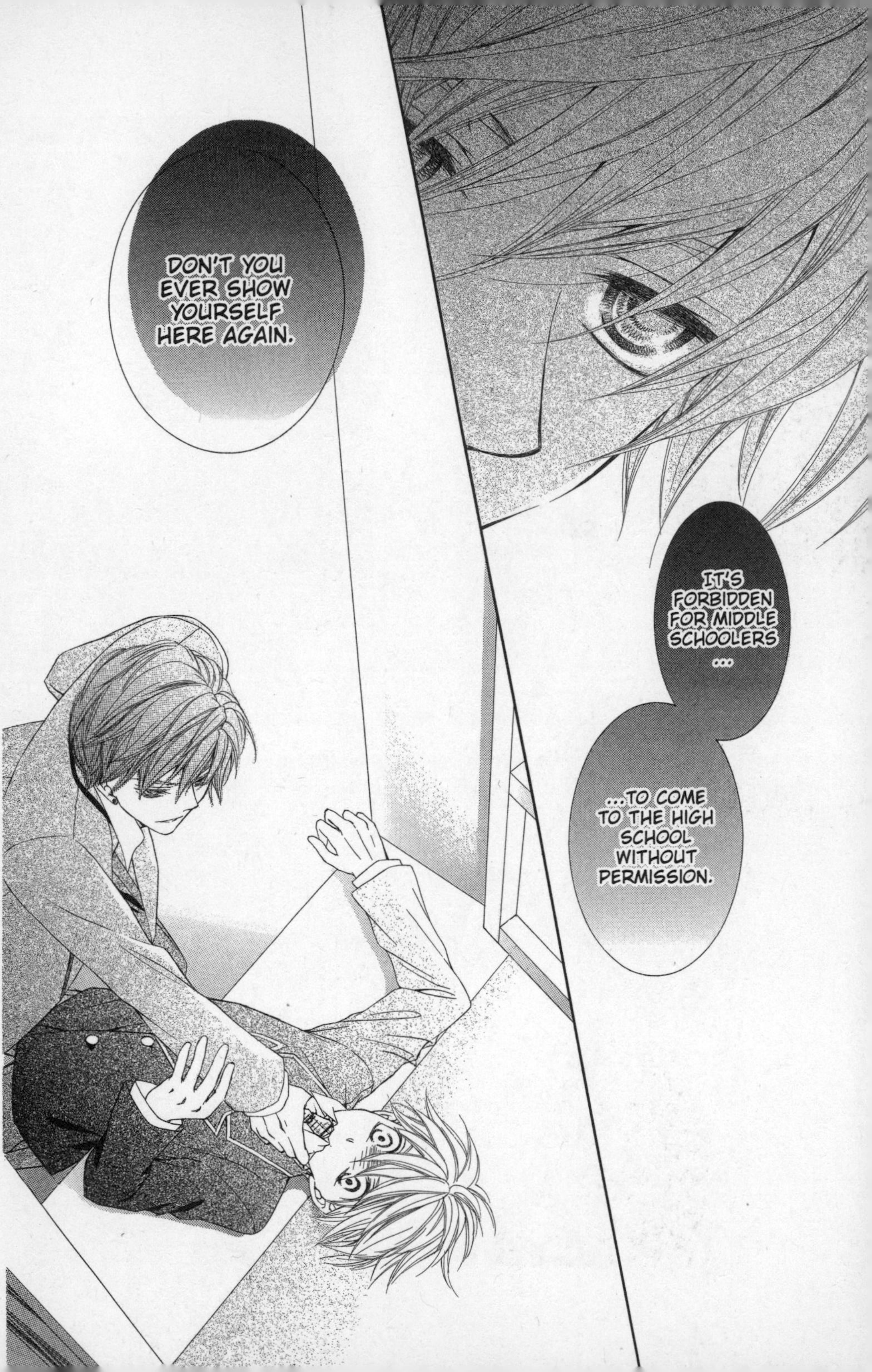
IT'S FORBIDDEN FOR MIDDLE SCHOOLERS ...
...TO COME TO THE HIGH SCHOOL WITHOUT PERMISSION.
DON'T YOU EVER SHOW YOURSELF HERE AGAIN.

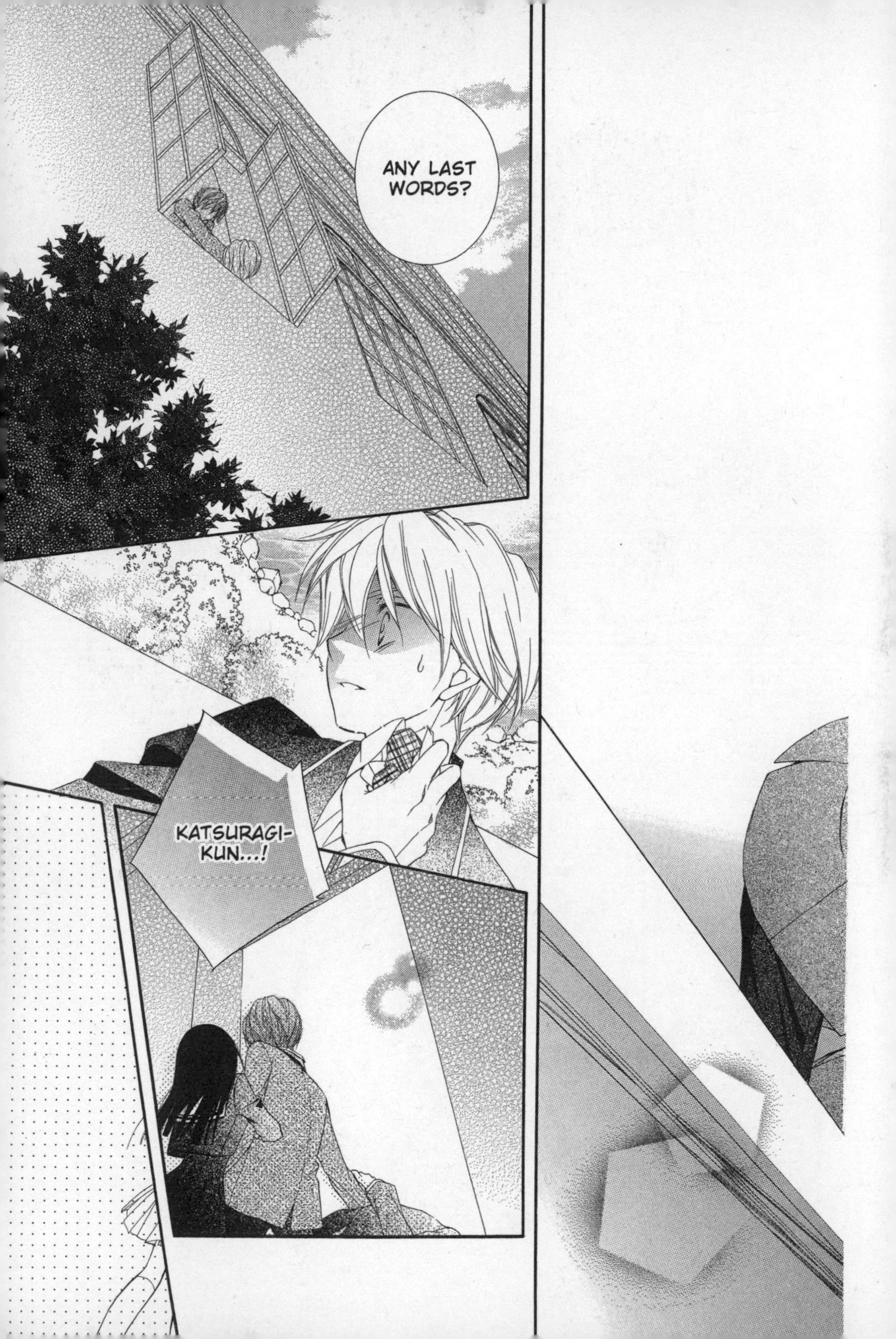
ANY LAST WORDS?
KATSURAGI-KUN...!

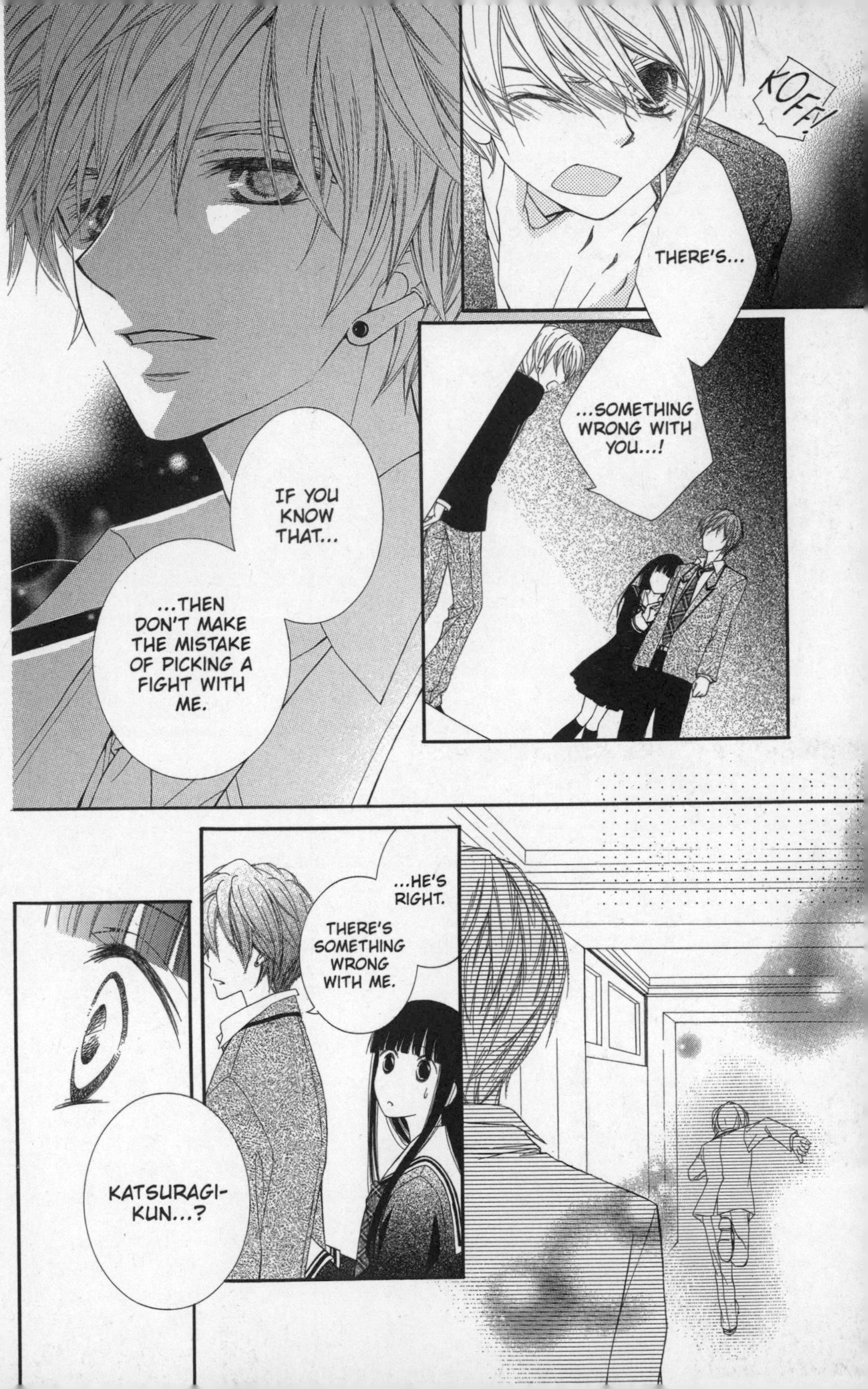
KOFF!
THERE'S...
...SOMETHING WRONG WITH YOU...!
IF YOU KNOW THAT...
...THEN DON'T MAKE THE MISTAKE OF PICKING A FIGHT WITH ME.
...HE'S RIGHT.
THERE'S SOMETHING WRONG WITH ME.
KATSURAGI-KUN...?

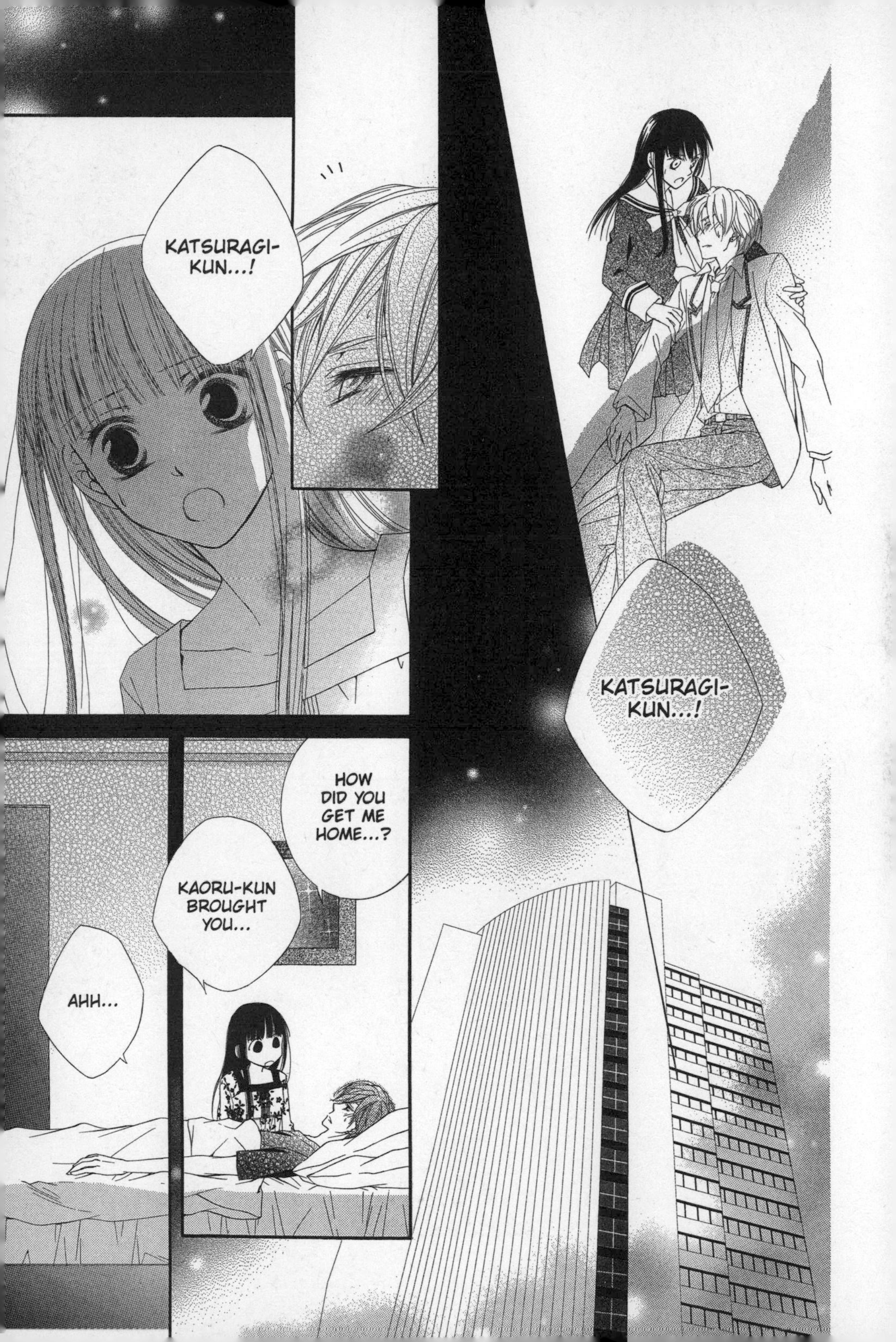
KATSURAGI-KUN...!
KATSURAGI-KUN...!
HOW DID YOU GET ME HOME...?
KAORU-KUN BROUGHT YOU...
AHH...

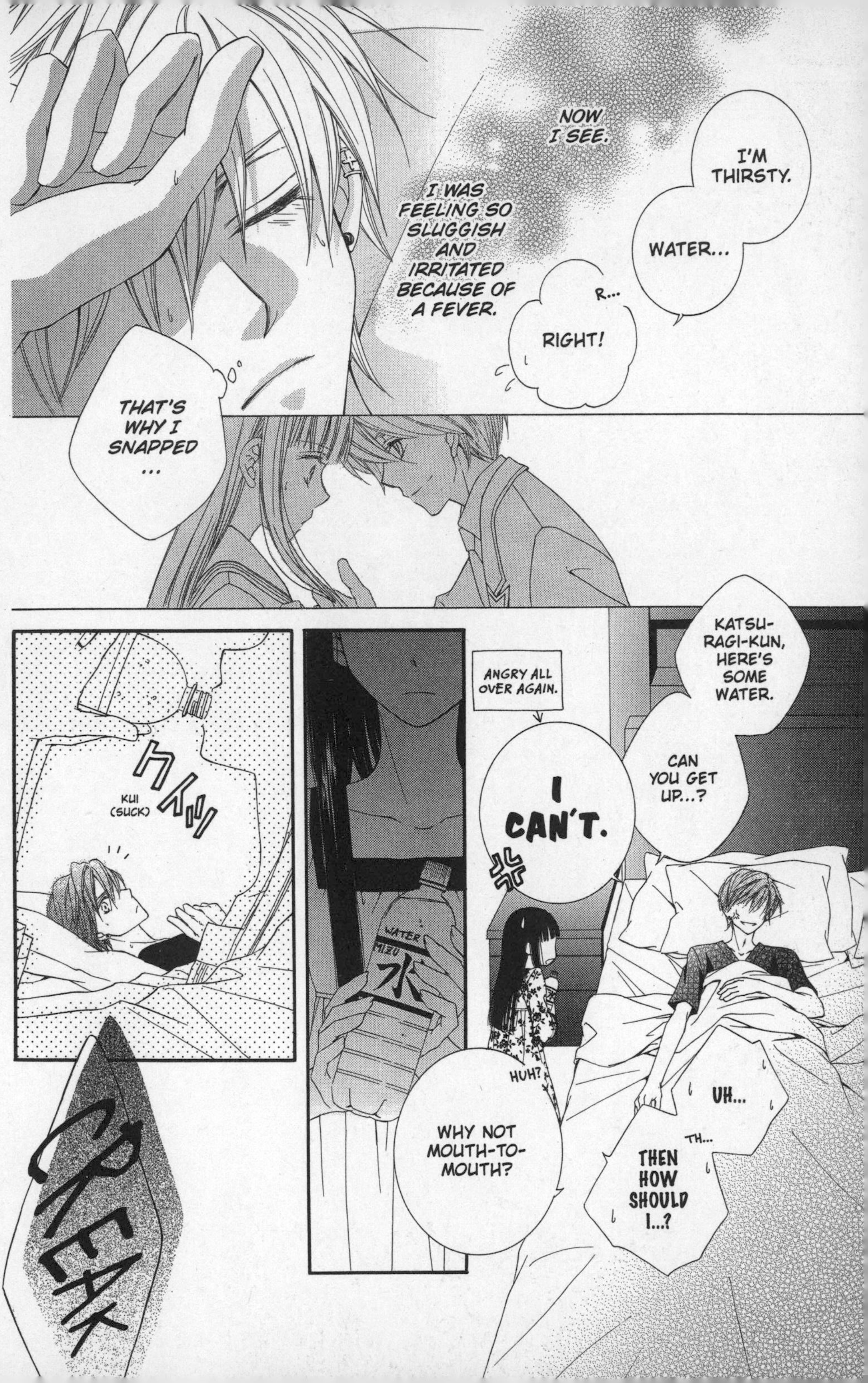
I'M THIRSTY.
WATER...
NOW I SEE.
R...
RIGHT!
I WAS FEELING SO SLUGGISH AND IRRITATED BECAUSE OF A FEVER.
THAT'S WHY I SNAPPED...
KATSU-RAGI-KUN, HERE'S SOME WATER.
CAN YOU GET UP...?
ANGRY ALL OVER AGAIN.
I CAN'T.
UH...
TH...
THEN HOW SHOULD I...?
HUH?
WHY NOT MOUTH-TO-MOUTH?
WATER
MIZU
水
KUI (SUCK)
CREAK

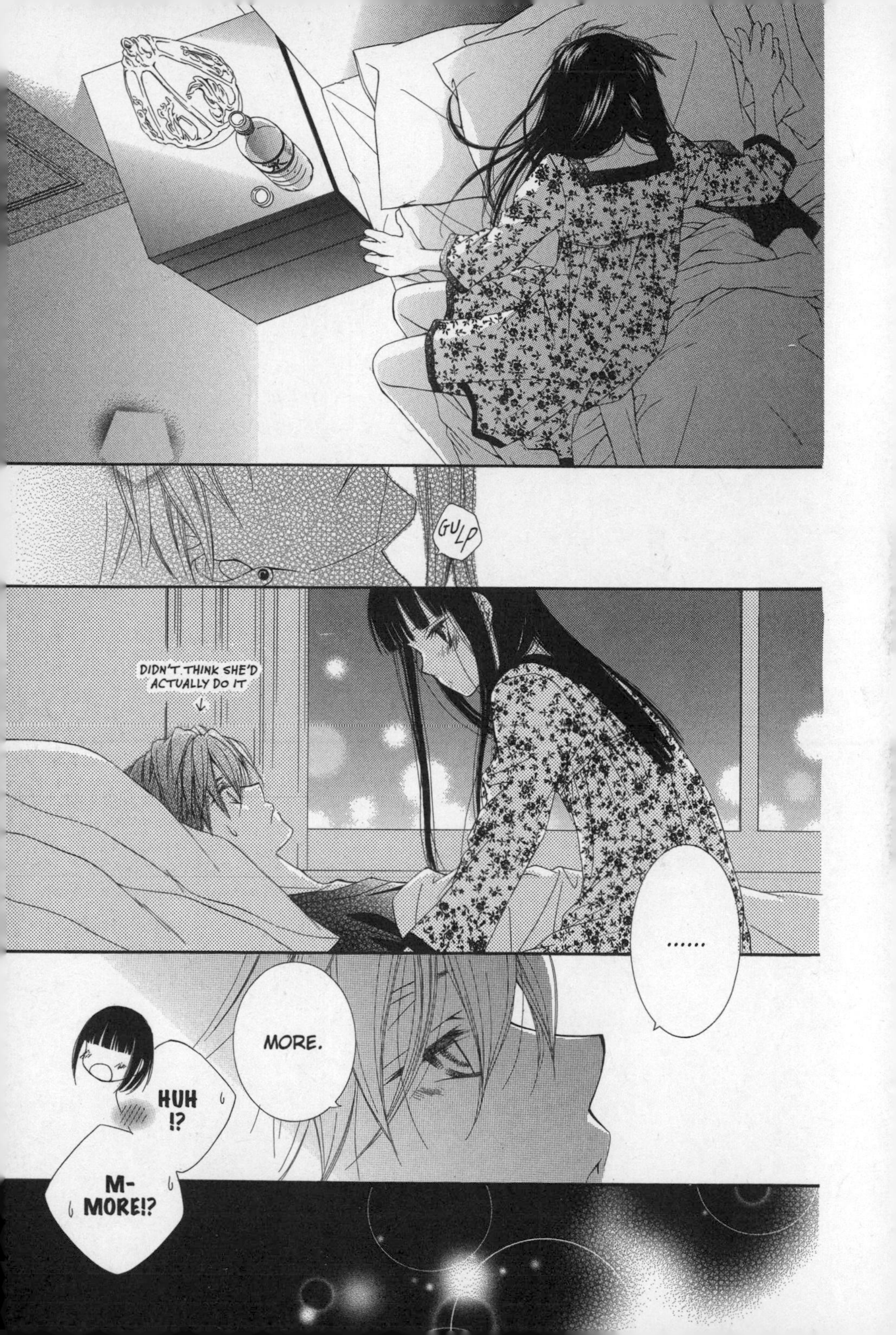
GULP
DIDN'T THINK SHE'D ACTUALLY DO IT
......
MORE.
HUH !?
M-MORE!?

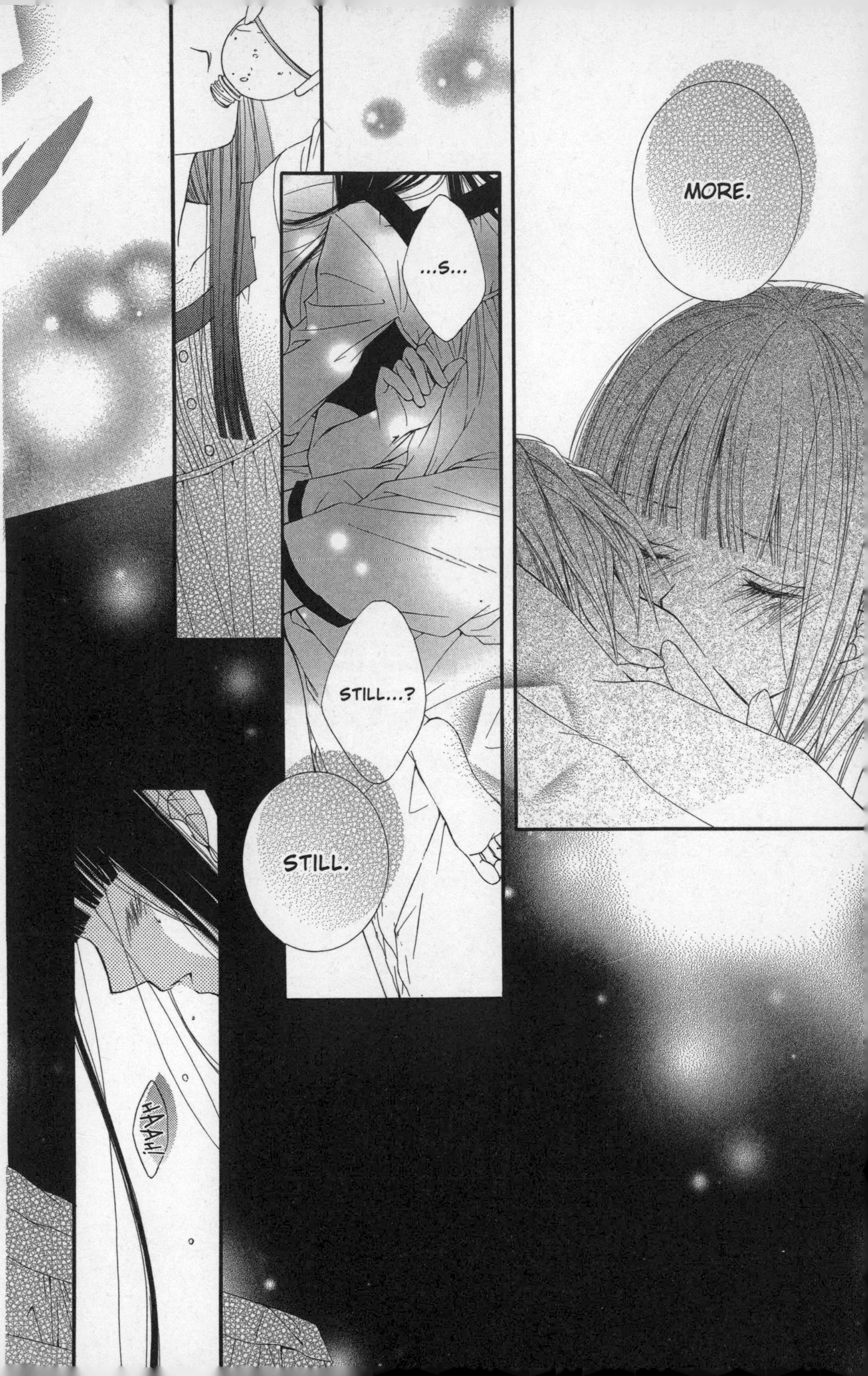
MORE.
...S...
STILL...?
STILL.
HAAH!

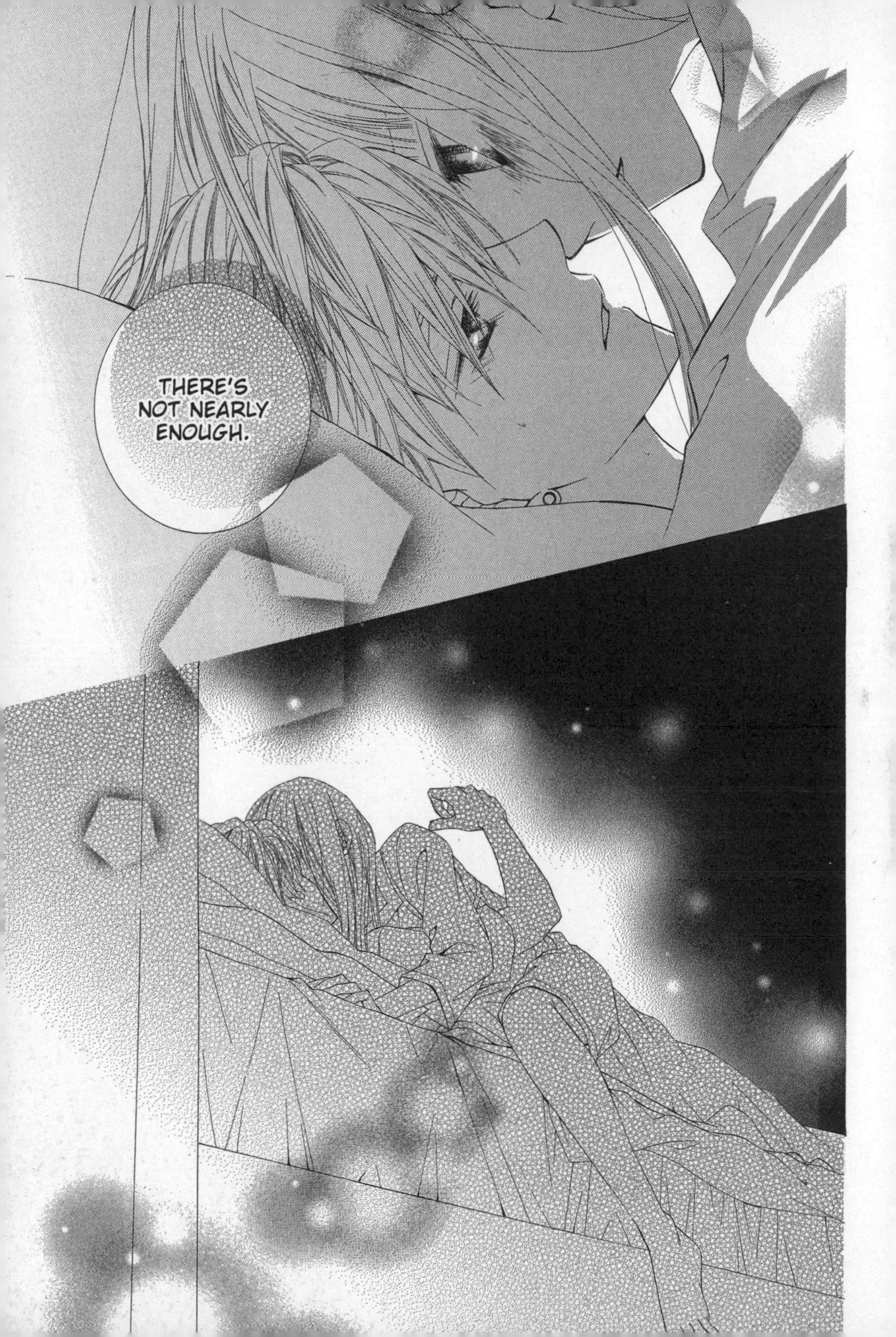
THERE'S NOT NEARLY ENOUGH.

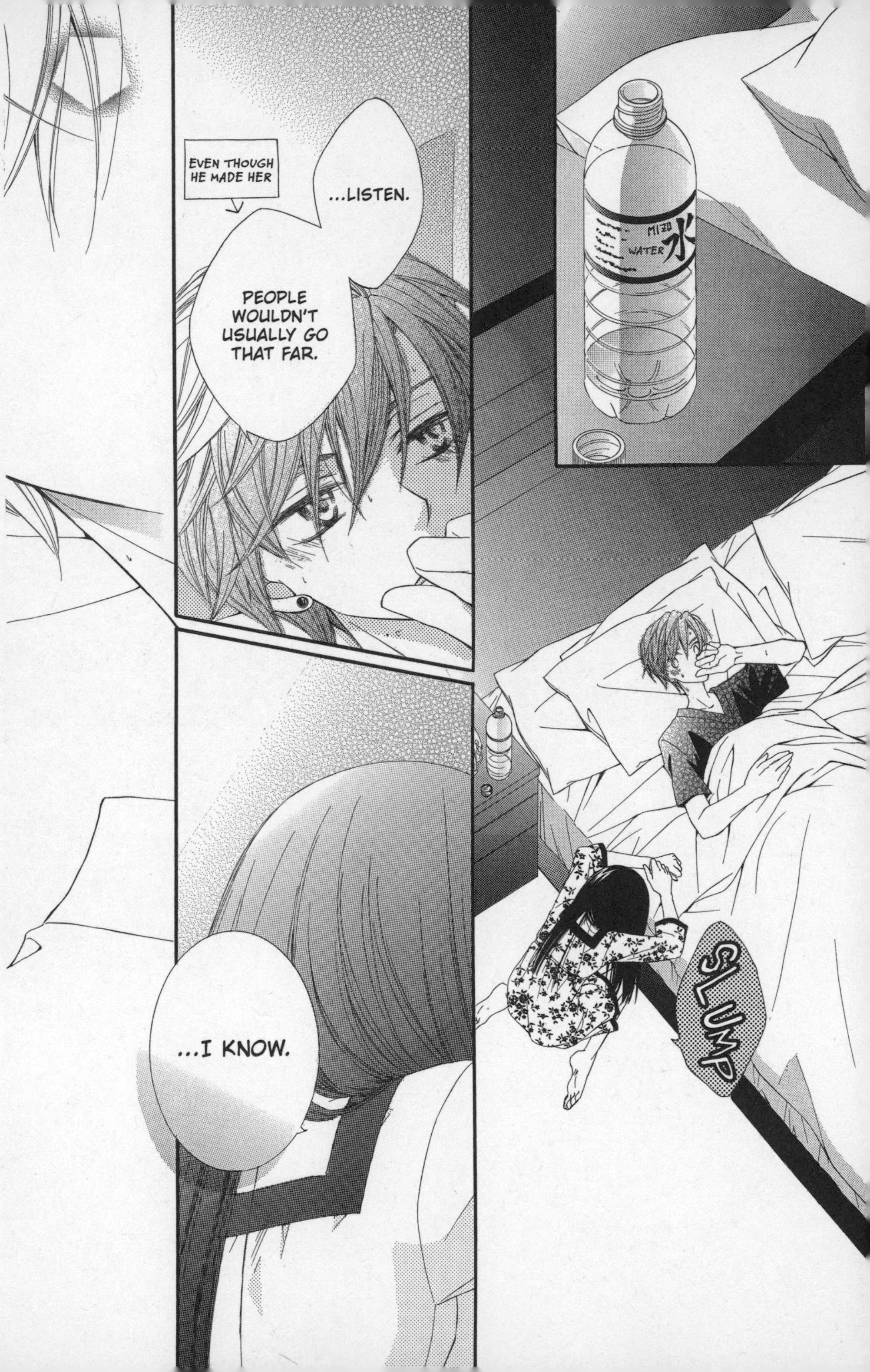
MIZU
WATER
水
SLUMP
EVEN THOUGH HE MADE HER
...LISTEN.
PEOPLE WOULDN'T USUALLY GO THAT FAR.
...I KNOW.

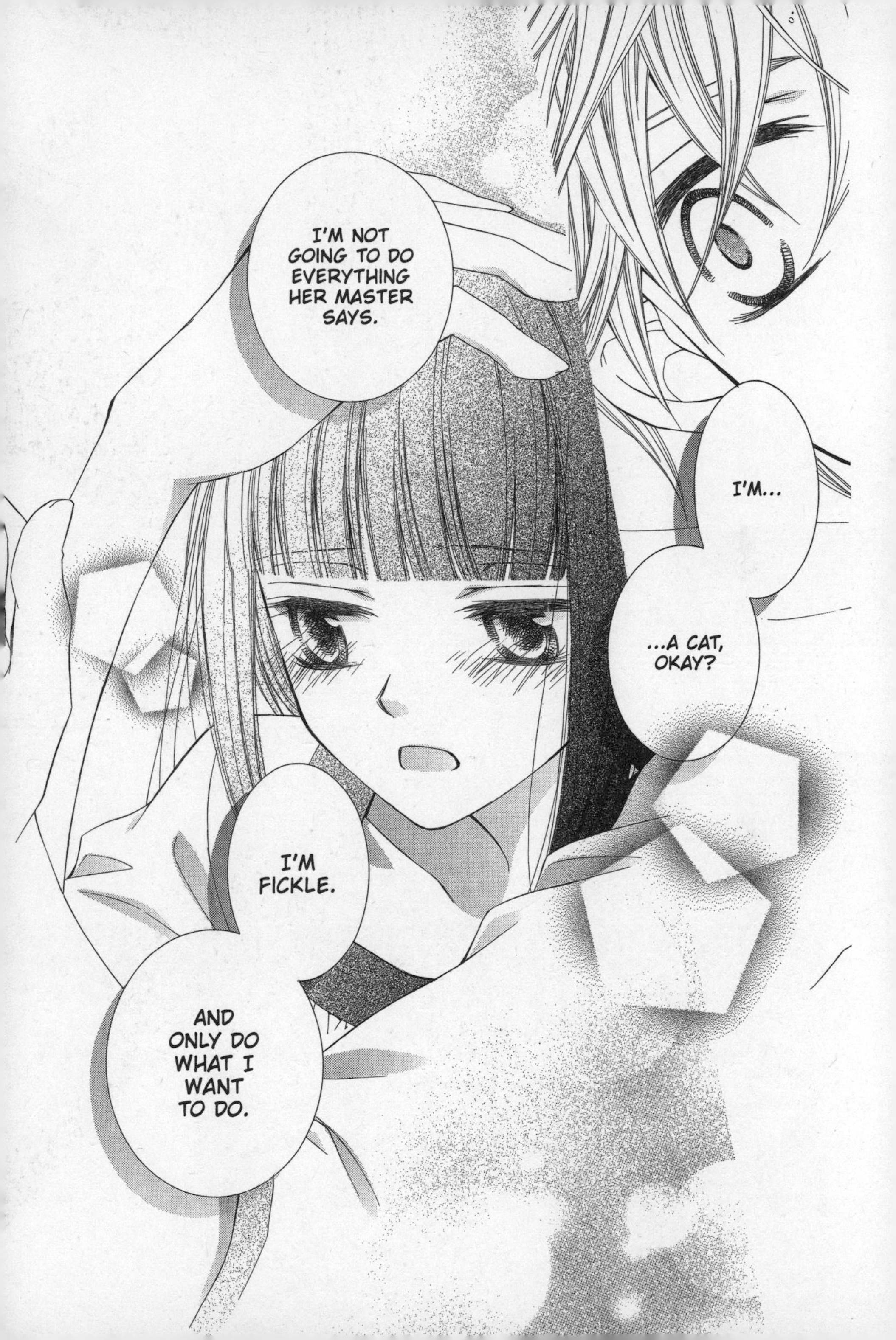
I'M NOT GOING TO DO EVERYTHING HER MASTER SAYS.
I'M...
...A CAT, OKAY?
I'M FICKLE.
AND ONLY DO WHAT I WANT TO DO.

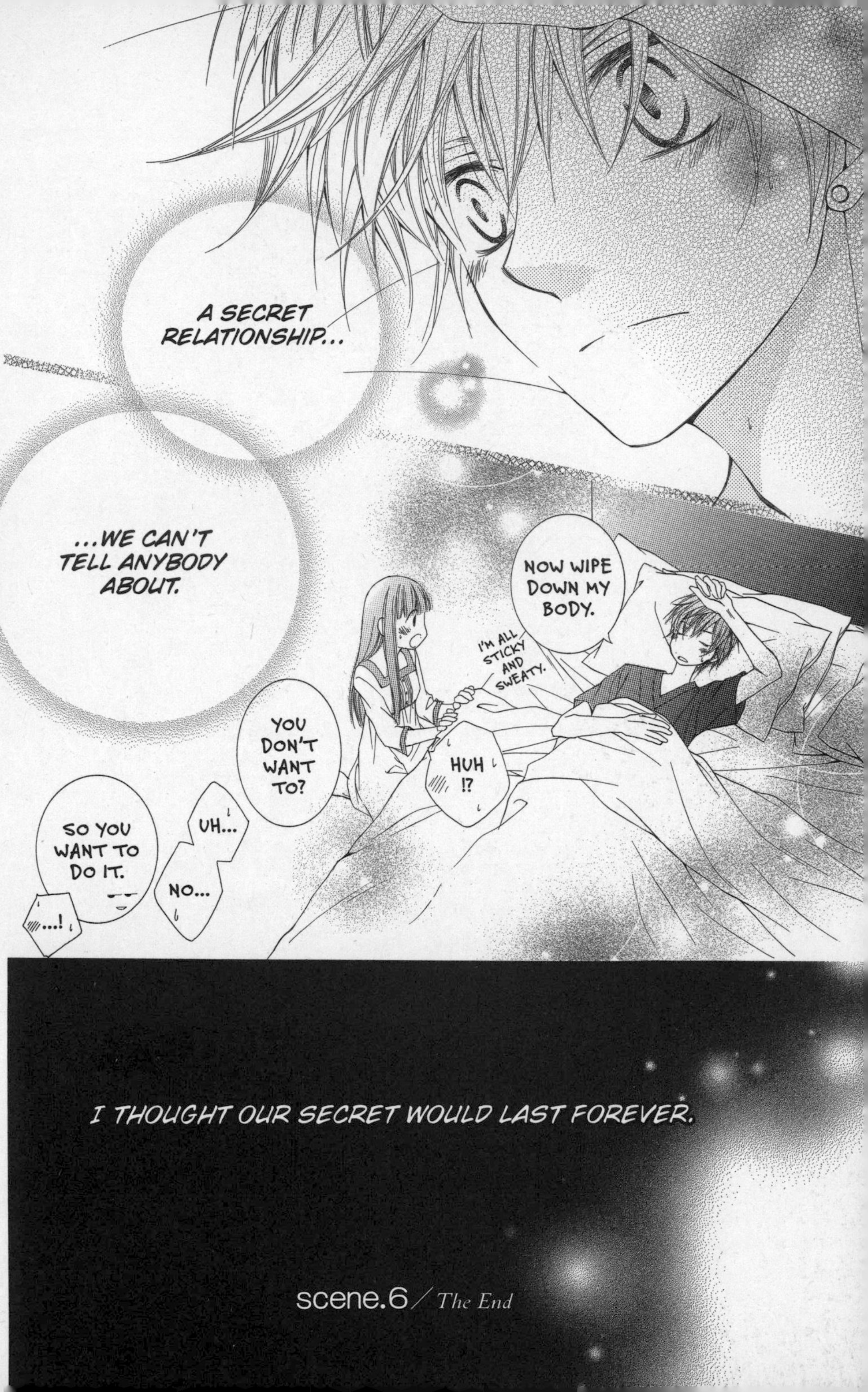
A SECRET RELATIONSHIP...
...WE CAN'T TELL ANYBODY ABOUT.
NOW WIPE DOWN MY BODY.
I'M ALL STICKY AND SWEATY.
HUH!?
YOU DON'T WANT TO?
UH...
NO...
SO YOU WANT TO DO IT.
...!
I THOUGHT OUR SECRET WOULD LAST FOREVER.
scene.6 / The End

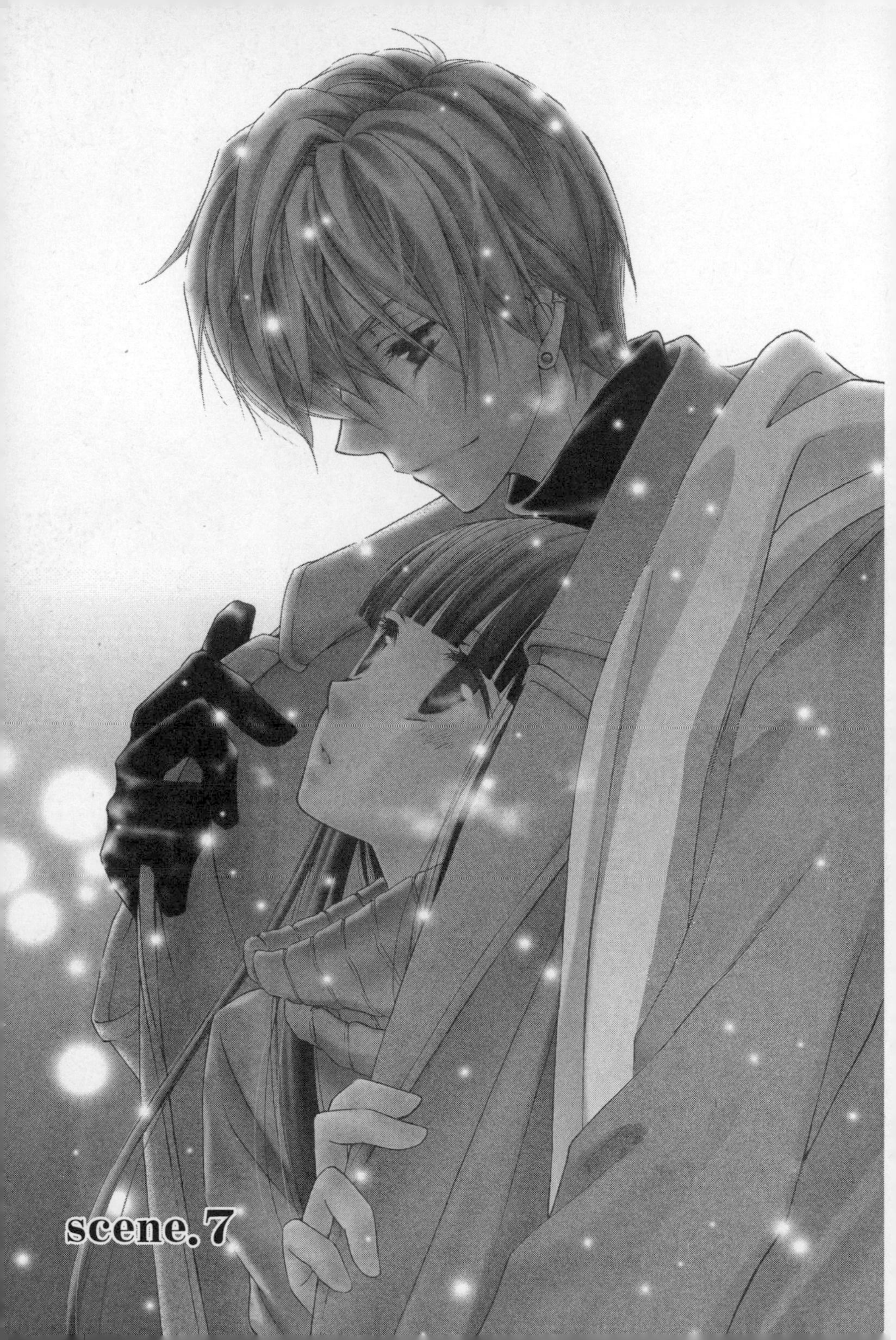
scene. 7

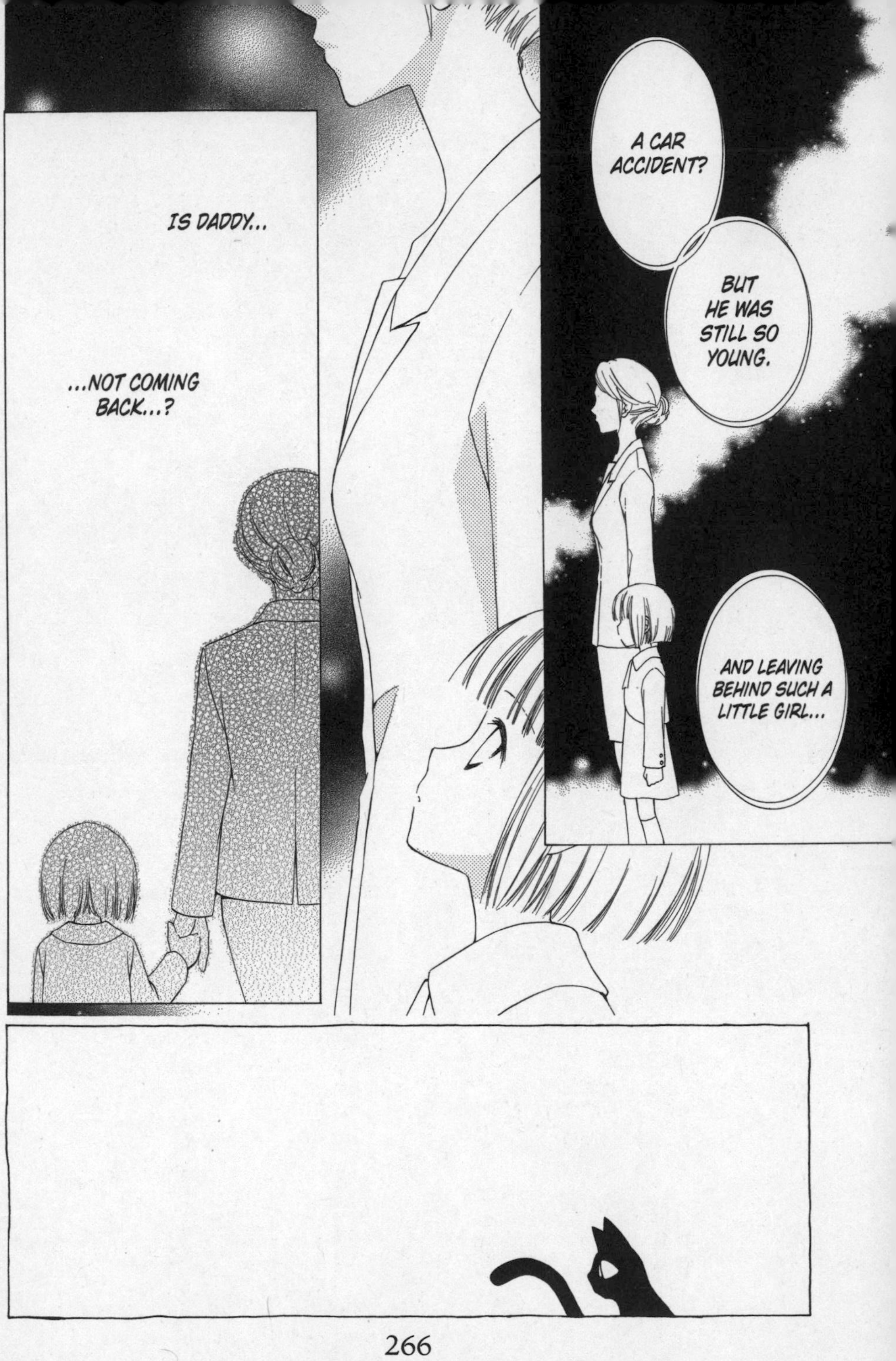
A CAR ACCIDENT?
BUT HE WAS STILL SO YOUNG.
AND LEAVING BEHIND SUCH A LITTLE GIRL...
IS DADDY...
...NOT COMING BACK...?

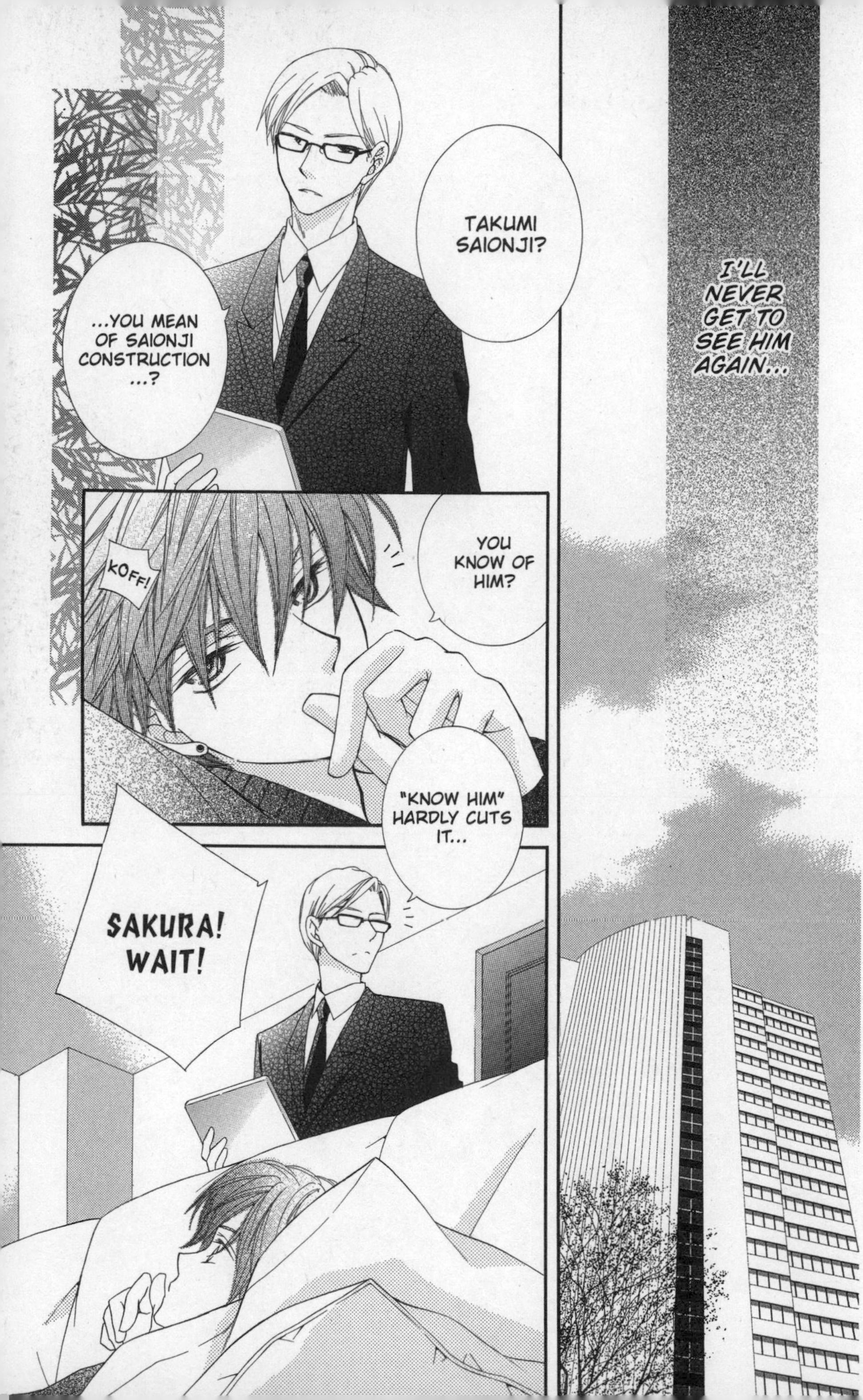
I'LL NEVER GET TO SEE HIM AGAIN...
TAKUMI SAIONJI?
...YOU MEAN OF SAIONJI CONSTRUCTION ...?
YOU KNOW OF HIM?
KOFF!
"KNOW HIM" HARDLY CUTS IT...
SAKURA! WAIT!

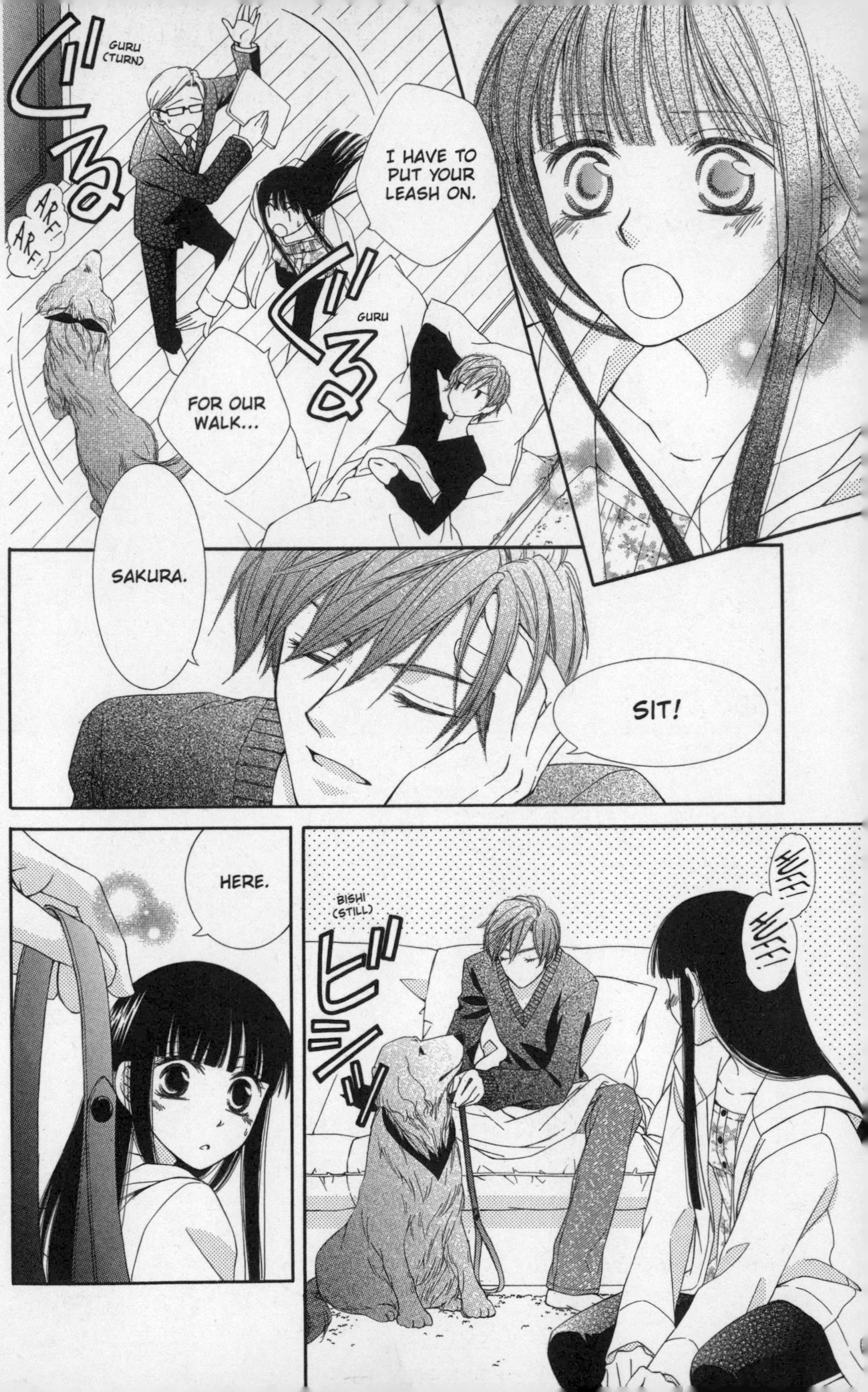
I HAVE TO PUT YOUR LEASH ON.
GURU (TURN)
ARF! ARF!
GURU
FOR OUR WALK...
SAKURA.
SIT!
HUFF! HUFF!
BISHI (STILL)
HERE.

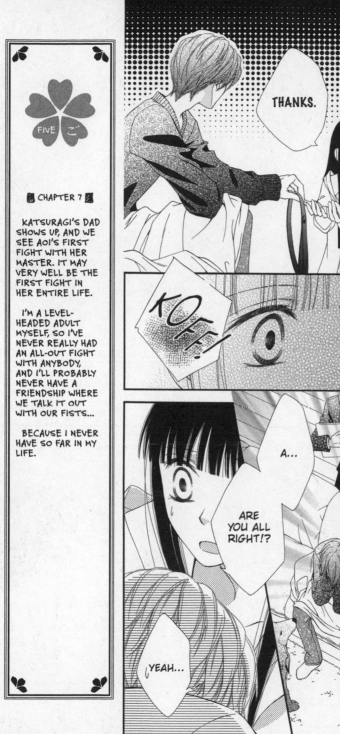

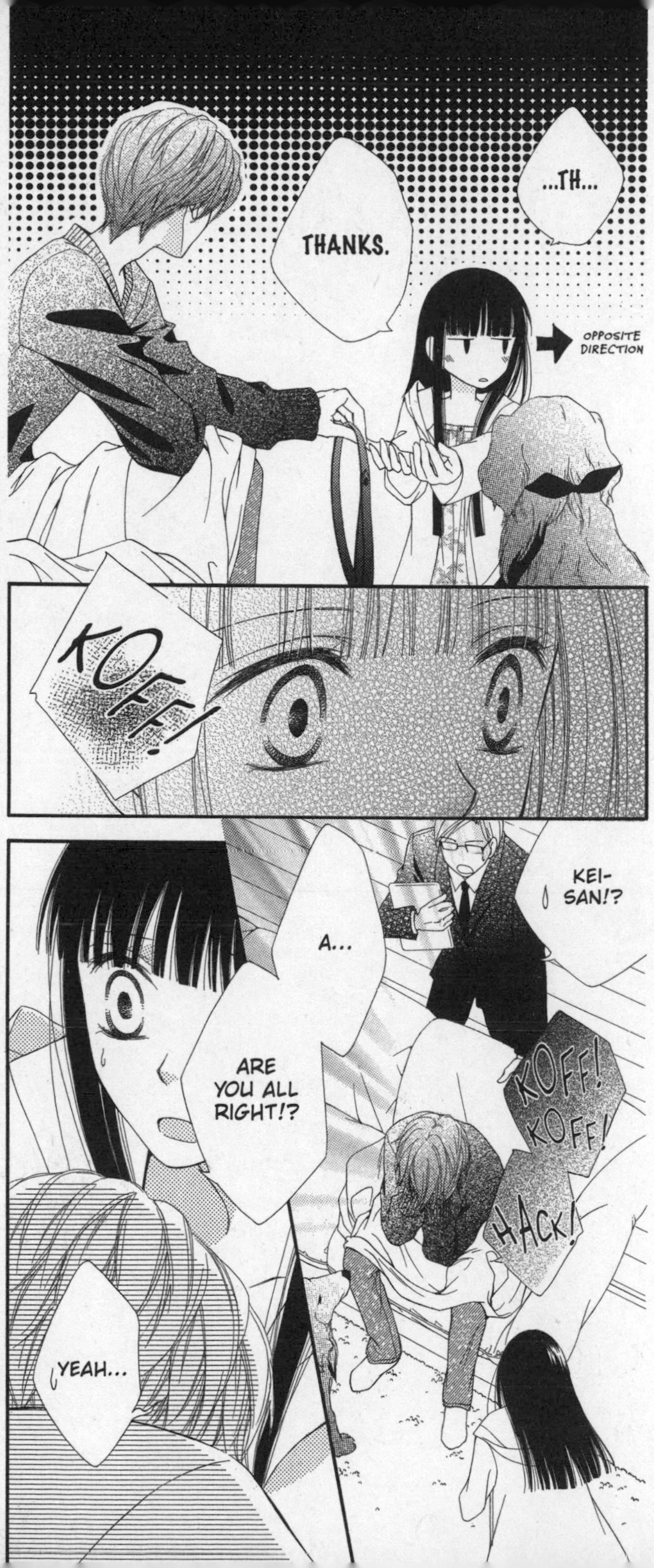
...TH...
THANKS.
OPPOSITE DIRECTION
KOFF!
KEI-SAN!?
A...
KOFF! KOFF!
HACK!
ARE YOU ALL RIGHT!?
YEAH...

FIVE ご

CHAPTER 7

KATSURAGI'S DAD SHOWS UP, AND WE SEE AOI'S FIRST FIGHT WITH HER MASTER. IT MAY VERY WELL BE THE FIRST FIGHT IN HER ENTIRE LIFE.

I'M A LEVEL-HEADED ADULT MYSELF, SO I'VE NEVER REALLY HAD AN ALL-OUT FIGHT WITH ANYBODY, AND I'LL PROBABLY NEVER HAVE A FRIENDSHIP WHERE WE TALK IT OUT WITH OUR FISTS...

BECAUSE I NEVER HAVE SO FAR IN MY LIFE.

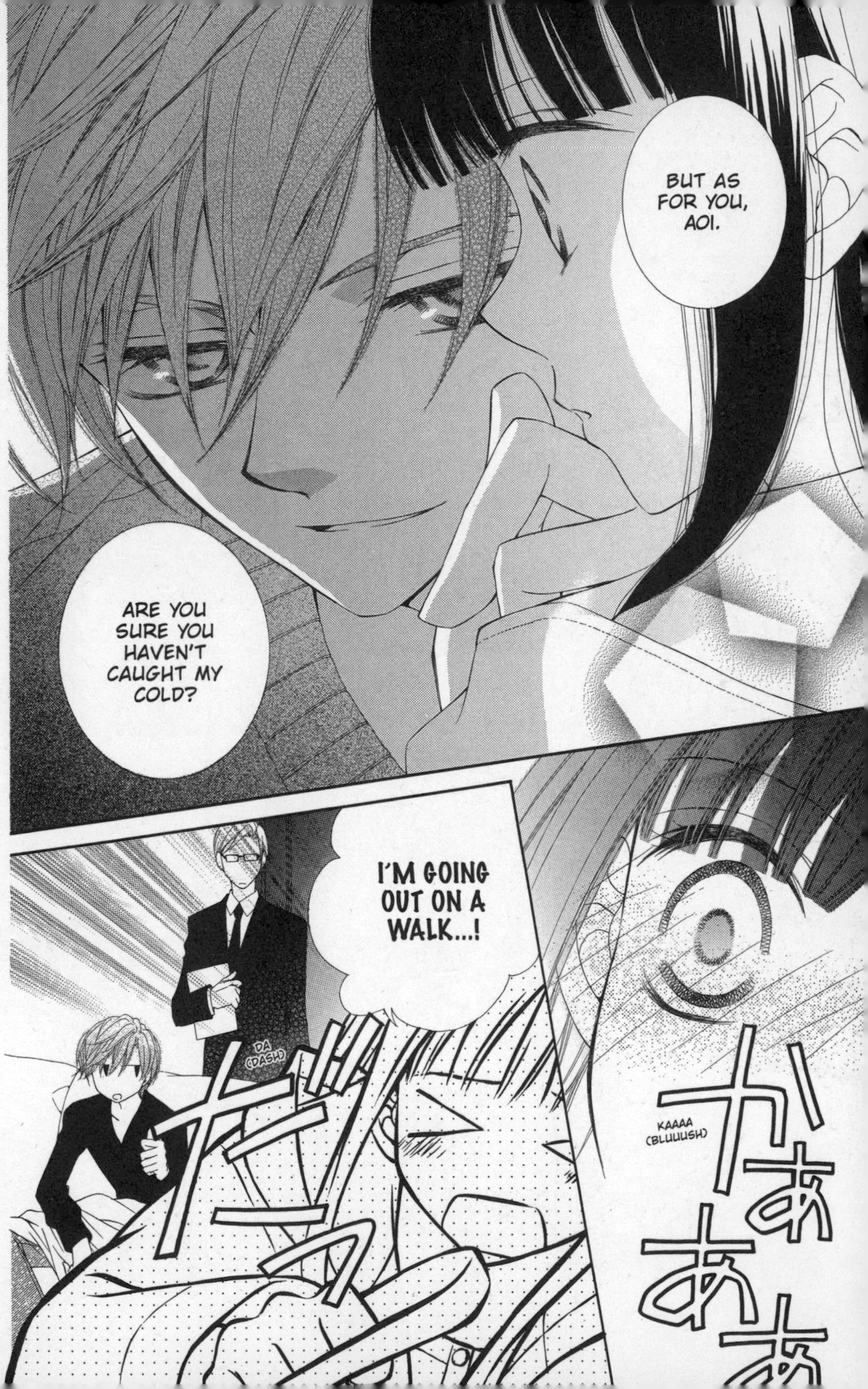
BUT AS FOR YOU, AOI.
ARE YOU SURE YOU HAVEN'T CAUGHT MY COLD?
KAAAA (BLUUUSH)
I'M GOING OUT ON A WALK...!
DA (DASH)

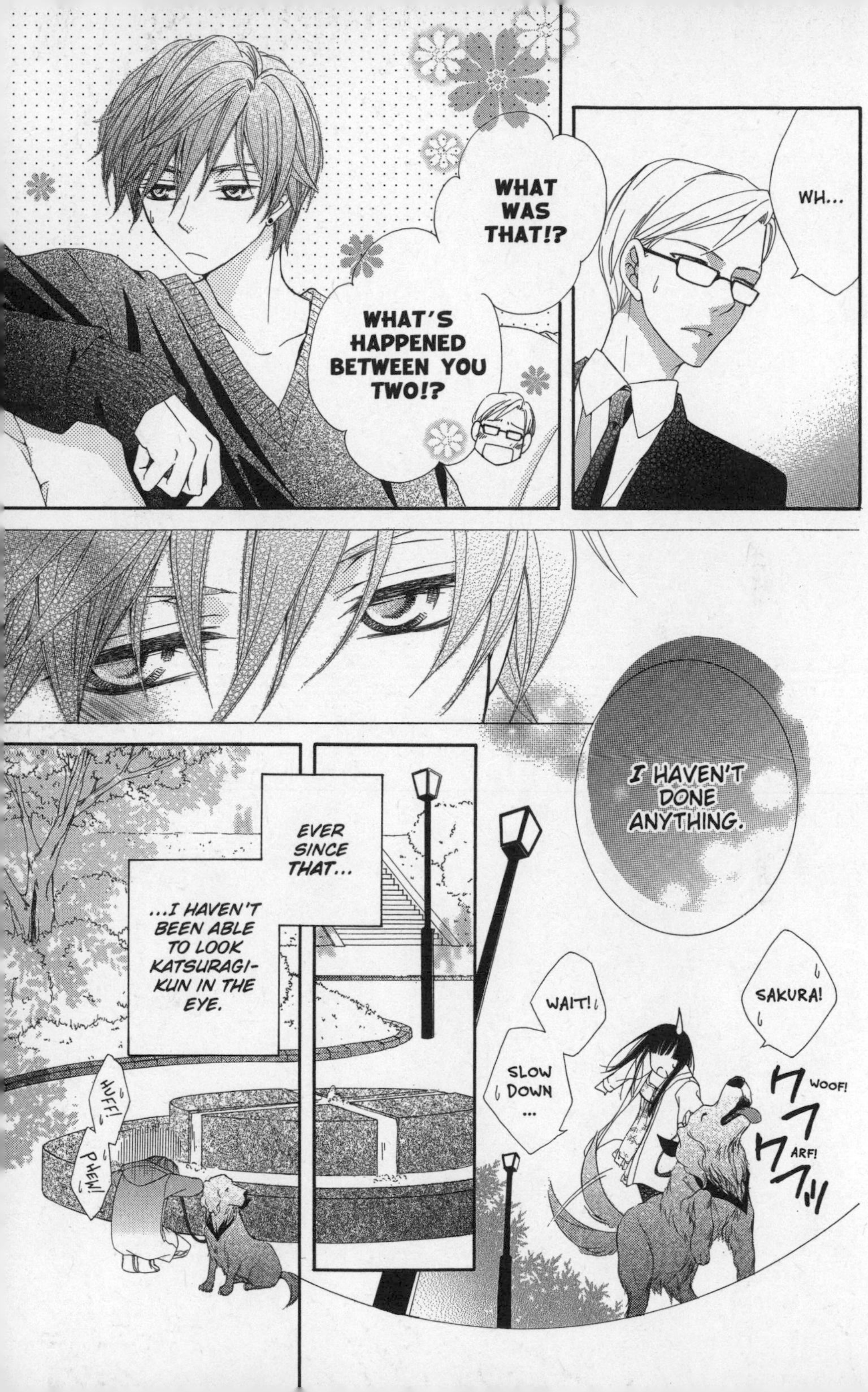

WH...
WHAT WAS THAT!?
WHAT'S HAPPENED BETWEEN YOU TWO!?
I HAVEN'T DONE ANYTHING.
SAKURA!
WAIT!
SLOW DOWN ...
WOOF!
ARF!
EVER SINCE THAT...
...I HAVEN'T BEEN ABLE TO LOOK KATSURAGI-KUN IN THE EYE.
HUFF!
PHEW!

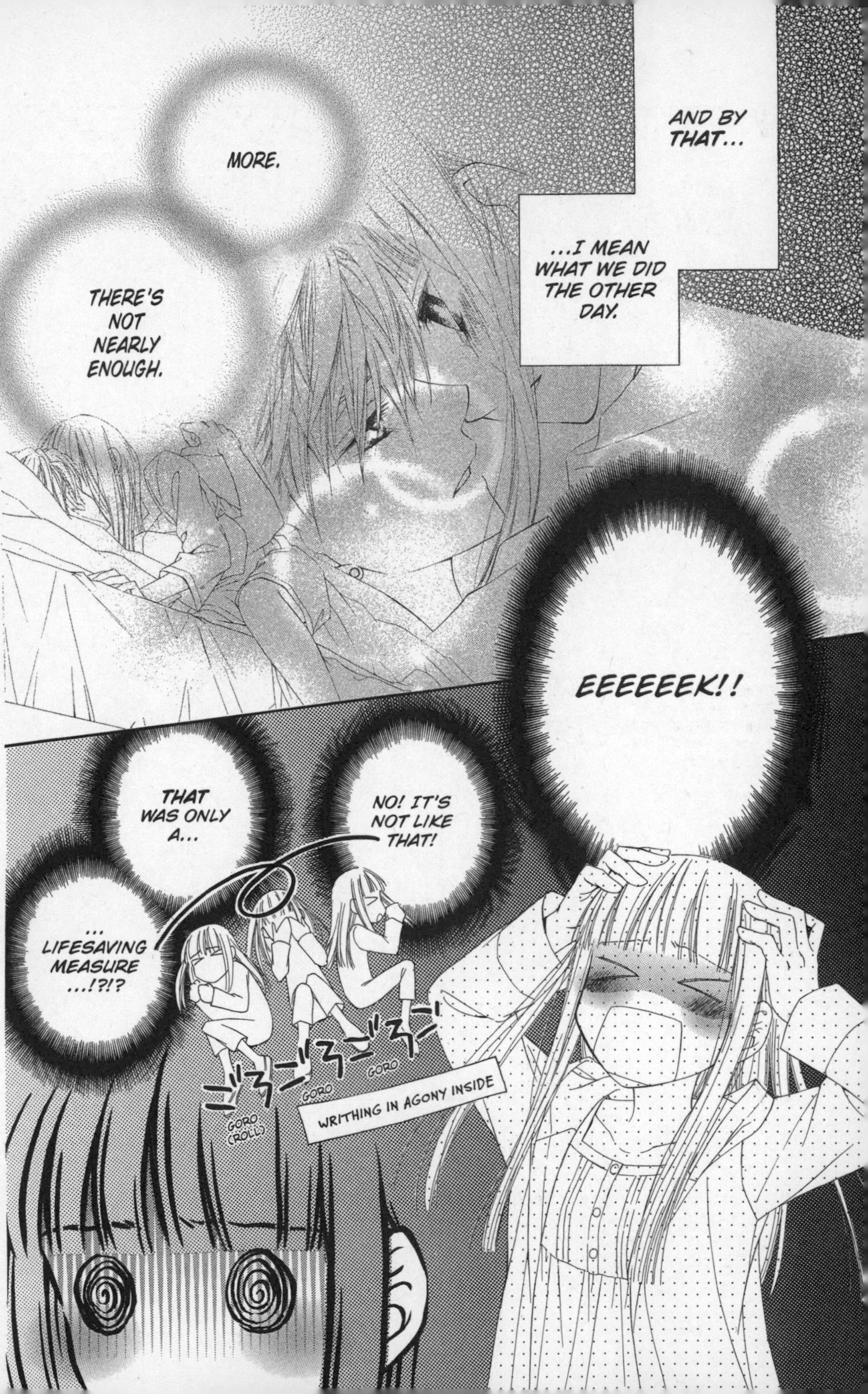
AND BY THAT...
...I MEAN WHAT WE DID THE OTHER DAY.
MORE.
THERE'S NOT NEARLY ENOUGH.
EEEEEEK!!
NO! IT'S NOT LIKE THAT!
THAT WAS ONLY A...
...LIFESAVING MEASURE ...!?!?
GORO
GORO
GORO (ROLL)
WRITHING IN AGONY INSIDE

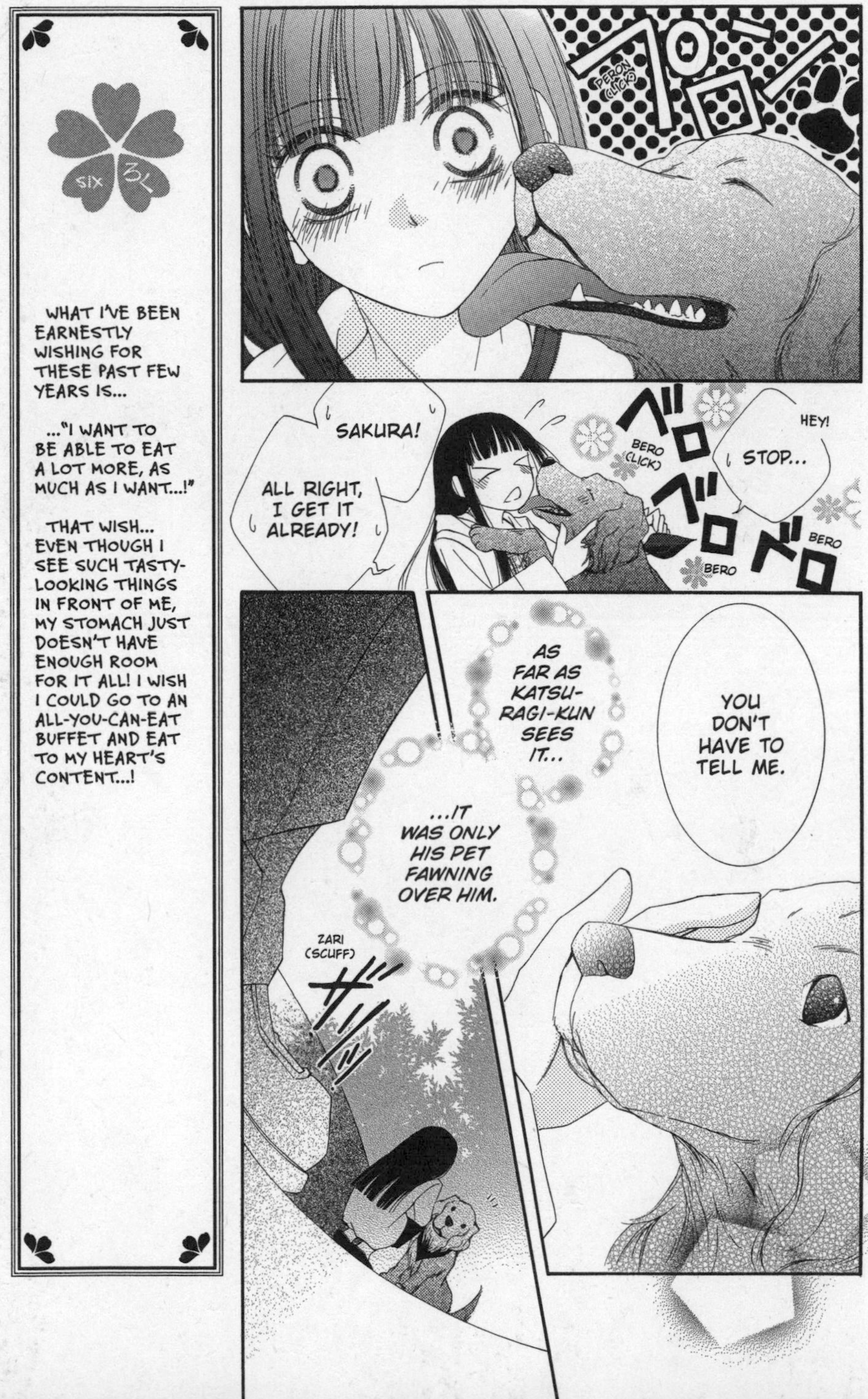
PERON (LICK)
HEY!
STOP...
BERO (LICK)
BERO
BERO
SAKURA!
ALL RIGHT, I GET IT ALREADY!
YOU DON'T HAVE TO TELL ME.
AS FAR AS KATSURAGI-KUN SEES IT...
...IT WAS ONLY HIS PET FAWNING OVER HIM.
ZARI (SCUFF)

six ろく

WHAT I'VE BEEN EARNESTLY WISHING FOR THESE PAST FEW YEARS IS...

..."I WANT TO BE ABLE TO EAT A LOT MORE, AS MUCH AS I WANT...!"

THAT WISH... EVEN THOUGH I SEE SUCH TASTY-LOOKING THINGS IN FRONT OF ME, MY STOMACH JUST DOESN'T HAVE ENOUGH ROOM FOR IT ALL! I WISH I COULD GO TO AN ALL-YOU-CAN-EAT BUFFET AND EAT TO MY HEART'S CONTENT...!

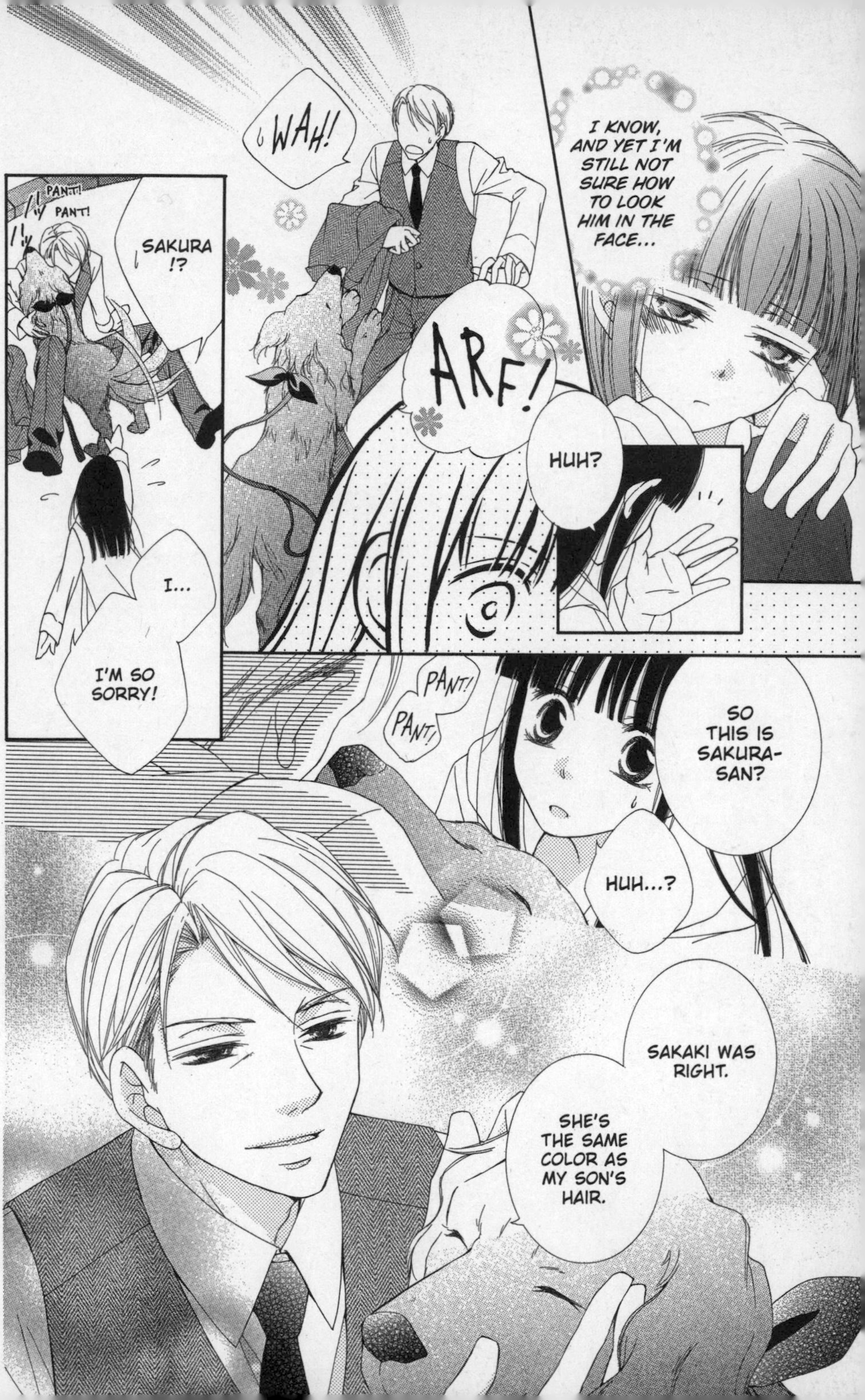

I KNOW, AND YET I'M STILL NOT SURE HOW TO LOOK HIM IN THE FACE...
HUH?
WAH!
ARF!
PANT! PANT!
SAKURA !?
I...
I'M SO SORRY!
PANT! PANT!
SO THIS IS SAKURA-SAN?
HUH...?
SAKAKI WAS RIGHT.
SHE'S THE SAME COLOR AS MY SON'S HAIR.

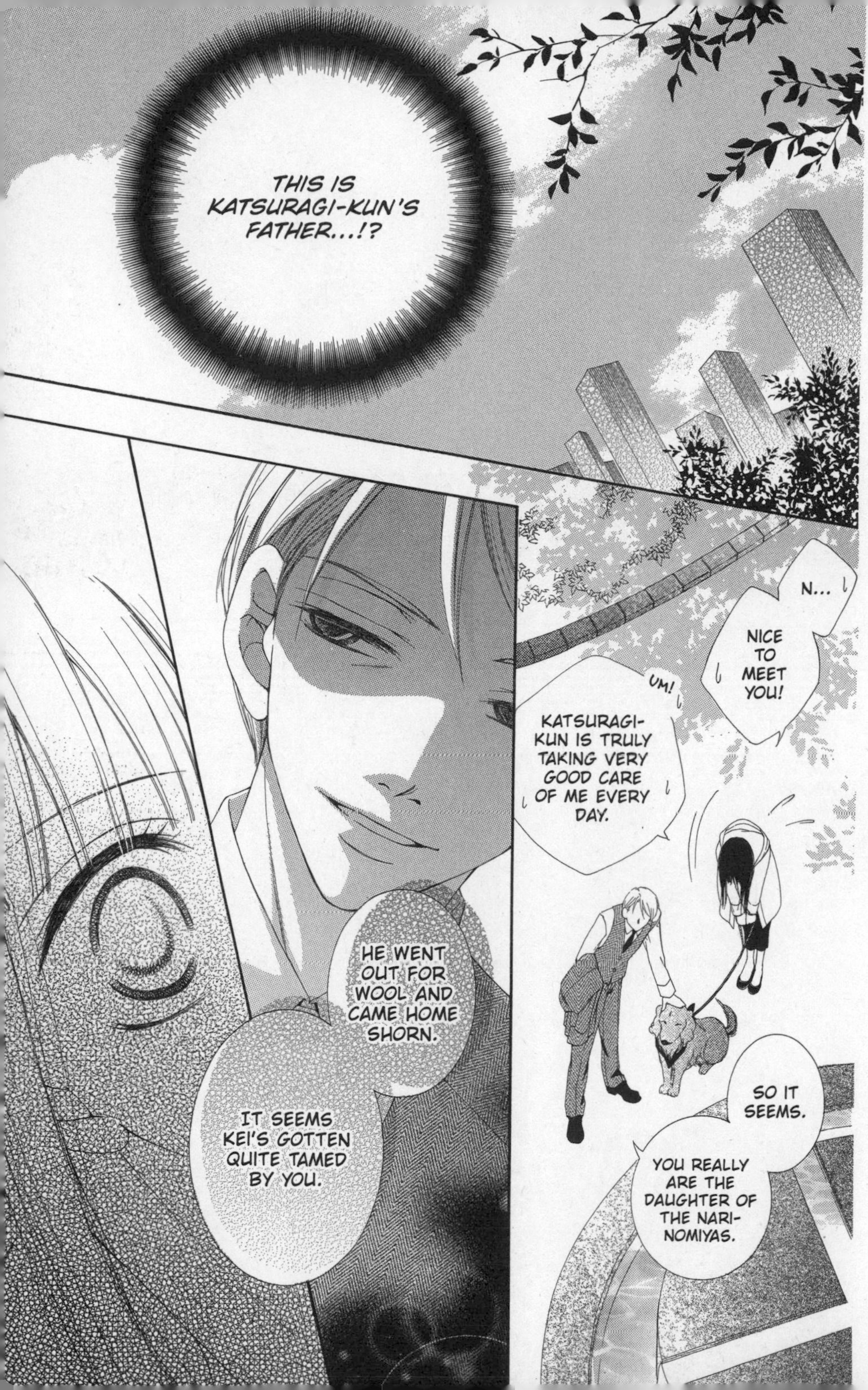
THIS IS KATSURAGI-KUN'S FATHER...!?
N...
NICE TO MEET YOU!
UM!
KATSURAGI-KUN IS TRULY TAKING VERY GOOD CARE OF ME EVERY DAY.
SO IT SEEMS.
YOU REALLY ARE THE DAUGHTER OF THE NARI-NOMIYAS.
HE WENT OUT FOR WOOL AND CAME HOME SHORN.
IT SEEMS KEI'S GOTTEN QUITE TAMED BY YOU.

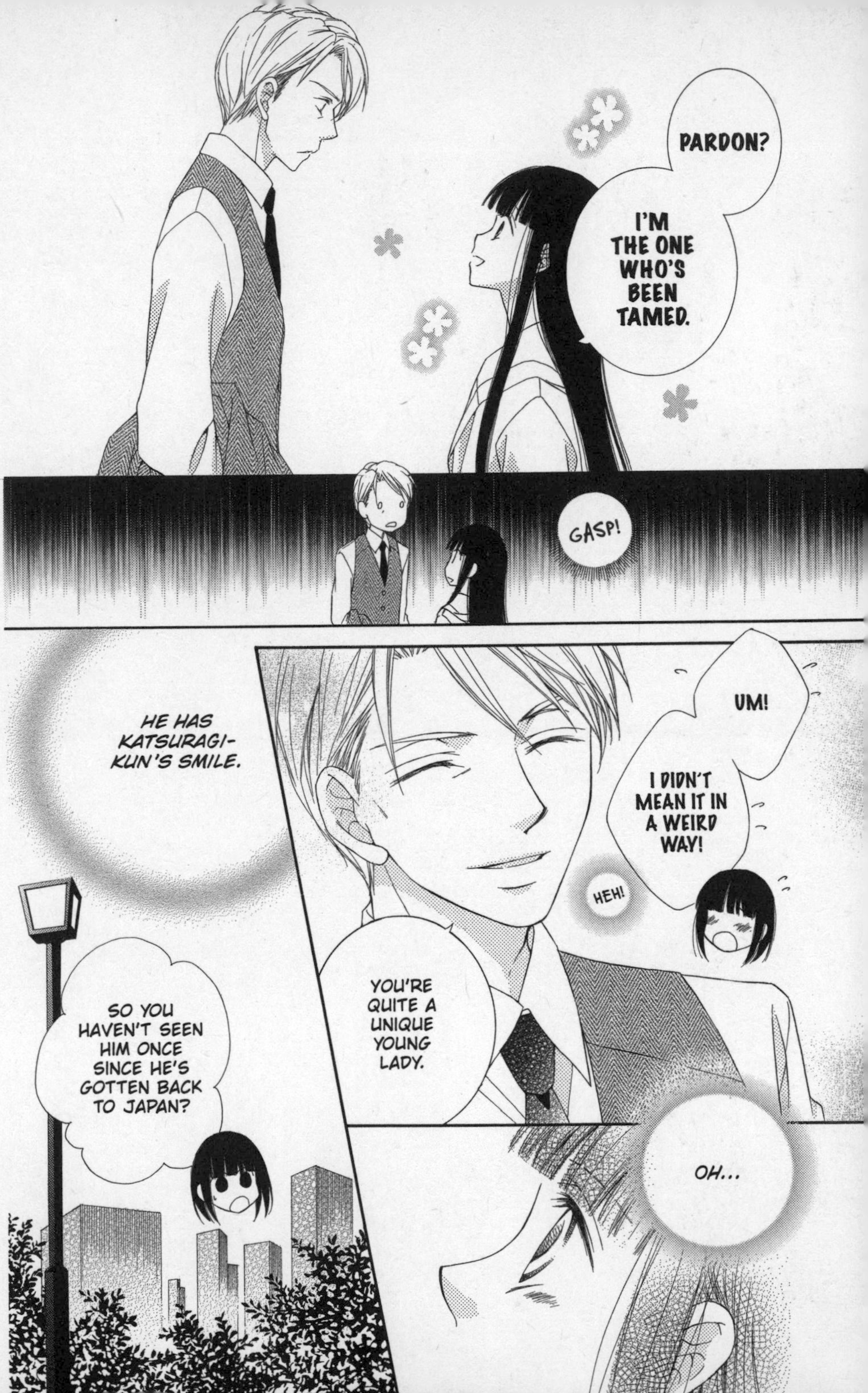
PARDON?
I'M THE ONE WHO'S BEEN TAMED.
GASP!
UM!
I DIDN'T MEAN IT IN A WEIRD WAY!
HEH!
YOU'RE QUITE A UNIQUE YOUNG LADY.
OH...
HE HAS KATSURAGI-KUN'S SMILE.
SO YOU HAVEN'T SEEN HIM ONCE SINCE HE'S GOTTEN BACK TO JAPAN?

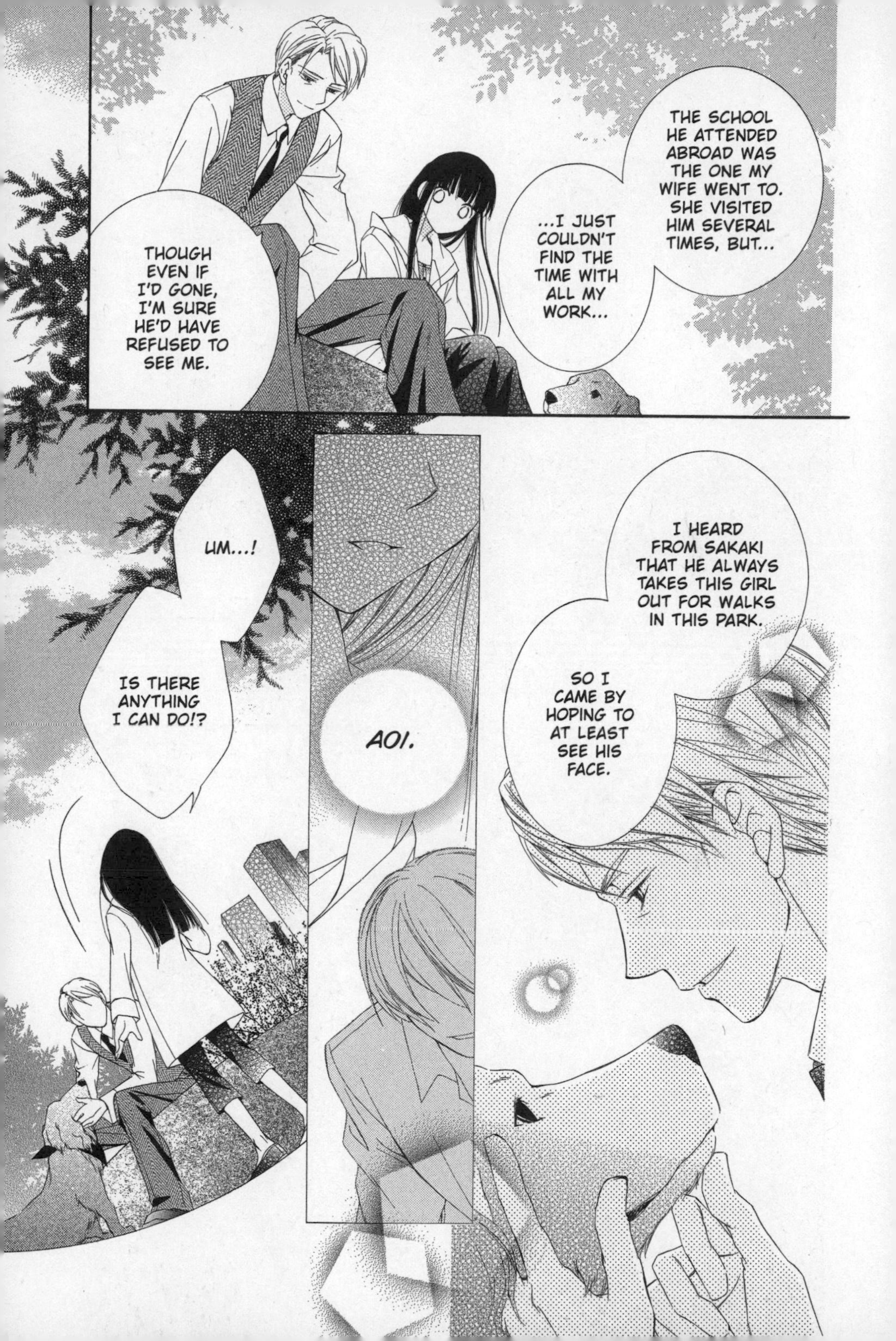
THE SCHOOL HE ATTENDED ABROAD WAS THE ONE MY WIFE WENT TO. SHE VISITED HIM SEVERAL TIMES, BUT...
...I JUST COULDN'T FIND THE TIME WITH ALL MY WORK...
THOUGH EVEN IF I'D GONE, I'M SURE HE'D HAVE REFUSED TO SEE ME.
I HEARD FROM SAKAKI THAT HE ALWAYS TAKES THIS GIRL OUT FOR WALKS IN THIS PARK.
SO I CAME BY HOPING TO AT LEAST SEE HIS FACE.
AOI.
UM...!
IS THERE ANYTHING I CAN DO!?

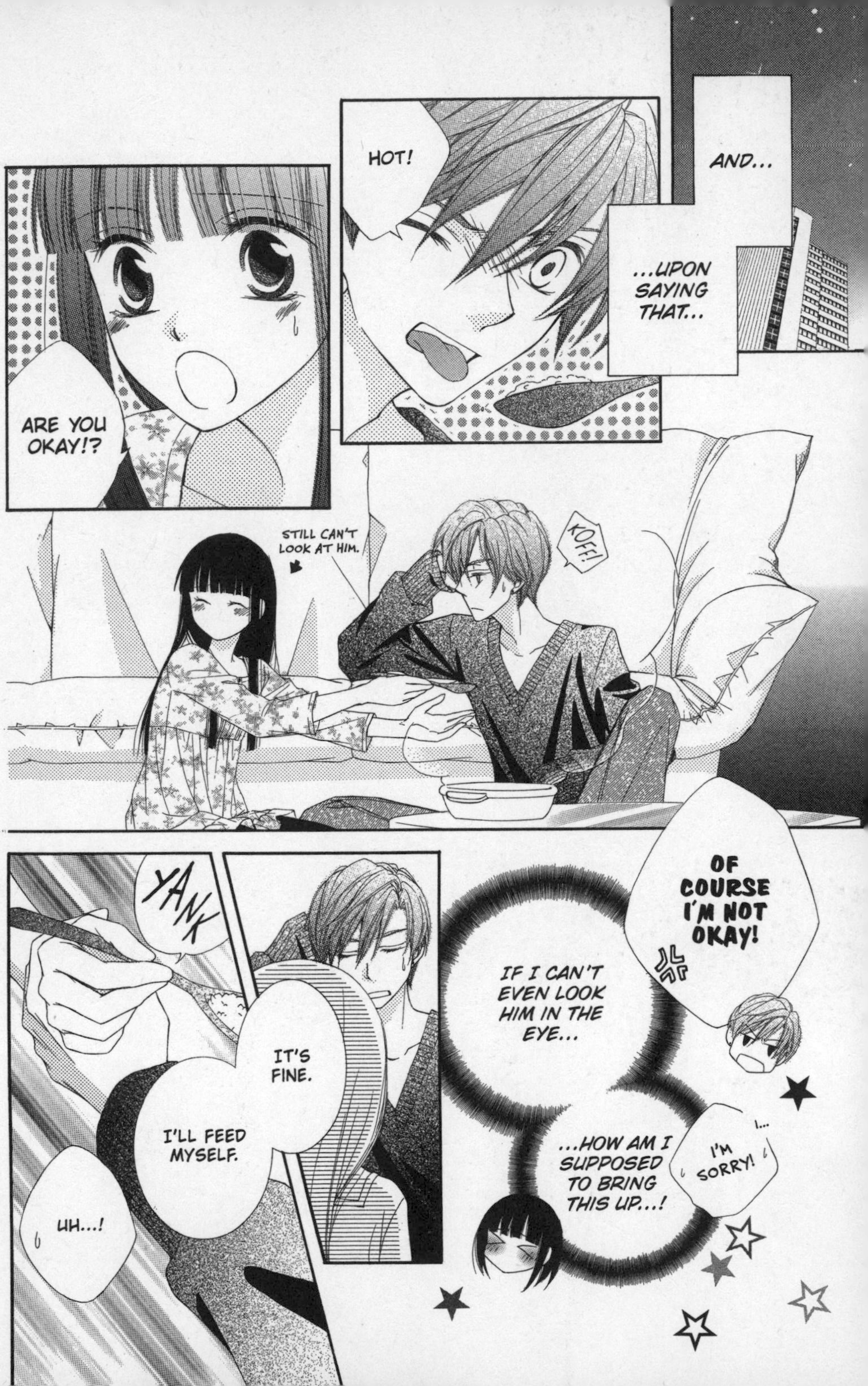
AND...
...UPON SAYING THAT...
HOT!
ARE YOU OKAY!?
KOFF!
STILL CAN'T LOOK AT HIM.
OF COURSE I'M NOT OKAY!
IF I CAN'T EVEN LOOK HIM IN THE EYE...
...HOW AM I SUPPOSED TO BRING THIS UP...!
I... I'M SORRY!
YANK
IT'S FINE.
I'LL FEED MYSELF.
UH...!

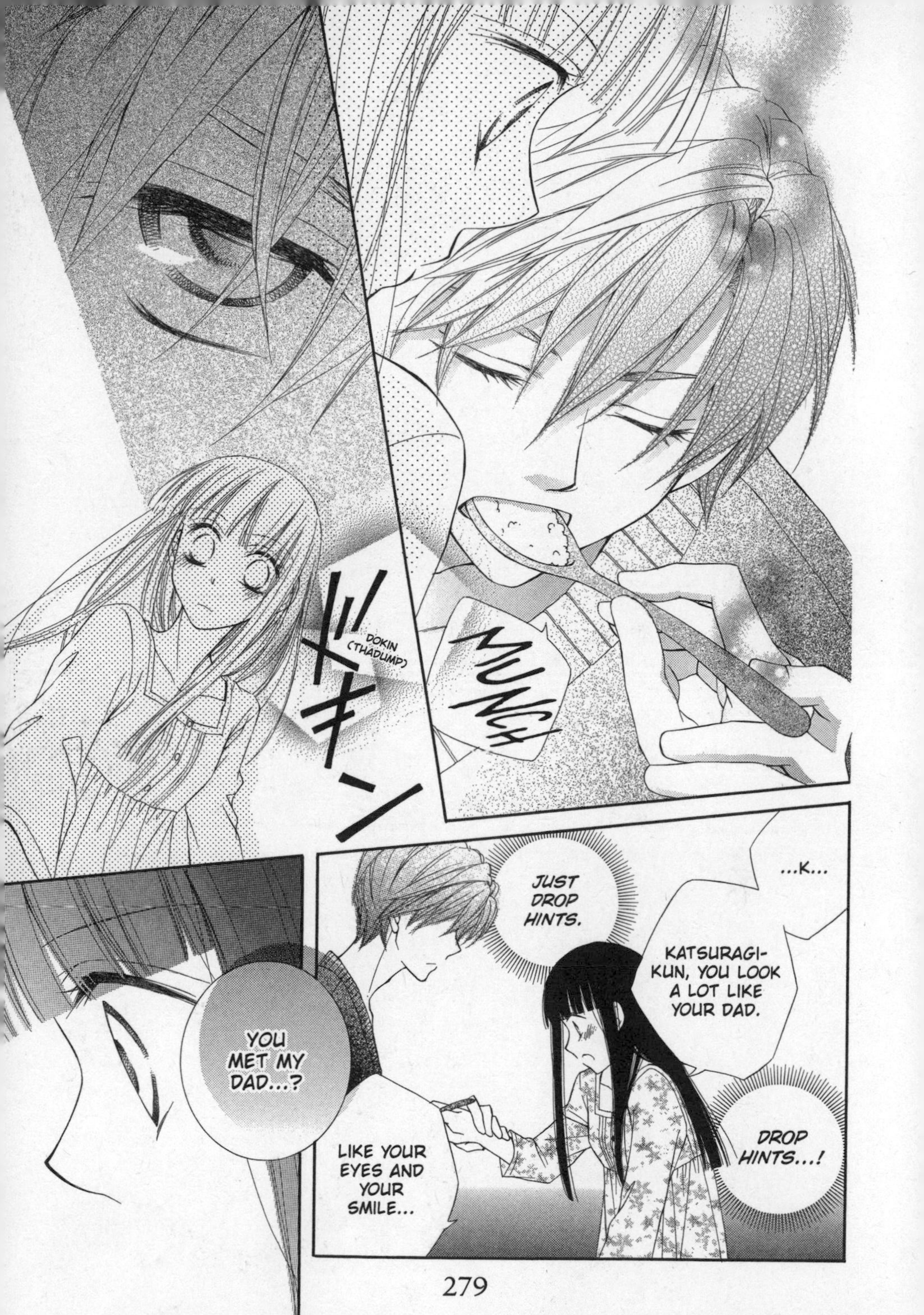
MUNCH
DOKIN (THADUMP)
...K...
KATSURAGI-KUN, YOU LOOK A LOT LIKE YOUR DAD.
JUST DROP HINTS.
DROP HINTS...!
LIKE YOUR EYES AND YOUR SMILE...
YOU MET MY DAD...?

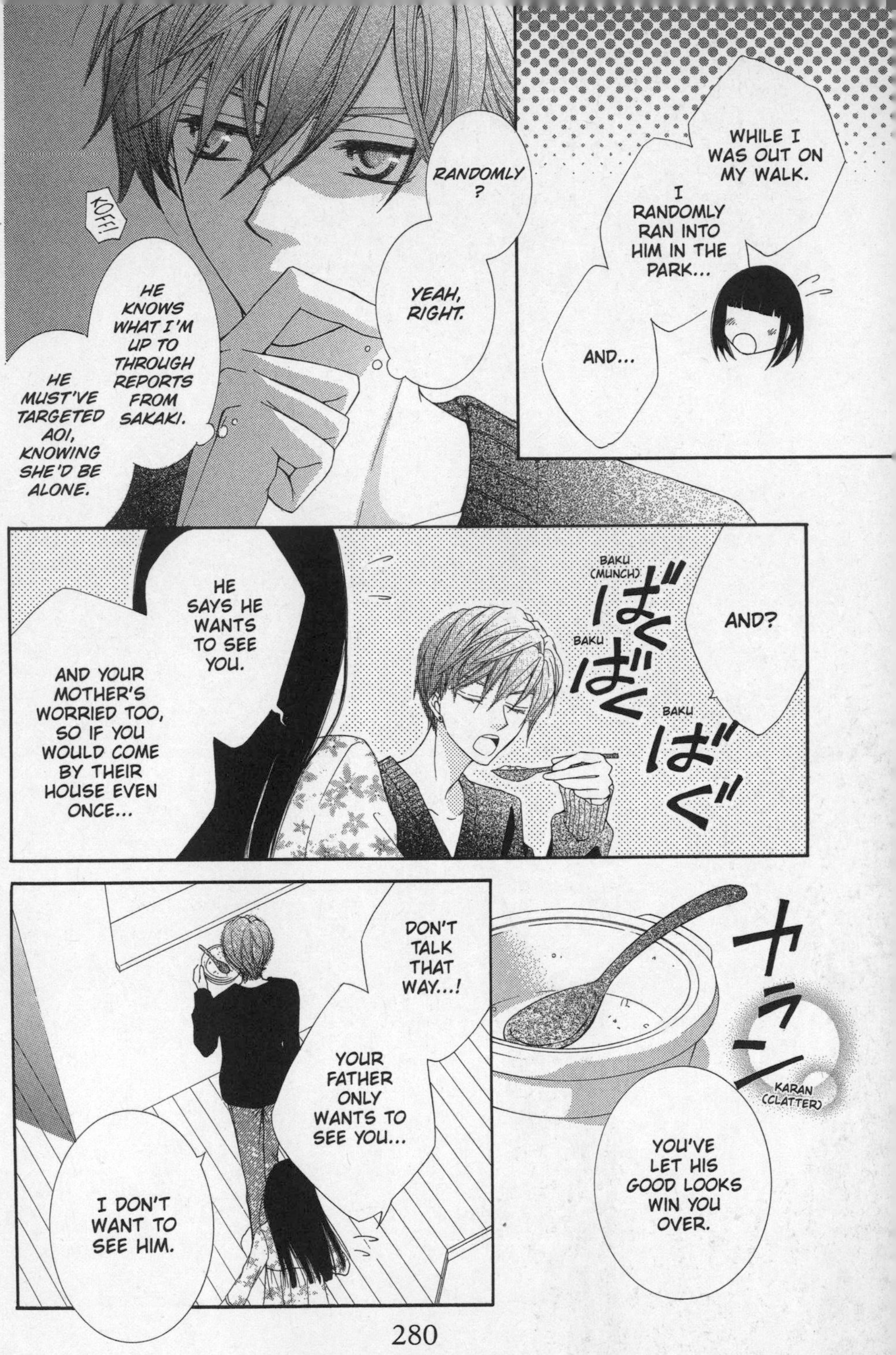
WHILE I WAS OUT ON MY WALK.
I RANDOMLY RAN INTO HIM IN THE PARK...
AND...
RANDOMLY?
YEAH, RIGHT.
KOFF!
HE KNOWS WHAT I'M UP TO THROUGH REPORTS FROM SAKAKI.
HE MUST'VE TARGETED AOI, KNOWING SHE'D BE ALONE.
AND?
ばくばくばぐ
BAKU (MUNCH) BAKU BAKU
HE SAYS HE WANTS TO SEE YOU.
AND YOUR MOTHER'S WORRIED TOO, SO IF YOU WOULD COME BY THEIR HOUSE EVEN ONCE...
カラン
KARAN (CLATTER)
YOU'VE LET HIS GOOD LOOKS WIN YOU OVER.
DON'T TALK THAT WAY...!
YOUR FATHER ONLY WANTS TO SEE YOU...
I DON'T WANT TO SEE HIM.

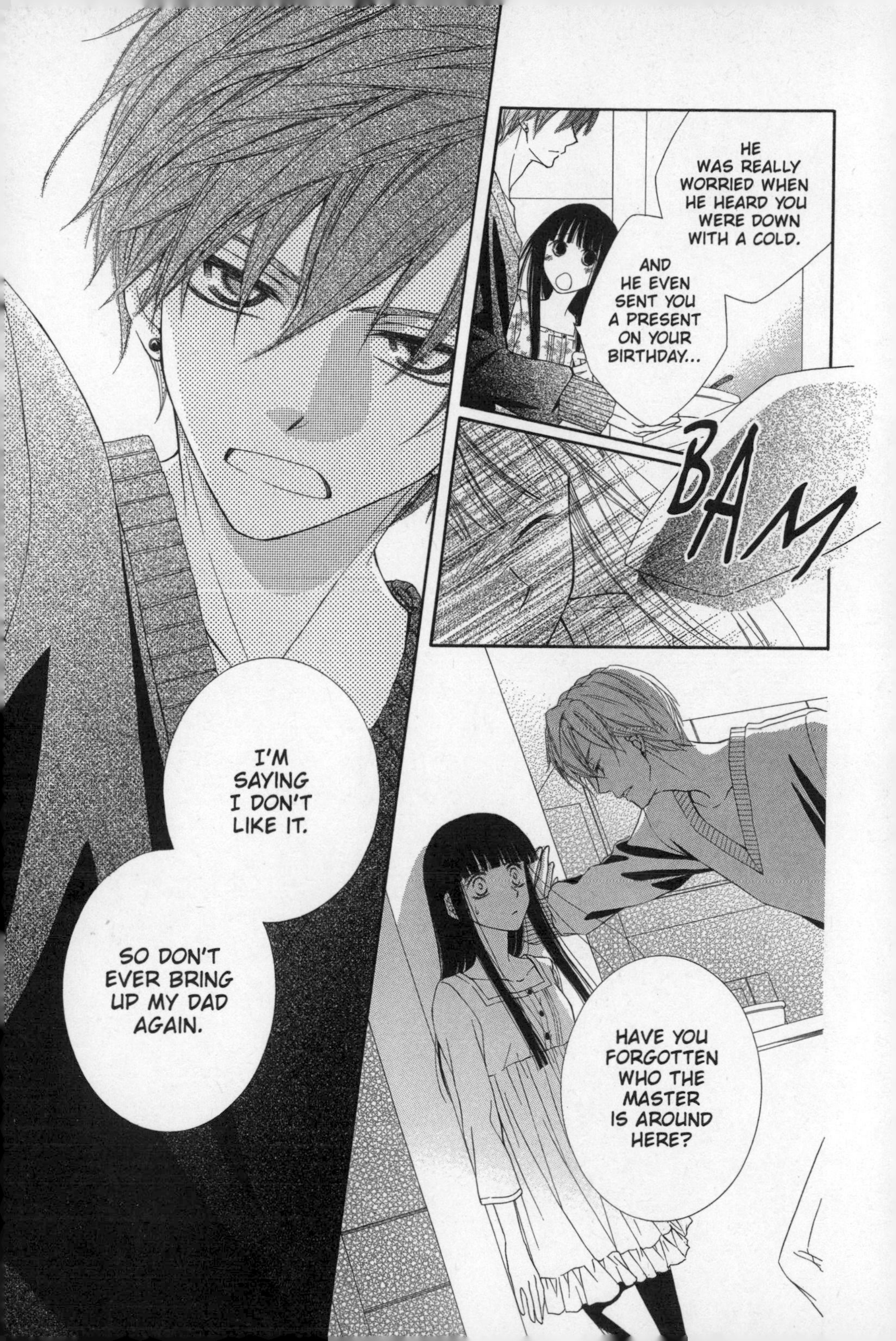

HE WAS REALLY WORRIED WHEN HE HEARD YOU WERE DOWN WITH A COLD.
AND HE EVEN SENT YOU A PRESENT ON YOUR BIRTHDAY...
BAM
HAVE YOU FORGOTTEN WHO THE MASTER IS AROUND HERE?
I'M SAYING I DON'T LIKE IT.
SO DON'T EVER BRING UP MY DAD AGAIN.

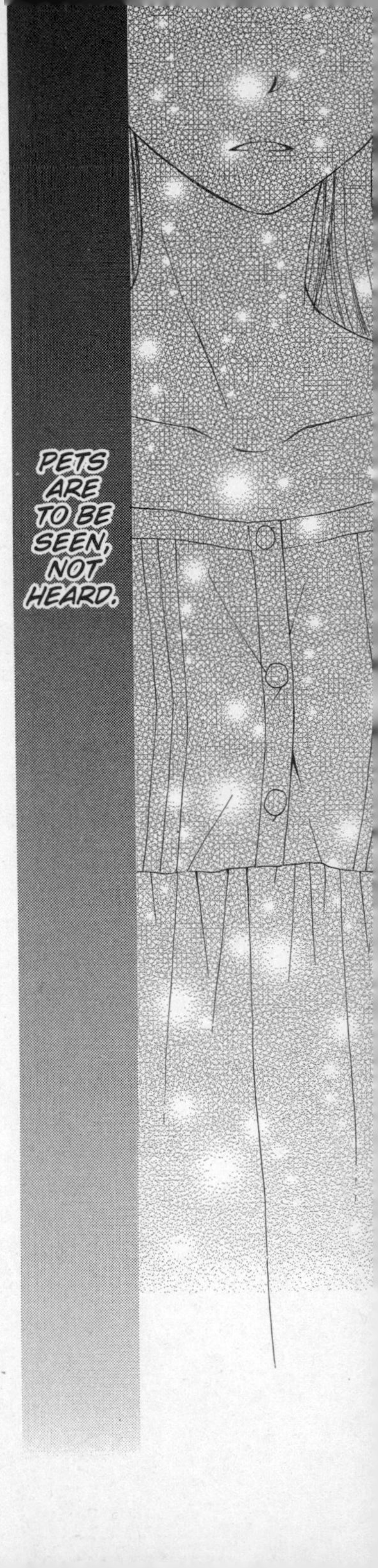
PETS ARE TO BE SEEN, NOT HEARD.

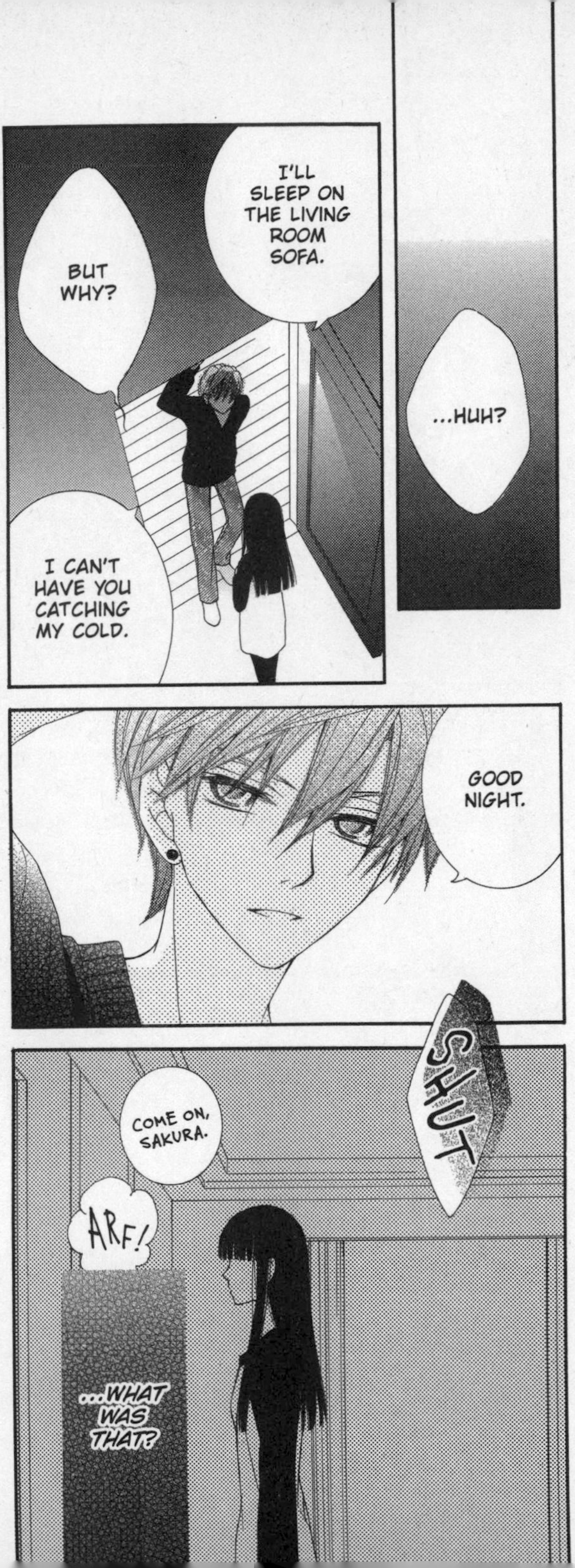
...HUH?
I'LL SLEEP ON THE LIVING ROOM SOFA.
BUT WHY?
I CAN'T HAVE YOU CATCHING MY COLD.
GOOD NIGHT.
SHUT
COME ON, SAKURA.
ARF!
...WHAT WAS THAT?

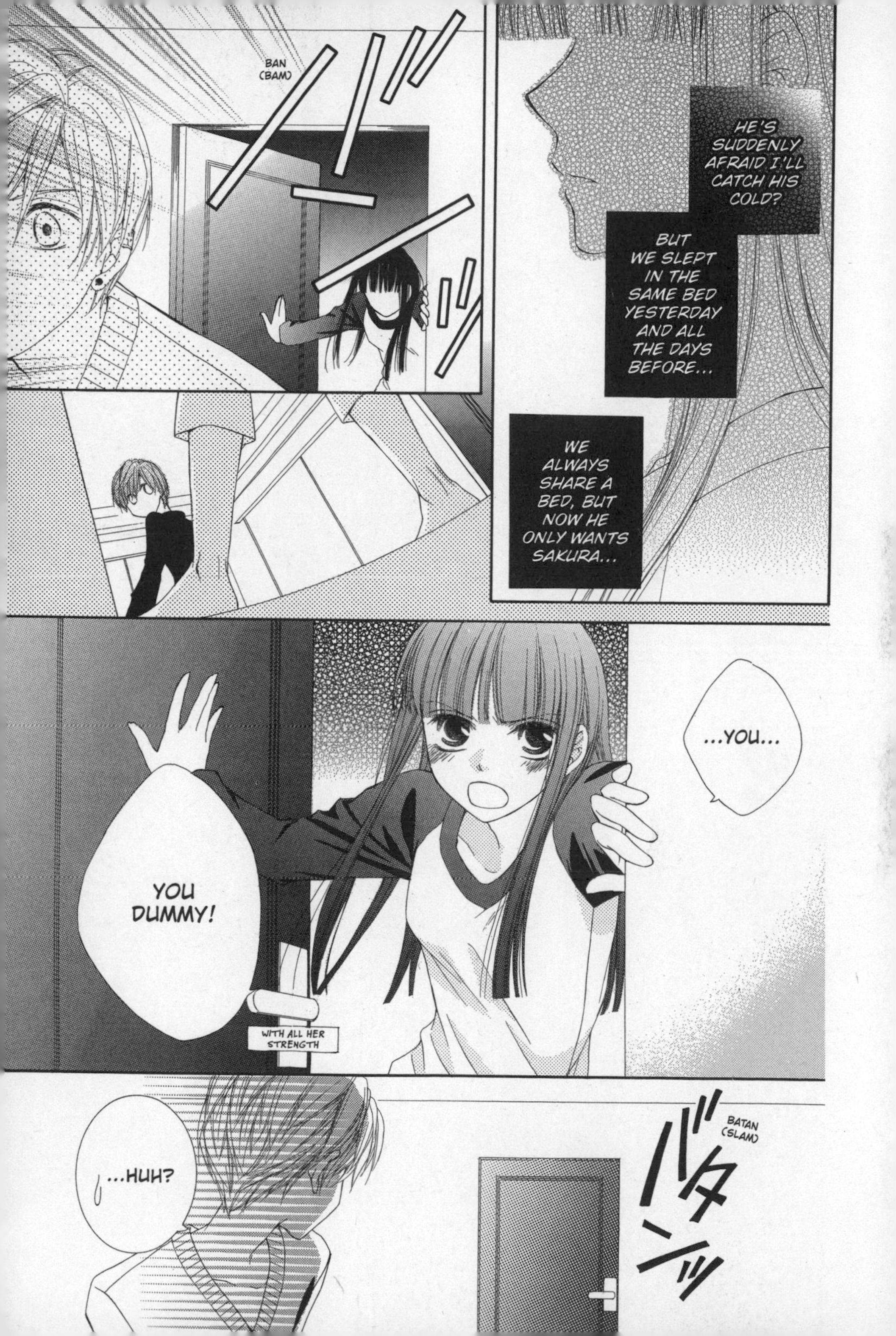

HE'S SUDDENLY AFRAID I'LL CATCH HIS COLD?
BUT WE SLEPT IN THE SAME BED YESTERDAY AND ALL THE DAYS BEFORE...
WE ALWAYS SHARE A BED, BUT NOW HE ONLY WANTS SAKURA...
BAN (BAM)
...YOU...
YOU DUMMY!
WITH ALL HER STRENGTH
BATAN (SLAM)
...HUH?

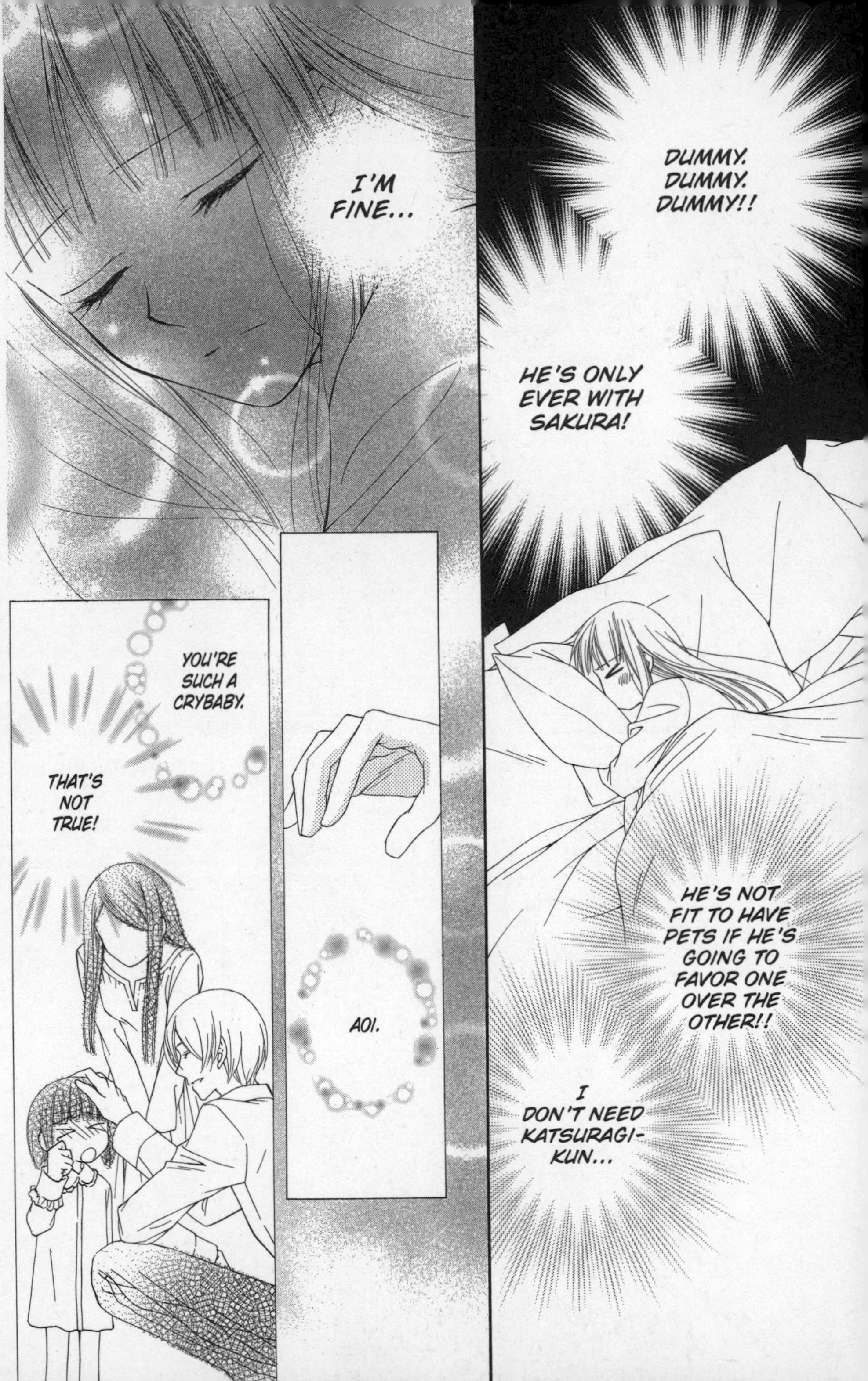
DUMMY. DUMMY. DUMMY!!
HE'S ONLY EVER WITH SAKURA!
HE'S NOT FIT TO HAVE PETS IF HE'S GOING TO FAVOR ONE OVER THE OTHER!!
I DON'T NEED KATSURAGI-KUN...
I'M FINE...
AOI.
YOU'RE SUCH A CRYBABY.
THAT'S NOT TRUE!

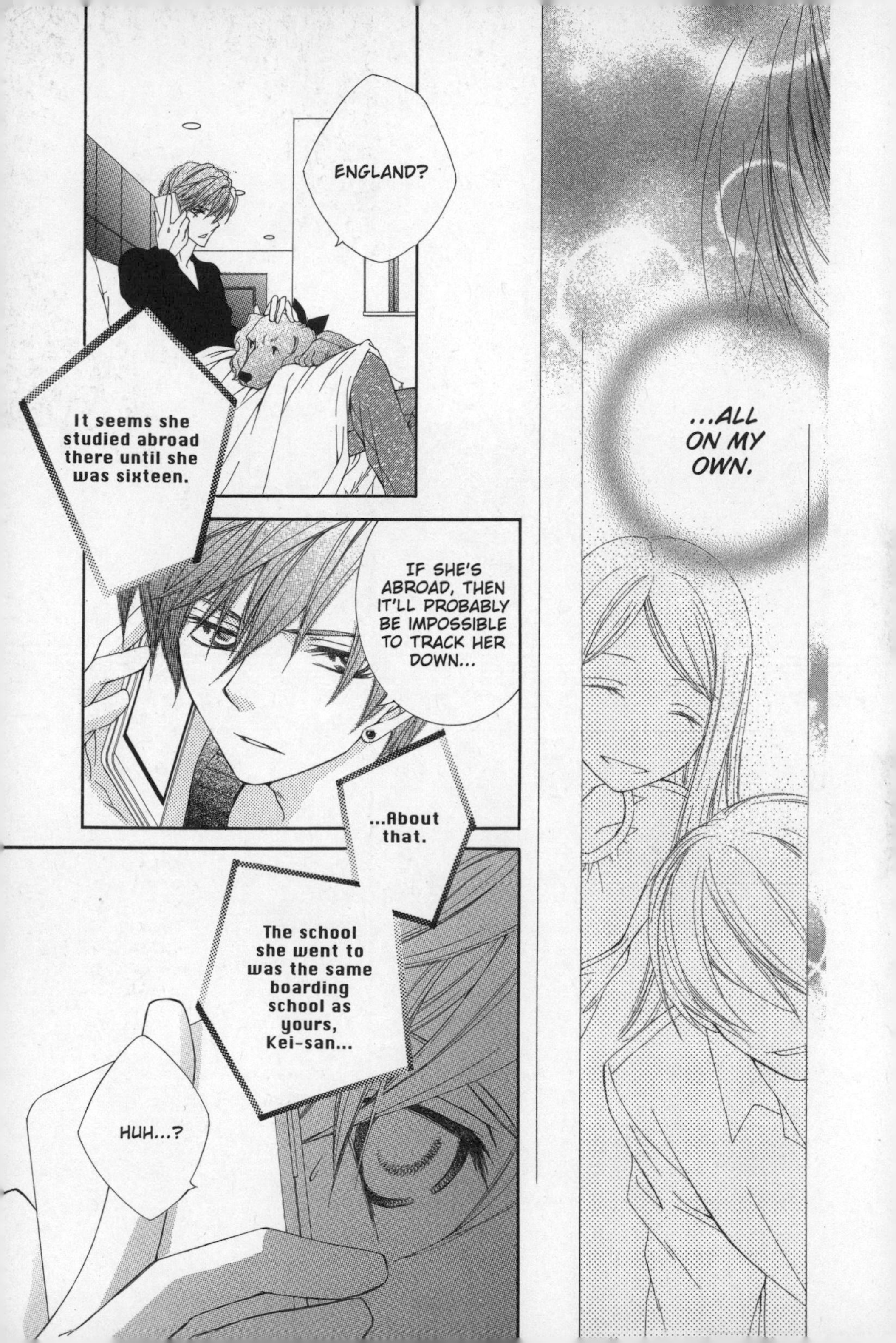
...ALL ON MY OWN.
ENGLAND?
It seems she studied abroad there until she was sixteen.
IF SHE'S ABROAD, THEN IT'LL PROBABLY BE IMPOSSIBLE TO TRACK HER DOWN...
...About that.
The school she went to was the same boarding school as yours, Kei-san...
HUH...?

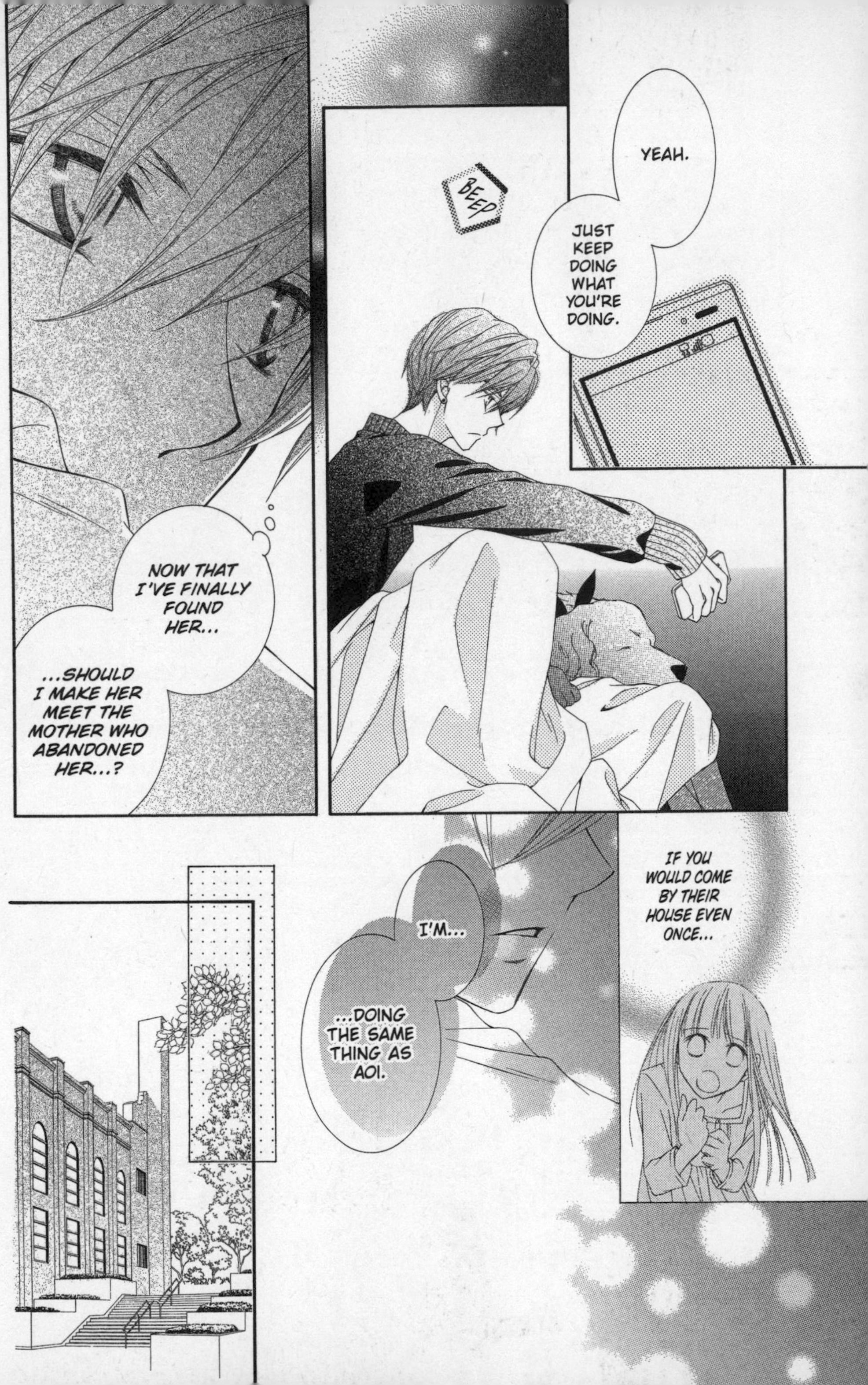
YEAH.
BEEP
JUST KEEP DOING WHAT YOU'RE DOING.
NOW THAT I'VE FINALLY FOUND HER...
...SHOULD I MAKE HER MEET THE MOTHER WHO ABANDONED HER...?
IF YOU WOULD COME BY THEIR HOUSE EVEN ONCE...
I'M...
...DOING THE SAME THING AS AOI.

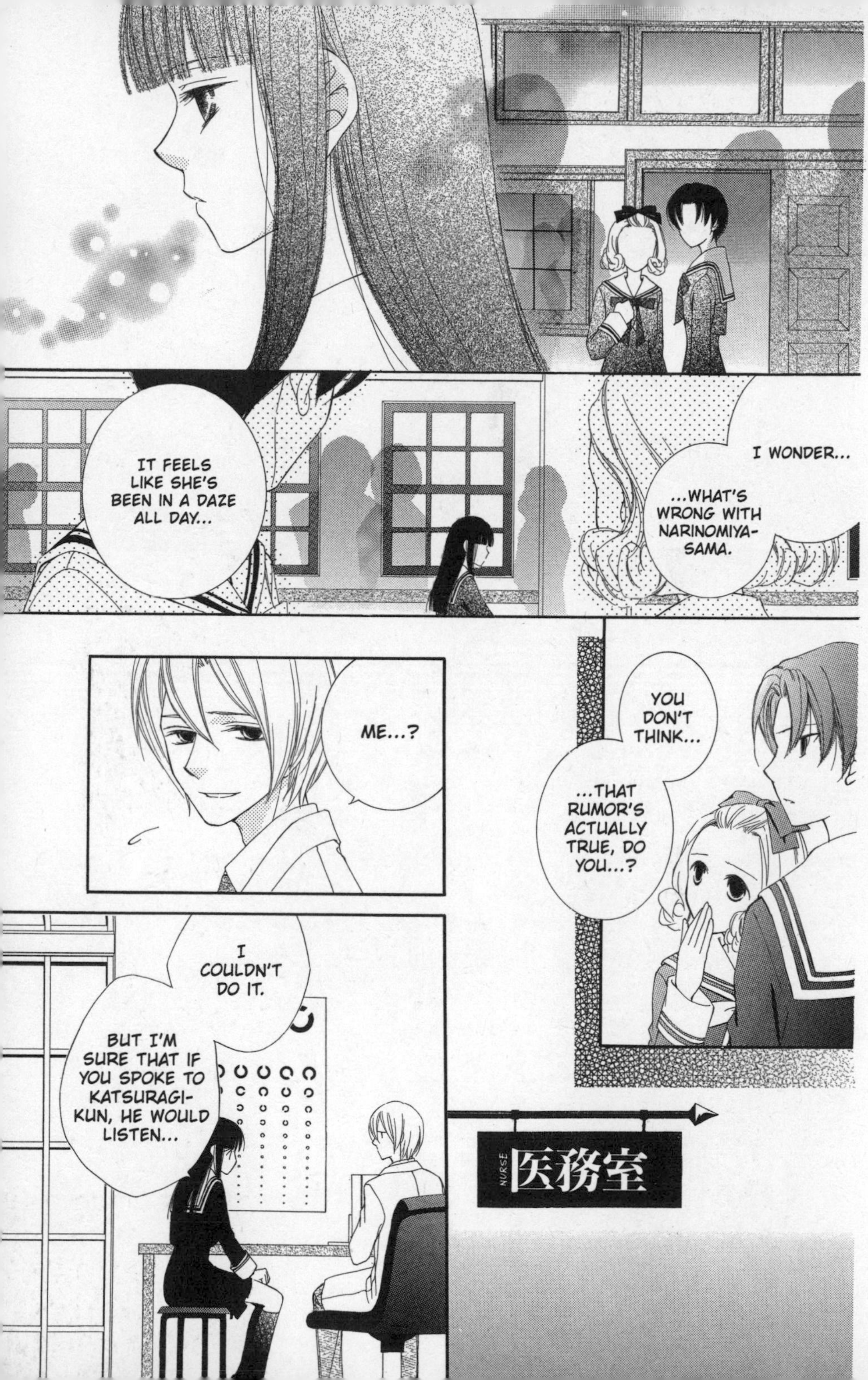
I WONDER...
...WHAT'S WRONG WITH NARINOMIYA-SAMA.
IT FEELS LIKE SHE'S BEEN IN A DAZE ALL DAY...
YOU DON'T THINK...
...THAT RUMOR'S ACTUALLY TRUE, DO YOU...?
ME...?
NURSE 医務室
I COULDN'T DO IT.
BUT I'M SURE THAT IF YOU SPOKE TO KATSURAGI-KUN, HE WOULD LISTEN...

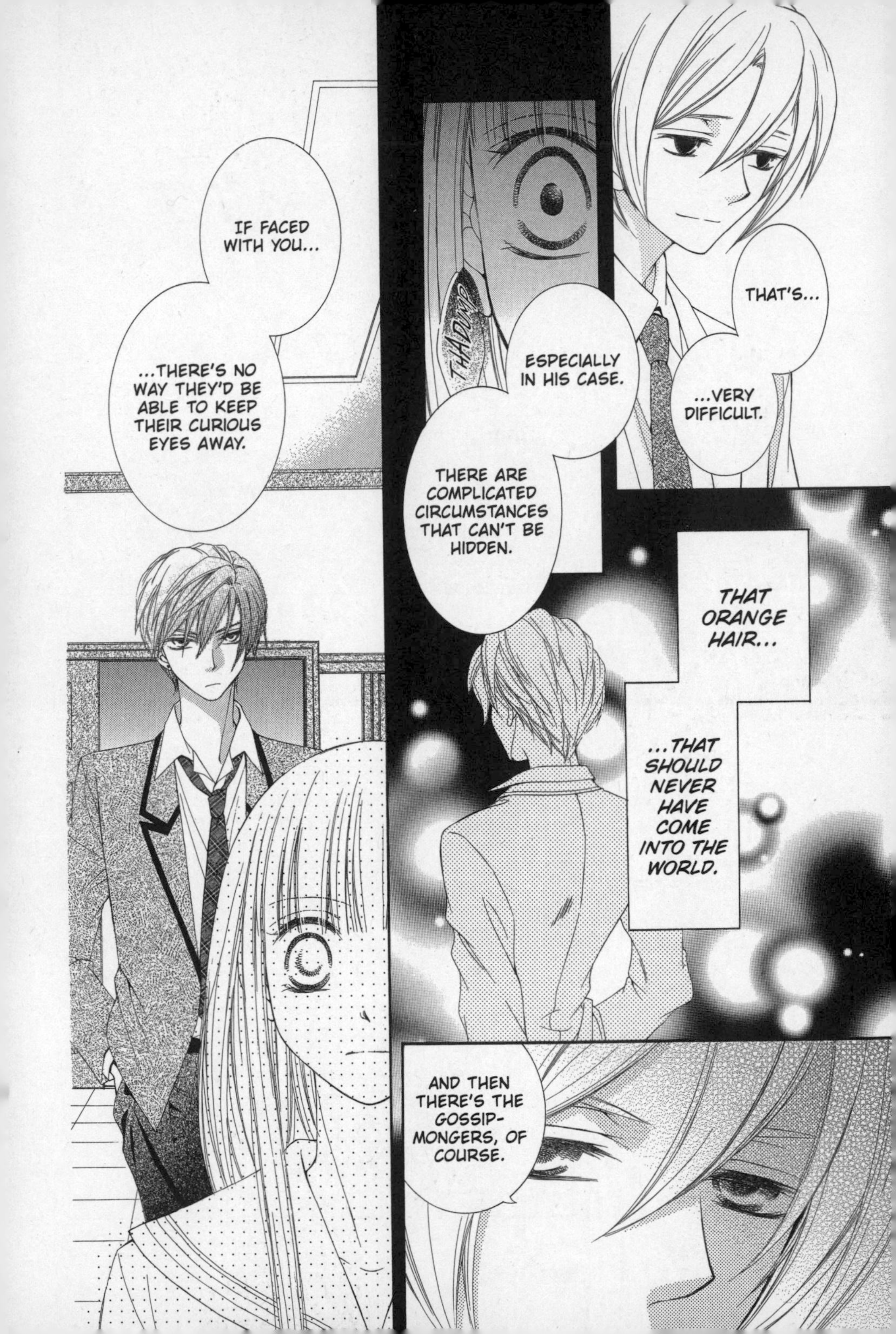
THAT'S...
...VERY DIFFICULT.
THADUMP
ESPECIALLY IN HIS CASE.
THERE ARE COMPLICATED CIRCUMSTANCES THAT CAN'T BE HIDDEN.
THAT ORANGE HAIR...
...THAT SHOULD NEVER HAVE COME INTO THE WORLD.
AND THEN THERE'S THE GOSSIP-MONGERS, OF COURSE.
IF FACED WITH YOU...
...THERE'S NO WAY THEY'D BE ABLE TO KEEP THEIR CURIOUS EYES AWAY.

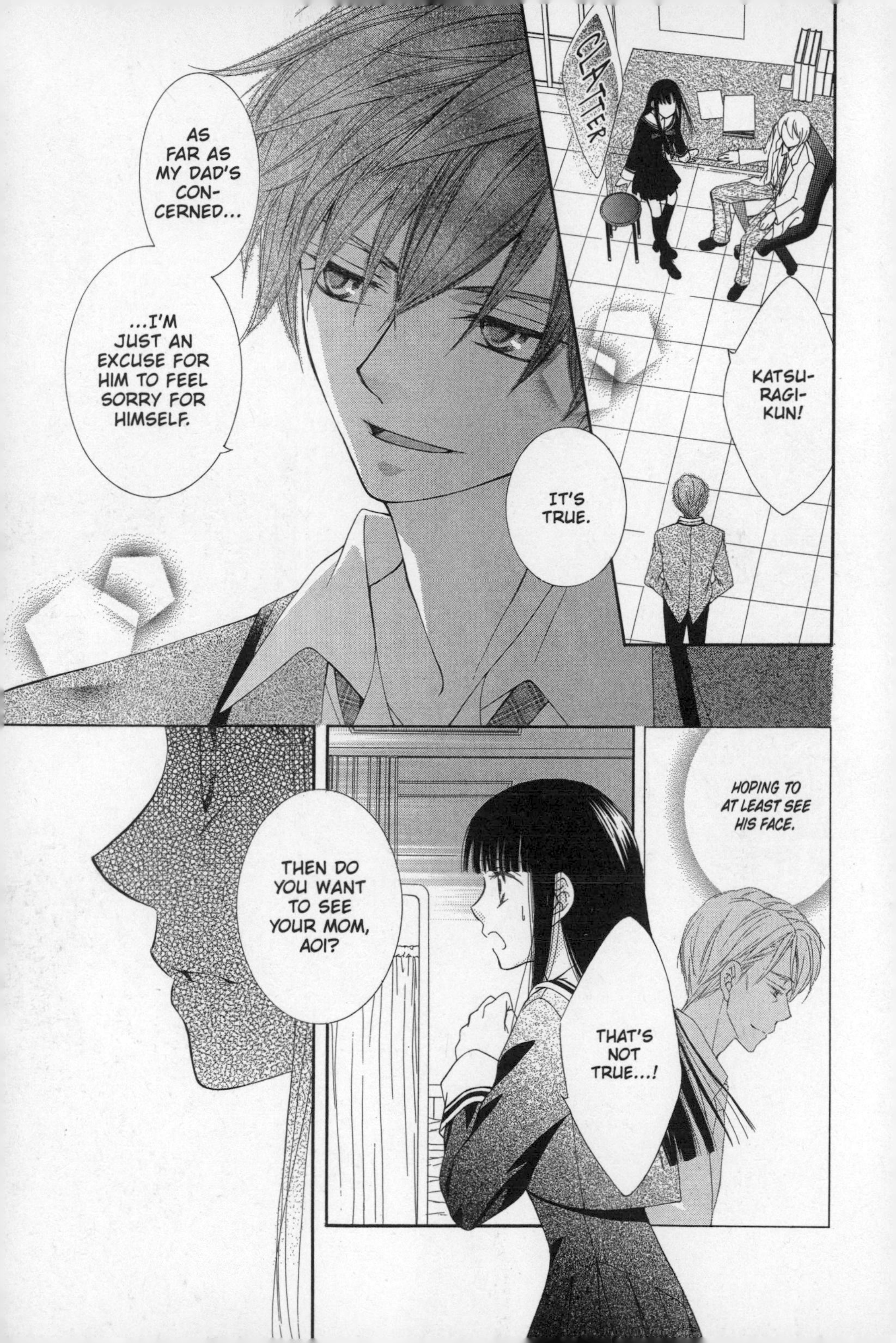
CLATTER
KATSURAGI-KUN!
IT'S TRUE.
AS FAR AS MY DAD'S CONCERNED...
...I'M JUST AN EXCUSE FOR HIM TO FEEL SORRY FOR HIMSELF.
HOPING TO AT LEAST SEE HIS FACE.
THAT'S NOT TRUE...!
THEN DO YOU WANT TO SEE YOUR MOM, AOI?

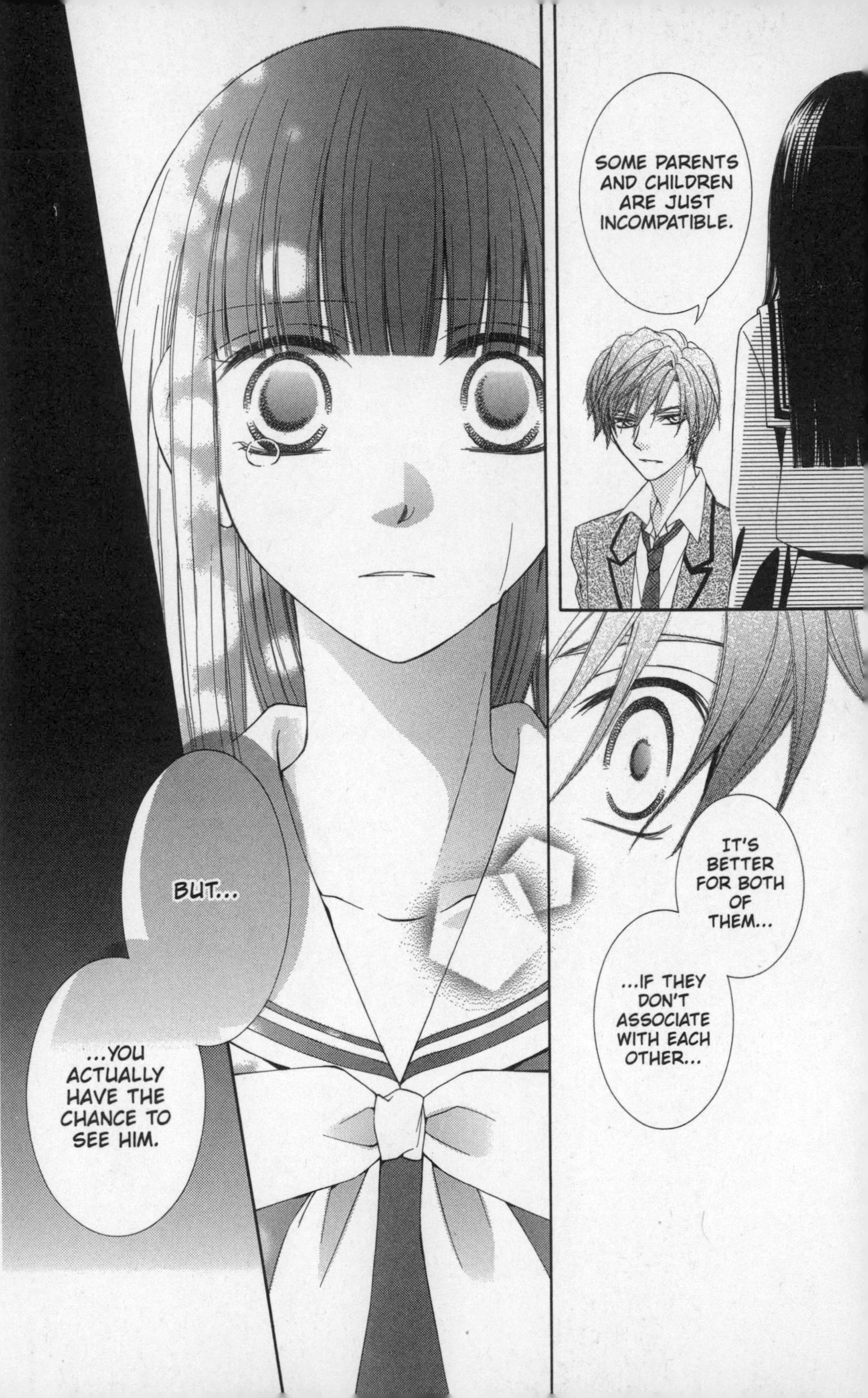
SOME PARENTS AND CHILDREN ARE JUST INCOMPATIBLE.
IT'S BETTER FOR BOTH OF THEM...
...IF THEY DON'T ASSOCIATE WITH EACH OTHER...
BUT...
...YOU ACTUALLY HAVE THE CHANCE TO SEE HIM.

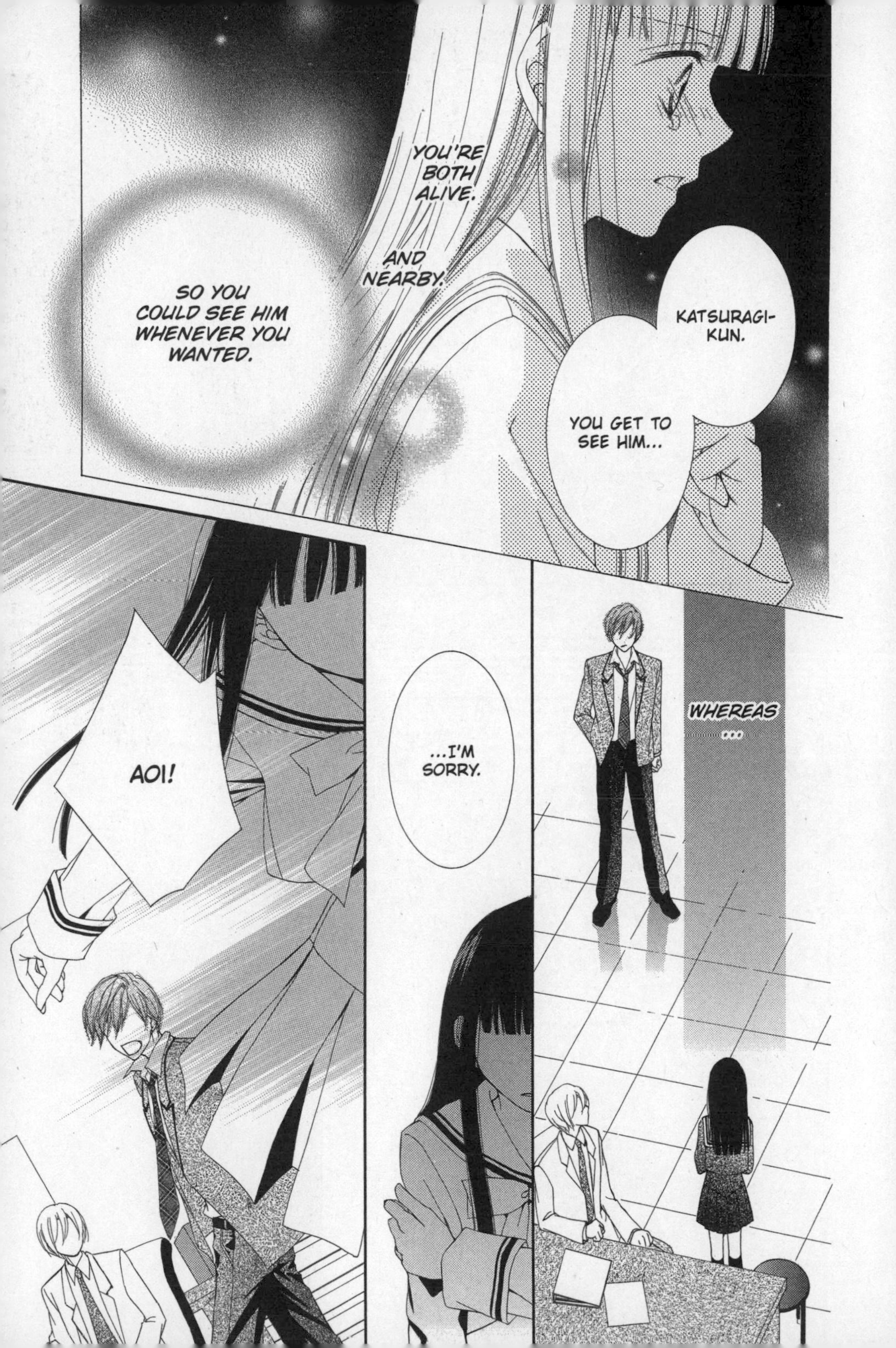
KATSURAGI-KUN.
YOU GET TO SEE HIM...
YOU'RE BOTH ALIVE.
AND NEARBY.
SO YOU COULD SEE HIM WHENEVER YOU WANTED.
WHEREAS...
...I'M SORRY.
AOI!

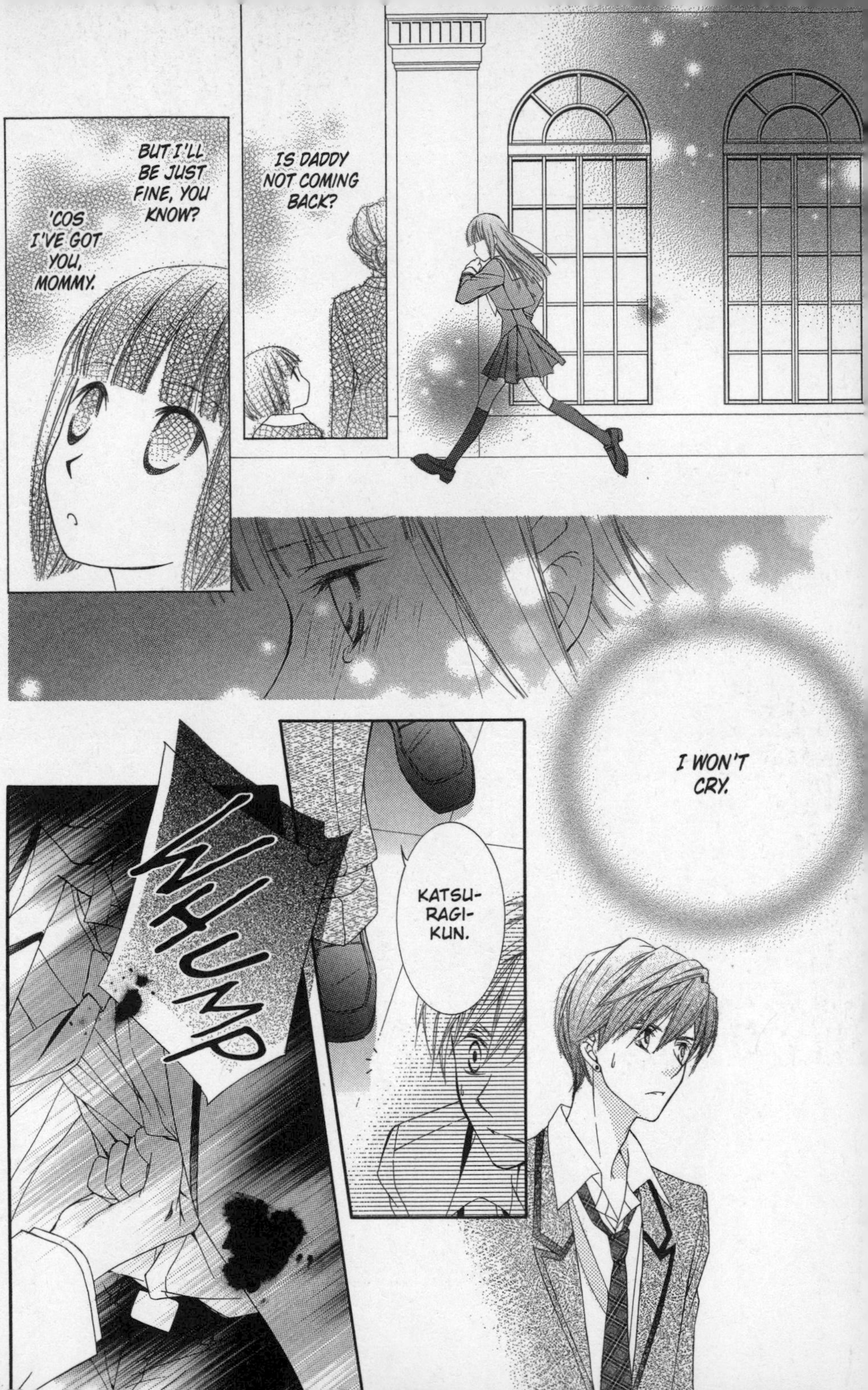
IS DADDY NOT COMING BACK?
BUT I'LL BE JUST FINE, YOU KNOW?
'COS I'VE GOT YOU, MOMMY.
I WON'T CRY.
KATSU-RAGI-KUN.
WHUMP

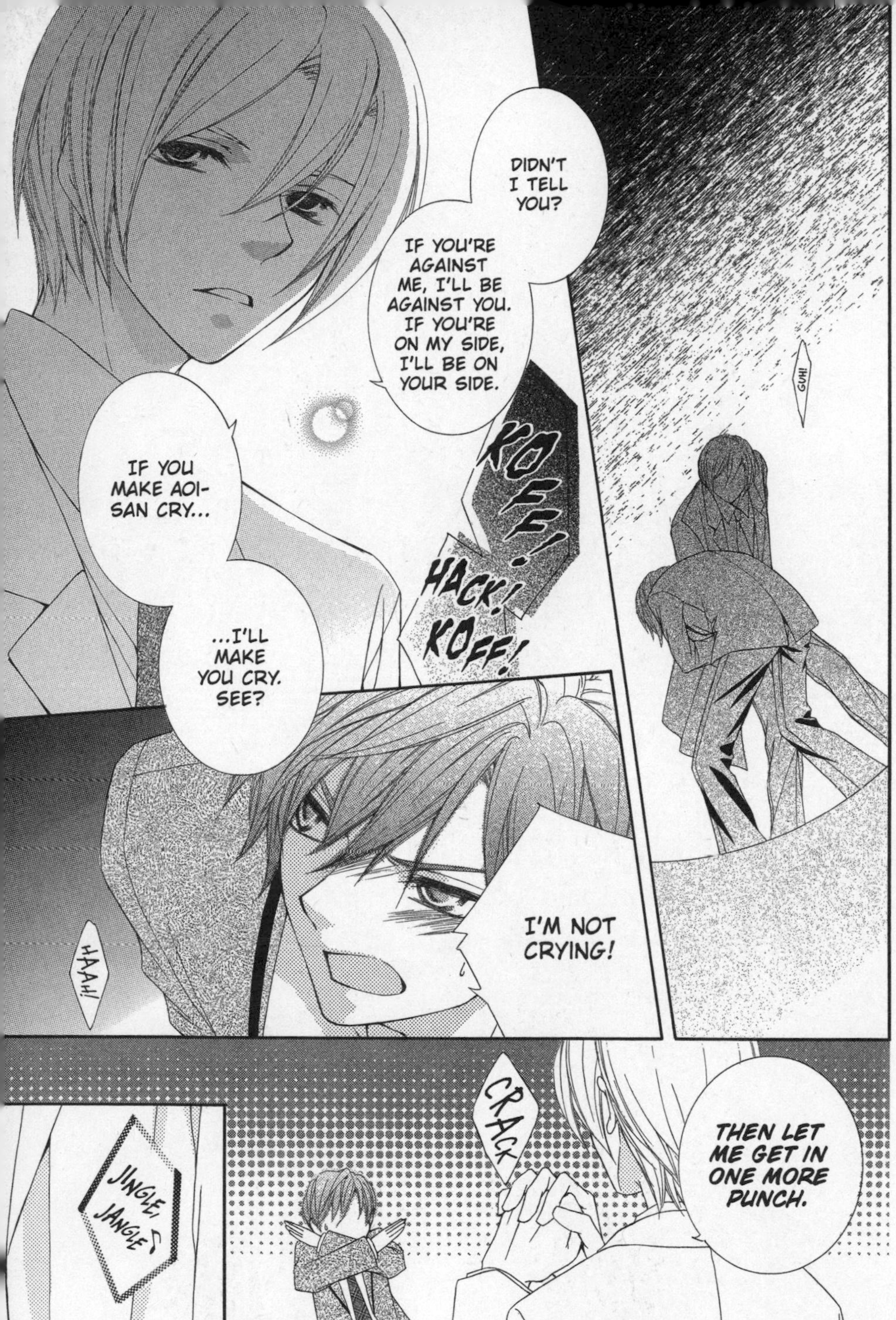
GUH!
KOFF! HACK! KOFF!
DIDN'T I TELL YOU?
IF YOU'RE AGAINST ME, I'LL BE AGAINST YOU. IF YOU'RE ON MY SIDE, I'LL BE ON YOUR SIDE.
IF YOU MAKE AOI-SAN CRY...
...I'LL MAKE YOU CRY. SEE?
I'M NOT CRYING!
HAAH!
CRACK
THEN LET ME GET IN ONE MORE PUNCH.
JINGLE, JANGLE♪

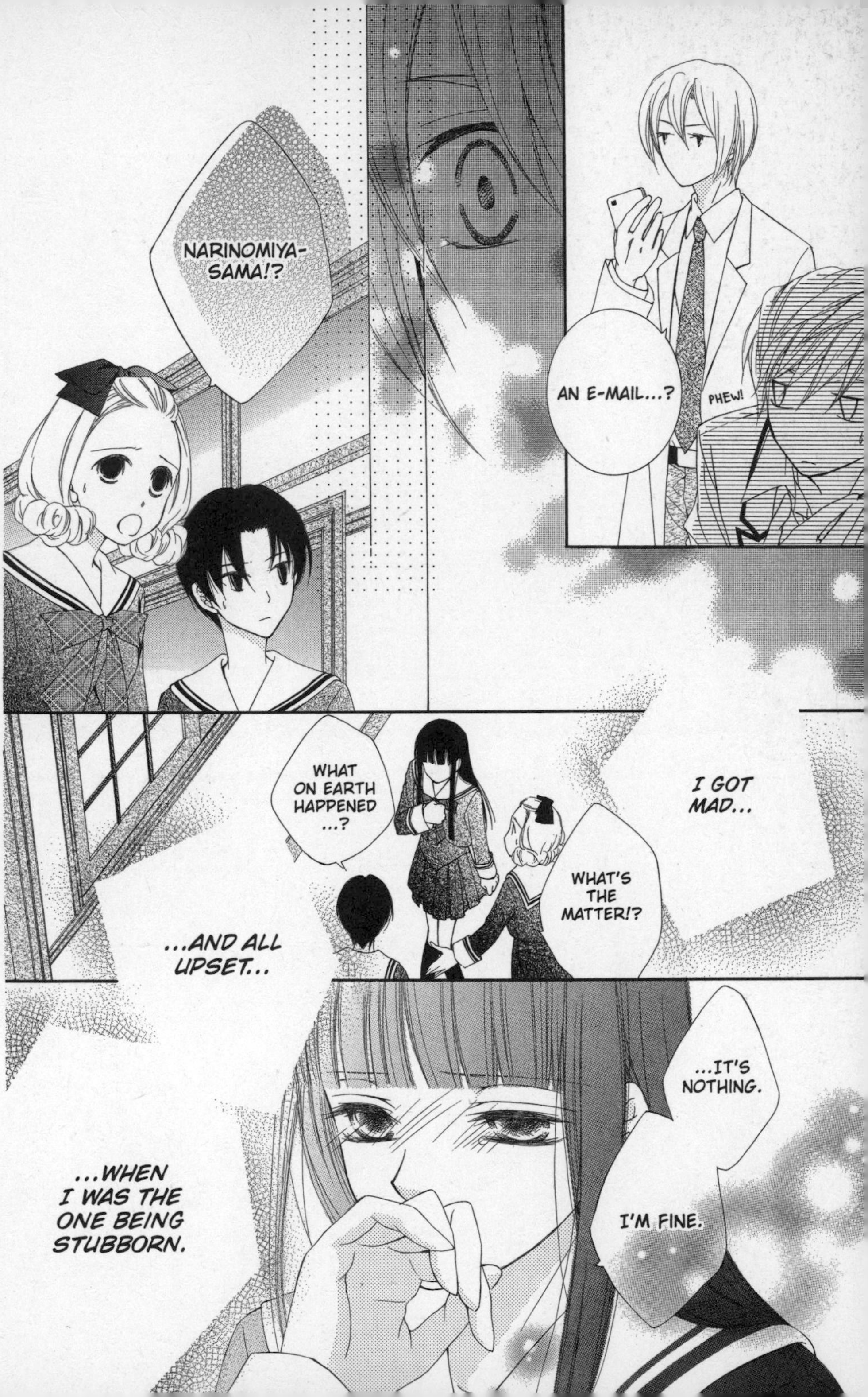
AN E-MAIL...?
PHEW!
NARINOMIYA-SAMA!?
I GOT MAD...
WHAT'S THE MATTER!?
WHAT ON EARTH HAPPENED ...?
...AND ALL UPSET...
...IT'S NOTHING.
I'M FINE.
...WHEN I WAS THE ONE BEING STUBBORN.

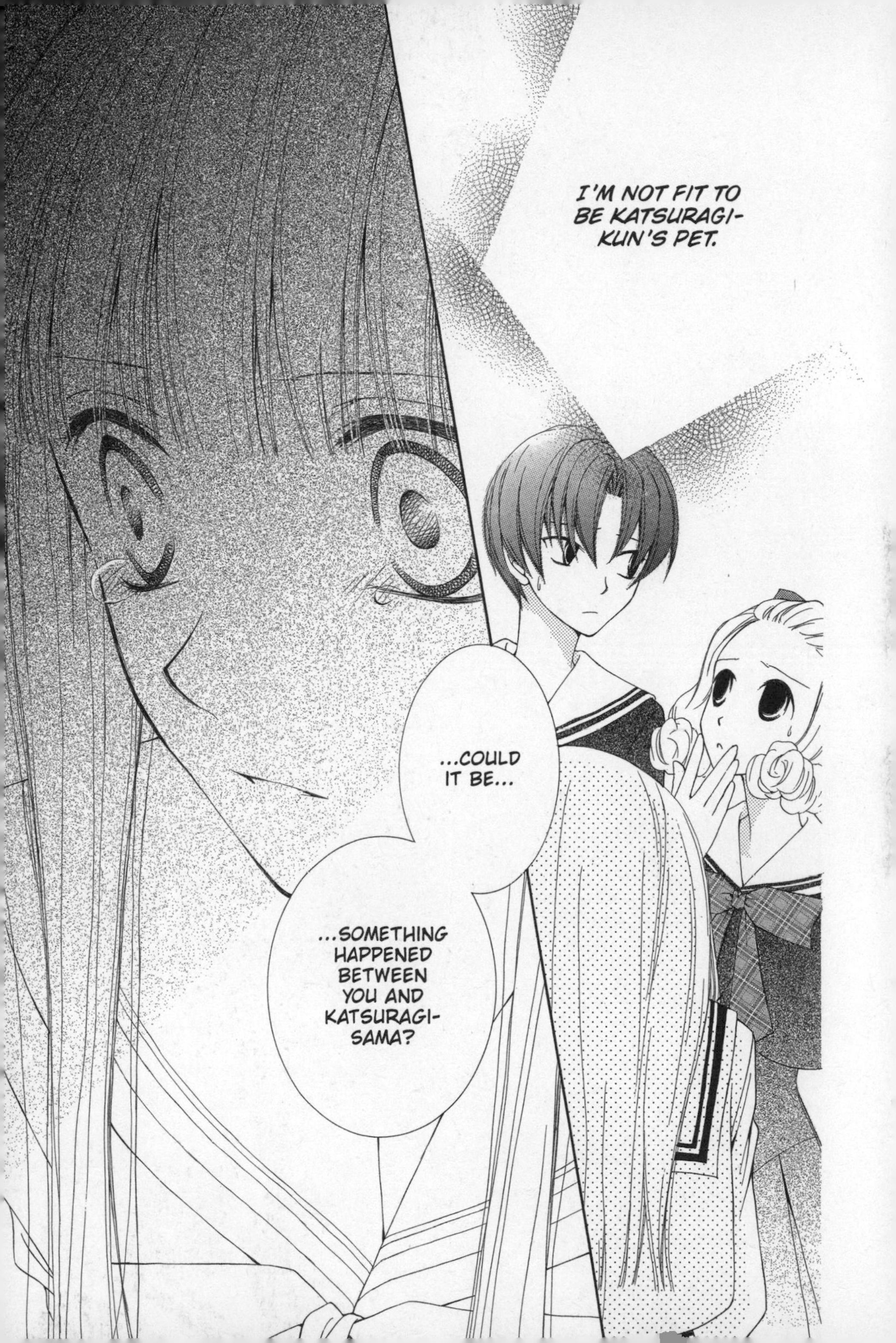
I'M NOT FIT TO BE KATSURAGI-KUN'S PET.
...COULD IT BE...
...SOMETHING HAPPENED BETWEEN YOU AND KATSURAGI-SAMA?

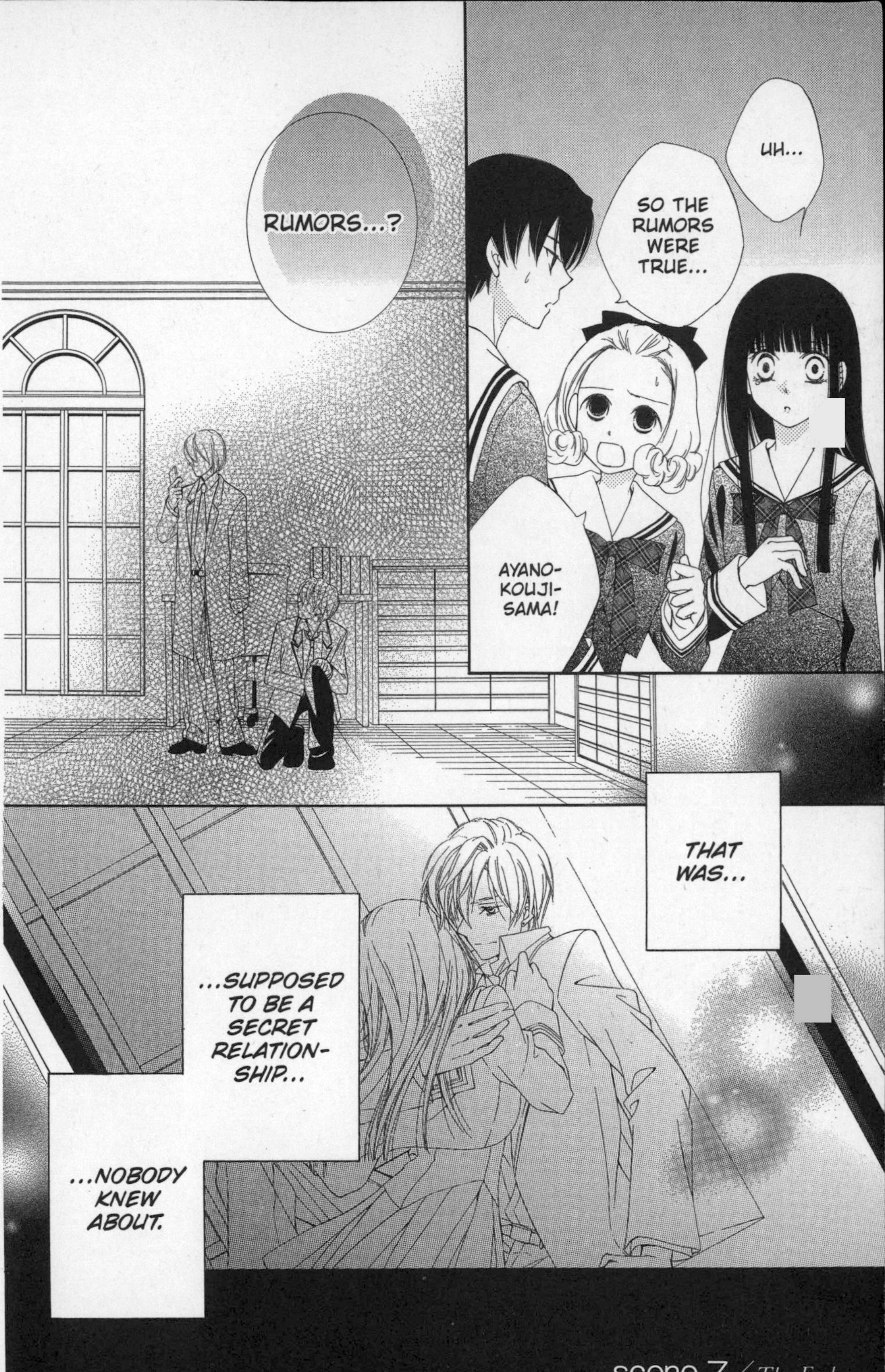
UH...
SO THE RUMORS WERE TRUE...
AYANO-KOUJI-SAMA!
RUMORS...?
THAT WAS...
...SUPPOSED TO BE A SECRET RELATION-SHIP...
...NOBODY KNEW ABOUT.

scene.7 / *The End*

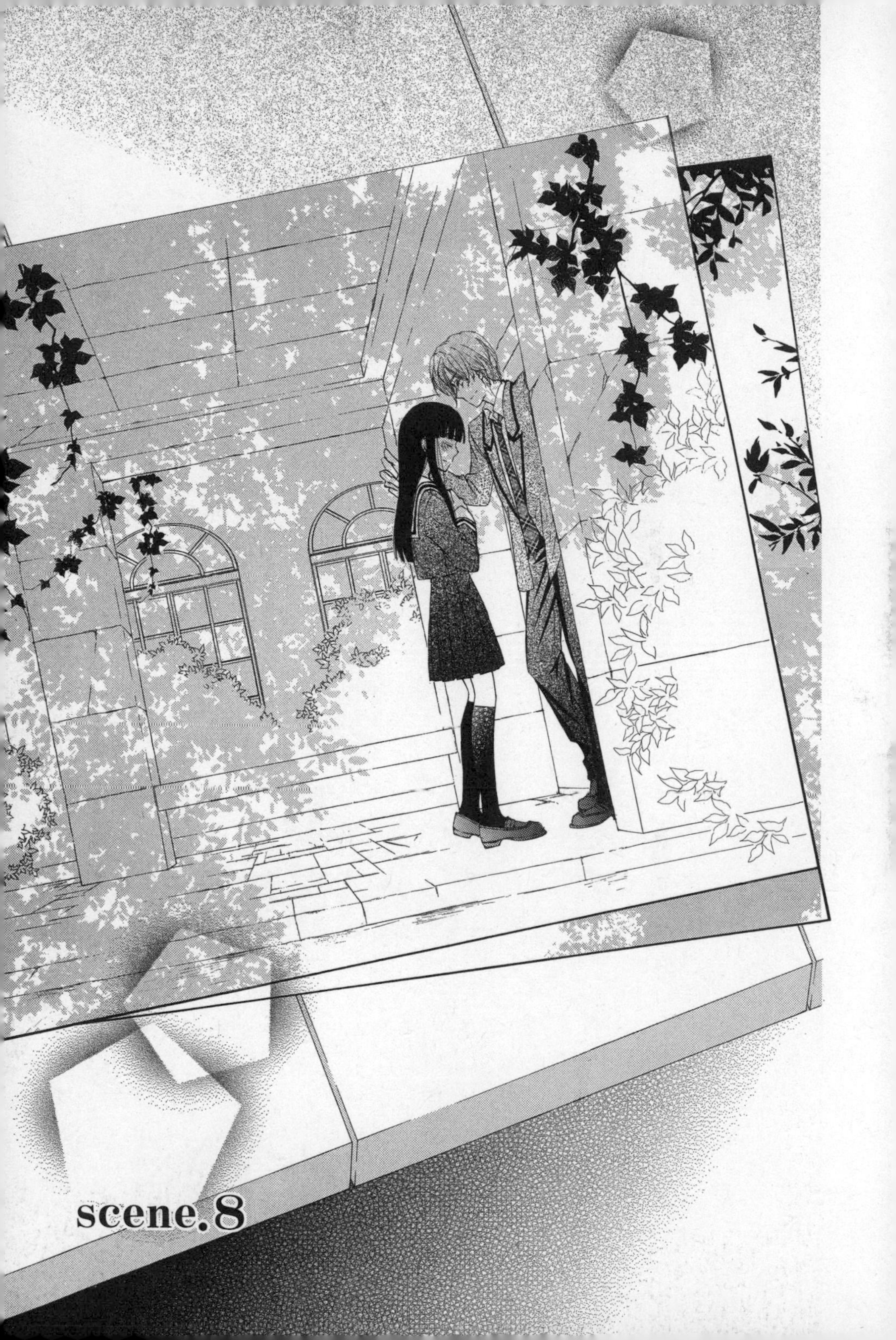
scene. 8

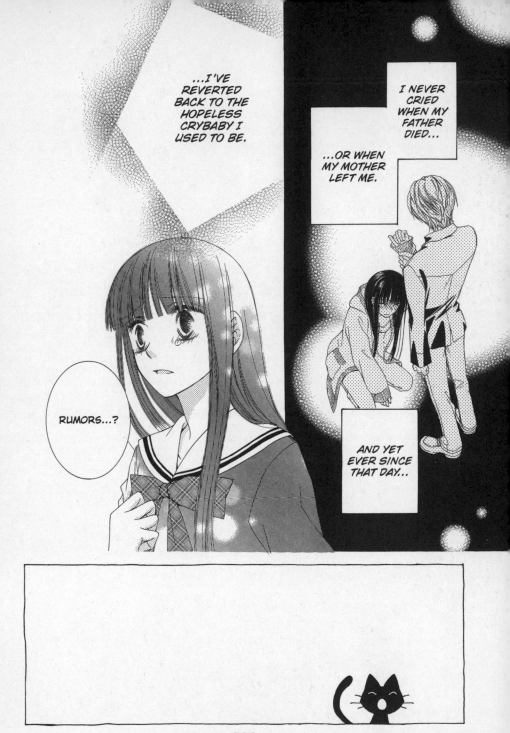

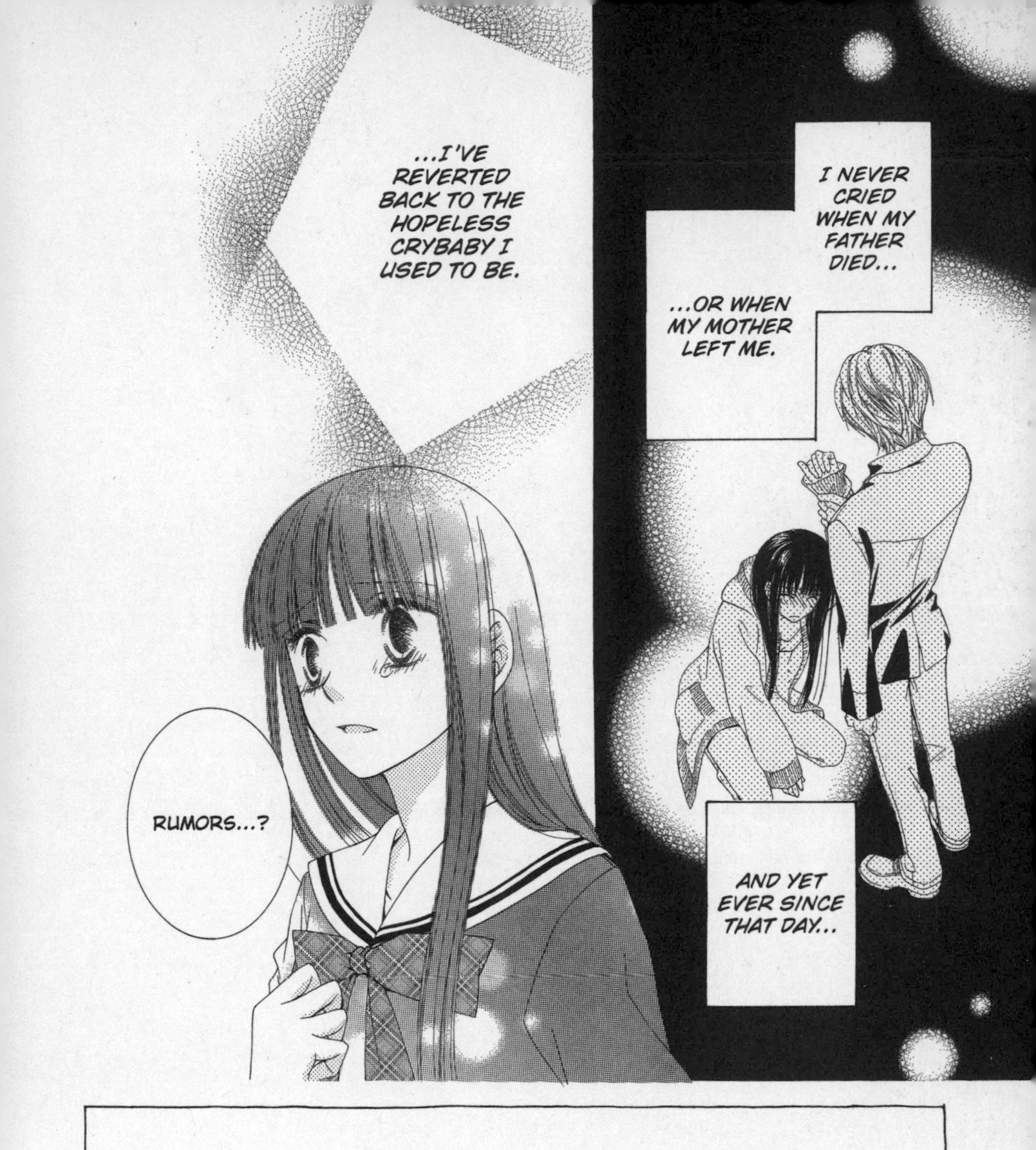
I NEVER CRIED WHEN MY FATHER DIED...
...OR WHEN MY MOTHER LEFT ME.
AND YET EVER SINCE THAT DAY...
...I'VE REVERTED BACK TO THE HOPELESS CRYBABY I USED TO BE.
RUMORS...?

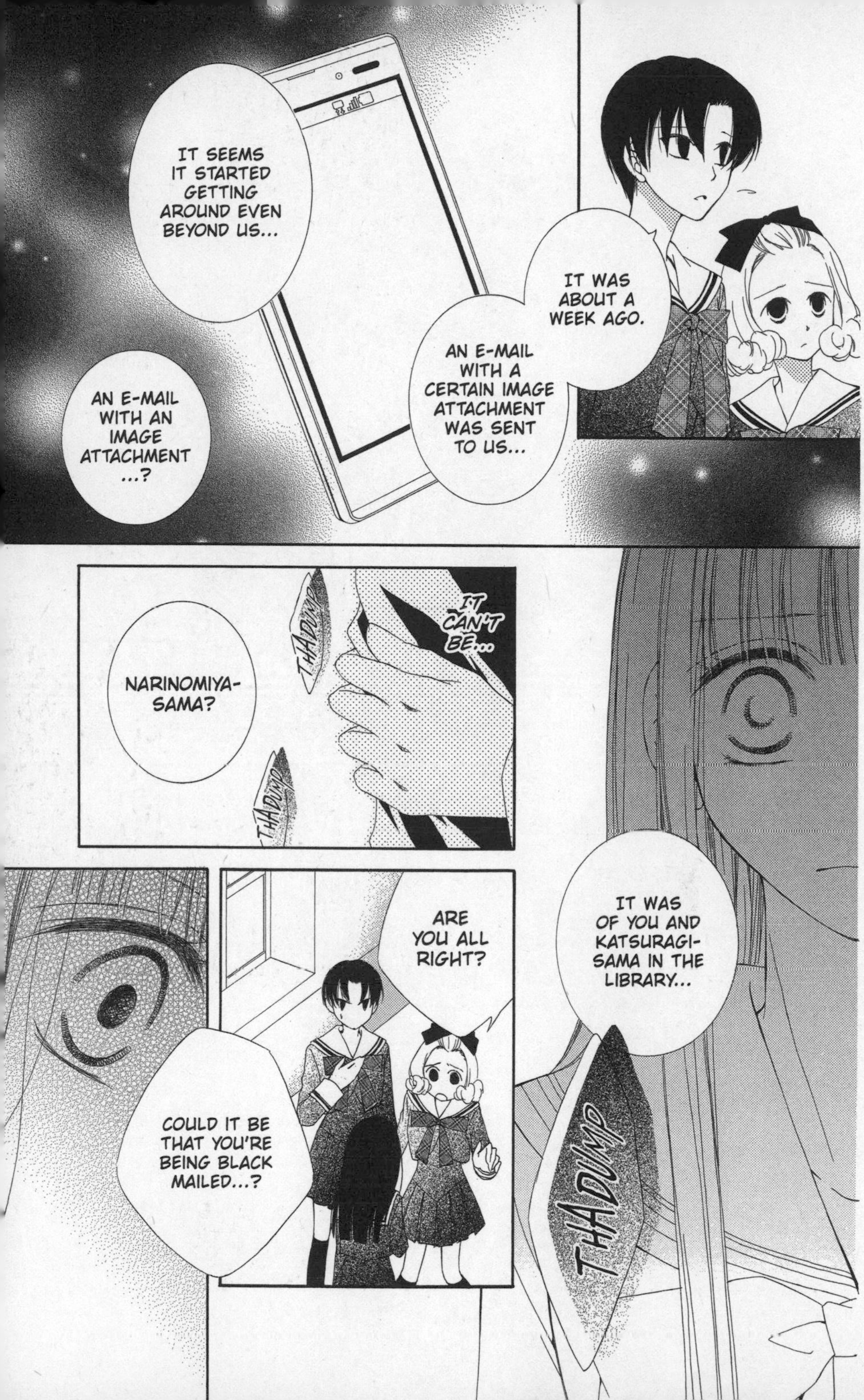
IT WAS ABOUT A WEEK AGO.
AN E-MAIL WITH A CERTAIN IMAGE ATTACHMENT WAS SENT TO US...
IT SEEMS IT STARTED GETTING AROUND EVEN BEYOND US...
AN E-MAIL WITH AN IMAGE ATTACHMENT ...?
IT WAS OF YOU AND KATSURAGI-SAMA IN THE LIBRARY...
THADUMP
THADUMP
...IT CAN'T BE...
NARINOMIYA-SAMA?
THADUMP
ARE YOU ALL RIGHT?
COULD IT BE THAT YOU'RE BEING BLACK MAILED...?

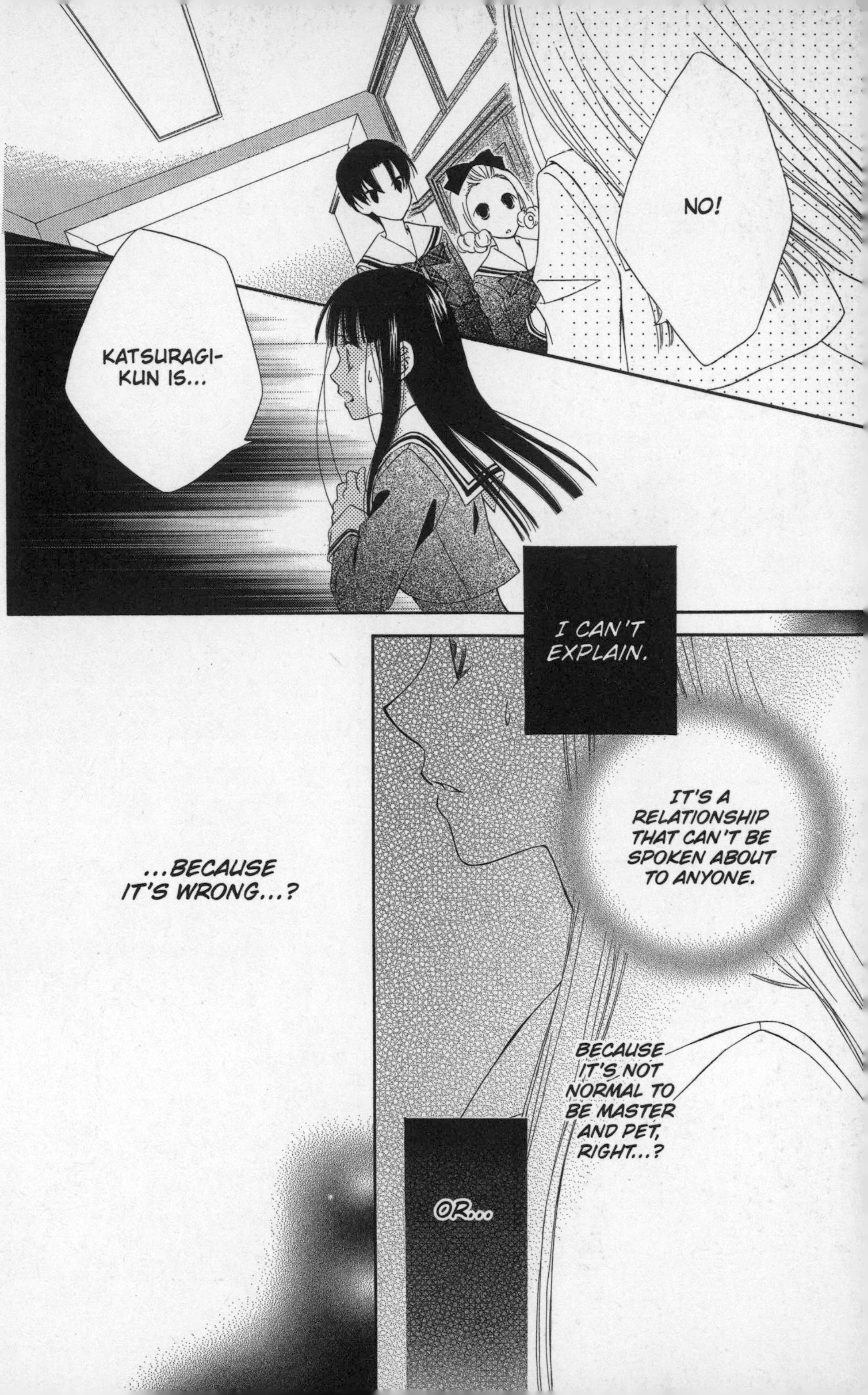
NO!
KATSURAGI-KUN IS...
I CAN'T EXPLAIN.
IT'S A RELATIONSHIP THAT CAN'T BE SPOKEN ABOUT TO ANYONE.
BECAUSE IT'S NOT NORMAL TO BE MASTER AND PET, RIGHT...?
OR...
...BECAUSE IT'S WRONG...?

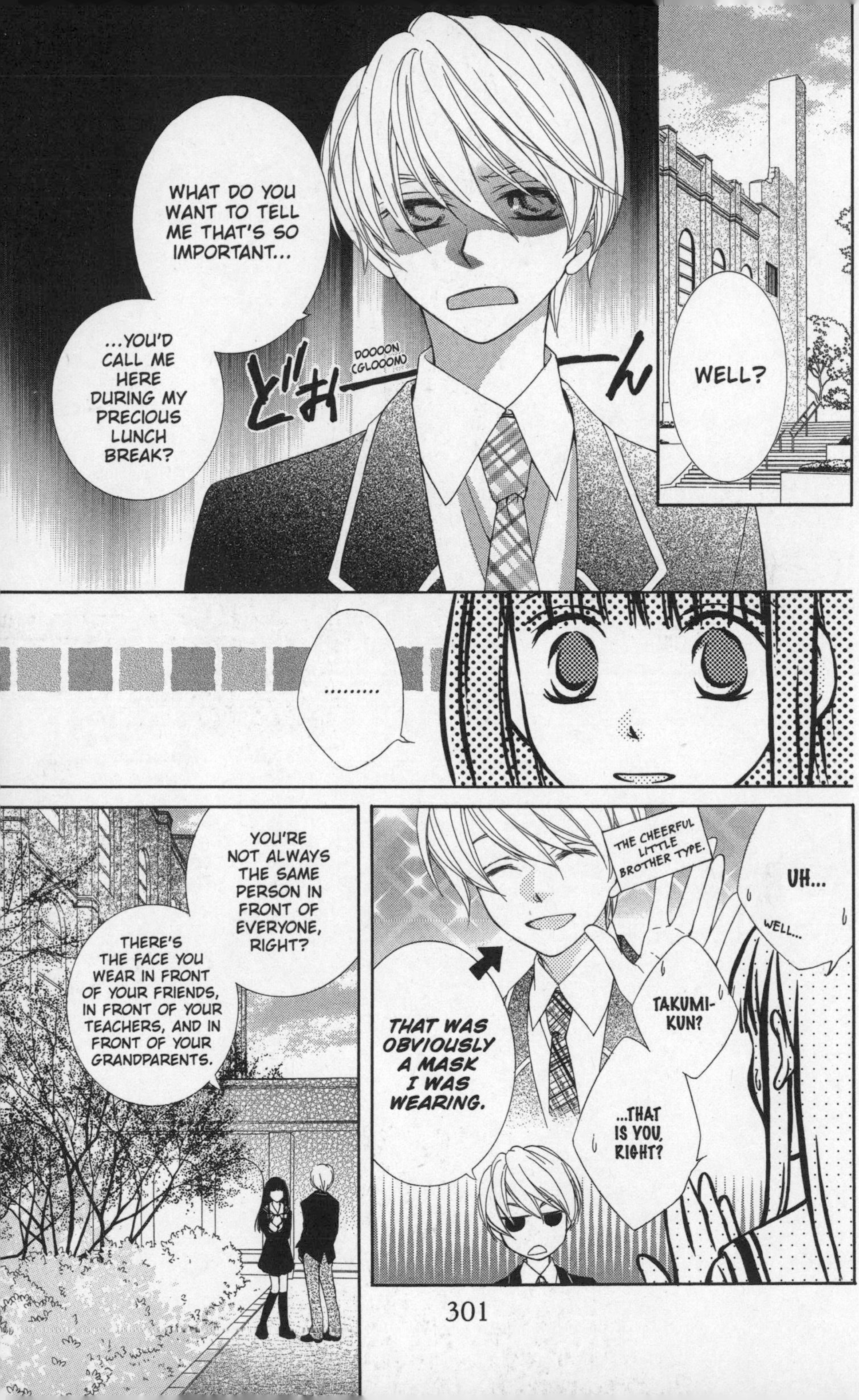
WELL?
WHAT DO YOU WANT TO TELL ME THAT'S SO IMPORTANT...
...YOU'D CALL ME HERE DURING MY PRECIOUS LUNCH BREAK?
DOOOON (GLOOOM)
....
UH...
WELL...
TAKUMI-KUN?
...THAT IS YOU, RIGHT?
THAT WAS OBVIOUSLY A MASK I WAS WEARING.
THE CHEERFUL LITTLE BROTHER TYPE.
YOU'RE NOT ALWAYS THE SAME PERSON IN FRONT OF EVERYONE, RIGHT?
THERE'S THE FACE YOU WEAR IN FRONT OF YOUR FRIENDS, IN FRONT OF YOUR TEACHERS, AND IN FRONT OF YOUR GRANDPARENTS.

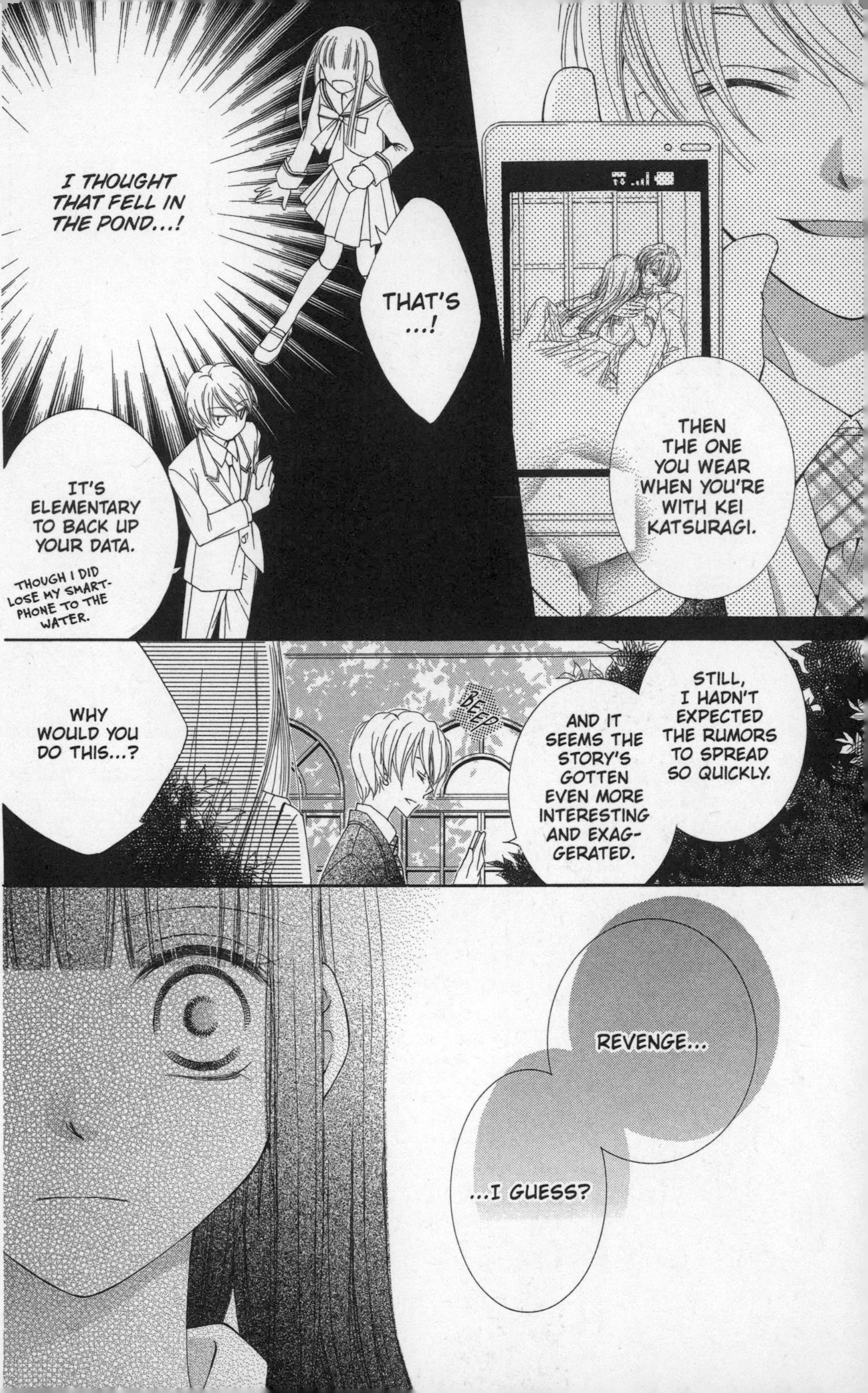
THEN THE ONE YOU WEAR WHEN YOU'RE WITH KEI KATSURAGI.
THAT'S ...!
I THOUGHT THAT FELL IN THE POND...!
IT'S ELEMENTARY TO BACK UP YOUR DATA.
THOUGH I DID LOSE MY SMART-PHONE TO THE WATER.
STILL, I HADN'T EXPECTED THE RUMORS TO SPREAD SO QUICKLY.
AND IT SEEMS THE STORY'S GOTTEN EVEN MORE INTERESTING AND EXAG-GERATED.
BEEP
WHY WOULD YOU DO THIS...?
REVENGE...
...I GUESS?

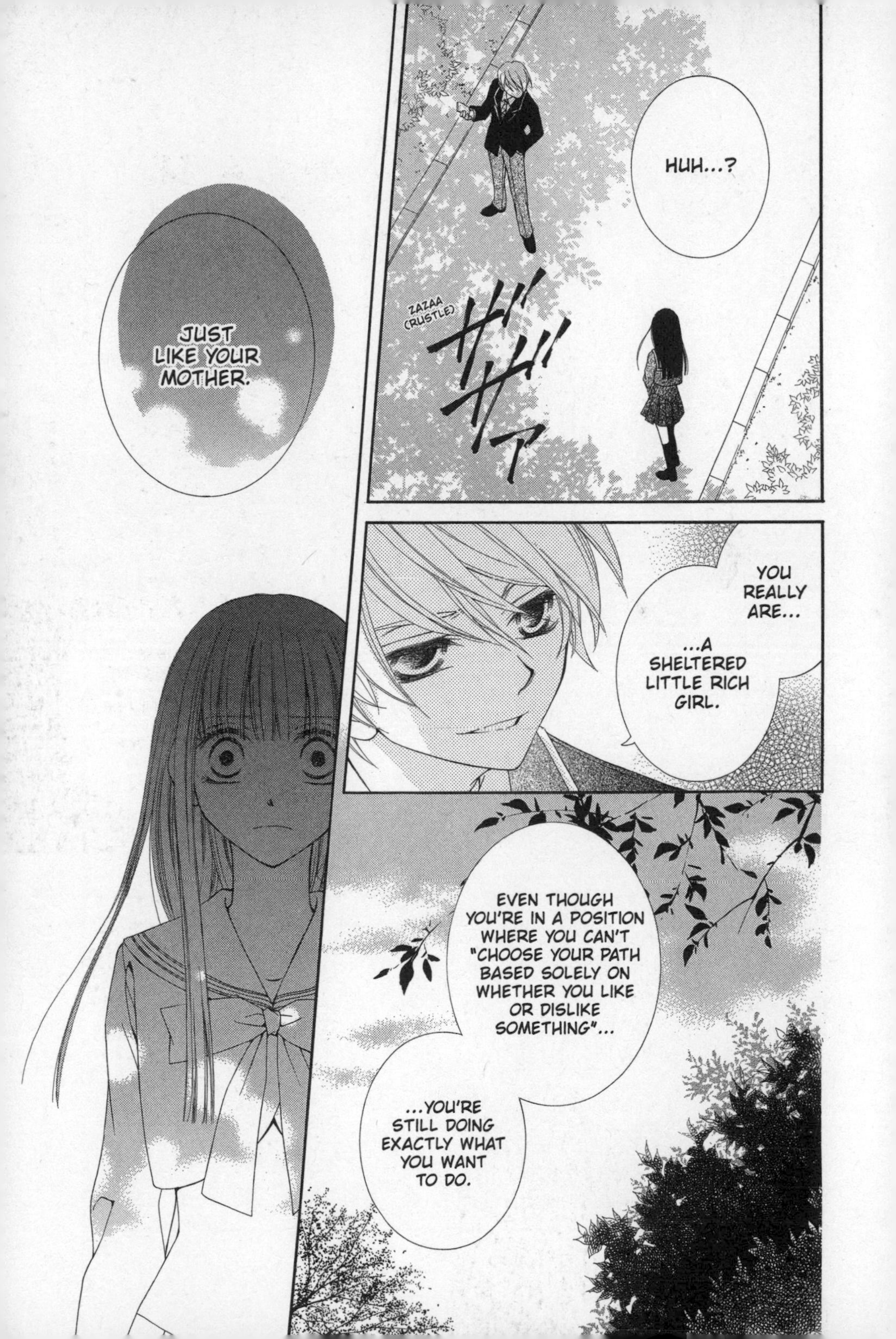
HUH...?
ZAZAA (RUSTLE)
YOU REALLY ARE...
...A SHELTERED LITTLE RICH GIRL.
EVEN THOUGH YOU'RE IN A POSITION WHERE YOU CAN'T "CHOOSE YOUR PATH BASED SOLELY ON WHETHER YOU LIKE OR DISLIKE SOMETHING"...
...YOU'RE STILL DOING EXACTLY WHAT YOU WANT TO DO.
JUST LIKE YOUR MOTHER.

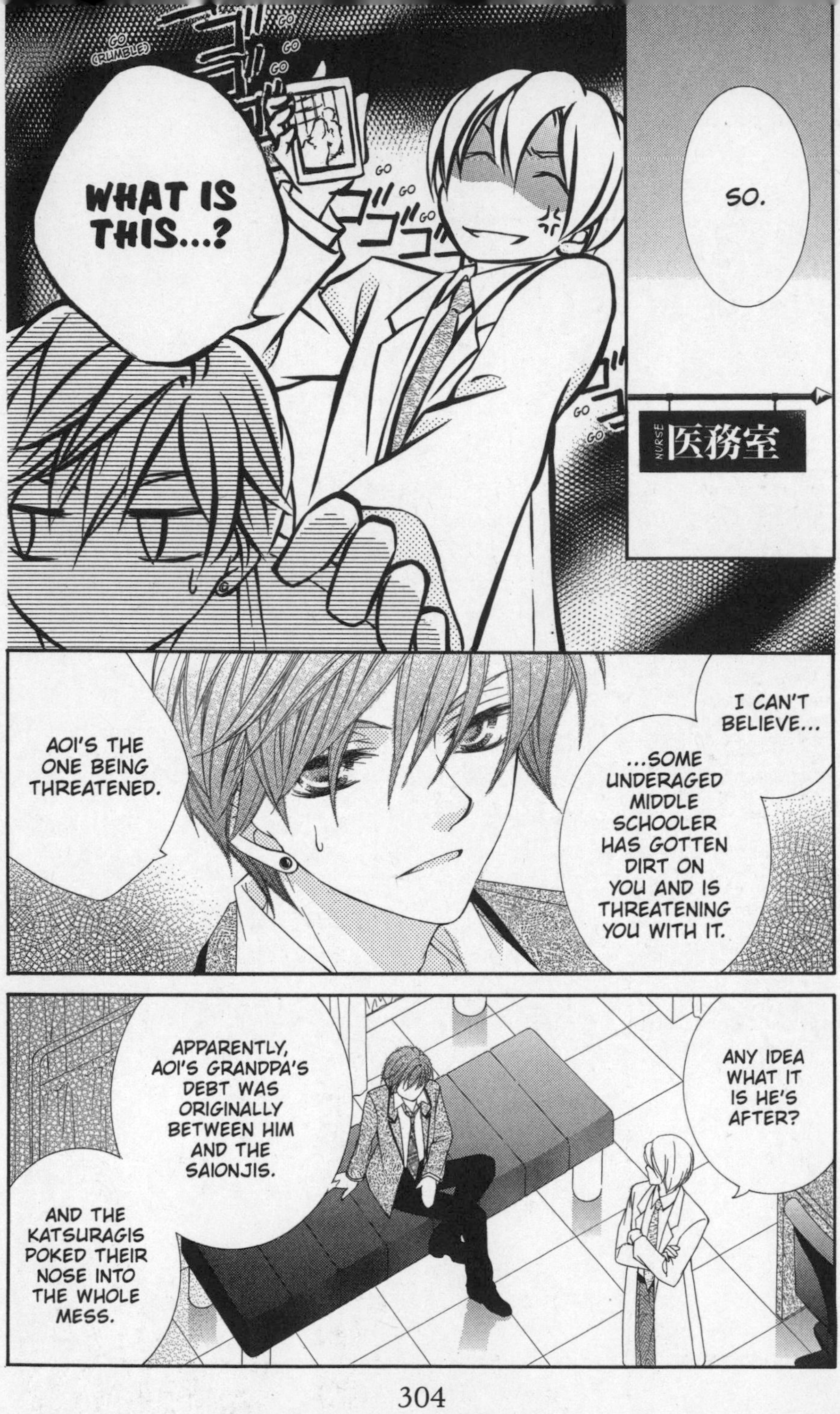
SO.
NURSE 医務室
GO GO
GO GO GO
GO GO GO (RUMBLE)
WHAT IS THIS...?
I CAN'T BELIEVE...
...SOME UNDERAGED MIDDLE SCHOOLER HAS GOTTEN DIRT ON YOU AND IS THREATENING YOU WITH IT.
AOI'S THE ONE BEING THREATENED.
ANY IDEA WHAT IT IS HE'S AFTER?
APPARENTLY, AOI'S GRANDPA'S DEBT WAS ORIGINALLY BETWEEN HIM AND THE SAIONJIS.
AND THE KATSURAGIS POKED THEIR NOSE INTO THE WHOLE MESS.

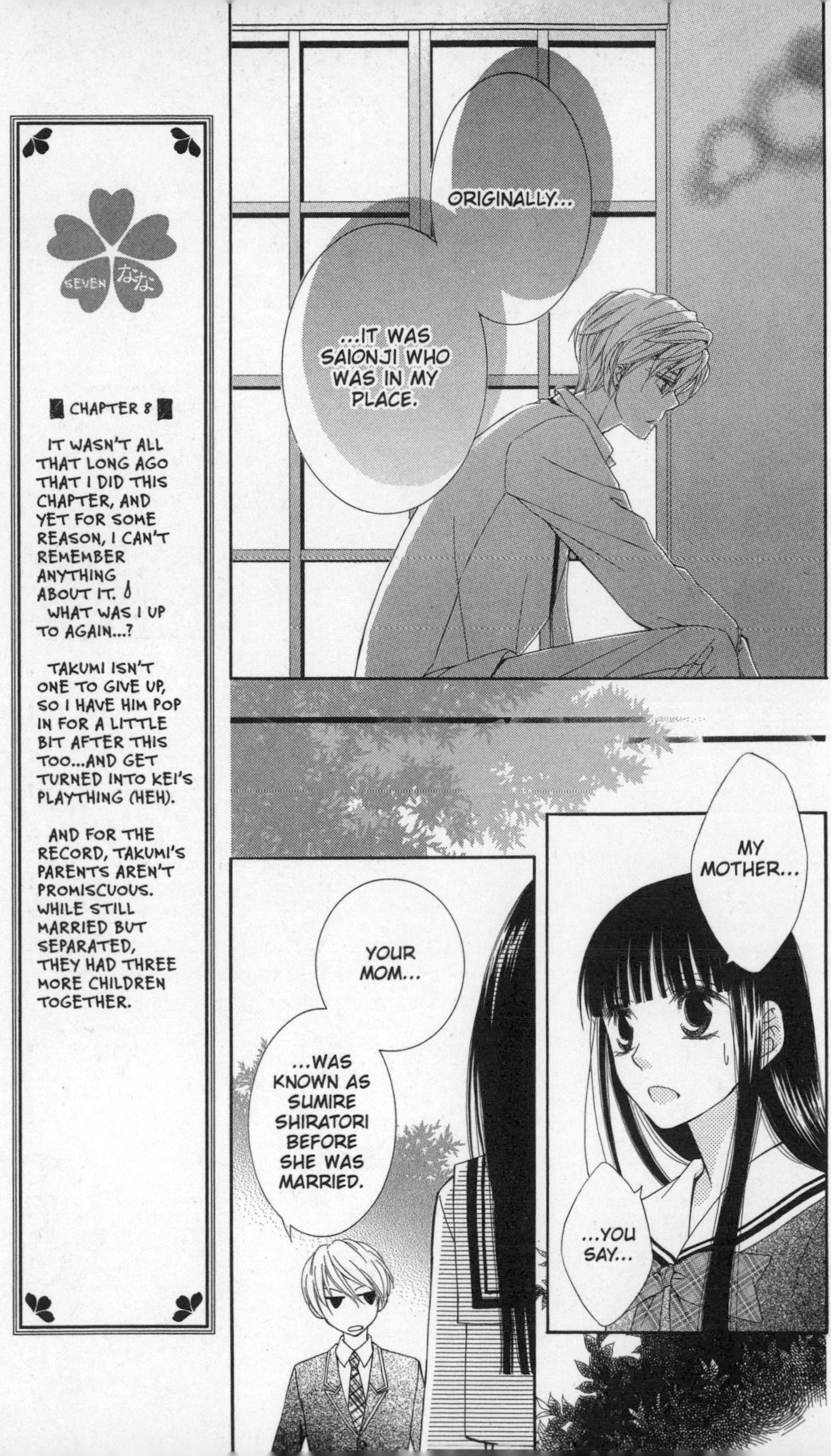
ORIGINALLY...
...IT WAS SAIONJI WHO WAS IN MY PLACE.
MY MOTHER...
...YOU SAY...
YOUR MOM...
...WAS KNOWN AS SUMIRE SHIRATORI BEFORE SHE WAS MARRIED.

SEVEN なな

CHAPTER 8

IT WASN'T ALL THAT LONG AGO THAT I DID THIS CHAPTER, AND YET FOR SOME REASON, I CAN'T REMEMBER ANYTHING ABOUT IT. WHAT WAS I UP TO AGAIN...?

TAKUMI ISN'T ONE TO GIVE UP, SO I HAVE HIM POP IN FOR A LITTLE BIT AFTER THIS TOO...AND GET TURNED INTO KEI'S PLAYTHING (HEH).

AND FOR THE RECORD, TAKUMI'S PARENTS AREN'T PROMISCUOUS. WHILE STILL MARRIED BUT SEPARATED, THEY HAD THREE MORE CHILDREN TOGETHER.

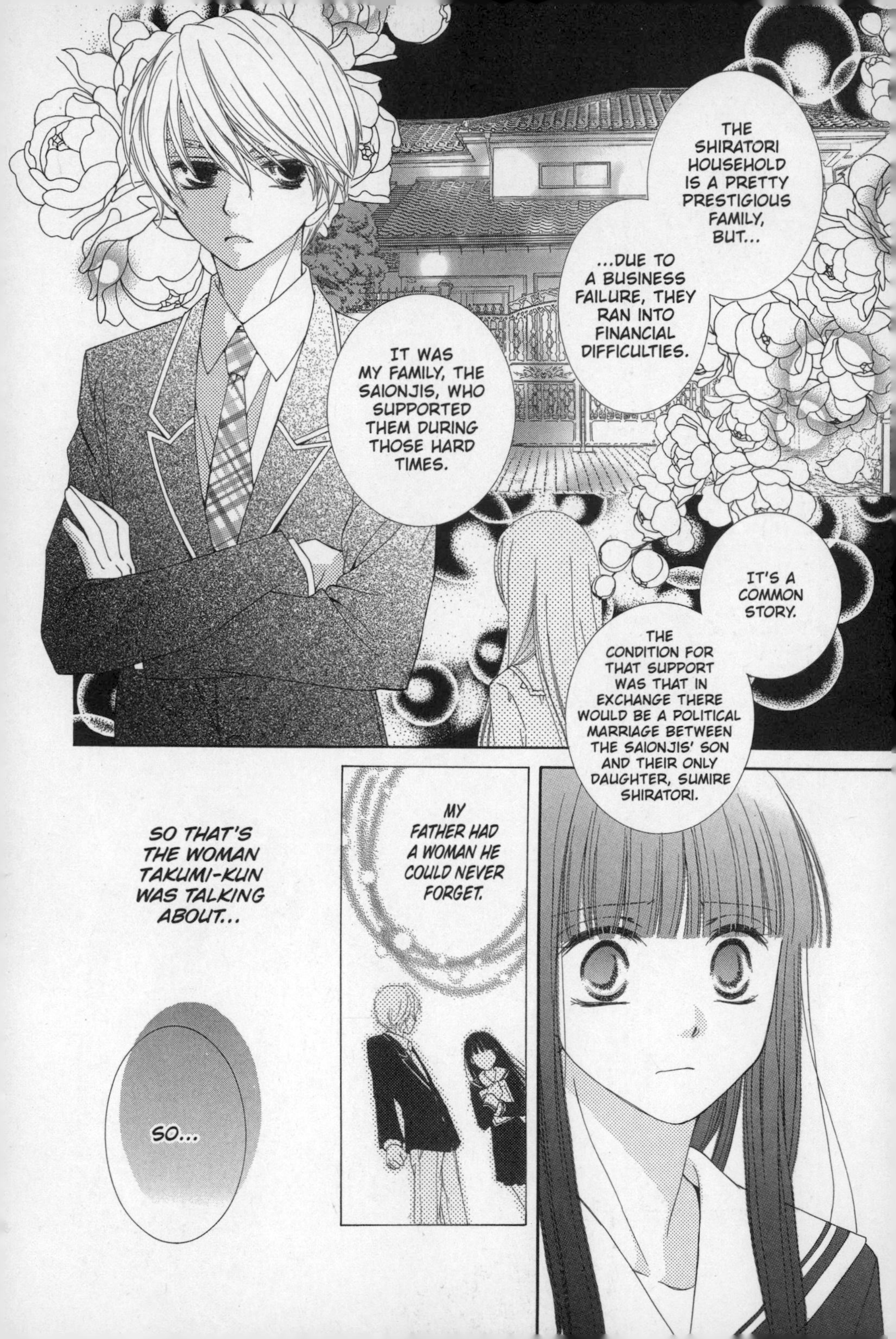
THE SHIRATORI HOUSEHOLD IS A PRETTY PRESTIGIOUS FAMILY, BUT...
...DUE TO A BUSINESS FAILURE, THEY RAN INTO FINANCIAL DIFFICULTIES.
IT WAS MY FAMILY, THE SAIONJIS, WHO SUPPORTED THEM DURING THOSE HARD TIMES.
IT'S A COMMON STORY.
THE CONDITION FOR THAT SUPPORT WAS THAT IN EXCHANGE THERE WOULD BE A POLITICAL MARRIAGE BETWEEN THE SAIONJIS' SON AND THEIR ONLY DAUGHTER, SUMIRE SHIRATORI.
MY FATHER HAD A WOMAN HE COULD NEVER FORGET.
SO THAT'S THE WOMAN TAKUMI-KUN WAS TALKING ABOUT...
SO...

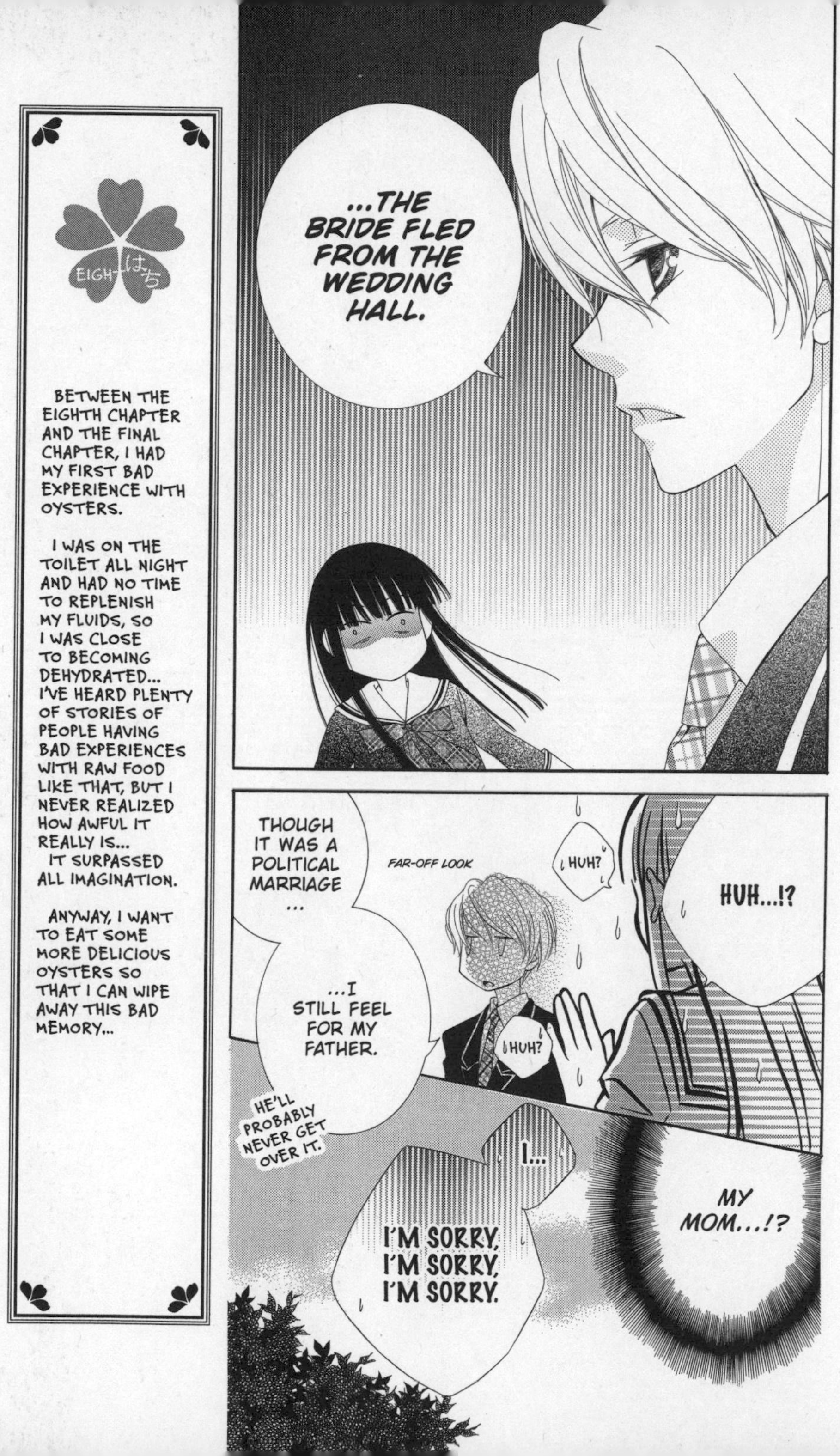
...THE BRIDE FLED FROM THE WEDDING HALL.
HUH...!?
HUH?
FAR-OFF LOOK
THOUGH IT WAS A POLITICAL MARRIAGE...
...I STILL FEEL FOR MY FATHER.
HUH?
HE'LL PROBABLY NEVER GET OVER IT.
MY MOM...!?
I...
I'M SORRY, I'M SORRY, I'M SORRY.

EIGHT はち

BETWEEN THE EIGHTH CHAPTER AND THE FINAL CHAPTER, I HAD MY FIRST BAD EXPERIENCE WITH OYSTERS.

I WAS ON THE TOILET ALL NIGHT AND HAD NO TIME TO REPLENISH MY FLUIDS, SO I WAS CLOSE TO BECOMING DEHYDRATED... I'VE HEARD PLENTY OF STORIES OF PEOPLE HAVING BAD EXPERIENCES WITH RAW FOOD LIKE THAT, BUT I NEVER REALIZED HOW AWFUL IT REALLY IS... IT SURPASSED ALL IMAGINATION.

ANYWAY, I WANT TO EAT SOME MORE DELICIOUS OYSTERS SO THAT I CAN WIPE AWAY THIS BAD MEMORY...

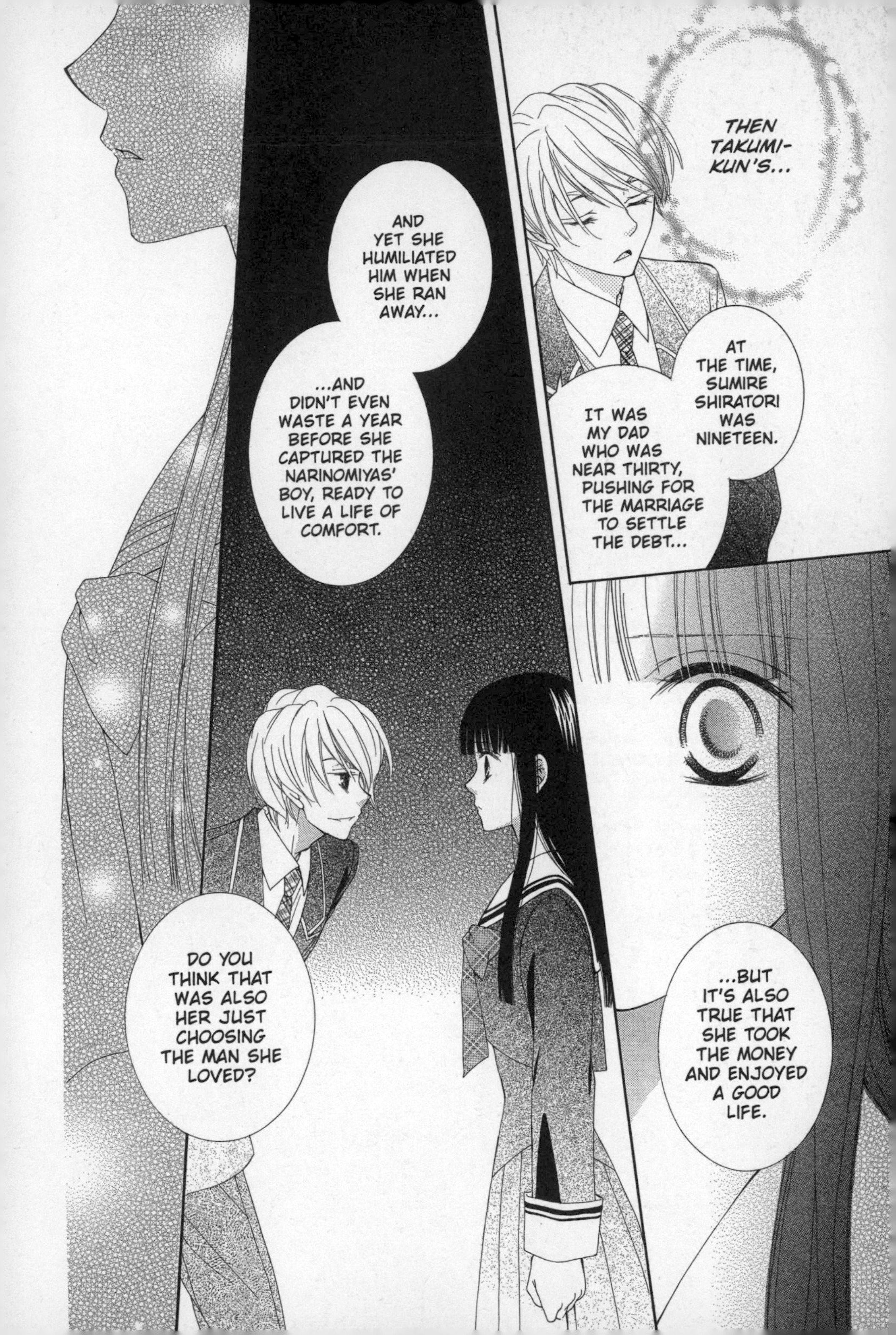
THEN TAKUMI-KUN'S...
AT THE TIME, SUMIRE SHIRATORI WAS NINETEEN.
IT WAS MY DAD WHO WAS NEAR THIRTY, PUSHING FOR THE MARRIAGE TO SETTLE THE DEBT...
...BUT IT'S ALSO TRUE THAT SHE TOOK THE MONEY AND ENJOYED A GOOD LIFE.
AND YET SHE HUMILIATED HIM WHEN SHE RAN AWAY...
...AND DIDN'T EVEN WASTE A YEAR BEFORE SHE CAPTURED THE NARINOMIYAS' BOY, READY TO LIVE A LIFE OF COMFORT.
DO YOU THINK THAT WAS ALSO HER JUST CHOOSING THE MAN SHE LOVED?

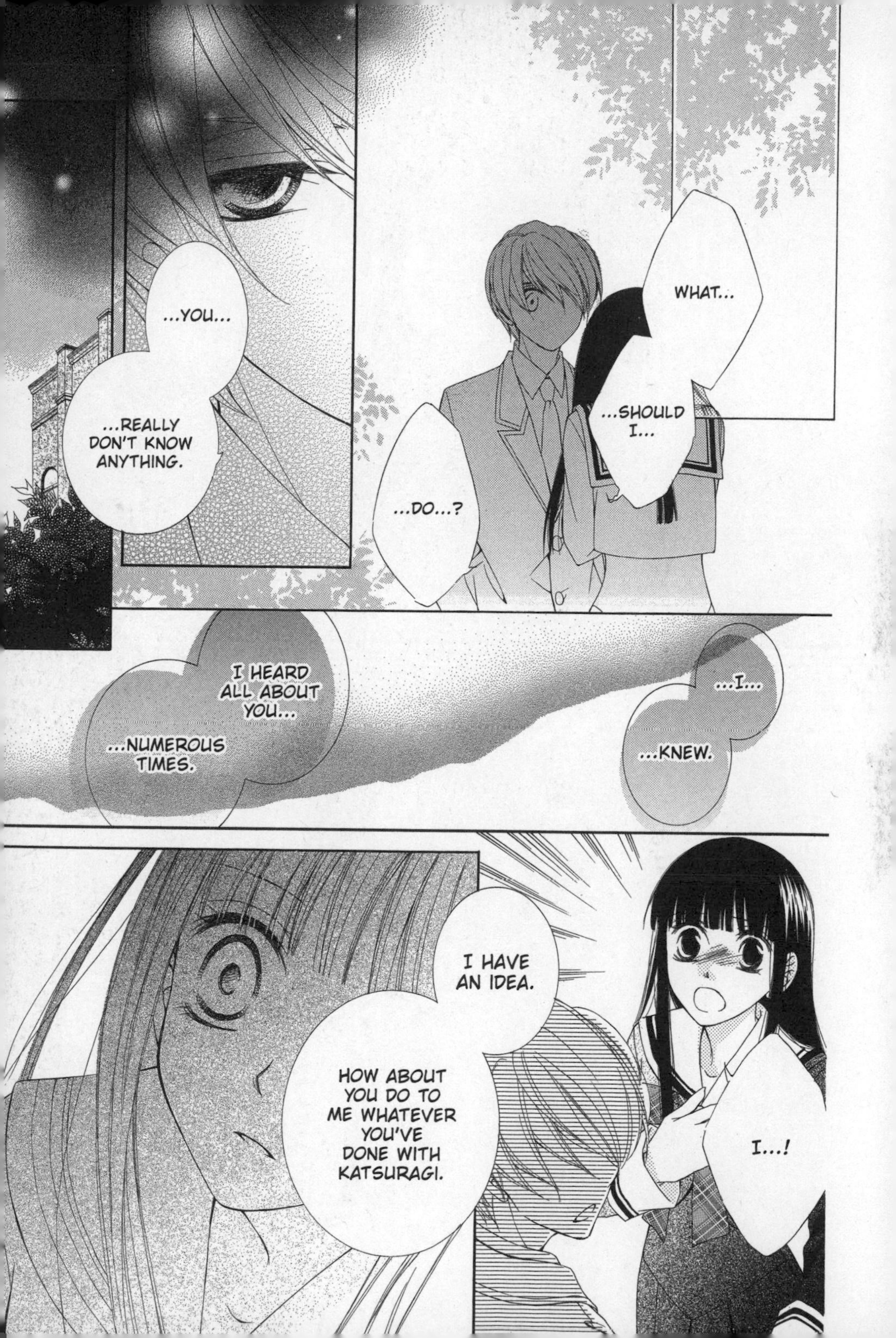
WHAT...
...SHOULD I...
...DO...?
...YOU...
...REALLY DON'T KNOW ANYTHING.
...I...
...KNEW.
I HEARD ALL ABOUT YOU...
...NUMEROUS TIMES.
I HAVE AN IDEA.
HOW ABOUT YOU DO TO ME WHATEVER YOU'VE DONE WITH KATSURAGI.
I...!

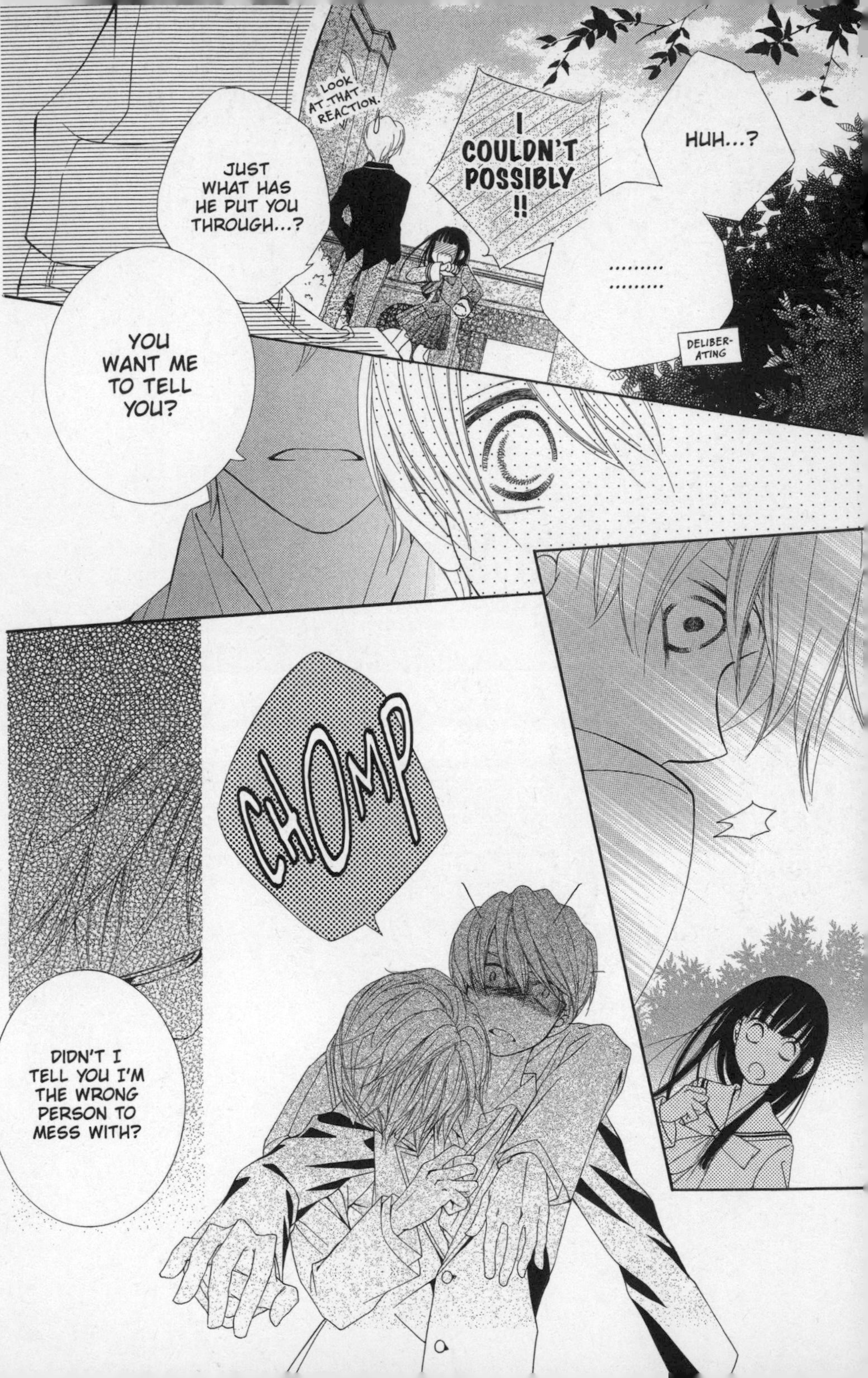
HUH...?
....
....
DELIBER-ATING
I COULDN'T POSSIBLY!!
LOOK AT THAT REACTION.
JUST WHAT HAS HE PUT YOU THROUGH...?
YOU WANT ME TO TELL YOU?
CHOMP
DIDN'T I TELL YOU I'M THE WRONG PERSON TO MESS WITH?

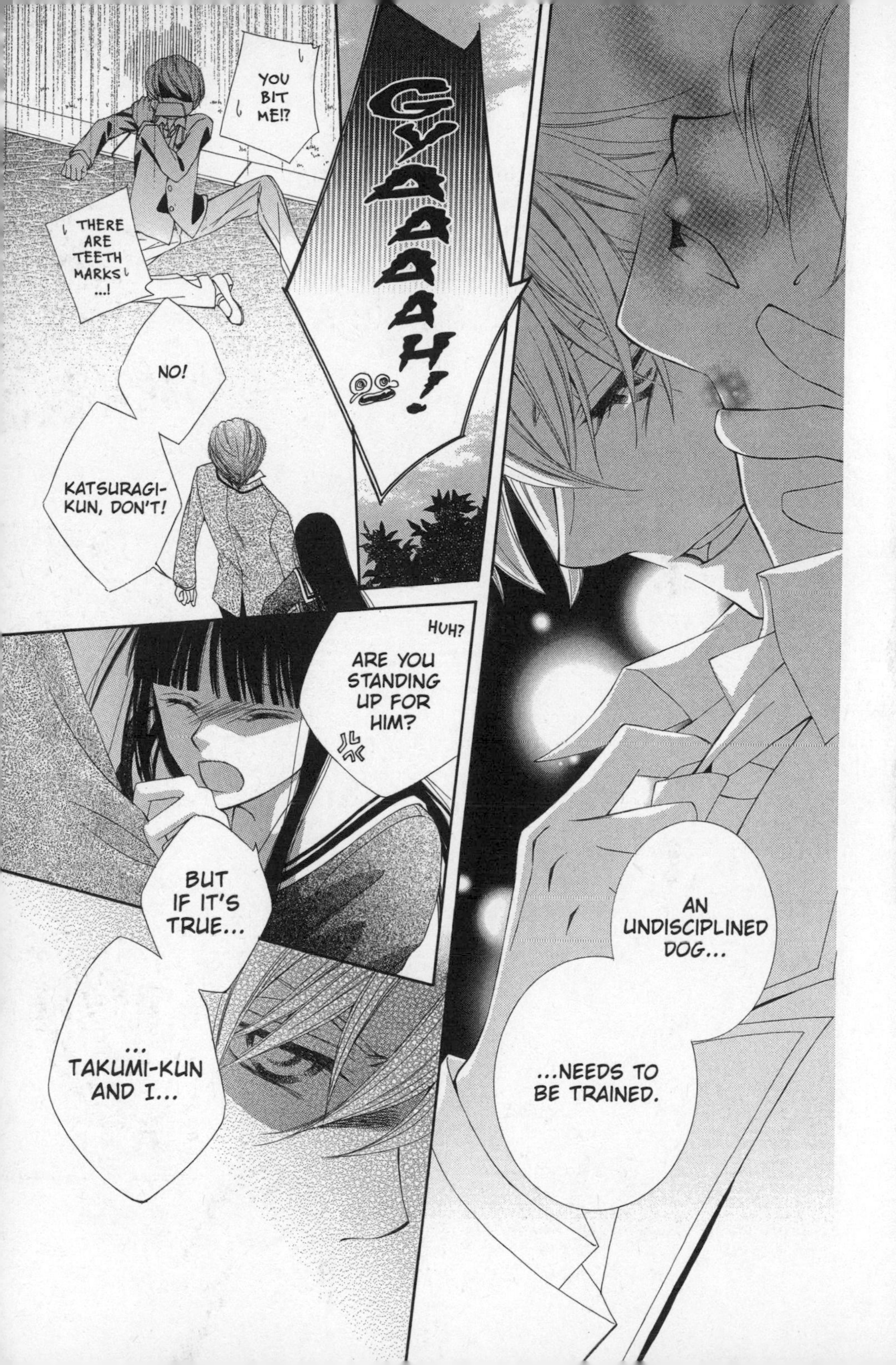
AN UNDISCIPLINED DOG...
...NEEDS TO BE TRAINED.
GYAAAAH!
YOU BIT ME!?
THERE ARE TEETH MARKS ...!
NO!
KATSURAGI-KUN, DON'T!
HUH?
ARE YOU STANDING UP FOR HIM?
BUT IF IT'S TRUE...
... TAKUMI-KUN AND I...

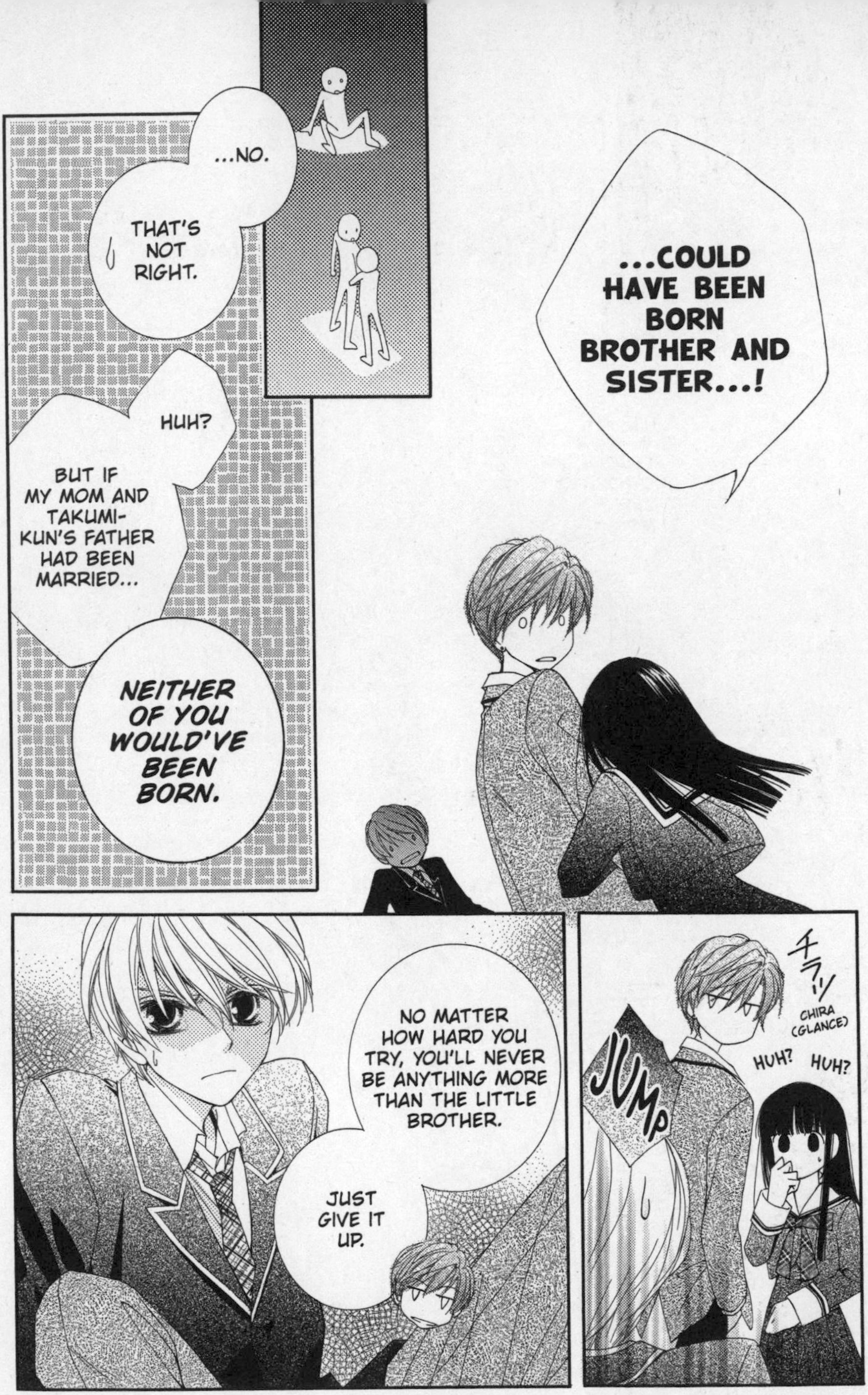
...COULD HAVE BEEN BORN BROTHER AND SISTER...!
...NO.
THAT'S NOT RIGHT.
HUH?
BUT IF MY MOM AND TAKUMI-KUN'S FATHER HAD BEEN MARRIED...
NEITHER OF YOU WOULD'VE BEEN BORN.
チラッ
CHIRA (GLANCE)
JUMP
HUH?
HUH?
NO MATTER HOW HARD YOU TRY, YOU'LL NEVER BE ANYTHING MORE THAN THE LITTLE BROTHER.
JUST GIVE IT UP.

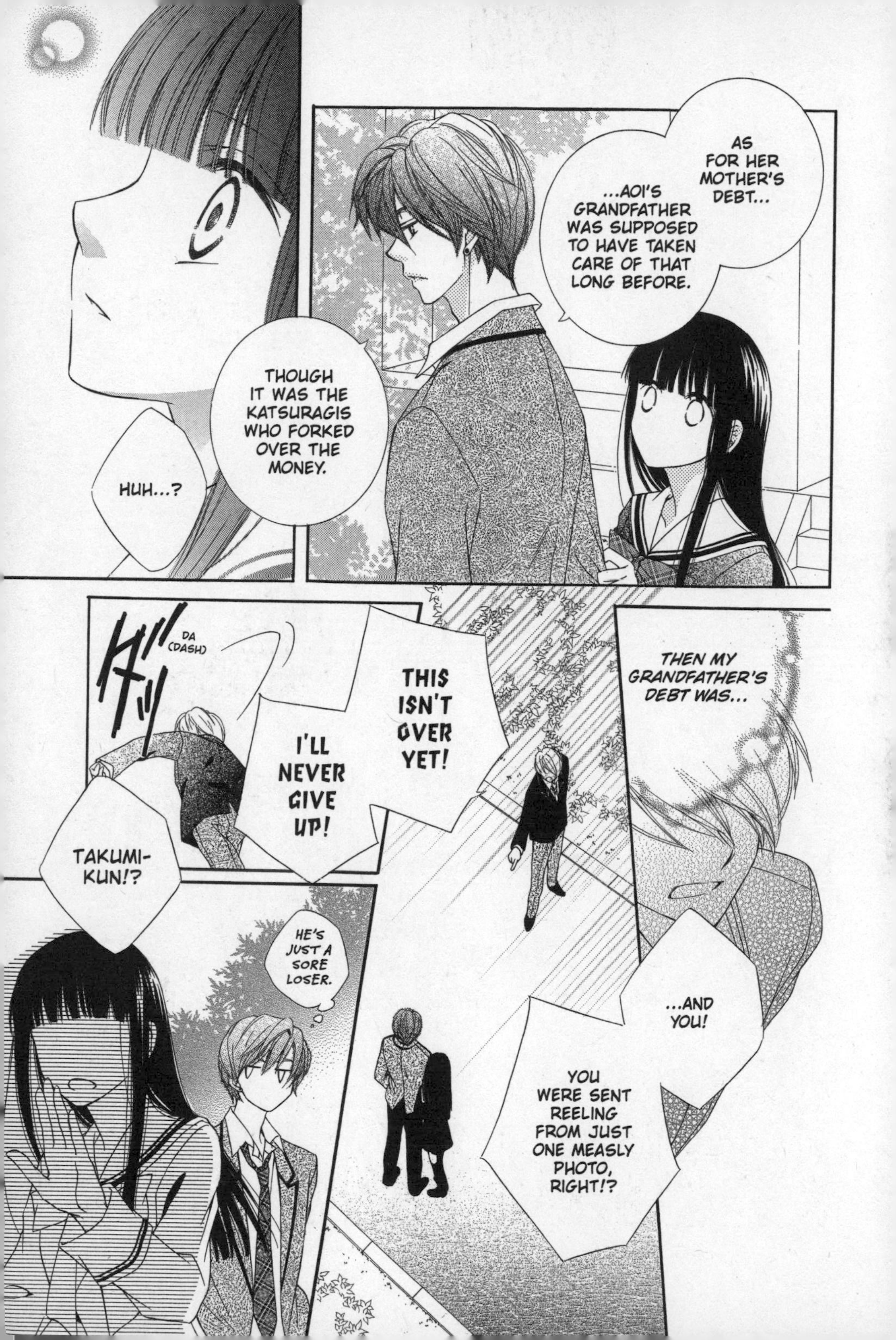
AS FOR HER MOTHER'S DEBT...
...AOI'S GRANDFATHER WAS SUPPOSED TO HAVE TAKEN CARE OF THAT LONG BEFORE.
THOUGH IT WAS THE KATSURAGIS WHO FORKED OVER THE MONEY.
HUH...?
THEN MY GRANDFATHER'S DEBT WAS...
...AND YOU!
YOU WERE SENT REELING FROM JUST ONE MEASLY PHOTO, RIGHT!?
THIS ISN'T OVER YET!
I'LL NEVER GIVE UP!
DA (DASH)
TAKUMI-KUN!?
HE'S JUST A SORE LOSER.

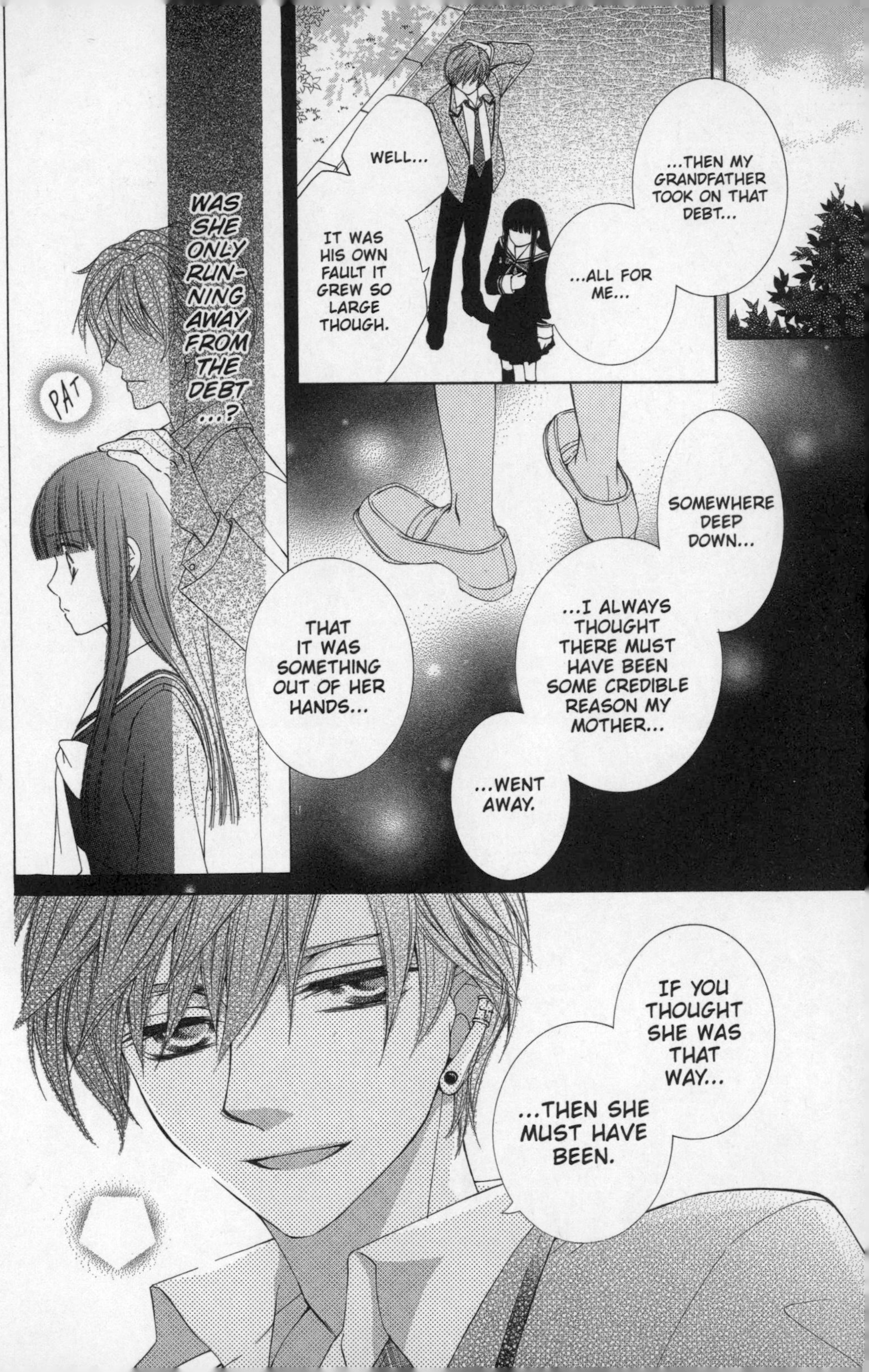
...THEN MY GRANDFATHER TOOK ON THAT DEBT...
...ALL FOR ME...
WELL...
IT WAS HIS OWN FAULT IT GREW SO LARGE THOUGH.
SOMEWHERE DEEP DOWN...
...I ALWAYS THOUGHT THERE MUST HAVE BEEN SOME CREDIBLE REASON MY MOTHER...
...WENT AWAY.
THAT IT WAS SOMETHING OUT OF HER HANDS...
WAS SHE ONLY RUN-NING AWAY FROM THE DEBT...?
PAT
IF YOU THOUGHT SHE WAS THAT WAY...
...THEN SHE MUST HAVE BEEN.

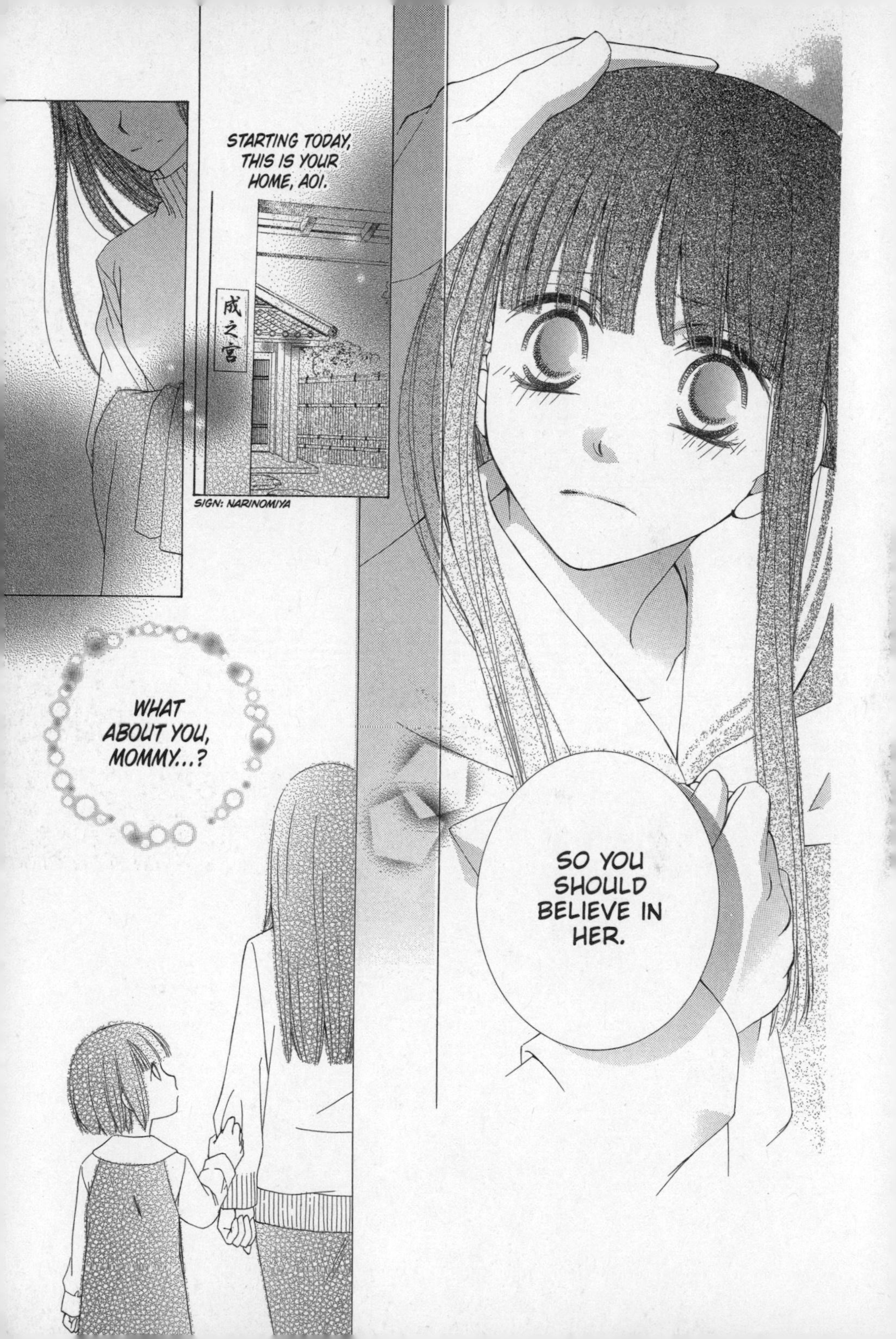
SO YOU SHOULD BELIEVE IN HER.
STARTING TODAY, THIS IS YOUR HOME, AOI.
成之宮
SIGN: NARINOMIYA
WHAT ABOUT YOU, MOMMY...?

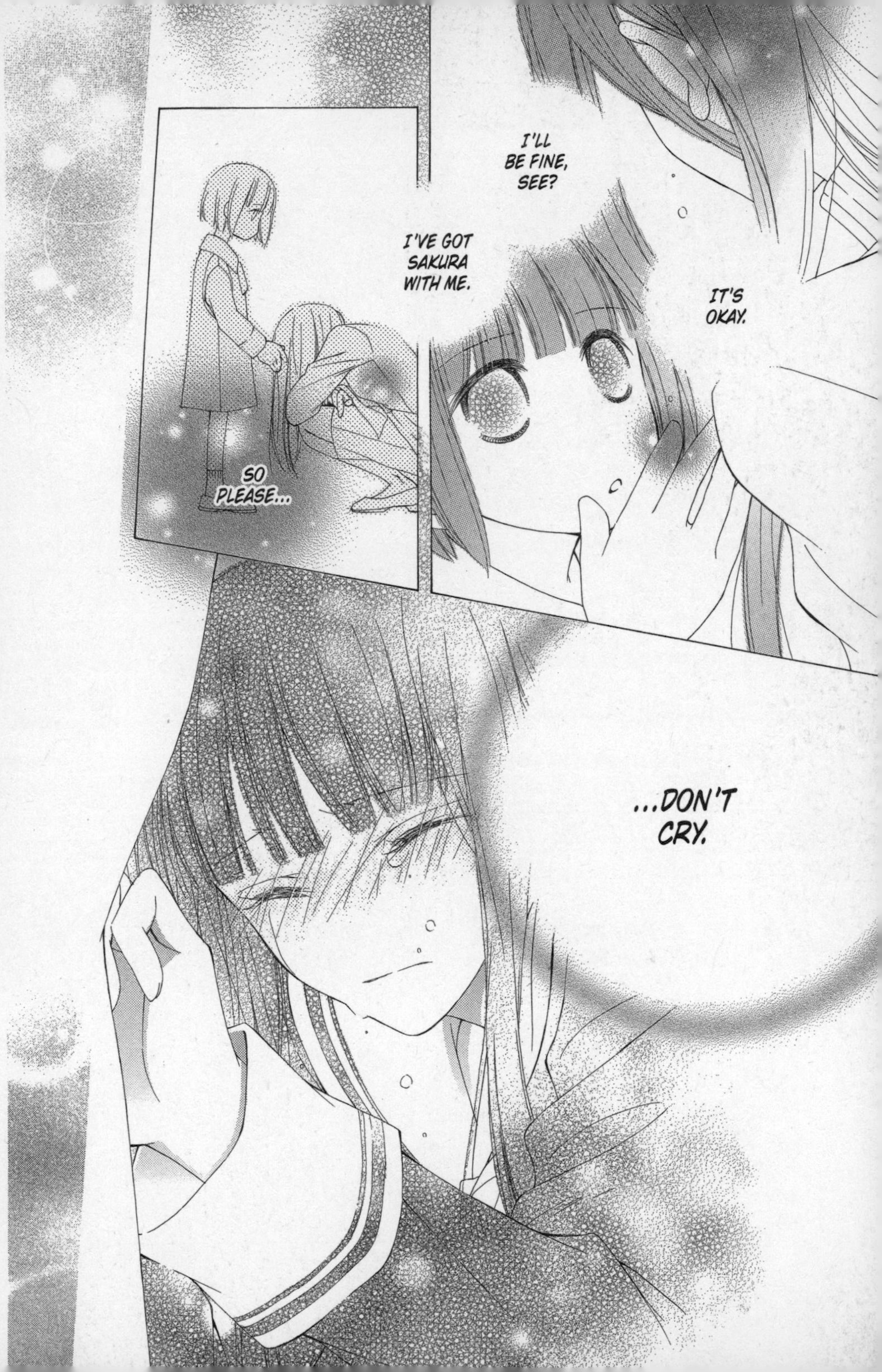
IT'S OKAY.
I'LL BE FINE, SEE?
I'VE GOT SAKURA WITH ME.
SO PLEASE...
...DON'T CRY.

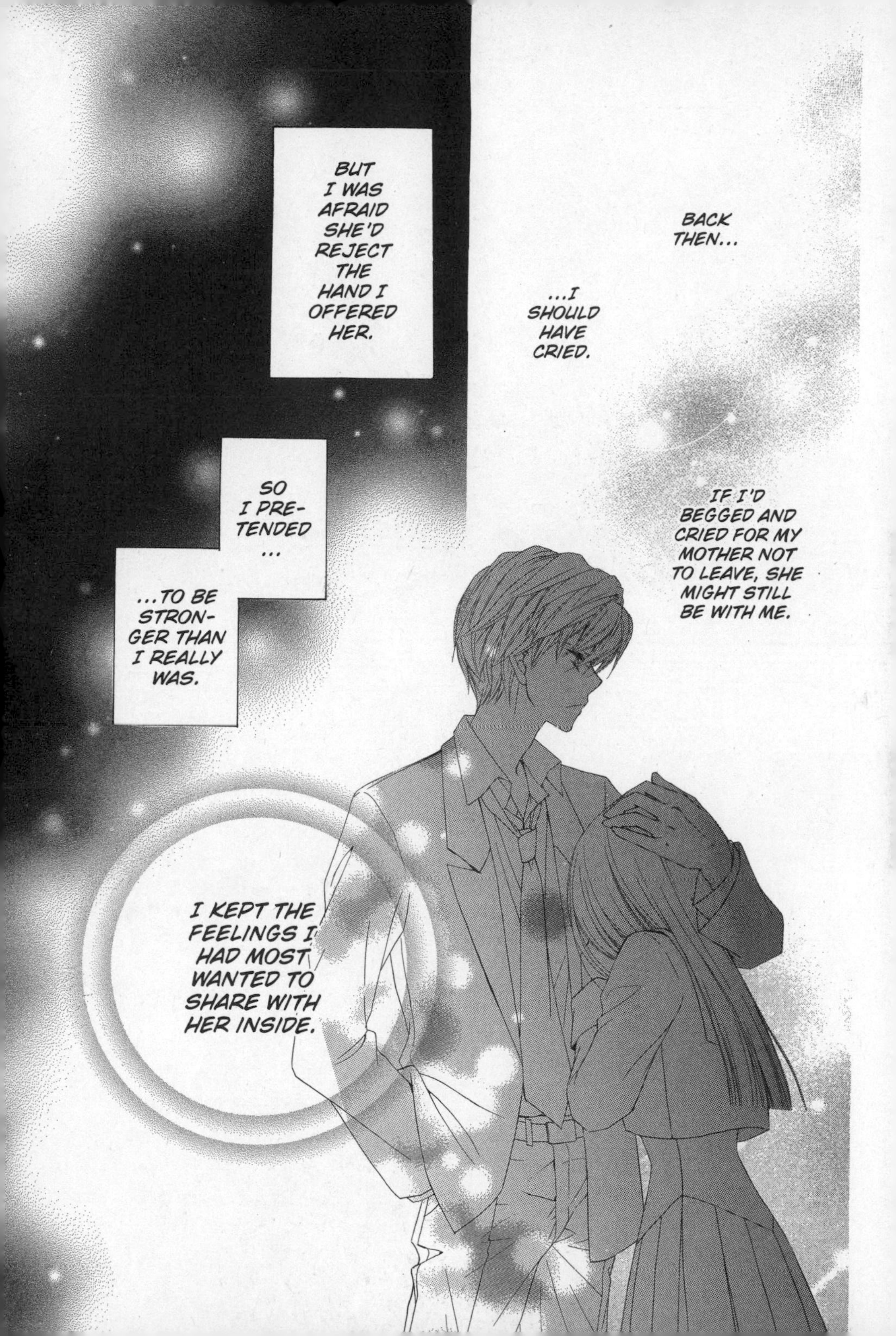
BACK THEN...
...I SHOULD HAVE CRIED.
IF I'D BEGGED AND CRIED FOR MY MOTHER NOT TO LEAVE, SHE MIGHT STILL BE WITH ME.
BUT I WAS AFRAID SHE'D REJECT THE HAND I OFFERED HER.
SO I PRETENDED...
...TO BE STRONGER THAN I REALLY WAS.
I KEPT THE FEELINGS I HAD MOST WANTED TO SHARE WITH HER INSIDE.

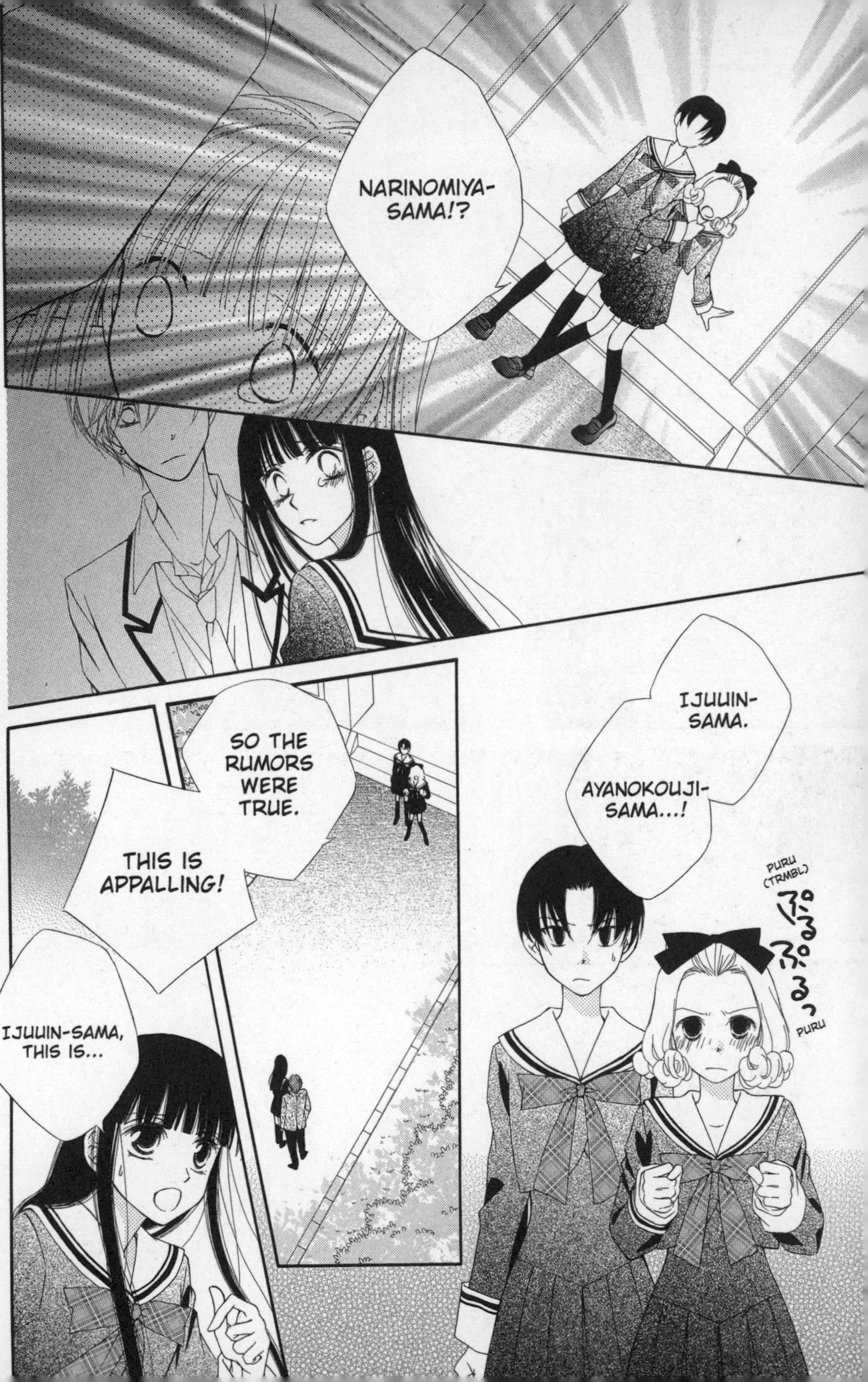
NARINOMIYA-SAMA!?
IJUUIN-SAMA.
AYANOKOUJI-SAMA...!
PURU (TRMBL)
ぷるぷるっ
PURU
SO THE RUMORS WERE TRUE.
THIS IS APPALLING!
IJUUIN-SAMA, THIS IS...

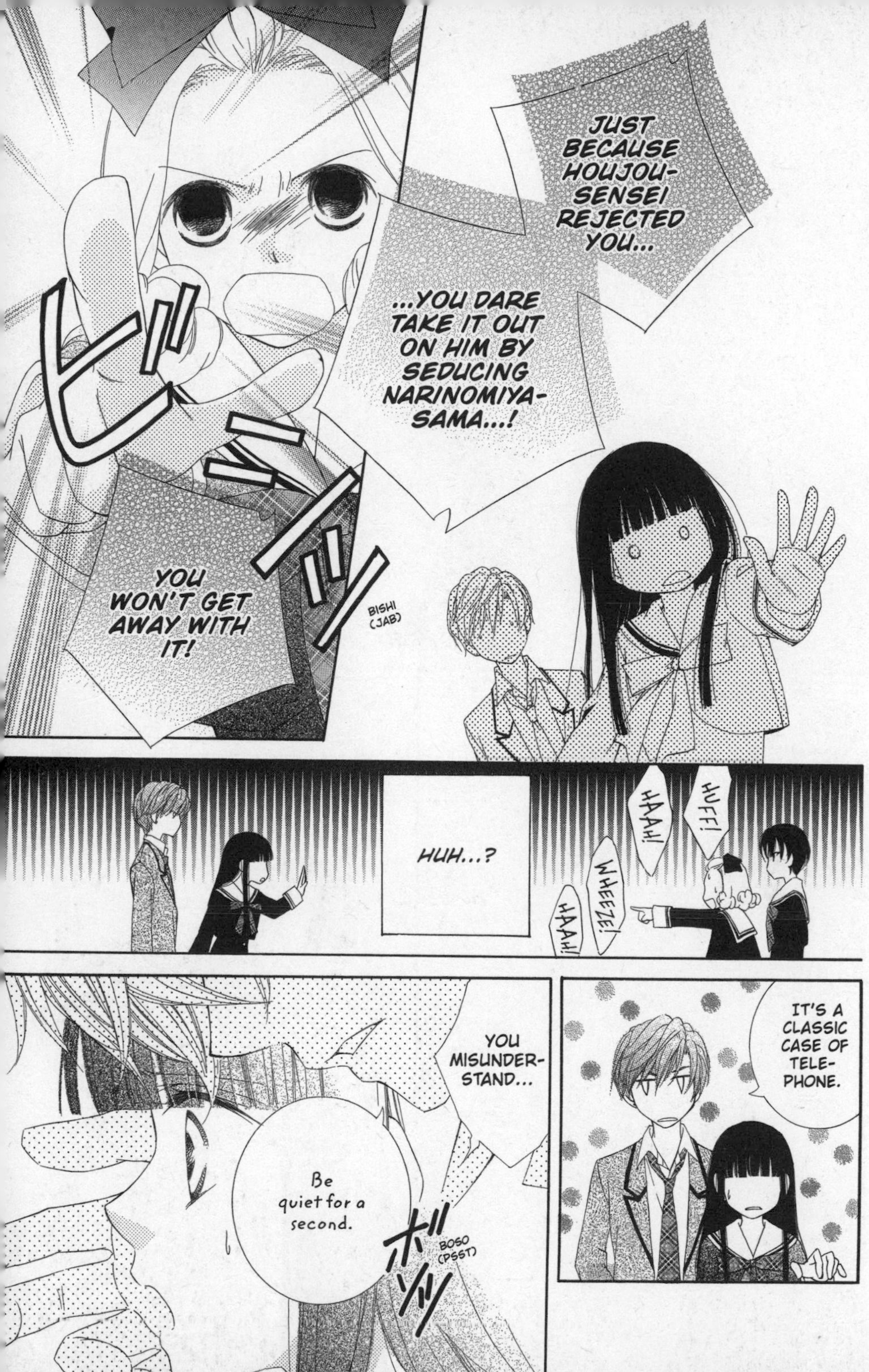
JUST BECAUSE HOUJOU-SENSEI REJECTED YOU...
...YOU DARE TAKE IT OUT ON HIM BY SEDUCING NARINOMIYA-SAMA...!
YOU WON'T GET AWAY WITH IT!
BISHI (JAB)
HUFF!
HAAH!
WHEEZE!
HAAH!
HUH...?
IT'S A CLASSIC CASE OF TELE-PHONE.
YOU MISUNDER-STAND...
Be quiet for a second.
BOSO (PSST)

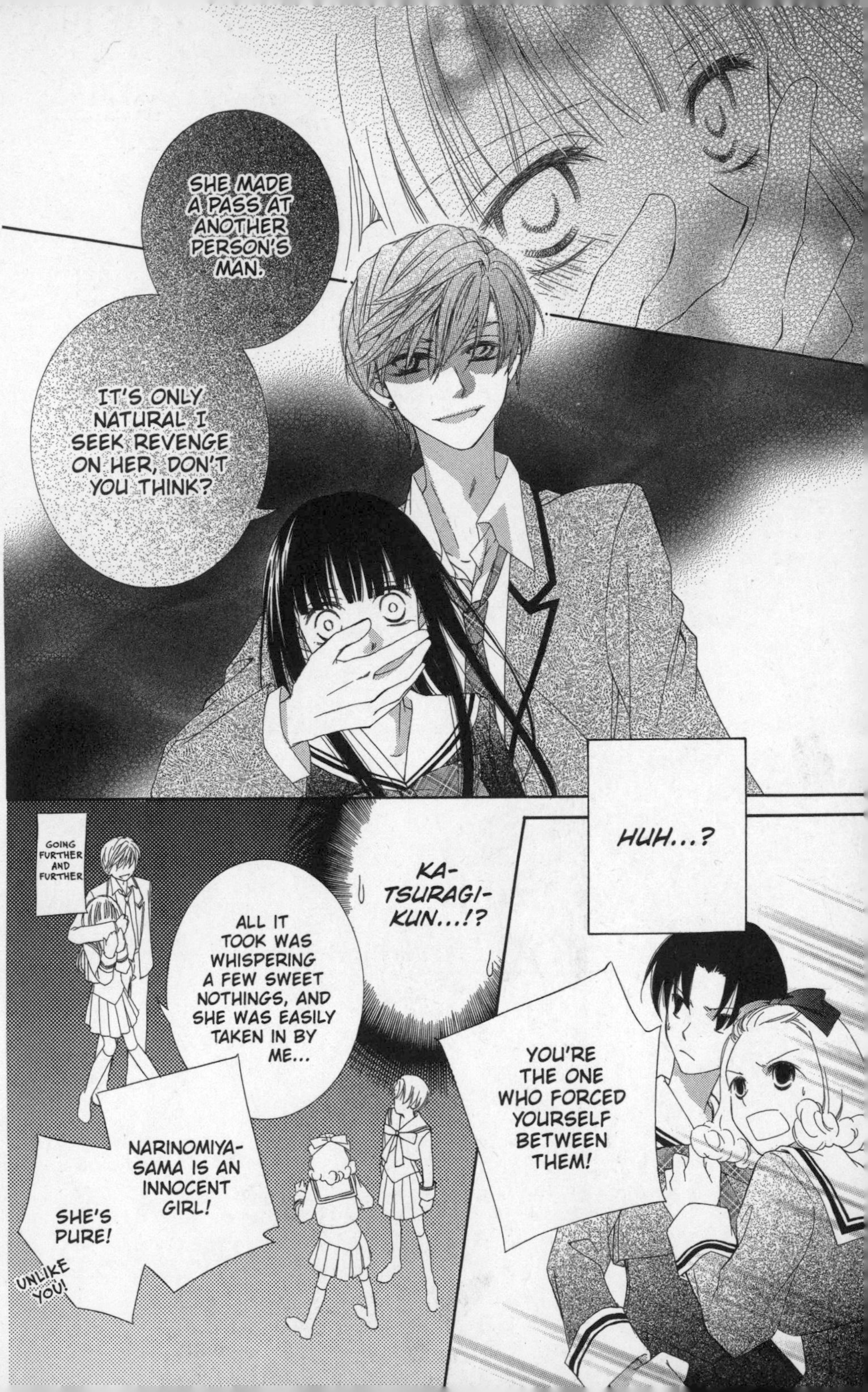
SHE MADE A PASS AT ANOTHER PERSON'S MAN.
IT'S ONLY NATURAL I SEEK REVENGE ON HER, DON'T YOU THINK?
HUH...?
KA-TSURAGI-KUN...!?
ALL IT TOOK WAS WHISPERING A FEW SWEET NOTHINGS, AND SHE WAS EASILY TAKEN IN BY ME...
YOU'RE THE ONE WHO FORCED YOURSELF BETWEEN THEM!
NARINOMIYA-SAMA IS AN INNOCENT GIRL!
SHE'S PURE!
UNLIKE YOU!
GOING FURTHER AND FURTHER

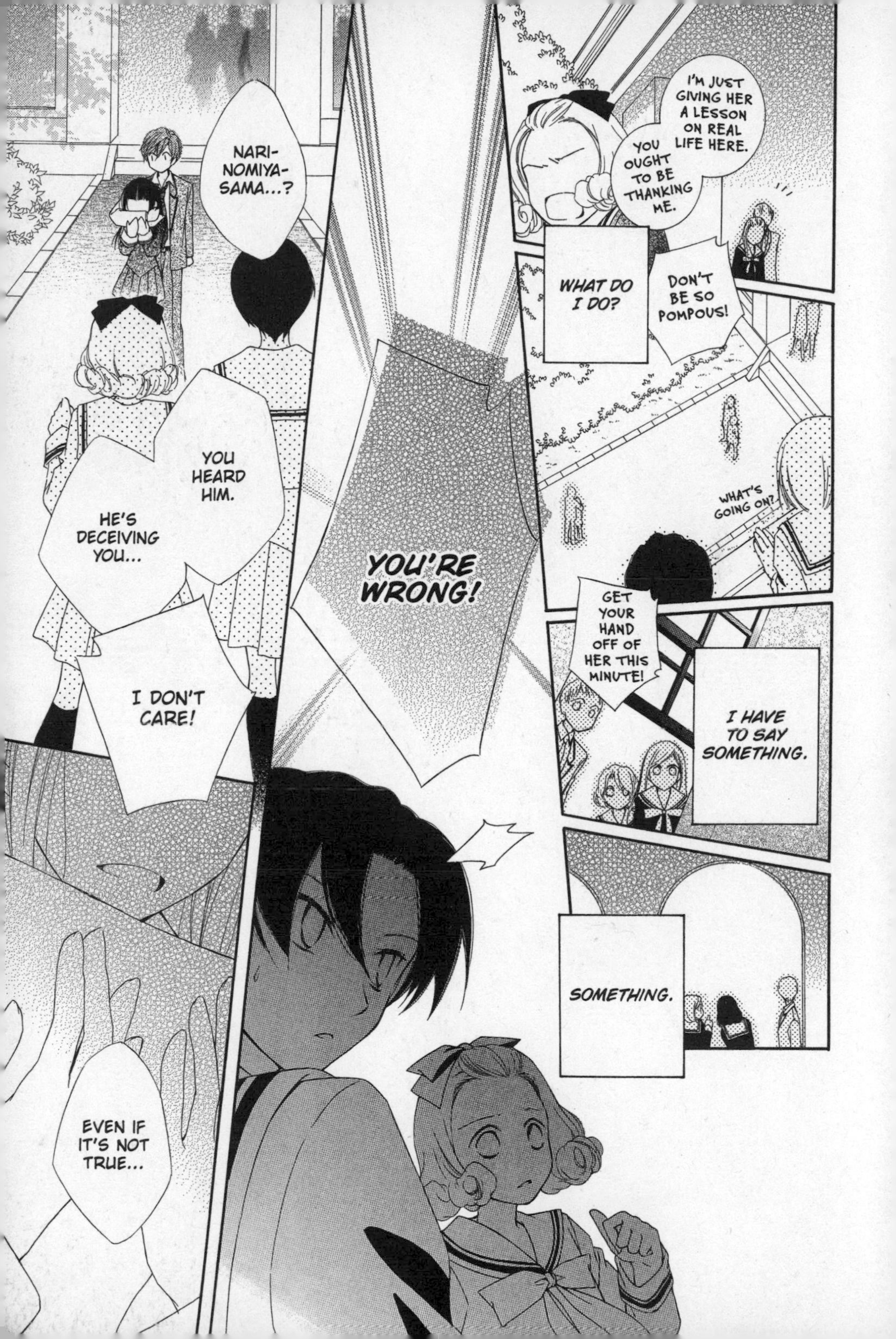
I'M JUST GIVING HER A LESSON ON REAL LIFE HERE.
YOU OUGHT TO BE THANKING ME.
DON'T BE SO POMPOUS!
WHAT DO I DO?
WHAT'S GOING ON?
GET YOUR HAND OFF OF HER THIS MINUTE!
I HAVE TO SAY SOMETHING.
SOMETHING.
YOU'RE WRONG!
NARI-NOMIYA-SAMA...?
YOU HEARD HIM.
HE'S DECEIVING YOU...
I DON'T CARE!
EVEN IF IT'S NOT TRUE...

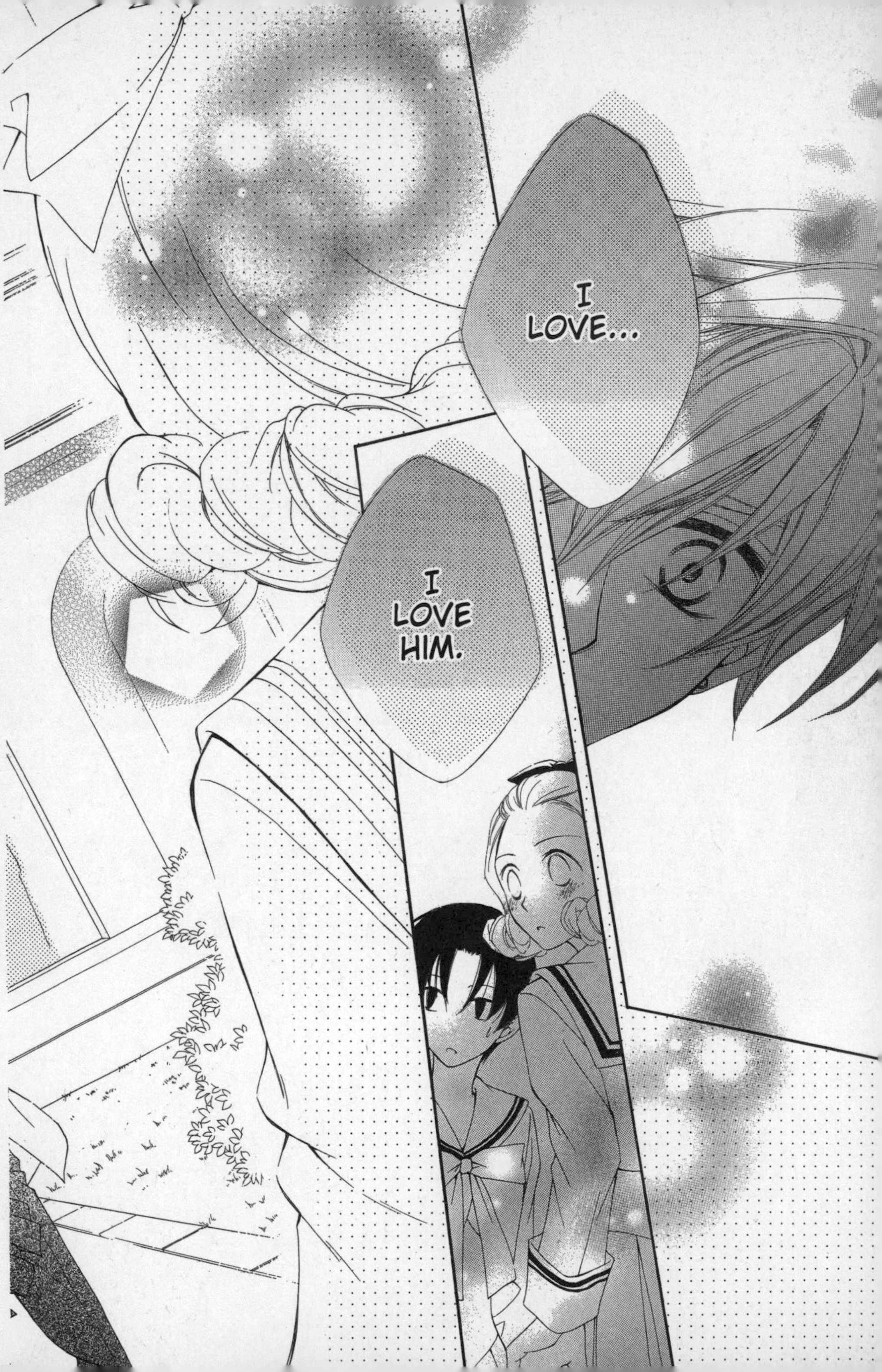
I LOVE...
I LOVE HIM.

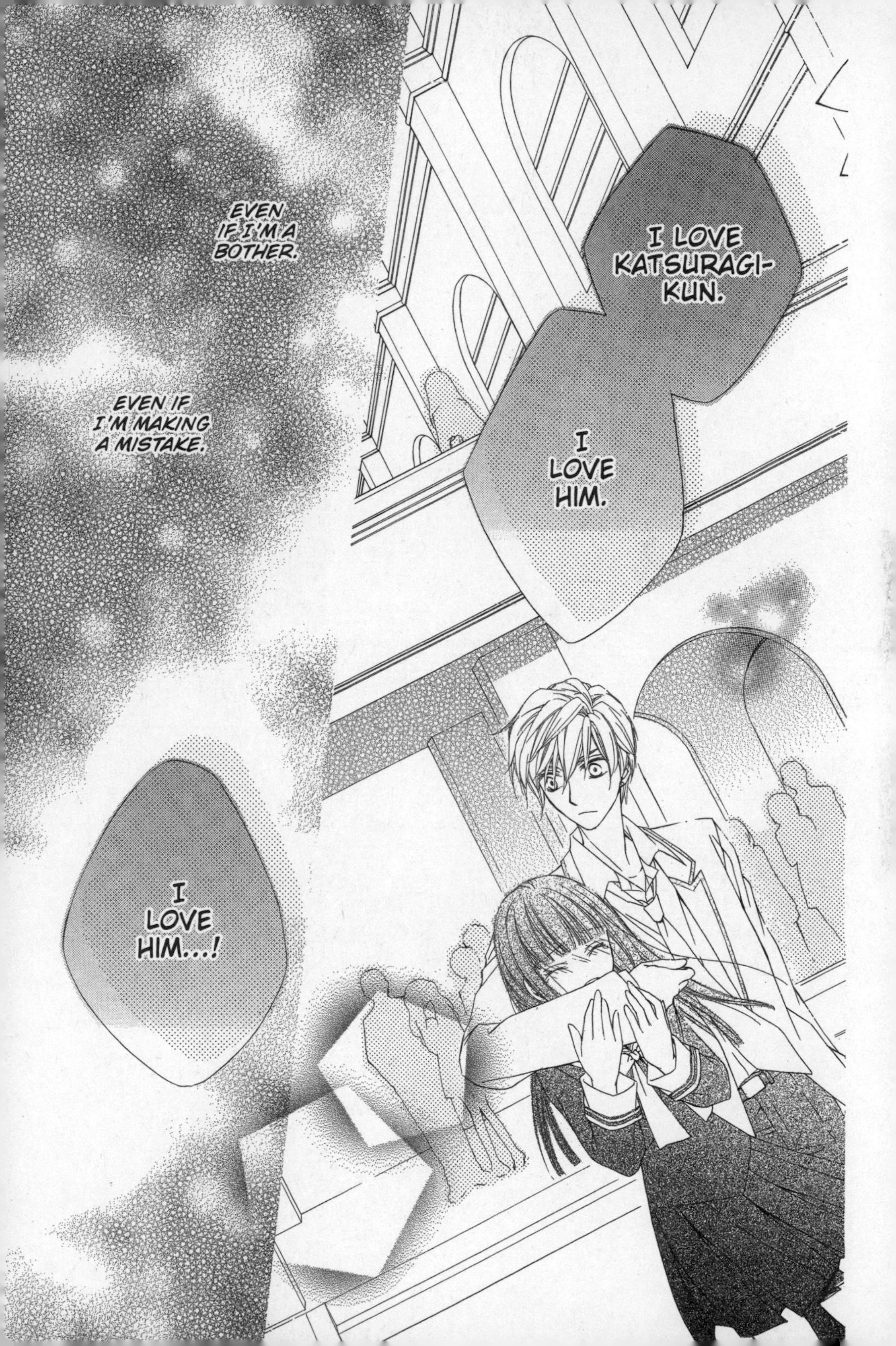
I LOVE KATSURAGI-KUN.
I LOVE HIM.
EVEN IF I'M A BOTHER.
EVEN IF I'M MAKING A MISTAKE.
I LOVE HIM...!

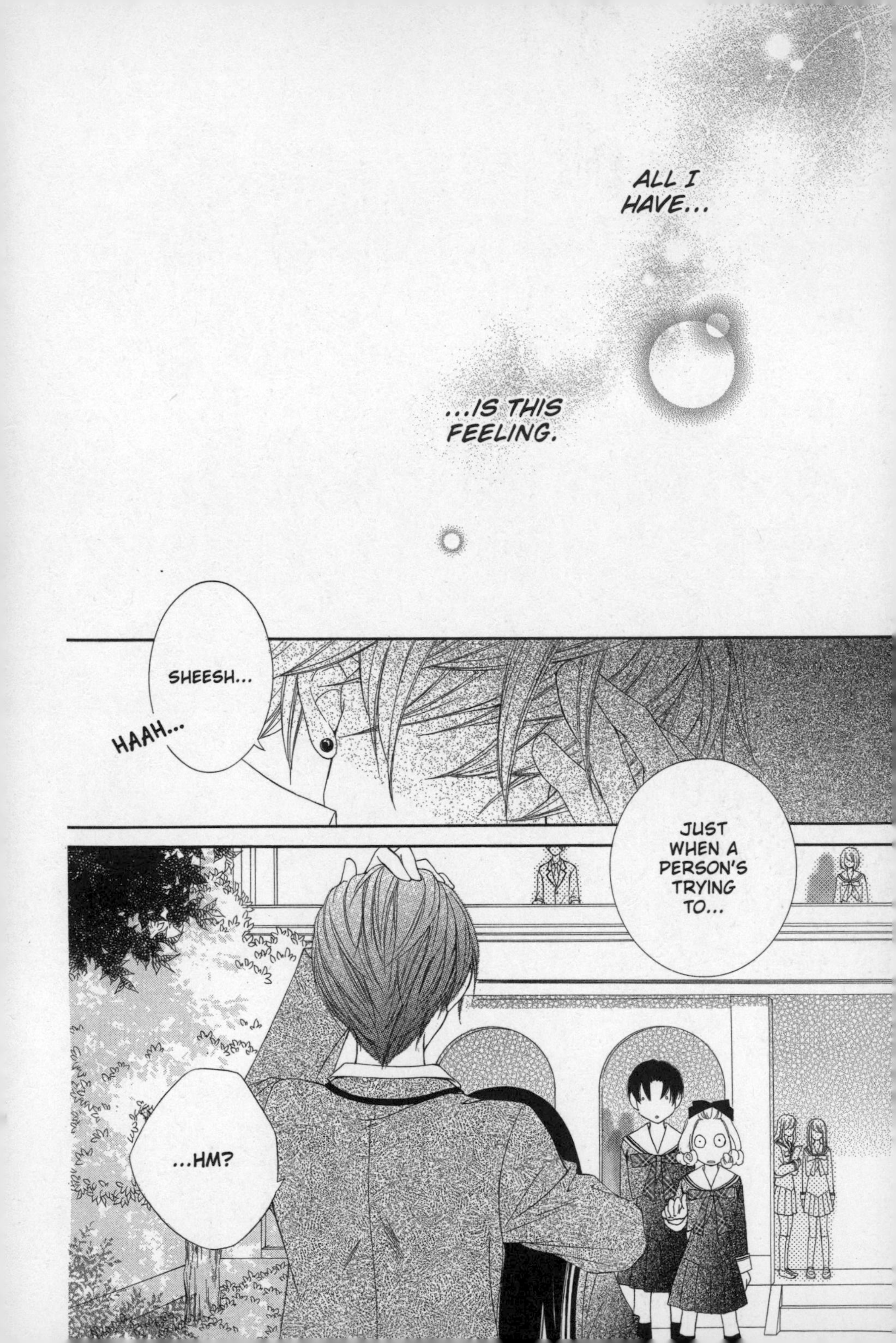
ALL I HAVE...
...IS THIS FEELING.
SHEESH...
HAAH...
JUST WHEN A PERSON'S TRYING TO...
...HM?

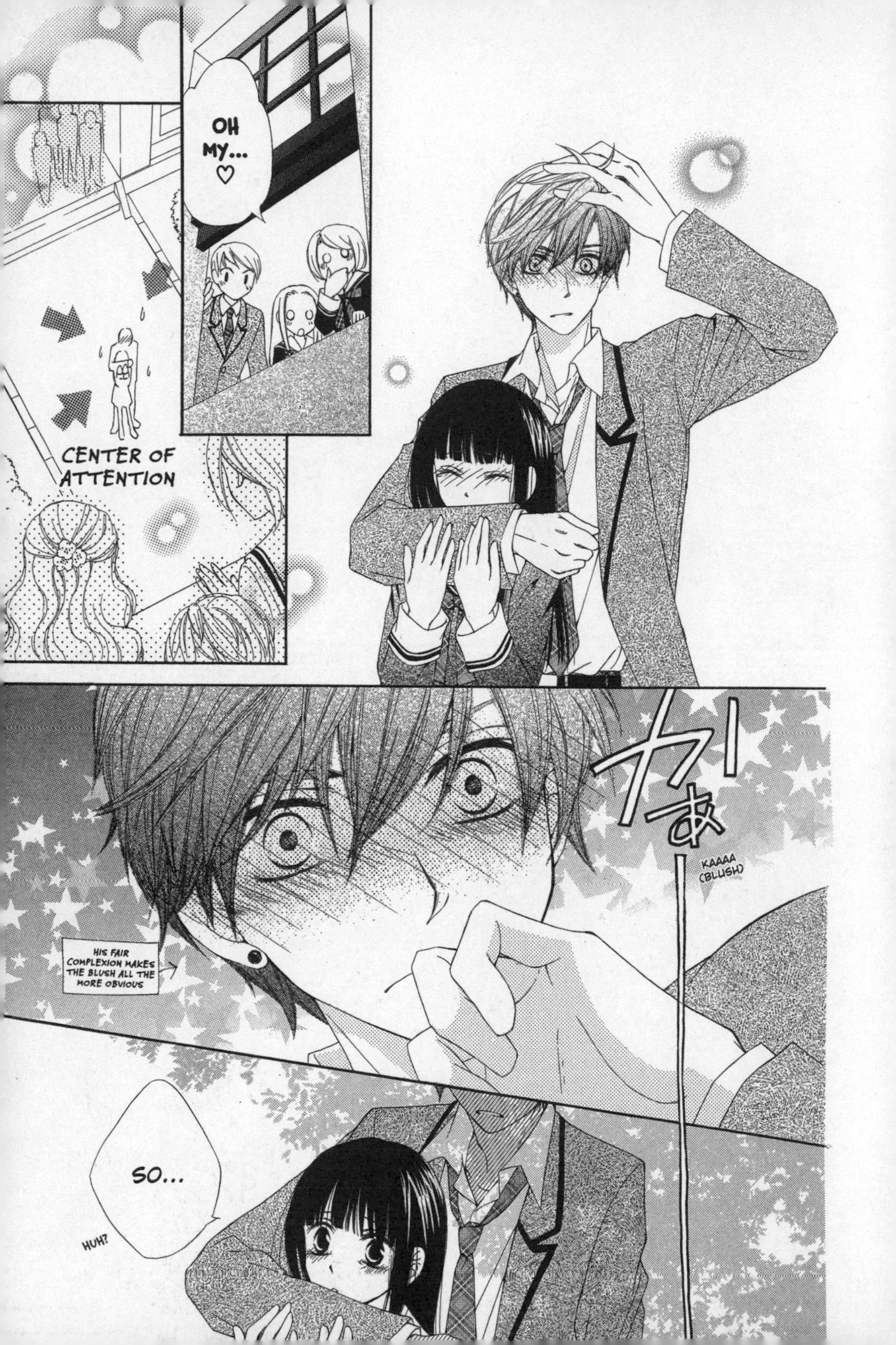

OH MY... ♡
CENTER OF ATTENTION
かぁ
KAAAA (BLUSH)
HIS FAIR COMPLEXION MAKES THE BLUSH ALL THE MORE OBVIOUS
SO...
HUH?

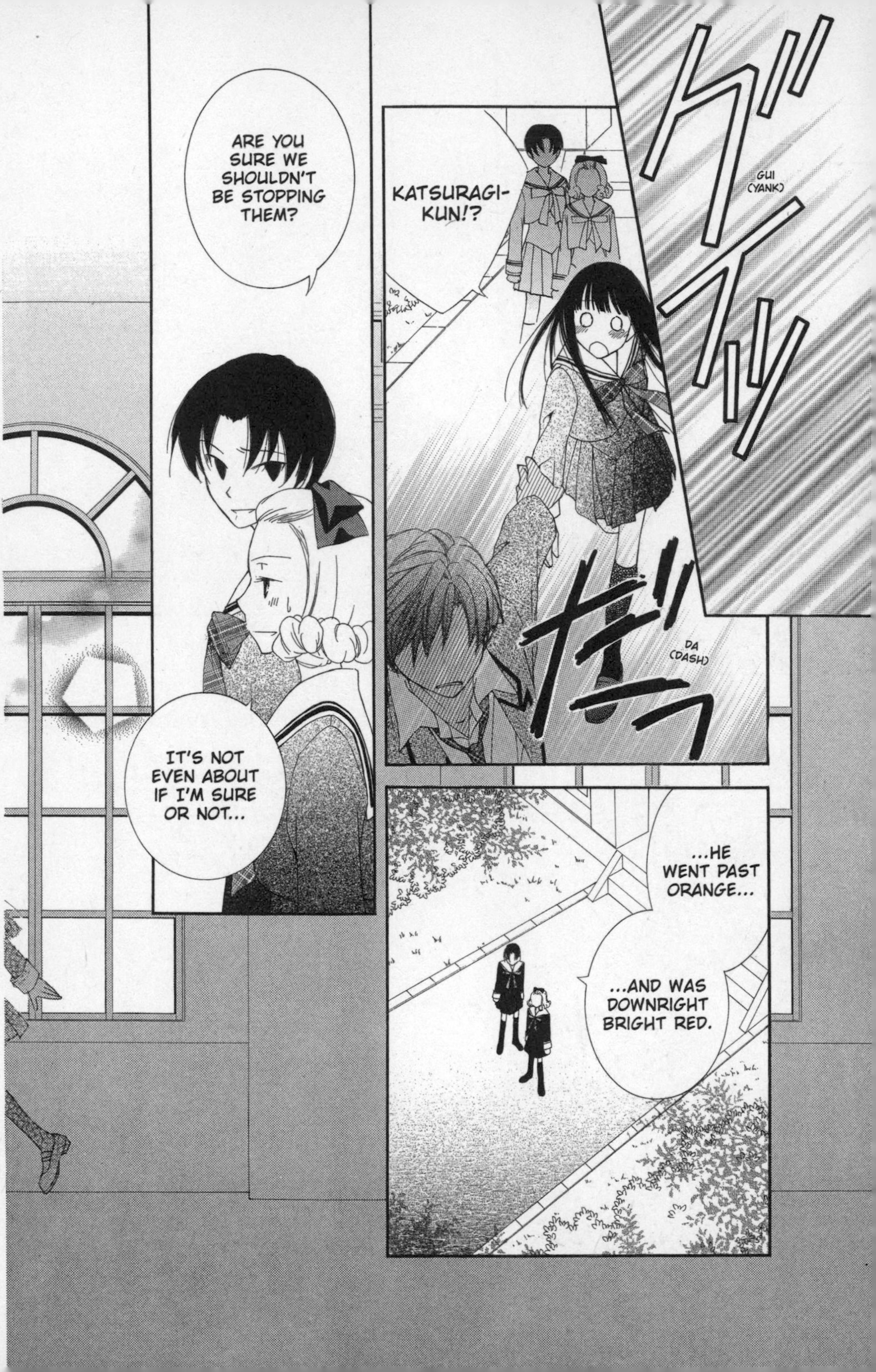
GUI (YANK)
KATSURAGI-KUN!?
DA (DASH)
...HE WENT PAST ORANGE...
...AND WAS DOWNRIGHT BRIGHT RED.
ARE YOU SURE WE SHOULDN'T BE STOPPING THEM?
IT'S NOT EVEN ABOUT IF I'M SURE OR NOT...

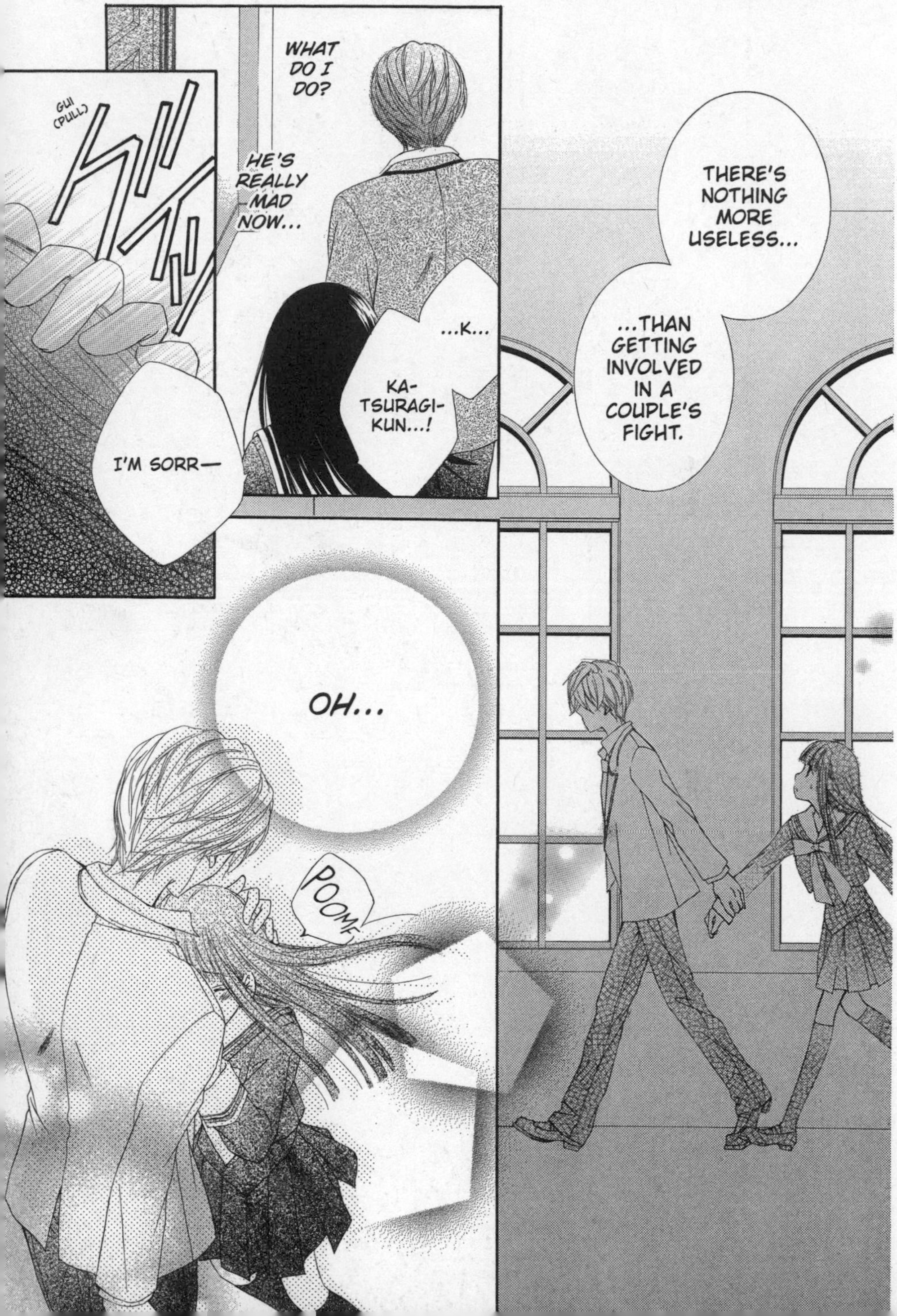
THERE'S NOTHING MORE USELESS...
...THAN GETTING INVOLVED IN A COUPLE'S FIGHT.
WHAT DO I DO?
HE'S REALLY MAD NOW...
...K...
KA-TSURAGI-KUN...!
GUI (PULL)
I'M SORR—
OH...
POOMF

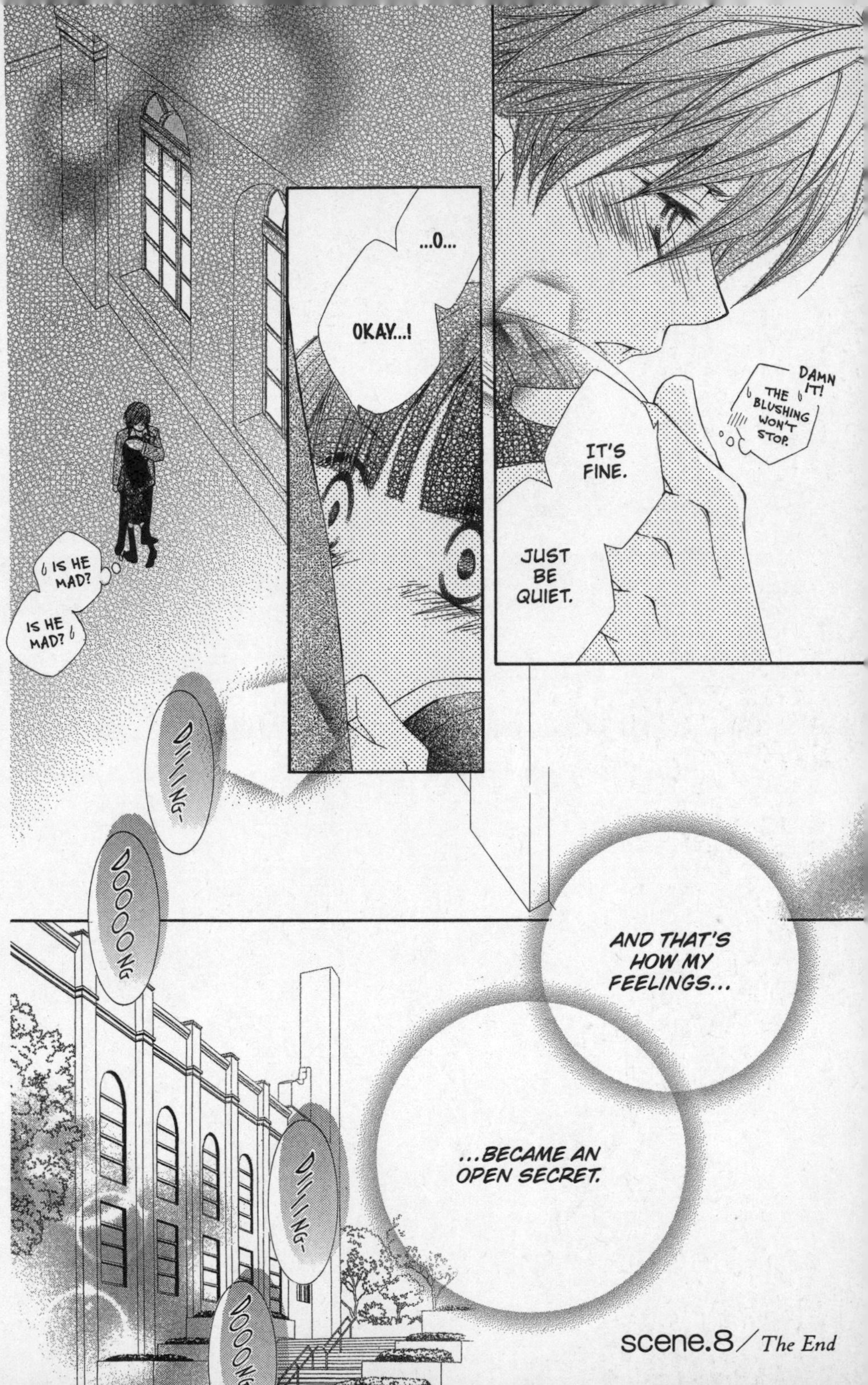
DAMN IT! THE BLUSHING WON'T STOP.
IT'S FINE.
JUST BE QUIET.
...O...
OKAY...!
IS HE MAD?
IS HE MAD?
DIIING-
DOOOONG
AND THAT'S HOW MY FEELINGS...
...BECAME AN OPEN SECRET.
DIIING-
DOOOONG

scene.8 / The End

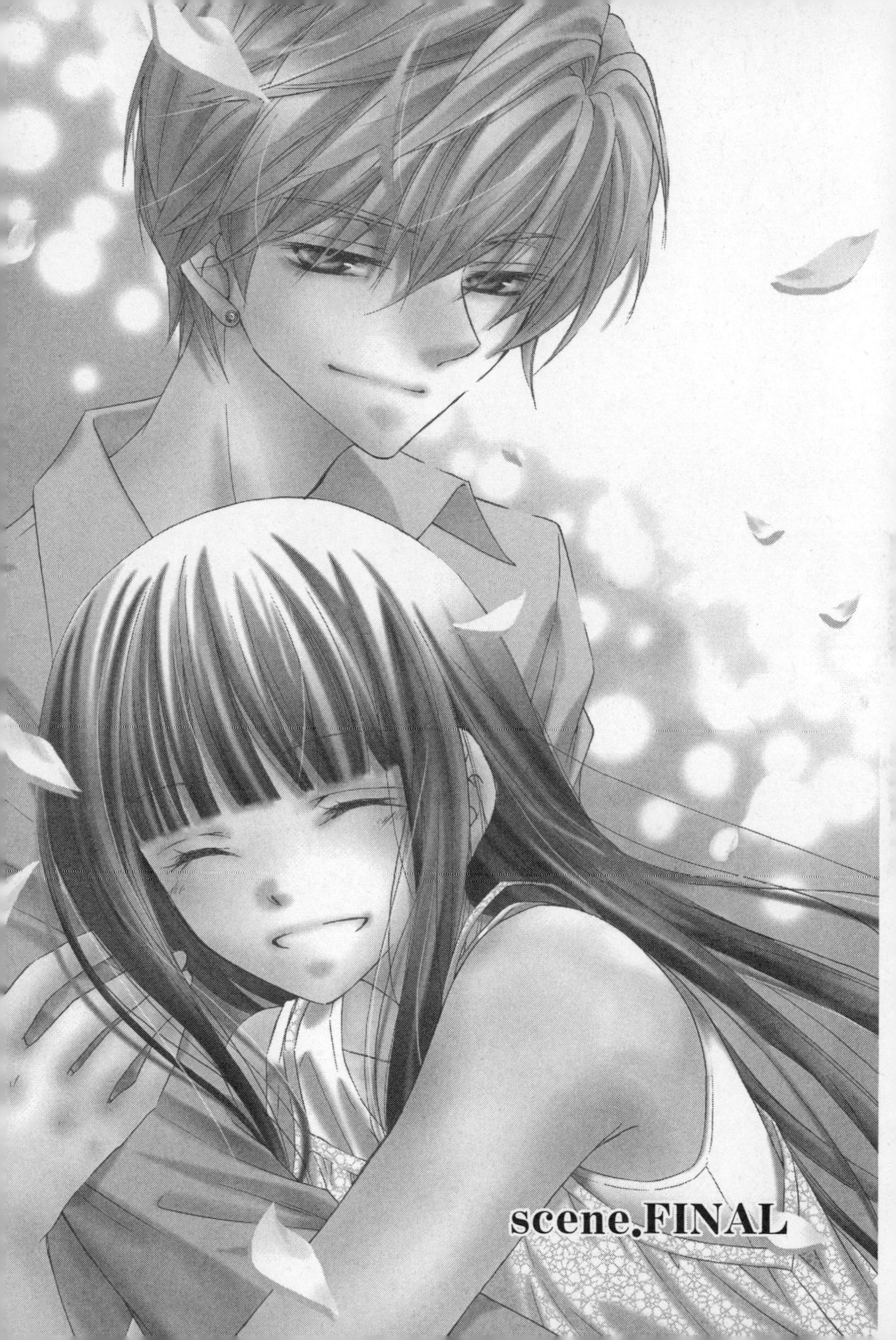
scene.FINAL

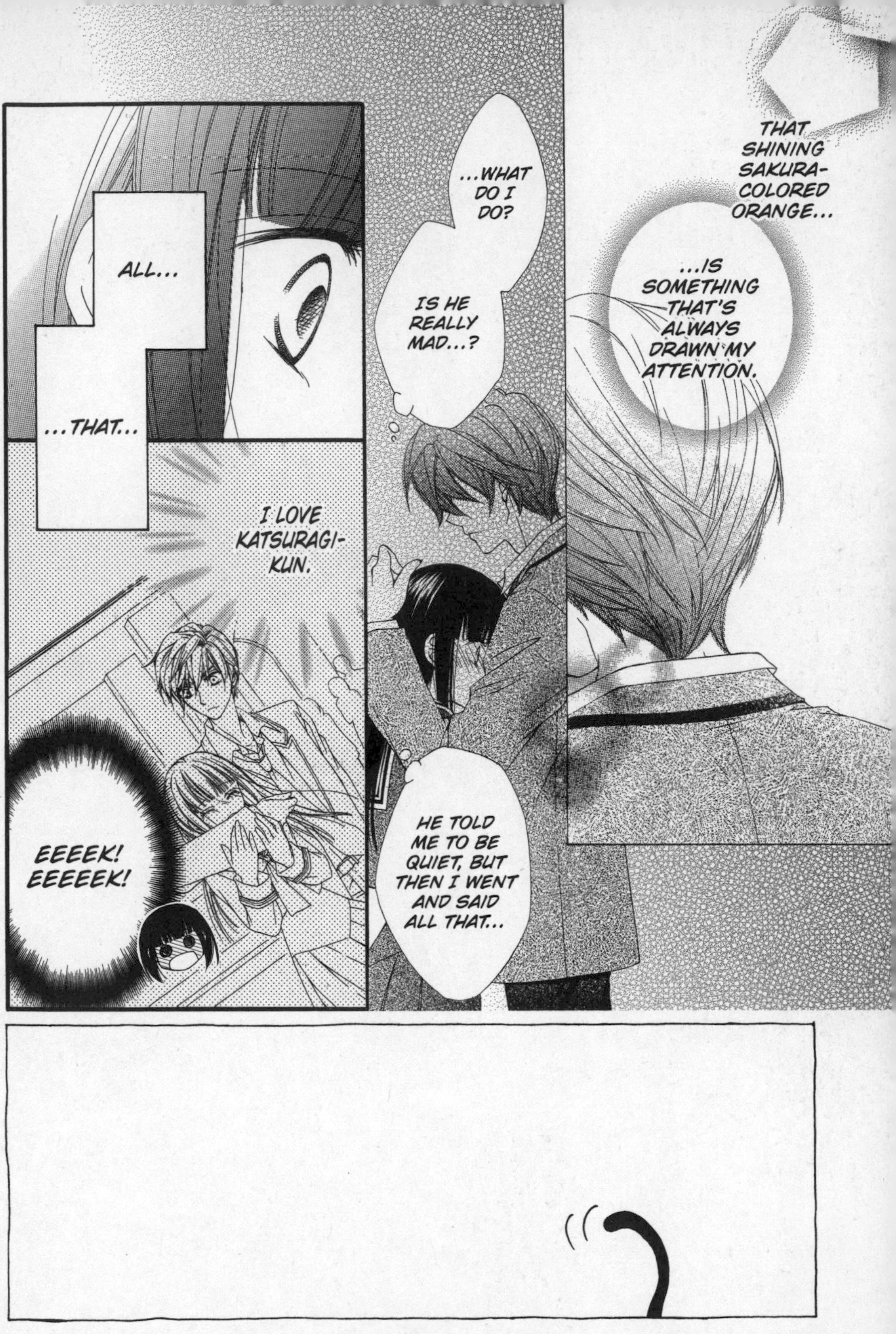
THAT SHINING SAKURA-COLORED ORANGE...
...IS SOMETHING THAT'S ALWAYS DRAWN MY ATTENTION.
...WHAT DO I DO?
IS HE REALLY MAD...?
HE TOLD ME TO BE QUIET, BUT THEN I WENT AND SAID ALL THAT...
ALL...
...THAT...
I LOVE KATSURAGI-KUN.
EEEEK! EEEEEK!

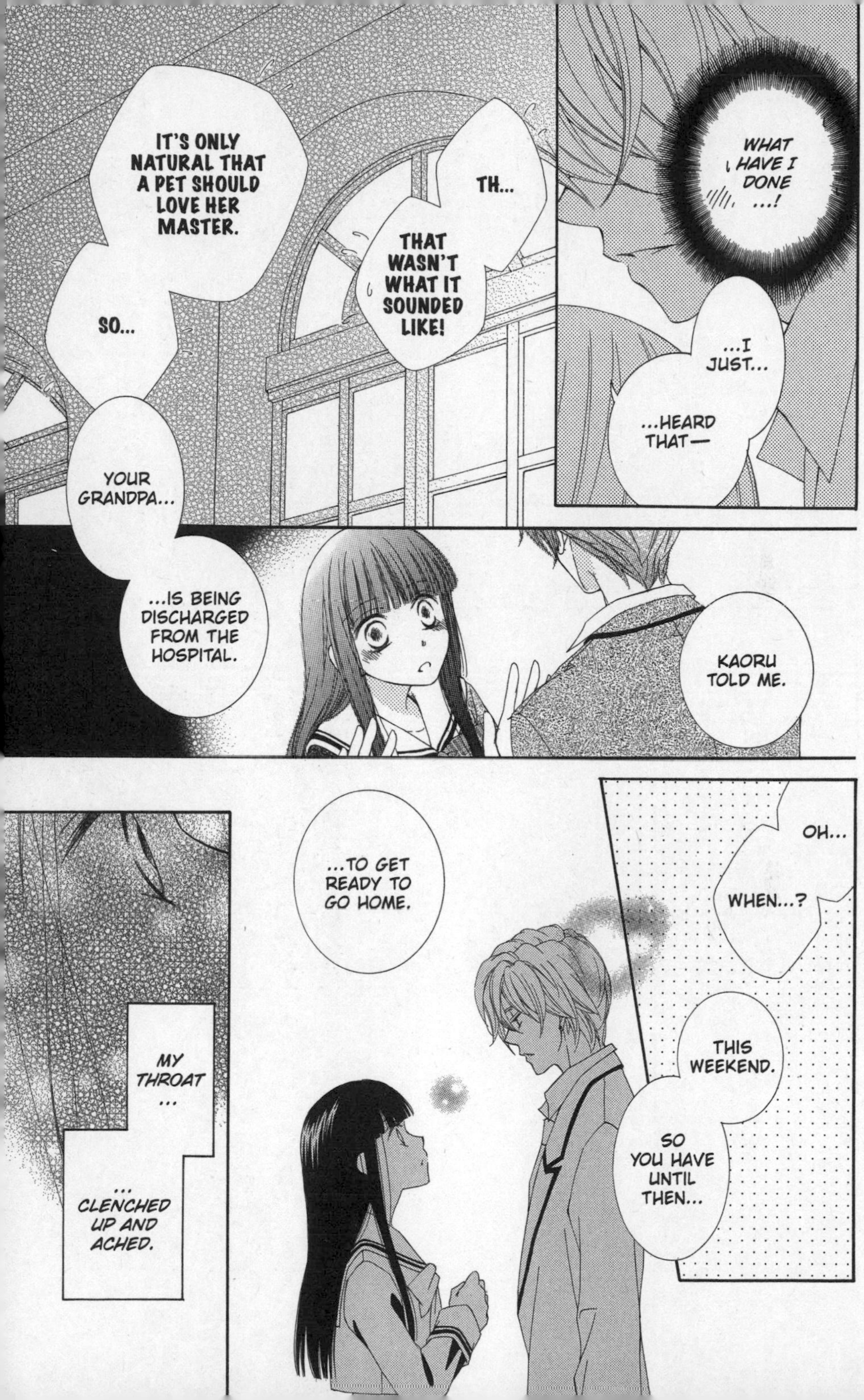
WHAT HAVE I DONE ...!
...I JUST...
...HEARD THAT—
TH...
THAT WASN'T WHAT IT SOUNDED LIKE!
IT'S ONLY NATURAL THAT A PET SHOULD LOVE HER MASTER.
SO...
YOUR GRANDPA...
...IS BEING DISCHARGED FROM THE HOSPITAL.
KAORU TOLD ME.
OH...
WHEN...?
THIS WEEKEND.
SO YOU HAVE UNTIL THEN...
...TO GET READY TO GO HOME.
MY THROAT ...
... CLENCHED UP AND ACHED.

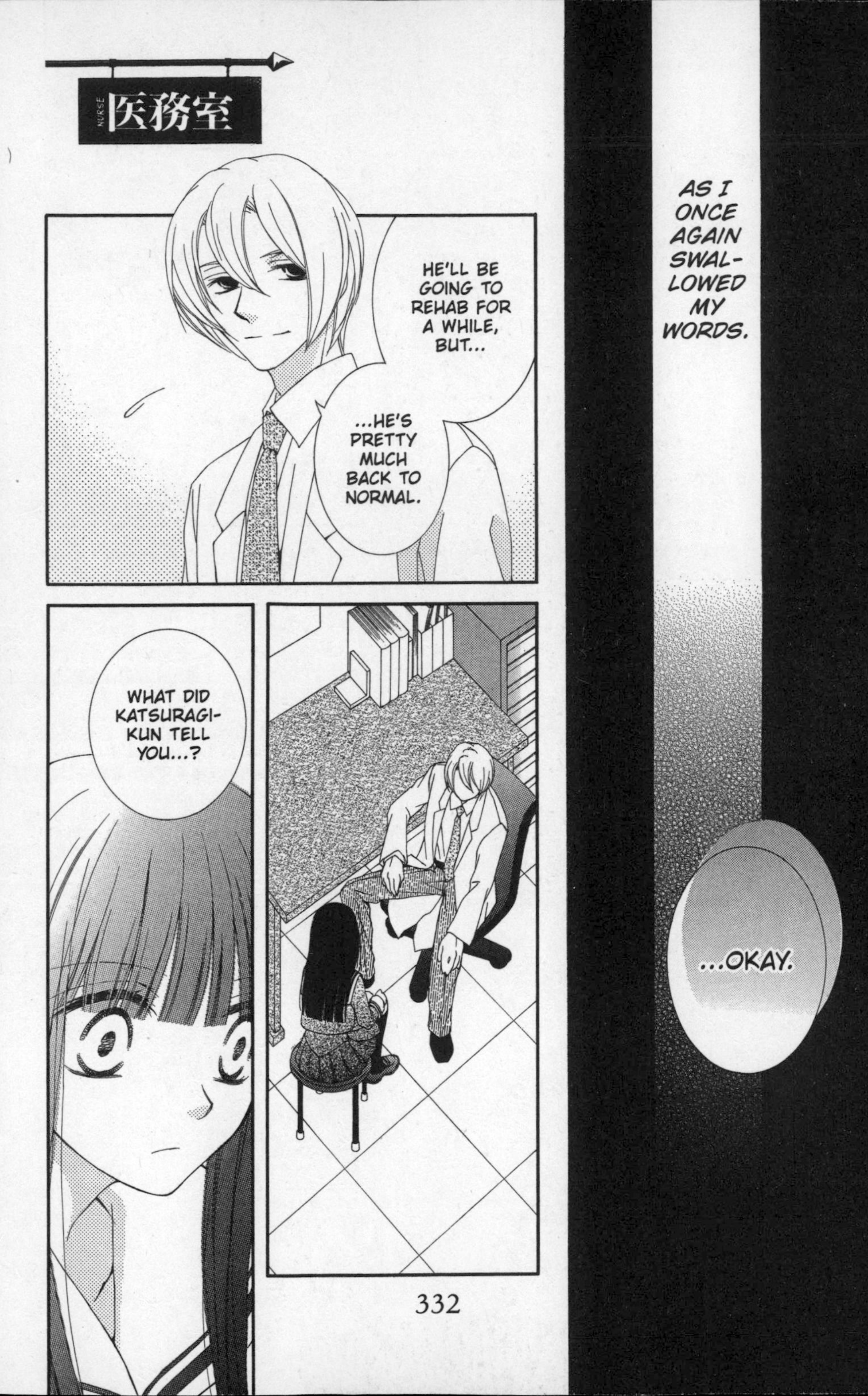
AS I ONCE AGAIN SWAL-LOWED MY WORDS.
...OKAY.
NURSE 医務室
HE'LL BE GOING TO REHAB FOR A WHILE, BUT...
...HE'S PRETTY MUCH BACK TO NORMAL.
WHAT DID KATSURAGI-KUN TELL YOU...?

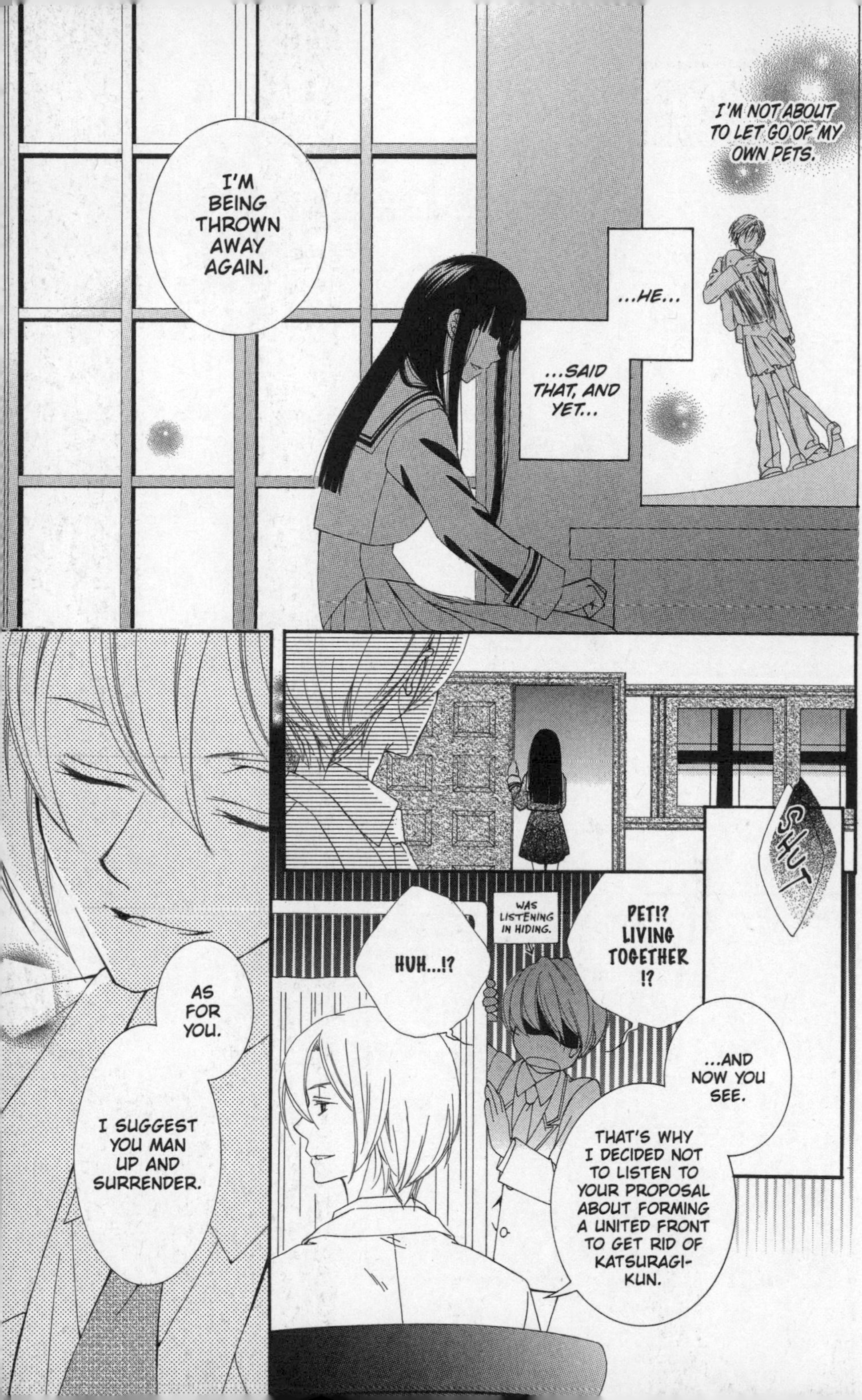
I'M NOT ABOUT TO LET GO OF MY OWN PETS.
...HE...
...SAID THAT, AND YET...
I'M BEING THROWN AWAY AGAIN.
SHUT
PET!? LIVING TOGETHER !?
WAS LISTENING IN HIDING.
HUH...!?
...AND NOW YOU SEE.
THAT'S WHY I DECIDED NOT TO LISTEN TO YOUR PROPOSAL ABOUT FORMING A UNITED FRONT TO GET RID OF KATSURAGI-KUN.
AS FOR YOU.
I SUGGEST YOU MAN UP AND SURRENDER.

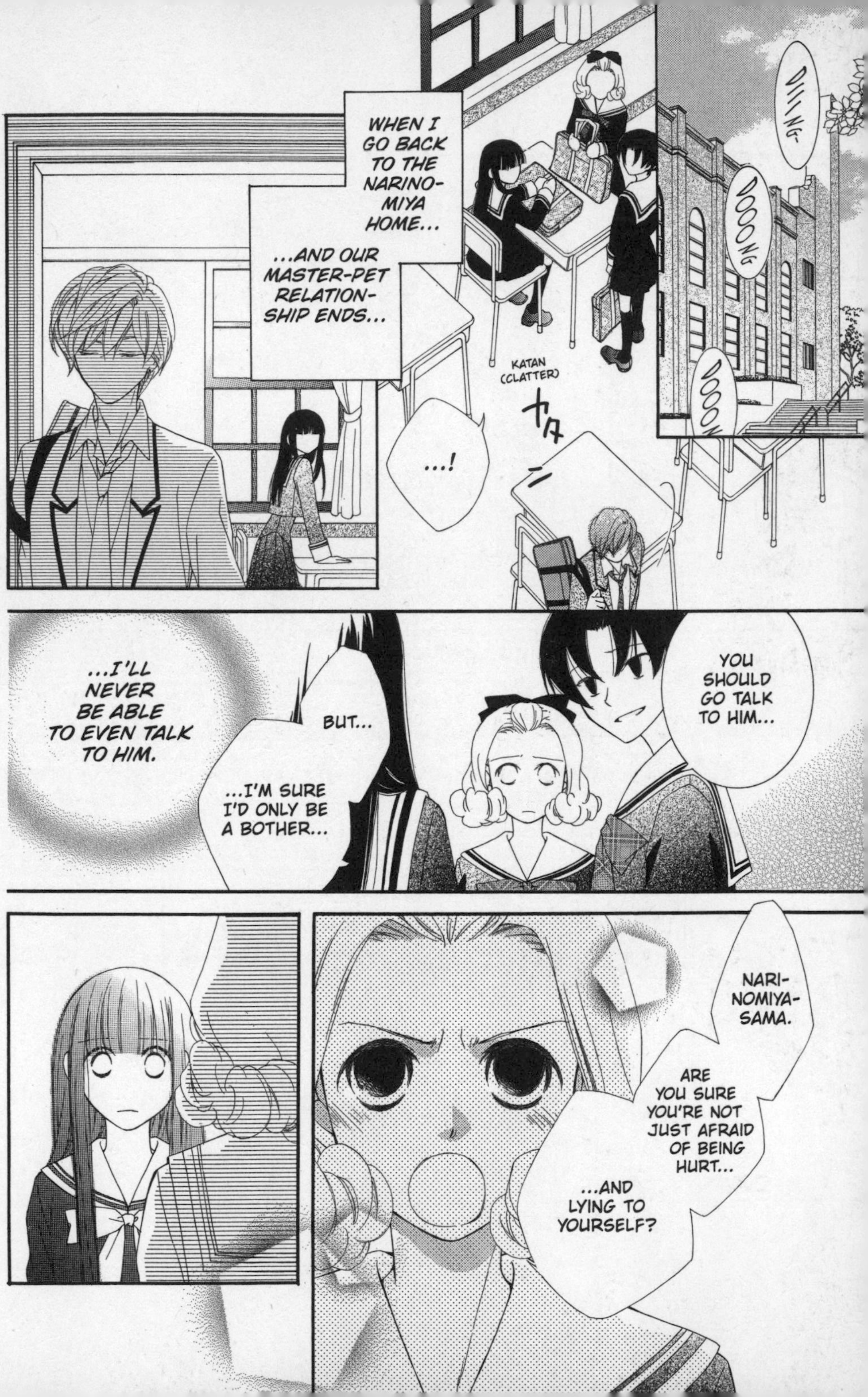
DIIING-
DOOONG
DOOON
WHEN I GO BACK TO THE NARINO-MIYA HOME...
...AND OUR MASTER-PET RELATION-SHIP ENDS...
KATAN (CLATTER)
...!
YOU SHOULD GO TALK TO HIM...
BUT...
...I'M SURE I'D ONLY BE A BOTHER...
...I'LL NEVER BE ABLE TO EVEN TALK TO HIM.
NARI-NOMIYA-SAMA.
ARE YOU SURE YOU'RE NOT JUST AFRAID OF BEING HURT...
...AND LYING TO YOURSELF?

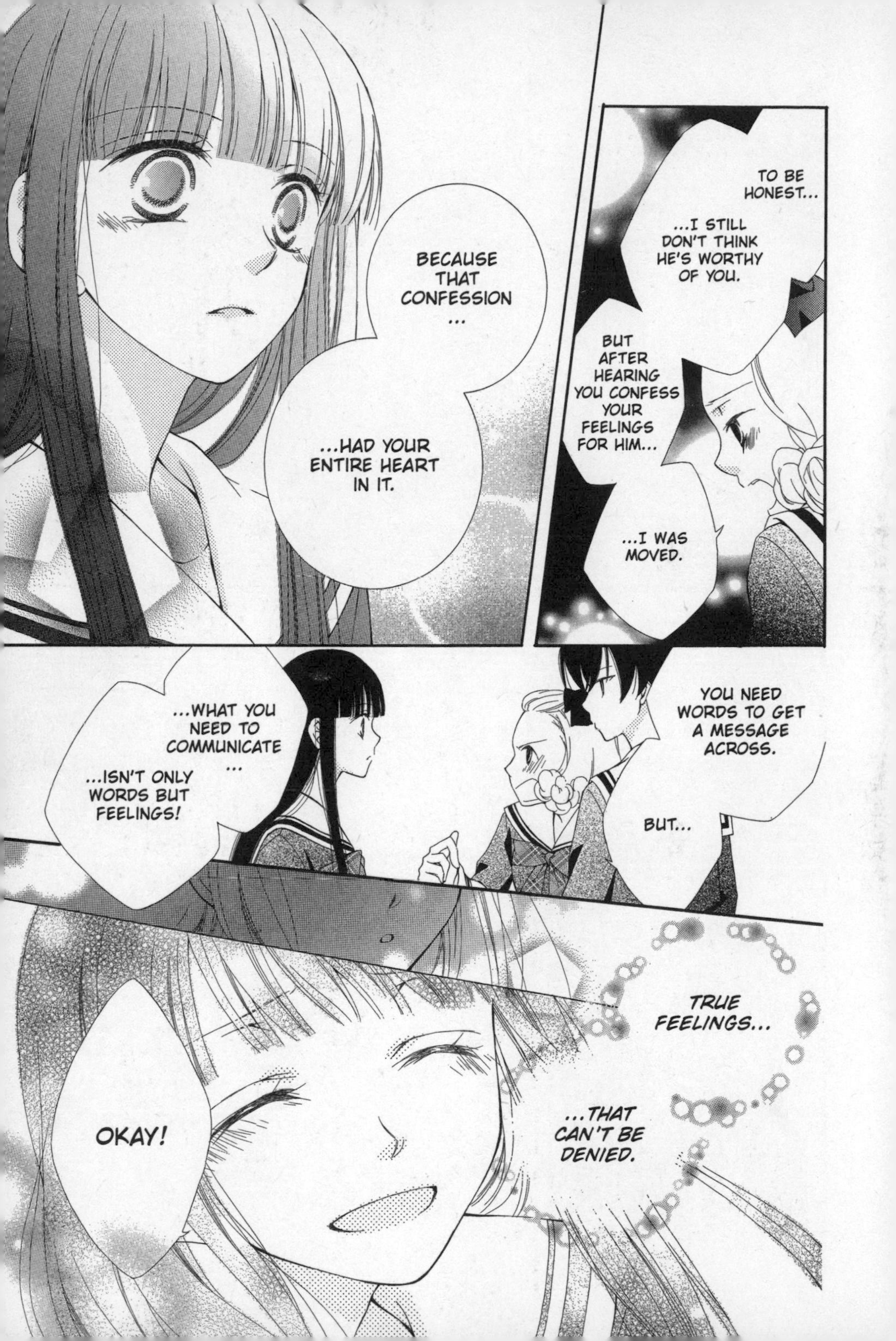
TO BE HONEST...
...I STILL DON'T THINK HE'S WORTHY OF YOU.
BUT AFTER HEARING YOU CONFESS YOUR FEELINGS FOR HIM...
...I WAS MOVED.
BECAUSE THAT CONFESSION ...
...HAD YOUR ENTIRE HEART IN IT.
YOU NEED WORDS TO GET A MESSAGE ACROSS.
BUT...
...WHAT YOU NEED TO COMMUNICATE ...
...ISN'T ONLY WORDS BUT FEELINGS!
TRUE FEELINGS...
...THAT CAN'T BE DENIED.
OKAY!

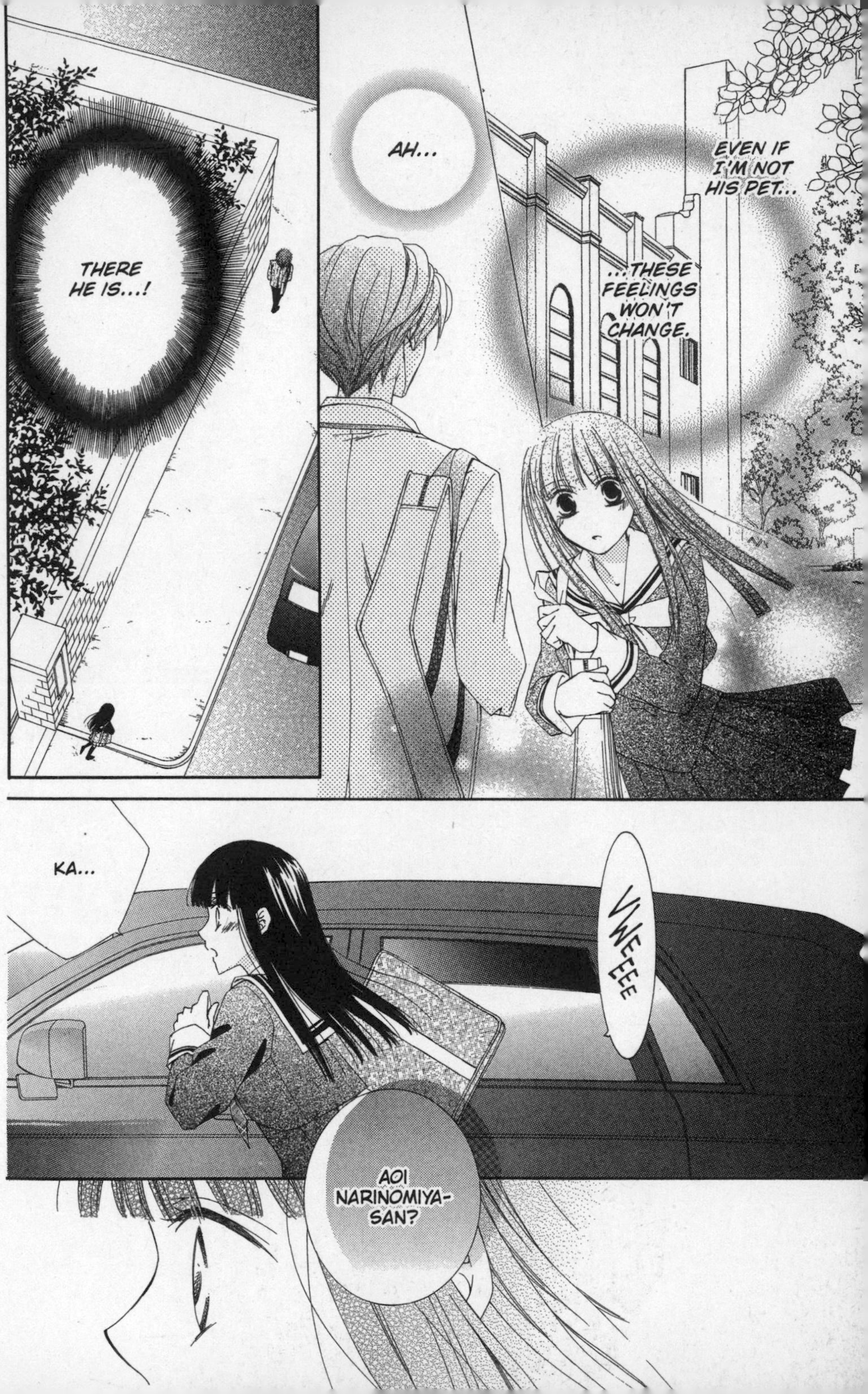
EVEN IF I'M NOT HIS PET...
...THESE FEELINGS WON'T CHANGE.
AH...
THERE HE IS...!
VWEEEE
KA...
AOI NARINOMIYA-SAN?

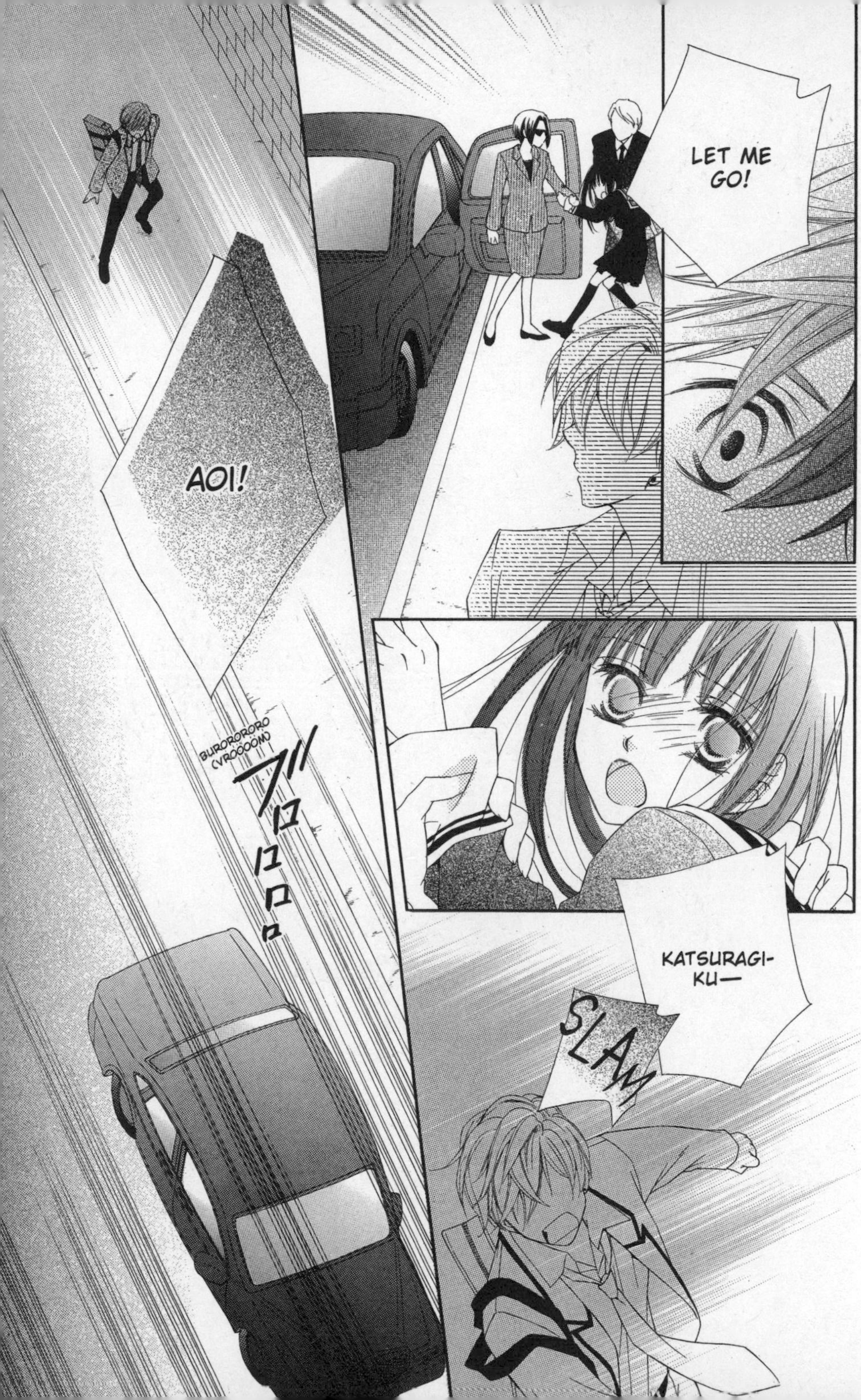
LET ME GO!
KATSURAGI-KU—
SLAM
AOI!
BURORORORO (VROOOOM)
ブロロロロ

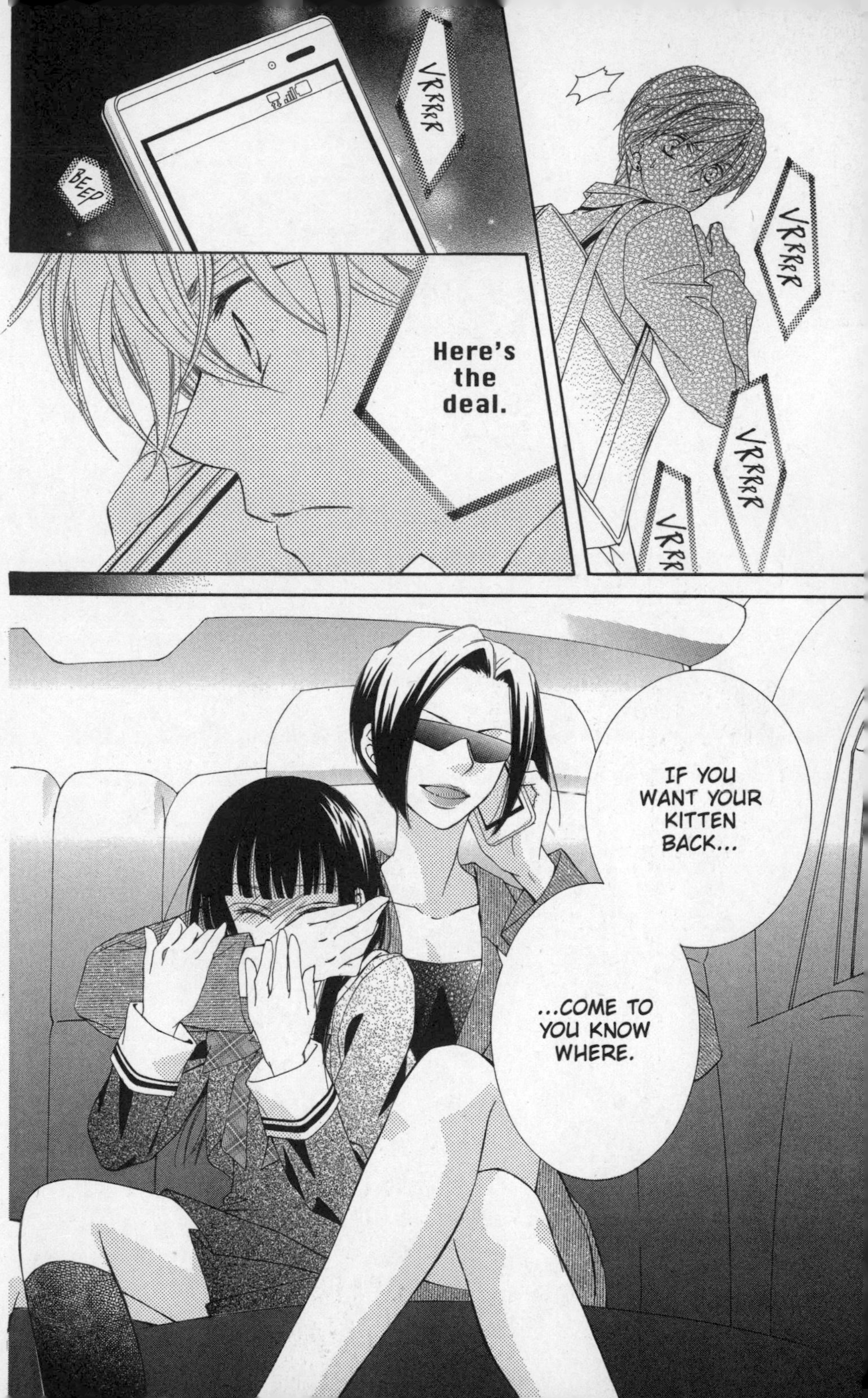
VRRRRR
VRRRRR
VRRR
VRRRRR
BEEP
Here's the deal.
IF YOU WANT YOUR KITTEN BACK...
...COME TO YOU KNOW WHERE.

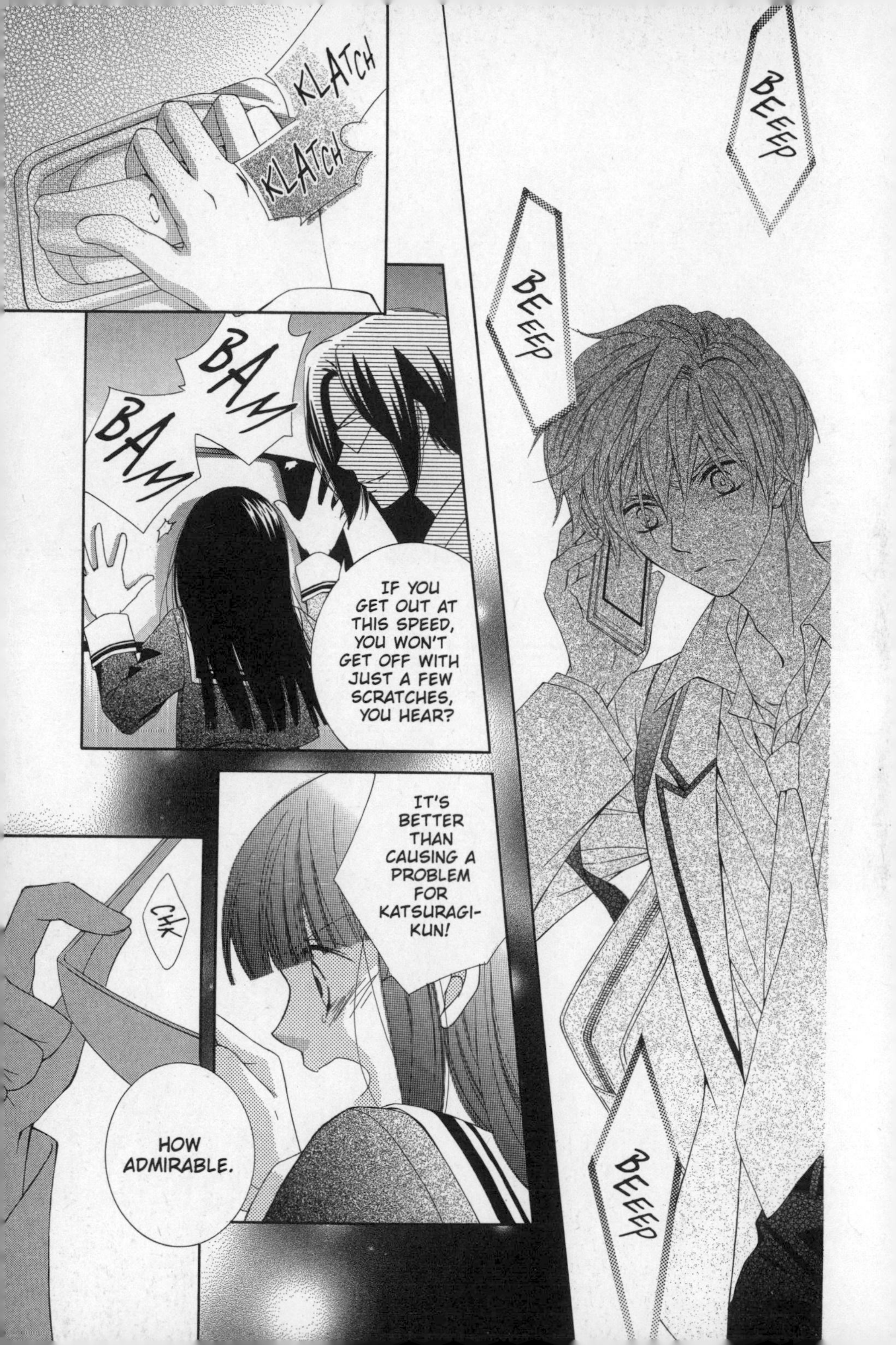
BEEEP
BEEEP
BEEEP
KLATCH
KLATCH
BAM
BAM
IF YOU GET OUT AT THIS SPEED, YOU WON'T GET OFF WITH JUST A FEW SCRATCHES, YOU HEAR?
IT'S BETTER THAN CAUSING A PROBLEM FOR KATSURAGI-KUN!
CHK
HOW ADMIRABLE.

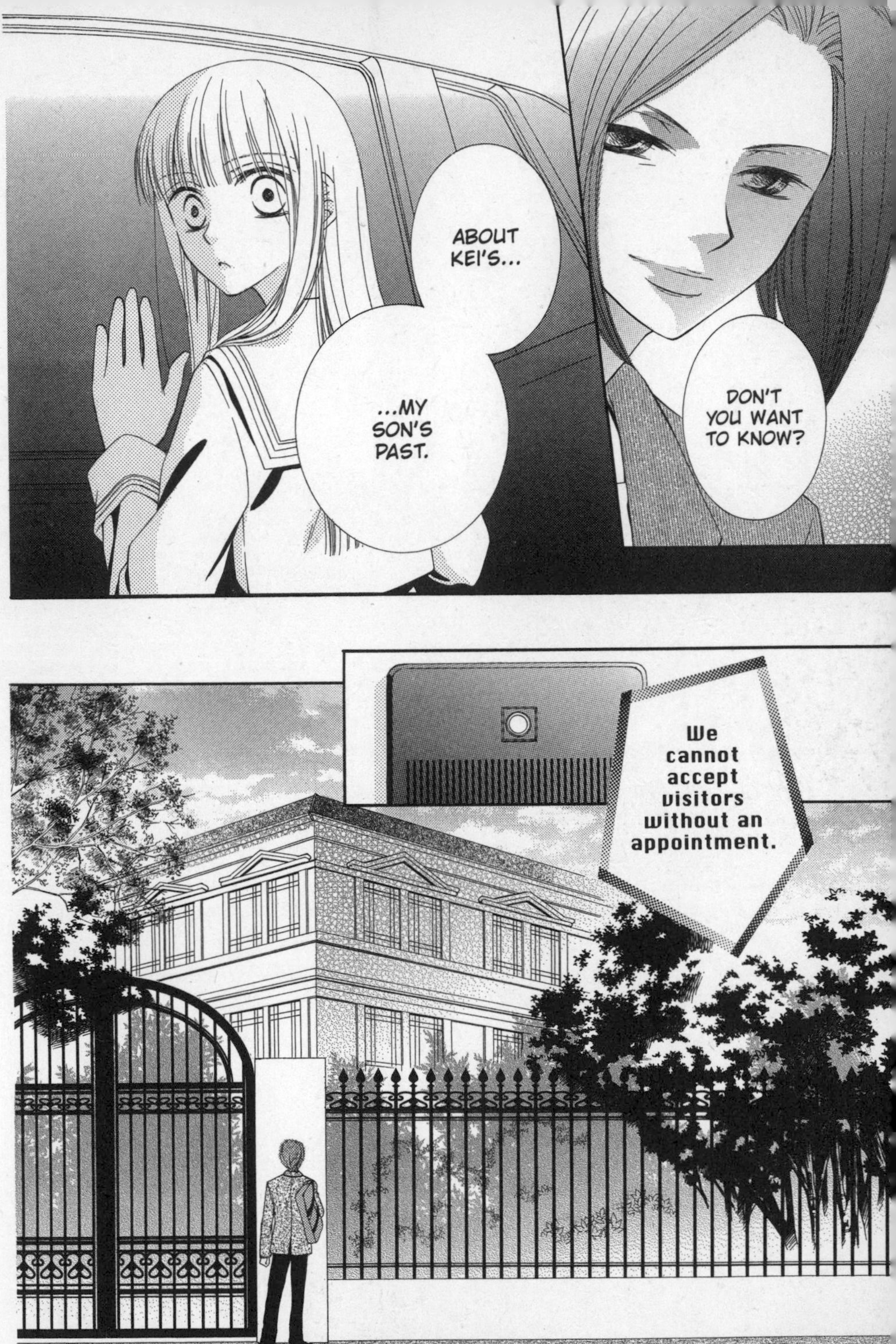
ABOUT KEI'S...
...MY SON'S PAST.
DON'T YOU WANT TO KNOW?
We cannot accept visitors without an appointment.

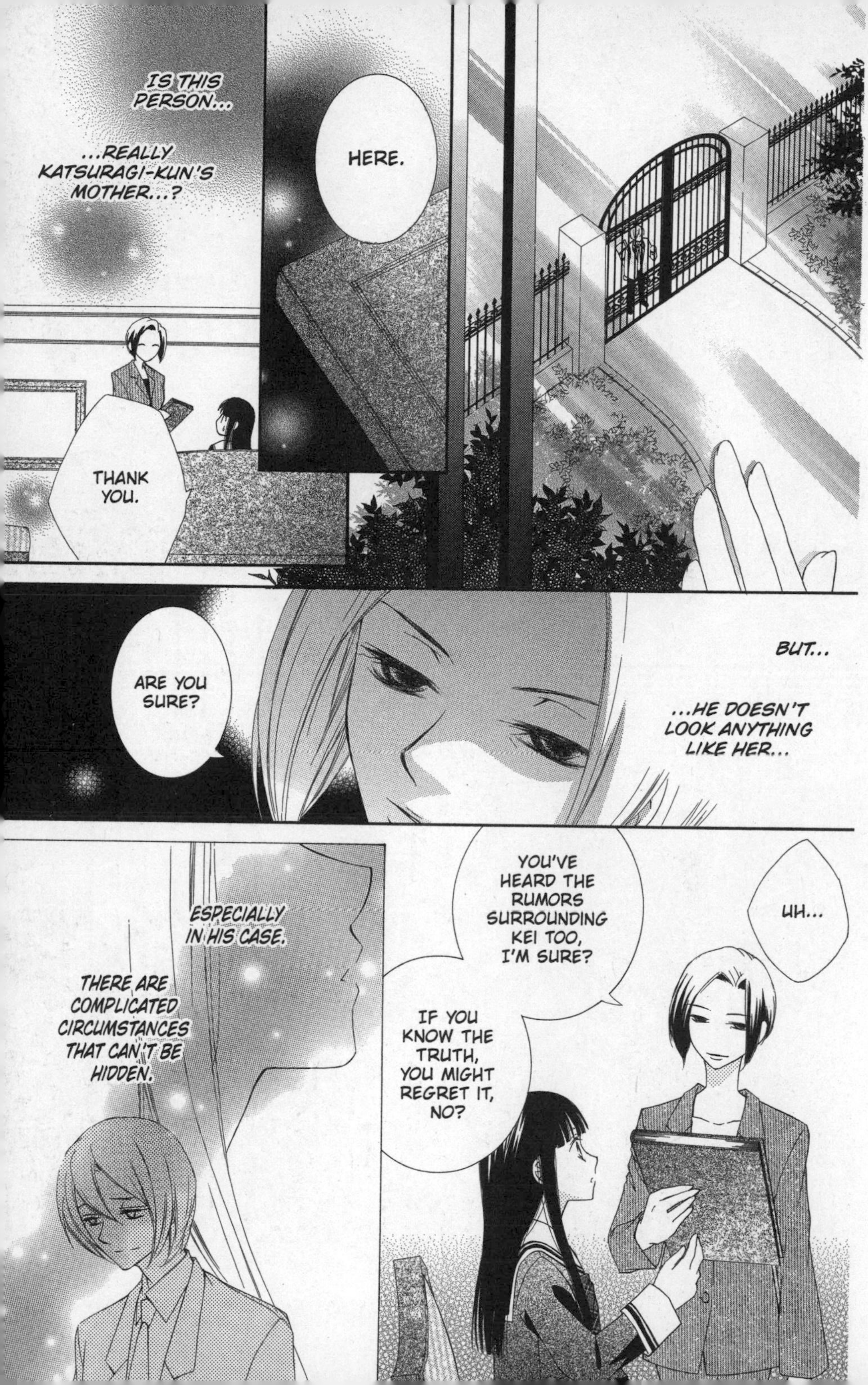
HERE.
IS THIS PERSON...
...REALLY KATSURAGI-KUN'S MOTHER...?
THANK YOU.
BUT...
...HE DOESN'T LOOK ANYTHING LIKE HER...
ARE YOU SURE?
UH...
YOU'VE HEARD THE RUMORS SURROUNDING KEI TOO, I'M SURE?
IF YOU KNOW THE TRUTH, YOU MIGHT REGRET IT, NO?
ESPECIALLY IN HIS CASE.
THERE ARE COMPLICATED CIRCUMSTANCES THAT CAN'T BE HIDDEN.

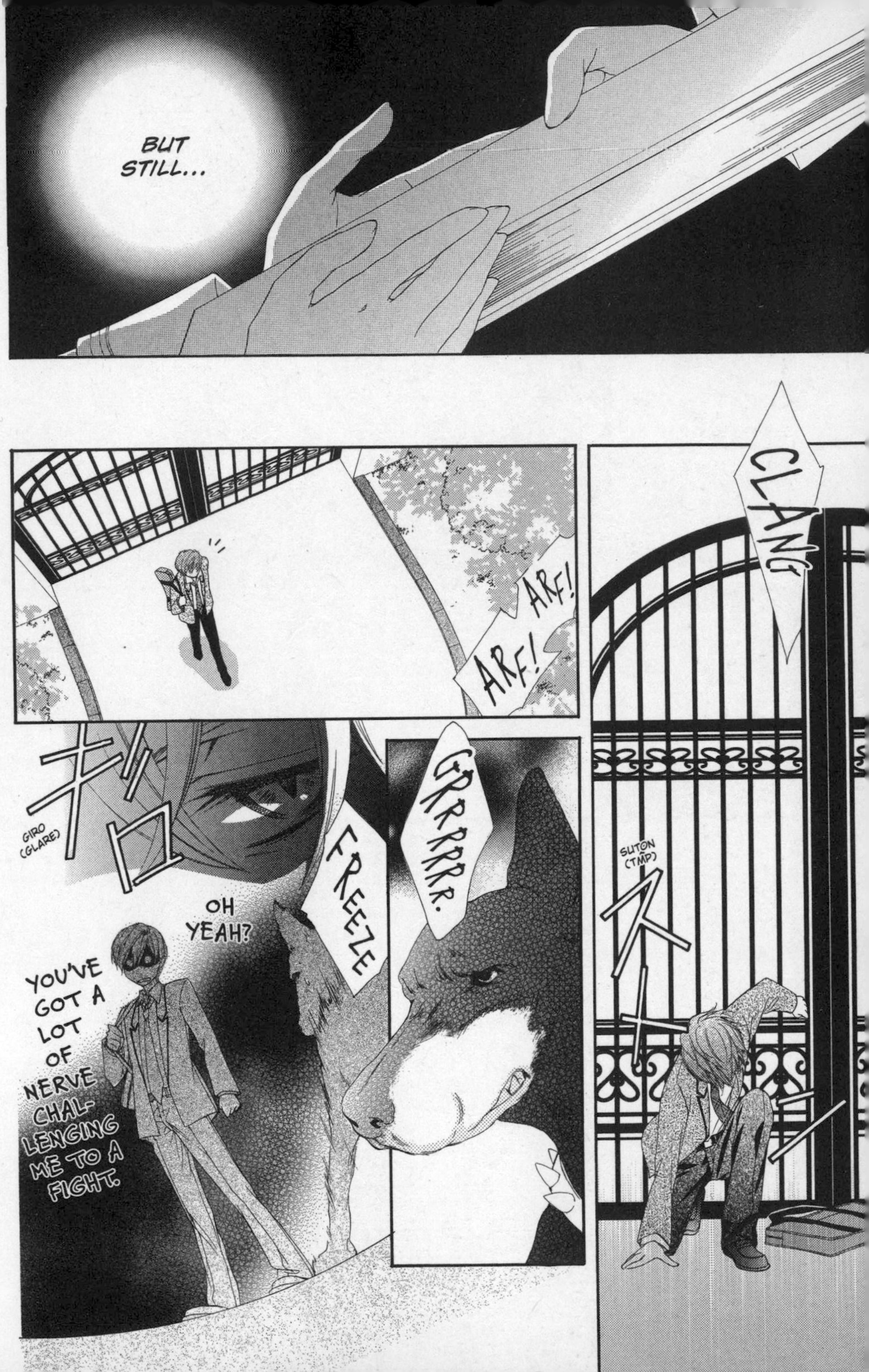
BUT STILL...
CLANG
SUTON (TMP)
ARF!
ARF!
GRRRRRR.
FREEZE
GIRO (GLARE)
OH YEAH?
YOU'VE GOT A LOT OF NERVE CHAL-LENGING ME TO A FIGHT.

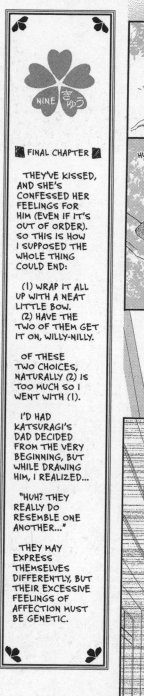

NINE きゅう

FINAL CHAPTER

THEY'VE KISSED, AND SHE'S CONFESSED HER FEELINGS FOR HIM (EVEN IF IT'S OUT OF ORDER). SO THIS IS HOW I SUPPOSED THE WHOLE THING COULD END:

(1) WRAP IT ALL UP WITH A NEAT LITTLE BOW.
(2) HAVE THE TWO OF THEM GET IT ON, WILLY-NILLY.

OF THESE TWO CHOICES, NATURALLY (2) IS TOO MUCH SO I WENT WITH (1).

I'D HAD KATSURAGI'S DAD DECIDED FROM THE VERY BEGINNING, BUT WHILE DRAWING HIM, I REALIZED...

"HUH? THEY REALLY DO RESEMBLE ONE ANOTHER..."

THEY MAY EXPRESS THEMSELVES DIFFERENTLY, BUT THEIR EXCESSIVE FEELINGS OF AFFECTION MUST BE GENETIC.

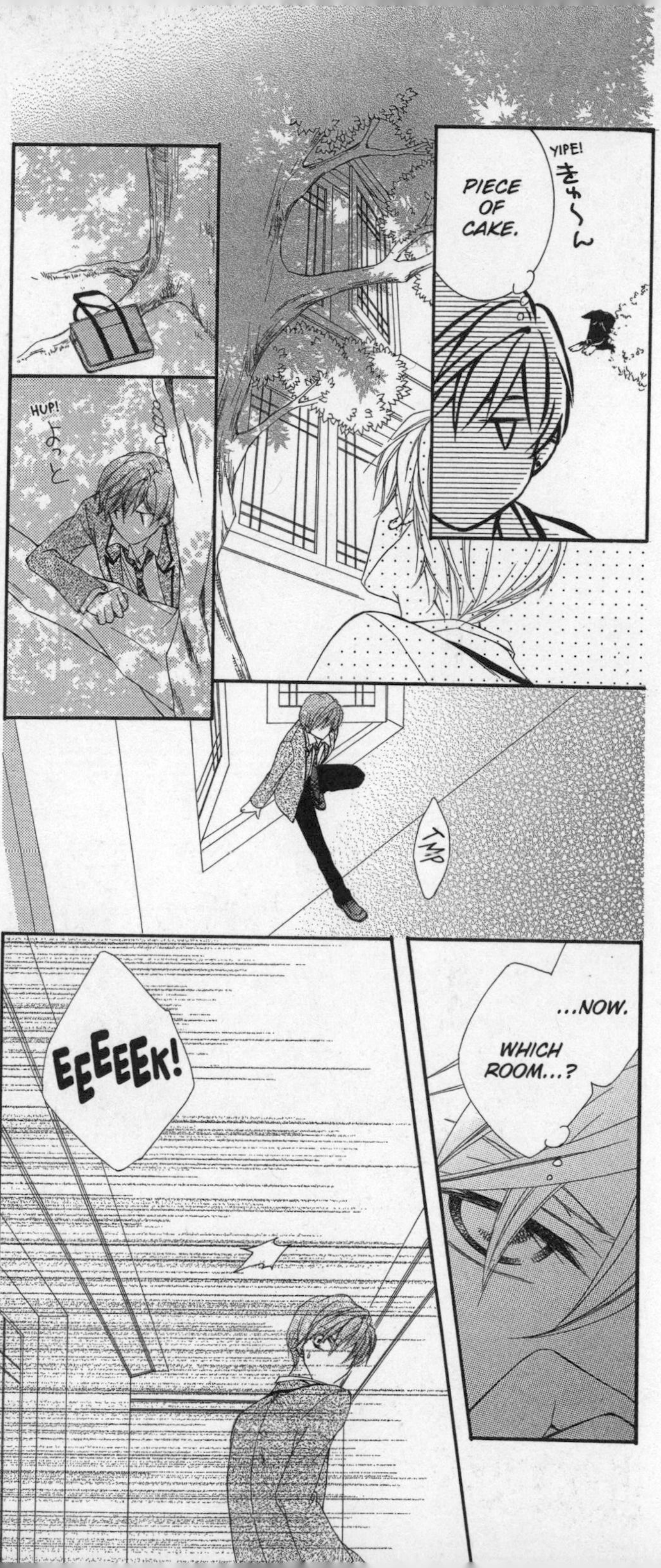
YIPE!
きゅ〜ん
PIECE OF CAKE.
HUP!
よっと
TMP
...NOW.
WHICH ROOM...?
EEEEEK!

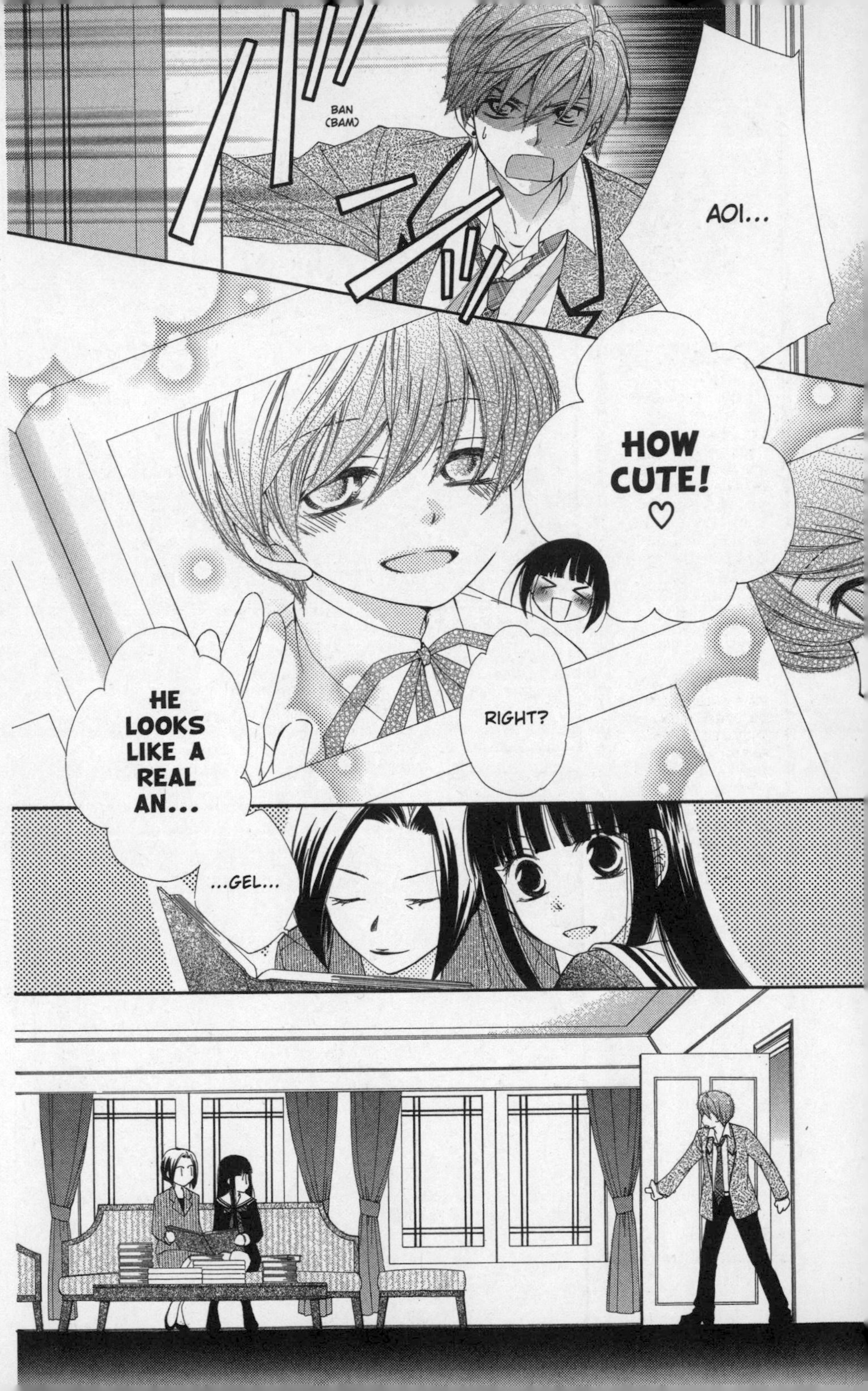
BAN (BAM)
AOI...
HOW CUTE! ♡
RIGHT?
HE LOOKS LIKE A REAL AN...
...GEL...

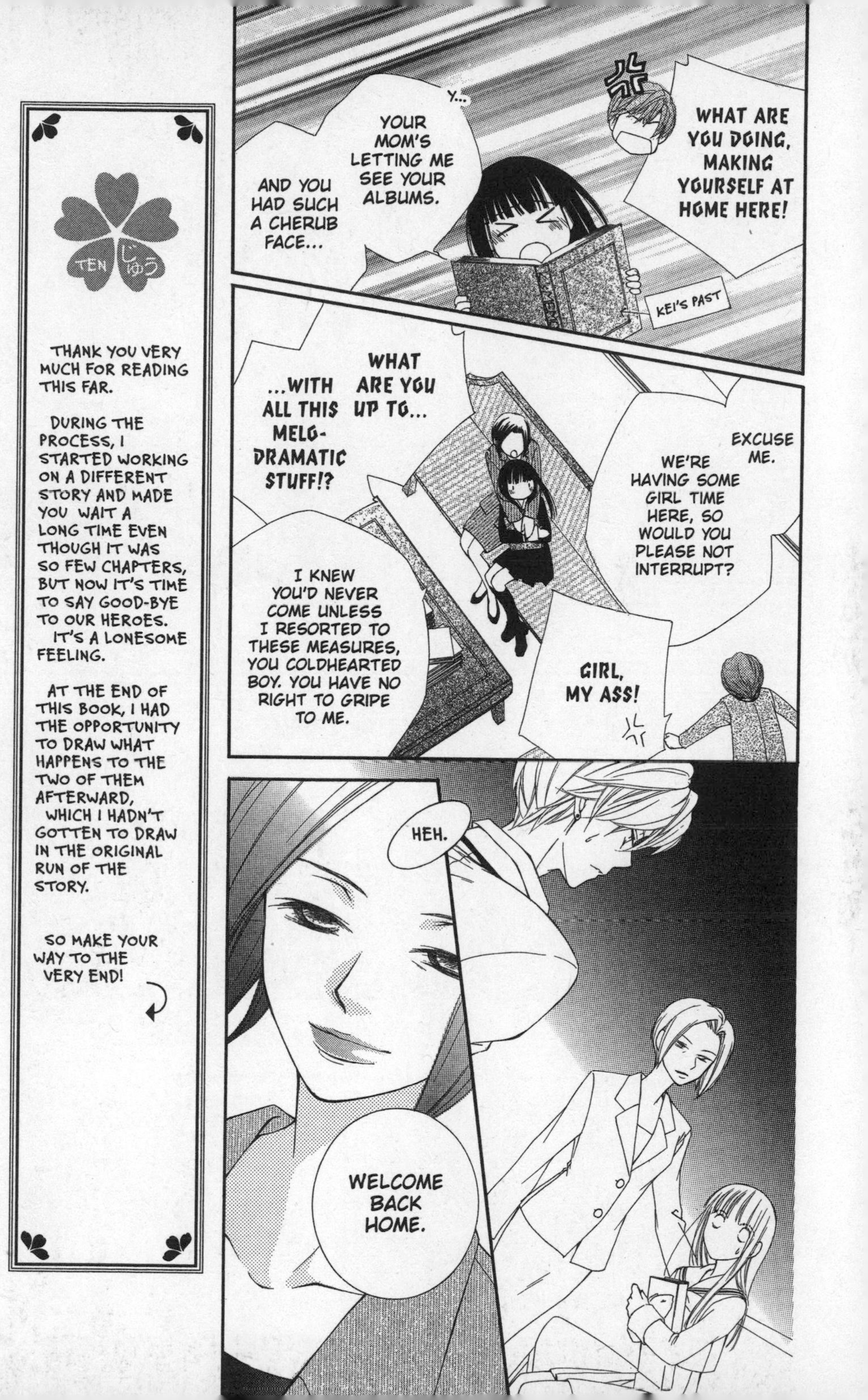
WHAT ARE YOU DOING, MAKING YOURSELF AT HOME HERE!
Y...
YOUR MOM'S LETTING ME SEE YOUR ALBUMS.
AND YOU HAD SUCH A CHERUB FACE...
KEI'S PAST
EXCUSE ME.
WE'RE HAVING SOME GIRL TIME HERE, SO WOULD YOU PLEASE NOT INTERRUPT?
WHAT ARE YOU UP TO...
...WITH ALL THIS MELO-DRAMATIC STUFF!?
GIRL, MY ASS!
I KNEW YOU'D NEVER COME UNLESS I RESORTED TO THESE MEASURES, YOU COLDHEARTED BOY. YOU HAVE NO RIGHT TO GRIPE TO ME.
HEH.
WELCOME BACK HOME.

TEN じゅう

THANK YOU VERY MUCH FOR READING THIS FAR.

DURING THE PROCESS, I STARTED WORKING ON A DIFFERENT STORY AND MADE YOU WAIT A LONG TIME EVEN THOUGH IT WAS SO FEW CHAPTERS, BUT NOW IT'S TIME TO SAY GOOD-BYE TO OUR HEROES.

IT'S A LONESOME FEELING.

AT THE END OF THIS BOOK, I HAD THE OPPORTUNITY TO DRAW WHAT HAPPENS TO THE TWO OF THEM AFTERWARD, WHICH I HADN'T GOTTEN TO DRAW IN THE ORIGINAL RUN OF THE STORY.

SO MAKE YOUR WAY TO THE VERY END!

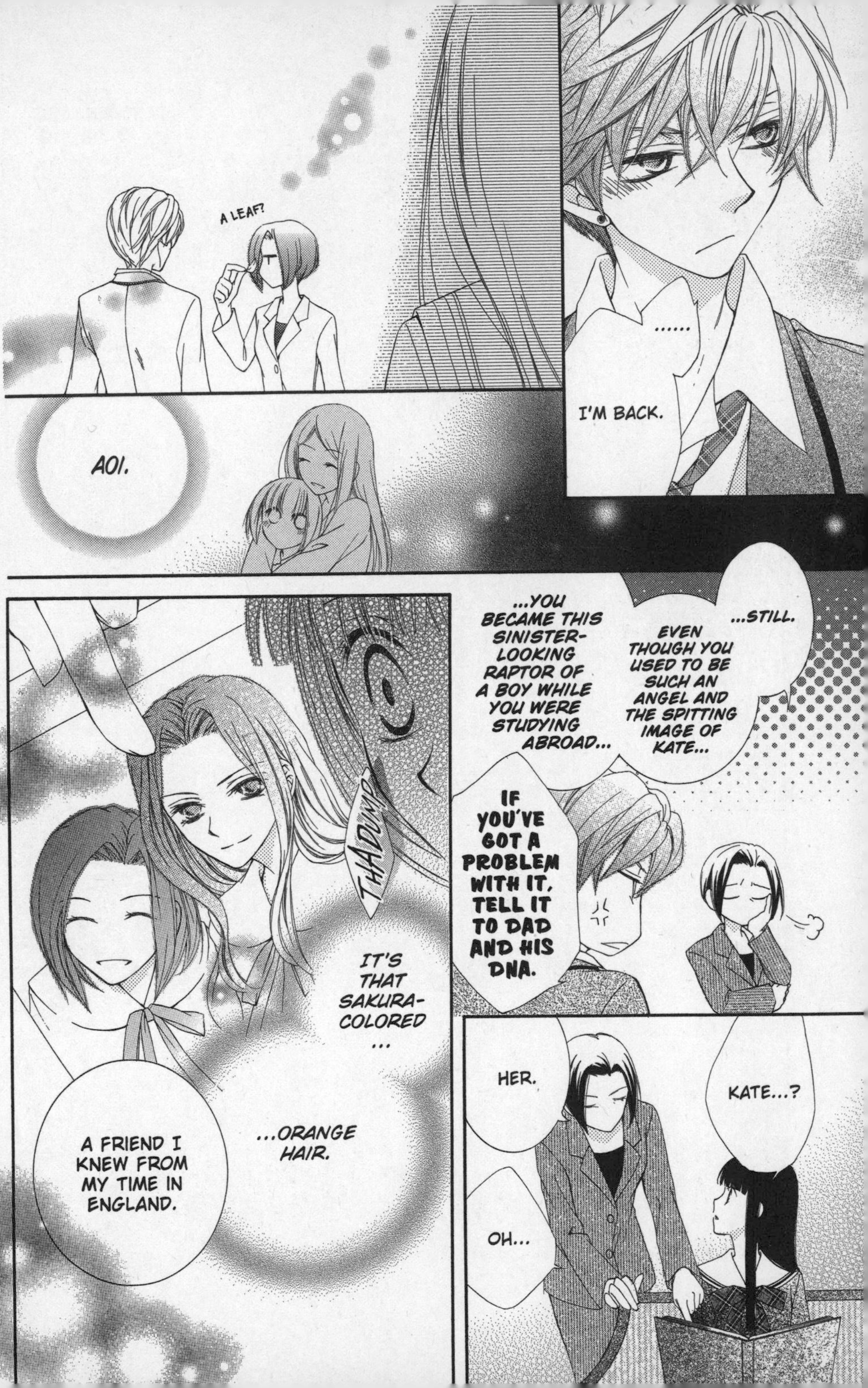
......
I'M BACK.
A LEAF?
AOI.
...STILL.
EVEN THOUGH YOU USED TO BE SUCH AN ANGEL AND THE SPITTING IMAGE OF KATE...
...YOU BECAME THIS SINISTER-LOOKING RAPTOR OF A BOY WHILE YOU WERE STUDYING ABROAD...
IF YOU'VE GOT A PROBLEM WITH IT, TELL IT TO DAD AND HIS DNA.
KATE...?
HER.
OH...
THADUMP
IT'S THAT SAKURA-COLORED...
...ORANGE HAIR.
A FRIEND I KNEW FROM MY TIME IN ENGLAND.

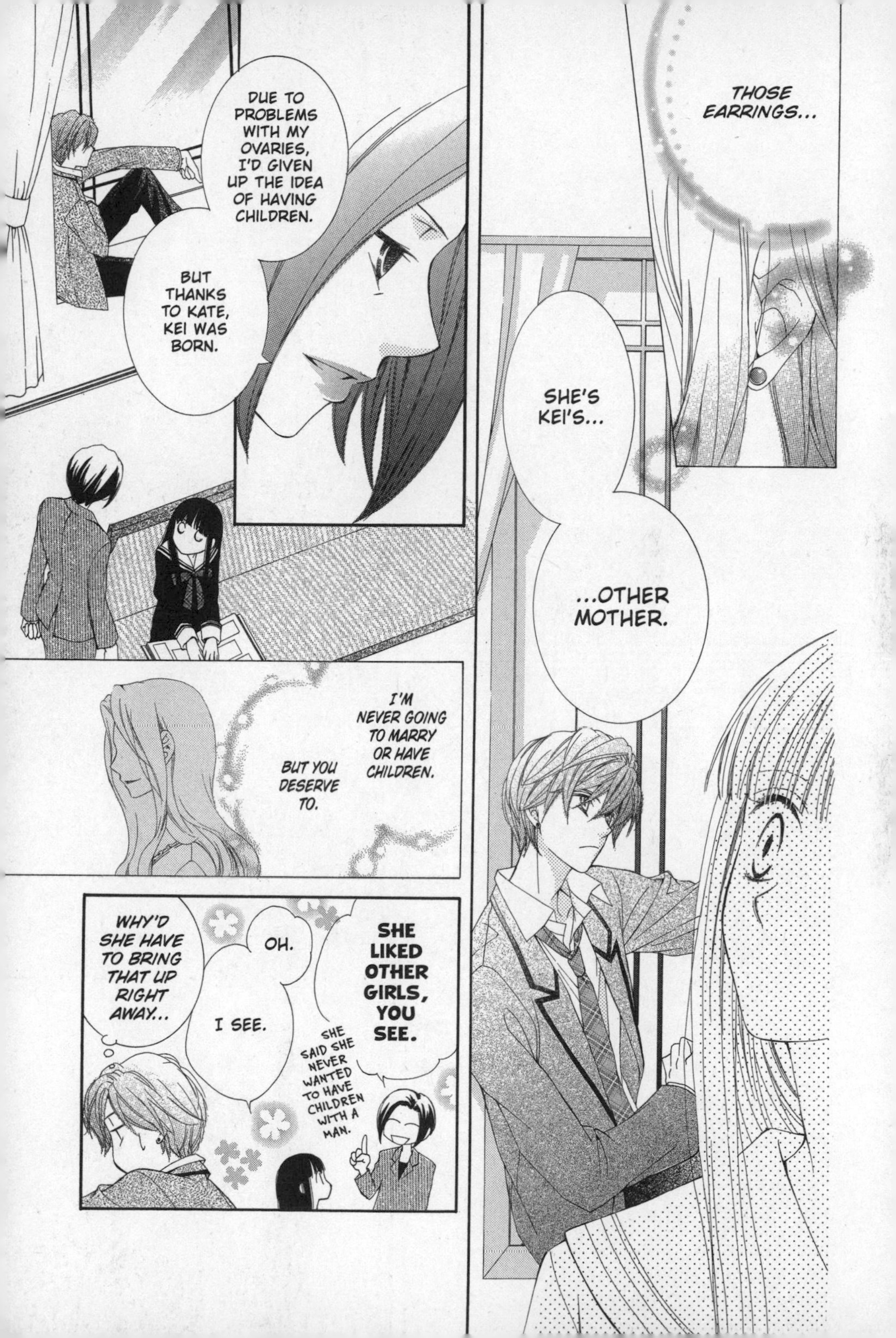
THOSE EARRINGS...
SHE'S KEI'S...
...OTHER MOTHER.
DUE TO PROBLEMS WITH MY OVARIES, I'D GIVEN UP THE IDEA OF HAVING CHILDREN.
BUT THANKS TO KATE, KEI WAS BORN.
I'M NEVER GOING TO MARRY OR HAVE CHILDREN.
BUT YOU DESERVE TO.
SHE LIKED OTHER GIRLS, YOU SEE.
SHE SAID SHE NEVER WANTED TO HAVE CHILDREN WITH A MAN.
OH.
I SEE.
WHY'D SHE HAVE TO BRING THAT UP RIGHT AWAY...

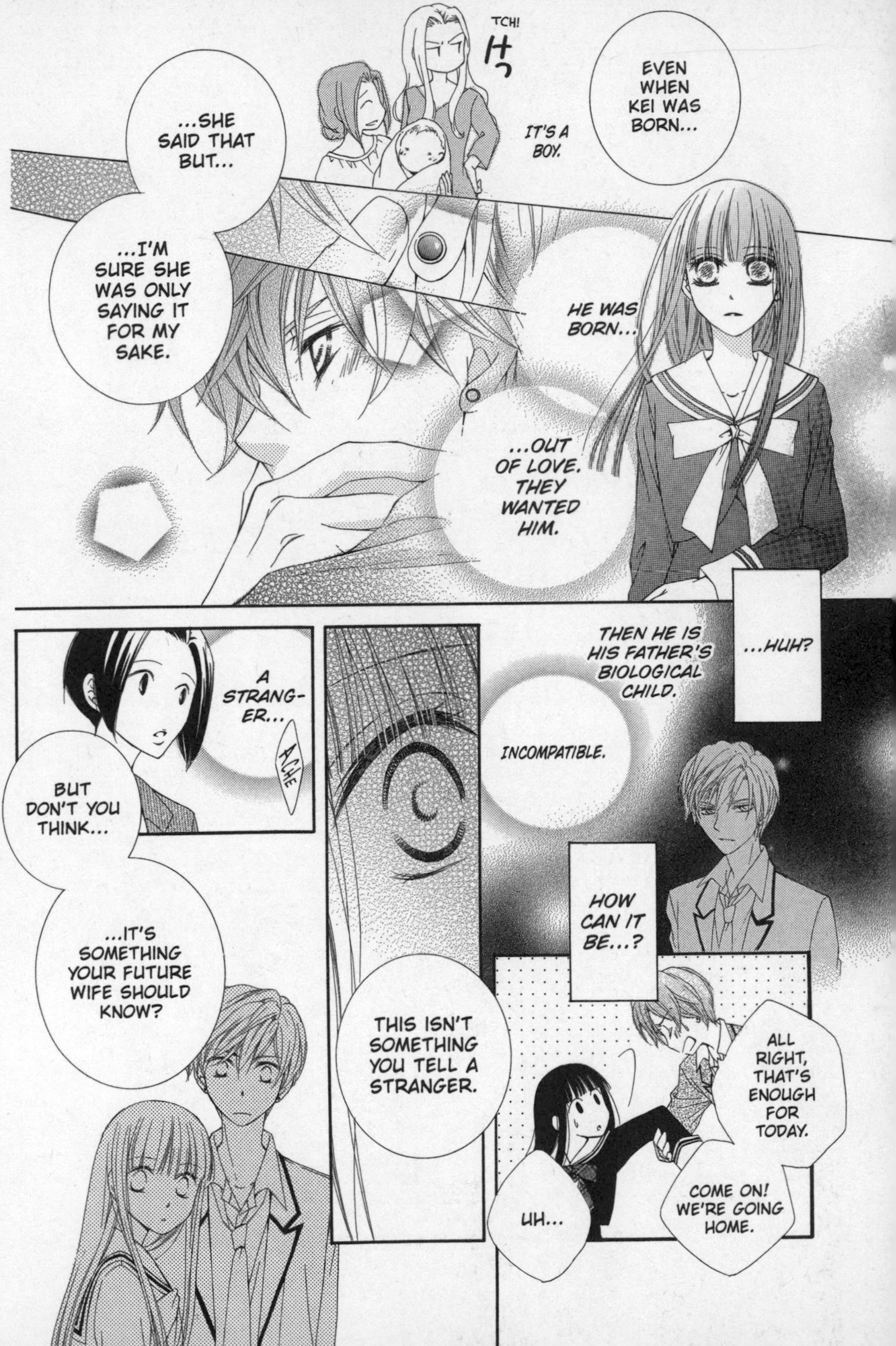
EVEN WHEN KEI WAS BORN...
IT'S A BOY.
TCH!
...SHE SAID THAT BUT...
HE WAS BORN...
...OUT OF LOVE. THEY WANTED HIM.
...I'M SURE SHE WAS ONLY SAYING IT FOR MY SAKE.
...HUH?
THEN HE IS HIS FATHER'S BIOLOGICAL CHILD.
INCOMPATIBLE.
HOW CAN IT BE...?
ALL RIGHT, THAT'S ENOUGH FOR TODAY.
COME ON! WE'RE GOING HOME.
UH...
THIS ISN'T SOMETHING YOU TELL A STRANGER.
A STRANGER...
ACHE
BUT DON'T YOU THINK...
...IT'S SOMETHING YOUR FUTURE WIFE SHOULD KNOW?

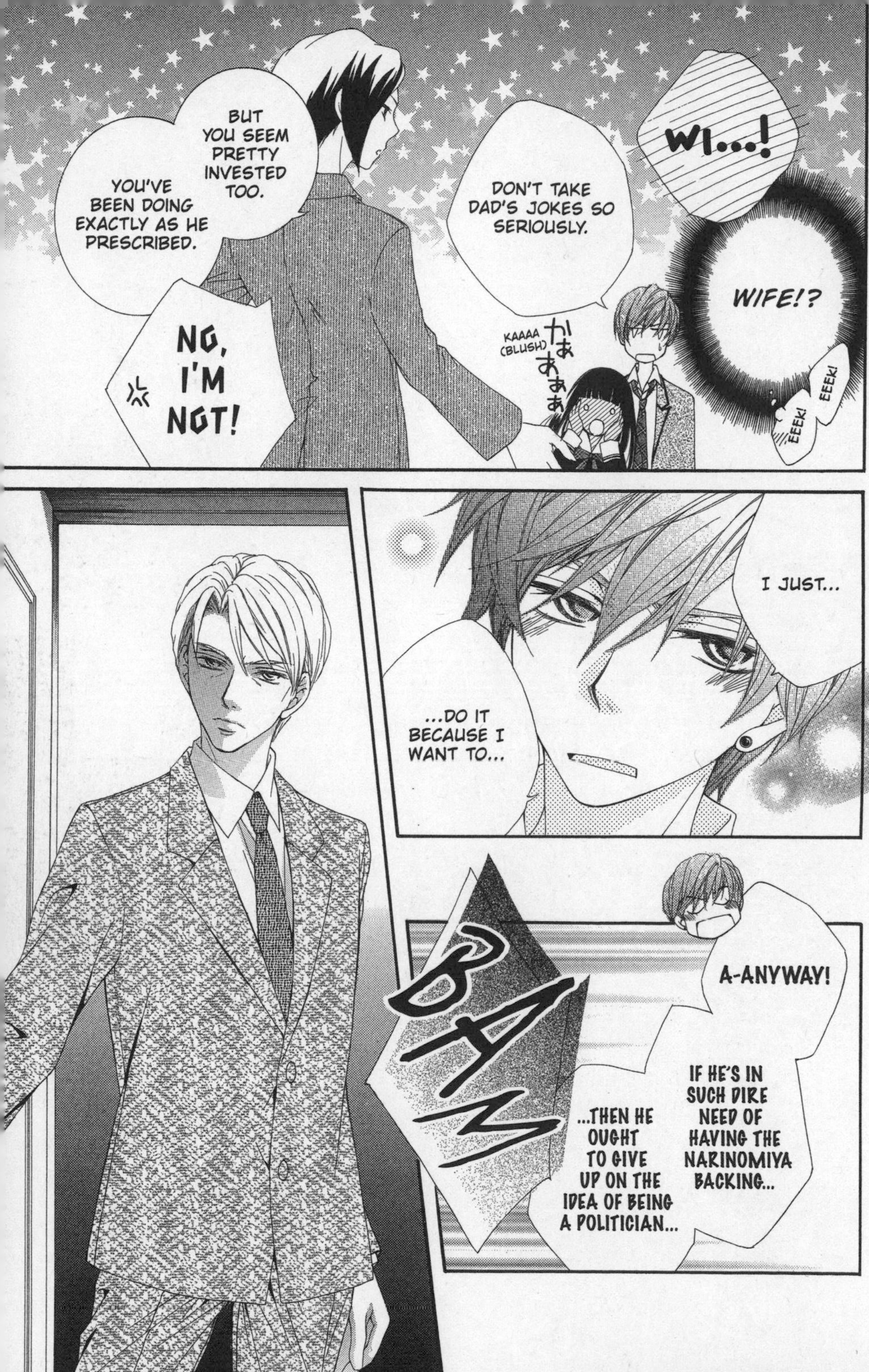
WI...!
WIFE!?
EEEK! EEEK! EEEK!
DON'T TAKE DAD'S JOKES SO SERIOUSLY.
KAAAA (BLUSH) かあああ
BUT YOU SEEM PRETTY INVESTED TOO.
YOU'VE BEEN DOING EXACTLY AS HE PRESCRIBED.
NO, I'M NOT!
I JUST...
...DO IT BECAUSE I WANT TO...
A-ANYWAY!
BAM
IF HE'S IN SUCH DIRE NEED OF HAVING THE NARINOMIYA BACKING...
...THEN HE OUGHT TO GIVE UP ON THE IDEA OF BEING A POLITICIAN...

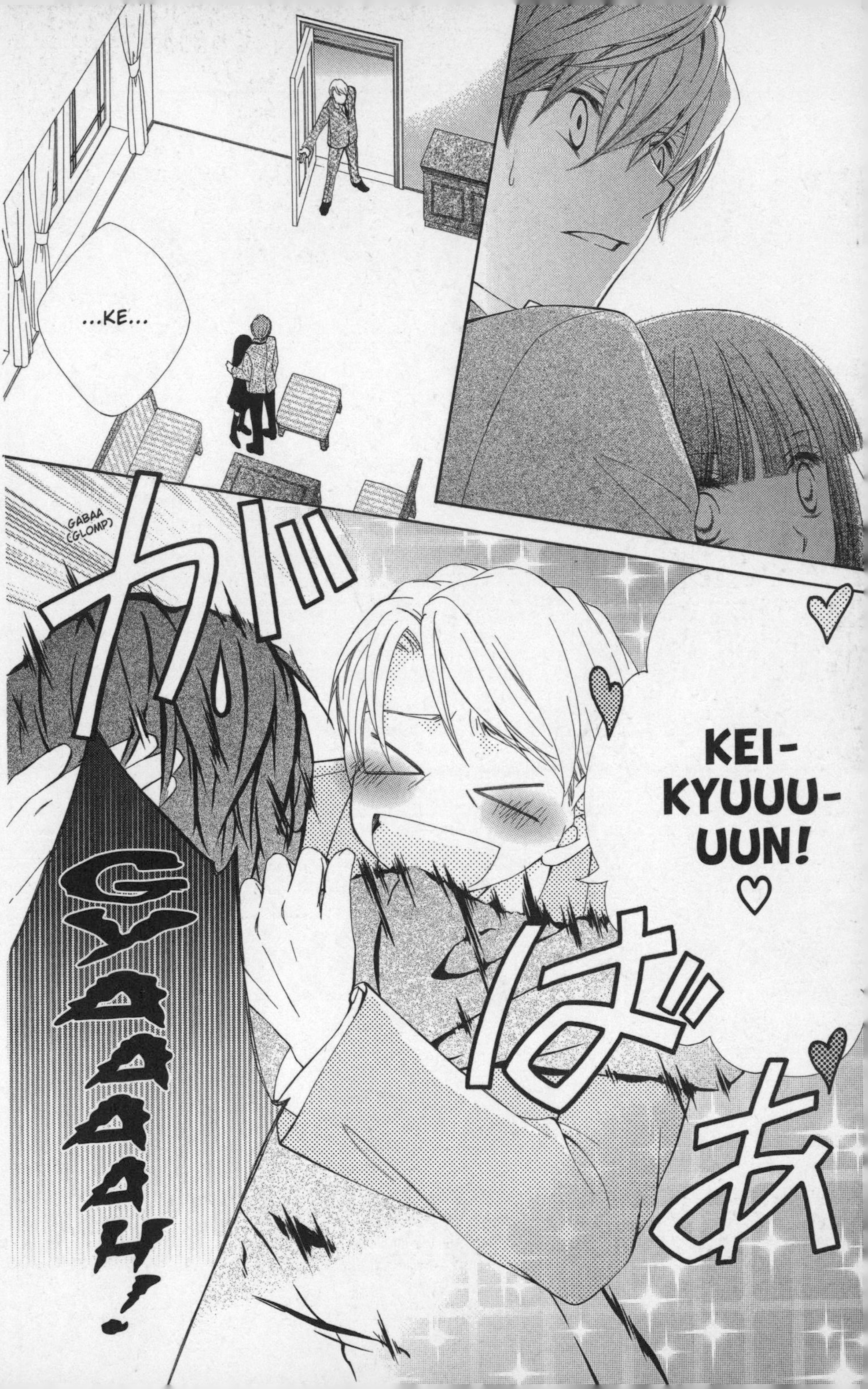
...KE...
KEI-KYUUUU-UUN! ♡
ガばあ
GABAA (GLOMP)
GYAAAAH!

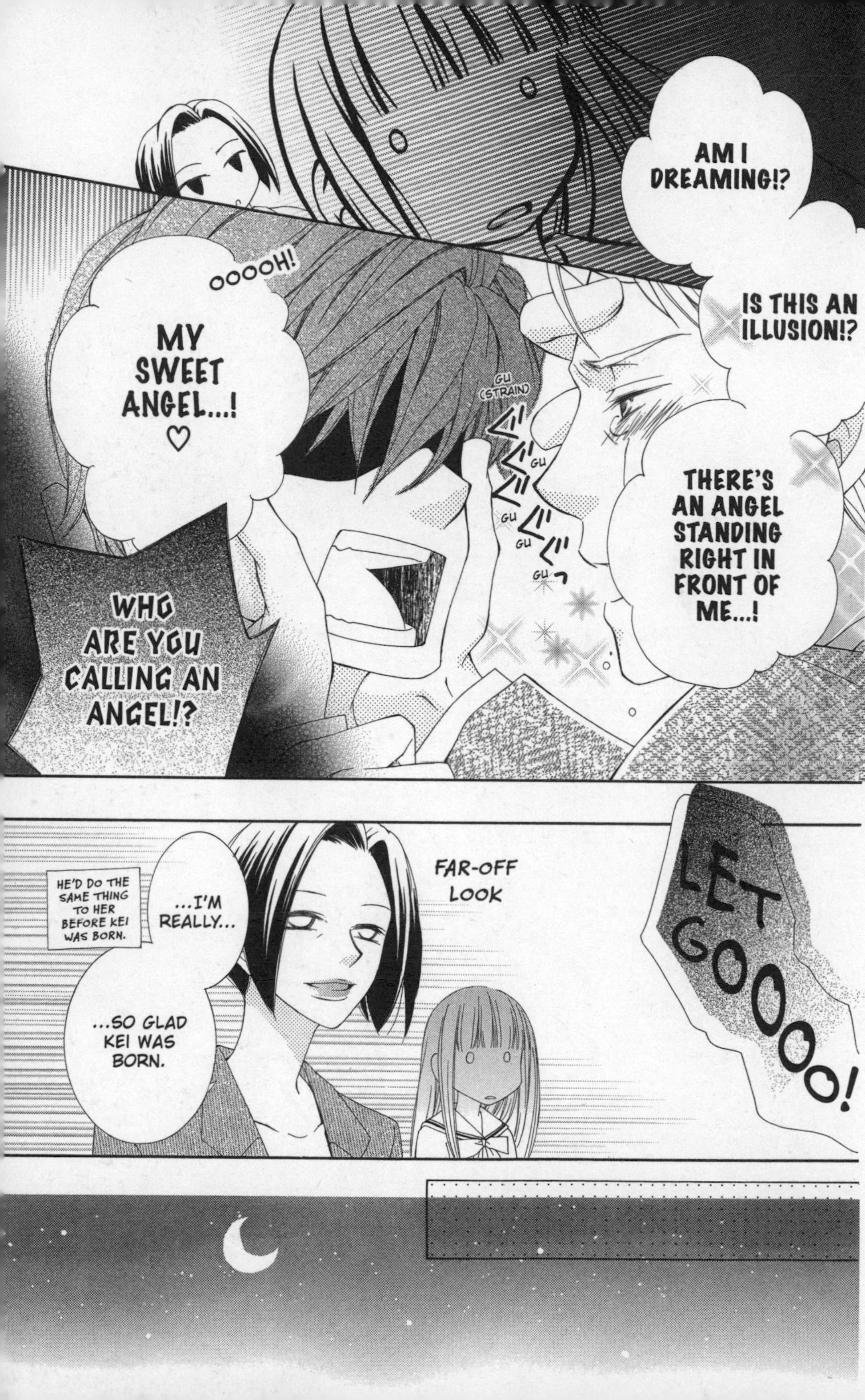
AM I DREAMING!?
IS THIS AN ILLUSION!?
THERE'S AN ANGEL STANDING RIGHT IN FRONT OF ME...!
OOOOH!
MY SWEET ANGEL...! ♡
GU (STRAIN)
GU
GU
GU
GU
WHO ARE YOU CALLING AN ANGEL!?
LET GOOOO!
FAR-OFF LOOK
...I'M REALLY...
...SO GLAD KEI WAS BORN.
HE'D DO THE SAME THING TO HER BEFORE KEI WAS BORN.

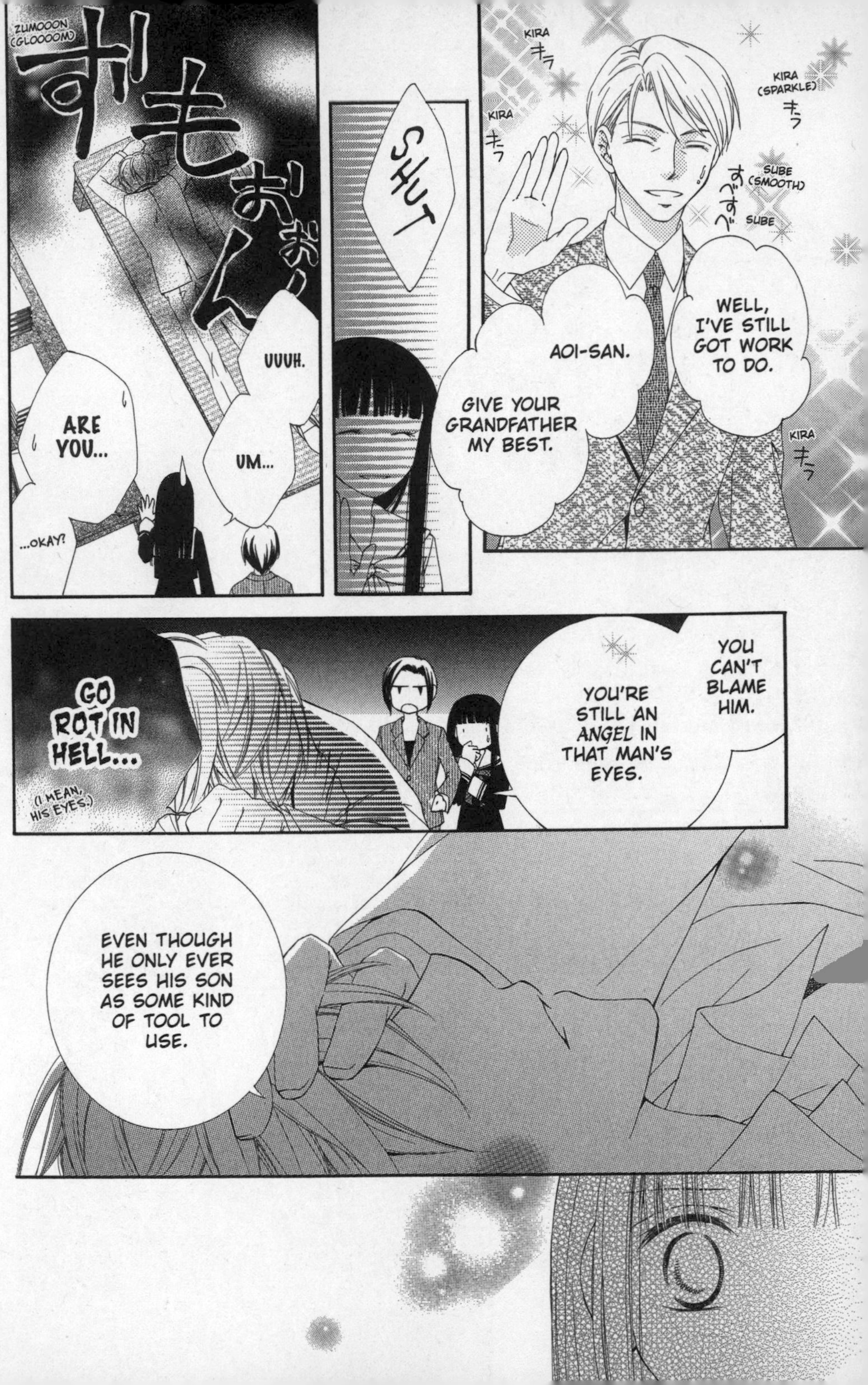
KIRA
キラ
KIRA (SPARKLE)
キラ
KIRA
キラ
SUBE (SMOOTH)
すべすべ
SUBE
WELL, I'VE STILL GOT WORK TO DO.
AOI-SAN.
GIVE YOUR GRANDFATHER MY BEST.
KIRA
キラ
SHUT
ZUMOOON (GLOOOOM)
ずもおおん
UUUH.
UM...
ARE YOU...
...OKAY?
YOU CAN'T BLAME HIM.
YOU'RE STILL AN *ANGEL* IN THAT MAN'S EYES.
GO ROT IN HELL...
(I MEAN, HIS EYES.)
EVEN THOUGH HE ONLY EVER SEES HIS SON AS SOME KIND OF TOOL TO USE.

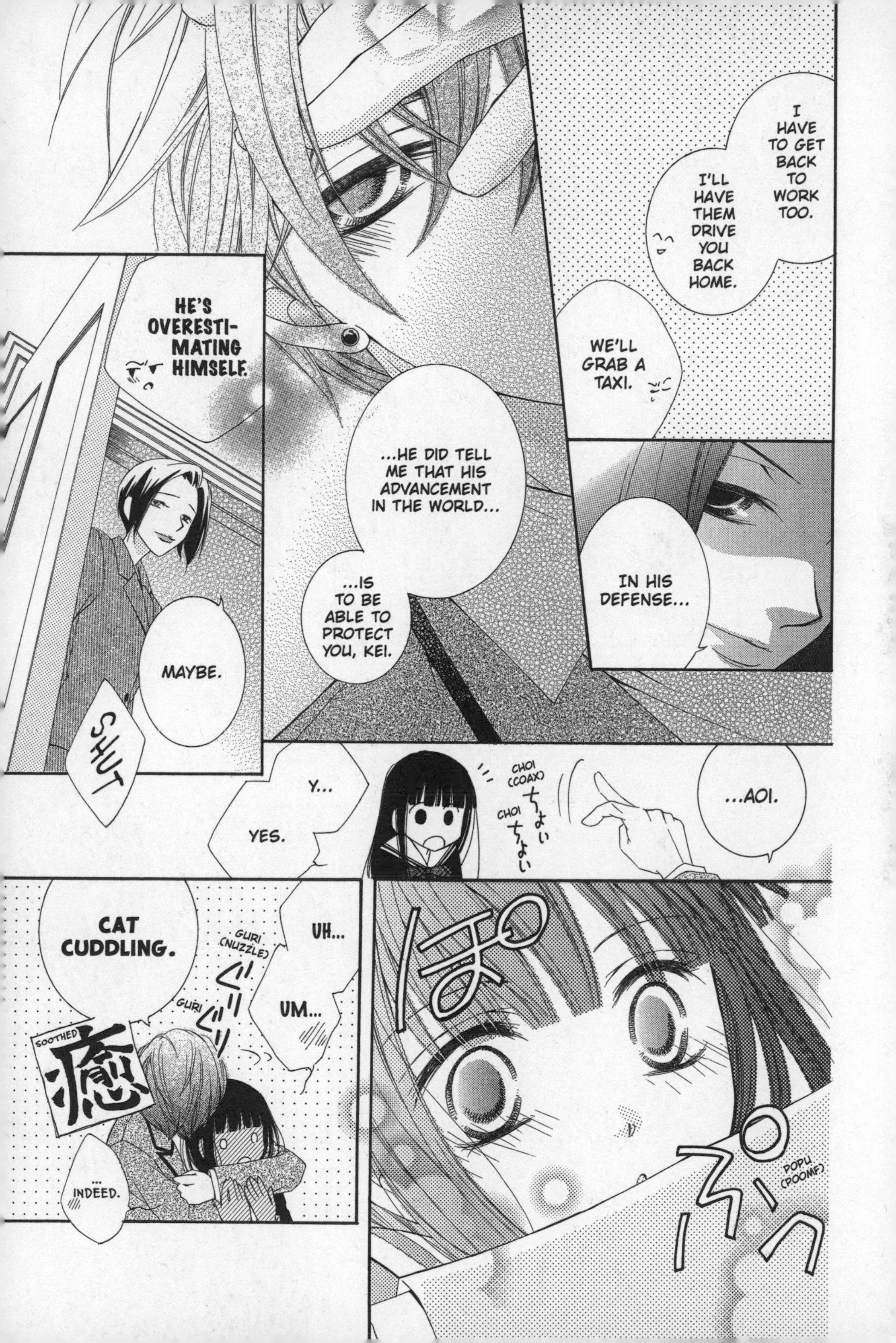
I HAVE TO GET BACK TO WORK TOO.
I'LL HAVE THEM DRIVE YOU BACK HOME.
WE'LL GRAB A TAXI.
IN HIS DEFENSE...
...HE DID TELL ME THAT HIS ADVANCEMENT IN THE WORLD...
...IS TO BE ABLE TO PROTECT YOU, KEI.
HE'S OVERESTI-MATING HIMSELF.
MAYBE.
SHUT
...AOI.
CHOI (COAX) ちょい
CHOI ちょい
Y...
YES.
ぽふっ
POPU (POOMF)
UH...
UM...
CAT CUDDLING.
GURI (NUZZLE) ぐり
GURI ぐり
SOOTHED 癒
...INDEED.

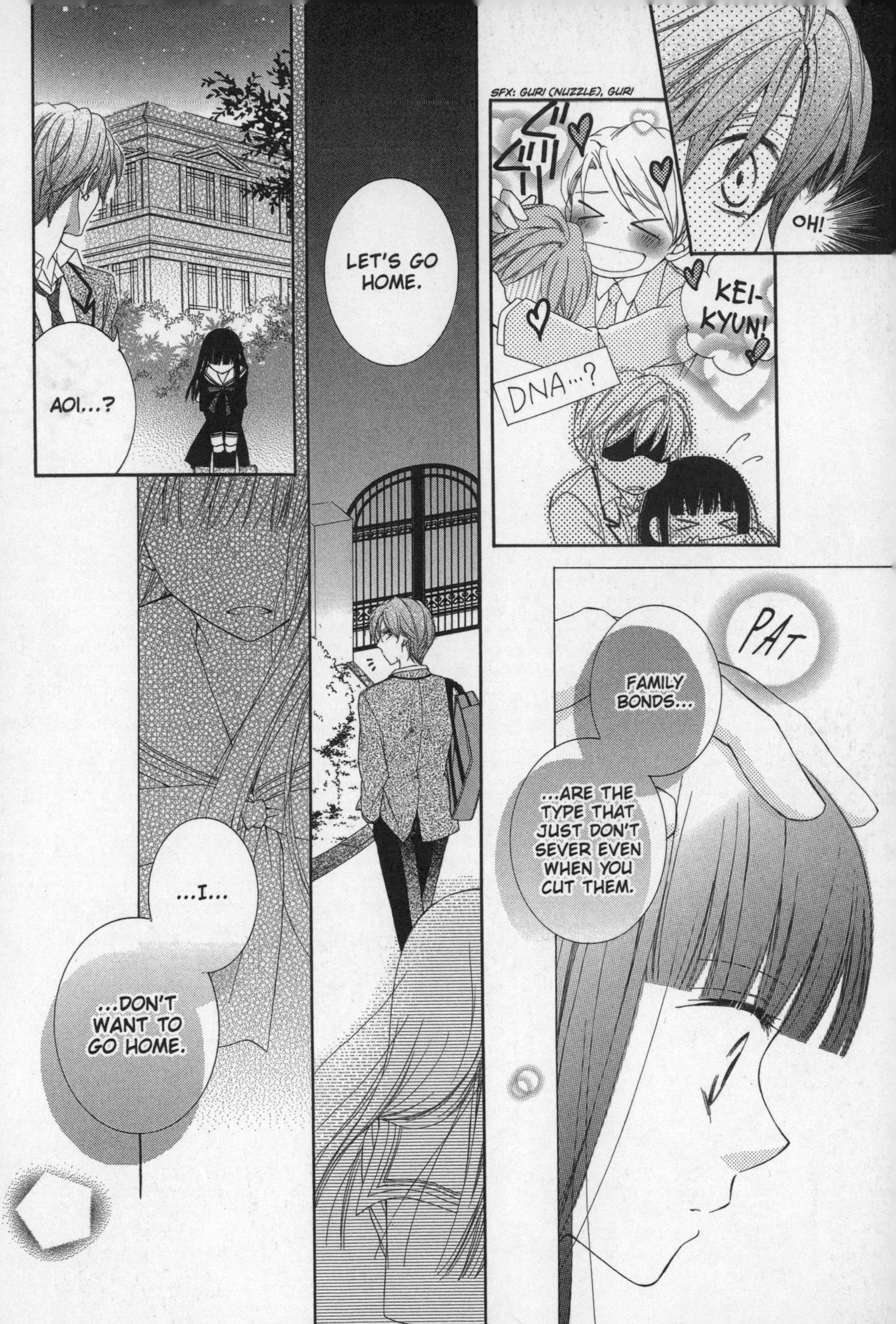
OH!
SFX: GURI (NUZZLE), GURI
KEI-KYUN!
DNA...?
PAT
FAMILY BONDS...
...ARE THE TYPE THAT JUST DON'T SEVER EVEN WHEN YOU CUT THEM.
LET'S GO HOME.
AOI...?
...I...
...DON'T WANT TO GO HOME.

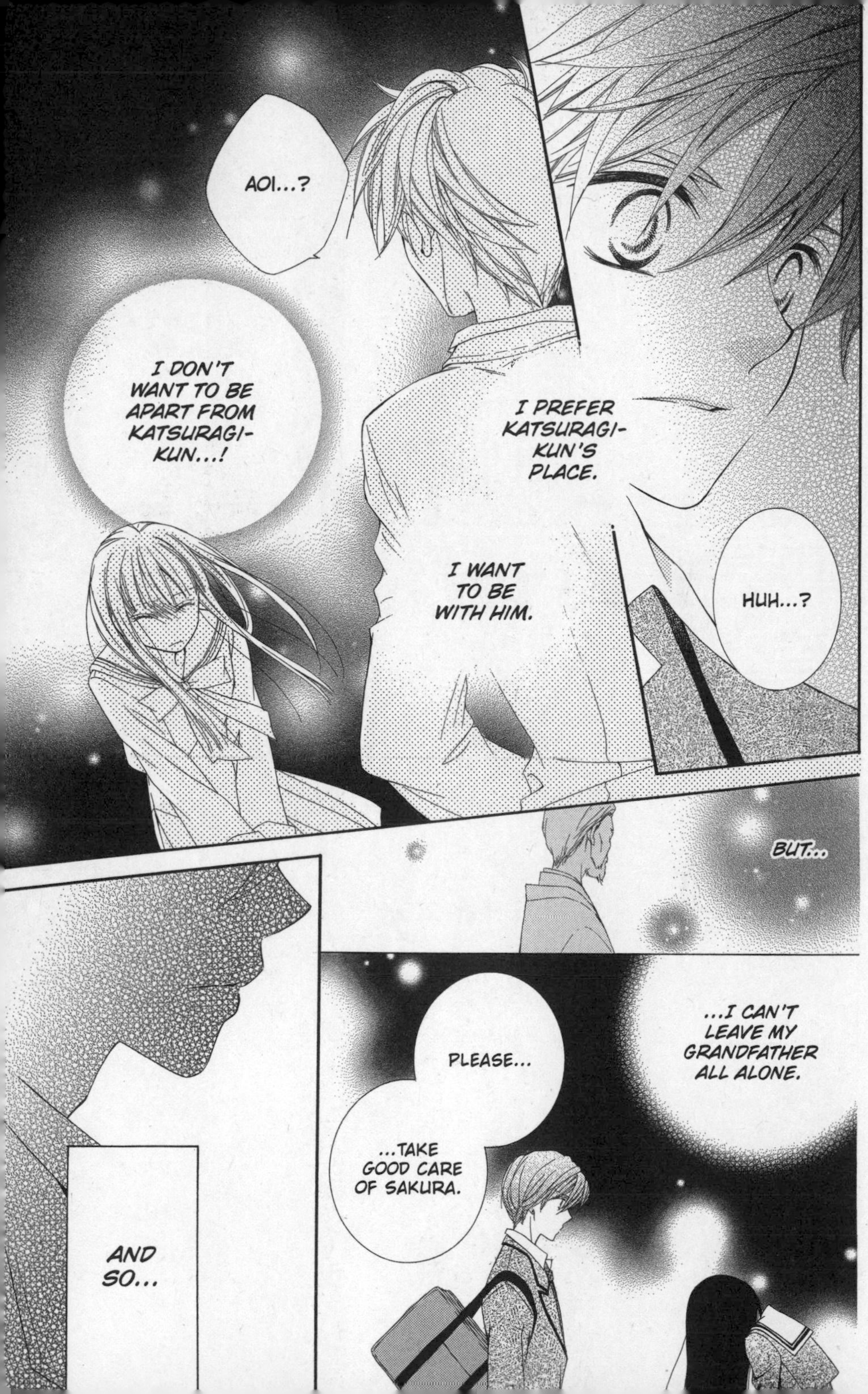
I PREFER KATSURAGI-KUN'S PLACE.
I WANT TO BE WITH HIM.
HUH...?
AOI...?
I DON'T WANT TO BE APART FROM KATSURAGI-KUN...!
BUT...
...I CAN'T LEAVE MY GRANDFATHER ALL ALONE.
PLEASE...
...TAKE GOOD CARE OF SAKURA.
AND SO...

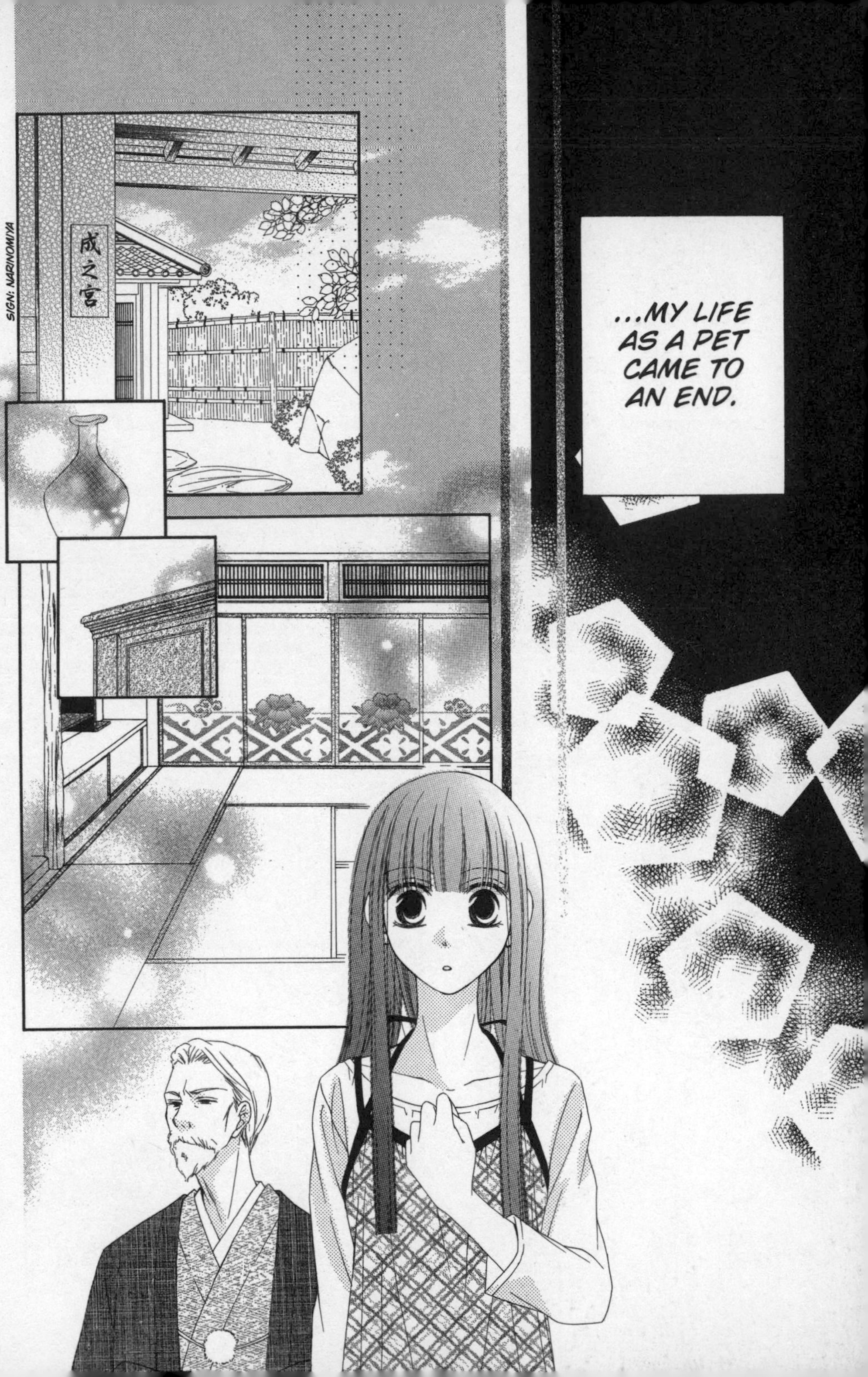
...MY LIFE AS A PET CAME TO AN END.
成之宮
SIGN: NARINOMIYA

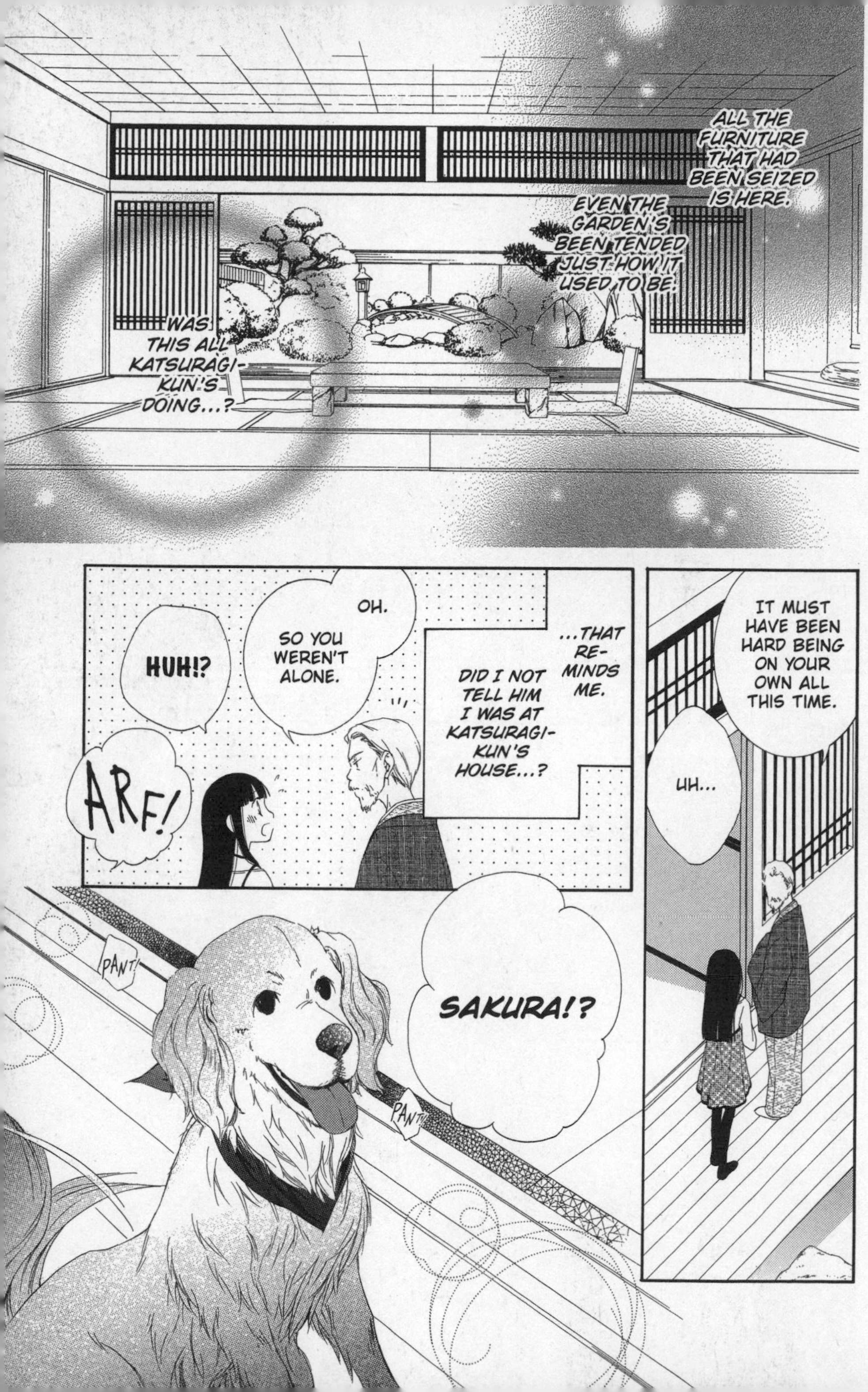

ALL THE FURNITURE THAT HAD BEEN SEIZED IS HERE.
EVEN THE GARDEN'S BEEN TENDED JUST HOW IT USED TO BE.
WAS THIS ALL KATSURAGI-KUN'S DOING...?
IT MUST HAVE BEEN HARD BEING ON YOUR OWN ALL THIS TIME.
UH...
...THAT REMINDS ME.
DID I NOT TELL HIM I WAS AT KATSURAGI-KUN'S HOUSE...?
OH.
SO YOU WEREN'T ALONE.
HUH!?
ARF!
SAKURA!?
PANT!
PANT!

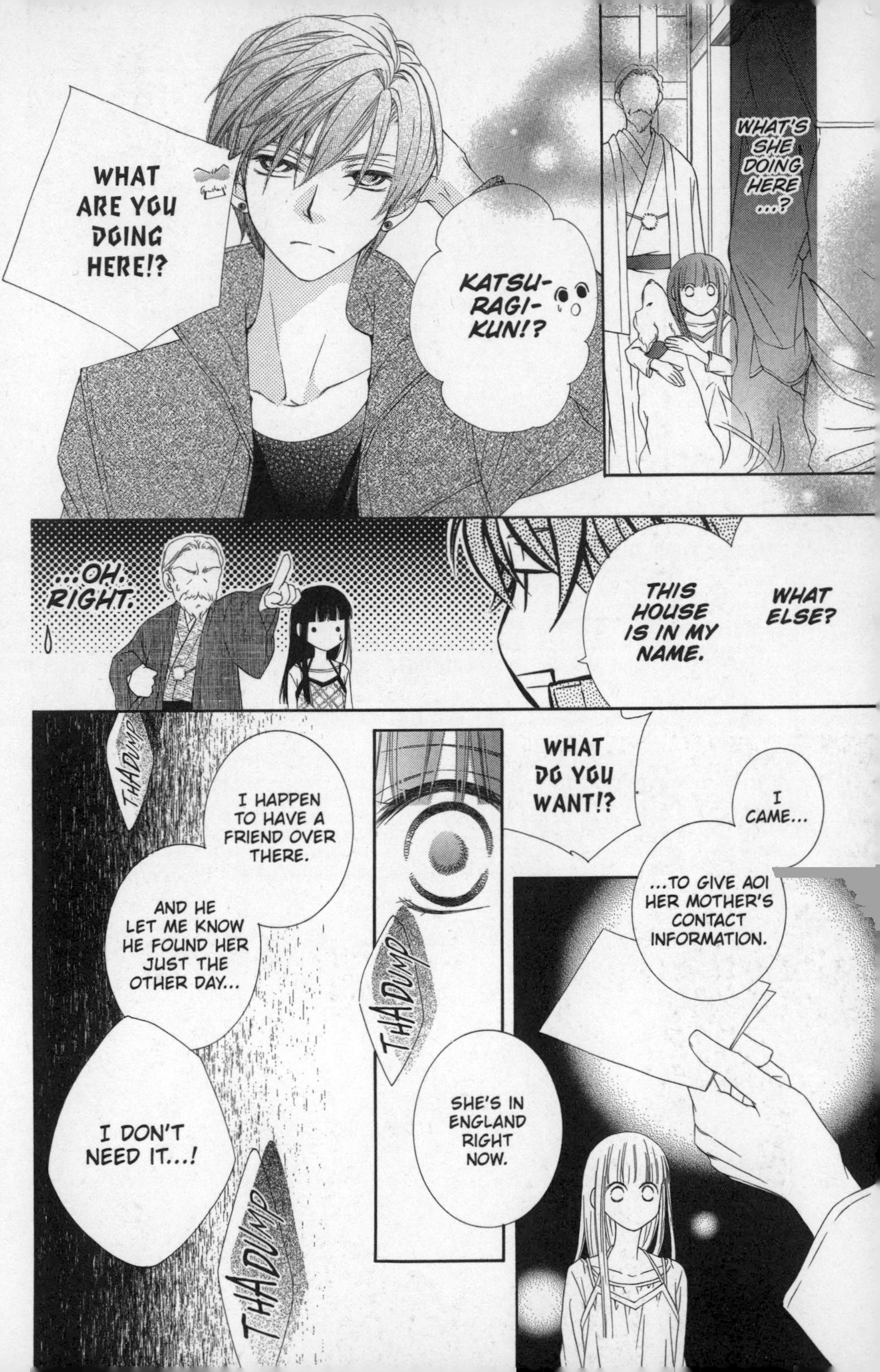
WHAT'S SHE DOING HERE ...?
KATSU-RAGI-KUN!?
WHAT ARE YOU DOING HERE!?
WHAT ELSE?
THIS HOUSE IS IN MY NAME.
...OH. RIGHT.
WHAT DO YOU WANT!?
I CAME...
...TO GIVE AOI HER MOTHER'S CONTACT INFORMATION.
SHE'S IN ENGLAND RIGHT NOW.
THADUMP
I HAPPEN TO HAVE A FRIEND OVER THERE.
AND HE LET ME KNOW HE FOUND HER JUST THE OTHER DAY...
I DON'T NEED IT...!
THADUMP
THADUMP

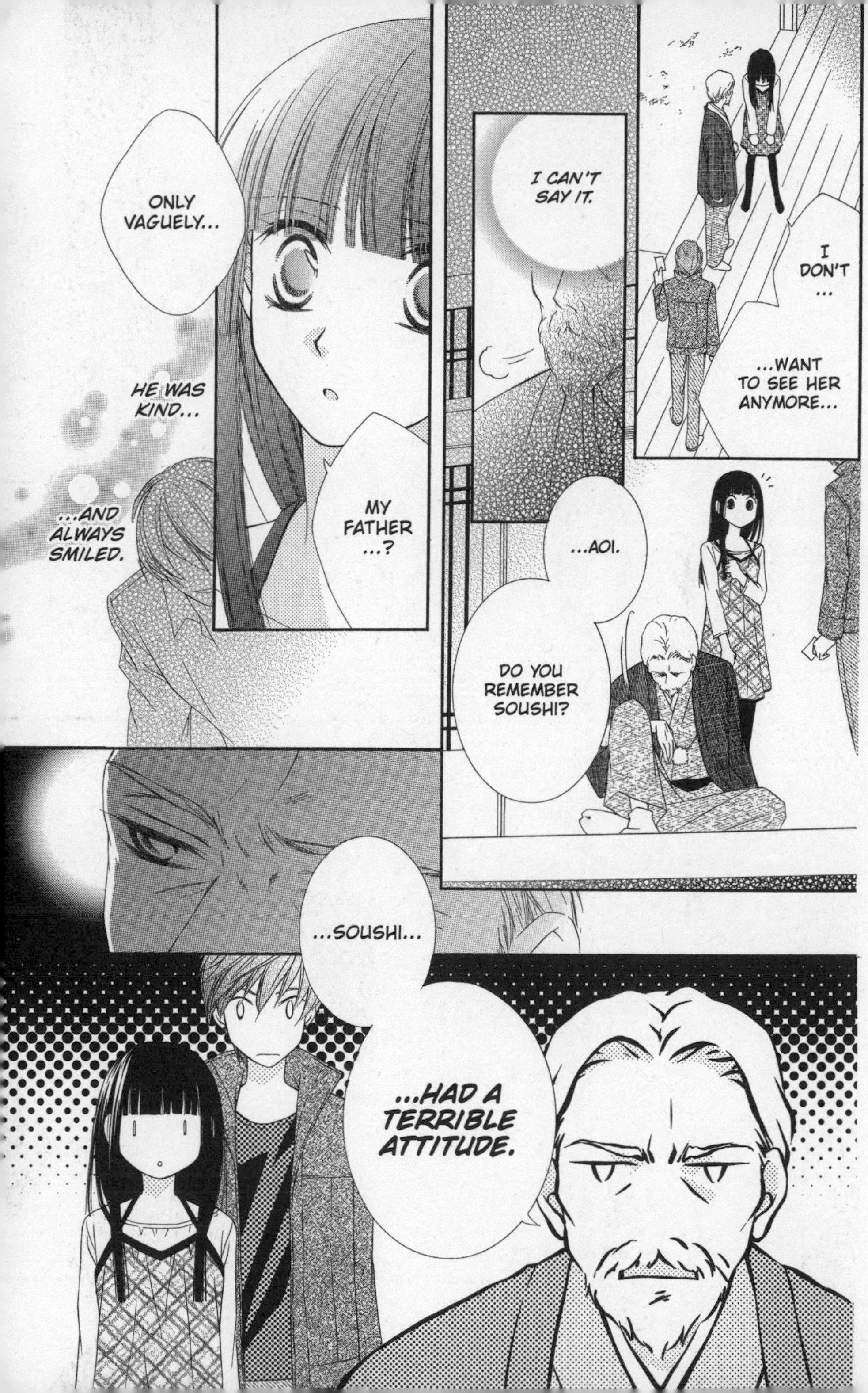

I DON'T ...
...WANT TO SEE HER ANYMORE...
I CAN'T SAY IT.
...AOI.
DO YOU REMEMBER SOUSHI?
MY FATHER ...?
ONLY VAGUELY...
HE WAS KIND...
...AND ALWAYS SMILED.
...SOUSHI...
...HAD A TERRIBLE ATTITUDE.

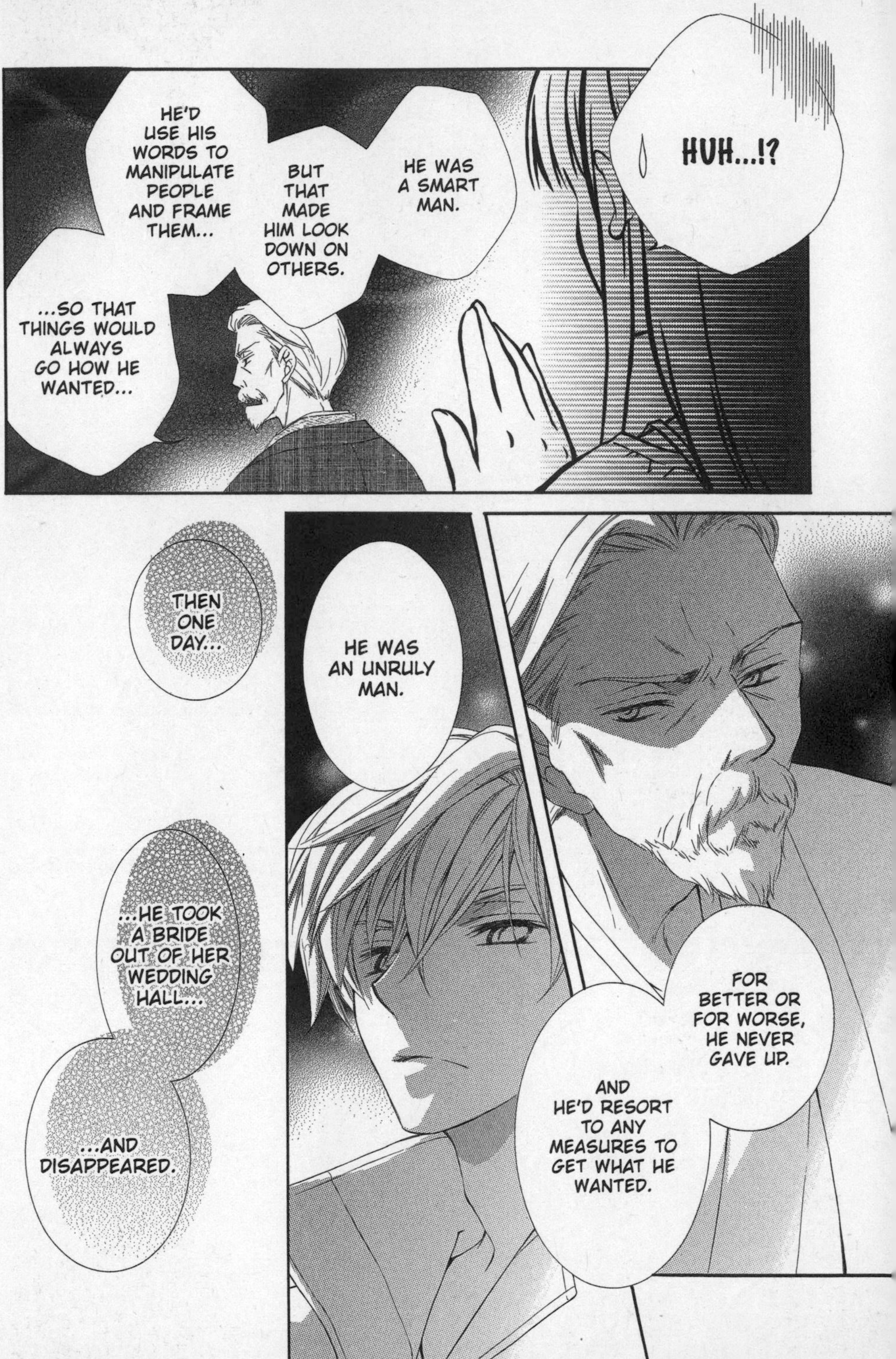
HUH...!?
HE WAS A SMART MAN.
BUT THAT MADE HIM LOOK DOWN ON OTHERS.
HE'D USE HIS WORDS TO MANIPULATE PEOPLE AND FRAME THEM...
...SO THAT THINGS WOULD ALWAYS GO HOW HE WANTED...
HE WAS AN UNRULY MAN.
FOR BETTER OR FOR WORSE, HE NEVER GAVE UP.
AND HE'D RESORT TO ANY MEASURES TO GET WHAT HE WANTED.
THEN ONE DAY...
...HE TOOK A BRIDE OUT OF HER WEDDING HALL...
...AND DISAPPEARED.

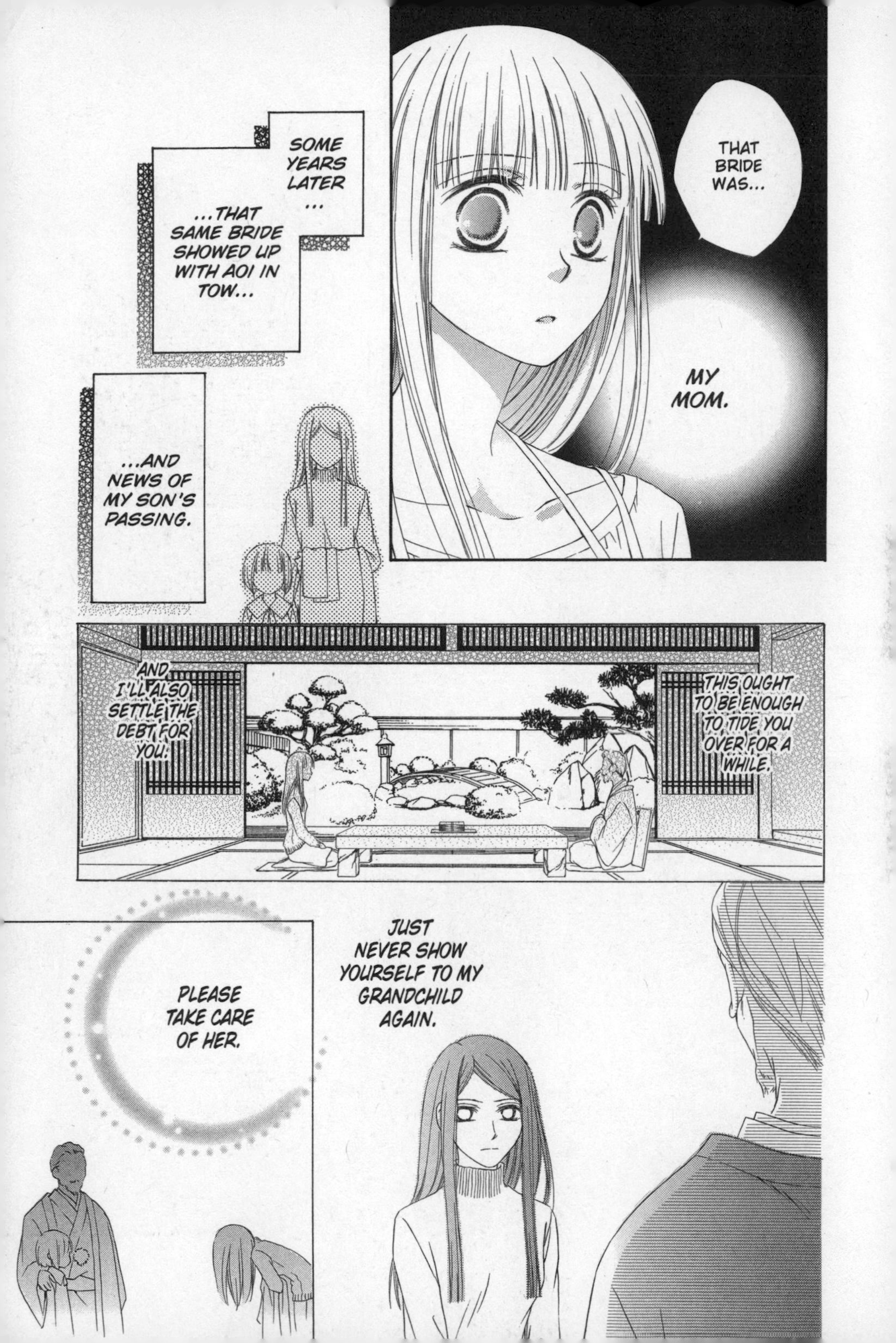
THAT BRIDE WAS...
MY MOM.
SOME YEARS LATER...
...THAT SAME BRIDE SHOWED UP WITH AOI IN TOW...
...AND NEWS OF MY SON'S PASSING.
THIS OUGHT TO BE ENOUGH TO TIDE YOU OVER FOR A WHILE.
AND I'LL ALSO SETTLE THE DEBT FOR YOU.
JUST NEVER SHOW YOURSELF TO MY GRANDCHILD AGAIN.
PLEASE TAKE CARE OF HER.

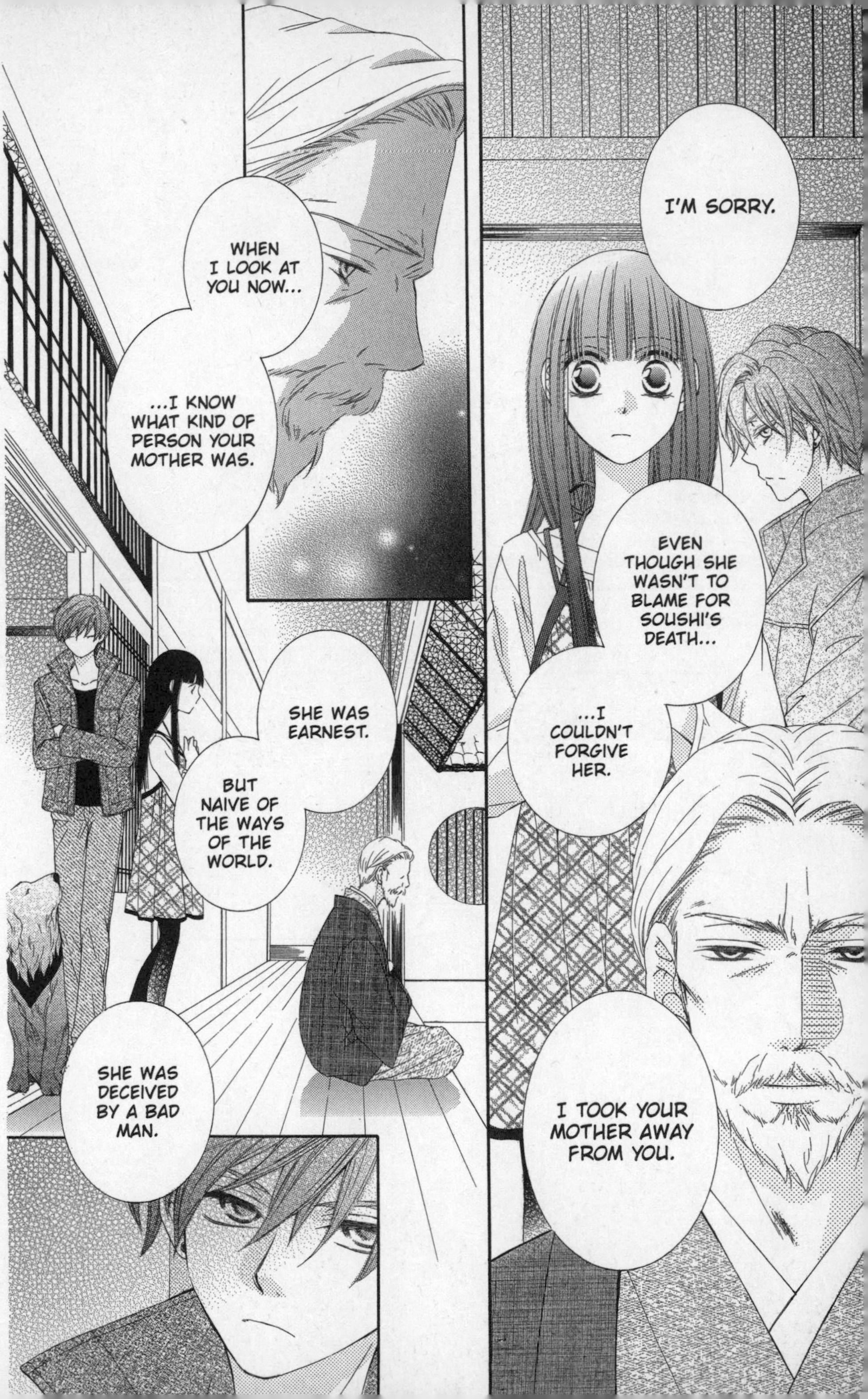
I'M SORRY.
EVEN THOUGH SHE WASN'T TO BLAME FOR SOUSHI'S DEATH...
...I COULDN'T FORGIVE HER.
I TOOK YOUR MOTHER AWAY FROM YOU.
WHEN I LOOK AT YOU NOW...
...I KNOW WHAT KIND OF PERSON YOUR MOTHER WAS.
SHE WAS EARNEST.
BUT NAIVE OF THE WAYS OF THE WORLD.
SHE WAS DECEIVED BY A BAD MAN.

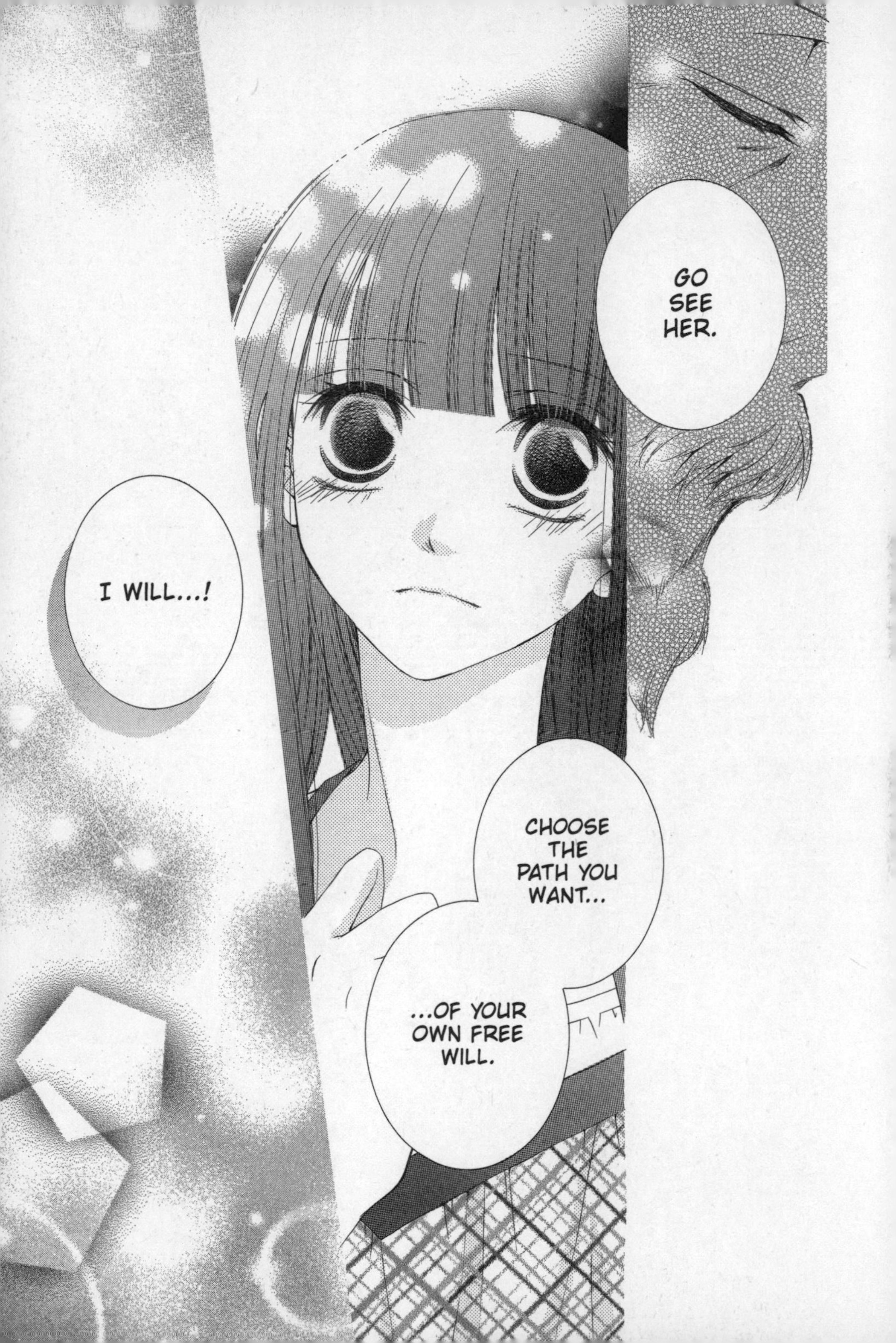
GO SEE HER.
CHOOSE THE PATH YOU WANT...
...OF YOUR OWN FREE WILL.
I WILL...!

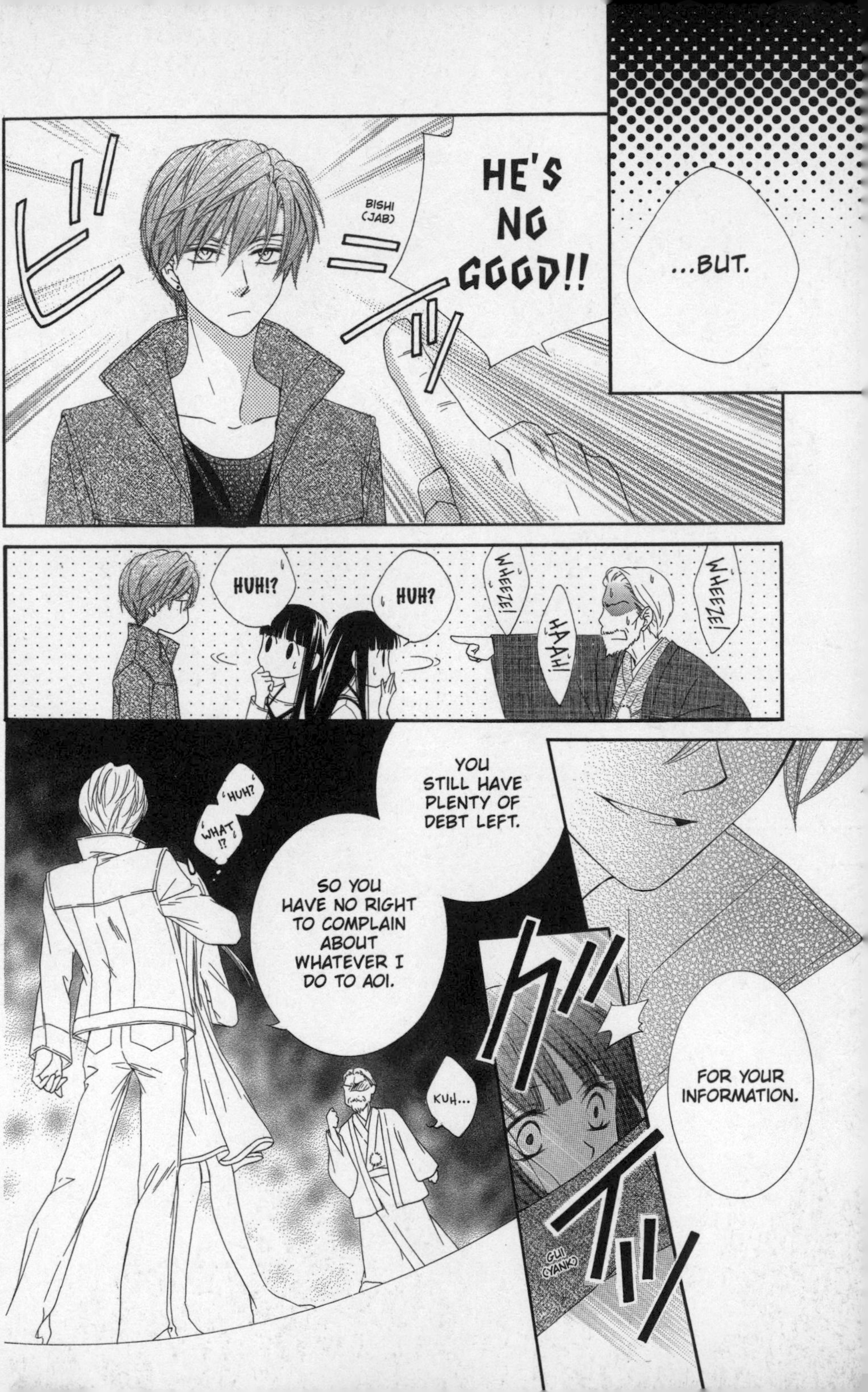
...BUT.
HE'S NO GOOD!!
BISHI (JAB)
WHEEZE!
HAAH!
WHEEZE!
HUH?
HUH!?
FOR YOUR INFORMATION.
GUI (YANK)
YOU STILL HAVE PLENTY OF DEBT LEFT.
SO YOU HAVE NO RIGHT TO COMPLAIN ABOUT WHATEVER I DO TO AOI.
'HUH?
WHAT!?
KUH...

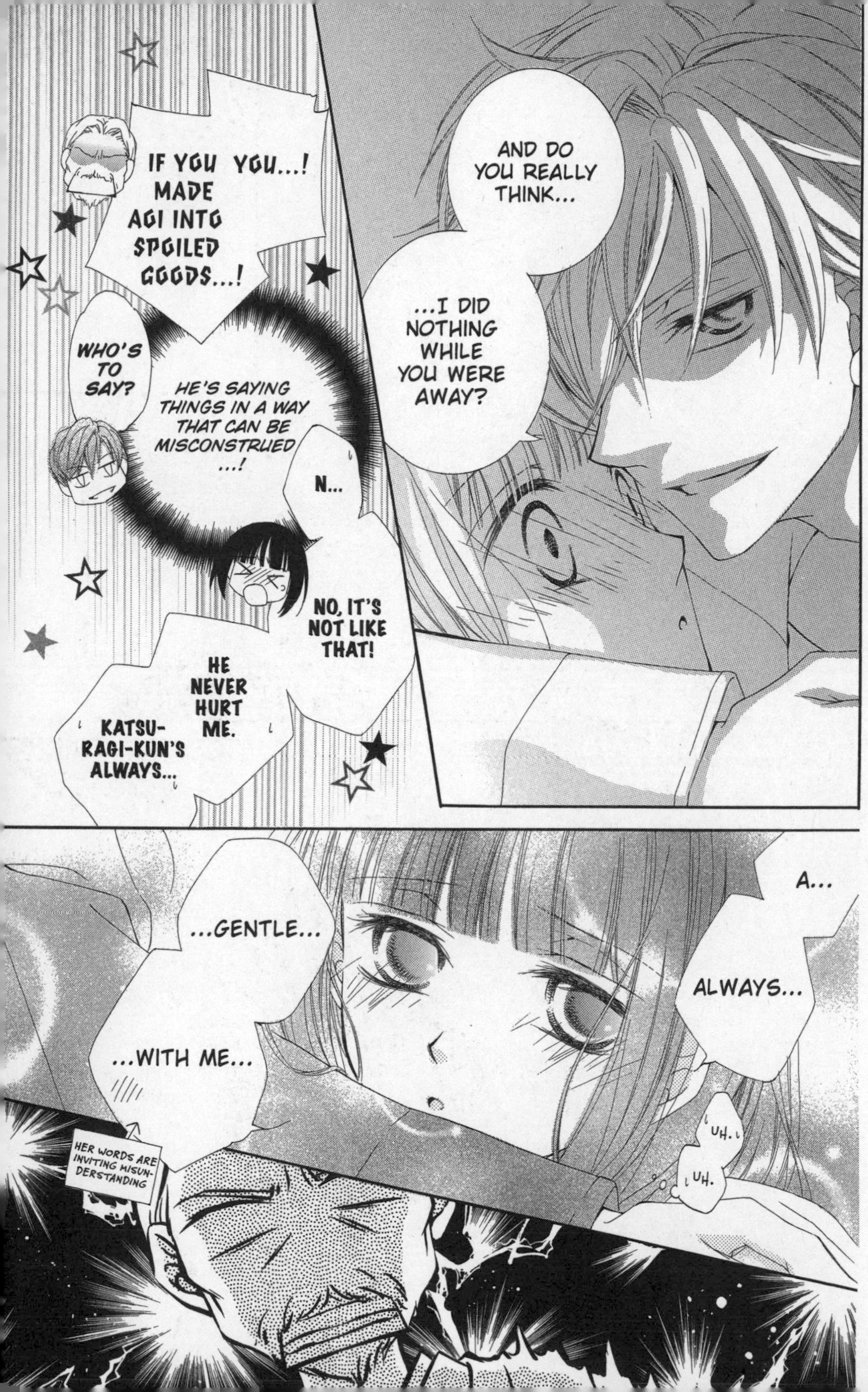
AND DO YOU REALLY THINK...
...I DID NOTHING WHILE YOU WERE AWAY?
IF YOU YOU...! MADE AGI INTO SPOILED GOODS...!
WHO'S TO SAY?
HE'S SAYING THINGS IN A WAY THAT CAN BE MISCONSTRUED ...!
N...
NO, IT'S NOT LIKE THAT!
HE NEVER HURT ME.
KATSU-RAGI-KUN'S ALWAYS...
A...
ALWAYS...
...GENTLE...
...WITH ME...
UH.
UH.
HER WORDS ARE INVITING MISUN-DERSTANDING

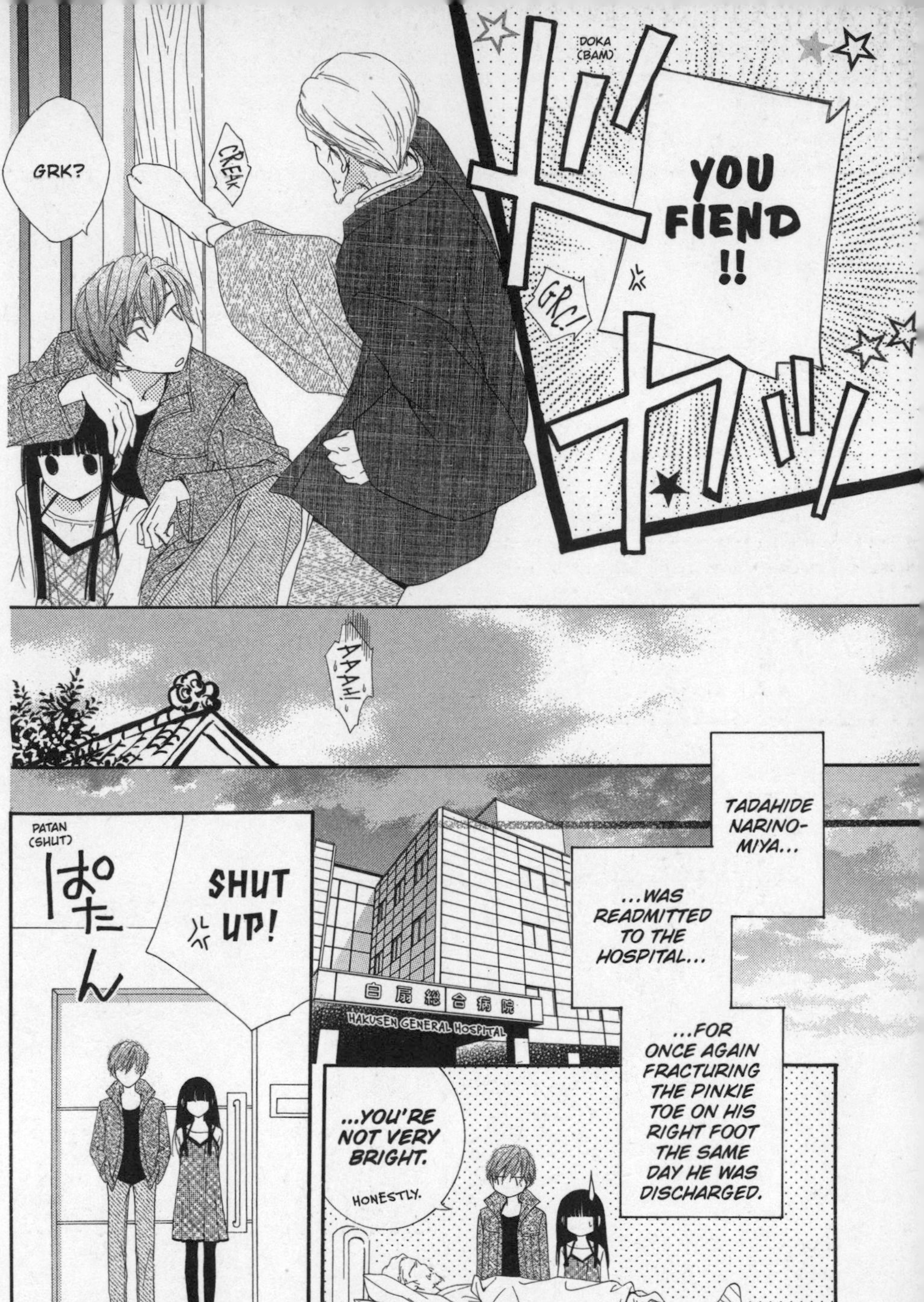
DOKA (BAM)
YOU FIEND !!
GRC!
CREEK
GRK?
AAAH!
TADAHIDE NARINO-MIYA...
...WAS READMITTED TO THE HOSPITAL...
白扇総合病院
HAKUSEN GENERAL HOSPITAL
...FOR ONCE AGAIN FRACTURING THE PINKIE TOE ON HIS RIGHT FOOT THE SAME DAY HE WAS DISCHARGED.
...YOU'RE NOT VERY BRIGHT.
HONESTLY.
PATAN (SHUT)
ぱたん
SHUT UP!

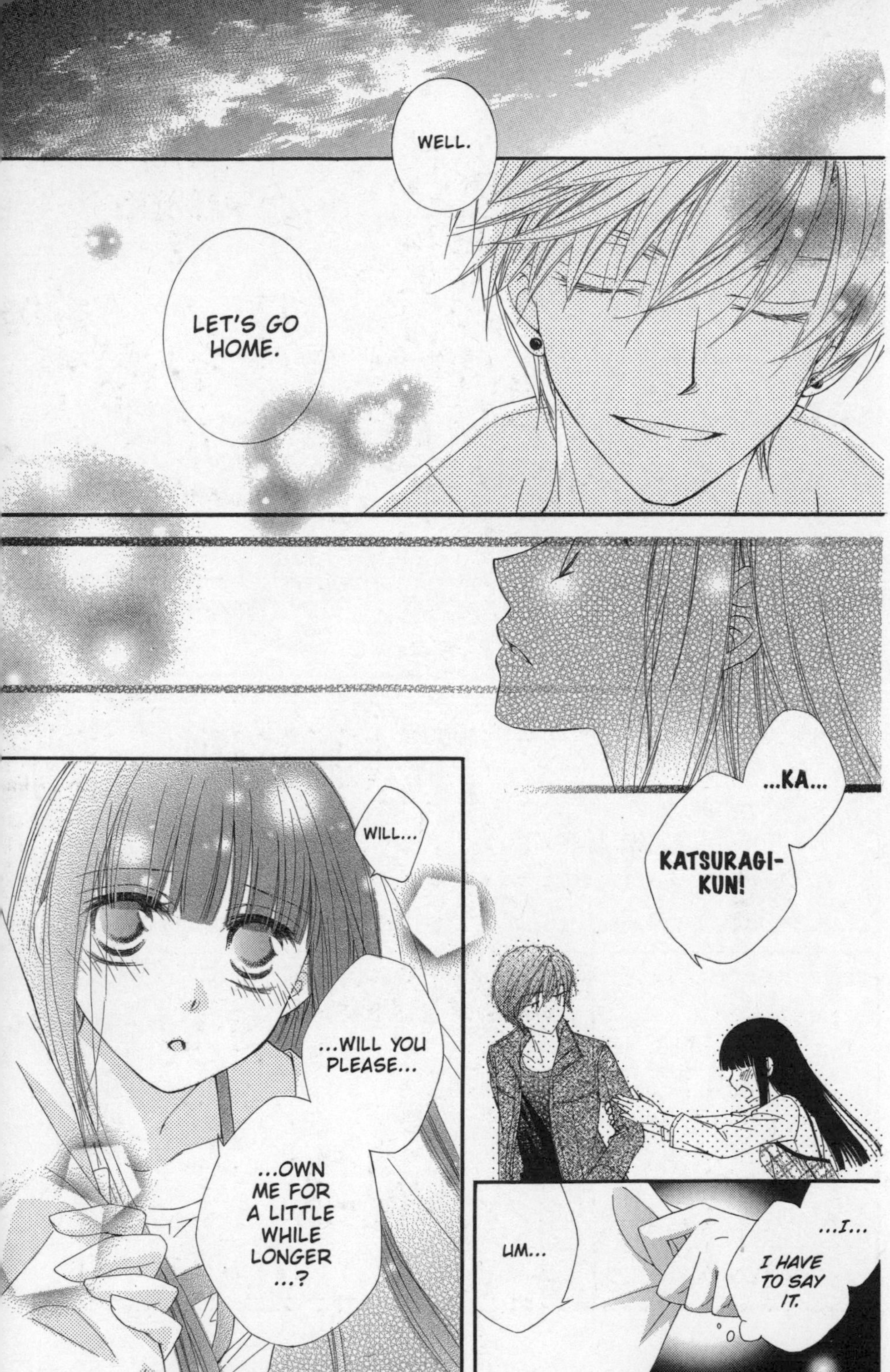
WELL.
LET'S GO HOME.
...KA...
KATSURAGI-KUN!
...I...
I HAVE TO SAY IT.
UM...
WILL...
...WILL YOU PLEASE...
...OWN ME FOR A LITTLE WHILE LONGER ...?

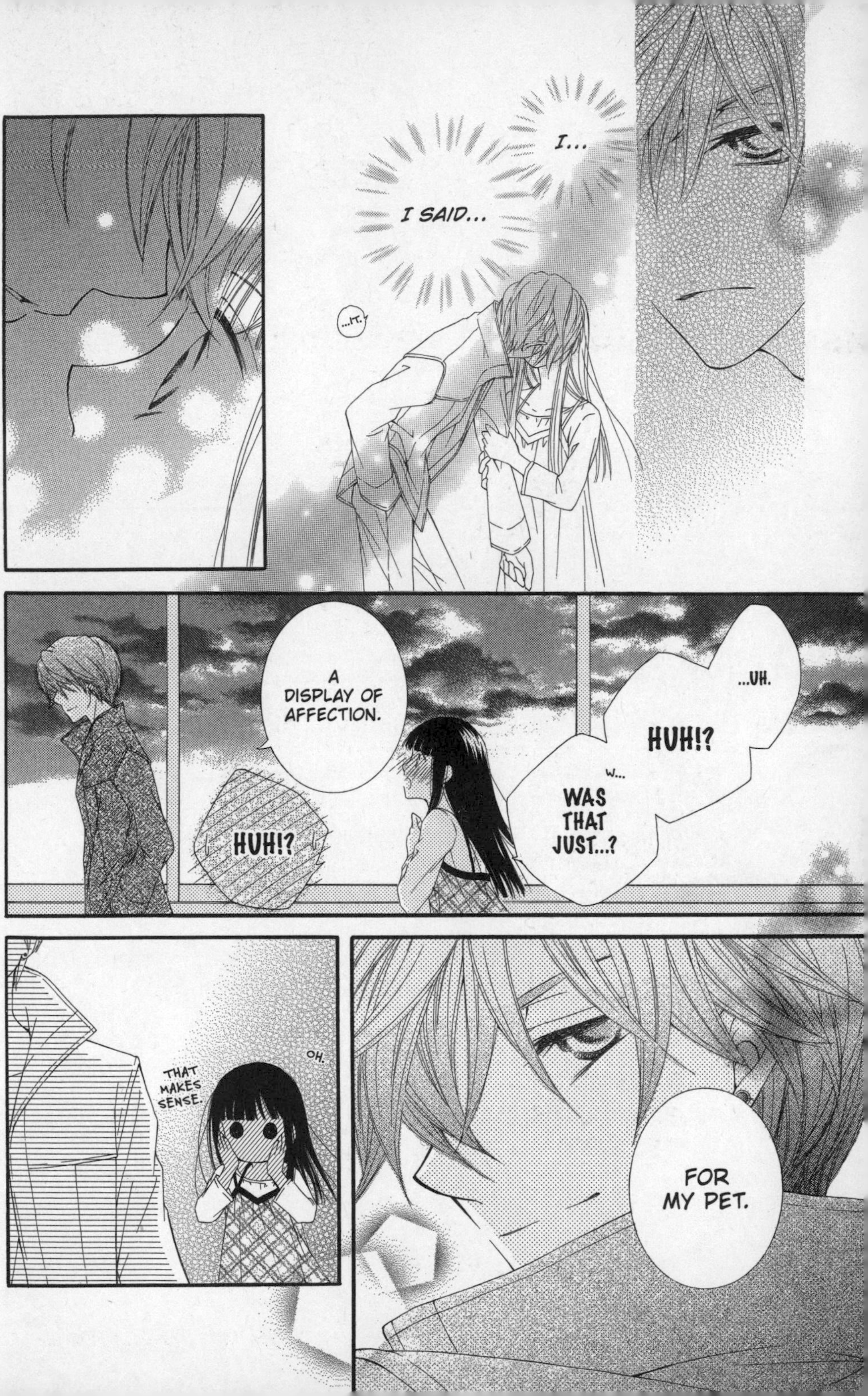
I...
I SAID...
...IT.
...UH.
HUH!?
W...
WAS THAT JUST...?
A DISPLAY OF AFFECTION.
HUH!?
FOR MY PET.
OH.
THAT MAKES SENSE.

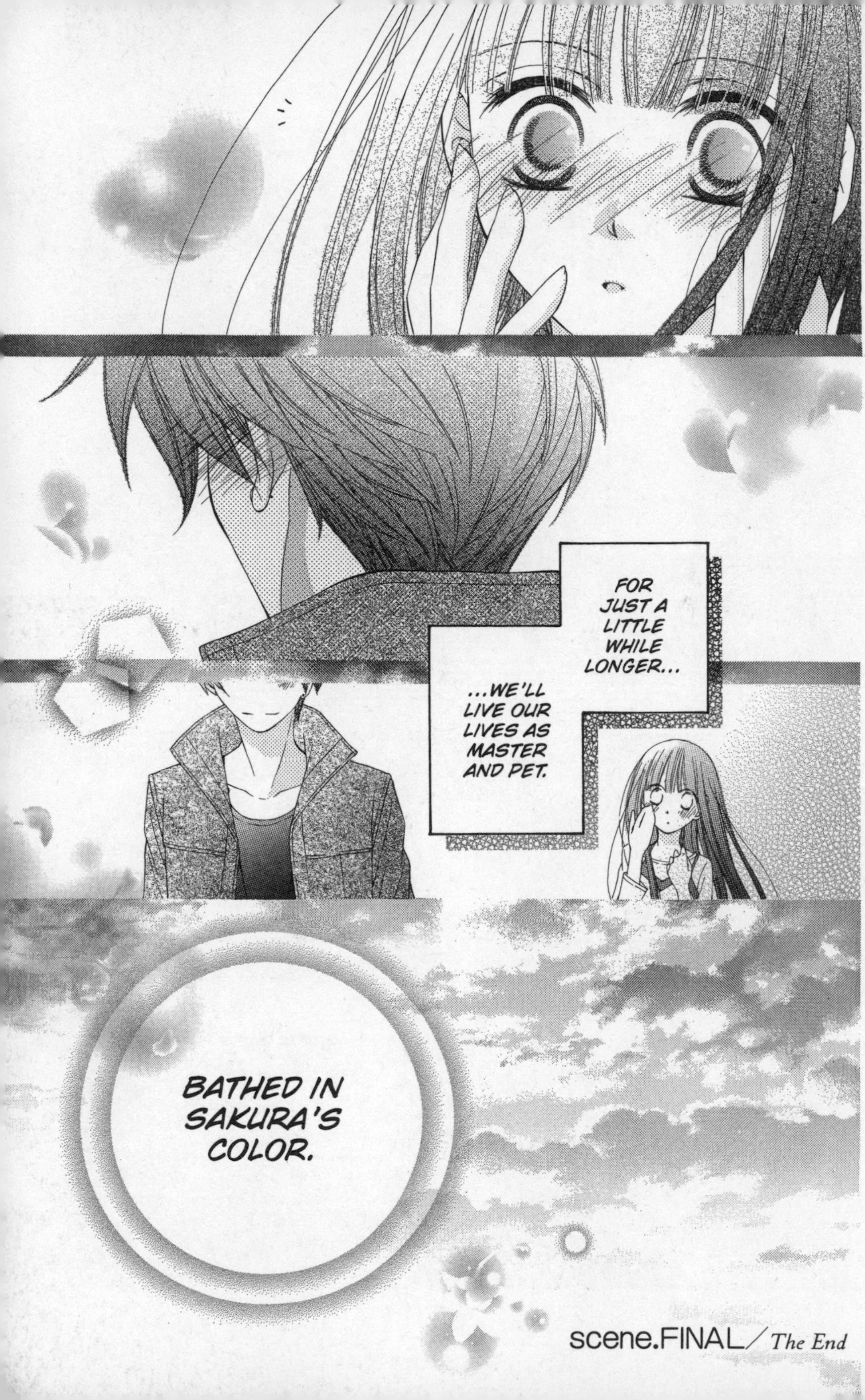
FOR JUST A LITTLE WHILE LONGER...
...WE'LL LIVE OUR LIVES AS MASTER AND PET.
BATHED IN SAKURA'S COLOR.
scene.FINAL/ The End

AFTERWORD

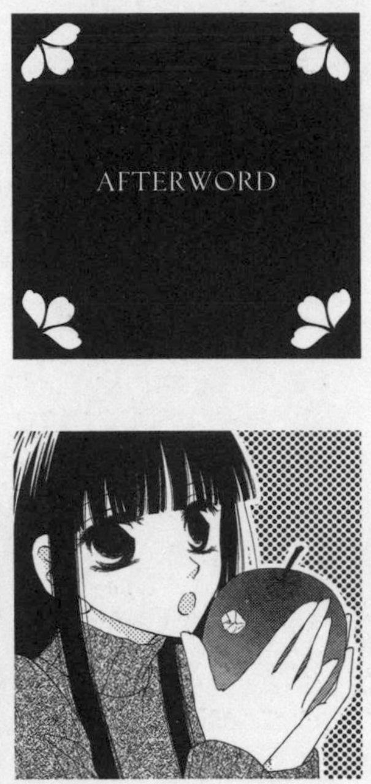

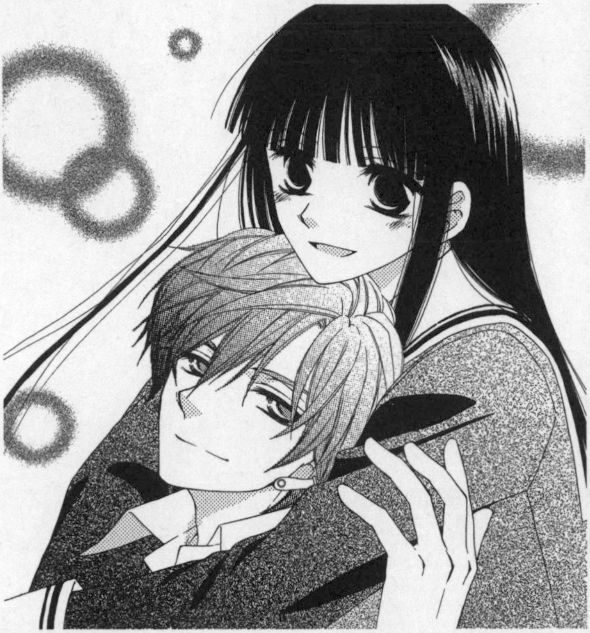

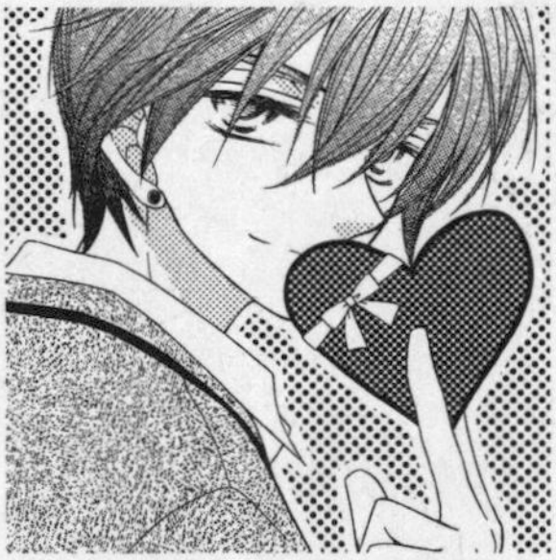

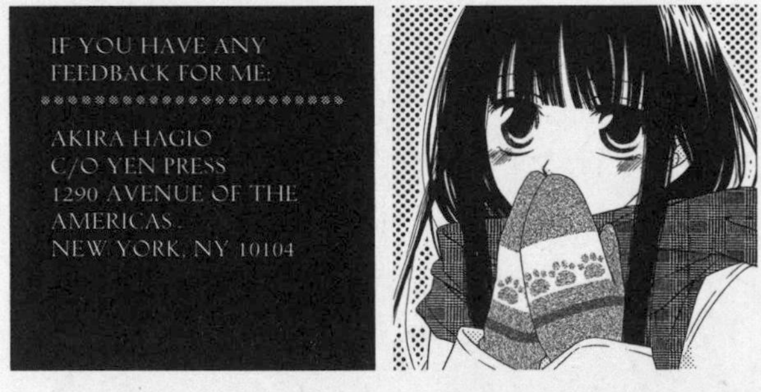

IF YOU HAVE ANY FEEDBACK FOR ME:

AKIRA HAGIO
C/O YEN PRESS
1290 AVENUE OF THE AMERICAS
NEW YORK, NY 10104

Special Thanks!

NANAU ICHIKAWA-SAMA, AYANE OOMIYA-SAMA, MOMO HACHIYA-SAMA, WATARU HIBIKI-SAMA, MEGURU ISHIKAWA-SAMA, GARO-SAMA, SUGAWARA-SAMA, MY SISTER, TOMO-CHAN, HII-SAN, ALL MY EDITORS, EVERYONE FROM THE EDITORIAL DEPARTMENT, EVERYONE INVOLVED IN THE PRINTING AND MARKETING OF THIS BOOK, AND YOU, FOR PICKING IT UP.

THANK YOU EVERYONE FOR SUPPORTING ME!

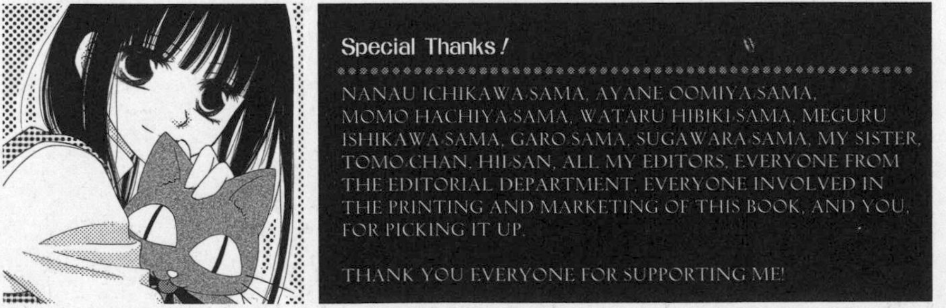

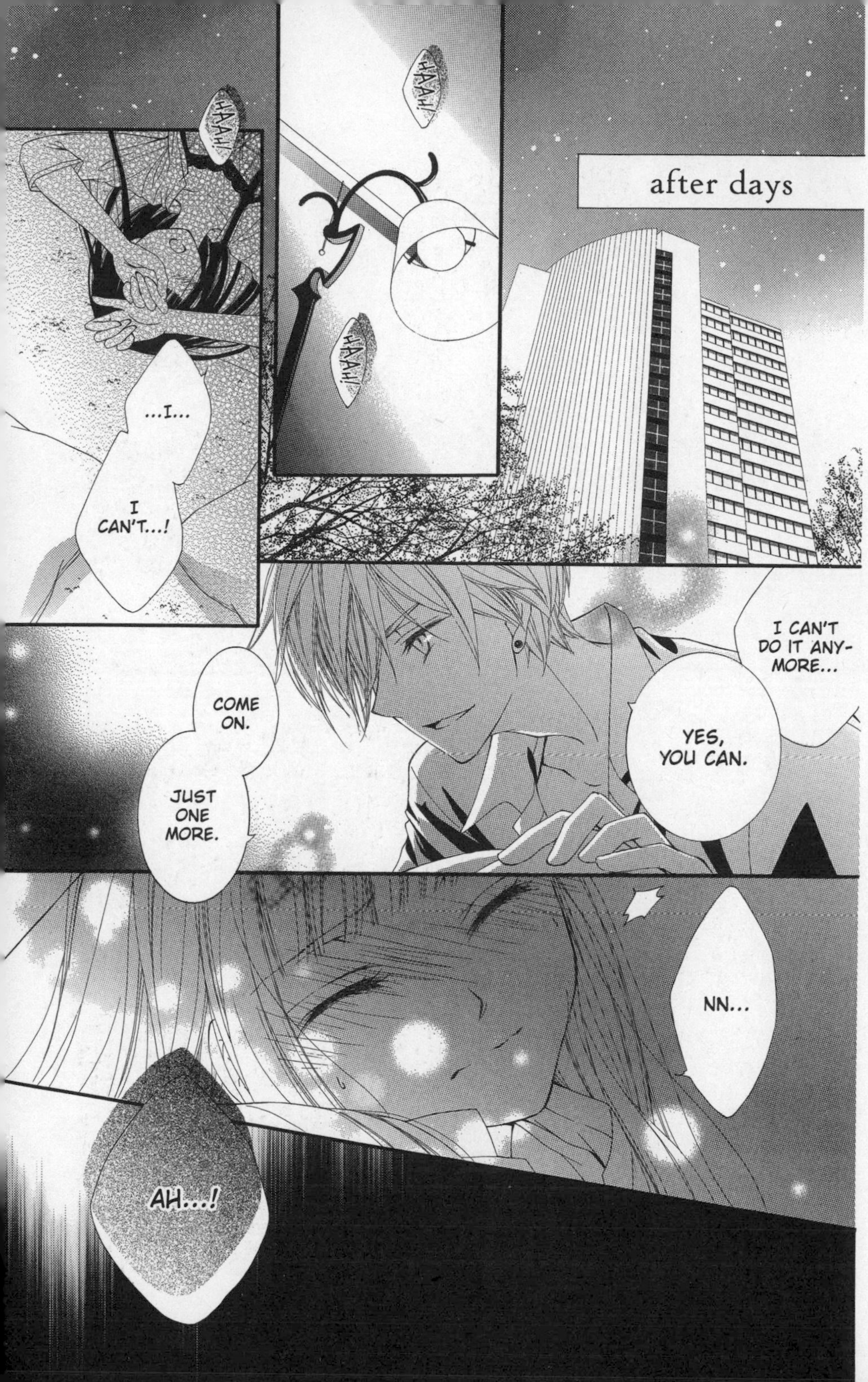
after days
HAAH!
HAAH!
HAAH!
...I...
I CAN'T...!
I CAN'T DO IT ANYMORE...
YES, YOU CAN.
COME ON.
JUST ONE MORE.
NN...
AH...!

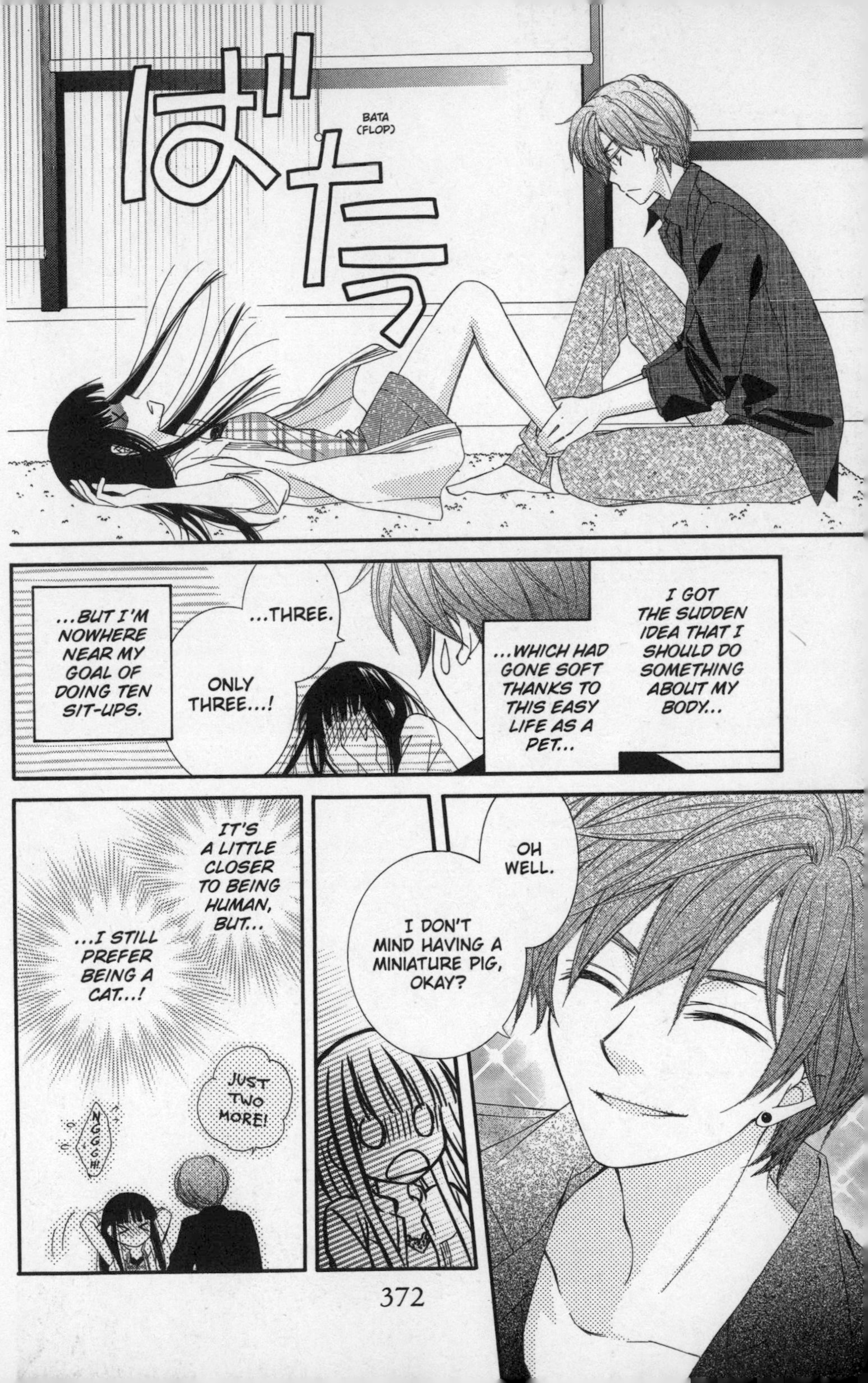
ばた
BATA (FLOP)
I GOT THE SUDDEN IDEA THAT I SHOULD DO SOMETHING ABOUT MY BODY...
...WHICH HAD GONE SOFT THANKS TO THIS EASY LIFE AS A PET...
...THREE.
ONLY THREE...!
...BUT I'M NOWHERE NEAR MY GOAL OF DOING TEN SIT-UPS.
OH WELL.
I DON'T MIND HAVING A MINIATURE PIG, OKAY?
IT'S A LITTLE CLOSER TO BEING HUMAN, BUT...
...I STILL PREFER BEING A CAT...!
JUST TWO MORE!
NGGGH!

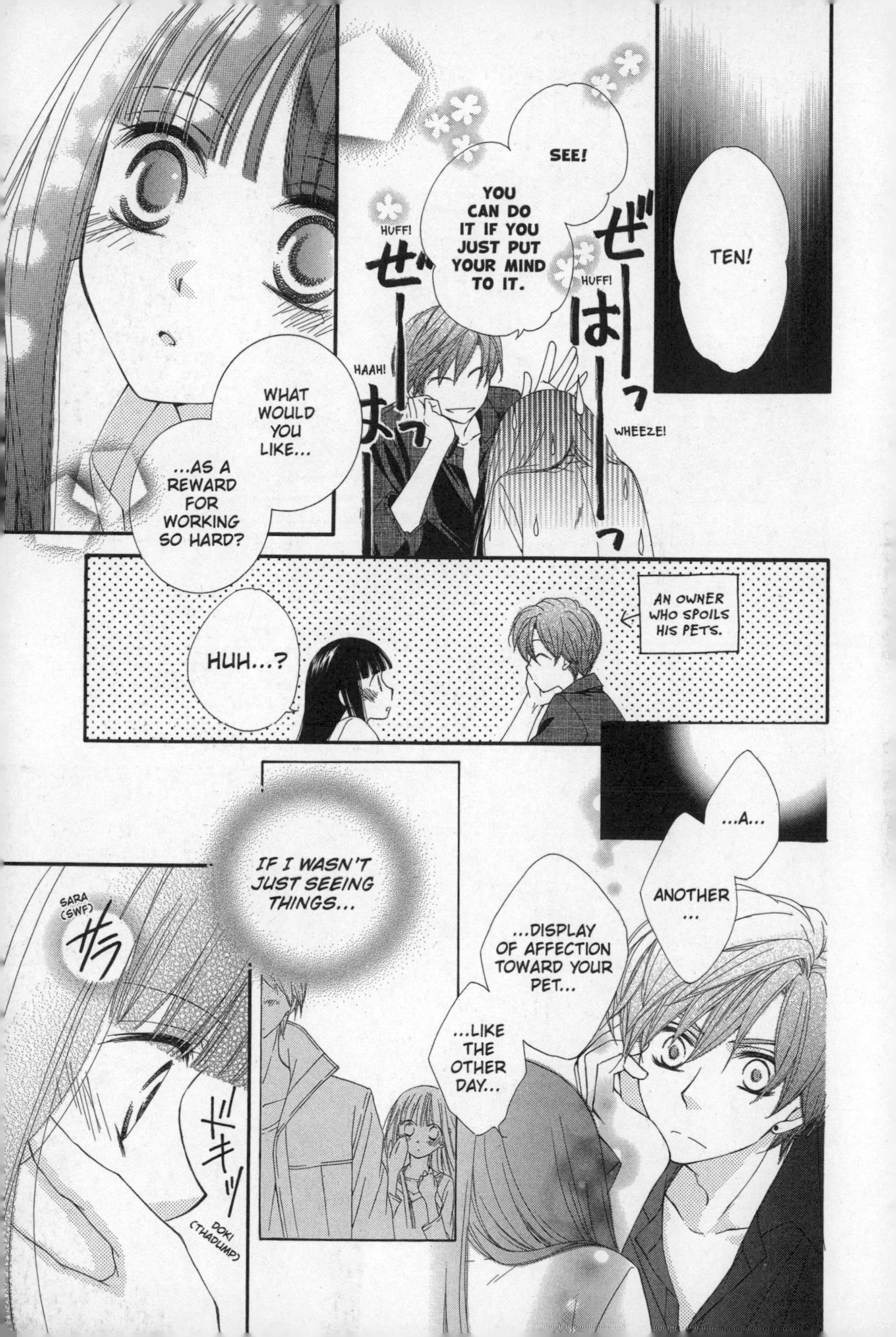
TEN!
SEE!
YOU CAN DO IT IF YOU JUST PUT YOUR MIND TO IT.
ぜーはーっ
HUFF!
WHEEZE!
ぜーはーっ
HUFF!
HAAH!
WHAT WOULD YOU LIKE...
...AS A REWARD FOR WORKING SO HARD?
AN OWNER WHO SPOILS HIS PETS.
HUH...?
...A...
ANOTHER...
...DISPLAY OF AFFECTION TOWARD YOUR PET...
...LIKE THE OTHER DAY...
IF I WASN'T JUST SEEING THINGS...
サラ
SARA (SWF)
ドキッ
DOKI (THADUMP)

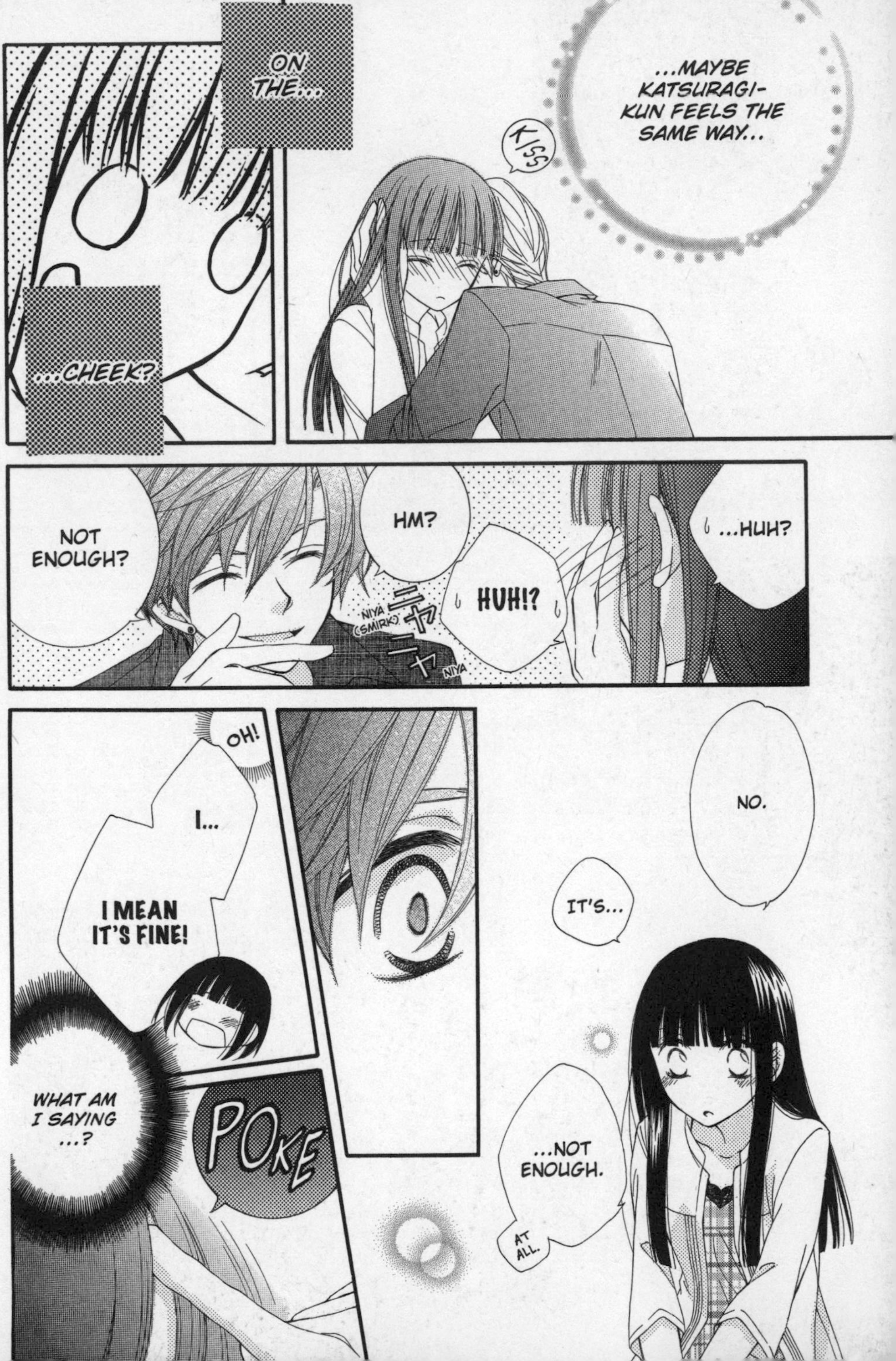
...MAYBE KATSURAGI-KUN FEELS THE SAME WAY...
KISS
ON THE...
...CHEEK?
...HUH?
HUH!?
HM?
NIYA (SMIRK)
NIYA
NOT ENOUGH?
NO.
IT'S...
...NOT ENOUGH.
AT ALL.
OH!
I...
I MEAN IT'S FINE!
WHAT AM I SAYING ...?
POKE

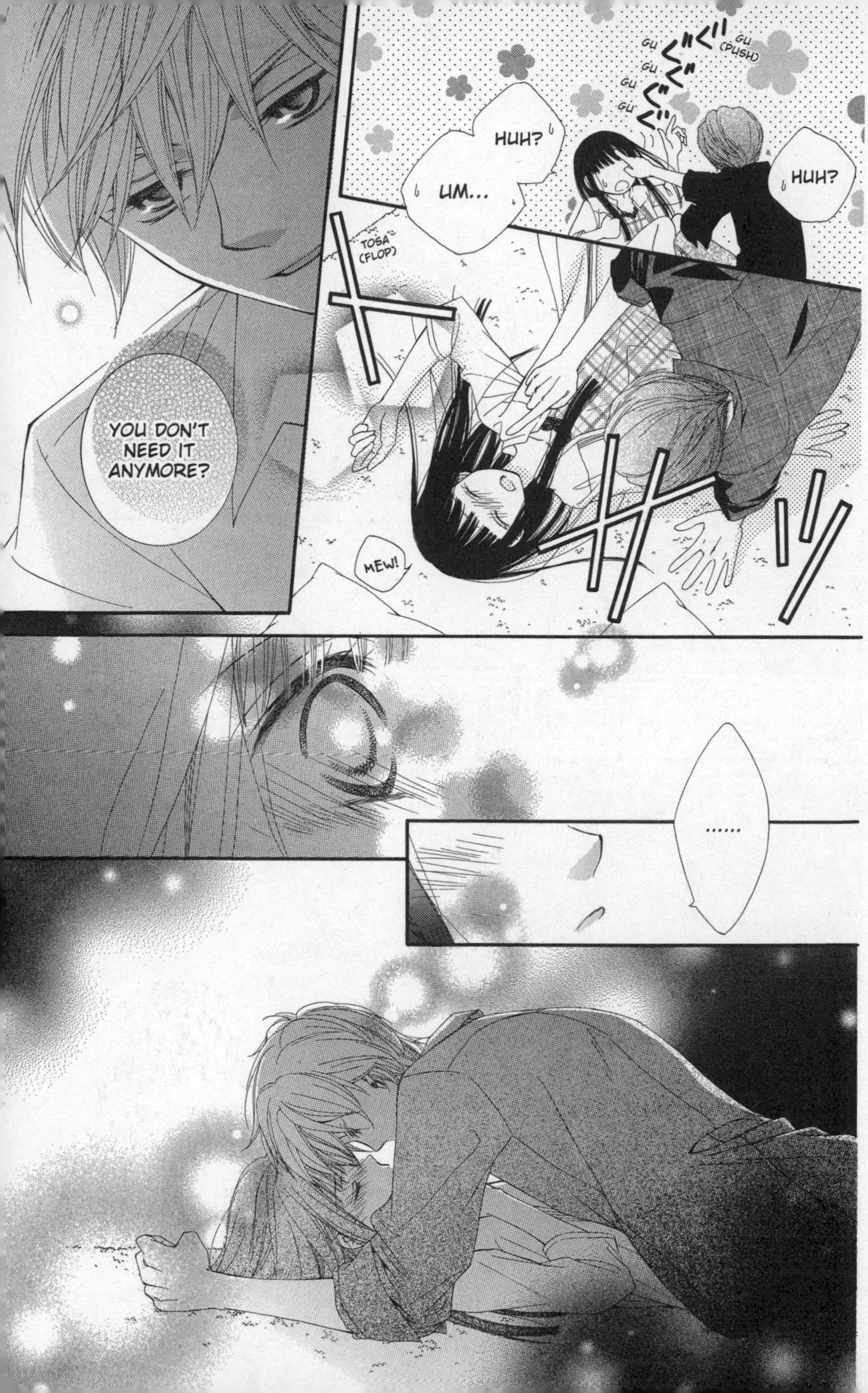

GU (PUSH)
GU
GU
GU
GU
HUH?
HUH?
UM...
TOSA (FLOP)
MEW!
YOU DON'T NEED IT ANYMORE?
......

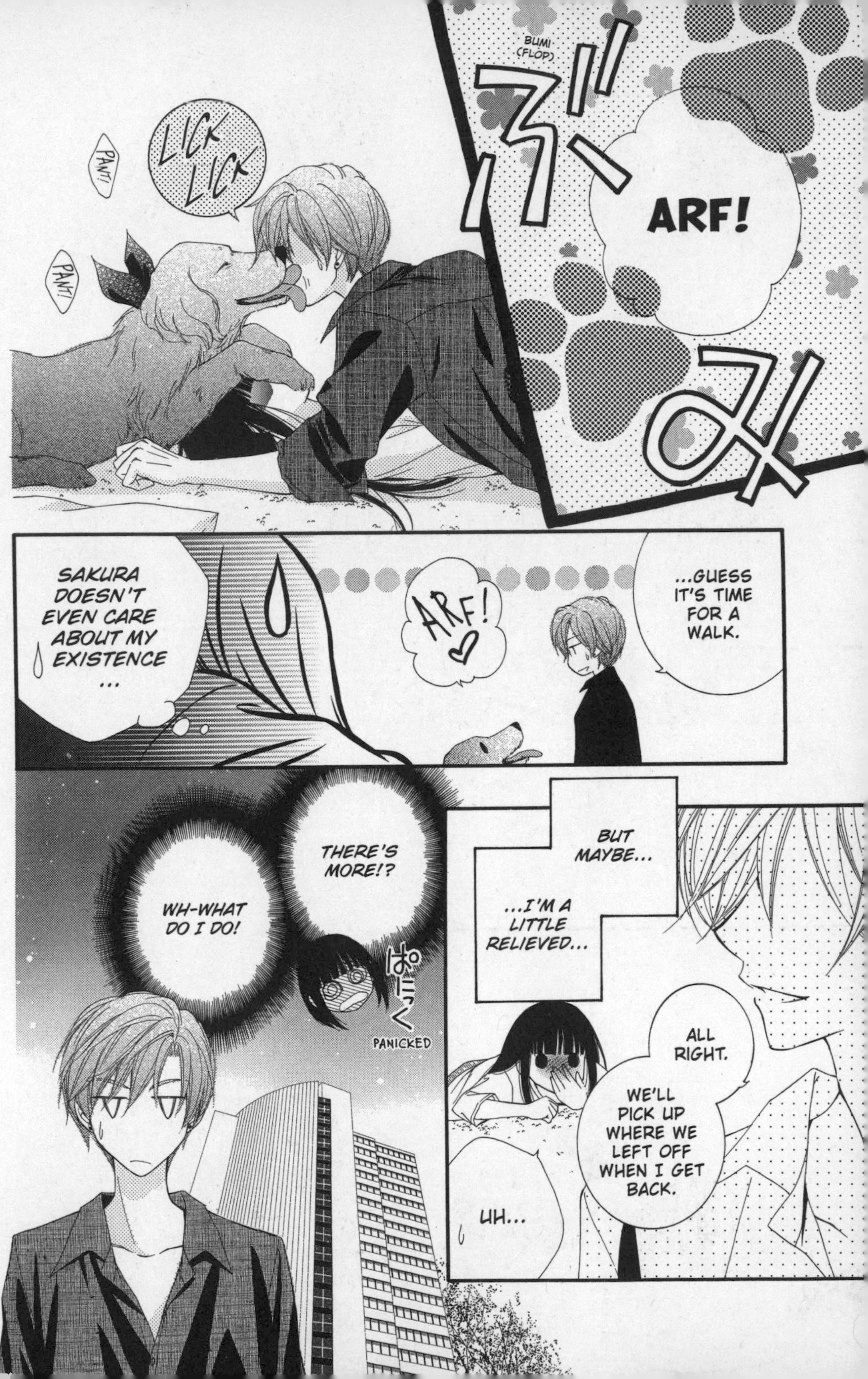
BUMI (FLOP)
ARF!
PANT!
PANT!
LICK LICK
...GUESS IT'S TIME FOR A WALK.
ARF! ♥
SAKURA DOESN'T EVEN CARE ABOUT MY EXISTENCE ...
BUT MAYBE...
...I'M A LITTLE RELIEVED...
ALL RIGHT.
WE'LL PICK UP WHERE WE LEFT OFF WHEN I GET BACK.
UH...
THERE'S MORE!?
WH-WHAT DO I DO!
PANICKED

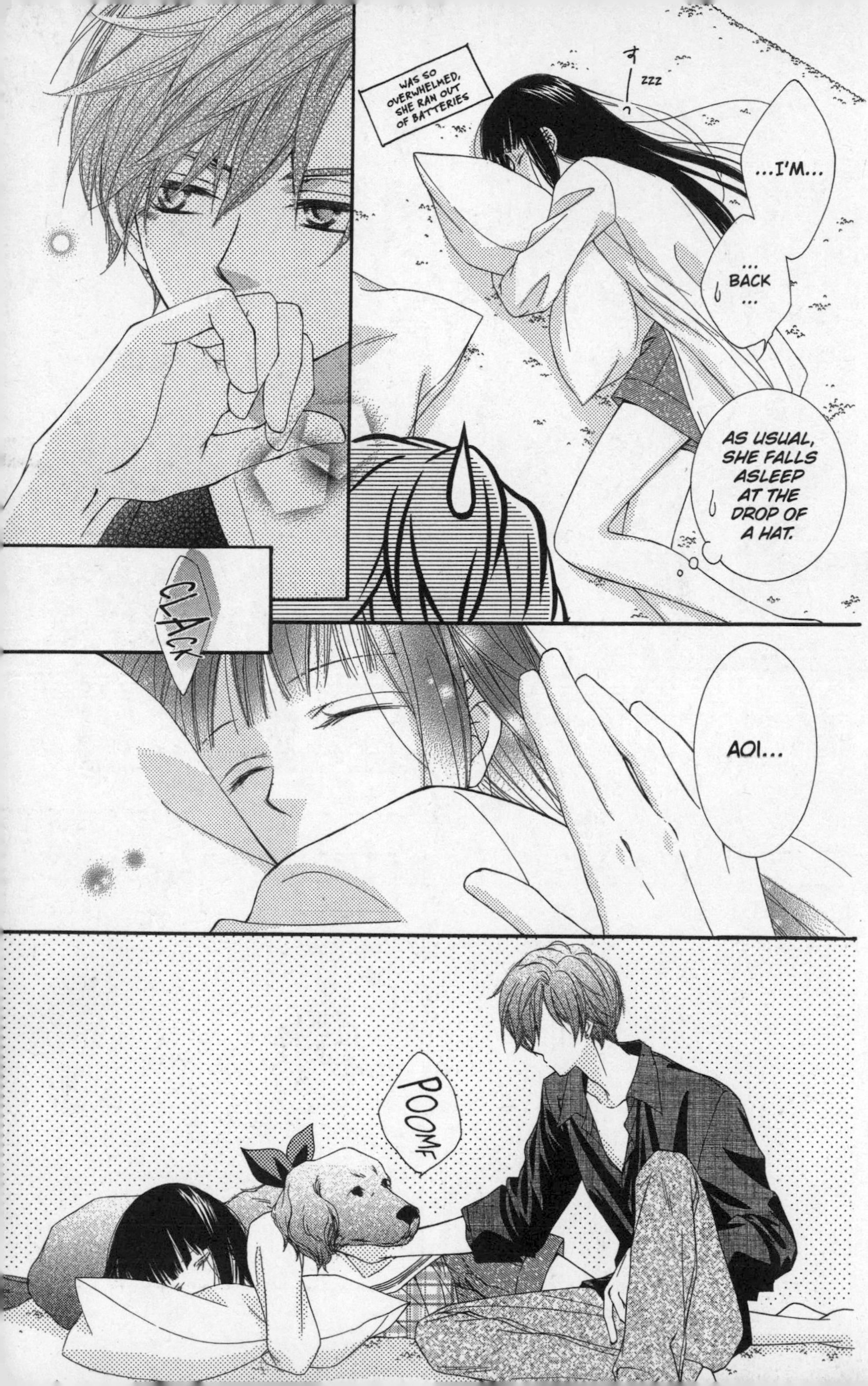

す
zzz
WAS SO OVERWHELMED, SHE RAN OUT OF BATTERIES
...I'M...
...BACK...
AS USUAL, SHE FALLS ASLEEP AT THE DROP OF A HAT.
CLACK
AOI...
POOMF

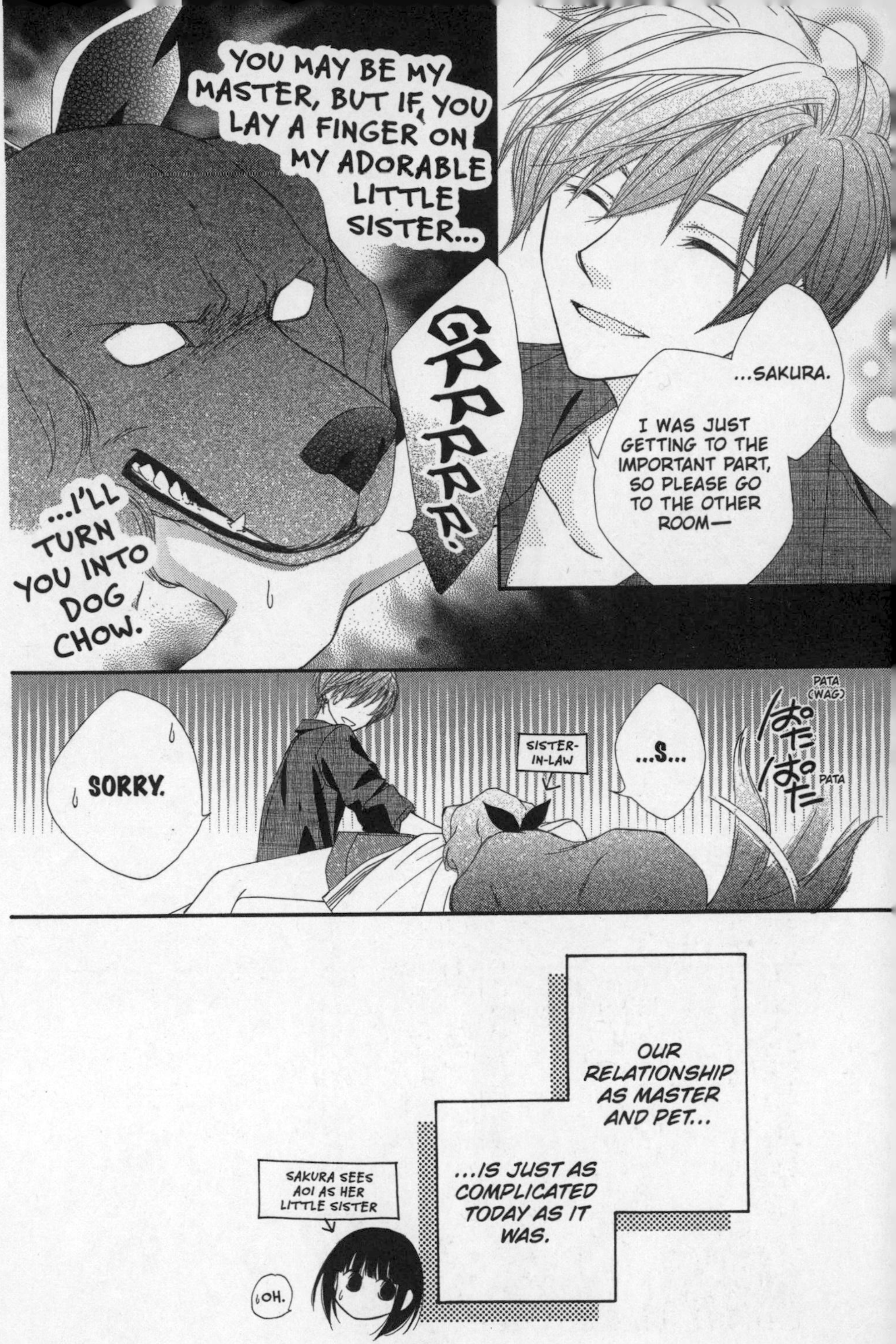
...SAKURA.
I WAS JUST GETTING TO THE IMPORTANT PART, SO PLEASE GO TO THE OTHER ROOM—
YOU MAY BE MY MASTER, BUT IF YOU LAY A FINGER ON MY ADORABLE LITTLE SISTER...
GRRRRR.
...I'LL TURN YOU INTO DOG CHOW.
ぱたぱた
PATA (WAG) PATA
...S...
SISTER-IN-LAW
SORRY.
OUR RELATIONSHIP AS MASTER AND PET...
...IS JUST AS COMPLICATED TODAY AS IT WAS.
SAKURA SEES AOI AS HER LITTLE SISTER
OH.

after days / *The End*

TRANSLATION NOTES

COMMON HONORIFICS:

no honorific: Indicates familiarity or closeness; if used without permission or reason, addressing someone in this manner would constitute an insult.

-san: The Japanese equivalent of Mr./Mrs./Miss. If a situation calls for politeness, this is the fail-safe honorific.

-sama: Conveys great respect; may also indicate that the social status of the speaker is lower than that of the addressee.

-kun: Used most often when referring to boys, this indicates affection or familiarity. Occasionally used by older men among their peers, but it may also be used by anyone referring to a person of lower standing.

-chan: An affectionate honorific indicating familiarity used mostly in reference to girls; also used in reference to cute persons or animals of either gender.

-senpai: A suffix used to address upperclassmen or more experienced coworkers.

-sensei: A respectful term for teachers, artists, or high-level professionals.

Page 71
Comecco is a snack food by Glico that is popular in Japan.

Page 94
Onee-sama means "older sister" in Japanese.

Page 121
The black cat logo refers to a popular delivery service in Japan called Yamato Transport. Their logo is a black cat mother holding her kitten by its neck, because their motto is that they will take care of your deliveries as preciously as a mother cat cares for its young.

Page 138
Washlette is a high-tech toilet by Toto that can warm the seat, activate a bidet on you, and maybe even play musical sounds to cover up the sounds of your business.

Page 183
Etsuko and Nakako are two different actresses who play housekeepers in two different Japanese shows. Etsuko played the elderly timid housekeeper from *Kaseifu wa Mita!* (*The Housekeeper Saw!*), while Nanako played a younger and more enigmatic housekeeper from *Kaseifu no Mita* (*I am Mita, Your Housekeeper*).

Page 185

Kotodama refers to the mysterious and powerful influence that words possess.

Hey! Say! JUMP is a Japanese idol group of men. The words "Hey! Say!" are meant to sound like the Japanese time period "Heisei," which began in 1989 and lasts to modern day, because all the members were allegedly born during this period, making them very young.

Showa Period
This is the period that came just before Heisei, lasting from 1926 until 1989. The joke here is that Editor H looks so young she wonders if he was born after 1989, but he assures her that he's a touch older than that.

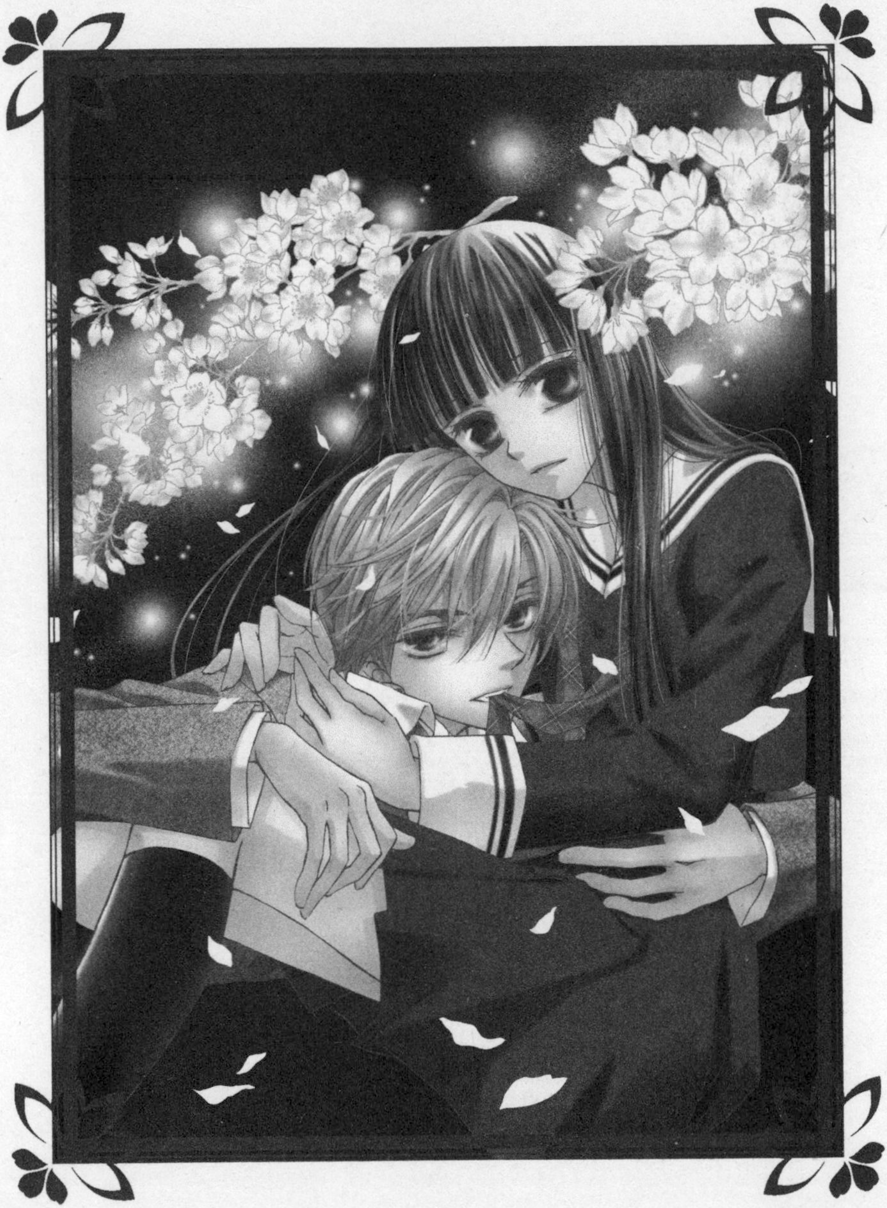

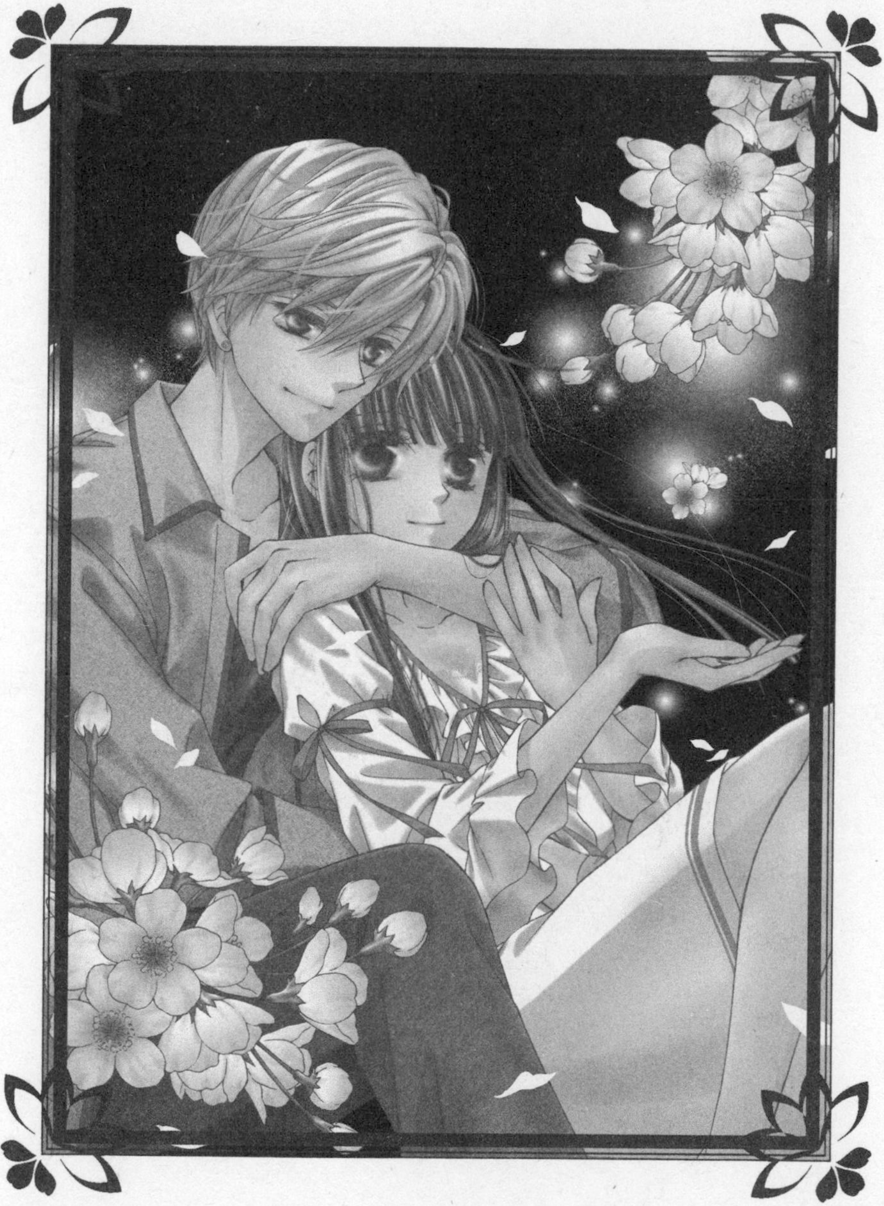

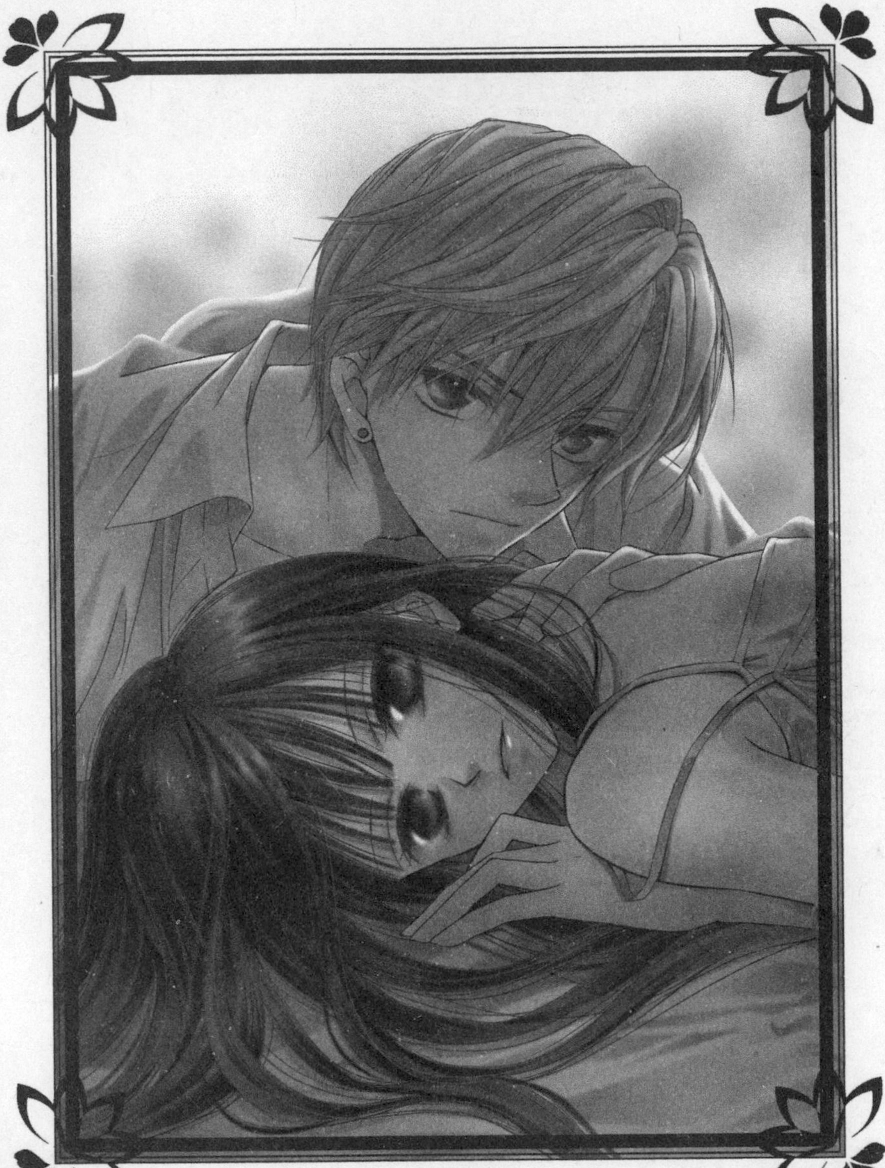

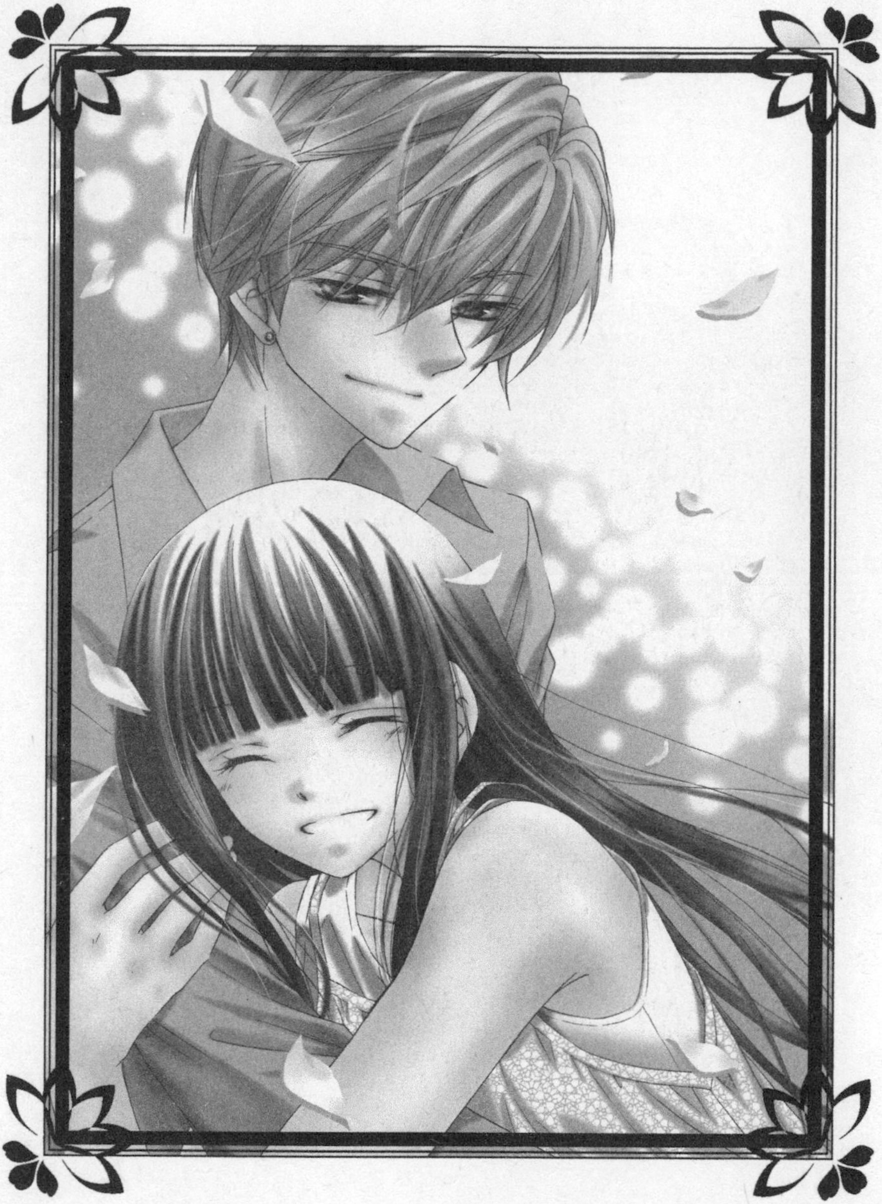

The Secret Sakura Shares
by Akira Hagio

Translation: Christine Dashiell   *Lettering: Bianca Pistillo*

SAKURA NO HIMEGOTO by Akira Hagio
© Akira Hagio 2012, 2013
All rights reserved.
First published in Japan in 2012, 2013 by HAKUSENSHA, INC., Tokyo. English language translation rights in U.S.A., Canada and U.K. arranged with HAKUSENSHA, INC., Tokyo through Tuttle-Mori Agency, Inc., Tokyo.

English Translation © 2015 by Hachette Book Group, Inc.

Yen Press
Hachette Book Group
1290 Avenue of the Americas
New York, NY 10104

www.HachetteBookGroup.com • www.YenPress.com

Yen Press is an imprint of Hachette Book Group, Inc.
The Yen Press name and logo are trademarks of Hachette Book Group, Inc.

The publisher is not responsible for websites (or their content) that are not owned by the publisher.

First Yen Press Edition: December 2015

ISBN: 978-0-316-35140-9

10 9 8 7 6 5 4 3 2 1

BVG

Printed in the United States of America